WINES

OF EASTERN NORTH AMERICA

WINES

OF EASTERN NORTH AMERICA

FROM PROHIBITION TO THE PRESENT
A HISTORY AND DESK REFERENCE

HUDSON CATTELL

CORNELL UNIVERSITY PRESS
ITHACA AND LONDON

First published 2014 by Cornell University Press
Printed in the United States of America

Design by Scott Levine.

Library of Congress Cataloging-in-Publication Data

Cattell, Hudson, author.
    Wines of eastern North America : from Prohibition to the present—a history and desk reference / Hudson Cattell.
        pages cm
    Includes bibliographical references and index.
    ISBN 978-0-8014-5198-0 (cloth : alk. paper)
    1. Wine and wine making—East (U.S.)—History. 2. Wine and wine making—Canada, Eastern—History. 3. Wine industry—East (U.S.)—History. 4. Wine industry—Canada, Eastern—History. I. Title.
    TP557.C384 2014
    663'.201—dc23   2013026057

Cornell University Press strives to use environmentally responsible suppliers and materials to the fullest extent possible in the publishing of its books. Such materials include vegetable-based, low-VOC inks and acid-free papers that are recycled, totally chlorine-free, or partly composed of nonwood fibers. For further information, visit our website at www.cornellpress.cornell.edu.

Cloth printing   10   9   8   7   6   5   4   3   2   1

To Linda, without whom this book could not have been written

CONTENTS

PREFACE AND ACKNOWLEDGMENTS

I HAVE WRITTEN THIS BOOK OUT OF BOTH INTEREST AND NEED. BACK IN 1976, WHEN I and my initial partner in L & H Photojournalism, H. Lee Stauffer (now Lee Stauffer Miller), first began publishing *The Pennsylvania Grape Letter and Wine News,* there was no information about eastern grapes, wines, or who was who in the industry available in the library. Although the first edition of Leon Adams's *The Wines of America* had been published in 1973, it would be late 1977 before I learned of its existence.

Because I needed to get background information to help with the editing of the *Grape Letter,* I made up my mind to research the past. As I began to learn some of the history of the industry, I realized that most people knew even less than we did. The result was the publication of our three booklets in the "Wines of the East" series between 1978 and 1980. For many years these booklets were considered the primary source of background information on the history of eastern grapes and wine. I was already hooked on the history of the industry in the East.

In 1981, Linda Jones McKee replaced Lee Miller as my partner in L & H Photo journalism. Together we founded the magazine *Wine East,* which was published from 1981 to 2008. For more than twenty-five years, day in and day out, we have followed the growth of the eastern grape and wine industry, writing about it, talking about it, and analyzing what was happening. As I traveled, I interviewed people about their history and did research in libraries whenever I had the chance. Much of what I discovered found its way into the pages of *Wine East.*

Normally, contributions of others to a book are reserved for an acknowledgments page. An exception must be made in this case. It is impossible to overstate the contributions Linda has made, and not only through our interaction during the everyday work on the magazine. Her travels for the magazine and her abilities as an expert observer helped build our factual knowledge and broad perspective of the industry. Linda contributed to the content of the magazine, edited everything I wrote—as I did for her—and handled both advertising sales and the magazine's design and production.

We also had our own special activities. Linda became involved in judging state, national, and international competitions. In 2002, her fascination with the wine industry took a new tack when she, along with Richard Carey, started Tamanend Winery in Lancaster, Pennsylvania.

My outside interests focused on the history of the eastern wine industry. Although Linda left the bulk of the historical research to me, her contributions to this book entitled her to be a co-author. She declined the offer. In recognition of what three decades of working together—and her friendship—has meant to me, this book is dedicated to her.

Over the years I have been fortunate enough to have known, and in many cases interviewed, nearly everyone who has played an important role in the development of the industry. The insights gained from having known these pioneers have been invaluable in my research and writing. Originally it was contemplated that this book would be completed in 2000, not necessarily because of the natural division between two centuries, but because the industry had matured to the point where it was rapidly expanding in numbers and the quality of its wines had earned the industry recognition both in North America and abroad. As time went by, however, and many of those who founded the modern industry passed away, additional information became available that could not be obtained during their lifetimes.

Philip Wagner left behind forty volumes of diaries (which he called "Daybooks") with handwritten entries from the early 1930s to shortly before his death in 1996. The nearly daily entries covered what he was doing in his vineyard and winery and also the contacts and conversations he had with visitors and those he visited. A professional journalist, Wagner's diaries were not only a window into the past but a way of identifying many other events in the more than sixty years he was a significant part of the industry. Additional notebooks covered entries made during his travels to California and Europe, and in another series he documented every wine that he made. The sheer amount of material in his notebooks and the immense value of his diaries made it necessary to take the time to go through them before completing the book.

Likewise, Dr. Konstantin Frank's death made much more information about him available, not as much in the form of documentary material as in the willingness of relatives and others to help in the reconstruction of his life. During his lifetime there was only sketchy and often contradictory information published about Frank. In the 1970s, for example, even the fact that he had his doctorate was widely questioned. Attempts to interview him usually degenerated quickly into a diatribe against the

French hybrids or a passionate espousal of the merits of the vinifera. I was fortunate enough to get one valuable interview with him, and that came in Virginia when no one else was around and I asked him to tell me about his childhood in Russia—and switched on my tape recorder. Well after the interview was over his thoughts were still far away and it was obvious that what he had told me was true to the best of his memory. Other than that, it has only been in recent years that it has been possible to assemble a reasonably accurate account of his life.

Also adding to the time it took to write this book was the decision to include a bibliography. I felt that it was important that readers know the sources of factual information for the book. Unfortunately, there was no existing bibliography to serve as a starting point. In constructing one from scratch, I decided to include not only items referred to in the text but, again with an eye to the future, other books and articles that might be useful to anyone working on a history or bibliography at a later date. Certain guidelines in the preparation of the bibliography are listed at the start of that section.

With several thousand wineries past and present in the East, and more than 10,000 people who helped build the industry, I know only too well how much has been left out of this book. If I were to make a list of all of the people in the industry who took the time to tell me their stories, answered my questions, or helped me in any number of ways, a list of acknowledgments would fill several pages—and would still leave someone out, I can simply say thank you.

The librarians at the New York State Agricultural Experiment Station at Geneva and the Horticultural Research Institute of Ontario (HRIO) have been an invaluable resource and a pleasure to work with. I thank Judy A. Wanner at HRIO for her assistance. After Judy was transferred from Vineland to the University of Guelph, Helen Fisher was able to provide me with valuable documents. At Geneva, Mary van Buren, Peter McDonald, Marty Schlabach, and Jeanne Samimy did everything they could to help me. Also at Geneva, I especially want to thank Mike Fordon, library coordinator at the Frank A. Lee Library for his interest in my project and his unfailing assistance in anything I requested, from locating documents and books to hunting down details for the bibliography.

A number of people took the time to read through parts of the manuscript and my thanks go to Laurie MacDonald, Tim Martinson, John McGrew, Gordon Murchie, and especially Lucie Morton who read much of the book. In addition, Ellie Butz, Lloyd Schmidt, Art Smith, and Chris Stamp contributed information on specific subjects.

At Cornell University Press, I could not have asked for better guidance than I received from Michael J. McGandy and Sarah Grossman. My thanks go to them and also to Karen Laun, senior production editor, who helped transform the manuscript into a book, and Scott Levine for his work on the cover. Lastly, for this computer-challenged author whose abilities go little further than word processing, I again thank Linda Jones McKee for her unstinting help throughout in preparing the manuscript for publication.

I have tried to give proper credit for the illustrations used in the book. Some of them, which were among the papers retrieved after Philip Wagner's death, are simply attributed to what I call the Philip Wagner collection and are included here with Susan Wagner's permission. The maps are the work of Susan Cottrel, a Lancaster, Pennsylvania, artist, and Bill Nelson, a professional cartographer.

Many of the items listed in the notes may not be readily available. At some point, all of my historical files will be donated to Cornell University's Eastern Wine and Grape Archive at the Carl A. Kroch Library in Ithaca or the Frank A. Lee Library in Geneva.

Finally, given the wide scope of this book, it is inevitable that errors will be found in what I have written. Any such errors are solely my responsibility.

Map 1: The shaded area indicates the states and Canadian provinces discussed in this book. To show the rapid growth of the eastern wine industry, the nine states and one province with the largest number of wineries in 2012 have the winery count followed by the 1985 count in parentheses. The latest winery count is courtesy of WinesVinesDATA, and the 1985 figures are from *Wine East* magazine.

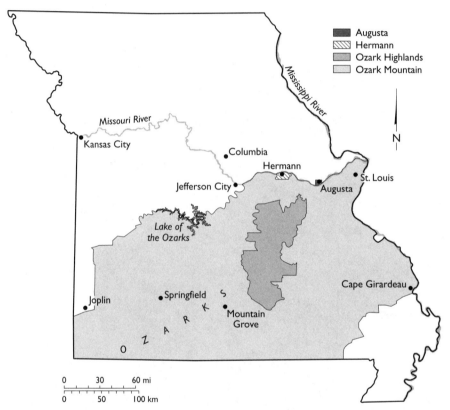

Map 2: Wine regions of Missouri. In 1980, the United States established American Viticultural Areas (AVAs,) that designate a grape growing region. An AVA is defined by its unique geographical features that affect the type of wine it produces. In Missouri, the Augusta AVA—the nation's first AVA—consists of 15 square miles, the Hermann AVA 51,200 acres, and the Ozark Highlands AVA 122,000 square miles. All three are within the Ozark Mountain AVA, which includes 3,520,000 acres in southern Missouri, northwest Arkansas, and northeast Oklahoma. (Regional boundaries are from Missouri Wine and Grape Board.)

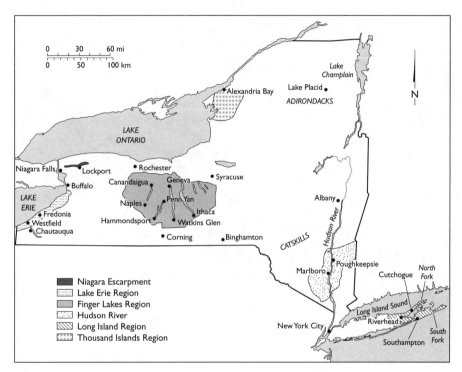

Map 3: Wine regions of New York State (boundaries from New York Wine and Grape Foundation). Wine regions shown on this map and those that follow are not necessarily AVAs.

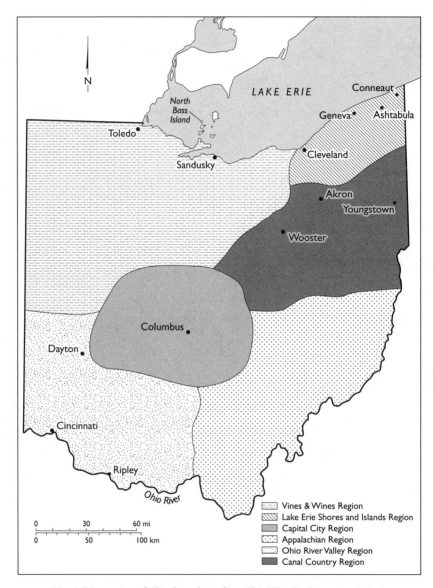

Map 4: Wine regions of Ohio (boundaries from Ohio Wine Producers Association).

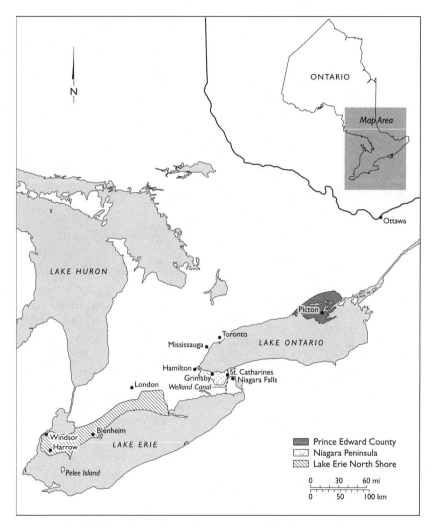

Map 5: Wine regions of Ontario (boundaries from Wine Council of Ontario).

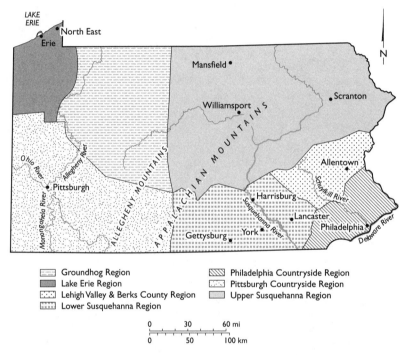

Map 6: Wine regions of Pennsylvania (boundaries from Pennsylvania Wine Association).

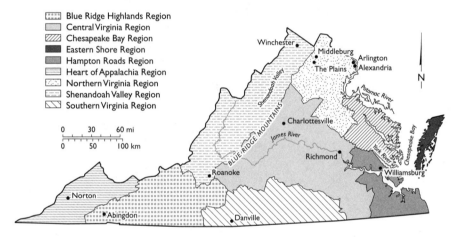

Blue Ridge Highlands Region
Central Virginia Region
Chesapeake Bay Region
Eastern Shore Region
Hampton Roads Region
Heart of Appalachia Region
Northern Virginia Region
Shenandoah Valley Region
Southern Virginia Region

0   30   60 mi
0   50   100 km

Winchester
Middleburg
The Plains
Arlington
Alexandria

Shenandoah Valley

BLUE RIDGE MOUNTAINS

James River

Charlottesville

Richmond

Potomac River

York River

Chesapeake Bay

Williamsburg

Roanoke

Norton

Abingdon

Danville

N

Map 7: Wine regions of Virginia (boundaries from Virginia Wine Marketing Board).

WINES
OF EASTERN NORTH AMERICA

INTRODUCTION

IN THIRTY-FIVE YEARS THE WINE INDUSTRY IN EASTERN NORTH AMERICA GREW AT a rapid pace from approximately 125 wineries in 1975 to more than 2,500 in 2010. During these years the East became an important wine region of the world as it was recognized that wine grapes could be profitably grown in the region and that outstanding wines made from them were winning prestigious awards in international competitions and finding widespread consumer acceptance. How this happened is the subject of this book.

The book focuses on the states and provinces where the modern eastern wine industry came into being following the end of Prohibition. In the 1940s and 1950s, a small number of dedicated grape growers, winemakers, and researchers in New York, Ohio, Maryland, and Ontario provided the spark that enabled the East to make quality table wines. As the result of their experiments in growing grapes in the difficult environments of the East—including subzero cold, diseases, and insect pests—interest spread to other states. New growers attended short courses in the more established growing areas in the East and took the information home with them. Winemakers and growers got to know each other, attended meetings, and joined organizations where they could interact with research and extension people. A sense of purpose and camaraderie helped the industry grow in states to the south and as far west as the Mississippi River.

One of these organizations was the American Society of Enologists (ASE), headquartered in California. The need for an eastern version of the ASE was recognized in 1974, and the following year the ASE formed an Eastern Section that would assist in the growth of viticulture and enology in a region that was quite different from California. About forty people attended the organizational meeting in 1975 and adopted a set of bylaws. Article IV defined the boundaries for the Eastern Section and stated that the "geographical area encompassed by the Section shall include all states east of the western boundaries of Minnesota, Iowa, Missouri, Arkansas and Louisiana, and the Canadian provinces east of the Ontario-Manitoba border."

It was within this geographical area that the growth of the eastern industry took place and, for the purposes of this book, constitutes "the East." Very little in the way of grape growing was taking place between the western boundary of the Eastern Section and the Rocky Mountains in 1975 and, when the industry developed there, there was little interaction with the East. It was not until the late 1980s that the first wineries opened in Kansas and Nebraska and the industry in those states reached out to become involved with the industry in the East. In 2010, the American Society for Enology and Viticulture, the now renamed ASE, allowed the Eastern Section to expand its boundaries to include "all U.S. states and Canadian provinces with territory east of the Continental Divide." The history of wine in Nebraska and Kansas is included in this book.

Readers may notice that more space is devoted to a few states such as New York than to other states. The wine and grape industry in these states started earlier and contributed more to the growth of the wine industry in the East. Each state, however, has a wine history, and appendix E discusses the early history of each state in alphabetical order.

From the start it was evident that the wines of the East would be quite different from the wines of California. For one thing, the native American grapes and French hybrids were rarely grown on the West Coast. For another, the wines made from the vinifera in the East tended to have considerably lower alcohols and higher acid levels because the East does not have a Mediterranean climate, and in many areas grapes do not develop high sugar content. There is a greater similarity between the wines of the East and those of France because the growing conditions in both regions are similar. But just as there is a difference between the wines of Bordeaux and Burgundy, there is also a difference between a Chardonnay or Seyval grown in New York and the same varieties grown in Missouri.

What has united the East as a region has been the difficulties and problems facing the grape grower, from cold climates in the north to Pierce's disease in the south. No wine region of the world has as many different grape varieties used for making commercial wines as eastern North America, and adding to this diversity is the availability of many different fruits and other agricultural products for winemaking. Research stations and extension agents have had to work with many variables, and this has also been a unifying factor.

Throughout the years, the East has had to depend on its own resources to build its industry. It was not until after World War II that modern sprays and methods of applying them made commercial growing of grapes for wine possible. The development of the industry was uneven because state laws and regulations delayed the start of wineries. Farm wineries opened in various states over a period of more than twenty years. There were hurdles that had to be overcome, including prejudice against drinking wine, strained relationships between growers and wineries, and trade barriers. This book describes some of the difficulties the industry has faced to reach today's level of success.

Readers in the United States may be surprised at how much Ontario has contributed to the industry in the United States. In the 1940s the first large-scale importations of the French hybrids took place in the Niagara Peninsula, the first commercial vinifera wine in the East was made there in 1955, and their emphasis on wine standards that led to the creation of Vintners Quality Alliance served as a model for similar organizations in the United States.

The history of wine in eastern North America is a colorful one and the results are a tribute to those who have made it possible to make world-class wines in the East.

CHAPTER ONE

PROHIBITION AND ITS AFTERMATH

PROHIBITION IN THE UNITED STATES AND CANADA GOES BACK TO THE TEMPERANCE movements that had their beginnings in the early eighteenth century and became a reality in the patriotic fervor of World War I.[1] Although both countries went through Prohibition at approximately the same time, they experienced it in somewhat different ways and emerged from it with their own sets of governmental controls that affected not only the way the wine industry in each country was to grow, but the rate at which it was to develop.

The modern history of the wine industry in the eastern United States and Canada got its start early in the twentieth century when Prohibition in the two countries came to an end, but the saga of grapes and wine in the East goes back many centuries before that. The fascinating history of those years is available in detail elsewhere, but a short summary here may be useful for readers not familiar with what happened in the past.[2]

Before Prohibition

The earliest reference to grapes in the New World dates back to about the year 1000 when Leif Eriksson and his Viking companions discovered wild grapes growing along the northeastern coast of North America. Their discovery of grapes is mentioned in *The Greenlander's Saga* and *Erik the Red's Saga* preserved in Iceland and confirmed by recent research.[3]

Other early explorers reported sighting grapevines: Giovanni da Verrazano along the North Carolina coast in 1524 and Jacques Cartier while sailing down the

St. Lawrence River in 1535. The first attempts to make wine were by the French Huguenots in Florida in the mid-1560s and by Spanish colonists on Parris Island, South Carolina, around 1568. Sir Walter Raleigh's Roanoke colony may have tried to make wine in the 1580s.

The first vineyard in Canada was planted in 1633 by Isaac de Razilly at Petite Riviere near LaHave in Nova Scotia.[4] By 1636, the Jesuits were making sacramental wines from grapes they found growing in the wild.

The initial permanent English settlement in North America came in 1607 at Jamestown, Virginia, and Captain John Smith described the nearly twenty gallons of wine made in 1609 from grapes the colonists found growing wild. The Pilgrims arrived in Plymouth, Massachusetts, in 1620, and it is not impossible that wine was served at the first Thanksgiving dinner in 1621.[5]

Vines from Europe began to arrive in the United States in 1619 when the Virginia Company sent vines with eight French vignerons to Virginia. Throughout the Colonial period vines were brought from Europe and attempts were made to grow grapes: the Massachusetts Company in 1630; Ambrose Gibbons in Maine, also in 1630; Lord Baltimore in Maryland in 1662; and William Penn in Pennsylvania in 1683. All of these early efforts ended in failure. The European vines of the *Vitis vinifera* had difficulty adapting to the harsh winters in the East and they had little resistance to diseases and insects found in the New World, particularly phylloxera, a root louse found everywhere in the soils of the East, but not in Europe. It would be centuries before the fungicides and techniques needed to control these insects and diseases would become available.

In 1786, the first commercial vineyard in the United States was planted north of Philadelphia in Spring Mill with the Alexander grape, a chance hybrid or "wildling" that had resulted from a cross between a wild vine and a vinifera vine brought over from Europe at an earlier date. The founder of this enterprise, a Frenchman by the name of Pierre Legaux, secured legislation in 1793 to establish a private stock company called the Pennsylvania Vine Company to finance the venture, and many prominent Americans of the day, including Alexander Hamilton and Aaron Burr, purchased stock. The Alexander grape consistently produced a good crop and made a wine superior to that made from wild grapes. In 1799, the founder of the Kentucky Vineyard Society, Jean Jacques Dufour, took it west to Kentucky, Indiana, and Ohio.

The discovery in 1802 of the Catawba grape, a chance hybrid originating in North Carolina, led to the start of the grape and wine industry based on Catawba in the Cincinnati area by Nicholas Longworth in 1825. By the late 1850s, there were more than 2,000 acres of Catawba planted in the Cincinnati area. These grapes made over 500,000 gallons of wine, more than a third of the wine being produced in the United States at that time.

The first commercial winery in Canada was founded in 1811 in Cooksville, Ontario, by Johann Schiller, an ex-soldier who had made wine in Germany. The wine he made from native grapes was primarily for himself and his neighbors, and by 1864 his property was bought by Count Justin M. de Courtenay who expanded the vineyards and later exhibited the wines he made in France. Two plantings on Pelee Island in 1866, one of thirty acres and another of fifteen acres, marked the start of grape growing there.

The discovery of other important grape varieties such as Isabella around 1816 and Delaware in 1849, and particularly the introduction of Concord by Ephraim Bull in 1853, led to rapid growth of the industry in both the United States and Canada. During the second half of the nineteenth century various states including New York, Ohio, Missouri, and New Jersey took turns being the largest wine producing state in the United States. It was not until the 1880s that the wine industry in California began to expand rapidly.

Wines from the East began winning international recognition when a Great Western champagne from New York State won a gold medal in Europe at the Vienna Exposition in 1873. At the same exposition a Cynthiana won the top award as the "best red wine of all nations."[6] Two Gold Seal champagnes from the Urbana Wine Company in New York won medals at the Paris Exposition in 1879 at the first head-to-head competition between American and French sparkling wines. In world expositions in Paris, Brussels, Chicago, and Philadelphia, eastern wines won award after award. Between 1873 and 1904 Stone Hill Winery in Hermann, Missouri, won eight gold medals. In Paris in 1900 the awards list included five wines from New York, two from Ohio, and one each from Florida, New Jersey, North Carolina, Virginia, and the District of Columbia.

Grape growing remained difficult in many parts of the East. In the 1860s, many vineyards in the Cincinnati area began to fail as vines succumbed to diseases for which sprays had not yet been invented. Conversely, the Concord vineyards did well in the harsh winters of the East. During the second half of the nineteenth century, early American hybridizers such as Edward Rogers and Thomas Volney Munson disseminated hundreds of new grape varieties by the end of the century. Efforts to grow the vinifera continued but met with little success.

Many of the American varieties of grapes had much stronger and often grapey flavors than the more subtle vinifera varieties from Europe. They also contained much less sugar and much more acid than the European varieties. Since making wine from American varieties required a large amount of sweetening, it was natural for wineries to produce sweet wines of all kinds, fortified wines, and sparkling wines where it was also possible to modify strong flavors. The continuing search for grapes that has marked so much of the history of grape growing and winemaking in eastern North America was based on the desire to find suitable grapes for making dry table wines.

The coming of Prohibition during World War I in Canada and just after World War I in the United States ended the first part of the history of grape growing and winemaking in eastern North America and wineries were forced to close. When Prohibition ended, the search for grapes that would make European-style table

Figure 1.1: The Stone Hill Wine Co. in Hermann, Missouri, won eight gold medals at world's fairs between 1873 and 1904 and incorporated the medals in their label design. This Dry Catawba label was in use in 1901. Courtesy of Jim Held.

wines resumed, this time with success. (See appendix A for more on the history of eastern wine grapes.)

Prohibition in the United States

In the United States, concern about the drinking of hard liquor led to the first state prohibitory law in Maine in 1851, which forbade the sale or manufacture of intoxicants in the state.[7] The temperance movement gradually came into being with the formation of the National Prohibition Party in 1869 and the birth of the Woman's Christian Temperance Union (WCTU) in 1874. In 1895, the Anti-Saloon League was founded, a well-organized political action group that would provide the leadership and lobbying required to get prohibitory legislation passed on a national level. By 1913, the League was calling for an Eighteenth Amendment to the Constitution, which would prohibit alcoholic beverages in the United States.

With the coming of World War I, and the declaration of war on Germany by the United States in 1917, prohibition was identified with patriotism. Many of the breweries were operated by people with German names who came from German backgrounds. Drinking their products was considered unpatriotic, and supplying alcohol to the troops was interpreted as a pro-German tactic. The Eighteenth

Amendment passed Congress on December 18, 1917, was ratified by the required thirty-sixth state, Nebraska, on January 16, 1919, and became effective at 12:01 a.m. on January 17, 1920.

The Eighteenth Amendment prohibited "the manufacture, sale, or transportation of intoxicating liquors" within, into, or out of the United States. What became known as the Volstead Act, passed by Congress over President Woodrow Wilson's veto on October 28, 1919, provided heavy penalties for violators and defined intoxicating liquors as anything containing one-half of 1 percent alcohol or more. Prior to the passage of the Volstead Act, there was some sentiment for exempting table wine and beer from Prohibition, but the Anti-Saloon League insisted on total victory. If they had been willing to accept a compromise, the results might have been very different.

Opposition to Prohibition was widespread and, except in the rural heartland of the United States where prohibitionist sentiment had the greatest popular support, the new laws proved to be largely unenforceable. It is estimated that 6 million wine-drinking immigrants from southern Europe alone had arrived in the United States between 1901 and 1915, and in the big cities with their large ethnic populations people saw no reason to give up wine as a part of daily life.[8] Many of them had also made wine in their native countries. In addition to contempt for the law, the effects of Prohibition included new social patterns such as the cocktail party, men and women drinking together in mixed company, and drinking in hotel rooms and the back seats of cars. The entire era will long be remembered for the beginning of widespread police corruption and the colorful and often lurid stories of the speakeasies, bootleggers, and racketeers as well as those who tried to enforce the laws.

Most wineries closed when Prohibition began, and those that remained open marketed sacramental and medicinal wines, tonics, and grape juice. People made alcoholic beverages any way they could and as cheaply as possible. For every moonshiner with an illegal still, there were many others who made their own beer or wine. Section 29 of the Volstead Act, inserted for the benefit of Virginia apple growers, permitted heads of households to make up to 200 gallons a year of nonintoxicating cider or fruit juice, and wine was tacitly considered to come under this provision. About 55 million gallons of wine were produced commercially in 1919. By 1925, legal commercial production dipped to just over 3.5 million gallons, but total wine production by commercial and home winemakers was on its way up to an estimated 150 million gallons by 1930.[9]

The demand for grapes for home winemaking in the East meant a boom period for California grape growers, and the number of acres of vineyards there more than doubled from 300,000 acres in 1919 to over 650,000 in 1928.[10] Thin-skinned wine grape varieties did not ship well, and Alicante Bouschet with its thick skin became a variety of choice. Moreover, its intense color lent itself to amelioration to the point where 600 to 700 gallons of wine could be made from a single ton of grapes.[11] Trainload after trainload of grapes arrived in the East and, in addition to what

Figure 1.2: Renault Winery in Egg Harbor, New Jersey, remained open during Prohibition. This poster promoted several varieties of tonics that were available "to relieve fatigue." In small type was a caution notice: "Do not refrigerate this product or it may turn to wine." When refrigerated, the medicinal elements would sink to the bottom of the bottle, leaving a 22% alcohol wine. Photo by author, 1980.

Figure 1.3: The cobweb-draped bottles in the cellar of Lonz Winery on Middle Bass Island in Ohio serve as a reminder of Prohibition nearly fifty years after it ended. Photo by author.

home winemakers paid for grapes, they spent an average of $220,000,000 a year on winemaking equipment and supplies, from presses and yeast to bottles and corks.[12]

Repeal came at 7:00 p.m. on December 5, 1933, with the ratification of the Twenty-First Amendment to the Constitution. Public opposition to Prohibition had been steadily mounting. Perhaps more important, from a political point of view, the onset of the Great Depression created a need for additional tax revenues, and legal alcoholic beverages could be taxed.

The text of the Twenty-First Amendment is short and, with the exception of a ratification clause, reads as follows:

> The eighteenth article of amendment to the Constitution of the United States is hereby repealed. The transportation or importation into any State, Territory or possession of the United States for delivery or use therein of intoxicating liquors, in violation of the laws thereof, is hereby prohibited.

What the Twenty-First Amendment did was to give each state the right to pass its own laws to control alcoholic beverages in any way it saw fit. The term "intoxicating

Figure 1.4: Prohibition became less and less popular as time went by and many different pins advocating Repeal were produced. Photo by John P. Herr.

liquors" was subject to different interpretations and different laws. From the beginning, largely due to effective lobbying by beer interests, a basic distinction was made between beer and spirits in many states. While hard liquor tended to remain tightly controlled, beer was made more readily available with fewer restrictions on sales and delivery. Wine had fewer adherents in those days and most states, with the notable exception of California, simply kept wine in the classification of an intoxicating liquor.[13]

Some states became monopoly states; some states remained dry until long after the end of World War II; other states adopted local option laws that have permitted some political subdivisions to remain dry to this day. With the Twenty-First Amendment being the only national law governing the control of alcoholic beverages, it is easy to see how today's jumble of individual state laws came into existence. When the federal government decided in 1986 that there should be a nationwide minimum drinking age of twenty-one, the presence of the Twenty-First Amendment made the government choose to enforce compliance by the blackmailing technique of threatening to withhold highway funds from any state that chose not to raise the minimum drinking age.

Commercial wine production resumed slowly in the United States after Repeal. In California where there was a favorable legislative climate toward wine, there was a rush to open wineries. But, after years of disuse, wineries had to be refurbished. There was a shortage of premium wine grapes, trained winemakers, and sound cooperage which, combined with the desire to market quickly, led to low quality wines being placed in the hands of consumers, who found them unpalatable.[14] As Philip Wagner put it, writing in *The American Mercury* in March 1933, "Prohibition proved merely to be a ban on *good* wines."[15]

Interest in wine elsewhere was low. Restaurants could not sell wine during Prohibition and, with the exception of home winemakers who continued to drink their own wines, the use of wine as an accompaniment to food had steadily declined. Without pressure on state legislatures to pass laws favorable for wine, it remained as tightly controlled as spirits. In later years, people who became interested in starting wineries would have the additional handicap of needing to seek changes in the law before they could proceed. In the eastern United States, then, the wine industry would have to start over again.

Prohibition in Canada

In Canada, as in the United States, the temperance movement got started in the early nineteenth century as a popular movement against the hard drinking of spirits and beer.[16] The success of the WCTU after it was founded in the United States in 1874 led to the establishment of the World WCTU in 1883. Just as the United States had its Anti-Saloon League, Canada had its Dominion Alliance, which by 1887 was considering the formation of a new political party.

The Canada Temperance Act of 1878, also known as the Scott Act, permitted any province to hold a plebiscite to decide whether liquor sales should end, and Prince Edward Island was the first to adopt provincial prohibition in 1907.[17] Aided by patriotic wartime sentiment, other provinces followed—Alberta, Manitoba, Nova Scotia, Saskatchewan, and Ontario in 1916; British Columbia, New Brunswick, Newfoundland, and the Yukon Territory in 1917; and a very reluctant Québec with its French and Roman Catholic heritage in 1918.

Encouraged by their victories in the provinces, prohibitionist forces continued to use World War I to further their cause. National prohibition was adopted on March 11, 1918, and remained in force until the end of 1919. This legislation prohibited the manufacture of intoxicating beverages, the importation of them into Canada, and the transportation of them into any part of Canada where their sale would be illegal.

Under the terms of the Canada Temperance Act of 1878, provincial prohibition was limited to banning the sale of intoxicating beverages. Thus, when national prohibition ended on December 31, 1919, the manufacture, importation, and transportation of intoxicating beverages again became legal even though control of sales remained with the provinces. Québec, which was least in favor of prohibition, voted by a nine-to-one margin to end it immediately and bring back the sale of light beer, cider, and wine.[18]

In Ontario the provincial government enacted the Ontario Temperance Act, which went into effect on September 15, 1916, and ended the sale of intoxicating beverages in bars, clubs, and stores. The grape growers in Ontario, however, had enough political influence to secure an exemption for native wine, and Ontario wine became the only legal alcoholic beverage that could be sold in the province. At the end of the war, with national prohibition about to be repealed, a referendum was held on October 20, 1919, in which voters overwhelmingly rejected the repeal of the Ontario Temperance Act. When the federal ban on manufacture, importation, and transportation ended, Ontario residents could import whisky and beer freely, and they did, mainly from Québec. When national prohibition was repealed, however, a law was passed permitting provinces to hold an election to prevent importation as well as sales. In Ontario the election was held on April 18, 1921, and as of July 19, 1921, it became illegal to import liquor and beer, and it became illegal to transport intoxicating beverages without a license to do so.

Wine remained the only legal alcoholic beverage in Ontario, but sales were restricted in various ways. For a time, wine could only be purchased at a winery in minimum quantities of a five-gallon keg or a case with no fewer than twelve bottles. Medical patients who needed treatment with higher concentrations of alcohol could obtain prescriptions for invalid tonics made from Ontario wines, which had been fortified to well over 30 percent alcohol. Doctors generally wrote prescriptions for twenty-ounce amounts, and in 1924 Ontario's 4,000 doctors issued 739,855 prescriptions for tonic wines.[19]

The consumption of native wine in all of Canada was 221,985 gallons in 1920–21, and ten years later Ontarians alone drank 2,208,807 gallons.[20] With Prohibition underway in the United States, there was an additional market for Ontario wines, and wine production in Canada went from less than 500,000 gallons in 1921 to more than 6 million gallons by 1929.[21] Many ingenious ways were found to export wine into the United States. Some boats on the Great Lakes carried papers showing that their cargo was destined for St. Pierre and Miquelon, or for Cuba, and a diligent boat captain could make as many as four trips a day. Ships going through the locks of the old Welland Canal could be surreptitiously loaded with quite a few casks of wine while tied up in a lock.[22] The demand in the United States was great enough that "anyone who could get a carload of liquor across the border could earn $75,000."[23]

From 1919 to 1925, the number of wineries in Ontario more than doubled, from twenty to fifty-one.[24] They bought out the entire grape crop in Ontario and half again as much from the United States.[25] The new wineries operated from converted barns, basements, garages—any place that someone who wanted to make wine could find. Wine quality was ignored in the rush to get product on the market. It was common for 600 gallons to be produced from a ton of grapes, and there was no limit on the amount of water or sugar that could be added. Sometimes so much water was added that colorants such as coal tar dyes and even formaldehyde were used to make the water look like wine.[26]

When provincial prohibition in Ontario ended in June 1927, what was known as "Operation Cleanup" began. An insight into the dimensions of the problem can be seen in the report of the Ontario Wine Standards Committee, established in November 1933:

> The most serious and far reaching effects following the granting of new winery licenses arose from the lack of exercising sufficient care to ensure that the new licensees possessed the proper plant and technical experience, or the finances to procure these, which are so necessary for the successful production of wine. While some of the permits fell into satisfactory hands, a number of them came into possession of men who should never have been permitted under a government license to sell to the public the product of their manufacture. Provided with improper and unsanitary quarters, inadequate equipment, and also lacking in the fundamental knowledge of fermentation or other phases of winemaking, it was only to be expected that these so-called wine makers would produce wines of poor quality.[27]

The Ontario Liquor Control Act ending provincial prohibition provided for a new Liquor Control Board of Ontario (LCBO), sworn in on April 6, 1927.[28] One stated purpose was to control the quality and sale of beer, wine, and liquor in the province. Winery sanitation was an immediate priority and the cooperation of the Department of Health was enlisted. Within three years, half of Ontario's wineries went out of business because they could not meet the requirement of having volatile acids of less than 0.25 percent.[29] The larger wineries were encouraged to take over marginal operations by being given the right to operate an additional retail store for each winery taken over.

With the formation of the Ontario Wine Standards Committee, the long-term process of improving Ontario wines began, an undertaking that was to continue for many years. Among other things, the committee recommended that no new winery licenses be issued. The prohibitionary experience from 1916 to 1927 left lasting memories. It would be decades before a new winery was licensed in Ontario. The legacy of huge quantities of bad wine and wineries not fit to be open led to a preoccupation with wine quality and standards that would eventually result in the premium Vintners Quality Alliance, which established wine standards of the 1990s.

Post-Prohibition in the United States

With the end of Prohibition, wineries in both the United States and Canada resumed making the same kind of sherries, ports, champagnes, sparkling wines, and red and white still wines that they had made before Prohibition. There were good reasons for doing so: there was a market for these wines, the grapes were readily available, and there were often commitments to growers that had to be honored. Some of the wineries in the United States that had stayed open during Prohibition making a variety of products from fresh grape juice to sacramental and medicinal wines returned to making the wines they had made before. Many wineries opened or reopened soon after Repeal, and for the most part, they were content to do things the traditional way.

The number of licensed wineries in Ontario was in the process of declining from fifty-one during Prohibition to nineteen in 1942 to a low of eight in 1970. As might be expected, Operation Cleanup resulted in an improvement of wine quality, as government regulations and a rigid inspection system led to the modernization of equipment and the development of winemaking standards and quality controls by individual wineries.

Some light wine was made in Ontario, but the market was for higher alcohol wines.[30] Edwin R. Haynes, winemaker at Château-Gai Wines in the 1940s, recalled that in those days all of the wineries fermented to high alcohols: "And when I say high alcohols, I'm saying 18–19 per cent alcohol.... If your fermentation didn't get above 16, you started it over again and got it up to 18."[31] Haynes went on to say that the highest verified alcohol by natural fermentation was 23½ percent by Gerry Kavanaugh at Turner's Winery in Toronto.

At the beginning of 1934, Ulysses Prentiss Hedrick, horticulturist at the New York State Agricultural Experiment Station in Geneva, reviewed the best grapes for making wine in eastern America in three articles that appeared in the *California Grape Grower*.[32] In general, the native grapes of choice for making fine white wines could all be said to be "fresh, light, clean, and have distinctive flavors and bouquets, similar and as good as German white wines." Catawba, Delaware, Iona, and Diana were particularly to be recommended. Dutchess was considered the best blender with Delaware and Catawba, though not very productive in the vineyard.

The chief varieties for making base wines for champagne were Catawba and Delaware; and, for blending with these, Iona, Diana, Elvira, Isabella, and Dutchess. Sparkling wines of the champagne type were, to Hedrick, what eastern wineries did best. Before Prohibition the Keuka Lake wineries annually produced 7,450,000 bottles of champagne, and more than three-quarters of the sparkling wines in the United States were produced in the East.

Hedrick was less enthusiastic about the red varieties. The best, though it needed a long growing season, was Norton. When well aged, he said, Norton could become a really great American red wine. Clinton, Eumelan, and Clevener were listed next. Ives was at its best when blended with Clinton or, even better, with both Clinton and Norton.

In 1936 a review of New York State dry wines by Harry E. Goresline of the United States Department of Agriculture, and Richard Wellington of the New York State Agricultural Experiment Station, appeared in *Wines and Vines*.[33] They identified the dry white wines of New York State as "mostly of the Sauterne, Riesling and Rhine wine types. These are produced by blending the wines of two or more varieties of grapes in such a way as to develop certain flavor characteristics." Three of the best grape varieties for making white wines were Catawba, Delaware, and Iona. Of the older white grapes, Dutchess "stands supreme for its wine making qualities."

The wine types for red wines were for the most part Claret, Burgundy, and Port. Clinton and Ives were described as the mainstay red grape varieties, though the authors stated that Norton had been grown successfully in New York State and that Isabella and Eumelan also made excellent wines.

For champagne making, and the authors considered the climatic and soil conditions of Keuka Lake to be practically ideal, the base wines were Catawba for delicacy and freshness, Delaware for body, and Elvira for neutral character. Varying quantities of Dutchess, Isabella, Iona, and Eumelan were then added to these.

As a summary of sorts, Goresline and Wellington noted that the red wines produced from native American grapes "possess qualities which are different from wines produced in warmer portions of the United States. The natural tartness and tannin content possessed by these grapes give the eastern wines the live and zestful flavor for which they are noted." The white wines "have considerable body, which seems to increase with age, and have a sprightly and 'live' flavor. They are light in color, capable of taking an excellent polish and have sound keeping qualities."

Hedrick offered a broader view:

> Out of the several species of native grapes found in eastern America, perhaps there are 500 or more cultivated varieties. There is no question but that these grapes offer a much wider range of distinct characters for wines than the thousand or more varieties of the Old World grapes. As yet, however, so few of them have been tried in wine making, and so few of the wine makers have experience and skill to make good wines, that no one knows what the possibilities of many native grapes are for winemaking. Much more is known about white wines and champagnes than of red wines from this native stock, it having been long ago demonstrated that a score or more of the native grapes make splendid champagnes and very good white wines.[34]

In both sets of articles, Hedrick, and Goresline and Wellington, were quick to point out that breeding experiments at the New York State Agricultural Experiment Station and elsewhere were developing promising grape varieties for winemaking in the future. At Geneva alone, according to Hedrick, there were between forty and fifty seedlings most promising for red wines and twice as many more for white wines.

On June 13, 1939, a New England dinner and tasting of eastern American wines was given for members of the Wine and Food Society of San Francisco at the St. Francis Hotel.[35] Accompanying such typical New England dishes as Finnan Haddie Canapés, Cape Cod Clam Chowder, Boiled Salmon with Lobster Hollandaise, Ostable Oyster Pie, Pan Broiled Turkey Wonolancet, Braised Dandelion, Parsnips Sauté, and Baked Indian Pudding were the following eastern wines:

Champagnes

Cook's Imperial American Champagne (American Wine Co., St. Louis, Missouri)
Crystal White Star Special Dry Champagne (M. Hommel Wine Co., Sandusky, Ohio)
Gold Seal Champagne (Urbana Wine Co., Hammondsport, New York)
Isle de Fleurs Champagne, Extra Dry (George F. Lonz, Middle Bass Isle, Ohio)
Great Western Special Reserve (Pleasant Valley Wine Co., Rheims, New York)

White Wines

Lake Erie Island Delaware Wine (George F. Lonz, Middle Bass Isle, Ohio)
Lake Erie Island Catawba Wine (George F. Lonz, Middle Bass Isle, Ohio)
Rhine Wine American (La Salle Wines and Champagnes, Farmington, Michigan)
Widmer's Hillside New York State Chablis (Widmer's Wine Cellars, Inc., Naples, New York)
Paul Garrett's Dry White Wine (Garrett & Co., Inc., Brooklyn, New York)

Meier's Ohio Sauterne (Meier's Wine Cellars, Inc., Silverton, Cincinnati, Ohio)
Taylor's New York State Sweet Catawba (The Taylor Wine Co., Hammondsport, New York)

Red Wines

Widmerheimer, Vintage 1934 (Widmer's Wine Cellars, Naples, New York)
Lake Erie Island Claret (George F. Lonz, Middle Bass Isle, Ohio)
Widmer's Hillside New York State Claret (Widmer's Wine Cellars, Naples, New York)
Paul Garrett's Dry Red Wine (Garrett & Co., Inc., Brooklyn, New York)
Meier's Ohio Burgundy (Meier's Wine Cellars, Inc., Silverton, Cincinnati, Ohio)

Port Wine

Dewey's Superior American Port (H. T. Dewey & Sons Co., Egg Harbor, New Jersey)

The various wine producers mentioned the names of the grape varieties used in their wines: Delaware, Catawba, Niagara, Elvira, Ives, Norton, Clinton, Clevener, Diogenes, Diana, Iona, Dutchess, and Eumelan. What did the members think of these wines? "To most of those present, the wines were a revelation because they were new to them and different in bouquet and flavor from those made in California and the European wine countries. These American wines are distinctly in a class by themselves and certainly proved interesting and delightful. They were presented under the most favorable conditions with a series of excellent dishes that brought out their every good point."

Both in terms of the varieties of grapes being used and the types of wines being made, the wineries in the East were moving ahead along the path established before Prohibition. The wines of the 1930s were popular and were to remain so for many years. Nevertheless, changes were coming, and they would involve both new grape varieties and new styles of wine. Three centuries of failure were about to end.

The search to find a way to make dry European-style table wines in the East in the 1930s began in three separate places. In Ontario it started in 1933 with the purchase of T. G. Bright & Company in Niagara Falls by Harry Hatch, a businessman who had the money and vision to succeed. A year later, in 1934, Charles Fournier left his native France to take the position of winemaker at Gold Seal Vineyards—then the Urbana Wine Company—in Hammondsport, New York. To the south, in Riderwood, Maryland, newspaperman Philip Wagner became increasingly interested in growing grapes and making dry table wines. Each started out unaware of the existence of the others; however, by the end of the decade they were poised for the breakthroughs that would come in the 1940s.[36] (See appendix C.)

Post-Prohibition in Canada

When Prohibition ended in Ontario in 1927, there was a sharp decrease in the demand for Ontario wines. Huge inventories of surplus wine built up in the wineries, and the coming of the Great Depression in the early 1930s compounded the problem of what to do with it. Much of the wine made by the newer wineries that had sprung up during Prohibition had turned to vinegar, and even in the more quality-conscious wineries the remaining stocks of wine were rapidly becoming oxidized and undrinkable.

In 1933, Canada's largest winery changed hands. T. G. Bright & Company, Ltd., in Niagara Falls had been founded in 1874 by a pair of lumber merchants, Thomas G. Bright and Francis A. Shirriff.[37] By the time of Prohibition it had grown to the point where its 4 million-gallon capacity made it the largest winery in the British Empire and one of the largest in the world. The buyer was Harry C. Hatch, who in 1926 had acquired Hiram Walker & Sons, a distillery that also represented some of the top wine shippers of the day in Europe.[38] Canadian wineries were making ports and sherries almost exclusively, but Hatch felt that there must be some way to develop a dry table wine industry. At stake was Brights competitive role in the markets of the British Empire.

Hatch lost no time beginning a rebuilding program. First, he disposed of the surplus wine that could no longer be sold as wine. He also began taking advantage of the LCBO's incentive to add retail outlets by purchasing smaller substandard wineries, closing them, and retaining the rights to the stores. In all, Brights acquired 13 additional outlets and a clear sales advantage in the days before the modern LCBO system of stores was set up.

Most important, Hatch began hiring top level employees with the technical knowledge to bring back professionalism to Brights. One of the first people hired was Dr. John Ravenscroft Eoff, a California-trained food scientist who had served with the United States Food and Drug Administration. His contributions to the wine program at Brights were substantial until he died in 1940, but he was soon overshadowed by the colorful and dominant personality of the person hired to be his assistant, Adhemar de Chaunac.

Adhemar de Chaunac has been described as a temperamental prima donna whose lack of tact and diplomacy combined with a supreme confidence in his own abilities to make him a person who could not—and would not—be ignored. Edwin Haynes, an Ontario winemaker who knew de Chaunac well, has said that while the former was strongly opinionated and said what he believed in no uncertain terms, he was often justified in his opinions. Conversely, he could be very nice, easy to get along with, and willing to help anyone. On ladies' night at the local chemists' society he insisted on taking care of the wine punch, and when he came to dinner at the Haynes' he invariably tossed the salad.[39]

Born in 1896 in southwestern France, de Chaunac came to Canada in 1907.[40] He returned to France in 1915 to serve in the French army during World War I. Early

Figure 1.5: Eleven years after Adhemar de Chaunac retired from Brights Wines in 1961, the Canadian Wine Institute paid tribute to his contributions to the industry by getting approval to name the French hybrid grapevine Seibel 9549 in his honor. A testimonial dinner was held for him at the Niagara Falls Club where he was presented with the award. In this photo, gathered around the newly named De Chaunac grapevine, are (*from left to right*) Philip Wagner, Adhemar de Chaunac, Jocelyn Wagner, Charles Fournier, and Richard Wellington. Photo by Richard N. Lein; Wagner Collection.

in 1918, he was captured by the Germans, but by October he had managed to escape and return to France. He returned permanently to Canada in 1919, completed his education as a chemist, and was employed in the dairy and yeast industries before being hired as chief chemist, or winemaker, at Brights in 1933.[41] As a team, de Chaunac and Eoff were able to add the professionalism that Hatch had envisioned and position Brights for a leadership role during the transition period leading to today's Ontario wine industry. De Chaunac was appointed director of research at Brights in 1944 and held that position until his retirement in 1961.

From the beginning of his tenure at Brights, de Chaunac had told Harry Hatch that an expenditure of $600,000 and twenty years in time would result in good table wines being produced at Brights. To underscore this point, de Chaunac made small experimental batches of dry table wine from Delaware and Catawba, two varieties that he felt lacked the heavy foxiness of other varieties. The results were so impressive that Harry Hatch gave permission to start production of the company's first table wines.

The first commercial release of a table wine in Ontario since the end of Prohibition was a 100 percent Agawam marketed in 1939 under the Manor St. Davids label.

When Harry Hatch bought Brights in 1933, he needed an accountant, and Meredith Francis Jones, who had been the accountant for the car manufacturer Willys-Overland, was hired to fill the position. Jones was attracted to Hatch's reorganization plan and soon became Hatch's right-hand man. After Hatch's death on May 8, 1946, Jones became the chief architect of the reorganization program, supervising the entire vineyard and winemaking operations at Brights. He moved rapidly from vice president to senior vice president and, from 1959 to 1963, president.[42]

Another early decision made by Hatch was to institute a research program that would lead to the production of grapes for dry table wines. Brights had always bought all of its grapes up to that time, and the grapes available on the Niagara Peninsula were primarily Agawam, Elvira, Niagara, and Concord, the varieties used for making ports, sherries, and sweeter wines. There were a few old plantings of Delaware and Catawba in Ontario, but they were in very short supply.

In 1934, Brights began its vineyard program with the purchase of 1,400 acres. Included in this acreage were 200 acres of Concord, Niagara, and some Worden belonging to Jacob Hostetter, and "Jake" was hired as vineyard manager. De Chaunac chose the grape varieties planted in 1934—Delaware and Catawba because they seemed to lack the foxiness of other varieties, and Elvira and Agawam primarily because Elvira could be treated by concentrating it to remove much of the foxiness. Dutchess, another variety with promise as a dry table wine, was added a little later.

The only French hybrid planted in Canada prior to World War II was Seibel 1000, or Rosette, which had arrived at Geneva in 1927 and planted at Brights in 1938. De Chaunac made an experimental batch of red wine from Rosette in the late 1930s and commented that this was the only variety he had tried that made an acceptable red wine.

Progress was slow in the vineyard at first. About 1939 Jacob Hostetter began grafting Delaware and Catawba on Clinton rootstocks to increase production after noticing that the vines were not as vigorous as he would have liked because of the heavy soils in the area. This was the first use of grafting in Ontario.

Watching what was happening literally in his own backyard was Jacob Hostetter's son George, who was twelve when Brights acquired his father's vineyard. George W. B. Hostetter—the W. B. stands for an ancestor, William Bligh, late of the H.M.S. Bounty—received his early education in vineyard management from his father. He recalls being sent out in the late 1930s to buy twenty-five tons of Delaware and, after driving all over the Niagara Peninsula, returning with a total of barely fifteen tons.

George Hostetter began his career at Brights on July 1, 1940, as an assistant to de Chaunac and worked full time in the propagation of grapes while attending college at the University of Toronto. He graduated in 1944 with a B.S. in agricultural science and in 1946 was named director of viticultural research, reporting to M. F. Jones.

Following de Chaunac's retirement in 1961, he was promoted to director of research and held that position until his own retirement on June 30, 1986.

Charles Fournier and Gold Seal

Charles Fournier was born into a cultured winemaking family in Reims, France, on June 15, 1902.[43] Even before he was born it was decided by his father and uncle that he would be named Charles after his uncle and would succeed him as winemaker at the champagne house of Veuve Clicquot Ponsardin. Accordingly, from the time he was a little boy, he worked in the vineyards and cellars. He received a degree in chemistry from the University of Paris, attended wine schools in France and Switzerland, and learned English and marketing in England. In 1926, he became chief winemaker at Veuve Clicquot, and in 1930 he was promoted to production manager.

In 1933, he was asked by Louis Oller, the proprietor of a large Spanish cork firm, to help look for a winemaker who would come to Hammondsport, New York, to rebuild Gold Seal Vineyards, then called the Urbana Wine Company. While visiting France in the fall of 1933, Edwin S. Underhill, Jr., Gold Seal's president, offered Fournier the job of winemaker and production manager. Fournier decided to take the job himself, not because of the challenge of making wine in the East, but because of the tragic death of his first wife who had fallen down a flight of stairs.[44]

Fournier began working at Gold Seal in 1934, and in later years he often told of his first impressions on arriving in the United States: "I had no idea of the climate and the grapes I would have to work with. It was a sultry 100° in the shade when I arrived in New York City. Then I tasted Concord, Catawba, Elvira and Isabella wines which, to say the least, gave me a shock. The winter that followed was the third shock! The temperature reached -14° Fahrenheit that winter, and another jolt came the following summer when 11 inches of rain fell in one night and it took two weeks to reopen the road from Gold Seal to Hammondsport."[45]

When he arrived at Gold Seal, Fournier was immediately struck by the distinctive champagne flavor certain grapes in the East developed in the most favorable locations. "The Finger Lakes region of New York, I found, was a unique upland where the traditional champagne flavor could be approached—not by the same soil and the same grapes—but by a combination of soil and grapes producing a similar bouquet through the champagne method and proper aging."[46] Catawba, in particular, acquired a taste quite similar to the French champagne flavor when made sparkling and aged in the bottle on the sediment. Delaware and Dutchess were two other varieties that worked well with Catawba.

One of Fournier's first projects at Gold Seal involved the promulgation of federal regulations to legalize use of the word "champagne" in the United States.[47] The new regulations took effect in 1934, stating that an American champagne had to be "a type of sparkling light wine which derives its effervescence solely from the secondary fermentation of the wine within glass containers of not greater than one gallon capacity, and which possesses the taste, aroma, and other characteristics attributed to champagne as made in the Champagne district of France."

To Fournier, using the name "champagne" in the United States was in no way intended as a reflection on French Champagne. In 1970 he wrote, "As a winemaker born in France but adopted by America I derive great satisfaction first, in having been a part of the success of the New York State champagne industry, and second, in having devoted my life to making sparkling wines worthy of the great French name *champagne*. I will continue to fight to protect it from those who would use it on the label of inferior foaming wine."[48]

Observing that Americans liked their champagnes somewhat fragrant and not too acidic, he decided to produce a champagne as close as possible to French champagne. He reasoned that such a champagne would appeal to those who bought French champagne either from snobbism or out of preference. The result was Charles Fournier Champagne made by blending such grape varieties as Catawba, Delaware, Dutchess, Elvira, Iona, and Isabella.[49]

The Charles Fournier Champagne, as Fournier later noted laconically, was "well-received." In 1950, the wine competition at the California State Fair in Sacramento was opened to wines from outside California for the first time since Prohibition. There were five medal winners in the "Bottle Fermented Champagne" class. Gold Seal won a gold medal for its Charles Fournier Brut and a bronze for its Gold Seal Brut. Brights in Ontario won a bronze for its 1947 President Canadian made by Adhemar de Chaunac. In the "Wine Awards" booklet issued by the State Fair the "Comment" appearing under the class read: "Best class of Champagnes entered at recent State Fairs. The opening of the competition to non-Californian wines has added greatly to the interest of this class." The success of out-of-state wines—the only other gold in the Bottle Fermented Champagne class had gone to B. Seppelt in South Australia—was apparently not to the liking of the Californians, for in 1951 the competition at the State Fair was once again closed to wineries outside California. No gold medals, one silver, and no bronzes were awarded in the Bottle Fermented Champagne class, and the "Comment" printed in the 1951 "Wine Awards" booklet was brief: "As a whole this group of wines was not up to expectations."[50]

Fournier also made sparkling burgundies using Ives, Clinton, Eumelan, and some Concords. A major triumph came with the development of Catawba Pink, a fruity rosé that appealed to the sweet preferences of many wine drinkers, and this wine, along with the champagnes and the sparkling wines paid the bills at Gold Seal.

CHAPTER TWO

❧

PHILIP WAGNER AND THE ARRIVAL OF THE FRENCH HYBRIDS

THE THIRD PLACE WHERE THE SEARCH BEGAN FOR WAYS TO MAKE EUROPEAN-STYLE dry table wines was Riderwood, Maryland, where Philip Wagner settled in 1931. More than any other individual in the 1930s and 1940s, he was responsible for the establishment of the modern eastern wine industry.

Wagner and the Early Years

Philip Marshall Wagner was born in New Haven, Connecticut, on February 18, 1904.[1] He moved to Ann Arbor, Michigan, that fall when his father, Charles P. Wagner, began a forty-three-year career as a professor in the Romance languages department at the University of Michigan. Wagner attended the University of Michigan, and when he graduated in 1925 he expected to go to work for the *Philadelphia North American* newspaper, where he had worked summers. However, the newspaper folded in May of that year, and Wagner started to work in the publicity department at General Electric Company in Schenectady, New York, where he was assigned internal writing tasks and external promotions. As he wrote later, here he spent "five of the most valuable years of my life in the world where the tangible material of our civilization is actually produced. The average newspaperman has little or no experience of that world. It isn't newsworthy except when something 'big' goes wrong."[2]

While at General Electric he wrote freelance articles for *Harper's,* the *Atlantic Monthly,* the *New Republic,* and other magazines that brought his writing to the attention of the editors at the Baltimore Sunpapers.[3] In 1930, he moved to Baltimore with his first wife, Helen Crocker, and their two young children to take the position of editorial writer at the *Evening Sun.* His newspaper career in Baltimore lasted thirty-four years. In 1936–37, he was assigned to the London bureau of the *Sun.* After his return he succeeded H. L. Mencken as editor of the editorial page of the *Evening Sun* from 1938 to 1943, and as editor of the editorial page of the *Sun* from 1943 to 1964.[4]

The editor of the *Evening Sun,* James Hamilton Owens, was interested in wine; Wagner rarely drank wine in Schenectady and did not become interested in wine until he moved to Baltimore and became a regular consumer. At that time Prohibition was still the law of the land and in order to have a source of wine one had to make it. Wagner and Owens began making wine together in the fall of 1931. Wagner would go down to the Baltimore and Ohio Railroad station where there was a long line of refrigerated cars with grapes from California. The grapes were sold directly out of the cars, mainly to Italians. It was also possible to buy grapes from New Jersey.

In 1932, Wagner described their faltering start:

> Our first mistake was last fall when we failed to realize the importance of getting started early. Beginning the second week in October I found in the markets: *white,* Thompson Seedless, which was selling too high ($2.75); Muscat, and Malaga. *Red,* Alicante, and Zinfandel, and of course Concord. We were a little disconcerted by the fact that none of these was mentioned anywhere in the Bible. Going blind, I got Alicante, 25 boxes @ $1.25.
>
> Our second mistake was to press them white-wine fashion. They yielded about 30 gals. of must. The weather was very cold, with no furnace heat, and the fermentation was very slow to begin. Mold developed on the surface to a thickness of half an inch. This appeared to sink as fermentation proceeded. First fermentation lasted several weeks. At the first racking the new wine had a musty smell, and was very raw and acid-tasting. Second racking took place at the end of February. Total 25 gal. We bottled 5 gal.; sound but musty-smelling. Wagners promptly drank their share; it deposited somewhat in the bottle.[5]

Wagner rented a 3.7-acre property in Riderwood, Maryland, which he subsequently bought in 1933. There were vines on the property, as he wrote in the spring of 1933:

> *The old vines.* First started on them in spring of 1932. I had not realized that there were any vines on the place; most of the posts and all of the wires were down; canes were 18 and 20 feet long, creeping off into the orchard. About 20 vines, assorted varieties. Those identified: Concord, Moore's Early, 1 Catawba, and about 4 of a very early-ripening, very

delicious sweet red variety with small fruit bunches and tending to early-browning leaf. Old vines the previous season had yielded little, partly because of their bad condition, partly because I did not spray.[6]

Owens and Wagner bought one hundred vines in the spring of 1933—fifty Bacchus, twenty-five Delaware, and twenty-five Diamond—and divided them. This was the start of his vineyard operation.

Wagner read everything about winemaking and grape growing that he could find, probably more in French than in English, and talked with anyone who might be able to help him. By May of 1933, he had finished writing his first book, *American Wines and How to Make Them,* which at that time became the only book in English on winemaking. Reading the book today, it is clear that it was a summation of everything he had learned. It is likely that Wagner wrote the book at least in part as a way of organizing his own thinking. Throughout his life he actively sought out the latest information on grape growing, grape varieties, and winemaking from libraries, research stations, scientists, and anyone who had more experience than himself. From 1932 on, he kept detailed records of how he made all his wines.

The favorable reviews of his book and its mention in 1934 in *The Complete Wine Book* by Frank Schoonmaker and Tom Marvel helped establish his wine credentials and opened doors.[7] Tom Marvel, a journalist with the Paris edition of the *New York Herald Tribune* when he met Schoonmaker by chance, visited Wagner and tasted his Clinton on May 21, 1934.[8] By 1935 Wagner had met Schoonmaker, a wine merchant as well as a writer, who was later to play an important role in marketing Wagner's wines.[9] André L. Simon, who had founded the Wine & Food Society (now the International Wine & Food Society) in England in 1934, and the first branch of the Society in Boston in December 1934, showed up with his press agent for dinner at the Wagners on May 12, 1935.[10] This meeting may have paid off, for on October 24, 1935, the Wine and Food Society of New York held a tasting of thirty-seven wines from California and the East at the Savoy Plaza Hotel, and Wagner was asked to write an introduction to the catalog of wines to be tasted that would be given out to each person attending. Wagner was later criticized for spending the first four paragraphs of the introduction on the poor quality of California wines sent East immediately after Repeal.[11]

Following the publication of his book, Wagner began to experiment with an increasingly broad selection of grape varieties. He discovered early that he liked the wine made from Delaware and that Cynthiana, Norton, and Clinton would not meet his standards. He made several early attempts to grow the vinifera, but with limited success. On April 7, 1934, grafted Carignane, Sirah, and Franken Riesling vines arrived from La Fata in California; on February 14, Cabernet Sauvignon, Merlot, Petite Verdot, and Chardonnay came from Frederic T. Bioletti, a California Experiment Station viticulturist. Of these vinifera plantings, only Chardonnay survived.

In 1936, Wagner was assigned to England for a year as the London correspondent for the *Sun.* By this time he had found references in his early reading to grapes grown in France known as the *hybrides producteurs directes* (HPD), or "hybrid direct producers." This is what the French hybrids were called in those days because they could be grown on their own roots rather than having to be grafted. While in England, Wagner visited the agricultural station at East Malling, southeast of London in Kent. There he was able to talk to people who were considering the potential value of the French hybrids for the British Empire, and to others who were working with what they called "cold country" vinifera. Although the researchers at East Malling were looking at the French hybrids for disease resistance, Wagner felt that the hybrids might be worth checking for winter hardiness to see if that characteristic might have been transmitted accidentally along with disease resistance. But it was the cold country vinifera that immediately caught his attention and in his next book, *Wine Grapes,* published in 1937, he urged that the cold country vinifera be tried in the East. This book was poorly distributed and soon fell by the wayside, much to Wagner's relief, because he almost immediately regretted writing about the cold country vinifera rather than the hybrids.[12]

Wagner returned to Riderwood in June 1937, and continued his search for grapevines. He looked into Thomas Volney Munson's experimental vineyards in Denison, Texas, and into the Missouri hybrids. Trips to Geneva and Fredonia, New York, put him in contact with Ulysses Prentiss Hedrick, Liberty Hyde Bailey, and, more helpfully, Richard Wellington. During these years and until well after World War II, the New York State Agricultural Experiment Station in Geneva was interested exclusively in Concords and table grapes, not in wine grapes. There was real concern at the Station that they might lose state funding if they were involved in any research having to do with wine. Richard Wellington could not be obviously involved in wine grapes at the Station, which did not prevent him from being interested in them and having his own test plot behind his home.

Wagner said later that on returning from England, "I made one of those typically amateurish discoveries, namely that a good many of the HPD were already here, growing obscurely in collections—not being used, not being studied, just collectors' items."[13] The first three French hybrids that he discovered with grapes on them were in Fredonia, New York, and were simply called Seibel 1XX, 2XX, and 3X. Their nametags were lost when they arrived sometime before 1913 and as a result were assigned temporary numbers. Nothing had been done with them, Wagner learned, because they lacked the flavor desired in a table grape, which was exactly what he was looking for in a wine grape. On a trip to Geneva he discovered a whole row of hybrids that nobody was interested in. Other vines were found in Elmer Snyder's collection in Oakville, California. Cuttings from these vines started arriving in Riderwood in December 1937.

On October 18, 1938, Wagner applied for a special permit to import twenty-five vines of Baco No. 1 from the hybridizer Maurice Baco. The permit was sent to Tom Marvel at Frank Schoonmaker and Company in New York who in turn forwarded the paperwork to the Bordeaux firm of Ed. Kressman & Co. These vines left France on February 16, 1939, arrived in Baltimore on March 31, and were taken to the Bureau of Entomology and Plant Quarantine in Washington, DC, where they were quickly inspected and forwarded to Wagner who planted them on April 2. The thousands of Baco No. 1 vines to be found in the East today can be traced back to this shipment of vines.[14] This was the first shipment of French hybrids to be introduced into American viticulture for wine production. The twenty-five vines themselves cost $1.15, but by the time shipping, customs, and other charges were added up, the total cost was closer to $20.00.[15]

In the spring of 1939 Wagner's first marriage was rapidly coming to an end as a strong romantic attachment developed between himself and Jocelyn Guttmacher, the woman who would become his second wife. Born Jocelyn McDonough in Portsmouth, New Hampshire, on August 14, 1901, she graduated from Vassar College in 1923 and the Smith College School of Social Work in 1925. In 1928, she moved to Baltimore and went to work for the Mental Hygiene Clinic of Maryland. She and her first husband, Dr. Manfred S. Guttmacher, had two sons.[16]

Wagner's first wife had worked with him in both the vineyard and home winemaking, but Jocelyn's enthusiasm for the grape and wine enterprise that Wagner had started equaled his. Her dedication helped form a lifetime partnership. All printed references to Boordy Vineyard, their nursery and winery, were followed by "J. and P. Wagner, Props."

Philip and Jocelyn Wagner were married on September 4, 1940. Two days later they visited the Maryland State Fair in Timonium and while visiting the horticulture section "decided on the spot" to enter a grape exhibit the following year. They did so on September 1, 1941, and were rewarded with a blue ribbon.[17]

On November 6, 1940, Wagner wrote: "The last few days I have been filled with the notion of establishing a wine-grape nursery. A list of not more than 12 highly recommended species [sic], a fairly good mark-up, directions for grape-growing, directions for wine-making, and catalogue of wine-making supplies....Start off with ad and article in House and Garden. Stress luxury angle—have your own chateau, bottled and labeled."[18] Two weeks later he plowed a strip of land 50 feet by 100 feet at the bottom of the meadow to be used as a grape nursery.

The Wagners ordered their first Boordy Vineyard stationery on July 8, 1941, a dollar's worth, printed in red on gray. When the stationery was delivered eight days later, Wagner had made up a list of the forty varieties then being grown (see appendix C) and was in the process of preparing a circular, which in effect was their first grape variety catalog. Wellington had suggested the prices: single vines—75 cents, 10 or more vines—50 cents each, and 50 or more vines—35 cents each. By the following day he had the circular written and the stencils made for mimeographing.

Inquiries from the first fifteen to twenty circulars distributed came in as early as August 1. The first actual order of vines, twenty Rosette, thirty-five Diamond, thirty-five Delaware, and one Baco No. 1, was shipped on December 31, 1941, to a man by the name of H. K. Benson at Stretch Island Winery in Grapeview, Washington.[19] "We are very pleased to have the nursery project seem real, at last," Wagner wrote in his *Daybooks*.[20]

Wagner was often asked where the name "Boordy" came from, but the origin remained a secret throughout his life. The *Staten Island Advance* (June 2, 1971) quoted him as saying, "It is not the ancestral name of the land. It doesn't mean anything. It just came out of the blue. I can't explain it. But it has a curiously authentic sound and it's easy to pronounce." The *Baltimore Sun* (July 1, 1981) reported that the Wagners "would sometimes suggest, tongue firmly in cheek, that the word would logically lie between "boor" and "boorish" in a dictionary, a fact they admitted was neither helpful nor placed their beverage in good company." The *Towson Times* (April 26, 1995) quoted them as saying, "We say that it's one of the fine, old Maryland place names of the future."

At the bottom of the 1941 grape variety catalog list the following note appeared: "Owing to limitations of space, I have been forced to sacrifice a good many varieties in the past, so that this list represents only those now being grown." More promising varieties were constantly coming along, and only one variety from the 1941 list, Baco No. 1, was still included in the Boordy Vineyard catalog in 1988.

How quickly new varieties could be added to his vineyard is illustrated by Wagner's encounter with Dr. Robert T. Dunstan in September 1941, which resulted in virtually doubling the number of varieties planted there. Dunstan was born on June 14, 1901, received his Ph.D. from the University of Wisconsin in 1928, and spent thirty-five years teaching Romance languages at Greensboro College in North Carolina.[21] As an adult he became interested in the muscadines growing wild in the North Carolina mountains. He began to plant different varieties of grapes in Greensboro and started a breeding program with the intent of improving the table grape varieties available in the Southeast, primarily in preventing the berries from splitting.

In 1938 Dunstan received a shipment of thirty French hybrids, including some Seibel and Seyve-Villard selections, and about twenty vinifera varieties from a friend who was a teaching assistant at Duke University. These were planted at Greensboro. A year or two later Dunstan notified various research stations of his acquisition and offered to make vines available to them. Among the people who received notification was Wellington at Geneva, who in the late spring of 1941 informed Wagner of their existence. The latter made arrangements to visit Dunstan when the vines were first fruiting, and in September he visited Dunstan in Greensboro and another grower of French hybrids, Joe R. Brooks, who lived near Asheville.

Dunstan later recalled Wagner's visit: "He came hot-footing to Greensboro. One of the most amusing pictures I remember of that is seeing him waltz up and down the rows of those French hybrid grapes that were new. My God, he was just absolutely beside himself; he was just delirious with joy."[22] For his part, Wagner listed thirty-eight important varieties he had seen in his notebook and added the following comment: "it is nothing less than a miracle that they should have this wonderful collection of wine grapes. Seeing their grapes was a thrilling experience; and their collections constitute a sufficient basis for a genuine viticulture east of the Rockies."[23] As soon as cuttings were available, Dunstan sent them to Wagner, who propagated them and sold them throughout the East from his nursery. Among the thirty-eight varieties were Aurore, Verdelet, Cascade, Roucaneuf, and Villard Noir. Dunstan recalled supplying Wagner with Seyval but this variety does not appear on the list of varieties Wagner looked at. Wagner's first reference to Seyval comes in September 1942, when he found a very promising reference to Seyve-Villard 5–276 in the U.S. Department of Agriculture (USDA) library and then discovered that the New York State Agricultural Experiment Station had that variety on its accession list.[24]

In the fall of 1941, the Wagners made eleven different wines. The winemaking operation was on a home winemaking scale, and less than 100 gallons were made in batches of two to three gallons, the largest being seventeen gallons of Baco No. 1. "It is too early to tell about any of them," he wrote at the time, "but it will be a fascinating winter as we discover them and [get] to know the possibilities of the various grapes."[25]

It was not long before these wines were evaluated. On May 9, 1942, fifteen people including Frank Schoonmaker and Tom Marvel gathered at Boordy Vineyard for a tasting of twenty-three wines, nearly all of them hybrids that had never before been used in the United States for winemaking.[26] These included Munson, New York, and French hybrids. Most of the wines had been made from grapes grown in Riderwood or the ones Wagner had made from grapes brought back from Geneva the previous September. Wagner summarized the outcome of this tasting as follows:

> As a result of this tasting, one thing stands out clearly. If eastern red wines are generally looked down upon by competent judges and the general public (and they are) it is mainly because eastern winemen and grape-growers have failed to explore the possibilities of growing better grapes. Some of the red wines in this [tasting], notably Seibel 6339, Baco, Seibel 1XX, and Seibel 5898 [later named Rougeon], were a revelation of all of us. The grapes from which they were made had ample sugar, low acid, excellent color, and all the other elements necessary [for] a 'balanced' table wine. When grown under proper circumstances, these grapes clearly require no 'adjustment' when made into wine, handle with ease, and yield wines far superior to those red wines made from the ordinary eastern grapes. To those should be added Seibel 1000 [Rosette], which is now being grown in a limited way in New York.[27]

This tasting marked the starting point at which the French hybrids began to be favored over other kinds of grapes in the effort to make dry European-style wines in the East. Very little was known about the French hybrids in the East when this tasting took place. Nothing was known about their stability of color, the ability of different varieties to develop bouquet, or what would happen to the balance of the wines as they aged. This tasting gave Wagner the incentive to concentrate more on the French hybrids in his nursery program. It would not be until another tasting in September 1945 that the wine industry in the East would begin to recognize the potential of the French hybrids and, again, it would be Wagner who would lead the way.

The idea of starting a winery had been considered by the Wagners for some time. With the arrival of more and more vines at Riderwood, Wagner was not only running out of vineyard space but accumulating more grapes than he could use. The start of a commercial nursery operation also meant a need for more wood to supply additional cuttings, and a search began for someone who might be willing to plant a vineyard for his use. On June 22, 1941, the Wagners went to look at land near Reisterstown owned by Fenwick Keyser. Two acres of land were suitable for grape growing, and negotiations were started to plant one of them initially. When 477 vines were planted on March 25, 1942, Wagner saw it as the first actual step being taken toward their commercial winemaking enterprise. Estimating that the first full vintage would be two and one-half to three tons in 1944, he wrote: "The problem now is to get going on the cellar, so as to be prepared for the vintage."[28]

On October 11, 1942, under the heading "Digging Wine Cellar," Wagner wrote:

> We have decided that it would be much more fun to try to build it ourselves. At least, I think I should be able to excavate, make the footings, lay the walls (concrete block, 8 x 8 x 16), and grade for pouring the floor. Dimensions, about 14 x 28 x 8 feet. Maybe even put on the joists, fill with rock wool, put in ceiling, and put on false roof. Cost of materials will be the determining factor. I don't know, maybe I bite off too much. I never seem to get anywhere.[29]

The first task was to dismantle the woodpile where the cellar would be located. Wagner began digging on November 8, "making a noticeable impression."[30] By November 12, he decided to expand the winery to 16 feet by 28 feet. Digging continued shovelful by shovelful through the winter and spring. The decision was made on August 1, 1943, to increase the size of the building to 21 feet by 32 feet, and the excavation work was completed on August 26. Concrete block work followed, and on September 7 the front wall was practically finished including putting the lintel over the window. The next day, "right after lunch, [Jocelyn] and I carved our 'cornerstone' in the lintel over the window, which was not yet hard, using a 16d nail to carve with. The inscription: 'Boordy Winery built by Jocelyn & Philip Wagner, 7 Sept. 1943.'"[31]

Again, doing most of the work themselves, the Wagners moved toward their 1944 harvest season deadline. The last of the roofing was laid on November 27, 1943;

Figure 2.1: This photo of Philip Wagner was probably taken around 1945 in the cellar of his winery, Boordy Vineyard. Wagner Collection.

July 1944, marked the end of the stuccowork and the start of clean up and painting; and on August 21 Wagner could record that everything was finished to make wine. On August 23, Keyser arrived with twelve bushels of Baco weighing 465 pounds, and at 7:00 p.m. the crusher was turned on to start the 1944 vintage in the new winery: "The winery looked cute as the devil, was all scrubbed and then sulfured this p.m. by [Jocelyn]. This actually starts us off with Boordy—our first contract grapes—and we are getting a huge bang out of it."[32] The Baco Noir would become the first commercial French hybrid wine in the East.

The Wagners received federal approval for a bonded winery on August 29, 1945. Also on that day Wagner received the first copy of his new book, *A Wine-Grower's Guide,* published by Alfred A. Knopf. This book was primarily concerned with grape growing and was the first to give a significant amount of information on growing the French hybrids in the East. Customers could now order vines and instructions on how to grow them. In their 1944–45 catalog published in late October 1944, the Wagners commented that they had provided vines for small vineyards in at least half of the states in the country.

Wagner often referred to the winery as a "pilot plant" started with the intent of showing that commercially acceptable wine could be made from new grapes in places where winegrowing had not previously existed.[33] Many of the early commercial wines were experimental and production in the late 1940s was only a few hundred gallons, less than 200 in 1945 and 543 in 1949. Production in the 1970s averaged between 6,000 and 7,000 gallons and was rarely more than 10,000 gallons during the Wagner years.

Wagner's friendship with Marvel and Schoonmaker paid off when it came time for the wines to be labeled and sold. Schoonmaker suggested labeling each of the two wines—Boordy White Wine and Baco Red Wine—as "A Frank Schoonmaker Selection." A back label with Frank Schoonmaker's signature was also prepared. Label approval came from Washington on June 29, 1947, and on July 9 the first tax-paid case of wine bearing "Serial No. 1" went to Schoonmaker, a sample case of 1946 Delaware.[34] The first order was for seventy-seven cases, which were shipped on August 6. A note in the *New York Herald Tribune* on September 3, 1947, announced the arrival of Boordy wines in the New York market and that they could be bought at Macy's, the Vendome, and Sherry Wine and Spirits. A similar announcement appeared in the *New York Times* on September 16.

Two other needs were met by the Wagners in these early years. The first was the difficulty in getting grape growing and winemaking equipment in a size suitable for family-scale operations. It was hard enough for the Wagners to find what they wanted, let alone being able to tell customers where they could buy it. On March 8, 1950, Wagner wrote to several Swiss firms for prices on such items as small crushers and presses with a view toward making a small catalog. Five weeks later, the Wagners prepared a return postcard advertising a grape hoe for $3.00 and asking recipients to indicate which items on a small list of vineyard and winery equipment they would like Boordy to stock.[35]

It proved to be unexpectedly difficult to find or import many of the items, and on July 25 the Wagners mailed out sixty-five copies of a "provisional" hardware circular listing about half the items to people who had returned the postcard. It was not until a year later that a new hardware catalog could be prepared and sent to their regular list of customers.[36]

The second need was for wine glasses.[37] Most of the readily available wine glasses were too small, poorly shaped, too elaborate, and too expensive. What the Wagners wanted was something of good size and simple shape, inexpensive, and made of clear glass or crystal that would withstand mechanical dishwashing. On May 23, 1950, with a major tasting coming up in mid-June, the problem of finding decent wine glasses had to be addressed. Jocelyn Wagner went to New York where she found six dozen glasses that would be suitable for the tasting, but the real find was a line of Julian Street glasses at the Morgantown Glassware Guild.[38] They were willing to make up eight-ounce glasses with a classical tulip shape and substitute a drawn stem for a cut stem and supply them wholesale to the Wagners for $3.20 a dozen.

Boordy Vineyard ordered many gross of these glasses over the years, supplying them in quantity both in the East and to the Wine Institute and the large wineries in California. This lasted until the Wine Institute decided to compete and began to supply similar glasses from another manufacturer in a cheaper quality of glass. The Wagners were able to order from Morgantown until shortly after the Kennedys moved into the White House. Then came a televised tour of the refurbished rooms in the White House hosted by Jackie Kennedy. One shot of a banquet room showed place settings with wine glasses that seemed identical to the ones being sold by Boordy. Not long after, Jocelyn Wagner called Morgantown to reorder glasses and was told that the company had no time to fill small orders such as hers. Ever since the broadcast, she was told, virtually every important department store was ordering this glass from them.[39]

By the end of 1950, Boordy Vineyard was the only commercial nursery selling French hybrid vines in the East, and would remain the sole source for a few more years. It was also a source of grape growing and winemaking equipment for the smaller operator, and whether in person or through Wagner's books, Boordy was the best place to get information on growing or winemaking. It is little wonder that anyone seriously interested in grape growing or winemaking during these years found that their path eventually led them through Riderwood, Maryland.

The Hybrids Come to Canada

The outbreak of World War II in September 1939 meant that grapevines could no longer be brought across the Atlantic Ocean from Europe. After the entrance of the United States into the war in December 1941, gasoline rationing made travel more difficult. Philip Wagner found himself limited to eight gallons of gas a week, and any long trip required that gas coupons be saved up in advance.[40] In 1941, the Wagners had made two trips to Geneva; in 1942, they had to decline an invitation to a tasting in Geneva on August 18, although they did ship some wines for that event.[41]

The first trip to the Finger Lakes that the Wagners were able to make after the imposition of rationing was in mid-September 1944, and was notable for the first meeting in person between Wagner and Charles Fournier. No tastings were scheduled on this trip, but there were undoubtedly opportunities for informal tastings of both Boordy and Finger Lakes wines.[42] The Wagners' second trip took place a year later, and this one did include a tasting.

September 21, 1945, is one of the key dates in eastern wine history. On the agenda that afternoon was an inspection of the vineyards at the Fredonia station, a substation of the main research station at Geneva, to be followed by a wine tasting. Among those present, in addition to the Wagners, were Hector Carveth, a Mr. Drake from Chateau Gay in New York, Adhemar de Chaunac from Brights, and a group from Geneva including Richard Wellington, George Oberle, and Nelson Shaulis and his wife Lillian. In all, there were thirty-two wines to taste, most of them made from New York numbered varieties. Unknown to anyone, Wagner had included some of his red French hybrid wines. There was total silence, Wagner later recalled—a stunned silence on the part of some—as it was generally realized for the first time that good wines could be made from French hybrid grapes.[43]

Adhemar de Chaunac was deeply impressed with the results of the tasting and returned to Brights determined to begin experimenting with the French hybrids. Harry Hatch had already committed Brights to finance a dry table wine program, and he and Meredith Jones gave their immediate approval to try growing French hybrid grapes. De Chaunac, J. R. Van Haarlem, then grape specialist with the Horticultural Research Institute of Ontario at Vineland, and George Hostetter began poring through the meager descriptions of vines in the catalogs published by the hybridizers in France.[44] A final selection was made and twenty French hybrid varieties and three vinifera varieties, most of them early maturing, were ordered (see appendix C for a complete list). The vines arrived on April 11, 1946, from Maclet-Botton in Villefranche, France.[45] As the person in charge of viticultural research, George Hostetter supervised the trial plantings.

The use of sulfur to control powdery mildew had been known for a long time, but it had always been applied at a time when the mildew had become evident. Hostetter theorized that trying different spray schedules might bring about marked improvement in the control of powdery mildew. Using sulfur as a clean-up spray after harvest on susceptible varieties and as a dormant spray before the start of the season worked.[46] The discovery that a spray had to be applied before powdery mildew was visible in order for it to be effective was a key to the success of the plantings at Brights.

While the Horticultural Research Institute of Ontario was also interested in growing the hybrids, there was a need for land to plant them on. The thirty-five-acre property on Cherry Avenue, which became the research vineyard, was purchased in 1946. The order for vines was sent late that year, and on January 28, 1947, the vines were shipped from Producteurs Directs Nouveaux de Seibel in Montboucher (Drôme), France. The packing list accompanying the shipment shows that approximately 7,200 cuttings of forty varieties were ordered at a cost of CAD$918.90 (about $924 1947 USD).

The original invoice dated January 28, 1947, still exists at Vineland (see appendix C for a complete list). Care of the vines was entrusted to Oliver A. Bradt, who was to spend more than thirty years as the grape specialist at Vineland. Bradt had joined the staff at Vineland Station in 1938 and shortly afterward took a leave of absence during World War II. He returned to the Station between the time the grapes were ordered and the time the shipment arrived and was offered the job of grape specialist. The memory of the arrival of the shipment remained vivid for many years:

> The shipment came in three big crates, and I remember unpacking them on a Saturday morning in April or May. The shipment had come by boat and it had taken longer than expected. The weather was warm, and we

Figure 2.2: George Hostetter became Director of Research at Brights Wines following the death of Adhemar de Chaunac in 1961. He was responsible for Brights vinifera program from the time the first vinifera vines arrived in the shipment of French hybrid vines from France in 1946. Photo by author.

didn't know whether the vines would survive. We had originally planned to put them in the vineyard, but they were in such poor shape that we put them out in nursery rows. The first case was so damaged that the tags had become separated from the vines, and we simply listed them as being from Case #1. It took us a while to get them sorted out according to the descriptions given in the catalogs.[47]

Most of the varieties survived, however, and all but two were listed some years later in field trial notes compiled by Bradt. Included in the plantings, and still to be seen in the research vineyard, is the original row of De Chaunac that came to North America.

When Harry Hatch died in May 1946, the ownership of Brights was left in the hands of the port and sherry people who were resistant to new ways of doing things. One of them was Earl Thomas, who was at Brights when Hatch took over and who was named general manager. Although Meredith Jones had an important voice in the company since the early 1940s, he had to wait until Thomas retired in 1959 before assuming the title of president. Jones knew that Thomas had no idea how to make better wine, and he, de Chaunac, and Hostetter decided to continue their work on better grapes and better wines for the long-term benefit of Brights. They

EXTRA QUALITY

PINOT

Canadian Champagne

Bright's

EST'D 1874

CONTENTS
26 FLUID OUNCES

PRODUCED BY T. G. BRIGHT & CO., LIMITED · NIAGARA FALLS · CANADA

Figure 2.3: The first commercial vinifera wine in the East was a 1955 Brights Pinot Champagne. It was followed by a Pinot Chardonnay in 1956. Courtesy of George Hostetter.

proceeded to do things on their own that they felt no one else in the company needed to know about.[48]

In addition to his work on establishing a spray program for Brights, Hostetter experimented with methods of pruning and thinning to avoid overcropping. In 1947 Brights became the first Ontario winery to provide growers with a professional viticulturist to assist them in the development of the most productive cultural practices. In 1939 or 1940, Jake Hostetter had started grafting Delaware and Catawba on Clinton rootstocks as a way of increasing production in an area with heavy soils. Experimentation with rootstocks remained a priority at Brights, and by the late 1940s they were able to supply growers with grafted vines.

Commercial plantings of the hybrids began with the planting of 40,000 vines in 1948. By 1952, Brights began commercial plantings with growers. The combination of new sprays and new methods of applying them made it possible for the vinifera to survive. The ten acres of Chardonnay planted on various rootstocks by Brights in 1951 was not only the first commercial planting of the vinifera in the East, but also the first successful vinifera vineyard. These plantings led to the first commercial vinifera wines to be produced in the East, a Brights Pinot Champagne in 1955 and a Pinot Chardonnay in 1956.

In 1949, Brights introduced its President Champagne, a méthode champenoise champagne made from Catawba, Dutchess, Delaware, and Rosette. In 1953 hybrids were added to the cuvée: Seibel 10868, Verdelet, Rayon d'Or, and Seyval Blanc. In 1950, Brights released the first nonlabrusca table wine in Canada, a Chelois and Rosette blend under the name of Manor St. Davids Claret. About the same time a Canadian Burgundy made from Foch was placed on the market. In 1953, Brights released two 7 percent sparkling wines, DuBarry Rosé and Winette. According to Brights, they were the first winery in the world to commercially produce and sell this type of wine.

From the 1930s through the 1960s, Brights pioneered the changes that were occurring in Ontario viticulture. Peter Chubb, a Toronto wine merchant, has been quoted by John Schreiner as saying in the early 1980s: "Everyone sells the varietal hybrids today but Brights did all the work."[49]

As befits a leader, Brights was willing to share its research findings with other Ontario wineries. In the early years when wines from the French hybrids were scarce and only Brights had a surplus, the winery was willing to sell bulk wines to its competitors. Schreiner notes that the purpose was both commercial and altruistic and quotes Hostetter: "We felt that if Brights was making something superior but others were not, we'd never convince the public that Ontario wines were other than garbage."[50]

The Hybrids Arrive in the Finger Lakes

In the mid-1950s the grape and wine industry in the Finger Lakes was much more limited geographically than it is today. Writing in *Gourmet* in 1957, Tom Marvel gave the following description:

> Vines are planted only along the shores of Lake Keuka and to a much lesser extent, Lake Canandaigua. The shorelines of most of the other lakes are too steep even for vines, so that the Finger Lakes wine district encompasses only a small portion of the Finger Lakes area. Furthermore, it is not a wine district as the term would be understood in Europe, where vineyards are broken up into small holdings and nearly everyone owns some vines and makes a little wine himself. There are but four important wineries in the whole lakes district, all of them most hospitable to the interested wine lover.[51]

Prior to Prohibition, vineyards and wineries extended over a somewhat broader area. In 1866, the Seneca Lake Grape Wine Company planted a 100-acre vineyard on Severne Point near Himrod and in 1869 produced 14,000 gallons of Seneca Lake wine.[52] The winery thrived until the advent of Prohibition forced it to close. When

Tom Marvel wrote his description in 1957, there were only a half dozen wineries, all of them along Keuka Lake and Canandaigua Lake. Wineries on Seneca Lake and Cayuga Lake would not open until the passage of the New York Farm Winery Law in 1976.

The oldest of the four important wineries was the Pleasant Valley Wine Company in Hammondsport, which was founded in 1860 by thirteen local businessmen and grape growers including Charles Davenport Champlin who managed the business.[53] The winery grew rapidly from its initial crush of eighteen tons and almost immediately decided to expand its product line to include champagne. By 1864–65, the winery was producing 20,000 bottles of champagne. When the champagne was ready to be marketed, Champlin sent a case to Marshall P. Wilder of Boston, a horticulturist and friend, asking his opinion about the champagne and if he might have a suggestion for naming it. At a dinner party at his club, Wilder poured the champagne and said with glass raised, "it is eminently proper to appropriate the entire western continent for its name. I therefore baptize it Great Western."[54] Great Western became a leading brand of champagne in the United States until Prohibition. During Prohibition Pleasant Valley survived by selling sacramental and medicinal wines. When Charles D. Champlin, the grandson of the founder, died in 1950, the winery was sold, first to a group in Pittsburgh in 1955, and then, at the end of 1961, to the Taylor Wine Company. The winery was managed as an independent division of Taylor by Greyton Taylor.

In 1880, a young cooper named Walter Taylor came to Hammondsport to make barrels for the wineries.[55] He bought a seven-acre plot and three years later purchased a seventy-acre farm. One day he inadvertently found himself in the wine business when a cash-strapped customer paid for his barrels in wine.[56] As the winery grew, three sons—Fred, Clarence, and Greyton—became involved in the business. The family acreage provided enough grapes until 1913 when the first grapes were purchased from local growers.

During Prohibition the Taylor Wine Company sold sacramental wines, table grape juice, and concentrated grape juice in barrels for home winemaking. For those who wanted to make the wine-types into legal wine at home, Taylor offered to send a specialist and his assistants to the home to help.[57] In 1955 the winery was reorganized from being a partnership to a privately held corporation with Fred Taylor as president and Clarence and Greyton Taylor as vice presidents. Fred Taylor became chairman of the board in 1964 and George A. Lawrence succeeded him as president. When Lawrence died in 1975, Joseph L. Swarthout became president and chief operating officer. On January 20, 1977, Taylor stockholders approved a merger with the Coca-Cola Company of Atlanta, Georgia.

Gold Seal Vineyards, Inc., was founded in 1865 as the Urbana Wine Company.[58] With the success of the Pleasant Valley Wine Company as an example, Urbana decided to make champagne, and by 1870 it was producing 120,000 bottles of "Imperial" champagne and 50,000 bottles of still wine. On July 12, 1887, the company applied for the trademark "Gold Seal," which replaced "Imperial." In 1881, the winery was reorganized as the New Urbana Wine Company, and in 1896 "New" was dropped and the company was again known as the Urbana Wine Company.

After Prohibition began, the company was sold to a new group that organized the company as the Gold Seal Products Company. The company was allowed to make sacramental wines and was later granted a permit to make champagne for the same purpose. They were also permitted to make wine for tonic medicines to be sold to the pharmaceutical firm of Smith, Kline and French. At the end of Prohibition the company's name was changed back to the Urbana Wine Company.

In 1929 the president of the company, Edwin S. Underhill, was killed in an automobile accident and was succeeded by his son E. S. Underhill, Jr., who hired Charles Fournier as winemaker and production manager in 1934. The company was sold in January 1951 to Thomas A. Holling and a group of Hammondsport and Buffalo investors.[59] Fournier was named president and Alexander Brailow became chief winemaker.[60]

The company was sold again in 1956 to the McKeown Timber Tech Corporation, which soon changed its name to Lawrence Properties Company. Louis A. Benoist, owner of Almadén Vineyards in California, headed Lawrence Properties and was elected chairman of the board of the Urbana Wine Company. A final name change occurred in 1957 when the winery once again became Gold Seal Vineyards, Inc.

In 1958, Gold Seal was sold to a New York group of investors. The controlling principals were Paul M. Schlem, later named chairman of the board, and Arthur Brody, who served under Schlem as executive vice president, secretary, and treasurer. It was during their tenure that the decision was made in 1962 to fire Dr. Konstantin Frank, who had been recruited by Fournier in 1953 to start a vinifera program at Gold Seal (see chapter 3). Fournier retired in 1967 but continued as honorary lifetime president until his death in 1983. In 1979 the winery was sold to J. E. Seagram and Sons, Inc.[61]

The fourth of the important wineries was Widmer's Wine Cellars, which was started by John Jacob Widmer in 1888 along Canandaigua Lake in Naples, New York.[62] In 1883 he borrowed money to buy land for vineyards and in 1885 built a house with a cellar that became the wine production and storage area. The founding date is considered to be 1888, the year he began selling wine to the residents of Naples.

In 1910 Widmer's son Will returned from the Royal Wine School at Geisenheim, Germany, and in 1924 he and his two brothers, Carl and Frank, took over the business. During Prohibition the winery produced unfermented grape juice and other nonalcoholic products as well as medicinal and sacramental wines. Will Widmer, the company's president, incorporated the winery in 1933. In the early 1940s Widmer's became the first New York winery to sell varietal wines.

Widmer's was sold in 1961 to George and Walter Todd of Rochester, New York, and Ernest Reveal was named president. The winery was sold three more times: to the R. T. French Company in 1969, to a group of local investors including some of

Widmer's management team in 1983, and finally to Canandaigua Wine Company in September 1986.

When Philip Wagner brought samples of wines he had made from the French hybrids to Fredonia in 1945 that impressed Adhemar de Chaunac so much, there was scant interest in the French hybrids in the Finger Lakes. De Chaunac, a chemist but not a winemaker by background, knew little about the French hybrids even though he came from France; and although Fournier was aware of the French hybrids from his winemaking days in France, he had not had meaningful experience with them.[63]

As was the case in Canada, Seibel 1000, later named Rosette, was the first French hybrid variety to be planted in the Finger Lakes. As early as mid-1942 Richard Wellington at Geneva wrote Wagner that Widmer's Wine Cellars had given him a good report on Seibel 1000.[64] According to Seaton C. "Zeke" Mendall, vineyard consultant for the Taylor Wine Company, a five-acre vineyard of Seibel 1000 along Keuka Lake north of Hammondsport had reached maturity when Taylor acquired the property in 1943.[65] Another planting of Rosette along Keuka Lake dating back to the 1930s was made by Gold Seal Vineyards.[66]

On September 14–15, 1944, when Wagner met Fournier in person for the first time, Fournier told him that he wanted to try out the hybrids and was reserving three acres for that purpose and wanted to order a sufficient number of vines immediately. Wagner's reply was that he could not fill an order that large. "He wants whatever we will let him have," Wagner wrote, "whenever we will let him have it."[67] Early in 1946, Fournier ordered a minimum of 1,000 vines each of Baco Noir and Rosette. The Baco part of the order, at least, was filled on March 4, 1947, and this planting of Baco Noir by the Urbana Wine Company was one of the earliest commercial plantings of the French hybrids in the United States.[68]

In his entry in the *Daybooks* for September 13–16, 1944, Wagner noted that Fournier, like Champlin, "depends chiefly on Catawba, Delaware, Elvira, what Dutchess he can get, and Isabella. And, I suspect, he tries to work off a good deal of Concords. They have to take the latter from the growers in order to get the others." With the exception of Fournier's order, there is no mention of interest in the French hybrids.

Two years later, Wagner was back in Geneva for a tasting of thirty wines, most of them made from French hybrids, and Wagner reported that the progress made since the tasting of 1942 was absolutely astonishing:

These were *real* wines—and everyone present was clearly impressed. My own belief is that this tasting represents a turning point in the attitude of these people on the value of new varieties—and that the swing to them will continue pretty steadily from now on. The situation now is that Fournier is definitely sold on them, and wants to go all out—that Champlin has some S. 1000 [Rosette] and will not be far behind—that Widmer now has his first S. 1000 coming in and will increase them, that Carveth and de Chaunac are sold—and that even Taylor is beginning to weaken (Celmar having ordered 50 S. 6339)![69]

Taylor did indeed catch up, as Wagner wrote in 1963: "Most of the eastern wineries and hundreds of amateurs have been experimenting with [the French hybrids] for two decades and producing good wine. Characteristically, Taylor was one of the last to inquire into them, but the first to take the plunge—to move from experiment to action."[70] When Greyton Taylor made up his mind to do something, he wanted to act as quickly as possible. Wagner recalled that Taylor came to him one day and asked what white hybrids he should plant. Wagner said his first choice would be Seyval Blanc, but that Aurore would also be worth a try. Because Seyval cuttings were in short supply, an impatient Greyton Taylor chose the more plentiful Aurore. This decision led to the hillsides of Keuka Lake being planted in Aurore rather than Seyval.[71]

While the demand for French hybrid vines was growing, they were not easy to come by. Philip Wagner with his limited facilities could supply only a certain amount of nursery stock, an estimated total of 16,000 cuttings in 1946.[72] In addition, embargo and quarantine regulations promulgated by the USDA in 1948 prevented direct importation from France or any other country in Europe without a required postentry quarantine for two years at USDA facilities in Maryland before being released.[73] Canada, however, was exempted from the quarantine, and the vineyards there had been mature for a longer period of time than in the Finger Lakes. During the late 1940s truckloads of prunings form Brights in Ontario crossed the border en route to nurseries and wineries in the Finger Lakes.

In 1975, Mendall, Taylor's vineyard consultant, reported that the acreage of French hybrids in New York had increased from approximately 35 acres in 1954 to more than 2,500 bearing acres in 1974, and that tonnage had increased from 104 tons in 1954 to more than 7,000 tons in the same time period.[74] Mendall also noted that Aurore had by then ranked fourth in acreage and production among all varieties in the Finger Lakes. This is scarcely surprising in view of a letter from Greyton Taylor to Wagner dated February 2, 1965, in which he said that Taylor is interested in 3,000 tons of Aurore a year and that steps are being taken to have growers plant between 50 and 60 acres a year. To do this, Taylor is making 175,000 cuttings a year and sending them to Foster Nursery for propagation.

In 1954, Greyton Taylor had written:

> A natural endowment of wines produced from Finger Lakes grapes is a distinctive flavor and bouquet, different from those of wines produced in other areas of this country and abroad. As a general rule, New York State wines are more full flavored, with a slight accent towards fruitiness (i.e., "grapeness").
>
> This the public has found to be a pleasant and agreeable change from usual wines. For our part, we happen to believe that since wine comes from grapes, wine should taste as though it did.[75]

The use of French hybrids was commented on by Mendall some years later:

> French hybrid wines are used mainly for blending with native grape wines. The hybrids are higher in sugar content although total acidity is about the same. Varietal wines made from these grapes are not as fruity. They offer opportunities to blend and produce new and different wines.
>
> A few hybrids have been marketed as varietals: Chelois, Baco Noir, Foch, Aurore, Seyval. As a group, the hybrids being grown in New York today are not used to best advantage as varietal wines. They are themselves somewhat improved through blending with native wines. The fruity character of the latter not only is acceptable but desired by most consumers of New York wines. Use of hybrids in blending wines allows the New York processor to vary the degree of fruitiness to an extent that he could never before attain.[76]

In 1965, Wagner gave a speech before the New York State Horticultural Society in which he stated that the hybrids account for about 9 percent of the New York State winery crush of 20,000 tons. The wineries also bring in around 11,000 tons from outside the state plus about 1.25 million gallons of blending wine from California.[77] He anticipated a greater demand for the French hybrids as a way of replacing the California blending wine being brought into the East. But he also mentioned some promising new French hybrids just becoming available from smaller producers. Growers near centers of population have found a surprisingly active market for these new varieties among amateur winemakers, he said. "Their successes in producing totally new wine types under Eastern conditions have been convincing enough to inspire a sharp change of direction in the industry."

CHAPTER THREE

❦

DR. KONSTANTIN FRANK AND THE PRO-VINIFERA CRUSADE

ONE OF THE MOST CONTROVERSIAL AND INFLUENTIAL FIGURES IN THE MODERN eastern wine industry was Russian-born Dr. Konstantin Damien Frank, who settled in Hammondsport, New York, in 1953.[1] Frank pioneered the growing of vinifera in New York and crusaded tirelessly to get others throughout the East to plant them as well. His fiery advocacy of the vinifera and his fulminations against the French hybrids won him strong supporters as well as opponents who thought he went too far. To anyone who would listen he carried the message that Americans deserve "only excellent" grapes.

Dr. Frank was fifty-two when he immigrated to the United States in 1951. Any meaningful understanding of this man must take into account his life in Europe and the background from which he came.[2]

Frank's Years in Europe

Despite being born in the Ukraine on July 4, 1899, Konstantin Frank did not think of himself as Russian. "I was not Russian, never," he would say emphatically. "I'm German. My great-grandfather left Germany in 1812 and organized in the Ukraine a village, Franksfeld." The name of the village was actually Franzfeld, Franz being the original family name (and subsequently translated into English as Frank).

German settlers were arriving in the southern Ukraine and Crimea in substantial numbers during this time. Franzfeld was one of many villages consisting entirely of Germans that were established throughout the region. These German settlers remained in their enclaves with little cultural interchange between themselves and the Ukrainian peasants.

Frank was born into one of these enclaves in 1899, and it is understandable why he should consider himself German rather than Russian. German was the language spoken at home and in the village, and the process of "Russification" only began during the student years away from the village. Frank's father was a well-to-do civil engineer who owned a large farm outside Odessa primarily for the breeding of livestock. He also grew grapes, but not commercially, and his son Konstantin was working in his father's vineyard from the time he was twelve, and making wine by the time he was fifteen. From time to time there would be talk at home of moving to the New World, specifically to Canada.

Frank was studying viticulture at the time of the Russian Revolution in 1917. This was followed by three years of civil war in Russia between the Reds and the Whites. The Franks were on the side of the Whites, who tried to prevent a communist takeover. When the Red Army proved victorious, Konstantin Frank's world had changed. Two of his brothers had been killed, and several other family members perished in the civil war and during the famine that followed. As the Reds took political control following the civil war, Frank continued his studies in viticulture and worked in the vineyard.

In 1924, Frank was appointed assistant professor of viticulture at the agricultural college level. By 1926, he was considered ready for bigger things. A vineyard nine miles long and four miles wide known as Trubetskoye near the Dnieper River had fallen on hard times after being ravaged by the phylloxera epidemic that had swept through Europe. Frank's job description was simple: restore the vineyards and fill up the cellars with wine. "I go there," Frank recalled years later. "Where they had planted Pinot Gris, I planted Pinot Gris—grafted, and where they had planted Pinot Chardonnay, I planted Pinot Chardonnay—grafted." Through the use of phylloxera-resistant rootstocks the vineyard was gradually restored and the cellars filled.

During the 1930s, Frank worked on what was to be his most significant invention, the grape plow. In Russia, where the temperatures during the winter can drop to -45° Fahrenheit, 90 percent of the vineyards were maintained by dropping the vines from the trellis and burying them during the winter. At Trubetskoye, this required a crew of 800 people a day working with shovels. In 1935, a prototype plow was used for the first time to cover four hectares of vines. The vines were not totally covered, however, and it took two more years to perfect a plow that would completely cover one hectare of vineyard in an hour. Still another year was needed to develop a plow that would uncover the vines at the same speed.

In 1939, the following notice appeared in *Yuzhnaya Pravda (Southern Pravda)* under the title, "Inventions by the Agronomist Comrade Frank":

> The senior agronomist of the grape growing Lenin sovkhoz in the Borislavsky district, Comrade Frank, invented last year a plow to cover

Figure 3.1: Dr. Konstantin Frank invented his plow for deep plowing in 1924. This photo was taken in a Russian vineyard in 1928 and shows three of the original four tractors used to pull the plow. Dr. Frank has his left hand on the wheel of the plow. Courtesy of Willy Frank.

grape vines. In the fall of 1938, this plow was used to cover 196 hectares of vineyards. The plow is drawn by a tractor and covers one hectare of vineyard per hour. Thanks to this invention of Comrade Frank, the sovkhoz saved 20,000 rubles. This year, he invented another plow to remove the cover from the vines, the productivity of which is the same as that of the covering plow. The use of the throw-outwards plow permits saving 50–60 rubles per hectare.

More than 45,000 of these plows were eventually made, and the modern plows in use today in most of the Soviet vineyards are based on the work of Dr. Frank.

In addition to the grape plow, Frank was responsible for inventing several machines for use in the vineyard including a mechanical digger, a mechanical planter, and a machine to mark planting locations. It was his first invention—a deep plow that could plow to a depth of four feet—that caused trouble with the authorities. The plans for the plow were drawn up in 1924 and called for four Ford tractors that had been donated to the Soviet Union to pull the plow. When it came time to test the prototype, there was a shortage of chain to attach the tractors to the plow. The result was that the last tractor in the line, which had been attached with a heavy bar, was torn apart. Frank faced charges of destroying one-quarter of the Ford tractors in the Ukraine. Only the intervention of a commissar who knew the value of Frank's work kept him from being tried as an enemy of the people.

During the late 1920s, Frank continued teaching, and his accomplishments were considered to be sufficiently meritorious that he was accepted by the Odessa Polytechnic Institute as a candidate for a doctorate. Significantly, the title of his doctoral dissertation was, "Protection of Grapes from Freezing Damage." He was awarded his degree in viticulture—though he also studied enology—in 1930. That same year, an International Congress was held in Tbilisi, and Frank was a speaker. He recounted his successes with the vinifera at Trubetskoye and pointed out publicly for the first time that there was no reason viticulturally to consider growing the French hybrids, which had already made their appearance in Russia.

World War II started in Europe in September 1939, but the Soviet Union did not become directly involved in the hostilities until the German armies invaded the country in June 1941. As the German troops swept eastward through Ukraine and Crimea, Konstantin Frank, his wife Eugenia, and their three children escaped westward to Austria, hiding in the coal bin behind a steam locomotive. In Austria, Frank managed an estate confiscated by the government to produce food. Although he was regarded with suspicion by the authorities, they chose to look the other way. When it became apparent during the closing weeks of the war that Soviet troops would be occupying Austria, once again the Franks fled, this time to southern Germany where the American army would be the occupying force.

When World War II ended in May 1945, Frank was appointed by the U.S. military occupation force as the manager of a large estate confiscated from the Nazis in Bavaria. In 1951, although he was assured of a continuing managerial job in Bavaria, he chose to move to the New World—not to Canada, because of immigration quotas, but to the United States.

In 1978, looking back at the end of World War II, Frank made the comment: "I was in trouble with the Russians; I was in trouble with the Nazis; I was in trouble with everyone who was left." It is not hard to understand why he felt this way. When hostilities broke out between the Soviet Union and Germany in 1941, the Franks and others with a German heritage were regarded with suspicion. How strong the German influence in the area remained at this time can be seen by the fact that the Crimean Soviet Socialist Republic lost its autonomous status in the Soviet Union in 1945 because of the collaboration between the Germans living in the area and the invading German armies during the war. Frank might have felt more at home in Austria, but the fact that he was a Russian national was enough to keep him under suspicion by the Nazis.

Frank had every reason to be satisfied with his accomplishments in viticulture in the Soviet Union; everything he had accomplished in his life was a triumph of his own will and by his own hands. The political changes that occurred during his life had made him a survivor, a man who could trust only himself and whose loyalties extended no further than to his own abilities and to his family. He was penniless when he arrived in the United States, but his assets were considerable: a will to work, a fighting spirit that would not admit the possibility of defeat, stubbornness in the face of obstacles, and a knowledge of viticulture that included the ability to grow the vinifera in cold climates. Above all, he had enthusiasm. "Without enthusiasm," he once said, "I would be dead." After what he had been through, there had to be a way to accomplish anything. He was prepared to feel that he belonged in the United

States, and he became a patriotic American who proudly identified his birthdate with Independence Day. But his experiences in Europe had left an indelible stamp on his personality, especially his will to survive and to win out, no matter how it had to be done or at what cost.

Frank, Gold Seal, and Vinifera Wine Cellars

Konstantin Frank arrived in New York City in mid-November 1951, with his wife and three children.[3] He had the added handicap of not knowing any English, although he could speak seven or eight languages. The family moved into a cold-water apartment on New York's Lower East Side and Frank began working as a dishwasher in a Horn and Hardart Automat. As soon as he had saved enough money to buy a one-way ticket to Geneva, New York, he traveled to the Finger Lakes and immediately started making the rounds of wineries and laboratories asking for work.[4] Personnel records at the New York State Agricultural Experiment Station show that he began work there on April 15, 1952, at the rate of $1.00 per hour.[5] The funding for his temporary position came from the Stuart Nursery Grant and the nature of work to be done was described as "propagation and field work in the nursery." On April 8, 1953, he began his second temporary job at Geneva under funding from the Concord grape grant at $1.25 per hour. His immediate supervisor was listed as Nelson Shaulis and the nature of work to be done described as "calculations, vineyard work." Frank found these tasks menial and referred to them in later years as "hoeing blueberries." During his nearly two years at Geneva he tried in vain to get someone to listen to his argument that the vinifera could be grown in New York State.

Fournier recalled how he first met Frank:

> One day I was at the Geneva station at a meeting. I was going in the hallway there and talking here and there when there was an older fellow there. I got to talk to him—I don't know why, I don't know how it happened, but I talked with him—and he began to get interested in talking with me and so I had plenty of time and the meeting was not going to start for half an hour later. He said: "Well, and what are you doing to make good wines here?" It was Dr. Frank. I just met him by luck. He began to talk to me about vinifera and growing them here and said, "I have been in Russia all my life and of course I left after the Revolution and the war, and here I am not doing anything of interest. But you can grow vinifera here. I grew them in the Ukraine with the same climate." I got immediately interested, and it had been my dream for a long time. So I got in contact with him immediately and came back to see him, and I said, "I'll take you to Gold Seal and give you whatever you need," and he assured me that we could do it.[6]

According to the *Geneva Daily Times,* Frank left Geneva in mid-March 1954. He resigned "in order to accept a position as consultant for the Urbana Wine Company in Hammondsport."[7]

Frank believed that the key to growing the vinifera was to find rootstocks that would accelerate both the ripeness of the grapes and the hardening of the wood. If the wood can be fully ripened off before the first freeze, he said, the vine would be able to withstand very low winter temperatures. The first job, then, was to find the right rootstocks. Fournier described the search:

> Dr. Frank and I began our tours of the northeast countryside and gathered wood from native grapes, especially of the riparia species. In a small convent in the Québec province of Canada, we discovered that the monk in charge of the gardens was growing Pinot grapes and he told us that one year out of three he would make a fairly good wine in spite of the extremely short growing season. He gave us some of the rootstocks he was using. With these, and with some interesting riparia we found right in our own backyard at Gold Seal, the great experiment started.[8]

It took five years and hundreds of thousands of grafts, Fournier recalled, to arrive at a list of successful combinations. In the fall of 1957 "our first plantings of Johannisberger Riesling and Pinot Chardonnay produced grapes that had more than 23% of sugar at the beginning of October plus an acidity high enough for very good balance."[9]

The first crop of Riesling and Chardonnay in 1957 together with their survival during the cold winter of 1956–57 led to the decision to start commercial plantings as soon as enough rootstock became available in their nursery. Vinifera acreage at Gold Seal increased to 70 acres by 1966 and 150 by 1977.[10]

As Philip Wagner had discovered a decade earlier, the shortage of propagating wood was a greater factor in slowing the growth of the industry than a lack of grapes. The Finger Lakes had the advantage that cuttings were available from Canada. Truckloads of brush and cuttings crossed the border from Ontario into New York state. Brights Wines in Niagara Falls, Ontario, shipped hundreds of thousands of cuttings southward, including large shipments to Fournier and Frank.[11] In November 1949, 500 cuttings of a dozen French hybrids were shipped to Fournier, and on January 12, 1951, Gold Seal ordered 2,000 cuttings each of Seibel 10868, Verdelet, and Seyval in addition to 3,000 cuttings of other French hybrids. Following Frank's arrival at Gold Seal, the vinifera began to replace the French hybrids: in December 1954, 300 cuttings of Pinot Noir, 300 of Pinot Blanc, and 200 of Müller-Thurgau were included in an order for 10,000 Chelois and 150 of other French hybrids.

In a 1961 article, Fournier reported that Frank, since he arrived at Gold Seal, had made over 250,000 grafts representing thousands of combinations of fifty-eight rootstocks with twelve vinifera varieties and many clones of each in nine soil conditions.[12] Only a few of the combinations showed the desired earliness and winter hardiness. As of 1961, only White Riesling, Chardonnay, and Muscat Ottonel were being grown in any quantity at Gold Seal as a result of satisfactory rootstock combinations being found.

The decision made in 1957 to expand the planting of vinifera led to the production of the first commercial vinifera wines in New York, a 1960 Pinot Noir and a 1960 Chardonnay.[13] A 1960 Johannisberg Riesling was almost certainly marketed as well.

Working for a big company like Gold Seal was not enough for Frank. He wanted to have his own land. Fournier had a friend, Felix Faber, who wanted to grow grapes but who had gotten into trouble and had to sell some of his land.[14] Fournier arranged for Frank to purchase the land and guaranteed payment to Faber. On July 13, 1956, Frank settled for 101.75 acres at a cost of $6,000.[15] The land for the vineyard was deep-plowed, probably in 1957, and the first vines planted in 1958.[16] By 1978 he had planted seventy acres of vines with each vine numbered and marked in his vineyard book.

Frank's purchase of his own land caused problems at Gold Seal. According to Fournier, Frank "just didn't want to work as a vineyard manager any more. He began to be very restive and to take days off without letting me know. Very difficult, very difficult."[17] By 1961 tensions were growing between Frank and Alexander Brailow over the former's demand that the vinifera be given priority in the winery. As Brailow put it later: "In his zeal he made demands that jeopardized the entire operation. The laboratory and all other facilities were expected to give first priority to his experiments. The final break came when he insisted that all our labrusca and hybrid vines be ripped out and replaced with vinifera. Then came an ultimatum, 'Brailow or me.'"[18] This created an impossible situation for Brailow, who was in charge of production. The problem came to the attention of the new owners of Gold Seal.[19] Fournier explained what happened next:

> One day one of the new owners decided to fire Dr. Frank and wrote a letter to me that Dr. Frank was fired, which made me mad because if anything was going to be done, I was the one to do it. Certainly I knew that Dr. Frank wouldn't stay any longer, and I was trying to get all the information I could on what he had done and put it down because he has only very very small records of what he had done, what the rootstocks were, etc.; and so when some charitable soul immediately told him that one of the owners was firing him, he got mad and never came back to Gold Seal again—ever, which of course bothered me a lot because I wanted to keep him involved some way because his knowledge and what he has done and what he could do were important to me.
>
> Dr. Frank went and built his winery and I was able to keep a fairly good relationship with him in spite of the big problem with Gold Seal. I got some information from him, but he was never very receptive to

Figure 3.2: This label was used on Dr. Frank's first wine, the 1962 Trockenbeerenauslese. The vineyard depicted on the label was not from New York. Judging from the costumes being worn, the location was probably in Germany. Author's collection.

working with me any more. It was probably the biggest blow I had since I was here. I had planned on him being a consultant, working with him, paying him as a consultant, and letting him work on his new winery as he wished. But it didn't work out that way.[20]

Frank's account of the separation was direct and to the point: "I left Gold Seal because it was sold to people who showed no interest in me or what I was doing. They were interested in money. They imported junk. I couldn't change them. I say goodbye. The next day I take a shovel and start digging the winery."[21] Frank left Gold Seal in early 1962.[22] His winery, Vinifera Wine Cellars, was bonded in June 1962, but a month before crush began, only the cellar had been dug for his own winery. Frank called his son Willy who lived in Long Island, and Willy rounded up four Swedish masons and headed for Hammondsport. Willy poured the mortar and in three weeks the roof was up. No more than fifteen minutes before the first grapes arrived, a used Vaslin press was moved into place for the first crush.[23]

One of the wines made from this 1962 vintage was a much praised Trockenbeerenauslese, which sold for $45.00 a bottle. Many accolades followed. A Chardonnay was served to Queen Elizabeth during her 1976 visit to Boston, and his wines were frequently served at the Governor's mansion in Albany and the White House in Washington.

Dr. Frank's Influence

Dr. Konstantin Frank's mantra that "only excellent will do" and that "Americans have everything else excellent and they deserve to have excellent grapes and excellent wines" marked his tireless and often outspoken advocacy of the vinifera. This alone would have guaranteed him an audience, but the fact that he was growing the highly desirable classic varieties of Europe despite the long historical record of not being able to grow them in the eastern United States was enough to bring home winemakers and wine enthusiasts to Hammondsport to see him.

A number of men in Ithaca, New York, in the early 1960s were interested in home winemaking. They bought grapes wherever they could and were always on the lookout for better quality fruit. Among them were Albert W. Laubengayer, Aldus Fogelsanger, and Harry Kerr, members of the Tompkins Oenological Society, who were to help found the Ithaca Oenological Union in 1966 and the American Wine Society a year later.[24]

After these home winemakers discovered Frank and bought juice and grapes from him, it became common practice for them to gather on Frank's back porch to discuss the wine situation in the United States. At that time imported wines were considered to be the only premium wines available. There was general agreement among those on the back porch that the prevailing view was wrong and that fine wines could be made in this country.

In 1967 a group of about a dozen of these winemakers met on Frank's porch and discussed forming a society that would promote both the consumption of American wines and the making of better American wines. On August 28, 1967, Frank sent out a general invitation to attend the "first convention" of *Vitis vinifera* growers and home winemakers at his Vinifera Wine Cellars in Hammondsport on the weekend of October 7 at 9:00 a.m. It read in part:

> The main purpose of the meeting will be to openly discuss the desirability
> of forming an American Food and Wine Society. This organization,
> composed of those individuals who are sincerely interested in the
> promotion and growth of superior quality domestic wines, would not be

a commercial venture in any way. Our objective would be to inform the general public of the ability and natural resources to produce excellent wines here in our own country. Too frequently they are erroneously led to believe that the only fine wines are imported. By showing what has been accomplished by a dedicated few, hopefully, people will not only recognize the excellence but demand expansion of domestic Vitis Vinifera wine production in the Eastern United States.[25]

Frank's invitation was sent to grape growers, winemakers, and anyone interested in consuming superior wines including doctors, salesmen, writers, and scientists. Approximately 200 people showed up on October 7, 1967, to hear Frank propose the formation of the American Wine and Food Society. After the decision had been made, a business meeting was held at which it was decided to elect temporary officers. Frank stood up and said, "I elect Al Laubengayer president." There being no objection, he proceeded to "elect" Aldus Fogelsanger treasurer and Harry Kerr secretary.[26] A formal organizational meeting was scheduled for December 3, 1967, at which time the name of the society was changed to the American Wine Society. Among those present were Mark and Dene Miller who opened their Benmarl Vineyards in Marlboro, New York, in 1971. In 1979, Dene Miller recalled the euphoria of that day.

> We were there. I don't remember everyone who was there that day, but I do remember many of the others: Charles Fournier, Walter Taylor, the Wiederkehrs who had come all the way from Arkansas; Bill Konnerth may have been there from Presque Isle; and Tom Clarke who became chairman of our region. Lou and Edith Meckes were with us and were also "founders." She was exceptionally qualified. She is the granddaughter of A. J. Caywood, hybridizer of the Dutchess grape. She is now about 85 years old and still lives on Caywood's old farm.
>
> After we all signed our founding agreement and paid our $3, Charles Fournier took us down to Gold Seal and gave us a personally conducted tour of that fine old winery. We tasted their champagne out on their terrace which overlooks Lake Keuka and felt we were celebrating a truly worthwhile beginning.
>
> It was an exciting day. Just about everyone stayed overnight and dined at the only restaurant in town. It had a nice setting, overlooking the lake.[27]

The convention, again according to Dene Miller, had immediate results:

> All of the founders worked very conscientiously for the cause in those days. Its purpose spread like wildfire. There really were very few organized "tasting" groups easily available to the masses way back in 1967. Our little group of three (the Clarks, Meckeses and us) mushroomed to a membership

of 30 by the following spring and almost 100 by the time the second annual conference was held at Painted Post. We held serious tastings throughout the year, always well attended. We had a tasting in '68 at our winery (when it was only two rooms, three years before we were licensed) and drew members from as far away as Philadelphia and New Haven.

Those first two annual conferences will always be the most memorable ones for us. We knew every member by his first name and from then on they felt like family.[28]

Harry Kerr kept minutes of the meeting for the Ithaca Oenological Society. "On arrival at the vineyard at 9:30 a.m., a goodly crowd was observed assembled from far and wide by invitation for the purposes of promoting the vinifera, sinking the French hybrids and as stated earlier, organizing a Wine and Food Society."[29]

Many of the participants were drawn to the conference more by interest in better American wines and food than by the cause of the vinifera. In *Wine: A Gentleman's Game,* Mark Miller noted that although it was amateur winemakers who provided the initiative for the formation of what was to be the American Wine Society, most of those attending were in the process of planting vineyards and opening wineries. He went on to say:

> Unfortunately the potential effectiveness of the incipient professionals in this group was to be severely hampered by the polarization of opinion into a diversionary controversy over which grapevines were the best. The most strident group, centered around Dr. Frank, adamantly insisted that only the old classic European vinifera varieties already identified with the world's most highly respected wines should be planted at all. Others more cautiously felt that, although these vines did indeed make superb wines in very special microclimates and particular soils, the very same grapes equally often made indifferent-to-frankly-bad wines in other environments. These winemakers, who identified with Philip Wagner, took the position that certain new crossbred or hybrid varieties seemed better suited to eastern climates and soils and in fact when grown in appropriate environments were capable of equal or better quality than the vinifera.
>
> It seemed that more invective was being generated than good wine, and this tempest-over-a-glass-of-wine was hampering what should have been a cooperative learning process. Both groups of antagonists were, of course, partly right and made some excellent wines to prove it.[30]

By the time of the first annual meeting on October 6 and 7, 1968, the American Wine Society had 140 members. Chapters had been founded in Maryland, Michigan, and eastern Pennsylvania with concentrations of members in fifteen other areas interested in organizing chapters.[31] When the second annual meeting was held a year later in Painted Post, New York, active membership had climbed to 329 and the number of chapters was steadily increasing with associated clubs as far away as North Carolina and Kentucky.[32]

Wine tastings in many cities helped recruit new members. The interest in wine and food was strong, but the dedication to the vinifera shown in 1967 began to erode as the membership increased. At the 1969 meeting in Painted Post, Frank was visibly upset by the attention being paid to the French hybrids.[33] A year later, at the third annual meeting in Erie, Pennsylvania, he asked for the opportunity to speak:

> Instead of writing me letters congratulating me about my accomplishments and hospitality, it would be better for you to center your attention on important matters. September 22, ten Geneva scientists and five from Washington visited me and were amazed at how Vinifera came through our worst winter. At the same time hybrids suffered. If you don't center on important matters, I will have to go my way alone. Americans who have the most of the best have the poorest wine in the world. Center attention here or I will have to resign my membership.[34]

Frank did, in fact, resign. However, at the next conference in College Park, Maryland, on November 5 and 6, 1971, it was announced that Frank was the recipient of the first American Wine Society Award of Merit, an honor that conferred life membership on him.

Both before and after the 1967 convention, people who were interested in growing the vinifera visited Frank, looked at his vineyards, listened to him explain how to grow the vinifera, and ordered vines for the following year. Frank referred to those who planted the vinifera after coming to see him as his "cooperators."

Among the earliest visitors to Frank were Dr. G. Hamilton Mowbray and Douglas P. and Marlene Moorhead who came to Hammondsport in late 1958 and planted vinifera vines purchased from him in the spring of 1959. Mowbray went on to open his own winery, Montbray Wine Cellars, in Silver Run Valley near Westminster, Maryland. The Moorheads later became partners in Presque Isle Wine Cellars in North East, Pennsylvania.

Other cooperators in the early 1960s included John and Cindy Moorhead from North East, Pennsylvania; Judge William O. Beach from Clarksville, Tennessee; Alcuin Wiederkehr from Arkansas; Arnie Esterer and Tim Hubbard from Ohio; Gary, Robert and Page Woodbury from New York; Harold E. Applegate from New Jersey; and, a little later, George and Cathy Mathiesen from Martha's Vineyard in Massachusetts; and Brother David Petri of St. Meinrad Archabbey in St. Meinrad, Indiana. Writing to Mowbray in 1963, Frank informed him that he had twenty-two cooperators.[35] This number increased steadily, but so did the standards for being considered a cooperator.[36]

Figure 3.3: Dr. Frank harangued the crowd in 1977 when the Vinifera Wine Growers Association held its Sixth Annual Wine Growing Seminar at Waverly Farm in Middleburg, Virginia. Photo by author.

Like many leaders of crusades, Dr. Frank attracted disciples. One early one was Edward Cloos, Jr., of Rochester, New York. On the occasion of the twentieth anniversary of the American Wine Society he was asked along with other charter members to comment on his early expectations of the organization and his opinion on the way it had developed. He replied:

> The principle on which the association was founded was to strive for great American wines and by no stretch of the imagination did that include hybrids.
>
> In New York State, led by Geneva scientists and some wine companies, hybrids became the major type in new plantings. This for years stifled vinifera development.
>
> Recent successes of small vinifera wineries, and realization that hybrid wines can't compete with California and European wines has shown the extent of the viticultural crimes of hybrid apologists.
>
> Early in the life of the AWS [American Wine Society], dedication to vinifera was dropped. The Society has filled an important role in the American wine scene, but not for me. I resigned in 1970 because it was no longer the organization Dr. Frank founded.[37]

Dr. Frank's most ardent disciple was undoubtedly Robert de Treville Lawrence, Sr., in Virginia, a founder of the Vinifera Wine Growers Association in 1973 and its journal, the *Vinifera Wine Growers Journal*, in 1974.[38] More will be said about him in later chapters.

The Toxic Scare

In the mid-1960s word spread in the East that wines made from the French hybrids were toxic.[39] French sources were quoted as saying that drinking hybrid wines brought about stomach upsets and other physiological symptoms. A 1951 report from a French physician, J. de Leobardy, was resurrected that attributed liver disorders to drinking wines made from either the French hybrids or from native American species. In 1960 Dr. Hans Breider, director of the Bavarian State Institute for Wine, Fruit and Horticulture in Würzburg, Germany, published a paper purportedly claiming to have verified the research done in France showing that liver damage was produced in chickens when hybrid wines were fed to them.[40]

Another Breider publication in 1965 detailed the results of an investigation in which wines made from the French hybrids were fed to seven strains of Leghorn chickens. He reported that as a result of his studies there was shown to be a high incidence of incomplete leg and foot bone development and some spastic conditions in the offspring of these chickens. In addition, he found that there were a significant number of broken eggs produced from chickens drinking hybrid wine.

By 1967, Breider was prepared to go further. In another article he claimed that there was a positive correlation between the hardiness of a vine and its parasites and pathogens. Juices and wines made from the hybrids were fed to hens and newly hatched chicks. Chicks produced from these hens, or the hybrid-fed chicks produced from the hens not fed the hybrid products, developed malformed legs and feathers as well as nervous system aberrations. The term biostatica was used to define the poisonous substances in the grapes that caused these conditions. Breider's finished report contained pictures of these crippled chickens.

Any evidence against the hybrids was, of course, welcomed by Frank. It is known that he received German research articles about the problem of toxicity of hybrid wines in 1965.[41] Word about the French hybrids spread rapidly in New York state, and the grim prediction was made that a whole generation of American wine drinkers would be doomed to bear deformed offspring.

It was extremist comments like this that led Dr. Willard B. Robinson, chairman of the Department of Food Science and Technology and coordinator of wine research at Geneva, New York, to become concerned. Robinson was a nutritional biochemist and knew there was little likelihood that the stories would be found to be true.

"I started reading these reports and hearing these stories," Robinson recalled in 1982. "We were using these hybrids in our breeding program, and I felt that we had better make very sure that there was nothing to all of this."[42] He decided to launch a full-scale investigation with all sorts of controls. One of the steps he took in 1967 was to hire Dr. Gilbert S. Stoewsand, a toxicologist and poultry expert, as an assistant professor of toxicology.

The reports from France turned out to be totally undocumented and relied, for the most part, on personal testimonials. Coming to grips with the German studies proved to be another matter. Stoewsand and Robinson agreed that the first step to be taken was the standard scientific step of trying to repeat the original researcher's work. The early results were predictable. First, there was the scarcely new discovery that a major effect of wine on newly hatched chicks was that they became intoxicated to the point of being unable to walk to their feeding troughs. Second, he found that chicks fed wine or juice did not grow as fast as chicks that drank water. The "empty calorie" effect came into play: the hybrid-fed chicks absorbed many calories without much nutritive value and had their appetites for ordinary chicken feed spoiled.

Try as he might, Stoewsand could not duplicate Breider's results. The next step was to go to Germany to visit Breider's laboratory at the Bavarian State Institute. He tried to find out how the experiments were conducted and, more important, he tried to find out the exact composition of the chicken feed used. By this time, Stoewsand was convinced that a liquid diet of wine or juice had to be balanced by a good solid diet if the chicks were to receive enough nutrition to survive.

Even though Breider would not see him, the trip had positive results. Stoewsand found out that Breider's work was subsidized by grants from chemical companies. In Breider's waiting room he found pictures of malnourished chicks in a science textbook that looked suspiciously like the pictures included with Breider's publication. These pictures illustrated the effect of severe riboflavin deficiencies on chicks. Perhaps most important, Dr. Elizabeth Wolf, a geneticist in Breider's laboratory, cooperated in furnishing samples of the feed and other helpful information. As Stoewsand wrote on October 30, 1989, "I must say that if it wasn't for the kind cooperation of Elizabeth Wolf... we would have never really explained Breider's results."[43]

Back in Geneva, Stoewsand began exhaustive studies on White Plymouth Rock chicks and Japanese quail. Along with grape juice and wine, the chicks were fed a sound nutritional diet including all of the required vitamins and minerals. In not one instance did these chicks develop any of the symptoms reported by Breider. Stoewsand and Robinson compared notes and agreed that Breider's experimental chickens developed a variety of chronic and acute nutritional deficiencies due to severe deficiencies of minerals, vitamins, and dietary protein.[44]

Outside the experiment station, charges were still swirling around the French hybrids. The controversy had gotten "hot and heavy," as Robinson described it. Before Stoewsand's results could be published, the whole matter escalated in importance. On January 13, 1971, Jack Anderson's syndicated column Washington Merry-Go-Round appeared in the *Washington Post* and in more than 600 newspapers around the country. Under the heading, "Wines Cause Deformities," Anderson wrote:

> The French hybrid wines, like those produced by many New York vineyards, cause such grotesque birth defects in chicks as crippled feet, "vulture beak," and ugly spine abnormalities. The hybrids, intended to eliminate the unpleasant "foxy" taste from New York wines without sacrificing the hardiness of American wines, are increasing in popularity. The hens that hatched the deformed chicks were fed French hybrid juice and wine in laboratories by Dr. Hans Breider.[45]

The publication of Anderson's column had instant repercussions. Dealers began taking New York wines off their shelves. Word that the French hybrids were toxic spread rapidly. Clearly, something had to be done, and fast. A bulletin was released under the title, "Review of Grape and Wine Toxicity Research," by G. S. Stoewsand and W. B. Robinson. It reviewed the problem, the nature of Stoewsand's research, and ended by saying: "From our data, we have concluded that non-vinifera or hybrid grapes contain no natural toxicants at levels high enough to affect healthy experimental avian species under an adequate plane of nutrition."

Two days after the Anderson article appeared, the *Washington Post* carried an article written by Paul Hodge, one of its staff members, that gave "equal time" to the Geneva Experiment Station.[46] Hodge noted that the Anderson article was immediately criticized by scientists and vineyard owners here as part of a "whispering campaign" by other wine growers to discredit the increasingly popular wine made from the French hybrid grapes.

There was also a statement from the Federal Food and Drug Administration that there was "no cause for alarm." Administration toxicologists had reviewed the German studies and had concluded that the studies had not demonstrated that hybrid grapes were toxic.

A retraction of sorts appeared in Jack Anderson's column early in February: "Studies by the New York State Experimental Station at Geneva, N.Y., dispute his (Breider's) findings but urge further investigations. The U.S. Food and Drug Administration, in a report made available to us, insists 'there is no cause for alarm based on toxicity.'"

Verification of Stoewsand's research was not slow in coming. A Swiss researcher, Dr. A. Schurch, published a report showing that in experiments with growing rats and chickens fed either hybrid juices or a vinifera juice, none of the animals exhibited any anatomical, pathological, or histological anomalies attributed to a specific treatment.

Nicholas H. Paul, ex-president of the Finger Lakes Wine Growers Association, recalled in 1985 that:

> At the height of his anti-hybrid campaign, the Jack Anderson column and so forth, I enlisted Charles Fournier to go as intermediary with me to call on Dr. Frank and beg him to tone down his attacks.

Figure 3.4: In 1982, at the end of his four-decade career at the Geneva Station, Dr. Willard B. Robinson referred to the refutation of the toxicity of chicks as one of the biggest contributions the Station had made to the wine industry. Photo by author.

> As you probably know, you didn't discuss things with him, you listened. We listened a long time to the litany of the indignities he suffered at Geneva and that is about as far as we got.[47]

Dr. Frank did not entirely give up talking about the toxicity of the French hybrids. In 1982, Fournier informed Wagner that Frank had quieted down quite a bit as far as his chicken and pigeon stories were concerned, although he could not resist mentioning them from time to time.[48]

The Vinifera-Hybrid Controversy

The start of the vinifera-hybrid controversy probably originated as the result of a number of articles published in 1961 by *Wines and Vines*.[49] In January, Charles Fournier reported on Gold Seal's success with Chardonnay and Riesling and the promising outlook for the vinifera. Keith H. Kimball of Great Western wrote in the April issue that the inherent tenderness of the vinifera and low minimum temperatures posed a real threat to commercial success with the vinifera. Fournier refuted Kimball's position in the August issue. Writing in the November 1961, issue, Philip Wagner reviewed what had been published and added:

In short, we have a real controversy here in the East. As an interested observer and good friend of all concerned, perhaps I may add a few remarks.

The first is that this is a controversy involving the very basis of our Eastern vineyards and the future character of the Eastern wines.

Second, it is a healthy controversy. Progress comes out of trial and error and much self-criticism.

Third, the vinifera controversy is only one aspect of a broader argument. In the New York Finger Lakes district, thinking on the future of Eastern wine-growing is in fact split four ways, and these four points of view have a way of shading into one another. It is a friendly argument even though it occasionally develops a cutting edge. All agree that in the end the decisions are going to be dictated by Nature and the Market.[50]

The four points of view recognized by Wagner were 1) the traditionalists who felt that such native American varieties as Catawba, Delaware, and Concord should remain the basis of their dessert and table wines; 2) the blenders, who felt that the traditional eastern varieties should be blended with California wines to achieve better overall balance; 3) the advocates of the French hybrids who felt that their mild aromas and flavors compared favorably with the vinifera with none of the risk involved in growing them; and 4) those whose objective was to produce a range of vinifera wines in the East as different from the vinifera wines of California as are the wines of northern Europe. A case could be made for all four points of view, Wagner wrote. "There is a very strong case for replacing the traditional viticulture with a viticulture based on the hybrids, and by some wine producers it has already been conceded and is being acted upon. And there is a case for the vinifera, when cultivated with the necessary expertise, as a source of premium wine of outstanding quality. The next decade or two are going to be exciting ones for the Eastern wine growers."

The antihybrid campaign had its origin in Europe. In France, for example, in the wake of the nineteenth-century phylloxera epidemic, the planting of French hybrids increased to more than 534,000 acres in 1929.[51] Then, in the early 1930s, a tremendous growth in the vinifera vineyards of Algeria led to a serious overproduction problem. The growers in Algeria and the Midi sought to have their overproduction problem resolved by limiting the production of the hybrids and, because they had sufficient political influence, the first antihybrid legislation was passed in 1935. In Germany the crusade against the French hybrids was joined by the chemical companies who knew that far less in the way of sprays and fungicides was needed to grow the hybrids successfully than was the case with the vinifera.

Although economic and financial considerations were responsible in France for the attempt to suppress the hybrids, any argument including grape racism was fair game for the provinifera forces. On March 31, 1935, the *Progres Agricole* of Montpellier, mouthpiece for the Official Viticulture of Midi, ran an article that indicates the level reached by antihybrid rhetoric:

> If the regions of polyculture begin producing wine, what will become of the regions which are devoted exclusively to the culture of the vine in the face of this competition?
>
> The wine of hybrids, issued from bastards, is also a bastard. It could possibly contain, like the vine from which it comes, the principal characteristics of its French parent; but aren't the other characteristics always dominant? Don't they have any influence? Don't they stain the honor of wine, as Oliver de Serres said—the black spot which inevitably marks the purity of a race?[52]

Wagner commented in a letter to Vernon L. Singleton at Davis on August 7, 1967:

> As you know, the issue is heavily political in Europe. These efforts to prove toxicity in non-vinifera wines are protectionist motivated, at least in Germany and are the ostensible basis for the exclusion from Germany of all wines including blends in which any trace of diglucosides can be found. In the meantime, of course, the Germans themselves are doing work with the hybrids.

The virulence of the antihybrid campaign in the United States mirrored what was going on in Europe. By 1971 the myth of the toxicity of the hybrids was beginning to be dispelled and there was the increasing realization that there were areas of the East where growing the vinifera was not practical or possible and that the French hybrids offered a very good substitute. On November 4, 1977, at the annual meeting of the American Wine Society in Arlington, Virginia, there was a last gathering at which Frank, Lawrence, Wagner, and others spoke. Wagner commented that any number of people growing hybrids also put in vinifera out of curiosity and hope:

> In other words, practical growers are remarkably free of doctrinaire prejudices. They see the problem in its true light, which is to discover the best grapes—aside from some lovely theory—that are capable of producing reliably in their location and yielding wine that may be priced competitively yet profitably.
>
> But in the 40 years of our experience growing grapes—and owing to those 40 years—we cannot in good conscience recommend a large planting of vinifera to anyone who can not afford the risk. To anyone who can afford the risk, all power to him. But not to the person who is thinking about retirement, has a few thousand dollars, and wants us to tell him to put in Cabernet Sauvignon.[53]

Practical considerations helped bring the vinifera-hybrid controversy to an end. However, many growers and would-be growers wound up choosing sides. Mark Miller has called Frank an anomaly, that he interrupted a trend toward an eastern viticulture based on the French hybrids. The vinifera would have eventually arrived in the East. It is arguable that the failure to build a solid industry before the vinifera were introduced brought about division when cooperative learning would have been more effective.

Chapter Four

Vineyards and Wineries before Farm Winery Legislation

Growing grapes in the East meant dealing with a difficult environment. Philip Wagner gave a memorable description of growing conditions in the East when he was the honorary research lecturer at the 1978 annual meeting of the American Society of Enologists in San Diego, California:

> In Maryland, I might say, conditions are ideal for experimental work with grapes. We are in the direct path of the Caribbean hurricanes, which usually drop 3 or 4 inches of rain on us the day before starting harvest. We are on the eastern, not the western, edge of the continental mass, meaning that we get all extremes of continental weather, which can favor us with from -14° to 76° in the same January. We alternate flood and drought, enjoy high humidity. Most of the diseases thrive here. We have no need to saturate a greenhouse with peronospora as they do at Geilweilerhof, to check mildew resistance, because the atmosphere is already saturated with it. We are perfectly equipped at no expense to test disease resistance, frost resistance, winter hardiness, hail resistance, phylloxera of course, bird damage, the effect of high winds, ripe rot and splitting.... No experimenter could ask for more. Anything that survives in Maryland is worth trial anywhere this side of the Arctic Circle.[1]

In 1945, Wagner's *A Wine-Grower's Guide* was the first book to provide guidance on growing the French hybrids. It took time for a full appreciation of the importance of these varieties to be realized. At first, a combination of their winemaking potential, cold hardiness, and disease resistance made experimenting with them seem worth considering, and this was reinforced when other attributes became known. A good example is a 1956 article evaluating the French hybrids written by Dr. Herbert C. Barrett, assistant professor of Plant Breeding at the University of Illinois at Urbana:

> One of the most interesting features found in the French hybrid varieties, and one of potential economic value, is the ability of many varieties to produce a commercial crop from secondary or tertiary buds in the event that frost or freezing has destroyed the primary bud or its developing shoot and flower clusters. In regions subject to unseasonable frosts in spring or extreme temperature changes in winter, there would be considerable value in such characters because it might mean the difference between a reduced but worthwhile crop or no crop at all. Few American varieties will produce anything beyond a few small clusterlets if the primary buds or shoots developing from these buds are destroyed.[2]

In addition to the availability of vines and equipment, and information on how to grow the French hybrids, articles pointing out their value were important in getting test vineyards started. As for the vinifera, with centuries-long history of failures, it was primarily a question of where it might be possible to grow them and if it would be profitable to do so.

Early Vineyards

In the 1950s and 1960s vineyard plantings and winery openings occurred at a slow pace. It was during these years that the influence of Philip Wagner and Konstantin Frank led to an increasing awareness of the possibilities the French hybrids and vinifera offered in making dry table wines.

It took time for there to be a change in the grape varieties grown and used by the large wineries in the East to make wine. These wineries had a ready market for the fortified and sparkling wines made from native American grapes, the grapes were readily available, and there were existing relationships with growers that made change difficult (see chapter 1). It is not surprising that some wineries became more enthusiastic about growing new varieties than others. In Ontario, for example, Brights played a leadership role in winemaking and grape growing using the French hybrids and vinifera while the other large wineries lagged far behind.

One winery where change came slowly was Renault Winery in Egg Harbor City, New Jersey. At the end of the 1970s the winery had 1,400 acres of grapes and produced 225,000 gallons of wine. The greatest quantity of grapes they used for wine remained unchanged from the past: Noah, the base grape used in their champagne, Elvira, Fredonia, Ives, and Catawba. Of the twenty-six wines on their wine list, 20 percent were blends utilizing French hybrids. Their varietal wines—Elvira, Noah,

Ives, and Catawba—all had a strong consumer following, and there was increasing demand for two sparkling wines that accounted for half of the winery's business, Blueberry Champagne, and Blueberry Duck.[3]

When Philip Wagner was preparing his "Profitable Wine Grapes for the North East" paper for presentation at the New York State Horticultural Society meeting on January 20, 1965, he contacted winery executives in the Finger Lakes and others for statistical information about grape varieties in their vineyards and what they saw as their requirements for the future. A letter from Fred C. Taylor at the Taylor Wine Company dated November 17, 1964, projected the winery's needs through 1970 as including 2,800 tons of Delaware, 1,100 tons of Ives, and perhaps 3,000 tons of Aurore. A December 28, 1964, letter from Greyton H. Taylor at the Pleasant Valley Wine Company stated that the winery was working on a line of 100 percent varietals including Delaware, Diamond, and possibly Isabella. Blends of French hybrids were being considered for a Vin Blanc Sec and a Vin Rouge. Diamond was singled out as a variety with considerable promise for new plantings.

In a letter dated December 29, 1964, Ernest Reveal at Widmer's Wine Cellars informed Wagner that Catawbas were already in short supply due to the popularity of Charles Fournier's Pink Catawba wine and that a shortage of Niagara was likely because of the rapidly increasing demand for Widmer's Lake Niagara. Reveal also looked for increased demand for Delaware and the Seibels. Charles Fournier at Gold Seal Vineyards responded on December 29 by saying that his winery was embarking on an extensive planting of Catawbas because their Catawba wine sales had increased at the rate of 75 percent a year for the past four years. The viniferas, which he stated as still requiring special care and offering special risk, would provide strong competitive advantage to wineries that could have them in commercial quantities.

A December 30, 1964, reply from Dr. John Einset, head of the Department of Pomology at the New York State Agricultural Experiment Station at Geneva, stated his belief that the big potential for the French hybrids would increasingly be realized through using them in place of the blending wines from California. The viniferas would have to bring $400–$500 a ton to compete with Delaware available at $200 a ton. Thus, of the native American varieties, increased plantings of Catawba and Delaware would be justified. Ives would continue to be much in demand until a substitute, perhaps a hybrid, could be found. Elvira was another variety that would likely be replaced by hybrid varieties.

A particularly interesting reply in a letter dated December 28, 1964, came from Douglas P. Moorhead at Presque Isle Wine Cellars in North East, Pennsylvania. After giving his opinion on a dozen varieties, he wrote:

> In summary, I would hesitate to recommend the planting of Delaware, Ives and Elvira to any grower in the northeast and would strongly advise not to plant Niagara or Clinton. Among the old eastern grapes, Catawba looks the best with possibly some room for Dutchess on good locations.

The hybrids must depend, unfortunately, almost completely on the present needs or desires of the wineries which doesn't leave much room for innovation or change, unless the grower wants to develop his own market like we are trying to.

I personally think that the greatest hope for the northeast is in a number of smaller wineries trying different lines than the big wineries in New York. Without them we are going to have another 50 years of Catawba, Niagara, Delaware and Elvira.

At the conclusion of his paper, Wagner stated: "There is a need for small-scale producers to pace the big commercial wineries, and I can assure you that the big fellows would welcome them. A few very small producers did the spadework in the case of the hybrids. They got a lot of fun out of it, and even made it pay. They had the processor's profit as well as the grower's profit, to help balance off the risk. Their successes in producing totally new wine types under Eastern conditions have been convincing enough to inspire a sharp change of direction in the industry."

Interest in planting the French hybrids had grown steadily from the time the Wagners established Boordy Vineyard in 1941. Within three years their nursery had supplied vines for customers in more than half the states in the United States. They freely offered their advice on how to grow the French hybrids, and that knowledge became widely available after the publication of Wagner's *A Wine-Grower's Guide* in 1945.

The French Hybrids in Ohio

Ohio is a good example of how a state got started on a wine grape program based on the French hybrids. The first French hybrids to arrive in Ohio were cuttings of Seibel 1000 (Rosette) obtained in 1941 by Mantey Vineyards in Sandusky and sent to Foster Nursery in Fredonia, New York, to be grafted on Couderc 3309 rootstock.[4] In 1954, Meier's Wine Cellars in Silverton, ten miles from Cincinnati, planted Baco No. 1 (Baco Noir), Seibel 5898 (Rougeon), Seibel 1096, and Seibel 4643 on North Bass Island (Isle St. George) in Lake Erie. The Ohio State University's Agricultural Research and Development Center (OARDC) planted Rosette at Wooster in 1956.

Grape production in the nineteenth century in Ohio reached a high of 28,000 acres in 1889 and then began a steady decline to less than 4,000 acres in 1968. Credit for the revival of the industry belongs to Henry O. Sonneman, president of Meier's Wine Cellars, who believed that knowledge of viticulture had progressed to the point where grapes could be successfully grown along the Ohio River. He lobbied hard for state support for the industry and finally won the cooperation of the Ohio Department of Agriculture, other state agencies, and Governor James Rhodes.[5]

In 1960, Dr. Roy M. Kottman, dean of the College of Agriculture at the Ohio State University and director of OARDC in Wooster, assigned Dr. James M. Beattie at the Research Center's Southern Branch at Ripley in Brown County to set up an experimental vineyard there. The initial research planting consisted of thirty-nine cultivars including twelve French hybrid varieties.[6] In 1963, Dr. Garth A. Cahoon joined the Research Center and was put in charge of the experimental vineyard.

This initial planting was successful, and in October 1964, Dr. Kottman formed a Grape Advisory Committee to broaden the experiment. In consultation with agricultural extension agents from fifteen counties along the Ohio River, it was decided to establish one-acre research-demonstration vineyards in each of these counties in cooperation with interested growers. At each location eleven cultivars were planted, selected from the thirteen best performing cultivars from the vineyard at Ripley.

Another scientist hired in 1963 was Dr. James P. Gallander, who in 1965 began evaluating the winemaking potential of all of these cultivars at the food technology laboratories in Wooster. Each year, chemical analyses and sensory evaluations were performed on about forty to fifty cultivars. Two of the best cultivars identified were Aurore and DeChaunac. Also given high ratings were Chelois, Chancellor, Villard Blanc, Seyval and Maréchal Foch.[7]

The cooperating growers signed five-year agreements, and by 1970 fourteen out of the fifteen had completed what they agreed to do. Half of the growers had increased the size of their vineyards, and by 1972 as a direct consequence of the research-demonstration project, seven new wineries were established in Ohio and one in Indiana. The first was Tarula Winery in New Clarksville, which Wistar A. Marting opened in 1967 after his vineyard had expanded to thirty acres and he needed to utilize his grapes. Valley Vineyards in Morrow opened in 1970 with more than forty acres, primarily French hybrids. Fittingly, the largest vineyard was Chateau Jac-Jan in New Richmond, which was owned by Meier's Wine Cellars and named after Henry Sonneman's children, Jack and Janet. That vineyard, containing between 90 and 100 acres, consisted mainly of French hybrids.

The Vinifera in Virginia

The Virginia experience differed sharply from that in Ohio because of the lack of government or university involvement and support when it was getting started. It was up to individuals in the private sector to decide the direction they wanted to take. The earliest plantings were French hybrids, but vinifera plantings quickly followed.

There were fifteen acres of grapes planted in Virginia in 1948, most of them table grapes, when Dr. George D. Oberle left his position as associate professor specializing in fruit breeding at the New York State Agricultural Experiment Station to become a horticulturist at the Virginia Polytechnic Institute (VPI) in Blacksburg. A test planting of twenty-eight French hybrid varieties was put in at

VPI and observations of their performance were made in 1950, 1951, and 1952, with the results being published in 1953.[8] Seyve-Villard 5-276 (Seyval), Seibel 13053 (Cascade), and Seibel 4986 (Rayon d'Or) were found to be the best adapted, four others fairly well adapted, and the remainder to be of doubtful promise or poorly adapted. No recommendations were made.

The test plantings at Blacksburg had no practical outcome, however, for the revival of grape growing in Virginia did not begin until the late 1960s and early 1970s. Wilbur "Bill" Garrett, editor of the *National Geographic,* planted seventy-five French hybrid vines he obtained from Philip Wagner in 1964, and Charles Raney, who later established Farfelu Vineyard, moved his first vines from Long Island to Flint Hill in 1967, bringing them to Virginia wrapped in burlap.[9] A planting of 3,000 vines followed. Robert de Treville Lawrence, Sr., ordered vines from Wagner in 1967 and planted fifty vines each of Seyval and Maréchal Foch at Highbury, his home not far from The Plains in April, 1968, and relied on Wagner for advice on how to grow them.

In 1972, Archie M. Smith, Jr., who opened Meredyth Vineyards in 1976, planted 2,300 vines near Middleburg under the guidance of Trenholm D. Jordan, an extension specialist in the Finger Lakes.[10] Other growers who later opened wineries and planted French hybrids about this time were Carl Flemer at Ingleside Plantation Vineyards in Oak Grove and Albert C. Weed at La Abra (now Mountain Cove) Vineyards in Lovingston.

Although the modern industry started with the French hybrids, it soon shifted to the vinifera. The person most responsible for the development of the vinifera industry in Virginia was Robert de Treville Lawrence, Sr., Dr. Konstantin Frank's most influential disciple.[11] Lawrence was born in Atlanta, Georgia, on June 21, 1915. He received an A.B. from the University of Georgia and worked for the Hearst papers in Atlanta before enlisting in the Air Force in 1941, where he rose to the rank of lieutenant colonel. In 1951 he joined the U.S. Department of State as a press attaché and public affairs officer, serving in many countries including Liberia where he became known as "Lawrence of Monrovia." He returned from overseas in 1965 and was assigned to the Voice of America in Washington until he retired in 1972.

Lawrence became interested in wine while he was abroad. In 1969, a year after he planted French hybrid vines at Highbury, he first heard about Konstantin Frank and wrote to him. He received his first vinifera vines from Frank and planted them in 1970. Frank also gave him instructions on how to grow them and told him about two Maryland growers who had planted vinifera, Dr. G. Hamilton Mowbray and Dr. Charles S. Singleton. In 1971 Lawrence planted 121 vinifera vines and added more in 1972.

Almost immediately, Lawrence became convinced that planting vinifera was both possible and desirable and began spreading the word about how profitable it could be to grow them. He felt that growers needed to have accurate information on how to grow the vinifera, and in a letter to the editor of the *Piedmont Virginian*

Figure 4.1: On August 30, 1980, the Vinifera Wine Growers Association awarded its Perpetual Monteith Trophy for the first time. The recipient was Dr. Konstantin Frank, who in this photo is flanked by Robert de Treville Lawrence, Sr., president of the VWGA, and Mrs. Elizabeth Furness, owner of Piedmont Vineyards which she had opened the year before on Waverly Farm in Middleburg, Virginia. Photo by author.

published on April 5, 1972, he stated that he had sent a letter to Governor Linwood Holton suggesting the establishment of a viticulture and enology department at VPI to assist farmers. In 1967, VPI offered no encouragement or assistance in planting wine grapes, and a VPI bulletin published in 1972 not only failed to mention vinifera but gave scant hope for the hybrids.[12] For several years Lawrence crusaded for funding from VPI and the U.S. Department of Agriculture (USDA) to provide programs to assist growers, and he did not hesitate to criticize them publicly for their failure to help the industry.[13] It would not be until after the Virginia Farm Winery Act was passed in 1980 that Dr. Leslie McCombs, professor of viticulture at VPI, would begin to offer courses and issue proceedings.

Interest in planting the vinifera grew rapidly. According to an article in its May 3, 1972, issue, the *Piedmont Virginian* was sponsoring the showing of a winegrowing movie about Dr. Frank's 1971 harvest on May 5 and that half a dozen residents of Fauquier and Rappahannock counties had already announced their intention of starting commercial wineries.[14]

An important addition to the list of vinifera growers came in 1973 when, at Lawrence's suggestion, Elizabeth Furness agreed to plant vinifera vines on her 500-acre Waverly Farm in Middleburg. That year, with Dr. Frank's assistance and encouragement, the first of thirty acres of Chardonnay and Sémillon, plus a little Seyval Blanc, were planted. She was seventy-five years old at the time, but that did not stop her from immediately becoming a home winemaker. For many years she hosted seminars and meetings at Waverly, and it was there in 1979 that she opened Piedmont Vineyards, the first commercial vinifera winery in Virginia.[15]

Lawrence invited Dr. Frank to come to Virginia to give a wine growing seminar on July 13, 1972, and a sizeable crowd gathered at Kinloch Farm near The Plains to hear him. It had also been arranged that during Frank's visit there would be a special wine tasting at the U.S. Department of State to honor both Frank and the wines he had made from 100 percent vinifera grapes. The event was held in the Van Buren Room on the eighth floor overlooking the Lincoln Memorial. Foreign Service officers and representatives from other federal government departments were treated to a blind comparison tasting of three of Frank's wines against three similar wines bought at the nearby Riverside Liquor Store. Frank's wines won high marks.[16]

In 1973 a second winegrowing seminar was held on July 14 with Dr. Hamilton Mowbray as the featured speaker. Mowbray had opened his own winery, Montbray Wine Cellars, in Westminster, Maryland, and Lawrence followed the seminar by organizing the "Piedmont Montbray Vinifera Wine School," a series of two-hour classes given by Mowbray on ten Mondays starting on September 10, 1973, which attracted fifty-two people.[17]

At the second class, Lawrence and Mowbray talked about the advantages of forming a Vinifera Wine Growers Association. A meeting was held in The Plains on October 4 to discuss the proposed organization and it was announced that Frank had agreed to serve as a consultant to the new organization. A week later the Vinifera Wine Growers Association was officially formed and Lawrence was elected president. It was pointed out that the new association could serve a valuable function by establishing a bi-annual publication that would generate, collect, and disseminate technical information on grape growing. Lawrence later said that the association's journal was intended to be "low tech" and would be a "fill-in" between *Wines and Vines* and the *Journal of the American Society for Enology*.[18]

The first issue of the *Vinifera Wine Growers Journal* appeared in the spring of 1974, and for many years Lawrence and the association promoted the vinifera with a singleness of purpose. People interested in growing the vinifera in many states subscribed to the journal, which helped promote the vinifera beyond Virginia. On August 28, 1976, the association held its first festival near The Plains to help finance the journal. As more and more vinifera were planted in the East, the journal gradually lost its revolutionary zeal.

The hybrids continued to be planted and the wineries making wines from them did well. Lawrence, however, was successful in shifting Virginia grape growing to the vinifera. By 1984, according to the Virginia Department of Agriculture and VPI, there were 963 acres of grapes in Virginia, 602 vinifera, 276 French hybrids, and 85 native American varieties.

Figure 4.2: Meredyth Vineyards opened in Middleburg, Virginia, on July 1, 1976. *Left to right:* Archie Smith, Jr., his wife Dody; and their son Archie, III, and his wife Suzelle. In the foreground is one of the winery dogs. Photo by author, 1977.

Early Wineries

Smaller wineries in most states did not open until after the passage of favorable legislation, usually in the form of farm winery laws. In a few states where there was no problem with the law, or where those who were interested in opening wineries chose to comply with existing laws, often at added expense, wineries opened at an earlier date.

One such winery was White Mountain Vineyards in Laconia, New Hampshire, founded by pharmacist John Canepa and his wife Lucille. In 1965, after searching for a good location to plant grapes, they planted 800 French hybrid vines on Governor's Island in Lake Winnipesaukee. They bought a farm near Belmont in 1968 and had seven-and-a-half acres in the ground by 1970. The winery was established in 1969 and the first sale was made to the New Hampshire state stores a year later.[19]

Meredyth Vineyards in Middleburg, Virginia was the result of a five-year plan drawn up in 1971 by Archie M. Smith, Jr., after the cattle market became erratic and he had to decide what to do with Stirling Farm, the land he had farmed since 1953. His son, Dr. Archie M. Smith, III, who was teaching philosophy at Oxford University at the time, suggested planting grapes. The decision was made to go ahead in a business-like way by figuring out how many vines had to be planted by 1975 in order to open a winery in 1976.[20] In 1972, 2,300 vines were planted on the first of sixty acres, and the Smith family went on to play an important role in the growth of the Virginia wine industry.[21]

Michigan did not require special legislation to open wineries after Prohibition, and wineries were being established in the state before Repeal. Two of them crossed the border from Ontario. St. Julian Wine Company in Paw Paw was founded in 1921 when Mariano Meconi, opened Meconi Wine Cellars in Windsor. In 1933 he moved the winery—now called Border City Winery—to Detroit where, at first, sacramental wines were made. Three years later he renamed the winery the Italian Wine Company and moved it again to Paw Paw where it would be closer to the source of grapes. During World War II when anti-Italian sentiment had developed in the United States, Meconi changed the name of the winery for the last time, choosing to honor San Giuliano, the patron saint of his birthplace, Faleria, Italy. By 1976 his son-in-law Paul Braganini and his grandson David Braganini were in charge of the winery and Charles Catherman had become the winemaker.[22]

The Windsor Wine Company in Ontario, owned by Morris Twomey, was relocated to Farmington in 1933 and was renamed La Salle Wines and Champagne. After Twomey died in 1963, the La Salle label was acquired by St. Julian.

Bronte Champagne and Wines Company was founded in 1933 by a dentist, Dr. Theodore Wozniak, who started his operation in Detroit eight months before the end of Prohibition. He made two products that had been recently legalized—3.2 percent beer and light wine. He subsequently moved the winery to Hartford, Michigan, and in 1979 sold it to Tabor Hill Vineyard and Winecellar in Buchanan.

Bronte was home to the first French hybrids to arrive in Michigan. In 1954, winemaker Angelo Spinazze brought in twelve vines of Baco No. 1 he had obtained from Ollie Bradt in Vineland, Ontario. These were followed by plantings of Aurore, Vidal, Maréchal Foch, De Chaunac, and Ravat 51. His first varietal Baco Noir was marketed as "Baco Dinner Wine" and did not sell well until he labeled it Baco Noir and turned it into a success. Spinazze is also given credit for starting the Cold Duck boom (see appendix D).[23]

Within two years of Repeal, nine wineries had opened in Michigan. Among them were Frontenac Winery, a family operation founded in Paw Paw in 1933 and sold in 1967; and Molly Pitcher Winery, which opened in Harbert in 1934 and was renamed Lakeside Vineyard after being sold in 1975.

Warner Vineyards in Paw Paw, which became the largest winery in the state after La Salle closed, was founded in 1938 by John Turner as Michigan Wineries, Inc. His son-in-law James K. Warner became president in 1951; in 1973 the name changed to Warner Vineyards; and in 1976 Turner's grandson followed as president. By the mid-1970s, the winery owned 250 acres of vineyards and was buying grapes from 400 growers. The storage capacity of the winery was about 3 million gallons.[24]

After the initial burst of winery openings after Prohibition, it was many years before another winery was bonded in Michigan. Two home winemaking couples—Leonard and Ellen Olson and Carl and Janet Banholzer—started Tabor Hill Vineyard and Winecellar in Buchanan in the early 1960s. They were convinced that they could grow premium wine grapes, and after two-and-a-half years of looking for a suitable site they purchased a farm on the south side of Mt. Tabor, six miles from Lake Michigan. They began planting vines in 1968 and by the time the winery was bonded in 1970 they had fifteen acres of vinifera and hybrid varieties. In addition, both couples had vineyards of their own, with the Banholzers experimenting with fifty-six varieties on their property. The Banholzers sold their interest in Tabor Hill in 1971 and a few years later opened their own winery, Banholzer Winecellars in Hesston, Indiana. The Olsons were producing 8,500 gallons in 1972 when the winery opened in July. In 1979 David F. Upton purchased Tabor Hill.[25]

Ohio was another state where small wineries did not need to have special legislation passed before they opened. The experiences gained by the test plantings in southern Ohio led to seven wineries being started in that part of the state. After the Civil War the grape and wine industry had shifted from southern Ohio to the northern part of the state, particularly along the southern coast of Lake Erie in the Sandusky area and four islands in Lake Erie: Kelley's Island, North Bass Island (Isle St. George), Middle Bass Island, and South Bass Island (Put-in-Bay). On these islands alone, at least 2,600 acres out of a total of about 5,700 acres were planted in vineyards.[26] Much of the vineyard acreage in this area remained intact during Prohibition with the grapes being used for juice.[27] Several wineries survived Prohibition in this manner including Meier's Wine Cellars, Mantey Vineyards, Lonz Winery, and Heineman Winery. The Steuk Winery near Sandusky, founded in 1855, closed at the start of Prohibition but maintained its vineyards throughout the thirteen-year era. Other wineries that opened right after Repeal were Dover Vineyards in Westlake, Catawba Island Wine Company in Port Clinton (doing business as Mon Ami Champagne Company), and Klingshirn Winery in Avon Lake.

Interest in growing grapes in northeastern Ohio started to increase in the late 1960s and a number of wineries opened there in the early 1970s. In addition to Markko Vineyard established by Arnie Esterer, one of Dr. Frank's cooperators, three others provided leadership for those who followed.

Chalet Debonné in Madison was founded in 1971 and opened its doors in 1972. The winery was started by Tony J. Debevc, a long-time grape grower, and his son Anthony P. Debevc, who had earned a degree in pomology from the Ohio State University and persuaded his father to add ten acres of French hybrids to the thirty acres of Concords that were already growing. By 1977 the winery was producing 15,000 gallons.[28]

Dr. Thomas Wykoff, an ear, nose, and throat specialist, started Cedar Hill Wine Company in Cleveland Heights. In 1974 he turned a beauty parlor into a French country style restaurant and winery. The restaurant, Au Provence, was on the first floor and the wine made in the winery underneath was called Chateau Lagniappe. Wykoff's outgoing personality and willingness to help other winemakers made him one of the best-known people in the eastern industry.[29]

Investment banker Willett "Bill" Worthy planted nine acres of vinifera and hybrids in Madison in 1973. He attributed his success with the vinifera to his practice of burying the vines during the winter. After selling his grapes to Cedar Hill Wine Company and others for several years, he opened his winery, Grand River Vineyard, in 1978.[30]

As was the case in Ohio, interest in grape growing in Missouri began in the 1950s and 1960s and grew to the point where wineries were opening by the early 1970s. Missouri had a thriving wine industry with more than 100 wineries when Prohibition forced them to cease operations, with the exception of St. Stanislaus Monastery in Florissant and one other monastery, both of which continued to make sacramental wines. When Prohibition ended, the demand was for sweet dessert type wines.

In 1943, Missouri created a Domestic Wine License that permitted small wineries to make up to 5,000 gallons of wine a year, enough that anyone could open a winery. Vineyards came first and in 1951 Axel Arneson planted the first French hybrids in Steelville. William B. Stoltz began planting Concords and other native American grapes near St. James in 1957, and in 1965 started to add French hybrids to his seventy-acre vineyard. By 1970 he had fifty-seven varieties, most of them experimental plantings, on what had become a ninety-two-acre vineyard. He opened Stoltz Vineyard Winery in 1968 but closed it a few years later, choosing to remain a grower selling his grapes.[31]

In 1963, at an Experiment in International Living program in St. Louis, journalist Clayton Byers had attended a lecture by Alexis Lichine that concluded with a tasting of Bordeaux wines. His interest aroused, he then read Lichine's book Wines of France and began visiting wineries in many states. With the goal of making the best possible wine out of Missouri grapes, Byers and his wife Nissel opened Montelle Vineyards in August 1969. In addition to leasing vineyards, the Byers started their own in 1970 including a research vineyard with nearly fifty varieties. At the end of the decade they had nine acres of vineyards and storage capacity for 5,000 gallons of wine.[32]

The first winery to open in Hermann was Stone Hill Winery in 1970. The original Stone Hill Winery on the property was founded in 1847, and after the Civil War it became the second largest winery in the United States with wine production of approximately 1,250,000 gallons. Between 1873 and 1904 the winery won eight gold medals at world fairs and expositions. During Prohibition the winery and vineyards were abandoned, and in 1936 the underground cellars on the property began to be used for the production of sixty-five tons of mushrooms a year. When Jim and Betty Ann Held bought Stone Hill in 1965, they already owned a four-and-a-half-acre Catawba vineyard in Pershing and were willing to make a commitment to preserve the historic property, restore the main building, and clean out the eight cellars. They began planting vineyards and in 1970 bonded the winery. By 1973 the limit on wine production had been raised, the Helds were producing 60,000 gallons of wine a year, and were purchasing grapes from their neighbors in addition to expanding the vineyards that had already reached twenty producing acres.[33]

James and Patricia Hofherr bonded their St. James Winery in St. James, Missouri, in 1970. He had earned a master's degree in microbiology from the University of Oklahoma and worked for both a brewery and winery before they made the decision to buy 155 acres in St. James that included 18 acres of Concords. Wine production in the first year was 10,000 gallons, and by 1980 they made 35,000 gallons and were rapidly expanding the vineyards.[34]

Early French Hybrid Wineries

Most people who grew grapes or opened wineries in the 1950s and 1960s were influenced by the advice they got from Philip Wagner or Konstantin Frank, or from someone who knew one of them. Wagner's books, his earlier start, and the fact that he had a nursery and could supply both vines and equipment meant that he was usually the first person the neophyte grower or winemaker heard about. What follows are brief profiles of a few of the earliest wineries that were based on the French hybrids and contact with Philip Wagner.

One of the earliest wineries to open after Philip Wagner's Boordy Vineyard in 1945 was High Tor Vineyards on the Palisades high above the Hudson River, thirty miles north of New York City. Everett Crosby, a radio and television scriptwriter and producer, and his wife Alma bought the seventy-eight-acre property known as High Tor in January 1950. The Crosbys had attempted to grow grapes in West Nyack but, as Everett put it in his autobiography, the vineyard was not successful because they planted the wrong varieties in the wrong place.[35] To give himself the best chance of success, he contacted Frank Schoonmaker for advice and was referred to Wagner, who sold him 3,000 French hybrid vines and gave him a great deal of help including information on winery design.[36] Crosby left it up to Wagner to select the grapes to be planted, and the varieties he received were purposely designed to ripen at different times to make harvest easier and to minimize the number of containers required. When the winery opened in July 1954, High Tor became the first commercial winery in New York to produce wine entirely from the French hybrids.

In Missouri the first French hybrids were planted by gynecologist Axel Norman Arneson, the founder of Peaceful Bend Vineyard in Steelville. His first experience with wine was helping his father make wine at home during Prohibition. His interest in wine was later reinforced by his travels through Europe. In 1951 he bought his first French hybrid vines from Wagner and planted them at his home. Three years later he purchased several hundred acres of land along the Upper Meramec River where the winery is now located and ordered additional vines from Wagner. An agreement between Arneson and the University of Arkansas in 1965 led to a university research project that involved the planting of eight acres of at least ten varieties of French hybrids on two hilltops on his farm. There is no record of what the research study entailed, but when it ended in 1972, Arneson was left with the vineyards, and he used the grapes that year to open his winery.[37]

Melvin S. Gordon, a successful businessman in the insurance industry in the Philadelphia area, became interested in wine while he was on vacation in Burgundy. When he returned to Pennsylvania he began making wine at home and then bought a farm in Birchrunville, a tiny hamlet west of Valley Forge in Chester County. He planted French hybrids acquired from Philip Wagner in the mid-1950s including Seyval, Aurore, Rayon d'Or, Maréchal Foch, Cascade, and Ravat Noir. The vineyards probably did not exceed four to four-and-a-half acres in size. He bonded his winery, Conestoga Vineyards, in 1963. Pennsylvania was a highly restrictive monopoly state and under the laws in effect at that time, he could only sell his wine to the state store system or outside the state. Worse yet, if he wanted to serve any of his wines, he was required to buy them from one of the state stores operated by the Pennsylvania Liquor Control Board. During the years he operated the winery, production was never more than 700 to 1,000 gallons. In 1974 he sold the winery to David Fondots and returned to the insurance business.[38]

Frederick S. Johnson, who had a long career in tropical agricultural development in many areas of the world, bonded his Johnson Estate Winery in Westfield, New York, in 1961. When he returned from managing Nelson Rockefeller's plantations in Venezuela and Ecuador in 1960, he was faced with the decision of what to do with 125 acres of Concords his father had left him. He decided to open a winery both as a way of maximizing the return from his vineyards and as a buffer in case the market for fresh grapes would collapse as it had in the past. Since he also felt that the future lay in dry table wines, he began replacing the Concords with French hybrid grapes. Like so many others, he went to Riderwood, Maryland, to consult with Philip Wagner on starting a winery operation.[39]

Walter S. Taylor was the grandson of Walter Taylor who founded The Taylor Wine Company in 1880 on Bully Hill, a steep hillside overlooking Lake Keuka. This property was sold in the 1920s when The Taylor Wine Company moved to larger quarters on the other side of Hammondsport. When the Bully Hill property again came up for sale in 1957, Walter bought it in cooperation with his father, Greyton H. Taylor; and in 1958 Bully Hill Farms was established on the seventy-acre property with its thirty acres of vineyards. In 1961 Walter went to work for The Taylor Wine Company. A year later when Taylor acquired the Pleasant Valley Wine Company, Greyton Taylor was named to manage it and Walter became the assistant managing director.

Greyton Taylor had long admired Philip Wagner and had become convinced of the value of the French hybrids. During the 1960s the Taylors at Pleasant Valley Winery worked closely with Wagner. Restoration of the old winery at Bully Hill began in 1964, sales of juice to home winemakers started in 1965, and in 1967 Walter

Figure 4.3: *Left to right:* Richard P. Vine, Greyton Taylor, and Walter Taylor grouped around a rack-and-cloth wine press at the Pleasant Valley Wine Company in Hammondsport, New York. Vine joined the winery as a cellar worker in 1961 and advanced rapidly to the position of winemaker and executive vice president by the end of the decade. A note with the photo, which was probably taken in October 1967 stated that this was the first time red wine had been fermented on the skins at the Pleasant Valley winery under Taylor ownership. Wagner Collection.

established Bully Hill Wine Company, which he thought of as an experimental winery based on the French hybrids. Walter was certain that these were the wine grapes to grow because of their resistance to cold and diseases and the quality of wine made from them. From that time on Walter was an advocate of the French hybrids and promoted them as avidly as Frank promoted the vinifera. In 1968 he hired Hermann Wiemer as his winemaker, and much of the credit for Bully Hill's success has been attributed to the quality of the wines he made.[40]

On April 20, 1970, Walter was fired by the board of directors of the Taylor Wine Company because of his public attacks on the company's winemaking practices. Taylor was using as much as 25 percent of California wines in its blends as a way of reducing acidity and increasing alcohol content. What Walter considered dishonest was that the winery was listing the wines as coming from New York state. Walter also objected to ameliorating wine with water to reduce acidity, and he was later to use the slogan "Wine Without Water" to promote Bully Hill Wines.

Greyton Taylor left Pleasant Valley Winery in protest to the firing, and father and son incorporated Bully Hill Vineyards on a 50–50 basis. By the end of 1970,

Bully Hill had 2,000 acres, 120 acres of vineyards and wine production of 6,000 cases. Greyton Taylor, however, died before the end of the year and their operation then belonged solely to Walter.[41]

Lucian Dressel's interest in growing grapes began in 1959 when he read one of Wagner's books while he was a student at Harvard. Two years later he called Wagner and went to Riderwood, Maryland, to meet him. In 1966 he and his wife Eva bought the dormant Mount Pleasant Winery in Augusta, Missouri, that had been founded in 1881 by Friedrich Münch, a Lutheran minister and grape breeder. The winery had closed in 1920 with the coming of Prohibition and the property had to be restored. Approximately twenty-five acres of the original vineyard site were planted with French hybrids and several Missouri grapes, one of them being Münch, a Munson hybrid named after the founder of the original winery. Mount Pleasant Vineyards was bonded in 1968 and opened in the same year.[42]

In the mid-1950s, when Mark Miller had become an established advertising and magazine illustrator, his wife Dene gave him a copy of Wagner's *A Wine-Grower's Guide*. This led him to buy ten vines from Wagner and to make wine. His hobby soon outgrew his home and he and Dene began looking for land where he could grow grapes. In 1957 they found an old vineyard property in Marlboro, New York, which had once belonged to A. J. Caywood, the developer of the Dutchess grape. They bought the forty-acre property in September of that year and named it Benmarl, combining "ben," the Gaelic word for "hill," and "marl," the word for the slaty soil found on the property. Relying on the advice of both Wagner and Professor Pierre Galet, whom he had met a year earlier in Montpellier, France, he ordered enough vines from Wagner to plant five acres of French hybrids. In addition, some Chardonnay vines from California were also planted. The vines were in the ground when Miller's art career took him and his family to Burgundy from 1960 to 1967. While in France, his interest and knowledge of wine expanded, and when he returned to Benmarl he continued to upgrade his vineyard and winery equipment. The winery was licensed in 1971 with his son Eric as winemaker. Taking a page from his years in France, he founded the Société des Vignerons in 1971 as a way of financing the vineyard and winery. Members bought "vinerights" to two vines, which entitled them to twelve bottles of wine each year.[43]

Dr. Frank's Cooperators

The widespread publicity that Dr. Frank received from his championing of the vinifera brought many growers and would-be growers to his home in Hammondsport. They looked at his vineyards and listened to him explain how to grow the vinifera. Sometimes they spent time working with him and more often than not ordered vines from him for their own vineyard. Frank called those who subscribed to his teachings his "cooperators."

One of Frank's earliest cooperators was Douglas P. Moorhead of North East, Pennsylvania, who first met Frank in 1958. Moorhead graduated from the Pennsylvania State University in 1956 with a B.S. in pomology and then served in the U.S. Army. While he was stationed in Germany in 1957 he visited vineyards along the Rhine and became particularly interested in the Rieslings grown there. Because his father was a Concord grower with 160 acres of vineyards, it was easy for him to decide that he would plant Riesling in the family vineyard when he returned in 1958. The vines he got from Frank were planted in 1959, and this was the start of an extensive involvement in wine grapes, which included French hybrids bought from Wagner. Five years later, in 1964, Moorhead and a friend, William Konnerth, opened Presque Isle Wine Cellars for the sale of home winemaking equipment, supplies, and grape juice. Moorhead became a leader in the campaign to have a farm winery act passed in Pennsylvania in 1968 (see chapter 5) and as a result, in 1970, Presque Isle Wine Cellars became a small commercial winery as well as a supplier of grape juice and winery equipment to amateur winemakers and small commercial wineries.[44]

In 1964, John Moorhead was encouraged by his cousin Douglas to grow wine grapes on the farm owned by him and his wife Cindy in North East, Pennsylvania. They started with Aurore, Seyval Blanc, Villard Blanc, and Chelois obtained from Philip Wagner, and in the same year they put in a test planting of Riesling and Chardonnay with the assistance of Frank. During these early years they would drive to Hammondsport every month or so to consult with him. Another important source of information for them was Brights Wines in Niagara Falls, Ontario. As the vineyard at Moorhead Farm expanded, the care that John Moorhead took with his grapes made them sought after by wineries as early as the mid-1970s. Although he never opened a winery, he remained one of Frank's closest cooperators.[45]

Arnie Esterer began reading about growing grapes and making wine while he was working as an industrial engineer at Union Carbide in Ashtabula, Ohio, and in 1967 he came across Frank's name. That same year he spent a week of his vacation working for Frank in his vineyard. In 1984 he commented on how important that week was:

> Dr. Frank did two or three things that were very important to me. He told me to buy a lot of land. I wanted 20 or 30 acres, but he said to buy 100. I wound up buying 130. I told him that I wanted to plant 2,000 vines. He said that was far too much and that he wouldn't sell or give that many to me. What he did was to restrict my growth and slow me down. Today I realize how right he was.[46]

The couple of hundred vines from Frank were planted in 1968. In that same year Esterer began his partnership with Tim Hubbard and purchased the land in

Conneaut, Ohio, that became Markko Vineyard. The winery was built in 1972 and the vinifera wines made that fall were the first commercial vinifera wines to be produced in Ohio.

In 1967 Robert Woodbury, his wife Page, and his brother Gary took over the family farm in Dunkirk in Chautauqua County, the westernmost county in New York.[47] At that time the farm was producing tree fruits and Concords. Gary Woodbury's interest in wine grapes began the year before when friends introduced him to Frank. The first vinifera grapes were planted in 1970, and by the time Woodbury Vineyards opened in 1980 there were twenty-five acres of vinifera, half their total acreage of wine grapes. In 1984 the first of seventy-five additional acres of vinifera were planted, two-thirds of which were Chardonnay. To oversee the vineyard expansion, Geisenheim graduate Markus E. Riedlin was hired as their research viticulturist.

Brother David Petri, the winemaker at St. Meinrad Archabbey and Theological Seminary in St. Meinrad, Indiana, became one of Frank's cooperators in 1973 when he was sent to Frank for a year to learn how to make dry table wines. For about seventy years the 160 residents of the monastery had been drinking the wines made from their ten acres of Concords, and they were ready for a change. Brother David returned from Hammondsport with Chardonnay, Merlot, and other vinifera vines that he planted at St. Meinrad. Unfortunately, temperatures plunged to -22° during the winter of 1976–77, killing the vinifera vines.[48]

As word about Frank got around, people who became cooperators came from greater distances. George Mathiesen, a vice president of Westinghouse Broadcasting, and his wife Catherine were both home winemakers from California who had spent summers on Martha's Vineyard in Massachusetts since 1965. In 1971 they learned that Martha's Vineyard, ten miles out in the Atlantic Ocean from Cape Cod, had a growing season similar to that in Burgundy and they decided to try their hand at growing grapes. Later that year they visited Frank and were offered help as well as vines they could plant. For the first year the Mathiesens visited him monthly to observe what he was doing. Their initial three-acre vineyard was expanded to twenty acres a year later. In 1973 their winery, Chicama Vineyards, was licensed and their first wine was sold in 1974.[49]

In Tennessee, Judge William O. Beach, known to everyone as Billy Beach, was given a winemaking kit for Christmas in 1962. In 1965 he visited Frank, who supplied him with grafted vines and added his name to his list of twenty-two cooperators. Beach increased his plantings slowly and had nearly an acre in the ground by the mid-1970s, all the while making wine at home. When his daughter Louisa became engaged to Edward M. W. Cooke in 1979, who became progressively interested in grapes and wine, Beach decided to open a commercial winery when he retired in 1982. He and his son-in-law planted six acres in 1982, six more the next year, and opened their winery, Beachaven Vineyards and Winery, in Clarksville on June 1, 1987.[50]

Two Different Outcomes in Maryland

Simply because some people became more closely identified with Philip Wagner and others with Konstantin Frank did not mean that they were tied exclusively to one or the other. Most growers in those early years started out by planting French hybrids because they were more readily available and easier to grow. More often than not they also tried growing the vinifera. Although they might have wanted to produce wines made from vinifera grape varieties, climate and other environmental factors usually determined what would grow best in their vineyards. Those who were able to grow the vinifera successfully often replaced the French hybrids with vinifera varieties, but not always. Personalities, taste, and economics also played a part.

There is an interesting example in Maryland where two growers went in two separate directions. Both were professors at Johns Hopkins University in Baltimore.

Charles Southward Singleton, Dante Professor of Italian, heard about the French hybrids from Philip Wagner and began planting vines bought from him around 1950.[51] He experimented with fifteen different varieties in his vineyard in New Windsor and found they produced very well on the heavy clay soils of Carroll County. For a short time he sold grapes to Wagner, but by 1954 he was intent on opening his own winery. Cároli Vineyards opened in 1954 and probably closed in 1962.[52] Singleton loved to grow grapes but was not temperamentally inclined to put up with governmental regulations and had a succession of problems dealing with regulatory authorities. Hastening his decision to close the winery was his discovery of Frank and the vinifera. He became a total convert to the vinifera, planted vinifera vines, returned to being a home winemaker, but did not reopen his winery.

G. Hamilton Mowbray, usually called by his nickname "Ham," earned his doctorate in experimental psychology at Cambridge University in 1953, and it was during his years in England that he first became interested in wine.[53] On his return to the United States he began a twenty-year career as a research psychologist in the Applied Physics Laboratory at Johns Hopkins University. He started making wine at home in 1956 and a year later discovered Wagner's winemaking book *American Wines and Wine-Making*. Singleton supplied Mowbray with a few French hybrid grape cuttings, which he planted at his home in Woodbine, Maryland. His first visit to Dr. Frank in late 1958 convinced him that the vinifera could be grown in the East. He bought 500 pounds each of Riesling and Chardonnay grapes and asked permission to buy cuttings from Frank for planting in the spring of 1959. His one-third of an acre at Woodbine soon became too small, and in 1964 he and his wife Phyllis bought a 100-acre farm in Silver Run Valley near Westminster, Maryland, and planted 600 vines there. When the winery was bonded two years later, Mowbray decided to call it Montbray Wine Cellars, using the original French spelling of his name.[54]

Wine production in the early years was around 1,000 gallons, and one of the first wines placed on sale was Seyve-Villard 5-276, better known today as Seyval.

Figure 4.4: G. Hamilton Mowbray and his wife Phyllis opened Montbray Wine Cellars in Silver Run Valley, Maryland, in 1966. In addition to running the winery, he was a lecturer on wine at several colleges, the operator of the Montbray Wine School, and a consultant to many winery start-ups in Maryland and Virginia. Photo by author, 1979.

Mowbray called it Seyve-Villard, using the hybridizer's name, and claimed that his 1966 release was the first varietal Seyval to be sold in the United States. On June 21, 1976, as the result of a visit to his vineyard by a French specialist, who reported that Mowbray's Seyve-Villard was of higher quality than anything produced by that variety in France, Mowbray was summoned to the French ambassador's residence in Washington to receive the French government's highest decoration for agriculture, the Croix de Chevalier de Merite Agricole. The fact that Mowbray was associated with French hybrids was galling to Frank, who in later years did not refer to Mowbray as one of his cooperators.

Mowbray made the first commercial ice wine in the United States in 1974 (see appendix D). In 1967 he was a founding member of the American Wine Society and remained a strong supporter of that organization. Over the years he was responsible for helping many growers in Maryland and Virginia get started.

Not every winery worked out as planned. In 1934, just after Prohibition in the United States ended, Château-Gai Winery in Niagara Falls, Canada, opened a winery called Chateau Gay in Lewiston, New York. Three years later the winery was bought by Dr. Hector Carveth and in 1966 was moved to a new location in Lewiston. A combination of a $2 million investment in the winery as well as in eighty acres of new vineyards left the winery overextended to the point where it closed in 1970. The equipment was sold and in 1971 the empty building was bought by Richard Vine, Edward Moulton, and others who reopened the winery and renamed it Niagara Falls Wine Cellar. The new venture was undercapitalized and folded in 1973.[55]

Some wineries have opened and closed leaving little trace of their existence. Leon Adams tells the story of one such winery, Woburn Winery, which was opened at Clarksville, Virginia, near the North Carolina border in 1940 by John June Lewis, a black veteran of World War I. Lewis initially learned about growing grapes as a boy from the owner of a nearby plantation where his mother had been born a slave. Later he had exposure to the vineyards of the Rhône Valley while serving with the U.S. Army of Occupation. When he returned to Virginia, he got a job in the lumber business and started saving money to buy his own farm. On Repeal, he began planting a ten-acre vineyard of French hybrids and labruscas, and by 1940 he had enough grapes to open his own winery. His winery produced 5,000 gallons, which were mostly sold to his neighbors.[56] The winery closed sometime after World War II.

Woburn Winery had long been out of business when Fedderman Wine Company opened in 1972 in Prattsburg, New York. Raymond Fedderman had probably never heard of Woburn Winery because his picture and the words "The First Black Winery in the United States" appeared on the labels of his wines.

Fedderman was a sharecropper who picked potatoes in Virginia before moving to the Prattsburg area and becoming a successful businessman.[57] In 1970, Walter S. Taylor gave him the idea of opening a winery. Construction began in April 1972, and when the winery opened on June 1, two wines were released—Irene Red and Rosalind White.

Financing became a problem, and it is not clear whether a bank loan, the failure of the Small Business Administration to guarantee a loan, or a combination of the two led to the winery's demise. In an article in the *New York Times* on November 16, 1973, Frank Prial wrote that "the Fedderman Winery is silent. The gleaming new bottle line is still, and the 5,000-gallon storage tank is empty. Hundreds of cases of wine rest on pallets, waiting for customers who never come."[58]

Ontario Wines before the Cottage Wineries

It would have been difficult for the image of Ontario wines to be any lower than it was after Prohibition. People remembered the bad wines made during that time, and they were unable to forget what defense attorneys kept saying, that wine was to blame for all antisocial and criminal acts.[59] These memories lingered even though within three years after the start of Operation Cleanup in 1934, half of Ontario's wineries had closed because they could not meet the newly imposed wine standards. The surviving wineries emphasized their adherence to technical, laboratory, and quality control standards. Together with equipment modernization programs, there was rapid improvement in the quality of Ontario wines.

To improve the image of their wines, the Ontario wineries formed the Canadian Wine Institute in 1940. The advertising of wine was not permitted in Ontario and public relations activities were seen as the most logical way to change the public's perception of Ontario wines. For the first time, emphasis was placed on the purity, quality, and palatability of these wines. The result was a slow increase in the consumption of Ontario wines, an increase that was also helped by the onset of World War II and a cutback in the importation of wines from abroad.[60]

After World War II, consumption of Ontario wines continued to rise, but this time the increase was due to higher sales of table wines. In July 1946, a check of sales by the Liquor Control Board of Ontario (LCBO) showed that less than half of 1 percent of all wines bought in Ontario were table wines. By 1968, table wines comprised 32 percent of the wines sold.[61] The shift to table wines was due in part to the many young Canadians who served in the armed forces in Europe and returned with some knowledge of wine. During the 1950s and 1960s larger numbers of young people traveled abroad and became familiar with wine.

In addition, tens of thousands of immigrants from southern Europe came to Canada in the 1950s and 1960s and brought with them their custom of drinking wine with meals. By 1970, Toronto alone had more Italians than the city of Florence, Italy.[62]

While many of the new arrivals made wine at home, the demand for table wines in the LCBO stores resulted in more wine sales. The Ontario wineries, however, were slow to take advantage of the consumer shift to table wines. They continued to make the fortified wines, ports, and sherries that were popular before

Prohibition and were still what the general public wanted to drink. In August 1962, Jordan Wines introduced Zing, a gin-flavored wine with 20 percent alcohol. The winery anticipated sales of 14,000 gallons; by the end of the year it was the largest selling wine in Ontario with 120,000 gallons sold. Sales reached 350,000 gallons the following year and other Canadian wineries started marketing their own versions with different flavors under such names as Zoom, Zip, Tiki, Riki, Whiz, and Zest.[63] The flavored wines were a fad that lasted until the end of the 1960s.

A Decade of Transition

A shift away from high alcohol fortified wines in the Ontario wine industry took place in the 1970s. It was a transitional decade that began with a boom in low alcohol sparkling wines and, more important, the start of meeting the demand for drier table wines.

In the spring of 1971, Andrés Wines in Winona introduced a low alcohol sparkling wine called Baby Duck. By 1974 it was Canada's biggest wine seller with annual sales of 9 million bottles. Its immediate success led to many imitators marketed under a variety of bird and animal names. This period of Ontario's wine history is sometimes referred to today in Canada as "our zoological era." Baby Duck was a blend of Concord and Niagara, carbonated to form 36–38 pounds of pressure at 50° Fahrenheit, a sugar level of 5 percent, and an alcohol content of just under 7 percent.[64]

The person responsible for Baby Duck and its success was Andrew Peller, who had emigrated from his native Hungary to Canada in 1927.[65] He started the Peller Brewing Company in Hamilton in 1946 and sold it for a considerable profit in 1953. An unsuccessful venture as owner of the *Hamilton News* led him to apply to the LCBO for a winery license. After being turned down repeatedly, he went to British Columbia and opened Andrés Wines in Port Moody in 1962.

In the mid-1960s, Andrés established plants in Calgary, Alberta, and Truro, Nova Scotia. His son, Dr. Joseph A. Peller, joined the company as president in 1965, and from 1965 to 1970 the Pellers again tried to get a license in Ontario and got no further than being promised temporary listings for their wines. After being advised that the best way to get a license in Ontario was to purchase a winery that already had one, Andrés bought Beau Chatel Wines, Ltd., which included their new winery premises in Winona, and took possession on January 1, 1970.

The first step in the development of Baby Duck occurred in 1967 when winemaker Guy Baldwin, assisted by Edward Arnold, developed Chanté, the first of Andrés light 7 percent sparkling wines. Chanté was sold as a red, white, or rosé and was given its name from the French word "to sing" because of the wine's light bubbly quality.

Andrés was the first Canadian winery to make Cold Duck, the 12 percent alcohol combination of champagne and sparkling burgundy popular in the United

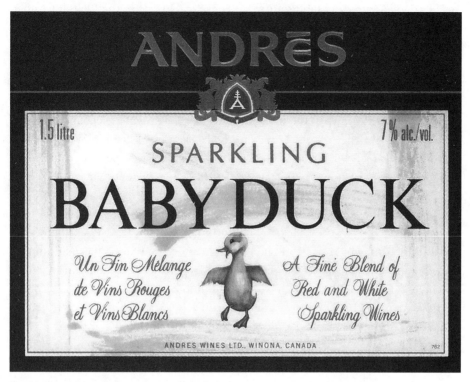

Figure 4.5: In what Canadians sometimes refer to as "our zoological era," low alcohol sparkling wines named after birds and animals dominated the wine scene in Ontario in the 1970s. The sales leader was Baby Duck, first introduced by Andrés Wines in 1971. By 1980, more than 60 million bottles had been sold in Canada, and many other wineries were marketing their own versions. Author's collection.

States in the mid-1960s. Cold Duck was so successful that Andrés tried to register "Cold Duck" as its own brand in Canada. It nearly succeeded, but it was blocked by Château-Gai Wines, which had developed a sparkling blend of Concord and white Elvira, and had begun selling its own Cold Duck in late 1971.[66] Cold Duck, however, was taxed at the $2.50 a gallon rate, and by blending red and white wines of the Chanté series Andrés would have an inexpensive low alcohol wine taxed at 25 cents a gallon that would appeal to consumers. A Concord and Niagara blend was introduced in Ontario in 1971. It was named Baby Duck and, according to Andrew Peller, "We took care to patent the name right away."[67]

Baby Duck was an immediate success and by 1980 it had sold more than 60 million bottles in Canada.[68] Other Ontario wineries were quick to put similar wines on the market under such names as Little White Duck, Luv-a-Duck, Fuddle Duck, Baby Bear, Baby Deer, Pink Flamingo, Gimli Goose, and Pussycat.[69]

The bird and animal wines, as they were often called, were largely responsible for the increase in retail wine sales in Canada from under $100 million to over $300 million during a ten-year period from 1968 to 1977.[70] Per capita consumption in Canada more than doubled during this same time period, from 0.5 gallons to 1.2 gallons a year. Sales of Baby Duck peaked in 1983.[71]

The demand for drier table wines that began in Ontario in the 1960s intensified in the 1970s. Both the wineries and the growers were out of touch with the marketplace.[72] What the growers had in the ground were largely red labrusca varieties, and the French hybrids that the wineries wanted were in limited supply. In 1931, shortly after Prohibition in Ontario ended, the importation of grapes from outside the province was forbidden and all wines had to be made from grapes grown in Ontario.[73] By 1975, when the wineries were unable to purchase enough grapes to make table wines, they sought help from the legislature. When the Wine Content Act of 1976 was passed on December 16, 1976, wineries were permitted to import grapes or wine to blend with Ontario grapes. No wine made in Ontario, however, could contain more than 30 percent of imported content.

Research at the Horticultural Research Institute of Ontario was conducted to assist growers. To identify the best sites for planting vineyards, Dr. John Wiebe headed an aerial infrared photography study in 1974. This study combined thermal infrared data obtained by cameras on Canadian Defense Department airplanes during nights of temperature inversions with maximum-minimum temperatures on the ground. Climatic maps of Ontario were available by 1979 as a result of this study.[74] Trickle irrigation research begun in 1972 by Dr. Robert A. Cline and completed in 1979 showed that it was possible to substantially increase yields using irrigation.[75] Cline's research was one of many projects designed to help increase grape production.

For growers during this time period there was no such thing as achieving a balance between supply and demand. A white wine boom that had started in the United States moved into Canada. The demand for ports and sherries plummeted and by the mid-1980s there was an almost total demand for white wines. The disparity between what was in the vineyards and what was desired by the wineries continued.

By the mid-1970s wineries were looking for drier table wines that would compete with the best-selling European imports such as Black Tower and Blue Nun. In 1977, Calona Wines in Kelowna, British Columbia, introduced Schloss Laderheim, a German-style white wine that blended various white hybrids with Thompson Seedless from California and was packaged in a brown Rhine bottle with a Germanic label.[76] Four years later it was the best-selling wine in Canada, just edging out Baby Duck. Similar off-dry blends were soon produced in Ontario with Château-Gai Wines introducing Alpenweiss in 1978. Other wineries followed with names like Hochtaler, Weinfest, and Baron Ludwig, all packaged in imitation of German, French, or Italian wines.[77]

The production of low alcohol wines was not original with Andrés. In 1950, for temperance reasons, the LCBO suggested to Adhemar de Chaunac at Brights that they look into the possibility of producing a 7 percent alcohol wine.[78] De Chaunac said it was possible, but there could be a problem with wine stability because of the low alcohol content. Brights suggested a joint project with the Fred Marsh Winery in Niagara Falls. To Brights complete surprise, the Fred Marsh Winery announced

Figure 4.6: After the first mechanical grape harvester arrived in Ontario in 1969, Niagara Peninsula grape growers got together and ordered twelve harvesters from New York. They are shown here when they cleared Canadian Customs on June 30, 1971. Photo courtesy of Jim Rainforth.

the release of a low alcohol wine called Winette. Their wine was made without de Chaunac's assistance and began to re-ferment in the bottle on store shelves. The wine had to be withdrawn and the Fred Marsh Winery had a disaster on its hands. In 1953 Brights bought the Fred Marsh Winery. Later that year Brights started selling de Chaunac's Winette in thirteen-ounce bottles and also introduced a 6.5 percent alcohol Du Barry Rosé d'Amour Sparkling Wine.

When the liquor monopoly was set up after Prohibition, low alcohol wines were taxed much lower than either table wines or sparkling wines. Meredith F. Jones, Brights' president, went to the LCBO and argued that even though Winette was a sparkling wine, it was a low alcohol wine and should be taxed at the lower rate. The LCBO agreed and the tax was lowered from $2.50 a gallon to 25 cents.[79]

While on a trip to Germany in 1972, George Hostetter at Brights was impressed with the low alcohol house wines that he found there. When he returned, Brights began to experiment with similar wines with an emphasis on combining the flavor they wanted with a low alcohol content. In 1977 Brights introduced its House Wine in red and white versions.[80] The white had 9 percent alcohol and 1½ percent residual sugar; the red had 10 percent alcohol and 2 percent residual sugar. National sales of the House Red and House White eventually exceeded a million gallons a year.

Other attempts were made to make up for the shortage of white wine grapes. In 1979 Brights began a research project whose goal was to make a white wine out of red De Chaunac grapes. This led to the August 1982 introduction of Brights Dry White House Wine, which utilized large quantities of De Chaunac. Another version of a white De Chaunac was made by Andrés Wines, a 100 percent varietal Richelieu De Chaunac Blanc.

Another response to the white wine grape shortage was the introduction of Interlude by Barnes Wines. Interlude was 95 percent Elvira that had the labrusca flavor removed by APV concentrators.

In 1949, Bright's was the first Canadian winery to market a méthode champenoise champagne, which was sold as Brights President Canadian Champagne. The champagne was originally made from the President grape, a Munson hybrid, but subsequently became a blend of Catawba, Dutchess, Delaware, Rosette, and Seyval Blanc. Brights then made a Pinot Champagne in 1955, a Pink President Champagne in the early 1970s, and in 1981 a brut version of their President Champagne. By 1977, the production of Brights President Canadian Champagne amounted to 2,500,000 gallons, one-third of Brights sales. One out of every three bottles of champagne sold in Canada was their President Canadian Champagne.

CHAPTER FIVE

❧

FARM WINERY LAWS
AND THEIR EFFECTS

ONE KEY TO THE GROWTH OF THE EASTERN WINE INDUSTRY WAS THE PASSAGE
of farm winery laws starting in the late 1960s and early 1970s by various state
legislatures. Although interest had been growing steadily in growing grapes and
making wine, the obstacles standing in the way of those who wanted to open
commercial wineries were formidable. License fees in many states were well over
$1,000 annually, state taxes on wine were as high as $1.50 a gallon, and sales of wine
by wineries were often restricted to licensed liquor stores, distributors, or wholesalers.

Farm Winery Laws Begin in the Eastern United States

In most states the laws governing the sale of alcoholic beverages had not been changed
since the end of Prohibition. In 1970, thirty-two states had legally dry areas. Out of
3,078 counties in the United States, 589 did not allow the sale of wine; in addition,
there were hundreds of towns and smaller districts that were dry.[1] Twenty states
restricted sales of alcoholic beverages to liquor outlets and forty-three states banned
such sales on Sundays. There were still two states, Oklahoma and South Carolina,
that prohibited restaurants from serving wine or any alcoholic beverage with meals.

The early farm winery laws were often passed under a variety of names such
as limited winery acts, small winery laws, native winery laws, or simply referred to
as farm winery legislation (see table 5.1). What these laws had in common is that
they were passed in the name of agriculture, not wine, and were sought by grape
growers who simply wanted to sell wine made from the grapes they grew on their
own property. There were differences from state to state in license fees, the amount

TABLE 5.1. Early farm winery laws

State	Type of legislation	Date
Alabama	Reduced license fee	1937
	Farm winery legislation	1979
Arkansas	Bonded Winery Act	1934
Connecticut	Farm winery legislation	1978
Delaware	Farm winery legislation	1991
Florida	Farm winery legislation	1979
Georgia	Farm winery legislation	1983
Illinois	Sales at winery permitted	1976
	Limited wine manufacturer's license	1987?
Indiana	Small Winery Act (Public Law No. 77)	1971
Iowa	Native Wine Law	After Repeal
Kansas	Farm winery legislation	1983
Kentucky	Small Winery Act (reducing license fee)	1976
	Farm Winery Law	1990
Louisiana	Native Winery Act	1990
Maine	Farm winery legislation	1983
Maryland	Class 4 Limited Winery Act	1976
Massachusetts	Farm winery legislation	1976
Michigan	One winery license for everyone	
Minnesota	Farm winery legislation	1980
Mississippi	Native Winery Law	1976
Missouri	Domestic wine license	1943
	Farm winery type legislation	1980
Nebraska	Farm winery legislation	1985
New Hampshire	Sales permitted at winery	1971
New Jersey	Farm winery legislation	1981
New York	Farm winery legislation	1976
North Carolina	License fee and tax reduced	1973
Ohio	A-2 license	After Repeal
Pennsylvania	Limited Winery Act	1968
Rhode Island	Farm winery legislation	1977
South Carolina	Farm winery legislation	1980
Tennessee	Grape and Winery Law	1977
Vermont	Reduced license fees	1971
Virginia	Virginia Wine Law	1930s
	Farm winery legislation	1980
West Virginia	Farm winery legislation	1981
Wisconsin	One basic winery permit for everyone	

of wine that could be made, or in other regulations, but the impetus for passage was always the same: to help local agriculture.

Pennsylvania was the first state to enact a farm winery law, the Limited Winery Act of 1968 (termed "limited" because the initial legislation limited the amount of wine a winery could make to 50,000 gallons a year). Pennsylvania was not the first monopoly state to permit wine to be made and sold where the grapes were grown— Ohio had exempted wine from its state monopoly and Michigan had exempted wines of less than 16 percent alcohol—but it was the first state to enact legislation to permit it.

The first step toward the passage of legislation in Pennsylvania began in 1964 when Douglas P. Moorhead and William M. Konnerth formed a partnership in North East, Pennsylvania, called Presque Isle Wine Cellars for the sale of home winemaking equipment, supplies and juice (see chapter 4). The idea of starting a winery had occurred to them, but under the law a winery could only sell wines out of state or if they wanted their wines sold in Pennsylvania, to the Pennsylvania

Figure 5.1: Marlene
M. Moorhead became
Douglas P. Moorhead's
partner in
Presque Isle Wine Cellars
in North East, Penn-
sylvania, in 1974 when
William M. Konnerth
retired from the business.
Photo by author, 1977.

Liquor Control Board (PLCB). It was clear to them that legislation was needed to make it legal to sell wine at the winery.

They began by organizing support for the legislation from growers and others in Erie County. By 1965 they had made enough contacts in the capital—Harrisburg— to win support from Secretary of Agriculture Leland H. Bull, who promised that the administration would help develop a wine industry and offered to set up a wine advisory council to bring all interested parties together. The Council was organized in 1967 with Moorhead as chairman. Also involved was George Luke, who together with two other growers, Blair McCord and George Sceiford, would later open Penn-Shore Vineyards. Erie County growers became increasingly supportive of this legislation out of concern that their area was becoming a one-crop economy based entirely on the Concord grape. Because they were dependent on out-of-state markets for the sale of their grapes, they had no economic leverage. Wine grapes would provide an independent market.

Proposed legislation was drawn up in the summer of 1967 that would permit limited winery license holders to produce table wines only from grapes grown in Pennsylvania in an amount not to exceed 50,000 gallons and to sell wine produced on the licensed premises to the PLCB, to individuals, and to hotel, restaurant, club, and public service licensees. The PLCB did not want to give up any part of its monopoly and opposed passage of the bill.[2] There was little other opposition, however, and the bill passed on the last day of the legislative session, July 17, 1968.

The first two limited wineries to open in Pennsylvania were Presque Isle Wine Cellars and Penn-Shore Vineyards, both in North East. They had their first crush in 1969, received their licenses on the same day, and opened in 1970.

The second state to enact a small winery bill was Indiana where Public Law No. 77, the Small Winery Act, was passed on April 8, 1971.[3] The two men most directly responsible for the legislation were Donald MacDaniel, an optometrist in Connersville, and William Oliver of the Indiana University Law School in Bloomington. MacDaniel had planted French hybrids purchased from Boordy Vineyard in 1958 and Oliver had acquired some French hybrids in 1966 from a vineyard in Kentucky. Both men were home winemakers. Modeled after Pennsylvania's Limited Winery Act, the Indiana bill set a maximum limit of 50,000 gallons a year and reduced license fees. Although wine had to be made from grapes, other fruit, or honey grown in Indiana, there was the additional provision that if the grapes, grape juice, fruit, or fruit juice, or honey was unobtainable in Indiana, a permit could be applied for to import the desired products.

Four months after the legislation passed, MacDaniel opened Treaty Line Winery near Connersville. In 1973, William and Mary Oliver opened Oliver Winery north of Bloomington.

Virginia's farm winery law, which became effective on July 1, 1980, replaced a multiple licensing system with a single license for a small winery. Previously, under a state law dating back to the 1930s, a license to produce 5,000 gallons or less cost $150, but the price increased to $1,500 if production was over 5,000 gallons. For $40 the winery could get a retail license to sell at the winery and for an additional $450 a license to sell at wholesale to distributors and retailers.[4] Under the new farm winery law, the license fee of $100 allowed the winery to sell at retail and wholesale without additional charge and the bottle tax on all wines produced and sold from farm wineries was prohibited.

In 1973, North Carolina passed a small winery law, which provided for a reduction in license fees from $1,000 to $100 a year, and a reduction in state tax from 60 cents to 5 cents a gallon. Interestingly, until 1979 the state's good intentions could be blocked by county alcohol beverage control regulations. When Duplin Wine Cellars could not sell wine because Rose Hill was dry, state legislation was required to permit this.

Mississippi passed a Native Wine Law in 1976 reducing the license fee from $1,800 to $10 a year and cutting the state tax from 35 cents to 5 cents a gallon.[5]

Winemaking was legalized in Alabama in 1936–37 when Prohibition was repealed. A license fee of $1,000 was established, but the fee was set at $25 if the fruit or produce used in making wine was grown in Alabama. However, this was the only advantage a winery had. There could be no tastings or retail sales at the winery. Sales could only be made to wholesalers or through the state stores. Moreover, a tax of 35 percent was imposed on the wholesalers' price.

Jim and Marianne Eddins had returned to Alabama from Maryland in 1971 where they had been growing grapes. After planting forty-nine acres of muscadines by 1978, they began trying to get Alabama's laws changed. With the help of a state senator and two consultants, one of whom was Richard Vine, proposed legislation was drafted based on Mississippi's Native Wine Law. To get the bill passed, they emphasized the agricultural aspect of wine production, and on June 6, 1979, Governor Fob James signed the Alabama Farm Winery Act. Sales were now allowed to consumers and retailers as well as to wholesalers, ABC stores, and outside the state. A 5 cent per gallon tax was established in place of all other state taxes. Free samples were not only permitted, but if they were less than six ounces, they were exempted from the tax. That same year the Eddinses opened their Perdido Vineyards in Perdido.[6]

Reducing license fees and lowering tax rates were common features in farm winery legislation. People who were interested in opening wineries and already growing grapes often waited for passage of farm winery legislation before making a final commitment to finance a winery. In Kansas, Robert G. Rizza, a pediatrician who planted grapes in 1978, knew that the laws had to be changed if the wine industry in his state was to become a reality, and he took the leadership in campaigning for a farm winery law.

Writing about it later, he said that there were three farm winery bills in Kansas that passed over considerable opposition before he was willing to make a $1 million investment in a winery.[7] The first farm winery bill in 1983 simply permitted farmers to make wine and sell it in bottles on their farms. Nothing was done about the license fee, which remained at $1,100 plus posting a $25,000 bond. In 1985 the second farm winery bill was passed dropping the license fee to $250 and the bond requirement to $2,000. Farm wineries could now sell to retailers. Rizza was still unwilling to invest in a winery until visitors to a farm winery could taste wine in a winery's tasting room.[8] Farm winery bill number three was passed in April 1988, and authorized a broad range of tasting and sales opportunities including off-premise consumption and wine judging and competition at the Kansas State Fair grounds.[9] Rizza never did open his winery, and the first farm winery license was issued to Jim Fair for the Fields of Fair winery in St. George, Kansas.

In New York, unhappiness on the part of existing growers was a contributing factor in the passage of that state's farm winery bill in 1976. Historically, the New York wine industry was based on native American varieties of grapes, especially Concords. Both before and after Prohibition the large wineries made and sold their ports, sherries, and sweeter red and white labrusca wines to consumers that had grown up appreciating them. Times were changing, however, and consumers began to prefer less strong grapey flavors in their wines. The large wineries recognized this change in taste and began bringing in bulk wines from California to blend with their own wines for flavor modification.[10]

It was only a question of time until the large wineries found that they needed to buy fewer New York grapes, and shortly before harvest in 1975 they notified growers that they would only purchase a small part of that year's grape crop. Growers started to look for alternate markets to sell their grapes. Some started to think about opening their own wineries, only to discover that the cost of a winery license together with an assortment of other fees would add up to a total of nearly $1,600 a year. Also discouraging was a provision in the alcoholic beverage law that allowed wineries to sell wine at retail on their premises but limited retail sales to 5 percent of the total gross sales the previous year. They turned to the state for assistance but made little headway.

This was not the first time farm winery legislation had been sought. Fifteen years earlier, in 1961, Mark Miller, the founder of Benmarl Vineyards in Marlboro, had tried to get legislation passed to lower license fees for small farmers who wanted to make and sell their own wine. The large wineries opposed the idea because small wineries represented potential competition, and the former knew they had the money and political influence to defeat any such proposal.[11] Farm winery bills were periodically introduced in the legislature in subsequent years but never made it out of committee.

The passage of the Farm Winery Act in 1976 was the result of a combination of events that started with the 1975 election of Governor Hugh L. Carey and the appointment of John S. Dyson as Commissioner of the Department of Agriculture and Markets. Dyson, who was interested in wine—he opened his Millbrook Vineyards in the Hudson River Valley in 1988—revived a farm winery bill that had died in committee in 1975. A task force headed by Assemblyman Daniel Welsh was created to assess the value of the bill. Mark Miller, who played a key role in the passage of the bill, was among those testifying. The Department of Agriculture and Markets, in what Frank Prial of the *New York Times* called a rarity, sent out press releases about some of the lesser known winemakers, and a tasting of twenty-six New York state wines was held at the Four Seasons restaurant in New York City on February 24.[12] Governor Carey sponsored a bill reducing the license fee for small wineries to $125. The Farm Winery Act passed and was signed on June 4.

Governor Carey also proclaimed November to be New York State Wine Month and announced a state-sponsored program to promote New York wine in stores and restaurants. Lieutenant Governor Mary Anne Krupsak took the wine and grape industry and its problems under her personal supervision.[13] In addition, the governor promised further help.

Governor Carey was as good as his word. In 1977, he requested and later signed a package of bills permitting Sunday sales, temporary permits to sell wine at fundraising and promotional events, a permit to establish a retail outlet away from the winery premises for tastings and sales, the abolishment of the 5 percent limitation on retail sales at the winery, the establishment of realistic fleet permit sales for the shipping of wine, and extending the ability to hold winery licenses to those holding brewer or distiller's licenses. Further, to encourage the development of domestic brandy, the distiller's license fee was lowered from $1,250 to $100. Farm

Figure 5.2: Governor Hugh Carey signed New York's farm winery bill in Albany on June 10, 1976. Mark Miller of Benmarl Vineyards, who helped draft the bill, is at the governor's left. Courtesy of Eric Miller.

wineries were also given permission to sell and manufacture grape products such as jellies, juices, and cooking sauces.

By 1978 seventeen states had passed laws to encourage the establishment of farm wineries, and by 1984 that number had increased to 23 (see table 5.1).[14] Sometimes passage of the legislation was accomplished in a spirit of cooperation; at others it was contentious. The story behind the passage of New Jersey's Farm Winery Bill in 1981 has been recounted by Dr. James R. Williams, who received the first farm winery license for DelVista Vinyards in Frenchtown in 1982.[15]

Williams and several other growers who were interested in starting wineries met in 1980 and formed the Hunterdon County Wine Growers Association. At that time New Jersey had two kinds of winery licenses. The first was a plenary license, which permitted unlimited production, additional sales outlets, and the use of out-of-state fruit. Plenary licenses were limited in number to one for every million people in the state. At that time the maximum of seven had been issued, and the only way of getting a license was to buy it from someone who had one (at a price well up in five figures). The other kind of license was a limited winery license allowing production of 5,000 gallons a year, did not permit any tasting of wine at the winery, and required that all wine be made from New Jersey fruit. The license was so restrictive that none had ever been issued.

When the farm winery bill was drafted, it was intended to replace the limited license bill. License fees would be cut in half, from $50 for less than 1,000 gallons to $200 for 1,000 to 50,000 gallons, the maximum production that a farm winery would be allowed. Farm wineries would have to be located on a minimum of three acres of land containing at least 1,200 vines under cultivation, and farm wineries could only make wine from New Jersey fruit. The wineries would be allowed to have free tastings of wine for visitors. In the hope that the plenary wineries would not oppose the bill, a benefit for all wineries was included: a reduced tax on wine production from 30 cents to 10 cents a gallon on wine made from New Jersey fruit. The plenary wineries did oppose the bill, but their proposal to limit the number of new farm winery licensees in the same way that plenary licensees were was rejected. The Hunterdon County Wine Growers Association had done its homework well, including getting the support of Secretary of Agriculture Phillip Alampi. The bill went on to be unanimously approved by both the Assembly and the Senate.

Williams ended an article he wrote in the *American Wine Society Journal* with several lessons from the New Jersey experience: "1) You must have the support of the Department of Agriculture to obtain farm winery legislation. 2) It is essential to obtain the support of a skilled and respected legislator to sponsor the bill. 3) Try to get the support of any existing wineries, but don't assume that they are totally on your side. 4) Get the support of wine organizations in the state and have members write to their legislators. 5) Once the bill is passed, be alert for attempts to modify it." The last point was important because some of the plenary license holders did attempt to modify the Farm Winery Law after it was signed by Governor Brendan Byrne.[16]

The lessons cited by Williams were important for anyone or any group that wanted to pass legislation involving wine. Invariably, legislation having anything to do with wine had to be presented as a benefit to agriculture. The often included provision that farm wineries make most or all the wine they produce from fruit grown in their own state underscored the state support for agriculture. Farm winery laws in many states, however, provided procedures where in the event of a natural disaster, grapes could be brought in from outside the state.

As time passed and the wine industry in the East grew larger and became more visible, it became easier to get passage of not only farm winery bills but other bills benefiting growers and wineries. In 1991, only two months was required to introduce, pass, and sign farm winery legislation in Delaware. The impetus for the legislation came from Margaret I. Raley, who later opened Nassau Valley Vineyards in Lewes. She and her father, Robert A. Raley, Jr., drafted the original bill and got it sponsored and introduced in the Delaware House by their representative, John Schroeder. When it was introduced, the Delaware Alcoholic Beverage Commission offered their assistance in rewriting the bill so that as few changes as possible would have to be made in existing Delaware law. Raley then handled her own lobbying, talking with forty-one representatives and twenty-one senators. The vote in the House was 33–1 and in the Senate 21–0. Governor Michael N. Castle signed the bill on July 5, 1991, and the winery opened on October 9, 1993.[17]

Figure 5.3: Grapes were planted at Truluck Vineyards in Lake City, South Carolina, in 1972, eight years before the passage of farm winery legislation. It was dawn and the mist was still rising when this picture was taken. Photo by author, 1982.

Liberalizing the regulatory environment usually required more than just the passage of the initial farm winery law. In New York the governor and the legislature worked together. It was quite different in Pennsylvania where the wineries had to fight for the additional help they needed. The Limited Winery Act that passed in 1968 over the strong opposition of the PLCB gave wineries the right to produce up to 50,000 gallons of wine a year and sell that wine on the winery premises, to the PLCB, and to hotel, restaurant, and public service licensees. Although the wineries were able to get the amount of wine they could produce increased to 100,000 gallons in 1970, sales of wine did not keep pace with production. In cooperation with the Department of Agriculture, the wineries asked the PLCB if off-premise sales would be allowed in urban areas or if bulk wine could be transferred from one winery to another. The answer was no. Wineries could only sell where the wine was made and therefore a winery would have to obtain another winery license.

The state's attorney general was then asked for his opinion, and in 1975 he stated that extensions of premises were permissible. The PLCB immediately proposed regulations that would require the extensions to meet federal requirements for bonded wineries. After a confrontational hearing with the PLCB in 1977, the wineries decided to go to the legislature for relief. The legislation that was introduced in 1979 marked the start of the changes wineries needed. In 1980, direct mail advertising was permitted and wineries were allowed to open on Sundays; in 1981, wineries could have three extensions of premises without production or bottling requirements; in 1983, small parcel delivery of wine was allowed. These were all fundamental freedoms that other kinds of businesses could take for granted, and for many wineries it made the difference between survival and success.[18]

New Wine Licenses in Ontario

The small wineries that began to open in Ontario in 1975 were called "cottage wineries." Their establishment was just as important for the growth of the wine industry there as the farm wineries were in the eastern United States. One major difference was that the start of the cottage wineries had less to do with promoting agriculture and much more with wine itself.

The Ontario Wine Standards Committee issued its report in 1934 while Operation Cleanup was continuing in the wake of Canadian Prohibition. It included the following recommendation: "For some years past the Liquor Control Board has refused to issue additional licenses to native wineries and at every opportunity has transferred the license from a winery whose products were unsatisfactory to better hands. It is highly desirable that this policy be continued."[19] The granting of licenses to F. W. Bayliss of Toronto and Victor Subosits in Welland in 1930 were the last to be issued until 1960, when a restricted form of license was granted to Strawa Honey Wines, Ltd., in Sarnia for the production of honey wines.[20] The first commercial license was issued to Inniskillin Wines in Niagara-on-the-Lake on July 5, 1975.[21]

The number of licensed wineries in Ontario declined from a high of fifty-one in 1925 to a low of eight when Major-General George Kitching became chairman of the Liquor Control Board of Ontario (LCBO) in 1970.[22] Kitching was not popular with the Ontario wine industry because he was perceived as favoring European wines and neglecting the Ontario industry. This was understandable because the shortage of table wines in Ontario led to the LCBO listing of as many as 1,000 new imports during his five-year term, and the Ontario wineries saw this as competition they had to overcome.

Kitching felt strongly that Ontario wines needed improvement. He was sympathetic to both Karl Podamer, who was seeking to open a champagne house, and Donald Ziraldo, who was applying for a winery license in 1973, when they sought his help in securing licenses. He wanted to be sure they would succeed if they were licensed, and for Ziraldo his assistance went so far as to have LCBO's accountants help draw up the cash flow projections that Ziraldo needed to take to his bankers.[23] To Kitching, Inniskillin became a pilot project and he even donated ten slightly damaged Portuguese barrels to help Ziraldo.[24]

Donald J. P. Ziraldo was born in St. Catharines in 1948 and graduated with a B.S. degree in agriculture from the University of Guelph in 1971. He and his brother Robert operated Ziraldo Farms and Nurseries, Inc., a family business specializing in fruit trees and grapevines. He met Karl J. Kaiser, his future partner, in 1971 when the latter came to the nursery to buy some French hybrid vines for his father-in-law's garden. They shared a bottle of Kaiser's homemade Chelois, became friends, and soon began thinking about opening a winery.

Kaiser was born in 1941 in Austria and had his first experience with grapes in 1954 when, as a secondary school student, he entered a Cistercian monastery and worked in their vineyard. Later, when he was teaching economics in the town of Zistersdorf, he helped with the vintage with his future wife's grandfather. He immigrated to Canada in 1969 following his marriage because his wife's parents lived in St. Catharines. Shortly after his arrival in Canada he earned a degree in chemistry at Brock University.

When Ziraldo applied for a winery license in 1973, he was fortunate in not only getting Kitching's assistance but also a $50,000 loan from the Ontario Development Corporation, a government agency. A provisional license was granted to Ziraldo and Kaiser in April 1974, enabling them to produce 10,000 gallons of wine. If all went well, their provisional license would be converted into a commercial license the following year. The first Inniskillin winery was located in an old packing shed at the family nursery, and the name Inniskillin was chosen because the nursery was located on land settled by a member of the Inniskillin Fusiliers after he served in the War of 1812.

Inniskillin received its commercial license on July 5, 1975. At first the winery was named Inniskillin House Wines, but the word "house" was soon dropped. A French enologist, Alain Rigaud, was involved initially but returned to France shortly after the winery opened. The first wines sold were made in 1974, 500 bottles each of Maréchal Foch and De Chaunac, and 5,000 bottles of Vin Nouveau, a blend of those two wines with Chelois and Chancellor. All of the first wines were red wines because no white grapes were available. In 1978 the winery moved to its present location two kilometers away from the nursery.

Inniskillin was a success from the start. Production increased to 12,000 gallons in its second year and reached 70,000 gallons in 1977. Everything they made sold out at premium prices, and in 1977 they ran out of wine before Christmas. In his book *Wines of Ontario,* William Rannie attributes the initial success to the novelty of a new winery's entry into the market and the praise heaped on the wines by the media.[25] Tony Aspler cites a public relations coup in February 1976, when Toronto wine writer Michael Vaughan took a parcel of wines to England where they were tasted by such notables as Harry Waugh, Michael Broadbent, and Hugh Johnson. When Johnson commented that "my favorite without doubt was the Inniskillin 1974 Maréchal Foch," the result in Ontario was an immediate sellout of Inniskillin Wines in Ontario and a huge leap in the winery's prestige.[26]

Ziraldo's original vision was that of "a premium estate winery producing varietal wines from grapes grown in the Niagara Peninsula."[27] It did not take long for Ziraldo's vision to be fulfilled, and the winery's success made Kitching's vision of a string of small wineries in southern Ontario come true as well.

The fact that Inniskillin was granted a license and that the winery was a success provided added incentive for people who wanted to open wineries. Allan and Charlotte Eastman, who founded Charal Winery and Vineyards in Blenheim, south of Windsor in southwestern Ontario, received their restricted license to make experimental wines in 1975. Their full production license was approved in 1977, the same year that their 1977 Pinot Chardonnay won a gold medal at the Wineries Unlimited competition in Lancaster, Pennsylvania. All of their wines were varietals and estate bottled.

Château des Charmes was founded in Niagara-on-the-Lake in 1978. Paul Bosc, Sr., was born in Algeria in 1935 and studied enology at the University of Dijon before immigrating to Canada in 1963. In that year, he became the winemaker at Château-Gai, and for the next fifteen years, he was instrumental in changing the winery's production in the direction of French hybrids and varietal wines.

John Labatt Ltd., the giant Canadian brewing company, acquired Château-Gai in 1973. That, coupled with seeing what Ziraldo was doing at Inniskillin, made Bosc decide to start his own winery with the goal of producing premium vinifera varietal wines. Château des Charmes got its start in 1978 when Bosc and St. Catharines attorney Roger Gordon planted fifty acres of vinifera, the largest single planting of vinifera in Canada at the time.

Newark Wines was opened in Niagara-on-the-Lake in 1979 by Joseph Pohorly. The winery's name was changed to Hillebrand Estates Wines in 1982 after Pohorly brought into the business the German investment firm of Scholl & Hillebrand.

By the end of the decade Ontario had eleven wineries. The small wineries that opened after Inniskillin were invariably interested in producing premium varietal wines. There was nothing new about making varietal wines in Ontario. Brights had made the first vinifera varietal in Canada, a 1956 Pinot Chardonnay. Their varietal Baco Noir, made from George's Clone that was discovered in 1955, won more gold medals in international competition than any other red varietal produced by Brights.[28]

Most of the wines made in Ontario before the first cottage wineries opened, however, were sold as proprietary wines even though they could have been sold as named varietals. A change came in 1974 when Paul Bosc, who was still at Château-Gai, replaced one of the winery's reds with a labeled varietal Maréchal Foch. Bosc himself touted his new red table wine in a series of three television commercials in 1975.[29] The wine sold out immediately. This shortage coupled with Inniskillin's success in England two years later made Maréchal Foch a much sought after wine for years. With the release of varietal Chardonnays, Rieslings, and Gamays planted in 1974, Inniskillin made a major contribution in establishing named varietals as quality wines in the minds of consumers.

CHAPTER SIX

THE INDUSTRY DEVELOPS IN THE 1970s

ENVIRONMENTAL FACTORS SUCH AS CLIMATE, DISEASES, AND PESTS WERE THE primary concern for those who wanted to grow grapes in those early years. Winemakers had to cope with manmade laws and regulations, and those interested in opening wineries often faced government restrictions that ranged from zoning ordinances to licensing. Finding ways in which existing laws could be changed and favorable legislation passed was sometimes more exasperating and difficult to achieve than growing grapes. Virtually everyone in those early days had to deal with both concerns.

Today, with the passage of time, it is difficult to understand how insurmountable the obstacles must have seemed to those who only wanted to make and sell wine. Progress was slow and sometimes minimal. For example, the Grape and Wine Law passed in Tennessee in 1977 reduced the annual license fee from $1,500 to $50 and the $1.10 per gallon tax on wine made from Tennessee farm products to $.05. Although wineries in any of the state's counties, dry or not, were given the right to sell up to 5,000 gallons a year at retail on their premises, a law was retained allowing only one gallon of an alcoholic beverage to be transported in a private vehicle through a dry area. In many instances this restricted sales of wine to one gallon per carload of people. It was not until 1983 that customers could buy up to five cases of wine and transport them anywhere in Tennessee. At that time the amount of wine wineries could sell retail was increased to 15,000 gallons or 20 percent of their annual production, whichever was greater. No limit was placed on sales to wholesalers. The limit on retail sales was increased in 1985 to 20,000 gallons or 20 percent of production. In 1995 the annual limit was increased to 40,000 gallons, but wineries wanting to increase retail sales to that amount had to get advance authorization from the Tennessee Alcoholic Beverage Commission. Wineries would have to show that they had either offered their wines to a distributor or that there would be a hardship to the winery or their growers if the authorization was not granted.[1]

Wholesalers and distributors frequently opposed legislation that they thought would cut into their sales. With their influence in the legislature and the dollars at their disposal for a campaign, they could place roadblocks in the way wineries wanted to do business. Until 1969, opposition from New York state liquor store owners prevented the major wineries in the Finger Lakes from selling wine at retail to visitors. Tastings and tours could be conducted, but when visitors asked to buy wine they were referred to a local retailer.[2]

New Hampshire did not pass a farm winery bill. The State of New Hampshire Liquor Commission was originally set up to handle bulk purchases and bulk sales, and it was neither easy nor profitable to handle a small New Hampshire winery's wines.[3] When John Canepa was issued a license to open his White Mountain Vineyards in 1969, it was under a liquor manufacturer's license that cost $750 a year. This license permitted him to sell his wines out of state or to New Hampshire's seventy-three state stores, but not at the winery. Canepa and the State Liquor Commission, which did not want to handle his wines, did not have a smooth relationship; and it took legislation to guarantee him shelf space for his product. In 1973, the legislature allowed him to sell wine to the public at the winery at an additional $250 license fee. Eight years later, in 1981, just before Canepa sold the winery, legislation was passed permitting direct sales to restaurants, private stores, and grocery stores. It was not until 1990 that the first separate winery license would be created at an annual cost of $1,140. Two years later that license became a "two-tier" license in that the cost for a winery producing under 1,000 cases was reduced to $100 while remaining the same for a winery making more than 1,000 cases.

However difficult it might have been to get the regulatory climate changed to the point where wineries could do more than just exist, time usually worked to the advantage of the wineries. As states became more accustomed to having small wineries within their borders and seeing the economic benefits in terms of tourist dollars and taxes from sales, attitudes changed markedly and legislatures and state agencies became much more amenable to helping their industries grow.

In state after state in these early years, high license fees and taxes, restrictions on sales outlets and local blue laws were only some of the obstacles that had to be overcome. Conservatives on the political right and religious fundamentalists continued their prohibitionist beliefs and were ready to oppose wine and wineries whenever the opportunity presented itself. Jerry K. Reed, who started the Tennessee Valley Winery in Loudon, Tennessee, vividly recalls the opposition surrounding the founding of his winery in 1984. He had obtained all of the permits needed to open the winery and had been assured of being in compliance with local zoning regulations. In an effort to show that he intended to be a good neighbor, he invited anyone who wanted to comment to come to a zoning hearing that was being held at his request. Two items were on the agenda, one having to do with a junkyard and the other with his winery. Of the 410 people who showed up, only 2 were interested in talking about the junkyard. The others let their opposition be known for five hours until a representative from the attorney general's office, who had been invited by Reed's banker, informed the crowd that Reed had met all of the necessary zoning and legal requirements and that there was nothing they could do to stop the winery from opening. This did not stop the opposition. Reed received hate mail, signs were attached to the winery's gates and fences, pentagrams were painted on the driveway to show collusion with the devil, and there were threats to put poisonous snakes in the mailbox. For many years afterward, Reed said, he opened the mailbox with caution.[4]

This was by no means an isolated incident.[5] Neo-Prohibitionism in many guises remained an ongoing problem for wineries and the wine industry right into the twenty-first century.

Winery Growth in the Early Years

The wine industry in the East started slowly and gained momentum with the passage of time. Table 6.1 shows the number of wineries in the eastern United States during the last quarter of the twentieth century.[6] There were 124 wineries in 1975, a number that doubled to 251 by 1980, and climbed to 656 by the year 1999. In 1975 there were thirteen states that had no wineries; by 1999 only six states had fewer than five wineries. Ontario had the same rapid growth (see chapter 12).

Not shown in the table are the figures for 1970 when there were fewer than one hundred wineries in the East, a third to a half of which were large wineries producing more than 100,000 gallons a year. The modest increase between 1970 and 1975 was in part due to the first farm winery legislation being passed in 1968 and the first farm wineries opening in the early 1970s.

The vineyard experiences in southern Ohio described in chapter 4 showed how a shared experience promoted the opening of wineries, and how the enthusiasm for planting vineyards led to the start of wineries in Virginia. For people who already had land they were farming, a common motivation to start growing grapes was a need or desire for diversification. Curiosity and the romance of wine led others to experiment with planting grapes and making wine.

The newcomers came from many different backgrounds. Some were scientists or professional people who were looking for a new career or perhaps a retirement occupation. Others were creative people, artists, writers, or poets, who wanted the challenges and rewards that came with making something unique with their own hands, and a quality wine was something that one could be proud of and win the recognition of others. The early 1970s, during and after the Vietnam War, witnessed

TABLE 6.1. Bonded wineries in the eastern United States

	1975*		1980*		1985*		1990*	1995*	2000**	2005**	2010**
State	Bonded wineries	BATF	Bonded wineries	BATF	Bonded wineries	BATF	BATF	BATF	TTB	TTB	TTB
Alabama	–	–	1	1	2	3	4	4	5	6	15
Arkansas	7	11	8	11	7	9	6	6	9	7	16
Connecticut	1	2	4	4	9	11	12	9	18	23	39
Delaware	–	4	1	1	1	1	–	1	1	1	2
Florida	2	4	3	5	7	11	7	5	13	34	75
Georgia	1	1	1	4	6	7	9	9	11	19	40
Illinois	3	8	3	7	3	13	7	11	25	64	128
Indiana	4	6	9	10	9	12	20	20	26	39	71
Iowa	10	14	13	13	16	19	16	10	13	36	99
Kansas	–	–	–	2	–	–	2	10	7	11	29
Kentucky	–	–	2	3	1	2	6	9	9	32	70
Louisiana	–	1	–	–	–	3	1	4	7	7	11
Maine	–	1	–	–	1	2	5	3	6	10	30
Maryland	2	4	7	11	9	15	17	14	12	19	57
Massachusetts	1	6	3	9	5	16	16	18	29	28	52
Michigan	10	10	15	21	16	29	31	28	59	88	182
Minnesota	–	2	2	2	3	4	5	7	14	20	52
Mississippi	–	–	4	4	5	6	4	4	5	5	4
Missouri	7	13	20	25	25	29	39	37	47	65	152
Nebraska	–	–	–	–	–	–	–	1	4	13	29
New Hampshire	–	1	1	1	–	1	1	3	5	8	34
New Jersey	4	15	9	12	12	18	21	21	23	33	62
New York	19	43	49	69	76	100	108	125	165	207	363
North Carolina	2	1	4	4	6	5	10	12	19	54	136
Ohio	26	32	39	44	42	49	46	47	60	100	172
Pennsylvania	11	14	23	29	42	52	60	52	70	104	179
Rhode Island	2	–	3	4	4	3	4	4	6	7	9
South Carolina	1	1	3	3	5	3	4	3	4	7	16
Tennessee	–	–	2	2	6	6	13	15	25	27	43
Vermont	–	2	–	2	–	1	4	4	8	9	31
Virginia	6	–	13	11	30	34	48	46	69	107	237
West Virginia	–	–	1	1	4	6	7	10	12	16	23
Wisconsin	5	5	8	11	11	9	12	13	17	31	80
TOTAL	124	201	251	326	363	479	545	565	803	1,237	2,538

*The bonded winery counts for 1975, 1980, and 1985 were compiled from several sources. The BATF winery count figures from 1975 to 1995 are for what they termed "Authorized-to-Operate: Wineries (Bonded)" and included distilled spirits plants and tax paid bottling houses. See note 6 for an explanation of these counts.
**The winery count in 2000, 2005, and 2010 are based on figures compiled by the Alcohol and Tobacco Tax and Trade Bureau (TTB), the successor agency of the Bureau of Alcohol, Tobacco and Firearms (BATF).

the emergence of a back-to-the-land movement. The idea of returning to a simpler life on the land seemed to be a welcome alternative to what some people saw as an increasingly dehumanizing world.[7]

These early vineyard and winery starts were usually financed by earnings from regular jobs, out of savings, or from accumulated wealth. What they had in common was the fact that their owners worked and lived in the East. They were aware of the wine industry in California and Europe and looked forward to the day when they would make wines as highly regarded as those coming from other wine regions of the world.

Figure 6.1: The vineyard at Rose Bower Vineyard & Winery in Hampden-Sydney, Virginia, was the subject of a film made in 1981 using winemaker Tom O'Grady's poetry (see note 7 in this chapter). Photo by author, 1989.

In those days, however, there was little interest in what was happening in the East in other wine regions of the world. Books written by established wine writers ignored the East or, at most, included a brief mention of New York. There were, to be sure, trained winemakers who came to the East from other countries, grapevines and vineyard and winery equipment were purchased for use in the East, but there was little investment in the East that originated in Europe or California. For the most part, the growth of the industry started slowly and came from within the East itself.

European Ventures in the East

Between the mid-1970s and mid-1980s, a few German, French, and Italian investors established vineyards and wineries in Virginia. Dr. Gerhard W. R. Guth, a German surgeon practicing in Hamburg, purchased a 1,500-acre dairy farm in True Blue, south of Culpeper, in 1974.[8] He invested in Virginia because farmland in Germany was three times as expensive as in the United States. His decision to plant grapevines was initially hobby related, but later led to the start of Rapidan River Vineyards.

Guth asked Dr. Helmut Becker at the German research station at Geisenheim to inspect part of a pasture he planned to fence off for a vineyard and make recommendations. Becker encouraged him to plant an experimental vineyard and also suggested that he engage one of his students, Joachim Hollerith, a recent graduate of the three-year viticulture and enology program. Hollerith's family had been growing grapes in the Rheinpfalz since the 1600s, and Hollerith had had three years of experience working in different vineyards.[9] Guth offered him the job of developing his vineyard and making wine in the German tradition. In April 1978, Hollerith, his wife Gitta and their son arrived at Guth's Island View Farm.

A two-and-a-half-acre high-density planting consisting mainly of Riesling was made in 1978. An additional seven-and-a-half acres were planted in 1979 and fifteen more in 1980. Between 8,000 and 10,000 gallons of wine were produced from the first vintage in 1981. In 1983, at the end of his second contract period with Guth, Hollerith left to become general manager of nearby Prince Michel Vineyards and to start planting their initial forty acres of vinifera. Guth's last years at Rapidan River Vineyards were increasingly complicated by marital problems and a succession of winemakers that lasted until the vineyards and winery were acquired by Prince Michel in 1985. When Hollerith left Rapidan River in 1983, there were twenty-five acres of vines in the ground, but he continued helping Guth out by planting twenty-five more acres because Jean Leducq, the owner of Prince Michel, knew that he would need them.

Prince Michel Vineyards was founded in Leon, Virginia, in 1983 by Jean Leducq of Paris, France.[10] Leducq's interest in wine and food began at an early age. His grandparents founded Le Grand Café in Paris; Auguste Escoffier, the most famous chef of his time and a noted cookbook author, was a friend of the family. After World War II he joined his family's industrial laundry business, which was to become the largest family-owned business in France, and formed the Elis group of companies, a multinational conglomerate. The acquisition of Rental Uniform Services brought him to Culpeper, and in 1983 he and Norman Martin, the founder of Rental Uniform Services, started Prince Michel Vineyards with a planting of forty acres of vines.

One of Leducq's friends was Prince Michel Poniatowski, minister of the interior under French president Giscard d'Estaing. Prince Michel was a famed wine connoisseur and a direct descendant of a king of Poland. A combination of their friendship and the intertwining of wine, France, and royalty led Leducq to name the winery after his friend.

Leducq initially asked Emile Peynaud to become a consultant, but he declined to take an active role because of his age. One of his students, Jacques Boissenot, accepted the role of consultant and Hollerith was recruited to begin planting the vinifera vineyards and serve as winemaker and general manager.

By 1985 approximately 110 acres had been planted, and in the same year Rapidan River with its fifty acres of vines was acquired. In 1989 Le Ducq Vineyards was established in California's Napa Valley and forty-one acres were soon planted there. The first wine was sold in 1984 and production climbed to 6,500 cases in 1986, 25,000 by 1989, 40,000 cases by 1992, and then leveled off at about 50,000 cases. In February 1990, Le Ducq Lot 87, a red meritage wine, was released at the then high price of $50 a bottle. A restaurant was opened in 1992. Four years later, in 1996, Jean Leducq and his wife established the Leducq Foundation to fund international cardiovascular research, with 100 percent of the profits from the sale of Prince Michel and Rapidan River wines being donated to the foundation.

The Italian investment in Virginia, Barboursville Vineyards, got its start when Cantine Zonin S.p.A., a wine company owned by the Zonin family of Gambellara (near Venice) wanted a hedge against political uncertainties in Italy. Virginia was chosen as a site because the climate there resembled that of their vineyards in Italy. Working with a London merchant banking firm, Western America Finance, they bought an 850-acre sheep farm in Barboursville, seventeen miles northeast of Charlottesville.[11] The farm was located on the site of the former Barboursville Plantation once owned by James Barbour, governor of Virginia from 1812 to 1814. His mansion, designed by Thomas Jefferson, was gutted by fire in 1884, and its picturesque ruins (often shown on Barboursville's labels) are a registered historic Virginia landmark.

Gabriele Rausse, who had recently graduated from the agrarian science school in Milan, was assigned the job of establishing a diversified agricultural operation at Barboursville and arrived there in April 1976. More than three thousand potted vinifera vines were planted in June. A very dry summer, an exceptionally cold winter, and a late spring frost the following year destroyed the vineyard. Rausse was ready to return to Italy and the London backers pulled out, but the Zonins decided to continue. In 1977, Rausse began a grafting operation and started a nursery with the intent of selling vines for 1978 delivery. For the next several years he sold as many vines as he could and planted the remainder. In 1980, 100,000 vines were sold and 6,000 vines added to their own vineyard.

In the fall of 1979 Barboursville made 2,000 gallons of wine, but most of it was still in the tanks when the winery burned to the ground late that fall. A new winery was built in 1980 in time for their first commercial vintage of 5,500 gallons. Winemakers in the early years were Gianmarco Arzenton, Claudio Salvador, and Adriano Rossi. In 1990, Luca Paschina, a graduate of the enology school at Alba, near Turin, was

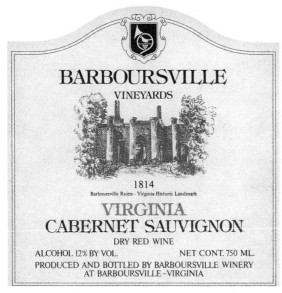

BARBOURSVILLE
VINEYARDS

1814
Barboursville Ruins - Virginia Historic Landmark
VIRGINIA
CABERNET SAUVIGNON
DRY RED WINE
ALCOHOL 12% BY VOL.   NET CONT. 750 ML.
PRODUCED AND BOTTLED BY BARBOURSVILLE WINERY
AT BARBOURSVILLE - VIRGINIA

JEFFERSON'S DREAM

Jefferson was a great lover of wine.
He designed the home of his
friend James Barbour in 1814, at
the time, Governor of Virginia.
With the help of Filippo Mazzei,
an Italian viticulturist, vitis vinifera
were planted on the Estate.
These first plantings failed. The
vineyards have been renewed and
with modern scientific technology
they are now extremely successful.
Jefferson's dream has become
a reality.

The 1979 vintage in the old property
of Governor Barbour, has produced
9350 bottles of Cabernet Sauvignon

This is bottle No.

BARBOURSVILLE WINERY INC.
Barboursville, - Virginia

Figure 6.2: The land on which Barboursville Vineyards is located was once the property of James Barbour, a former governor of Virginia. Thomas Jefferson designed Barbour's home in 1814, and after the mansion was destroyed by fire in 1844, the ruins were preserved as a Virginia historic landmark. Many of the winery's labels depict the ruins including this label used on the few bottles that survived a 1979 fire at the winery. Author's collection.

sent to Barboursville as a consultant in time for the harvest. When he returned to give his report to the Zonins, he was immediately sent back to Barboursville as general manager and winemaker. By 2000 the winery had 120 acres of vineyards and he was making 32,000 cases of wine.[12]

Apart from these three European ventures, there were surprisingly few attempts from Europe to establish vineyards and wineries in the East. A short-lived French enterprise occurred in 1985 when representatives of Les Vignes de France, a large white wine cooperative in Lussec, Bordeaux, came to the Finger Lakes to explore the possibility of buying grapes and making wine that would be sold in the major wine markets of the East. In addition to taking advantage of the overall health of the economy in the United States, they believed they could avoid the problem of having Bordeaux wines "cook" in their containers while crossing the ocean and also reduce their storage time in warehouses. They retained Gene Pierce, a grower and vice president of Glenora Wine Cellars, as a broker to buy the grapes. Originally it was thought that the New York State Agricultural Experiment Station would be the site of the winemaking experiment, but the project was too extensive and Glenora offered them the use of its own facilities.[13]

What was called Glenora's "French Connection" resulted in a white wine called Château Liberté, a blend of 20 percent Chardonnay, 40 percent Seyval Blanc, and 40 percent Cayuga White. In 1985, 1,000 cases were made and test marketed the

Figure 6.3: Rob Deford, III, proved that winery growth can occur after a winery changes hands. In 1980, Philip and Jocelyn Wagner sold their winery, Boordy Vineyards, to the Robert B. Deford family, which moved the winery to Hydes, Maryland. Rob Deford, Jr., took over the active management of the winery, and turned it into one of the largest wineries in the state. Photo by author, 1995.

next year. Between 6,000 and 10,000 cases were made in 1986 and there was talk of building a joint venture winery. In the fall of 1987, however, it was announced that the joint project would end with another 6,000 to 10,000 cases being made at Glenora. Les Vignes de France was then expected to build its own 30,000-case winery in the Finger Lakes, but that winery did not materialize.

California exhibited little more interest in the East. In 1980 there were rumors that Paul Masson Vineyards was planning a vineyard operation in Virginia.[14] An experimental vineyard was probably planted. Paul Masson Vineyards subsequently started a Canadian operation in Lincoln, Ontario. The $2.9 million winery opened on June 18, 1985, and closed two years later.

Although winery starts that originated in Europe and California were not common in the East, many trained winemakers came from overseas and went on to play prominent roles in the development of the eastern industry. Among those were Charles Fournier at Gold Seal; Adhemar de Chaunac at Brights; Hermann Wiemer at Bully Hill and his own winery, Hermann J. Wiemer Vineyard; and Jacques Recht at Ingleside Plantation Vineyards in Virginia.[15] Recht also consulted for many wineries in the East and had more than 125 technical winemaking articles published that aided the growth of the industry in the East.

Developments in New York

With its large wineries, industry pioneers like Konstantin Frank and Charles Fournier, and the magnitude of the research contributions of the New York State Agricultural Experiment Station, New York exerted an influence far beyond its borders. It had the added distinction of being the second largest wine producing state in the United States by a wide margin. In 1980, when California had 90.3 percent of the nation's wine production, New York had 7.3 percent while no other state had as much as 1 percent.

The modern wine industry in the East had its base in New York. Although each state had its own wine history (see appendix E), the grape and wine history of New York is worth detailing not only in its own right, but as a way of better understanding the growth of the industry in the East.

Renaissance in New York

Four large wineries dominated the New York wine industry in the years following Prohibition. The Taylor Wine Company, the Pleasant Valley Wine Company (which was acquired by Taylor at the end of 1961), Gold Seal Vineyards, and Widmer's Wine Cellars were all original members of the Finger Lakes Wine Growers Association that was founded in 1932 to work for the immediate modification of the Volstead Act to include light wines and the ultimate repeal of the Eighteenth Amendment.[16] Until the enactment of the Farm Winery Act in 1976, these wineries had the money and the political influence to stop the passage of any legislation they felt would be against their interests.

After Prohibition, the New York wine industry continued to be based on native American varieties of grapes to make the ports, sherries, and sweeter labrusca wines for consumers who had grown up appreciating them. It took time, but by the 1960s the Finger Lakes wineries were increasingly planting the French hybrids and experimenting with the vinifera.[17,18]

The annual reports of the Finger Lakes Wine Growers Association in the late 1960s and early 1970s paid tribute to the close cooperation that existed between growers and wineries that enabled the industry to show a steady pattern of growth. Growers, however, did have their own concerns, and on April 22, 1965, an organization called the New York State Wine Grape Growers was formed. One of the issues they wanted to deal with was price: when grapes were delivered, the wineries would simply put them on the scales and then tell the growers what they would pay for them. There were also quality and quantity issues associated with delivery schedules. In addition, the growers felt that an organization could help them in marketing and could represent them in the legislature. Eastman Beers was president, Zeke Mendall was treasurer, and LaMont "Monty" Stamp was secretary.[19] A committee was formed to begin a discussion with the wineries.

Through 1968, grape purchases were invariably initiated through a verbal agreement between the grower and winery, and a handshake was regarded by both parties to be absolutely binding. At this time, growers were finding it increasingly difficult to get bank financing without written contracts. The Taylor Wine Company issued formal contracts for the first time prior to the 1969 harvest. Pleasant Valley and Gold Seal followed quickly and then Widmer's in 1973.[20]

Another trend that started in the 1960s was a marked shift on the part of consumers toward drier table wines. The larger wineries recognized the change in taste and saw the need to produce wines with less strong grapey flavors. Winemakers at the time were allowed to use sugar and water to ameliorate up to 35 percent of the volume of the finished product and they began bringing in bulk wines from California to blend with their own wines for flavor modification. Coinciding with this shift was a changing consumer preference toward white wines that left the wineries with a surplus of red grapes and not enough white varieties to meet the demand.

Large grape harvests in 1974 and 1975 resulted in an inventory of wine at Taylor that was much greater than ever before. This, combined with the fact that between 20 percent and 25 percent of the wine used in Taylor's wines came from outside New York, helped create the large surplus.[21] The other large wineries found themselves in a similar situation.

In August 1975, Widmer's notified its growers that it would only buy part of their crop and wound up buying 80 percent. Taylor bought all they had contracted for in 1975, but in November amended the contracts they had with their more than 400 growers to permit the company to buy less than a full crop in 1976. Allocations continued through the 1970s. There was another record harvest year in 1978, and the following year Taylor bought only 40 percent of the red French hybrids and 50 percent of the Concords.

Two other major changes in the industry were taking place at this time. First, the ownership of the large wineries was changing. Following the death of the last of the Taylor brothers (Fred C. Taylor had died in 1968, Greyton in 1970, and Clarence in 1976), The Taylor Wine Company and its subsidiary Pleasant Valley were acquired by the Coca-Cola Company of Atlanta, Georgia, and soon became part of its new wine division, The Wine Spectrum. Will Widmer had died in 1968 and the ownership of Widmer's changed three times between 1961 and 1983. Gold Seal was sold to Joseph E. Seagram and Sons in 1979.

The second change was the passage of the Farm Winery Act. Farm winery legislation had been sought at various times since 1961, but the large wineries were able to block it whenever it was proposed. In 1976 it passed, aided in part by the grape surplus and the start of winery allocations. Within seven years of the signing of the farm winery legislation, forty-seven farm wineries came into existence and the New York wine industry started in a new direction. But, in the meantime, there was

Figure 6.4: Alex Hargrave and his wife Louisa spent two years looking around the country for the most promising place to start a vineyard. Based on climate and soils, they finally bought an old potato farm on the East End of Long Island in 1973. During the twenty-five years that passed before they sold the winery, they were credited with pioneering the wine industry on Long Island. Photo by author, 1981.

more pressure on the growers who were largely dependent on the large wineries as a market for their grapes. The ensuing crisis is described in chapter 9.

Long Island

Some of the most spectacular growth was to occur on Long Island. With a long growing season and winter temperatures that seldom go below 0° Fahrenheit, the eastern end of Long Island had long seemed to be an ideal place to grow the vinifera. The humid summers that encouraged fungus diseases, however, were a serious problem that continued until modern fungicides were developed.[22] It was not until the early 1960s that a farmer in Cutchogue, John Wickham, successfully grew cold sensitive table grape varieties. His experience as a grower was one factor that led Alex and Louisa Hargrave to plant the first commercial vinifera wine grape vineyard on Long Island in 1973.[23]

The Hargraves began looking for suitable vineyard land after he completed graduate work in Chinese history and language at Harvard University and she had graduated from Smith College majoring in education. After looking for land on both coasts, Professor John Tompkins at Cornell University suggested they look at the North Fork of Long Island. In 1973 they bought sixty-six acres of land in Cutchogue and planted seventeen acres of Cabernet Sauvignon, Pinot Noir, and Sauvignon Blanc that same year. By 1981 they had fifty-five acres of grapes, adding Chardonnay, Merlot, Sémillon, and Riesling. Hargrave Vineyard opened its doors in 1976.[24]

The Hargraves were instrumental in getting the Long Island industry started. David Mudd planted one acre of vinifera in 1974 and went on to plant thirty-six acres more in addition to starting a vineyard management and consulting business that played an important role in the development of the industry. Inquiries about planting vinifera began piling up at the Suffolk County Cooperative Extension office, and the Hargraves provided extension agent William J. Sanok with the vineyard space he needed to conduct experiments with pruning and vine training systems. Sanok was also able to get the New York State Agricultural Experiment Station in Geneva to begin conducting variety trials at Cornell's Horticultural Research Laboratory in Riverhead.

By the late 1970s there were eight growers on a commercial scale on Long Island. Wineries followed: Bridgehampton Winery on the South Fork in 1983 and Lenz Winery and Pindar Vineyards on the North Fork in the same year. Pindar Vineyards—founded by physician Herodotus Damianos—planted 200 acres by 1986 and produced 40,000 cases of wine, doubling both by the year 2000.

In 1986 there were thirty-five growers, 1,800 acres and sixteen wineries; and by 2000 there were forty-nine growers, 3,000 acres, and twenty-five wineries. A major boost for growers came in 1987 when Alice V. Wise became the viticulture extension specialist at Cornell Cooperative Extension in Suffolk County. A year later, an international Bordeaux Symposium was held on Long Island. What was happening on Long Island began to attract national attention. The November 30, 1988, issue of the *Wine Spectator* had a color photograph of Alan Barr and his South Fork winery Le Rêve on the cover along with the words "Long Island Has Arrived" in large type. Inside was not only a twelve-page article by James Laube but another six pages rating eighty Long Island wines.[25] This was the start of extensive publicity for Long Island's wines.

The First American Viticultural Areas

American viticultural areas (AVAs) got their start during the 1970s. They were an "appellation of origin," a term referring to the place of origin of a wine, or where the grapes used in making the wine were grown. Appellation of origin laws had their start in France in 1905 in the wake of the phylloxera epidemic. With many French vineyards devastated and abandoned, there were shortages of grapes, particularly from the famous wine regions of France. New vineyards were planted, often in marginal locations with varieties that turned out to be the wrong ones for the area. Sugar and water were then added to the pomace to make the wines palatable. These wines, in addition to inferior wines brought in from elsewhere in the Mediterranean, were widely sold as coming from the well-known wine regions. To counter this widespread fraud, the first "Appellation d'Origine" laws were passed to guarantee the geographical place of origin of the wine.

Geography alone, however, did not guarantee wine quality, and in 1935 the first laws of the "Appellation d'Origine Controlee" (AOC) system were passed to ensure wine quality standards by regulating such viticultural and winemaking practices as the varieties of grapes that could be grown, the maximum yields per acre that could be harvested, and alcoholic content of the wine. In the French AOC system, the more specific the name or appellation, the more tightly controlled the standards were likely to be.

The term "appellation of origin" was also used in North America. In the United States, prior to the establishment of AVAs in the 1970s, the regulations of the Bureau of Alcohol, Tobacco and Firearms (BATF) stated that in order for a wine to be entitled to an appellation of origin, at least 75 percent of its volume had to be derived from fruit grown in the place or region indicated by that appellation. In no way was the term "appellation of origin" to be considered an indicator of wine quality. Even after AVAs were established, there was only the requirement that 85 percent of the grapes used come from the named AVA. The closest the United States came to a designation of quality was allowing the term estate bottled to be used on a label to specify that the grapes used to make the wine came only from vineyards owned or leased by the winery. Again, though no quality standards were to be implied, consumers tended to infer that an estate bottled wine would be a wine of above average quality, and this was often the case.

On July 17, 1975, the BATF announced that it was considering rulemaking to provide definitions of the terms "appellation of origin" and "viticultural area."[26] BATF stated that it had "long recognized many diverse and sometimes ill-defined geographical areas as being entitled to distinctive appellations of origin based upon the statutory requirement that it approve labels for wine sold in interstate commerce." It had also become aware "that considerable confusion exists within the industry and among the general public with reference to the term 'viticultural area.'" Since there was a requirement "that vintage wine be labeled to show the viticultural area in which the grapes were grown, and that the wine be fermented in the same state in which the viticultural area is located...there may exist an implication in that wording that a viticultural area is some area smaller than a state, but the term is not elsewhere defined."

To end the confusion, BATF stated that a viticultural area or appellation of origin for a domestic wine would mean 1) the United States, 2) a state, 3) a county, or 4) a region or place within a state precisely defined by geographical boundaries and formally established by the state as a winegrowing area. At that time BATF believed that individual states were in the best position to evaluate their own wine growing areas. Estate bottling would be permitted on the label only if the wine was produced by the bottling winery entirely from grapes grown within five miles of and on property owned by the bottling winery.

On August 23, 1978, BATF published Treasury Decision ATF-53, which provided for the establishment of definite viticultural areas and for the names of approved viticultural areas to be used as appellations of origin on wine labels. BATF had now determined that viticultural areas would be established by Federal regulation and the procedures for proposing an AVA were outlined. Use of the viticultural area appellations by wineries would be optional in most cases but would be required if a winery wanted to label its wine as estate bottled. On September 22, 1978, the new regulations took effect and October 12 was established as the first date on which petitions could be submitted.

The first petition submitted was on behalf of an AVA in Missouri to be named "Augusta."[27] At that time there were two wineries in Augusta—Mount Pleasant Winery opened by Lucian W. and Eva B. Dressel in 1968, and Montelle Vineyards founded by Clayton Byers and his wife Nissel in 1976. Dressel was immediately attracted to the idea of an appellation. He and Clayton Byers prepared the petition and drew up the proposed boundaries of the AVA, which consisted of about fifteen square miles in and around Augusta in St. Charles County. Dressel then took the petition to Washington, DC, himself and was on the steps of the U.S. Treasury Building when it opened for business on October 12, the first day petitions would be accepted for filing.[28]

Wine quality was a major consideration in Augusta when the petition was drawn up. By the end of the year, the Board of Trustees of Augusta had established a Wine Board to set strict standards for Augusta wines. BATF, however, made it clear that approval of a viticultural area would be based on whether the area under consideration was viticulturally different from the surrounding areas and not on whether the wines were better than in other areas.

On July 17, 1978, BATF published a notice proposing the establishment of an Augusta AVA. A deadline of August 16 was set for written comments. Several people requested a hearing, and on September 24 BATF published a notice of a public hearing to be held in Augusta on November 1. The hearing was held in the American Legion Hall by a panel of five BATF members chaired by Thomas

George, chief of the Regulations and Procedures Division. Thirteen witnesses were called, all but two of them supportive of the Augusta AVA petition.

On June 20, 1980, BATF approved "Augusta" as the nation's first AVA. "Napa Valley" became the second AVA approved on January 28, 1981. By December 2012, a total of 206 AVAs had been approved in all parts of the United States, primarily because wineries needed to have an AVA designation on their labels if they wanted to call their wines estate bottled (see appendix G for a list of the AVAs approved for the East).

Wine Standards in Augusta

From the time that the petition for the Augusta AVA was filed with BATF on October 12, 1978, wine quality was a concern in Augusta. At the public hearing held by BATF in Augusta on November 1, 1979, Augusta's mayor Melvin Fuhr said:

> While the Federal viticultural area establishes strict standards to insure that wine bearing the name Augusta has indeed been made from the unique grapes of the Augusta area, it does not seek to control the other factors that affect the quality of the wine, such as grape growing and winemaking practices.
>
> Recognizing this need, the Board of Trustees of the special charter town of Augusta meeting December 4, 1978, established the Augusta Wine Board, the first such wine board ever established in the United States, consisting of 5 members which are: Howard K. Nason, Michael W. O'Reilly, Colonel Richard L. Lodge, Mrs. Lee Lapointe and Steve Casagrande.
>
> The Augusta Wine Board has been chosen from the Greater St. Louis, Missouri area who [sic] are distinguished in their own fields, as well as being experienced wine tasters. These members cannot have any association with the wine business, other than their love of wine. The Board will meet several times a year to consider wines presented to it. The wines will be tasted and evaluated to determine if the standards of quality of the Board have been met.
>
> These standards far exceed the present state and federal requirements, and are similar to the strict standards imposed on the finest wines of the regions of Europe. Indeed, in one notable regard, these standards exceed those of Europe since few of those regions require any final tasting of the wine to see if it passes the ultimate test of the senses.
>
> Wines grown within the Augusta viticultural area which meet the strict standards of the Board, will be recognized by a unique seal which will appear on the label. The seal consists of a wreath of grape vines enclosing a great horned owl, which has long been the symbol of the

town of Augusta, and signifies wisdom and strength, two elements which come in very handy in winemaking, as well as life in general.[29]

On May 27, 1979, the Augusta Wine Board adopted a set of bylaws and basic standards for vineyards, wineries, and wines. Four of the members of the Wine Board were members of the Commanderie du Bordeaux, and it is not surprising that the standards resembled those in effect in France. The standards covered such matters as grape production per acre, minimum sugar levels, irrigation of vineyards, amelioration of wine, and acceptable levels of free SO_2.[30] In addition the Wine Board appointed vineyard and winery advisers to check on compliance with the standards.

By the time BATF gave final approval to the Augusta AVA, the Augusta Wine Board had already approved seven wines as having the right to carry the official "Owl Seal," which by this time had been redesigned to feature a stylized great horned owl. In its ruling, BATF had found it necessary to emphasize that it was not approving wine quality:

> ATF does not wish to give the impression that by approving the Augusta viticultural area, it is approving the quality of wine from that area. ATF is approving the Augusta area as being viticulturally different from the surrounding areas, not better than other areas. Any commercial advantage which Augusta wineries may gain can only be substantiated by consumer acceptance of Augusta wines. ATF may not disapprove a viticultural area because consumers may find wines from that area appealing. By approving the Augusta viticultural area, ATF is allowing producers of Augusta wines to claim a distinction on labels and in advertisements as to the origin of the grapes used in the production of the wine. ATF will not allow producers of Augusta wine to claim that their wines are better because they originated from an approved viticultural area.[31]

The Augusta Wine Board met twice a year, and after each meeting a list of wines evaluated and the results of the evaluation were submitted to the Augusta Town Clerk. Certification of compliance to the established standards was then given to the Town of Augusta Board of Trustees.

Establishing quality standards with an accompanying quality seal had already been thought about in the East (see chapter 12). The Augusta Wine Board, however, was the first to implement such a program with a provision for enforcement.

Chapter Seven

❧

Building the Infrastructure in the 1970s

If it were possible to identify one single factor that contributed most to the growth of the eastern wine industry, it would have to be the character of the people who were responsible for its start. Very little would have happened if it had not been for the individual motivation, perseverance, and the desire to succeed that were an important part of the makeup of those involved in growing grapes and making wine.

Growing grapes and making wine is hard work, and it takes self-starters willing to prune vines in the dead of winter or spray vines at exact times in the summer heat to have a chance at success. The early pioneer growers were independent-minded people who forged ahead in the direction they thought would have the best chance of working. Long before there was any real knowledge of the importance of site selection, people planted grapes on the land they had available. If they were unlucky enough to plant in frost pockets, they had immediate and continuing problems; but if they were fortunate and planted in a favorable microclimate, they had a jump-start on success. The choice of grapes to grow was more often than not based on the kind of wine the individual grower liked to drink, because there were no recommendations on the varieties of grapes for a particular climate or site.

Viticulturist Lucie Morton has pointed out that each vineyard and winery had to be its own research station.[1] The fact that many growers were trying many different approaches helped reduce the amount of time spent in experimentation, but a major reason for success was the acquisition of the knowledge of where and how to grow grapes, what kinds of grapes to grow, how to make wine that was not only drinkable but wine that others would buy. Effective spraying depended not only on the kinds of spray to use but the timing of those sprays.

As a larger number of people began growing grapes, assistance became increasingly available from various sources: state universities, county or regional extension agents, field days, short courses, industry conferences, and publications. Also, societies and other organizations started to provide more information on growing grapes and making wine in a new wine region.

Basic Grape and Wine Research

Two major agricultural experiment stations in the East were responsible for much of the basic research involving grapes and wine in the twentieth century. One was the Horticultural Research Institute of Ontario (HRIO) at Vineland Station, Ontario, sometimes simply referred to as the Vineland Station. The other was the New York State Agricultural Experiment Station (NYSAES) at Geneva, New York, often called the Geneva Station. At both stations grape research began with table and juice grapes. Interest in wine grapes came later, and wine research and programs were often started in response to industry needs. Grape breeding programs at both stations led to the naming of new grape varieties that proved to be important in the East.

The Horticultural Research Institute of Ontario

The Horticultural Experiment Station got its start in 1906 when a farm at Vineland Station was given to the Ontario government by Moses F. Rittenhouse for "experimental work in tender fruits."[2] Thirty-two varieties of grapes were planted in 1908 and an additional thirty-one a year later. The immediate purpose behind the plantings was to delineate trellising systems and to provide information to growers.[3] The grape breeding program began in 1910 with the objective of developing table grapes with skins sufficiently tough to withstand shipping damage when sent west to Winnipeg or east to the Maritimes.

A shift in interest to wine grapes came during Prohibition when wine was the only legal alcoholic beverage permitted in Ontario and growers in the province had a need for wine grape varieties. Major progress in developing new wine grape varieties, however, did not come until after 1947 when new genetic material became available with the arrival of the French hybrids at the station.

In March, 1931, the Ontario minister of agriculture received a suggestion from the wine industry that a wine research laboratory be established at Vineland. A year later, part of the basement in the Administration Building was reconditioned as a processing laboratory. By 1943, growers and wineries were pushing for a more substantial laboratory, and in 1947 construction began on a new facility, the Horticultural Products Laboratory, which opened in the summer of 1950. On December 1, the station was renamed the Horticultural Research Institute of Ontario

Figure 7.1: Oliver A. "Ollie" Bradt was responsible for grape research at the Horticultural Research Institute of Ontario from 1947 when the first French hybrids arrived at the Vineland Station to 1978. Photo by author, 1978.

with the goal of integrating all horticultural research in Ontario in one institution, The stations at Simcoe and Bradford became substations of Vineland.

Thirty years later, on April 1, 1977, as part of a budget-cutting move by the province of Ontario, the station and three technical agricultural colleges were turned over administratively to the University of Guelph in Guelph, Ontario. The station officially became the Vineland Campus of the University of Guelph's Department of Plant Agriculture, but more often called by its original name, the Horticultural Experiment Station, Vineland. The wine program was deemphasized and, while the grape breeding work was continued, the grape program turned increasingly to soil management and vineyard environmental stewardship.[4]

Consistent leadership at Vineland during the early years was supplied by Dr. E. Frank Palmer, a grape breeder who served as the station's director from 1916 to 1956. The assistant director, J. Roelef van Haarlem, was a hybridizer of grapes and peaches from 1923 to 1942. When Brights Wines authorized Adhemar de Chaunac to bring in a large shipment of French hybrids in 1945, Palmer was immediately interested. The station did not have the land available to plant them, and thirty-five acres were purchased in 1946, some of which could be used for vineyards.

Palmer asked Oliver A. Bradt, who had taken over the peach work from van Haarlem, if he would assume the grape research as well; and he also asked van

Haarlem to work with de Chaunac on creating a list of vines to be ordered from France for planting at Vineland.[5] When the vines arrived in 1947, Bradt was responsible for their care. (See appendix B about the naming of the French hybrids.)

Bradt used the French hybrids in his breeding program, which resulted in crossing and naming several wine grape varieties: Vincent in 1967, Ventura in 1974, and Veeblanc in 1977. He also named Veeport, a labrusca variety suitable for port, in 1961, and Festivee, a table grape, in 1976.[6] When he retired in 1978, K. Helen Fisher succeeded him as research scientist and viticulturist, and the first wine grape named by her was Vivant in 1982. In 1995 she named L'Acadie in conjunction with the Nova Scotia grape and wine industry and, also in the same year, Vintinto, a teinturier variety, in cooperation with biochemistry scientist Tibor Fuleki at the station, who wanted the variety named primarily for research purposes.[7]

Emil T. Andersen came to Vineland in 1967 as chief research scientist in charge of production and breeding. A major research project taken on during his tenure was a study headed by John Wiebe in the mid-1970s on the use of infrared photography during temperature inversions to delineate frost-prone and frost-resistant areas in Ontario.[8] This study resulted in the "Grape Climatic Map" that identified potentially favorable grape growing areas along the north side of Lake Erie from Niagara-on-the-Lake to Windsor.

In the Horticultural Products Laboratory, which opened in 1950, Ralph F. Crowther was responsible for evaluating the winemaking potential of new grape varieties being grown in the experimental vineyard at Vineland. One of his early successes was the development of the Crowther-Truscott submerged-culture *flor* sherry-making process for making the Spanish fino-type sherry, a process that completely changed sherry making in both Canada and the United States.[9] During the mid-to-late 1970s, Fuleki developed the Vineland Flavour Index, a method of screening grape seedlings for labrusca flavor component using analyses of methyl anthranilate and total volatile esters to arrive at an index number. Seedlings with an index of over 14 would be likely to have a labrusca flavor character. The vinifera and French hybrid varieties tested had values below 8. Conversely, Concords averaged 416.[10]

Microbiologist Angus M. Adams succeeded J. H. Lloyd Truscott as director of the Horticultural Products Laboratory in 1970. One of his major contributions was his insistence that wine research at Vineland be related to what was needed by the wine industry. He was one of the principal advocates for wine standards in Ontario, and during his tenure the Ontario Wine Standards Tasting Committee was set up in conjunction with the Wine Council of Ontario and the Liquor Control Board of Ontario.[11] Richard V. Chudyk, who later succeeded Adams as laboratory director, developed methods of forecasting grape quality. His statistical analysis of Ontario's grape crop over a period of years led to the development of grape quality standards and the eventual grape-quality pricing system in Ontario based on sugar content.[12]

Changes in the quarantine laws in both the United States and Canada have made it more difficult to transport grapevines across their common border and thereby

Figure 7.2: Dr. Angus M. Adams, director of the Horticultural Products Laboratory at the Vineland Station from 1970 to 1981, was a major advocate for wine standards in Ontario before the advent of the VQA. Photo by author, 1978.

created a problem for those who wanted to obtain new varieties of grapes. Until the United States Quarantine Act of 1912 was revised in 1980, only grapevines from Europe had to pass through quarantine. Philip Wagner and others who brought cuttings into the United States illegally in the 1930s and 1940s did so to prevent them from being detained at a quarantine station where there was a good chance they would not survive. Grapevines from Canada were exempted from quarantine, and some of the earliest plantings of the French hybrids in the Finger Lakes took place in the 1950s when truckloads of cuttings crossed the border after pruning was completed in Canadian vineyards.[13]

Canadian quarantine procedures were also undergoing revision around 1980. The result was that grapevines could not be brought into the United States from Canada without a phytosanitary certificate from Canadian authorities, and Canadian authorities would not issue such a certificate until the vines were indexed—that is, checked for viruses. This led to instances of grapevine smuggling, sometimes by car, sometimes by boat across Lake Erie.

The quarantine laws in both countries have limited the number of new varieties of grapes that cross the border. New Canadian varieties such as those being named by Helen Fisher and new hybrid varieties from Minnesota must now pass through quarantine before being permitted entry even for field testing in the other country.

The New York State Agricultural Experiment Station

The New York State legislature passed legislation establishing the New York Agricultural Experiment Station in Geneva on June 26, 1880, but the station did not officially become operational until March 1, 1882, when Dr. E. Lewis Sturtevant took office as its first director.[14] It remained an independent institution until July 1, 1923, when the legislature transferred the administration of the station to the New York State College of Agriculture at Cornell University, now the New York State College of Agriculture and Life Sciences. At the same time "State" was added to the name of the station.[15] In 1948 the New York State Agricultural Experiment Station also became a statutory college in the State University of New York.

Research in the early years centered on dairy cattle and milk, with swine and poultry being added by 1895. Animal husbandry was discontinued at the station in 1929 and dairy research was transferred to Ithaca in 1943. Starting in 1882, experiments began on vegetables, field crops, and fruit, but by 1896 fruit crops had become the primary research interest in the horticulture department.

In the early years two horticulturists at Geneva were primarily responsible for grape research and breeding.[16] The first was Ulysses P. Hedrick, best remembered today as the author of *The Grapes of New York* in 1908 and as the director of the Station from 1928 to 1938. The second was Richard Wellington, who helped Hedrick write *The Grapes of New York* and other books in that series on fruits. Wellington was in charge of the fruit breeding program and until his retirement in 1953 was responsible for naming thirteen grape varieties in addition to many other fruits.[17]

By 1982, when Geneva celebrated its centennial, forty-six grape varieties had been named at the Station, forty-five of them table grapes, although a few of them were used for wine such as Alden, Canada Muscat, New York Muscat, and Steuben. In 1972, Cayuga White became the first grape to be named as a wine grape. Cayuga White was a cross between Seyval Blanc and Schuyler and was known as GW 3 (Geneva White 3) when it became part of a 1964 variety trial that included ten white and ten red varieties developed at Geneva. Widmer's Wine Cellars became the first to plant Cayuga White commercially in 1970, vinify it in 1974, and release it as a commercial wine in 1977. Two more wine grape varieties were scheduled to be released during the centennial year. GW 7, a sister seedling of Cayuga White, was named Horizon, but the second variety, NY 65.533.13, which, for the lack of a name became simply known as the Gewürztraminer hybrid, was withdrawn because stem pitting virus was found in some of the test vines. Following years of research when the virus was found to be a nonissue, the variety was finally named Traminette in 1996. This variety has become one of Geneva's most popular releases.

Along with Wellington, George D. Oberle and John Einset were two other fruit breeders who were particularly interested in grapes. In 1980, Bruce I. Reisch took over responsibility for the grape breeding program in addition to the genetic engineering program.

During his thirty-six-year career as viticulturist at the station that began in 1944, Nelson J. Shaulis helped transform the way grapes were grown in New York and elsewhere.[18] Among his major contributions was the development of the Geneva Double Curtain training system for vines, initiated in 1960 and published in 1967.[19] He was also heavily involved with the development of the mechanical grape harvester, work on which began in 1957. E. Stanley Shepardson in the Department of Agricultural Engineering in Ithaca and the Chisholm-Ryder Company in Niagara Falls, New York, cooperated on the engineering, and James Moyer in the Food Science Department performed grape quality studies.[20] The first mechanical harvester came into commercial use in New York in 1968. When Shaulis retired in 1979, he was succeeded by Robert M. Pool, who had been hired to continue the plant breeding program after Einset retired in 1974. Pool then moved over to the viticulturist position.

Prohibitionist sentiment remained high in rural western New York after Repeal, and politicians in New York and nationally were reluctant to approve any alcohol-related project.[21] In the 1930s there was one enology-related achievement when Donald K. Tressler, head of the chemistry department, developed the Tressler Sherry Baking Process, a controlled oxidation of wine by a baking process that could take grapiness out of Concord wine and turn it into a very acceptable sherry. The process was patented in 1939 and by 1973 saved the industry more than $25 million in production costs.

Terry E. Acree in the food science department has attributed the start of the wine program at Geneva to the vision of four men who were working at the station in the 1950s and got together once a week to play bridge, drink wine, and discuss the prospects for wine and winemaking in New York.[22] They were chemist Willard B. Robinson, pomologist John Einset, entomologist Edward H. Glass, and plant pathologist Alvin J. Braun. They were convinced that their region's horticultural characteristics, weather features, and the presence of large bodies of water that could ameliorate the cold climate in winter was all that was needed to make New York a perfect place to make fine table wines that would be every bit as good as those produced in the Rheingau, Burgundy, or Champagne. What had to be done was to adapt existing technology to deal with winter hardiness. They saw the need for a professor to be hired who would be dedicated to making wines and could make wines as a support function for the horticulture department so that problems related to the culture of grapes in New York could be addressed directly in terms of the needs of the winemaking industry. Robinson in particular was fascinated by the idea of having an undergraduate major in viticulture and enology.

These four scientists did not socialize directly with each other very much, according to Acree, and they mostly represented different attitudes and politics. What they all agreed on was that they were living in a beautiful place to develop a healthy wine industry. Their names were not nearly as important as the fact that they represented four different fields of research at the station. A critical moment for them came late in the 1950s when Dr. Frank successfully planted a substantial acreage of Riesling because it provided experimental evidence that their vision had substance.

It would be 1964 before their vision would start becoming a reality, with Willard Robinson assuming a leadership role. Robinson earned his Ph.D. at the University of Illinois in 1943 and became interested in wine in 1952 when he began a study of objective methods for measuring and describing the color of wine.

Donald W. Barton became director of the Station in 1960. Two years later, with his active support, several attempts were made to interest wine grape processors in working with Geneva researchers to solve industry-wide problems related to New York. It took a year and a half to convince them that they not only needed and wanted an expanded grape research program, but that they were willing to support a request for a $50,000 appropriation from the state for wine and grape research. The grape component would be the development of new wine grape varieties.

Robinson and David Hand, the head of the Food Science and Technology Department, established the Wine Technical Advisory Panel.[23] The Panel, which included researchers from Geneva and winemakers from a key group of five wineries, met regularly to keep updated on new developments and to review unsolved problems and suggest possible solutions.[24] In addition to the $50,000 appropriation from the state, annual grants of $11,000 to $15,000 came from the industry.

Hand retired in 1967 and Robinson became department chairman. He believed that "any successful industry, no matter what it is, needs a back-up with scientific expertise to attack any problem that may arise of a technical nature."[25] He wasted no time building a team of specialists who would be in a position to solve any problems related to grapes or wine that might come up. Almost immediately he hired toxicologist Gilbert S. Stoewsand to work on the alleged toxicity of the French hybrids. Acree recalls that when he was hired in 1968, Robinson told him that he would not only be allowed but would be expected to work on matters related to wine. He might have to do it covertly at first, but approval would come. By 1972, according to Acree, sixteen of twenty-one professors in the department were working on projects related to wine. Most of these projects were bootstrapped to other nonwine projects. Whatever funds Robinson had available would be given to laboratories for projects related to wine. There was still resistance at the state level to funding anything involving alcoholic beverages, but this ended in 1976 with the signing of the New York Farm Winery Act.

After 1967 the wine program at Geneva moved rapidly forward. Improving the quality of New York wines was the top priority and Robinson's initiatives were aimed in that direction. The first New York Wine Industry Workshop was held in 1971 for commercial winemakers and for a time, with the interest in winemaking growing, amateur workshops were held in alternate years. Another of Acree's memories is that when he was first hired, Robinson allowed him to buy $1,000 worth of wines from the Rheingau, Champagne, and Burgundy—the areas that he believed New York

For Experimental Use

New York State Agricultural
Experiment Station, Geneva, New
York State College of Agriculture

A Statutory College of the State
University of New York at Cornell
University, Ithaca

Figure 7.3: The New York State Agricultural Experiment Station used this label in the late 1970s to identify its experimental wines. Author's collection.

would be competing against. "We sat down as a group for an entire week tasting, analyzing and just becoming familiar with the sensory attributes and chemistry of those wines."

The search for new grape varieties continued. Although it had been shown that the vinifera could be grown in New York, there was doubt that they could be successfully grown on a commercial basis. In 1955 Einset and Robinson made the first wine samples from a variety that would be named Cayuga White in 1972. By the time it was released, Geneva had a winemaker, Joe Bertino, who was making 500 gallons of experimental wines from grape varieties being tested at the station, and vineyard and tasting panel evaluations were being printed as "Vineyard and Cellar Notes." In 1973, Robinson was quoted as saying, "In our breeding program we're getting closer and closer to the vinifera flavor every year. Last year we named a new grape variety, Cayuga White, that produces a high quality dry table wine very much like the German White Riesling."[26]

When Robinson retired in 1982, the Station had hired its first extension enologist, Thomas H. E. Cottrell, and the vision of the four men who got together in the 1950s was well on its way to being realized. Donald F. Splittstoesser expanded the wine program when he succeeded Robinson as the next department chairman, and a major milestone occurred when Thomas Henick-Kling was hired in April 1987. Henick-Kling, a wine microbiologist who was trained in Germany, Oregon, and Australia, increased the role of the station in the New York wine industry through applied research and extension services (see chapter 13).[27]

Other Research and Extension Programs

Research was also conducted on the federal level. One of the best-known researchers in the East was Dr. John R. McGrew, research plant pathologist at the U.S. Department of Agriculture's (USDA) Agricultural Research Center in Beltsville, Maryland. Originally he was hired for work on strawberry viruses in the early 1950s, but much of his research then centered on breeding for black rot resistance in grapes. In 1968 he was assigned the task of improving a USDA extension bulletin for farmers interested in growing grapes in the East, and while he was in the process of revising it, he joined the American Wine Society. He became an active member of the organization, a frequent contributor and technical adviser to its publications, and was always available for advice on grape growing and winemaking.[28]

Research and extension programs were established in many states to assist people interested in growing wine grapes and making wine. One of the earliest programs involved the grape variety trials that began in southern Ohio in the early 1960s. The scientists who oversaw the project were Garth A. Cahoon and James F. Gallander. Cahoon earned his Ph.D. at the University of California in 1954 and left his position as assistant horticulturist at the University of California at Riverside in 1963 to join the Ohio State University's Agricultural Research and Development Center in Wooster as an associate professor working in the areas of fruit crops and nutrition. Gallander joined the faculty at Wooster after receiving his Ph.D. at Ohio State in 1963 to work in the areas of food processing and research in apples, peaches, and strawberries. Cahoon was responsible for the experimental vineyard and Gallander for the winemaking potential of the grapes grown there. Neither scientist was hired specifically to work with grapes, but research and extension of grapes and wine became a major part of their careers.

What kinds of wine grapes to grow and where to grow them was the most basic immediate need of those getting started in the industry. In Pennsylvania, Carl W. Haeseler began serving as extension pomologist in thirty-three counties while completing his Ph.D. at the Pennsylvania State University in 1962. When his thesis adviser, Dr. Harold K. Fleming, retired in 1966, Haeseler succeeded him at Penn State's Erie County Field Research Laboratory in North East and in 1967 planted the first wine grapes at the research station. Other trial plantings followed in the eastern part of the state, at Landisville in 1971 and Biglerville in 1972. Winemaking trials began in 1970 when Robert B. Beelman, who had done his graduate work under Gallander at Ohio State, joined the Penn State faculty at the main campus at State College. Another key researcher at the North East facility was entomologist Gerald L. "Skip" Jubb. Next to the problems of choosing grape varieties and site selection, disease and pest control ranked high on the list of viticultural concerns.

Gordon S. "Stan" Howell, Jr., received his Ph.D. from the University of Minnesota in 1969 and was immediately hired by Michigan State University as extension specialist in small fruit culture in the horticulture department. His interest in wine grapes started in 1970 when he learned about research going on in Ohio and other eastern states with climates similar to Michigan. The opportunity to grow grapes other than Concords came in 1972 when the Michigan Wine Institute funded a viticulture research program to determine the potential for growing wine grape varieties including the French hybrids in different areas in Michigan.[29] As a visiting scientist at the New York State Agricultural Experiment Station in 1975, he had the opportunity to learn more about growing wine grapes from Nelson Shaulis and received encouragement from him.

As programs started in other states, the emphasis was less on variety trials and more on other areas of viticulture and enology. For example, Bruce Zoecklein left his graduate teaching and research position at California State University–Fresno in 1980 to become Missouri's state extension enologist; and a year later, Larry Lockshin, who had a degree in pomology from Cornell and was extension horticulturist at Southwest Missouri State University, left that position to become Missouri's state extension viticulturist. A summary of the progress being made in Missouri was published early in 1982 and reflected their work in such areas as the development of a computer model to aid in site selection, soil analysis, grafting, bitartrate stabilization, and malolactic culture trials.[30]

Zoecklein left Missouri in 1985 to become Virginia's state enologist, professor of food science and technology at Virginia Tech, and the leader of its Wine/Enology Grape Chemistry Group. Much of his work with Virginia Cooperative Extension was done in collaboration with Tony Wolf, professor of horticulture, who arrived at Virginia Tech in 1986.

Most of the scientists in these early years were hired to do research rather than extension. At Geneva, pomologists had 100 percent research appointments, but they were always willing to answer questions from growers and participate in extension efforts such as taking part in winter fruit meetings held by state extension agents.[31] Haeseler's job description called for him to spend 75 percent of his time on research and 25 percent on extension, and Howell's time was to be spent 80 percent on research and 20 percent on teaching. The job of education was primarily left to extension agents.

Pennsylvania had a system of county agents who were responsible for working with the public. They could call on university researchers whenever they needed help in answering questions about a particular crop. Haeseler was the specialist in grapes and in 1971 he began meeting with county extension agents to give them in-service training. Most agents were very willing to let growers talk to Haeseler directly, and he enjoyed working with growers. It was not long before growers began to contact him directly rather than consulting their extension agents. Not only did he take time from his research, but he devoted much of his personal time to provide growers with the assistance he felt they needed. An unfortunate but understandable result was a delay in his being promoted to the rank of full professor.[32]

In New York, two early grape specialists with Cornell University Cooperative Extension began their careers as county agricultural agents. Gilbert C. Smith was hired as the Yates County agricultural agent in 1944 and in 1968 became the first Finger Lakes area grape specialist. Trenholm "Trenny" Jordan became the assistant county agent for Chautauqua in 1951 and in 1970 Cornell appointed him cooperative extension grape specialist for western New York State.[33] In 1974, following Smith's retirement, Thomas J. Zabadal, who had completed his Ph.D. in plant physiology from Cornell, was named the second Finger Lakes grape specialist.

Assistance for growers also came from the private sector. Wineries had much to gain by providing practical assistance to growers who would be supplying them with grapes. Brights Wines in Ontario made professional viticultural help available to growers starting in 1947. In March 1960, the Taylor Wine Company in Hammondsport, New York, published *The Planting and Care of Young Vineyards in the Finger Lakes Area of New York State,* written by its vineyard consultant, Seaton C. "Zeke" Mendall. Stating that this guide should be used in conjunction with the revision of Cornell's Extension Bulletin 805, *Cultural Practices for New York Vineyards,* and his 1957 publication, *Vineyard Practices for Finger Lakes Growers,* Mendall outlined the reasons for his new publication in the introduction. "Due to the fact that The Taylor Wine Company has instituted a vineyard expansion program and many growers are planting vineyards for the first time, it was felt, by the writer, that some informative material, supplementary to that already available through the County Extension Services, was needed." He went on to say that individual problems that could not be solved through available literature should be brought to the attention of a consultant or their county agricultural agent.

William M. "Bill" Konnerth, Douglas P. Moorhead's original partner in Presque Isle Wine Cellars in North East, Pennsylvania, knew there was a need for winemaking information when they started selling juice and winery supplies in 1964. To provide this information, as well as to publicize their operation, he gave talks on winemaking throughout Pennsylvania, New York, and Ohio. In 1966 the first edition of his booklet *Beginner's Book of Winemaking* was published, and by April 1977, it was in its seventh printing. From 1964 to 1976 he wrote a newsletter, "Cellar Notes," which included practical articles on enology and viticulture as well as essays on any number of subjects from wine and food to wine drinking and taxation, that went to as many as 300–400 subscribers at the height of its popularity.[34]

Starting in 1970, Allentown College of St. Francis de Sales in Center Valley, Pennsylvania, looked for a way to increase enrollments in their chemistry courses. A new faculty member, Frank J. Gadek, who had received his Ph.D. in organic chemistry in 1969 and who had become interested in wine as a graduate student, suggested enology and in January 1973, gave a lecture and demonstration on winemaking. More than 100 people showed up and said that they would attend a practical laboratory course. In the fall of 1973, Allentown College offered its first science of enology course, and between 1973 and 1978 there were 168 attendees. Other courses were added and were attended by people from eighteen states and Canada. By 1980, more than 300 people had attended his courses.[35]

Research and extension bulletins were effective tools for communicating with growers and winemakers. They were particularly useful for researchers whose time allowance for extension was limited. Workshops and conferences were ways of bringing together a group of experts and a larger number of people wanting practical information on grape growing and winemaking. Two early conferences attracted people from a wide geographical area. The First Pennsylvania Wine Industry Conference was held on November 20–21, 1968, at Penn State's J. Orvis Keller Conference Center in University Park and was sponsored by the extension and research divisions of the University's College of Agriculture and the Pennsylvania Grape Council. In 1972 the first Ohio Grape—Wine Short Course was organized by the Ohio Agricultural Research Development Center in Wooster. Both conferences brought in a range of speakers from around the East and sometimes from California, and each published an annual volume of proceedings. After a few years, industry began to become involved with the organization of the conferences, the Pennsylvania Wine Association with the Pennsylvania conference and the Ohio Wine Producers Association with the Short Course in Ohio.

The Rise of Industry Publications

Five major trade publications were available to the grape and wine industry in the East for most of this period. Two of them originated in California, *Wines and Vines,* founded in 1919, and *Practical Winery and Vineyard,* first published as *The Practical Winery* in 1980. Three periodicals were started in the East in the mid-1970s: the *Southeast Grape Letter,* which later became *The Pennsylvania Grape Letter and Wine News* and then *Wine East; Eastern Grape Grower,* which evolved into *Vineyard and Winery Management;* and *The Vinifera Wine Growers Journal.*[36]

In January 1974, the first issue of the *Southeast Grape Letter* was published by Howard J. Miller, Jr., an advertising executive in Lancaster, Pennsylvania, who was also a grape grower. The two-page newsletter that was intended to give basic information to growers in southeastern Pennsylvania became a four-page newsletter and was renamed *The Pennsylvania Grape Letter* in 1975. In August 1976, it was bought by Hudson Cattell and H. Lee Stauffer, partners in L & H Photojournalism, a firm specializing in educational public relations, and renamed *The Pennsylvania Grape Letter and Wine News.* Cattell's background included a liberal arts education at Wabash College in Crawfordsville, Indiana, an M.A. from the University of Wisconsin, and five years' experience as publications manager with the Science Press. Stauffer had an undergraduate degree in journalism from Penn State and was working for a Lancaster advertising agency when she met Cattell. In 1979 she married Eric Miller and moved to Benmarl Vineyards in New York. It then became necessary to find a replacement for her in Lancaster.

Linda Jones McKee joined L & H Photojournalism in January 1980. In addition to holding degrees from Carleton College in Minnesota and New York University, she had a strong background in public relations and was a former editor of *Antiques Collecting* magazine. Her interest in the eastern wine industry began immediately and developed rapidly. At that time the eastern wine industry was expanding, and Cattell and McKee made the decision to convert the newsletter into a magazine and rename it *Wine East*. The first issue in the new format was published in May 1981, and from the start the intent was to focus its editorial content exclusively on the grape and wine industry in eastern North America.[37]

J. William Moffett, who founded *Eastern Grape Grower* in 1975, graduated from the University of Minnesota in 1963 with a B.A. in communications. He worked for a short time at the *Minneapolis Star and Tribune* and then became a field editor for the college division of the publishing firm of Charles Scribner's Sons. In 1970 he bought a farm in Hector, New York, and grew twelve acres of grapes, which he sold to the Canandaigua Wine Company. When Charles Scribner's Sons closed its college division in 1974, Moffett began thinking about starting a technical magazine for grape growers. The first issue of *Eastern Grape Grower* was published in February 1975.

In November 1974, Hope Merletti began working for Moffett as a part-time secretary. She had studied dietetics at the University of Buffalo and had become interested in writing while she was a student there. Her plans for writing were shelved, however, when she quickly became involved as operations manager for the magazine and as the coordinator for the first Wineries Unlimited, a technical seminar and trade show, in 1976. In 1977 she became a full partner in the business, and in 1981 she and Moffett were married.

The magazine was renamed *Eastern Grape Grower and Winery News* in August 1977, and after experimenting with planning and holding events for consumers, the decision was made to reposition the magazine. Effective with the May–June 1986 issue, the magazine was renamed *Vineyard and Winery Management* and the process of turning it into a national trade publication began.[38]

The Vinifera Wine Growers Journal was edited by Robert de Treville Lawrence, Sr., and was published by the Vinifera Wine Growers Association in the Plains, Virginia (for more on the history of the journal, see chapter 4). The first issue was dated spring 1974, and for most of its existence it came out quarterly. In addition to publishing news of the association and technical articles on grape growing and winemaking, technical articles were reprinted from other sources. The winter 1989 issue was the last under Lawrence's editorship. John J. Baxevanis, of the Department of Geography at East Stroudsburg University in East Stroudsburg, Pennsylvania, succeeded him and served as editor until publication ceased in the winter of 1991 (see chapter 9).

Older than any of the three preceding publications was the *American Wine Society Journal,* the official organ of the American Wine Society (AWS). The society was founded by Dr. Konstantin Frank in 1967 (see chapter 3 for details), and the first issue of the *American Wine Society Newsletter* was published without a volume number in February 1969. The second issue, Vol. 1, No. 2, dated spring 1969, was published under a new name, *Vintage.* Following the publication of the winter 1973 issue (Vol. 5, No. 4), the name was changed once again. Philip Seldon, a New York wine writer, had started a new magazine called *Vintage* and the American Wine Society, not having the money to fight for their name in court, decided to rename their publication the *American Wine Society Journal.* The editorial content of the journal was intended to be read by the membership and contained articles written by members, news of the society, and other information of interest to home winemakers.

Organizations Supporting Wineries

In its earliest years, the American Wine Society was important because it was the only organization in the East that brought people together. Although its membership at the start consisted almost entirely of professional and amateur winemakers, it was not long before it included grape growers, researchers, and professional people interested in or involved with wine as well as consumers. One result was the start of other organizations by people who came together and interacted at the society's annual meetings.

One organization that traces its beginnings directly to AWS is the Society of Wine Educators. Its first president, Robert J. Levine, has described how it happened.[39] In the early 1970s there was an increasing number of members whose main interest in wine was the study, appreciation, and tasting of wine. Among them was a small number who taught wine appreciation courses. Levine brought them together and formed Wine Appreciation Instructors Committee, which became a formal subcommittee of the Education Committee within the society. Later, at the annual meeting of AWS in Toledo, Ohio, on November 6, 1976, they presented a session on what winemakers could learn from a wine appreciation course, and to everyone's surprise more than 100 people came to hear their presentation. Such enthusiastic response led to a business session to set the stage for future activities in AWS and also to the birth of the Society of Wine Educators on August 12–15, 1977, when nearly 150 people interested in wine education met at the University of California at Davis.

The American Society for Enology and Viticulture was founded in California in 1950 as the American Society of Enologists (ASE). The idea of forming the Eastern Section as a chapter of ASE dates back to the evening of December 5, 1974, when three friends got together at The Pride, the rathskeller of the Nittany

Lion Inn on the campus of the Pennsylvania State University.[40] It was the first day of the Seventh Pennsylvania Wine Conference, and the three who were attending the conference were Andrew C. Rice of the Taylor Wine Company, Robert Beelman from Penn State, and Vernon Singleton from Davis. Singleton, who that year was ASE's first vice president, was an enthusiastic supporter of forming chapters within the society. A week later Rice met with Joseph Swarthout, president of the Taylor Wine Company, who agreed to underwrite the expenses of forming a chapter. Rice also met with Willard Robinson, who was not only enthusiastic but agreed to let the Geneva Station serve as a home base if the chapter were to be started. An organizational meeting of more than forty people interested in forming the Eastern Section was held on August 22, 1975, and on November 8 the national ASE approved the formation of its first chapter.

When the first annual meeting was held at Behrend College in Erie County, Pennsylvania, on August 13–14, 1976, the Eastern Section had 165 members. In 1984, prior to the Eastern Section's ninth annual meeting, the national ASE changed its name to the American Society for Enology and Viticulture. Key events in the history of the Eastern Section include the formation of the Eastern Section Enology and Viticulture Library Center at the Geneva Station following the signing of a formal memorandum of understanding by Cornell University on December 23, 1978, and the Eastern Section on January 30, 1979.

In 1997 the Eastern Section was instrumental in the establishment of the Eastern Wine and Grape Archive by Cornell University at the Kroch Library in Ithaca for the preservation of historical documents related to the history of the grape and wine industry in eastern North America.[41] Both the center and the archive received annual funding from Eastern Section. A student scholarship award program was developed in 1979 and the first scholarship was awarded to Renee Romberger for her 1980 academic year at Penn State.[42] The first student paper competition was held in 1985 with Peter Braell at Cornell University receiving the award.

A group of winemakers met in the office of Bert Sanderson of Dundurn Wines in Hamilton, Ontario, in the hope that "someday all technical members of the Wineries, so joined together, would provide a medium of free exchange of technical information and ideas on problems of general interest to the Canadian Wine Industry."[43] The result was the formation of the Canadian Society of Oenologists on April 1, 1952. The first annual meeting was held in June of the same year. In 1966 there were sixty-six members. That number dwindled to fifteen active members in the mid-1970s, but after a period of inactivity the society was revived in April 1980, under the leadership of George Hostetter of Brights Wines.[44] Annual meetings resumed in May 1981, and the membership continued to grow. By 1987 there were 166 members.

Many other organizations were formed on the state, provincial, and local levels, and their numbers proliferated as more people became attracted to the grape and wine industry. In general, technical knowledge was developed by professionals, transmitted to extension agents and those motivated individuals who were willing to spend time and effort in getting the best information possible, and then made available to beginners who wanted to get started and needed to have someone show them how to do it. Interest in growing grapes and making wine spread rapidly and took many forms as, for example, the accelerating interest in wine appreciation and home winemaking that took place at the American Wine Society starting in the mid-1970s.

CHAPTER EIGHT

WINERY EVENTS AND
MARKETING IN THE 1970s

How to grow grapes and make wines that their customers would buy were the main concerns of those who opened wineries in the 1970s. Marketing was a secondary concern that was primarily addressed by including tasting rooms in the winery planning. In addition, events held at the wineries and by others interested in wine helped contribute to building the infrastructure needed for the future growth of the industry.

Winery Events

Winery events in the 1970s included tastings of various kinds, wine competitions, and festivals. Competitions usually were conducted as closed events, but wineries then used the competition results to help promote their wines. Other events such as festivals were open to the public and encouraged people to interact with the wineries and their staff.

Tastings

The most basic way of experiencing wine is to taste it. When a bottle of wine is opened at home or in a restaurant, the initial sip, however cursory, is a form of evaluating the wine, if only to see if the wine is to one's liking. Wine tastings in a more organized form have long been a part of the eastern wine scene and have been held for many reasons. Tastings can be both educational and fun as, for example, the 1939 New England dinner and tasting of eastern wines for members of the Wine

Figure 8.1: The tasting room at Good Harbor Vineyards in Lake Leelanau, Michigan, was typical of those in the late 1970s and early 1980s. Photo by author, 1981.

and Food Society in San Francisco (see chapter 1). Wine clubs and wine societies hold meetings where the entire program revolves around a wine tasting. Most of these tastings are intended only for their members, but sometimes one of these events can have an importance that transcends the place where the tasting was held.

One such tasting took place early in 1977 for the Beverly Wine and Food Society of Chicago. Five Johannisberg Rieslings were tasted blind without any indication of the country of origin. Those attending were asked to identify which one of the Rieslings came from Germany. When the scores were tallied, the 1974 Riesling from Mazza Vineyards in North East, Pennsylvania, was the wine identified as coming from Germany and won out over two Australian Rieslings, one from California and, of course, the actual German wine. One of the people at the tasting was Ruth Ellen Church, the wine critic for the *Chicago Tribune,* who devoted one of her widely syndicated columns to the tasting.[1]

"You didn't know that Riesling grapes would grow in Pennsylvania?" she wrote. "Because Mazza Vineyards are so close to Lake Erie, not only Riesling but Chardonnay, Gamay, Pinot Noir and Traminer, as well as a battery of French-American hybrids are cultivated there." The result was important publicity for not only Mazza Vineyards but the emerging Pennsylvania wine industry as a whole.

Tastings with a more serious purpose in mind have been held that have been instrumental in shaping the development of the entire eastern industry. One such event was the May 9, 1942, tasting held by Philip and Jocelyn Wagner at Boordy Vineyard to determine the winemaking possibilities of various varieties of grapes. This tasting, which first identified the French hybrids as varieties of grapes that should be investigated further, led to a second tasting on May 15, 1943, which was held to find winter hardy varieties that could produce wines without foxiness.[2] This, in turn, led to the September 21, 1945, tasting at Fredonia, New York, where it was generally realized that the French hybrids could make good wines and led directly to the first large importation of French hybrid vines into the East (for more on these tastings, see chapter 2).

Tastings of small lots of wines made from new varieties continued in many places. In Lewiston, New York, on August 9, 1948, a tasting of fifty-three wines was held by a group calling itself the Eastern Wine Growers. *Wines and Vines* described the event:

> It became a habit among those wine men most interested to meet together occasionally for a highly informal tasting of small lots of wine made from these new [French hybrid] varieties. The whole thing has remained spontaneous and highly informal. There is no set organization whatever, and both meeting place and participation vary from year to year. The early tastings promptly discouraged mere dilettantes, for they were devoted largely to discarding varieties manifestly unsuitable for one reason or another. The tastings are in no sense competitive contests, for the material of which these wines are made are grape varieties whose possibilities are still not fully determined. Self-criticism is the rule, and the sole concern of the participants is the search for better wine quality.[3]

Among the papers of the late John Einset (housed at Cornell University's Eastern Wine and Grape Archive) were references to other early tastings. There was a wine tasting meeting in the cellar of the Urbana Wine Company on September 19, 1947; a "Tasting Bee" wine tasting meeting held in Niagara Falls, Canada, on June 28, 1949; and a New York Wine Testing Association tasting hosted by Philip Wagner on June 19, 1950.

Research stations at Vineland and Geneva established tasting panels that were convened periodically to evaluate the wine potential of varieties grown in their experimental vineyards and under test in the wine cellars. Annual tastings at the Horticultural Products Laboratory at the Vineland Station began in the 1950s. Einset kept a report of the seventeenth annual meeting on August 19, 1967, when nineteen wines were examined. There were thirty-three tasters from sixteen groups

Figure 8.2: A tasting at Pleasant Valley Winery in Hammondsport on July 28, 1952. Jocelyn Wagner is in the middle, and to her right is Charles Fournier. Wagner Collection.

including eight Canadian and two New York wineries. Einset and Willard Robinson represented the Geneva Station. At the start of the meeting, Vineland research scientist Ralph F. Crowther discussed the nineteen wines to be tasted during the morning and afternoon sessions. Later in the day, Ollie Bradt discussed the vineyard characteristics of the grapes used to produce the wines.

Similar research tastings were held annually at the Geneva Station, probably beginning in 1958. The results of the wine samplings and vineyard evaluations for the current year and previous years were bound in booklets titled "Research Circulars" and, later, "Vineyard and Cellar Notes."

It takes many years of experience to discover which grape varieties will make the best wine in any region. Starting in 1969 and continuing for more than a decade, members of the Baltimore and District of Columbia chapters of the American Wine Society met each year at Montbray Wine Cellars to compare their skills as winemakers. This evaluation of varietal wines helped speed the process of discovering the best wine grapes for their particular region. In 1985, Dr. John R. McGrew studied the results of these tastings over the eleven-year period from 1974 to 1984, and assembled data on nearly 800 wines made by approximately 120 winemakers comprising 5,000 individual judgments.[4] One surprising statistic was that Riesling outscored Chardonnay by an average rating of 12.39 to 10.82. Another finding was that red hybrid varietals had a relatively poor showing, although blending red hybrids appeared to improve wine quality.

In June 1980, the *Pennsylvania Grape Letter and Wine News* held a tasting for a small number of people interested in the problems and prospects of aging eastern wines. Most of the twenty-one wines tasted were between six and nine years old, although some were more than ten years old, the oldest being a very drinkable 1964 Gold Seal Chardonnay. The tasting was revelatory in that contrary to what the tasters expected, the white wines had aged better than the reds.[5]

The first Wineries Unlimited was held in Lancaster, Pennsylvania, on November 30, December 1 and 2 in 1976 and brought together 204 winery owners, winemakers, and newcomers from twenty-two eastern states and two Canadian provinces. Winemakers could sample a variety of eastern wines and mentally compare them with their own. The 1976 Wineries Unlimited was the first time that personnel from sixty-four wineries had gotten together in one place and it was the first opportunity for many of them to sample and evaluate other winemakers' wines. For many winemakers this was a major learning experience.[6]

For new wineries, their tasting rooms were a way of finding out which wines would appeal the most to consumers in their areas. In the late 1970s, New York's Canandaigua Wine Company expanded the new line of premium varietal table wines under its own label. In 1979, visitors to its first tasting room at Sonnenberg Gardens in Canandaigua were given the opportunity to participate in preference tastings, which gave the winery a good insight into consumer tastes. These tastings proved to be popular, and while the wines on their wine list were the initial subject of the tasting, it was not long before experimental blends developed by their winemakers were included to gauge consumer reaction.[7]

Tastings also helped get legislation passed that was beneficial to the industry. On July 9, 1979, the Pennsylvania Wine Association sponsored its first tasting for members of the House Liquor Control Committee and their staff. Fourteen of the state's twenty wineries brought their wines. The tasting was the first opportunity for many of the legislators to meet the owners of Pennsylvania's wineries and to sample their wines. They displayed a lively interest in the state's grape and wine industry and its potential. Many legislators commented that they were impressed by the number of wineries that were represented. For their part, the winery owners were just as impressed by the number of legislators attending and the interest they showed.[8]

An event that received considerable media coverage in the greater Philadelphia area was a wine tasting held on April 13, 1977, by the Archdiocese of Philadelphia to select the wine to be sent to Rome for the ceremonies marking the canonization of the fourth bishop of Philadelphia, John Neumann. A traditional part of the canonization ceremony involves presenting the pope with wine from the new saint's home district. Bishop Neumann's diocese in the 1850s included most of Pennsylvania and southern New Jersey, and one wine from each state was to be selected for delivery to Rome. Eight wineries, five from Pennsylvania and three from New Jersey, were represented at the tasting that took place at the South Mountain Winery in Philadelphia. Only red wines could be submitted and, not surprising for that era, all of the wines were either 100 percent Baco Noir varietals or blended wines in which Baco Noir was the principal component. The highest scoring wines were the Rare Red Wine from South Mountain and a blended Baco Noir from New Jersey's Antuzzi Winery in Delran.[9]

Competitions

Frank J. Prial wrote in the *New York Times Magazine* in 1989, that "wine competitions evolved from agricultural fair events. They took their place alongside the pumpkin judging and the three-legged race. As wine became a bigger and bigger business, the competitions were seen more as promotional events for the fairs and marketing tools for the wine makers."[10] With California in mind, and the long history of competitions there, he went on to say that in America competitions as a big media event grew out of two industry needs: recognition and reassurance, individually and collectively.

It took time for the eastern wine industry to reach the point where winning medals and awards became an important part of promotion and marketing. Tastings of the kinds described earlier in this chapter were a necessary precursor to competitions for commercial wines. A few of the older and larger wineries were the first to enter competitions held outside the East in Europe and notably in Sacramento at the California State Fair Competition in 1950. It is very likely that 1977 was the year in which commercial wine competitions first caught people's attention in the East.

In 1976, the first year that Wineries Unlimited was held, there was no competition. There were no ratings, no awards, and winemakers had the opportunity to compare their wines with those made by other winemakers in the East. The following year, Wineries Unlimited held its first competition for eastern wines only at the Host Farm Resort Motel in Lancaster, Pennsylvania. More than 230 wines were entered, and the sixteen judges awarded fifteen gold medals. Each of the gold medal wines was designated a "Host Eastern Wine Selection" and was stocked in the four Host Enterprise resorts in the Lancaster and Harrisburg areas until the 1978 competition was held.[11]

Another important 1977 competition in the East was the first American Wine Competition held in conjunction with the Maitre des Tastevin's Wine and Cheese Festival held at the Washington, DC, Armory in October. The six-day wine and food extravaganza featured daily seminars, films, lectures, exhibits, and demonstrations by world-famous wine and food experts. The competition itself, which was billed as the first to be open to wines from the entire United States, was no less spectacular. Forty-six judges were brought in from around the world for a 6-day triple blind judging. Seventy-four wineries entered the competition, twenty-three from the East. More than 600 wines were entered and nationwide seven gold medals, thirty-one silver medals, ninety-one bronze medals, and ninety-four honorable mentions were awarded. Forty-seven awards were given to eastern wines. The East won no golds, but did take six silver medals: Antuzzi's Winery (New Jersey) and Meredyth Vineyards (Virginia), both for Seyval Blanc; Markko Vineyards (Ohio) for a 1973

Chardonnay; Tabor Hill Vineyard (Michigan) for both a 1975 and a 1976 Riesling; and Wiederkehr Wine Cellars (Arkansas) for a dry sherry.[12]

The publicity surrounding these competitions did much to call attention to the idea of holding competitions for commercial wines in the East. Even earlier was the First National Home Winemaker's Competition held at the Westbury Hotel in San Francisco on February 23, 1973. The competition was made possible by the issuance of Revenue Ruling 72-272 by the Internal Revenue Service, which for the first time allowed home winemakers to file an application for authorization to remove and transport wines from their homes for the purpose of entering them in organized exhibitions and competitions. Each entrant had to file an application in advance with the Internal Revenue Service and secure the necessary authorization before moving his wines from home to the place where the specific event was being held.[13]

The First National Home Winemaker's Competition attracted over 170 entries from twenty-six states and had several hundred spectators. In addition, five television stations, numerous national magazines, and several newspaper and radio syndicates spent hours interviewing judges and contestants.[14]

State competitions got their start in the mid-1970s. In Pennsylvania the first commercial wine competition open to all wineries in the state was held in the small town of North East in September 1975. The competition was sponsored by the North East Community Fair Association; and the fair's president that year, Gerald "Skip" Jubb, an entomologist at Penn State's Erie County Research Laboratory in North East, was responsible for the competition which drew twenty-six entries from across the state.[15]

The Indiana State Fair held its first commercial competition in 1976. Commercial wines competed in two groups, one exclusively for Indiana wines and the other for wines from anywhere in the United States. Accounts of the competition held on August 13 reported that the judging involved 135 judges, 180 support people, 226 commercial wines, and more than 600 amateur wines from fifteen states.[16]

Other early state competitions held for the first time in the late 1970s and the early 1980s were the Michigan State Fair Competition in 1977, both the New England Wine Competition and the New York State Fair Competition in 1980, and the first Virginia Wine Competition in 1982.

Wine Festivals

Two of the earliest festivals in the East were held in the mid-1940s by Philip and Jocelyn Wagner at Boordy Vineyards in Riderwood, Maryland. Their first Fête de Vendange took place on Sunday, September 24, 1944, just after the first crush in their new winery, and Philip recorded the event: "Bright, with some clouds, very crisp. We had our *Formal Dedication and Fete de Vendange,* which was a great success. About 24 people, luncheon on the lawn (delicious) and lots of Delaware and Delicatessen—with vermouth instead of cocktails. Broke up about 4:30 p.m."[17]

Figure 8.3: *From left to right*: Mark, Dene, and Eric Miller stand in front of a recently planted vineyard at Benmarl Vineyards in Marlboro, New York. Photo by author, 1977.

The second Fête de Vendange was held a year later on Sunday, September 30, 1945, a month after the winery had officially opened: "Gray, cold, raw. *Party*—the vintage festival, in weather appropriate to this awful season. But we had a swell time—27 people, wonderful food including 3 of J's cheese cakes, good wine (Del. 1944 and S. 1000 1944), an open fire, and a cheerful, friendly atmosphere. All over by 4:30 p.m."[18]

The French tradition was also a meaningful one to Mark Miller, who founded Benmarl Vineyards in Marlboro, New York, because of the years he spent in France. In the winery's early days, a "Vendange Picnic" was held on the first two Saturdays in September. The winery also celebrated La Fête du Muguet in tribute to a Gallic rite of spring, which is traditionally celebrated by offering a bouquet of "muguet des bois" (lilies of the valley) to those one loves.[19]

Festivals by definition can be held on special days or at times of religious or other celebrations marked by feasting, ceremonies, or other observances. In the spring of each year, Markko Vineyard in Conneaut, Ohio, held a traditional "Blessing of the Vines," a brief service in the vineyard with hymns and prayers to celebrate the new growing season, a time for the rededication of growers to their vines and their hopes for a fruitful harvest. The event brought together growers, winemakers, and friends from northeastern Ohio and was followed by a tasting in the vineyard where the participants could drink a little wine and look forward to a good year of wine and fellowship.

Although festivals sometimes focused on a special occasion to be celebrated, the most common reason for holding festivals was to promote the winery and sell wine. Winery owners learned early that festivals would draw people to the winery. Bucks Country Vineyards in New Hope, Pennsylvania, was established in 1973 and held its first Sangria Festival in 1975. In 1978 its festival calendar called for a May Wine Festival with square dancers, a June Sangria Festival featuring the José Greco Dancers and Musicians, a July Italian Festival with several folk dance groups, an August Polish Festival with folk dancers, and an Oktoberfest celebration with Bavarian Schuhplattlers.[20]

All kinds of entertainment are offered to attract crowds to festivals: musical acts, performers of various kinds, arts and crafts, and a variety of food booths are common draws, but the grape stomp has always been one of the most popular attractions at festivals. Tabor Hill Winery in Buchanan, Michigan, held its ninth festival in 1981. Advance publicity for the festival listed two special events, both involving grape stomping. On Saturday, September 12, it was the "Largest number of people stomping grapes in one barrel at one time: 1980 Record: 57; 1981 Record: ?" On Sunday, September 13, it was the "World's Largest Competitive Grape Stomp: See 160 teams in wild and crazy grape-stomping competition!!"

Mount Hope Estate and Winery in Cornwall, Pennsylvania, held its first Renaissance Faire in 1980 as a one-day demonstration of modern day jousting. This led to a re-creation of medieval life. In 1982 several chapters of the Society for Creative Anachronism brought with them a large number of authentically costumed lords, ladies, friars and knights; and the Amateur Jousting Club of Maryland added jousters, pages, and dead body removers. New attractions were added each year, and in 1986 the Renaissance Faire was listed among the top ten Events in Pennsylvania by the state's Department of Commerce.

One of the largest festivals in the Midwest has been at Valley Vineyards in Morrow, Ohio, which got its start in 1970. Crowd estimates have approached 100,000 for the three-day celebration on the last weekend of September. Attendance in 1992 was estimated between 50,000 and 60,000 and, to give some idea of the size of the event, there were twenty-two acres of parked cars and 2,000 cases of wine expressly bottled for the festival.[21]

The oldest continuously running festival to be held in the East is the Niagara Grape and Wine Festival, which got its start in St. Catharines, Ontario, as a one-day event on October 4, 1952.[22] Credit for the idea of a festival goes to George Hostetter of Brights Wines who had been looking for a way to promote wine. At a 1951 meeting at the University of Guelph, Hostetter met Bevis Walters, an agricultural journalist in southwestern Ontario who had experience organizing festivals in Australia. Walters expressed an interest in organizing a festival if funding could be secured. The Ontario Grape Growers' Marketing Board and the Canadian Wine Institute each contributed $1,500 to finance a parade, folk dancing, and "Big Nite Out," a celebration and dance at which the first Grape Queen was elected by the amount of applause she received.[23]

Over time the festival grew from three events taking place on one day to 200 or more events over the course of 10 days. Winery tours, open-air wine gardens, wine and cheese parties, and many other events were added along the way. In addition to the Grande Parade, the Pied Piper Parade for children was started in 1962 and later drew about 3,000 participants. In 1956 the first Grape King was crowned, honoring the grower judged to have the finest vineyard in the Niagara Peninsula.

In the early years the word "wine" could not be used in the title of the festival, and it was known as the Grape Festival or, later, as the Niagara Grape and Vintage Festival. Nor could wine be served, and it was a number of years before the provincial government allowed wine consumption at licensed public festival events. Over the years, the Niagara Grape and Wine Festival became a major promotional event for the Niagara Peninsula, the city of St. Catharines, and the Ontario grape and wine industry. As many as 500,000 spectators line the streets of St. Catharines for the Grande Parade, ten times the number who reportedly attended the first parade, and overall attendance has been estimated at more than 750,000.

In the United States, regional or statewide festivals were a logical outgrowth of the festivals held by individual wineries. An individual winery or winery organization might take the lead in planning or organizing a festival for the benefit of a group of wineries, but it was often an outside sponsor that would take on the task of setting up a festival as a fund-raising event or to promote tourism. The first Maryland Wine Festival, for example, was the idea of John Barker, the public information and tourism officer for Carroll County, who formed a small committee to organize the event at Union Mills on September 29, 1984. Nine wineries participated and approximately 4,500 people attended.[24]

Marketing and Sales Efforts

When the first small wineries in the East opened, their owners of necessity concentrated on the basics of grape growing and winemaking. The majority of them had no background in marketing and no immediate reason to give a lot of thought to what they would have to do to sell the wine they were making. Almost all of them had regular jobs or other sources of income and did not have to depend on income from the winery to make a living. Some naively assumed that once they had wine to sell, people would automatically come to buy it.[25] It was not uncommon to hear people say that they were only going to make dry wines because that was what they themselves liked to drink. A year or two after their wineries opened, a visitor would find that their wine lists would contain a majority of sweeter wines. When reminded of their original intent, the proprietors would explain that they got tired of having people come to their tasting room and walk out without finding anything they liked or wanted to buy.[26]

Selling wine at the winery was the easiest and cheapest way to sell wine. Many early wineries were located in barns or other buildings where the wines were made, and sometimes the tasting bar consisted of a couple of boards placed on top of sawhorses or barrels located near the entrance. These were later replaced with more elaborate tasting bars often located in areas that were partitioned off or in separate buildings.

As was the case with winemaking, laws and regulations governed the marketing of wine. Even in tasting rooms, there were often restrictions as to what kinds of crackers, cheese, or other finger foods could be served with wine samples, or what kinds of nonwine items or foods could or could not be sold in the tasting room. Selling wine by the glass or in open bottles for consumption on the premises was invariably a matter to be decided legally.

Distribution of wine away from the winery premises depended in many cases on changes in the law. Apart from the three-tier system involving wholesalers and distributors, the transportation and delivery of wine, the ability to open off-premise sales locations and regulations governing the sale of wine were all matters controlled by the individual states, and each state had its own laws and regulations.

Most small wineries producing a few thousand gallons of wine were dependent on their local markets for sales. Locating a winery within easy driving distance of a population center meant that people could be attracted to the winery for an afternoon or evening open house, tasting, or festival. It also meant that the winemaker could hold a tasting or speak at a meeting or social function without spending a lot of time traveling. Word of mouth, publicity in local media, newsletters, and brochures were all effective ways of bringing people to the winery to buy wine without incurring a lot of expense on promotion. As opposed to larger wineries that utilized distributors and wholesalers, the small wineries could keep all of the money they received from the sale of their wines.

Wineries in the Finger Lakes, for example, had a more difficult marketing problem because they were located in a sparsely populated area with larger cities such as Rochester and Syracuse being a considerable distance away. There were a minimum number of restaurants, overnight accommodations, and other tourist attractions in the 1970s and early 1980s. As the tourist infrastructure improved and the number of wineries in the Finger Lakes increased, so did the number of visitors to the Finger Lakes wineries, from 217,000 in 1985 to 1,077,000 in 1995 and 2,879,000 in 2003.[27]

Wineries with production facilities away from highways found ways to make their sales facilities more accessible to customers. Sometimes it was accomplished by simply moving the tasting room to a more visible part of the property; Chicama Vineyards, located on Martha's Vineyard ten miles out in the Atlantic Ocean south of Cape Cod, furnished visitors to the winery with lists of places on the mainland where they could buy Chicama's wines. As laws were passed that allowed wineries to open tasting and sales rooms away from the winery, it became easier to sell wines in metropolitan areas and at tourist sites.

Generating Publicity

Publicity has always been a key component of marketing. Festivals were a highly visible way of attracting attention on a broader scale, but they were not the only way in which wineries got widespread publicity. Very different marketing success strategies in the 1970s helped generate state and national attention for two New York State wineries.

Benmarl Vineyards and the Société des Vignerons

Mark Miller, who established Benmarl Vineyards in 1957 in Marlboro, New York, realized that wine was not part of everyday life in the United States and that if he wanted to raise money and gain support for his winery, he would have to dramatize it and its wines.[28] As an artist living and working in Burgundy in the 1960s, he had become a member of the Confrérie des Chevaliers de Tastevin, a brotherhood formed for the promotion of Burgundian wines through medieval pageantry and monthly feasts to which celebrities and other well-known people were invited. Miller knew that these guests became strong supporters of the region and its wines.

With this experience in Burgundy in mind, he created Benmarl's Société des Vignerons in 1970 and invited his friends and Benmarl customers to become members of "a small cooperative grape growing association formed to produce the finest possible wines for our own members exclusively." In the first issue of the Société newsletter, he described how it would work:

> Our members, who bear the title of "Vigneron," are able to produce as much wine as they wish by the purchase of as many "Vinerights" from the Société as they require. One Vineright represents two actual grapevines and produces for its owner one case of wine each vintage year. The Vigneron is responsible for his own vineyard which he maintains by employing the cooperative's experts [Benmarl and Mark Miller] to manage his vines and make his wines. The cost for this maintenance is shared by all members who pay a fixed annual sponsorship fee for each Vineright.[29]

Initially, the cost of the vineright was set at $130 and the annual sponsorship fee at $30. The response was so encouraging that 500 additional vinerights were offered to sponsors for the 1971 vintage.

It was romantic to be called a vigneron, and the case of wine to which each vigneron was entitled was called the "droit de Seigneur." Each spring, vignerons were invited to a tasting at Benmarl to select the wine they wanted to have, and the wine would be bottled with a special Société label that included the member's own personal signature.

The romantic and unusual nature of the Société gave it elite status that attracted many prominent people, including many members of New York's "400." National publicity ensued and in the early 1980s membership peaked at about 1,400. By that time the price of the vineright had risen to $500 and the annual sponsorship to $50. Members were also invited to special dinners and other events.

Walter Taylor vs. the Taylor Wine Company

Walter S. Taylor, the owner of Bully Hill Vineyards in Hammondsport, New York, was brilliant, eccentric, and flamboyant. He could be charming when he wanted to be, never shied away from controversy, and was stubborn when it came to sticking up for what he believed in. Early in his career he worked for his family-owned Taylor Wine Company and the Pleasant Valley Wine Company it had acquired. When he criticized the Taylor Wine Company publicly and at length for what he considered to be dishonest practices in labeling its wines, he was fired in April 1970 (see chapter 4). Walter then built Bully Hill into one of New York's best-known small wineries through a combination of personal showmanship—he was a first cousin of P. T. Barnum of circus fame—artwork, eye-catching labels, and promoting popular causes such as ending the depletion of the ozone layer and the melting of the polar ice cap. Nor did he end his attacks on the Taylor Wine Company. He went as far as to have a railroad tank car hauled up on a hillside above Keuka Lake where it would be in plain view to protest shipments of wine from California to be used in blending with New York wines rather than the hybrids that were available in the Finger Lakes.[30]

The much-publicized feud between Walter and the Taylor Wine Company began shortly after the Coca-Cola Company of Atlanta purchased the Taylor Wine Company in January 1977.[31] In May of that year Walter announced that Bully Hill would introduce a new "Walter S. Taylor" line of 1976 vintage wines with family portraits on the front label together with "Walter S. Taylor" in large type. Previously, Walter's name was only on the back label. The Coca-Cola Company, always diligent in taking legal action to end any infringement on its trademarks, filed suit to prevent Bully Hill from using the name Taylor "in connection with any labeling, packaging materials, advertising or promotional material, or infringe on Taylor trademarks or engage in acts of unfair competition." On August 10, 1977, Judge Harold P. Burke of the U.S. District Court in Rochester handed down a decision that banned Bully Hill's use of "Taylor."

Walter's first response was to have his employees and others take black markers and obliterate the Taylor name on labels. In a tasting in Rochester he enlisted people to help him ink out his name on the bottles. He then proceeded to have his name covered over on bags, boxes, winery signs, and even on the door to his office. To anyone who would listen, he charged that Coca-Cola and the Taylor Wine Company had stolen his name and heritage. One slogan was, "They may have our name,

Figure 8.4: Walter S. Taylor was always willing to explain to visitors how the Taylor Wine Company was persecuting him by robbing him of his name. Photo by author, 1978.

Figure 8.5: As the result of a 1977 District Court decision, the name Taylor was banned wherever it was associated with Bully Hill Vineyards. His name on winery labels was inked out, and even the sign above the winery door was covered up. Photo by author, 1978.

but they do not have our souls." A decision handed down on May 22, 1978 stated that portraits and likenesses of Taylor family members could not be used on Bully Hill labels. Walter responded by putting a black slash across their faces and then "raccoon" masks over their eyes. When Taylor received an injunction against that, Bully Hill began used one eye on the portraits, the so-called Cyclops labels. Portraits of people not connected with the winery appeared on labels, including the likeness of a prostitute, and the name "Walter St. Bully" was used on labels.

The legal battle between Walter and the Taylor Wine Company attracted nationwide attention and comparisons were frequently made to David and Goliath. When the ban on family likenesses on the labels was issued, Walter appeared on television in New York City wearing a Lone Ranger mask and telling viewers that "they won't even let me use my own face." The mutilated labels on Bully Hill wines were attention-getters and many stores had difficulty keeping the wines in stock. When Bully Hill released new wines, the defaced labels had already been given approval by the Bureau of Alcohol, Tobacco and Firearms and Bully Hill's publicity continued. The labels became collectors' items and it was possible to trace the history of the court fight through the labels.[32]

The Taylor Wine Company sought to have Walter held in contempt of court, and in 1981 he was fined $11,000 and ordered to turn over all offending material including artwork to the Taylor Wine Company. Walter complied. The offending material was loaded onto two manure spreaders for delivery and as many as 100 supporters formed a motorcade that wound its way through downtown Hammondsport to deliver labels to Taylor's front door.[33] Walter also tethered a goat, on which the words "Bully Hill" had been painted, to the bed of a flatbed truck. The winery returned the goat to Walter, and this inspired what was to become Walter's best-known slogan: "They have my name and heritage, but they didn't get my goat." The goat, which was given the name "Guilt Free," appeared on Walter's labels, and goats became a tradition at Bully Hill.

Walter filed a suit in 1981 that challenged Coca-Cola's takeover of the Taylor Wine Company in 1977. The courts dismissed the case in 1986 and an appeal to the U.S. Supreme Court ended matters when on November 15, 1988, the Court declined to review the case. Years earlier, in 1983, Coca-Cola had sold the Taylor Wine Company to Joseph E. Seagram and Sons.

Wine sales soared as a result of the feud with the Taylor Wine Company. Walter's promotional instincts and his marketing skills had enabled him to take advantage of every opportunity that was handed to him. In various interviews, Walter stated that sales in 1976 were approximately $600,000 and that they had reached the $2 million mark in 1988.

CHAPTER NINE

GROWING PAINS IN THE 1980s

Most of the controversies that arose in the eastern wine industry in the 1970s centered on laws and regulations that wineries in the various states needed to have passed or changed in order to be in business. A wider range of controversies developed in the 1980s. Four of them are discussed in this chapter: a confrontation between two states over a competing appellation; a major crisis involving growers and wineries; two rival festivals in a legal battle; and, in Ontario, a free trade fight against the United States and Europe. These were growing pains, certainly, but in each case had an outcome that strengthened the industry.

The Two Shenandoah AVAs

A major AVA (American viticultural area) controversy between Virginia and California began on September 18, 1980, when the Amador County Wine Growers Association in California petitioned the Bureau of Alcohol, Tobacco and Firearms (BATF) to approve Shenandoah Valley (California) as an AVA in order for the wineries in that state to use the estate bottled designation.[1] Because an AVA had to be distinguishable by geographical features rather than political boundaries, the Amador County Association had little choice but to file for a Shenandoah Valley AVA rather than their more widely known Amador County name.

When the BATF published the notice of the proposed Shenandoah Valley AVA in the *Federal Register* on April 13, 1981, and wineries in Virginia found out about it, there was a storm of protest from Governor John N. Dalton and other top political figures who charged that California was trying to swipe one of Virginia's proudest names.

The media recognized a good story when they saw it. A headline in the *San Francisco Chronicle* read "Virginia Chokes on Amador Wine," and the story in the *Santa Rosa Press-Democrat* ran under the title "Wine War on with Virginia." Virginia newspapers used such headlines as "Grapes of Wrath" and "Our Valley and Theirs." Wire services picked up the story and Channel 2 in Oakland traveled to Virginia to provide coverage.

To further complicate matters, Virginia and California each had a winery named Shenandoah Vineyards. Shenandoah Vineyards in Edinburg, Virginia, was owned by James and Emma Randel, and Shenandoah Vineyards in Plymouth, California, was owned by Leon Sobon. Both wineries had been licensed within two weeks of one another in 1977, in BATF's Philadelphia regional office and in its San Francisco regional office, respectively. It was some time before this duplication was noticed and BATF then required each winery to make a label change by using "Virginia" or "California" in large letters to avoid confusion.

Shenandoah Vineyards in Edinburg, Virginia, filed its own petition for a Shenandoah Valley AVA in Virginia in August, an action that gave the BATF competing petitions to deal with. The bureau indicated that it would consider both historical and viticultural evidence. The final decision on December 23, 1982, gave Virginia a Shenandoah Valley AVA without requiring a state name and California a California Shenandoah Valley AVA.

Virginia's wine marketing specialist Lou Ann Ladin summed up the outcome: "Virginia was surprised to find California had a Shenandoah area, but California was surprised to hear Virginia had a wine industry. It did us a lot of good."[2]

Virginia Festival Rivalry

Wine festivals in Virginia date back to 1976. The story of the principal Virginia festivals is detailed here at some length because the events surrounding these festivals form an important part of Virginia's wine history.

The oldest wine festival in Virginia was held by the Vinifera Winegrowers Association on August 28, 1976, just a few weeks after the first commercial wineries opened in the state. It was not held to benefit Virginia wineries but to raise funds for the publication of the association's journal. The event was called the Bicentennial Festival and included a tribute to Thomas Jefferson. In addition to the Festival Center located in a field midway between Middleburg and The Plains, there were tours of three vineyards, audio-visual showings at the Middleburg Community Center, and the fifth annual seminar at Piedmont Vineyards.[3]

The Vinifera Wine Growers Association (VWGA) moved the festival to Piedmont Vineyards in 1978. For the first few years the brochure for the event simply referred to it as "Wine Festival," but by 1982 it was called "The Virginia Wine Festival." In 1983 the festival was held on August 27, an unbearably hot day that sent the festival into the red.[4] The financial loss set off a conflict that ended up in court.[5]

Robert de Treville Lawrence, Sr., the association's president was quoted as saying that in 1981 and 1982 the festival made $10,000 but "suffered." Elizabeth "Sis" Worrall of Piedmont Vineyards and the festival chairwoman, said that the concession stands had to be guaranteed and had to be paid $3,000–$5,000 when the crowd did not consume the food. The festival report stated that the festival made only $3.64. Lawrence demanded a full accounting; Worrall said that Lawrence had not turned in 200 ticket receipts. Worrall was appalled when Lawrence "slapped" a subpoena on her and promptly seceded from the festival.

The result was a split and the creation of two separate wine festivals. The two rival organizations set their dates, the VWGA choosing their traditional late August date; and the new group, the Virginia Wineries Association, setting August 11 for theirs. The Vinifera Association had been using the Virginia Wine Festival name and an argument arose over the use of the name. After a long court battle in May, Judge Shore Robertson ruled that neither could use the name, but could choose any other name. The Virginia Wineries Association opted for the Virginia Wineries Festival, which was held at Piedmont Vineyards. The Vinifera Association chose Vinifera Wine Festival and in 1984 elected to have the festival center midway between Middleburg and the Plains at Byrnley Farm, the home of Jack Kent Cooke, owner of the Washington Redskins.

In 1985 the Virginia Wineries Festival moved to Commonwealth Park in Culpeper and set July 20 as the date for the festival. The Vinifera Wine Festival moved to Valley View Vineyards in Middleburg. The feuding had not come to an end, however. Worrall and Robert and Phoebe Harper, proprietors of Naked Mountain Vineyard in Markham, decided to continue holding a festival at Piedmont Vineyards even though the Virginia Wineries Festival had moved to Culpeper, and they set August 17, 1985 as the date for their Middleburg Wine Festival. Lawrence referred to his festival as the Annual Middleburg Wine Festival and court proceedings began once again to seek an injunction on trademark infringement.[6] The injunction was granted and there was a second round in court where the injunction was found to have been violated. Skirmishing over the use of the name Middleburg continued until 1990.

The Virginia Wineries Festival continued to be held at Commonwealth Park until 1988 when it moved to the Northern Virginia 4-H Educational Center in Front Royal and then in 1992 to Great Meadow near The Plains as "Vintage Virginia '92—The Eleventh Annual Virginia Wineries Festival." The Vinifera Wine Festival continued to be held at Valley View Vineyard until it moved to Great Meadow in 1991.

Meanwhile, the VWGA made some major changes. Treville Lawrence retired as president at the annual meeting on August 26, 1989, and was succeeded by Gordon W. Murchie of Alexandria, Virginia.[7] Lawrence, who had previously announced his retirement as editor of the association's journal, agreed to stay on until a successor was found. On January 1, 1990, John Baxevanis of Stroudsburg, Pennsylvania, assumed the position of editor.

When Lawrence retired in 1989, he offered to give the VWGA sponsorship of the festival for one more year, 1990, to enable it to continue publishing the journal and to give the association time to find alternate funding sources for the publication. This arrangement was subsequently continued for another and final year. By this time Lawrence had already formed another corporation, The Virginia Wine Festival, Inc., and the 1992 festival was actually conducted under Lawrence's corporate name.[8]

Murchie had felt for some time that the Vinifera Wine Growers Association was moving away from its long-term program objectives and saw that the imminent control of the festival moving over to a new corporation headed by Lawrence was a real threat to the association's source of funding. The summer 1991 issue of the journal carried the notice that the election of officers and board of directors would take place during the 1991 festival and that approval would be sought to increase the membership of the board from seven to twelve. It was also stated without naming anyone specifically that prospective board candidates were suggested and discussed at the board of directors' meeting held at Oasis Vineyard on July 7.

When the elections were held, Murchie was reelected president and Lawrence, treasurer. Anita Murchie, Gordon's wife, was elected secretary. Seven newcomers were elected to the board. On August 22, 1992, the Vinifera Wine Growers Association sent a letter to all Virginia wineries notifying them "that the VWGA is under new management, a new Board of Directors, and a renewed mandate to promote the interests, growth, marketability, legislative protection, and public support of the Virginia wine industry." The letter also stated that as of the close of the upcoming 1992 festival, the VWGA would no longer be associated with nor support the activities of the Virginia Wine Festival, Inc. The VWGA intended to sponsor—in 1993—a major festival at Great Meadow, a wine competition, and "at least one major wine seminar on legislation, tax and other regulatory constraints placed on the wine industry and what can be done about them."[9]

In 1993, Lawrence advertised that his Virginia Wine Festival, Inc. would hold its eighteenth festival on July 10–11, 1993, at Morven Park in Leesburg. A VWGA logo was used in the advertising, and it was announced that the three traditional VWGA awards would be presented—the Perpetual Monteith Trophy, the Jefferson Loving Cup and the Wine-Grape Productivity Tray.

The VWGA felt it was necessary to take legal action against Lawrence and his corporation to protect its interests and filed for an injunction in the Circuit Court of Loudon County. On June 30, a Final Injunction (Chancery No. 15043) was agreed to by both parties stipulating that Lawrence could not use the name "Virginia Wine Festival" with or without a numbered designation, nor could it use the VWGA logo. In addition, no competition or award could be used that was called the "Jefferson Loving Cup" or the "Wine-Grape Productivity Tray."

Lawrence renamed his festival the Eastern Wine Festival and held it as scheduled on July 10–11.[10] The VWGA held its annual Virginia Wine Festival on August 28 and 29. On January 1, 1994, Murchie was able to write the following to the membership of the Vinifera Wine Growers Association:

> With a serious legal challenge to the very existence of the VWGA, the sudden resignation of the VWGA *Journal* editor, and loss of membership records, dues payments, etc., the new Board was faced with a simple choice, either disband the organization and let a long history of service to the wine consumer public and industry dissolve or, enter into a legal battle to win back the VWGA's identity, logo and control of its traditional annual wine events.... That legal battle has now been won, and we successfully conducted, in July of 1993, the 12th Annual Virginia Wine Competition, the largest and best in our history, and an equally successful 18th Annual Virginia Wine Festival at Great Meadow, The Plains, Virginia, on the 28th and 29th of August, 1993, which had 40 participating wineries, the largest number of Virginia wineries ever gathered at a single festival!

Both of the festivals held at Great Meadow continued to do well. In 1994 the Virginia Wine Festival attracted 15,000 visitors and the Virginia Wineries Festival 36,000. Under Murchie's leadership the VWGA expanded its membership and played an important role both in Virginia and nationally in pushing for favorable wine legislation on Capitol Hill. Murchie, who had become executive director of the National Wine Coalition in 1993 (see chapter 11), became a leader in many aspects of Virginia's wine industry in the years that followed.

Crisis for Finger Lakes Growers

Wine sales and grape prices began to slide in the Finger Lakes in 1980. Consumer purchases of labrusca wines were declining and the low price of European imports made the situation worse. By 1978, the Wine Spectrum had created a new brand, Taylor California Cellars, and its advertising dollars were being diverted to support it.[11] From 1981 to 1984 the average price for wine grapes fell from $305 to $182 a ton.[12]

The situation did not change when the Coca-Cola Company of Atlanta announced in October, 1983, that it was selling the Wine Spectrum, including the Taylor Wine Company, to Joseph E. Seagram and Sons. Taylor's announcement that it would reduce 1984 purchases by approximately 15,000 tons, one-third of what it normally bought, and would in addition eliminate the purchase of Concords altogether, led to about 200 angry growers picketing Taylor. Things would only get worse. On December 11, 1984, Taylor announced that all contracts were being canceled for both Taylor and Gold Seal and that all 1985 purchases would be made on the open market. Prices reached a low of $105 a ton for any grape variety. The financial hardships that resulted were enormous. The *Wine Spectator* in its March 16–31, 1986, issue ran a special report on the crisis in New York's vineyards with a photo on the cover of a vineyard being torn out with a bulldozer. At least 50 percent of the wine grape vineyards in the Finger Lakes were abandoned or destroyed.[13] Bankruptcies and foreclosures were commonplace. Neil Simmons, a Bluff Point grower, recalls seeing seven of his neighbors going bankrupt during this period.[14]

On April 30, 1987, saying that "the market…has not developed as we expected," Seagram's sold the wineries it had purchased from the Wine Spectrum plus Paul Masson, which it had bought in 1955, to a new company, Vintners International.[15] The new company formed by Paul M. Schlem and Michael P. H. Cliff posted heavy losses in 1989 and 1990 and, according to Zeke Mendall at the end of 1990, was "selling off everything possible just to meet interest payments."[16] In 1994 all of the companies Vintners International had bought from Seagram's were acquired by the Canandaigua Wine Company.

The 15,000 tons of grapes that growers had no market for were often just left to hang. Two cooperatives, one in the Finger Lakes and the other in western New York, were formed, but neither really helped, according to Monty Stamp.[17] Another way of using surplus grapes was to start a winery. Stamp was one of the growers who had foreseen what might happen as early as the 1970s, and in the 1980s when interest rates were high and prices were falling he planted wine grape varieties that he could use himself. His first vintage was in 1988, and Lakewood Vineyards was opened in Watkins Glen in 1989 as a family operation after he was able to convince his son Chris to leave his position as enology specialist at the Ohio Agricultural Research Development Center and return home to become their winemaker.

The New York State Wine Grape Growers had not been idle during this period of turmoil. In the late 1970s they had started to think about securing a marketing order to finance research and promotion.[18] They hired Juanita Spence as their office manager to help get a marketing order approved, and in late 1981 approval was given for the production areas in the Finger Lakes and western New York. The marketing order was expected to generate funding of $150,000 a year and now that there was a funding source, James Trezise, director of corporate communications at Conrail, was hired as executive director of the New York State Wine Grape Growers effective February 14, 1982.

Almost immediately the marketing order was contested by two lawsuits, one filed by three growers in western New York and the other by the Taylor Wine Company. On June 18, 1982, the marketing order was ruled invalid and the funding canceled. The New York Department of Agriculture and Markets appealed the ruling. During the appeals process, the office of the New York State Wine Grape Growers was kept open, and Trezise was supported financially by contributions from individual members that enabled him to continue working.

Another organization, the New York Association of Wine Producers, had been formed in 1980 for the purpose of securing legislation to fund research and promotion. Bertram Silk, vice president of operations for the Canandaigua Wine Company, was largely responsible for its organization and served as its president. After the marketing order was overturned, the New York Association of Wine Producers and the New York State Wine Grape Growers agreed to cooperate on programs of mutual interest and to create an umbrella organization, the New York Wine Council. The marketing order appeal was lost on May 26, 1983, and in June the Council was formed with Trezise as president and Juanita Spence its manager.

Although the New York Wine Council was intended to be involved in promotional activities, the immediate needs were in the areas of organizational development, fundraising, and legislative support. In 1983, Trezise wrote a letter to all wineries asking for their wish list of legislation they would like to see passed. The importance of educating the legislators was obvious to Trezise. He spent twenty-six weeks in Albany making the case for state support for a deserving industry. "I was on the same schedule they were," he said later. "When they went to Albany, I went to Albany; when they went home, I came home."[19] Very often he was accompanied by members of the industry on visits to legislators.

Six months of lobbying paid off with three important pieces of legislation being passed in 1984. Most important for the growers was that they could sell wine coolers in grocery stores. Wineries were given the right to hold tastings in liquor stores. In what Trezise has called the "winery deregulation act," wineries were allowed to sell wine by the bottle at fairs and farmers' markets and to distribute each other's wines. Wineries were also permitted to increase the number of satellite stores they owned from one to five and could locate them anywhere in the state.

Both the provisions for wine coolers to be sold in grocery stores and the new satellite stores were bitterly fought by the New York liquor lobby. The satellite stores were opposed because they could operate in the same way as the winery tasting rooms, and this meant they could be open on Sundays. At that time the liquor stores could not—and did not want to—be open on Sundays. The liquor lobby lost on both issues, and it was the first time since Prohibition that the liquor lobby had been defeated.

Legislation establishing the New York Wine and Grape Foundation as a private nonprofit trade association passed in May 1985. The first year's budget was set at $2 million, after which the funding would continue for four years but would decrease each year on a declining matching fund ratio of state to industry funds.[20] Seventy percent of the money disbursed was to go for research and 30 percent for promotion. A thirteen-member board of directors was to be appointed by the governor and legislative leaders. It took several months to complete the formation of the board. Silk was named chairman and Gene Pierce of Spring Ledge Farms vice chairman. The board appointed Trezise to be the foundation's president, and he and Juanita Spence, who was appointed as manager, assumed their duties on November 1, 1985.

Figure 9.1: The staff of the New York Wine and Grape Foundation in 1994 included (*from left to right*) Karyl Hammond, Teresa Knapp, Susan Spence, and James Trezise. Photo by author, 1994.

The legislation passed in 1984 and 1985 was a milestone in the history of grapes and wine in New York State. An omnibus bill was passed in 1993, but the major step in the development of the industry had already been taken. Foundation projects such as the financial support of New York's wine trails helped bring the industry together (see chapter 10). An industry that was already growing grew faster.

The four large wineries that had dominated the Finger Lakes wine scene during the years following Prohibition had been changing ownership. By 1994 all of them had been acquired by the Canandaigua Wine Company of Canandaigua, New York.

The Canandaigua Story

No account of the modern eastern wine industry, let alone New York state, would be complete without mentioning the rise of the Canandaigua Wine Company from the time Marvin Sands bought it as a small bottling plant in 1945 to the time it became the largest winery in the United States sixty years later.[21] The Canandaigua story began with Marvin's father, Mordecai E. "Mack" Sands, who founded his Car-Cal Winery in Greensboro, North Carolina, in 1936, naming the winery after the two states that were his most important sources of fruit. He based his operation on the formula used by Captain Paul Garrett, who before and after Prohibition had made his wine Virginia Dare the bestselling wine in the United States.[22] Garrett had recognized the value and appeal of the Scuppernong flavor and after careful thought had named the wine after the first child born of English parents in America. By 1919 he had seventeen plants in six states with a production capacity of 10 million gallons. Mack Sands created a 20 percent alcohol dessert wine he called Old Maude that was eventually to sell 20 million bottles annually.

Marvin Sands was born in 1924 and served in the U.S. Navy from 1943 to December 1945. Several months before Marvin was released, Mack Sands contacted his mentor, "Little Joe" Applebaum, who had hired him after Prohibition in 1933, to try to find a way to get his son Marvin into the wine business. Little Joe had a bulk wine plant called Canandaigua Industries that he was willing to sell. Marvin bought the plant and 500,000 gallons of wine in exchange for a two-year note for $500,000. No sooner had the deal gone through that Marvin discovered he had problems. The federal authorities were investigating Little Joe and the winery for suspected adulteration of the wines. To make matters worse, there was a precipitous drop in wine prices to as low as twenty-five cents a gallon and there was no way he could pay off the note when due. Marvin knew the importance of keeping his reputation intact and, when Little Joe refused to renegotiate the note, borrowed the money from a Rochester bank. It was a struggle for survival but Marvin was determined to succeed. He was selling bulk wines to other wineries, but he decided he needed to diversify by selling his own wines under his own brand name.

A number of attempts were made to establish a brand, but the breakthrough did not come immediately. In 1948, Mack Sands joined his son at Canandaigua after his Car-Cal Winery closed. Mack was put in charge of southern operations, and in 1951 he established Richard's Wine Cellars in Petersburg, Virginia, naming the winery after Marvin's son, Richard. In 1954, Marvin and his sales manager Robert Meenan came up with the idea of Americanizing the French pronunciation of rosé as a way of appealing to American consumers. Meehan came up with the name of a Broadway show and Richards Wild Irish Rose was born. The wine was a fortified rosé with 20 percent alcohol content and a brilliant red color. With Meenan's advertising experience—he had been aware of Garrett's success with Virginia Dare and Mack's with Old Maude—and the production capability of Richard's, sales of Wild Irish Rose climbed dramatically from $500,000 in 1954 to $2 million in 1955, 3 million by 1957, and $10 million by 1963. Canandaigua now had the money to expand.

Mother Vineyard Wine Company, a muscadine winery in Manteo, North Carolina, was acquired in 1956 and Tenner Brothers Winery in Patrick, South Carolina, in 1965. With Tenner Brothers came the largest Scuppernong Vineyard in the world, more than 300 acres. According to Richard Sands, Canandaigua acquired the rights to the name Virginia Dare on a royalty basis from the Guild Wine Company of Lodi, California, in 1965. Marvin and Mack Sands could not have been

Figure 9.2: When Widmer's Wine Cellars turned 100 in 1988, Canandaigua Wine Company's top executives came to Naples, New York, on April 30 to celebrate the centennial of the winery they had acquired two years earlier. The speaker in this photo is United States Senator Alphonse D'Amato. In back of him are (*from left to right*) Marvin Sands, chief executive of Canandaigua Wine Company; Charles E. Hetterich, Jr., president of Widmer's; Richard Sands, president of Canandaigua; and Robert Sands, Canandaigua's chief counsel. Photo by author.

prouder: "They had both revered Captain Garrett and his innovative spirit, and they had admired how he had turned Virginia Dare into what was, back then, the best-selling wine in America."[23]

Canandaigua made its entry into the premium sparkling wine market in 1969 with the purchase of the Hammondsport Wine Company. A California presence was established in 1974 when Canandaigua bought Bisceglia Brothers Wine Company in Madera. Profits soared again in the mid-1980s when the winery introduced the Sun Country brand of wine coolers. Acquisition of the large Finger Lakes wineries began in 1986 with Widmer's Wine Cellars (with Manischewitz brought over to Widmer's from the just purchased Monarch Wine Company the same year). The wineries and brands previously acquired by Vintners International, Taylor, Great Western, and Gold Seal, became part of Canandaigua in 1994.

A long list of other acquisitions followed, including such well-known wineries as Almadén Vineyards, Inglenook Vineyards, Franciscan Vineyards, Simi Winery, Mount Veeder, Estancia, and Ravenswood. There were also a number of notable acquisitions from abroad including BRL Hardy and Vincor International. With the purchase of Robert Mondavi Corporation in 2004, Canandaigua became the largest winery in the United States.

Canandaigua changed its name to Constellation Brands, Inc., in 2003. Marvin Sands was president of the company until 1986 when Richard Sands became president (and CEO from 1993) and Marvin became chairman. Robert Sands, who was seven years younger than Richard, joined the company in 1986 as chief legal counsel. After Marvin's death in 1999, Richard Sands became chairman. In 2007, Robert assumed the position of president and CEO while Richard remained chairman.

In the mid-1950s, shortly after Richards Wild Irish Rose was introduced, Gallo first released Thunderbird, a 21 percent alcohol wine made with white port and lemon juice.[24] Both wines sold well to winos in the ghettos of big cities. When queried about wine quality in a large winery as opposed to a small winery, Marvin Sands said that the issue was not about large wineries versus small wineries.[25] "The issue is that when we make a wine here, we commit. We buy the necessary equipment, we commit the equipment, and we have the capital resources to do it. If the wines have to be made in small lots under controlled temperatures, we can do that. If continuity of taste is important as in the Rose line, we can do that too. I don't think quality can be attributed on the basis of small or large, but on the basis of commitment." He added: "When you talk about quality, we take a look and try to determine what it is that people want to drink, what the taste is, what the characteristic of the product is, and then we try to meet the demand." At the time he made this statement in 1981, the Rose line accounted for 65 percent of the winery's production of more than 18 million gallons, and Sands knew that he had accomplished it through commitment.

Progress and Turmoil in Ontario

If the 1970s were a decade of transition, the 1980s were a decade during which a stable base was established for the future of the Ontario wine industry. It was not an easy period to live through. On the one hand, progress was made through an increasing commitment to the improvement of wine quality; on the other hand, there was the challenge and turmoil caused by trade agreements between Canada and the United States and Europe that adversely affected the Ontario grape and wine industry. Paradoxically, the trade agreements that ended the preferential treatment of Ontario wines in the marketplace, and which were perceived as threatening the survival of the industry, were in large part responsible for positioning the industry for its success in the 1990s.

The concerns about the quality of Ontario wines and the actions taken to improve them included the Wine Content Act of 1976 that set stricter standards for Ontario wine, the formation of the Ontario Wine Standards Tasting Committee in 1978, and the creation of the Vintners Quality Alliance by the industry that began with informal discussions in 1982 and led to the drafting of "Rules and Regulations" by the end of the decade.

There was also deep concern about the viability of the Ontario wine industry. Sales of Ontario wine had begun to slip after the provincial government gave permission for an increase in imported wines from 30 percent to 70 percent. The Ontario wineries, which had held a 55 percent share of the Liquor Control Board of Ontario (LCBO) sales in 1982, slid to a 39.5 percent share of the market six years later.[26] In the spring of 1984, the Minister of Agriculture and Food Jack Ridell announced the formation of the Ontario Wine and Industry Task Force to analyze problems and examine opportunities for Ontario's wine and grape industries.[27] Jack W. Tanner, professor emeritus of the Department of Agriculture at the University of Guelph, was named chairman of the task force, which became known as the Tanner Task Force. In addition to Tanner, there were seven other members: three growers, three from wineries, and one from the LCBO.

The Tanner Task Force released its report on May 12, 1986, stating:

> So long as foreign governments continue to subsidize their wine and grape industries, some degree of protection, through preferential pricing, will be necessary if our industry is to survive; however, the long term viability of the industry cannot be secured by preferential pricing alone. As customers become more sophisticated, quality will become the most compelling factor. It is urgent that Ontario table wines become recognized by consumers as being equivalent in quality at a lower price or better in quality at the same price. To be recognized as such, this must be so in fact. To that end, it is essential that, for table wines, the use of labrusca grapes and the use of stretch be phased out; major new plantings of hybrid and vinifera grapes occur, with research, education and extension backup; and grapes be purchased on a sugar standard.[28]

There were twenty-nine recommendations in the report covering such subjects as research, vineyard plantings, bulk wines, and standards. The labruscas were the subject of Recommendation 5, which stated "that the industry should begin immediately to phase out the production of labrusca grapes for use in table wines, including light table wines. After December 31, 1995, labrusca grape would no longer be permitted in table wines."[29] Recommendation 6 called for the provincial government and the industry to support the development and expansion of the grape juice industry to fully explore the utilization of labrusca varieties for nonalcoholic products.

It was stated at the start that the report was based on the assumption that unrestricted free trade, the talks of which were already underway, would not transpire. "In the event that it does, it would negate the value of the Report in that, under total free trade, the industry would be placed in dramatic jeopardy."[30] Unfortunately, the assumption was wrong.

Free Trade and GATT Problems in Ontario

Two international trade disputes in the 1980s threw the Ontario grape and wine industry into disarray. The first was the start of talks between Canada and the United States on a free trade agreement that would end the differential treatment of wines entering Ontario from the United States; and, shortly afterward, a challenge from the European Economic Community (EEC) under the General Agreement on Tariffs and Trade (GATT) that would do the same for wines entering Ontario from Europe. Under Ontario law, the LCBO could give preferential listings to wines produced in Ontario. Its mark-up for Ontario wines was 58 percent; for Canadian wines outside Ontario, 105 percent; and the foreign mark-up, 123 percent. The main threat to the Ontario industry was that the competitive pricing advantage they had would come to an end.[31]

In Canada, international trade in wine involved both the federal and provincial governments. The authority to control imports into and exports from the country was vested in the federal government. In the case of wine, the provinces had jurisdiction over the distribution and sale of all wine, including imported wine once it arrived in the province. Free trade agreements between Canada and other nations, therefore, were a matter for the federal government to decide.

In the mid-1980s the trade deficit in the United States was increasing and along with it protectionist sentiment in the U.S. Congress. At this time, import restrictions were on the rise and duties were imposed on softwood from Canada. As a way of protecting its interests and securing its access to markets in the United States, Canada initiated talks on a free trade agreement. President Ronald Reagan and Prime Minister Brian Mulroney met in Québec City in March 1985, and subsequently held a summit meeting in Ottawa in April 1987. One outcome, in addition to the hype that the United States and Canada were about to create the world's largest free-trade zone, was that an agreed-upon deal had to be ready to present to the U.S. Congress by October 3, 1987. Moreover, the final pact signed by the two countries had to be ready for consideration by Congress on January 2, 1988. Final approval would also be required in Canada.

Less than two hours before the deadline on October 3, Canada's trade minister Pat Carney and U.S. secretary of the treasury James Baker reached an agreement. Negotiations had been held behind closed doors, and when the details of the proposed pact became known the next day, the complete elimination of tariffs over a seven-year period brought immediate reactions from the grape and wine industry.

Brian Nash, chairman of the Ontario Grape Growers' Marketing Board charged that the grape growers were sold out and predicted that it would be the end of the road for many of Ontario's grape growers. Jan Westcott, executive director of the Ontario Wine Council, stated that the wineries felt like they had been sacrificed and that the $30 million grape industry would be gone within a year. David Diston, Brights vice president, said that his winery would likely have to become a blender and bottler of wine rather than a wine maker.[32]

Ontario premier David Peterson found himself in a particularly tight spot. He was reminded that during the recent provincial elections he had promised to protect Ontario's grape growers and winemakers and he was urged to refuse to go along with the pact. Business and steelmakers, however, supported the agreement while labor and agriculture were against it. From Ottawa, Prime Minister Mulroney was urging Peterson's support.

Adding to the pressure that October was the issuance of a preliminary ruling by a GATT panel that found that higher price mark-ups on imported wines in provincial liquor stores was an unfair trade practice. Ontario was faced with losing preferential mark-ups not only with the United States but also with the EEC.[33]

It was necessary for Ontario to think seriously about its situation, and there was much to consider in addition to the economic consequences of losing the preferential mark-ups. The Free Trade Agreement would require the United States and Canada to treat each other's products as if they were their own. In addition to the LCBO stores in Ontario, there were about 350 privately owned winery stores, and the United States wanted its wineries to be able to operate its own stores in the province.[34] This was unacceptable, and it was mandated that as of October 4, 1987, any new wineries in the province would be restricted to only one sales outlet, the one it could get on its premises when it opened. The stores that the existing wineries already had were grandfathered in, and this resulted in inequities that led to marketing consequences that were still causing problems in 2010.

With higher prices for Ontario wines now inevitable, the LCBO wanted assurance that Ontario wines would be of sufficient quality so they would be saleable in competition with imported wines. Quality was already a concern in Ontario. The Vintners Quality Alliance was in the final stages of drawing up its rules and regulations and the Tanner Task Force had emphasized the compelling need for quality in Ontario wines. Originally, the Task Force had recommended that labrusca grapes not be permitted in table wines after December 31, 1995. Now, however, the LCBO decided that it would no longer sell wines with labrusca content. As a result, the effective date for banning the use of labrusca grapes was moved up to September 1, 1988. If the labruscas were banned from table wines, the financial consequences for growers would be severe. Mulroney had already taken the position that anyone injured by free trade would be compensated by the government, and Peterson was determined to fight on behalf of the grape and wine industry.

On November 22, 1987, the government of Ontario, the Ontario Grape Growers' Marketing Board, and the Wine Council of Ontario submitted a "Framework for a Response to the GATT Panel Ruling" to the federal government in Ottawa. The "Framework" represented a commitment that all three entities were willing to make as Ontario's response to the GATT panel's ruling and moved far beyond the issues of mark-ups, stores, and LCBO listings over which they would have no control.

During a twelve-year period, Ontario wineries would commit to the purchase of a minimum of 25,000 tons a year of grapes grown in Ontario. Price negotiations between growers and wineries would continue under the auspices of the Farm Products Marketing Board, and a mechanism developed to establish specific support levels by grape variety so that wineries could buy grapes at prices that would be competitive with the price of imported grapes from the United States. A "Grape Industry Adjustment" program was outlined that included the removal of 8,000 acres of vineyard land not suitable for quality grape production. Government financial assistance would be provided for the removal as well as funding other programs to improve grape quality and production.

Looking beyond the borders of Ontario, the "Framework" also called for the federal government to challenge the subsidy practices used by the EEC and eliminate interprovincial trade barriers. Efforts by the industry to export wine to other countries should also be encouraged.

The final resolution of the trade disputes was not easy and took time. The question of whether the federal government had the constitutional power to ensure compliance by the provinces held up the acceptance of both agreements.

An unsuccessful attempt was made by the federal government to negotiate a settlement with the EEC on the issue of wine. The EEC rejected it, and on March 12, 1988, GATT issued its final report, which set a date of December 31 for Canada to state what it was going to do about the price mark-ups imposed by ten of its provincial liquor boards. Failure to comply could mean retaliation by the twelve members of the EEC.

President Reagan sent the Free Trade Agreement to the U.S. Senate for approval on July 25, 1988, where it was ratified in September. Approval was less certain in Canada, however. The Liberal Party, which was the majority party in the Canadian Senate, stated it would not approve the Agreement unless Mulroney called a general election that would likely determine the issue. If the Liberal Party won, Mulroney would be defeated and approval of the agreement would almost certainly fail. A win for Mulroney's Progressive Conservative Party would signify majority support and both the House of Commons and the Senate would no doubt approve.

National elections were held on November 21, 1988, and Mulroney's party prevailed. On December 17, 1988, the GATT agreement between Canada and the EEC was signed in Brussels, Belgium. The House of Commons approved the Free Trade Agreement on December 24, the Senate voted favorably on December 27, and in a formal ceremony on December 30, royal assent was given by Canadian governor-general Jeanne Sauvé to clear the way for the Free Trade Agreement to become effective at midnight on Saturday, December 31, 1988.

Vintners Quality Alliance

Canada began to develop its Vintners Quality Alliance (VQA) system in Ontario in the 1980s. It had its start as a voluntary appellation of origin system along the lines of the French AOC (appellation d'origine contrôlée) system and was intended to set standards for Ontario's finest wines.

Wine quality standards in Ontario originated shortly after the end of Canadian Prohibition in 1927. Only beer and liquor had been banned in the province and large quantities of wine were made for local consumption or export to the United States with little or no concern for quality.[35] So much bad wine was made during this period that quality standards were imposed by the passage of the 1927 Ontario Liquor Control Act. More than half of Ontario's wineries were put out of business because they could not meet the standards.

Quality standards for wine have been part of the Ontario wine scene ever since. In 1934, the Ontario Wine Standards Committee was created by the Ministry of Agriculture, and this led to the establishment of research facilities and a small winery at the Horticultural Research Institute of Ontario at Vineland. In the early 1950s, the Canadian Wine Institute established a quality standards committee that conducted formal tastings of the wines of member wineries, and the LCBO set up its own laboratory to analyze wines and hold its own tasting sessions.

The passage of the Wine Content Act of 1976 on December 16 by the Ontario legislature resulted in stricter standards such as limits on the use of chemicals and preservatives, volatile acidity, and the acceptable time between harvest and delivery of the grapes. In 1978, to carry out the intent of the Wine Content Act, the Ontario Wine Standards Tasting Committee was formed, which established a tasting panel with members from industry and government who were tested and qualified for their ability to taste wine.[36] Under this program, all Ontario wines had to be approved by the panel before being listed by the LCBO. Standards were also set for various types of wines including a new "Ontario Superior" designation.[37] On June 30, 1981, the first tasting was held to evaluate wines for the Ontario Superior designation. One of the criteria for this highest designation was that the wine had to be made from French hybrid or vinifera grapes.

The work of the tasting panel established by the Ontario Wine Standards Tasting Committee continued until the end of 1986. At that time the industry-created VQA tasting panel took over.

During the harvest of 1980, under the supervision of the Ontario Department of Agriculture, grapes were tested at every winery for sugar levels, pH, and total acidity by taking a sample from every four tons brought into the winery.[38] One result of this testing program was to establish a system of bonuses and penalties for a number of grape varieties according to their sugar levels at harvest.[39]

The concerns about wine quality led to considerable discussion in the industry as to what was needed, a consortium or a set of rules and regulations, and whether it should apply to wines or wineries. Donald Ziraldo, then president of Inniskillin Wines, is generally credited with providing the leadership to create an alliance of wine producers that would be committed to quality wine production.

In 1982, Ziraldo had received a 200-case order from a Burgundy shipper for Inniskillin's 1980 Maréchal Foch. Before the wine could be delivered, the French government notified him that shipments had to conform to the EEC's appellation of origin regulations. This meant that the Niagara Peninsula would have to be approved as a recognized viticultural area.[40]

Given this incentive, Ziraldo organized meetings in the Ontario wine industry to discuss a voluntary independent alliance. The focus on developing ways to meet standards for international trade led to an industry decision that individual wines rather than wineries would be the focal point. It was decided to explore the possibility of setting up an appellation of origin system by which consumers could identify the wines of Ontario based on the origin of the grapes from which they were produced.

A long series of arduous meetings on what was to become the Vintners Quality Alliance took place until the end of 1986. Agreement on standards became very difficult because at any given meeting the winemakers might have come from Germany, France, or Fresno, each with strong and often conflicting opinions of what constituted highest quality. Arguments were frequently resolved by looking at the appellation systems in Italy, France, or Germany.

When it came to the organization of tasting panels, it was generally recognized that an independent outside group was needed to assure the integrity of the tasting results. It was also necessary to get the influential critics in downtown Toronto to accept the concept if the VQA system was to have any chance of success. With some reservations it was decided to recruit the assistance of the LCBO and ask it to provide the tasting panel. It was agreed that the LCBO senior tasting panel would be the group to determine whether wines were of VQA quality or not. The competency and professionalism of the panel turned out to be one of the keys to the success of the VQA system. The process of drawing up the VQA rules and regulations began in January 1987. Leonard Pennachetti of Cave Spring Cellars and Leonard Franssen of the LCBO wrote the initial draft, which was then circulated among the wineries for revision.

The VQA was set up as a corporation with an eight-person board of directors that consisted of four winery representatives and four outside members, including one from the LCBO, a grape grower, a third from research, and a fourth either from the academic world or the hospitality business. The number of winery representatives was later raised to six and then to eight as the number of wineries increased. Funding was limited to an assessment of five cents a bottle on every bottle of VQA wine produced, regardless of the size of the bottle.

The VQA Board of Directors met formally for the first time on December 19, 1988, and Ziraldo was named chairman of the alliance. The initial draft of the "Rules and Regulations" was approved by the board on September 15, 1989, and the final draft on June 27, 1990. On March 18, 1991, the Board announced that Peter Gamble had been appointed to the position of VQA's first executive director.

Chapter Ten

❧

Winery Promotion in the 1980s

Cooperative marketing by wineries was on the increase in the 1980s. Among the important efforts was the establishment of wine trails where tourists were given instructions or other incentives to encourage them to visit more than one winery on a trip.

One of the earliest appearances of wine trails in the East came about when the *Pennsylvania Grape Letter and Wine News* published a four-page insert called "Wine Trails of Pennsylvania" in its April 1979 issue.[1] There were twenty wineries and five extensions of premises in the state at the time, and the wineries submitted information including directions, addresses, and hours for the directory insert. The wineries were grouped into five arbitrarily chosen geographic areas for the convenience of anyone wanting to visit several wineries in one day.

New York led the way in the formal establishment of wine trails, and the first was the Cayuga Wine Trail in the Finger Lakes in 1983.[2] This idea has been credited to Mary Plane, who with her husband Robert founded Plane's Cayuga Vineyard in Ovid. Six wineries on the west side of Cayuga Lake from Seneca Falls to Ithaca agreed to cooperate in marketing, and five of them founded the Cayuga Wine Trail. Their first project, as was true of virtually all wine trails, was to create a brochure. In 1984 they prepared a press release to publicize the awards won by their member wineries at the 1984 International Eastern Wine Competition sponsored by Wineries Unlimited. Their first cooperative events, a barrel tasting and a "Summer Wine and Food Fest" were held a year later.

With funding assistance from the New York Wine and Grape Foundation, eight wineries inaugurated the Keuka Lake Wine Route on June 18, 1986, and later that year eleven wineries formed the Seneca Lake Wine Trail. Other wine trails followed, and a decade later there were six trails in New York state.

One of the earliest and most important impacts of the wine trails was to extend the tourist season by two to three months. In the Finger Lakes this meant that instead of ending on Columbus Day, it continued through the end of the year. The influx of visitors was accompanied by the opening of bed and breakfasts and other tourist services and this, in turn, led to the expansion of the tourist industry in the Finger Lakes.

A typical wine trail event would feature a themed wine and food pairing with a different food and wine being served at each winery on the trail on the same day. A particularly successful event begun in November 1992 was the Seneca Wine Trail's "Deck the Halls," where visitors were given a grapevine wreath, a ribbon, and a recipe book at the first winery they visited. There, and at each of the other wineries on the trail, they could receive a unique ornament for the wreath and taste a wine and food pairing from the recipe book. The first year 300 people were expected, but 700 showed up. It became necessary to limit the number of tickets sold, and in 1993 the event was expanded to two weekends in November with 900 tickets being made available for each weekend. By 1997, tickets were sold out six months in advance after being placed on sale in mid-January at $30.00 for an individual and $45.00 for a couple.

The New York Wine and Grape Foundation, established in May 1985 by the state legislature, had an initial budget of $2 million. On February 25, 1986, the foundation's board appropriated $657,860 for nineteen research projects, $150,000 for table grape promotion, and $100,000 for "wine country" tourism. The promotion funds given to wineries were on a matching basis, and one of the first disbursements was to assist in the founding of the Keuka Lake Wine Route. Also developed from the initial funding was the "Uncork New York" slogan and logo.

About one-third of the foundation's budget went for research, primarily at Cornell. However, in recognition of the importance to the industry of linking wine and health, it has contributed in a number of areas including support of research being done by Curtis Ellison and his colleagues at the Boston University School of Medicine in Boston and the development of the Mediterranean Diet Pyramid by the Oldways Preservation and Exchange Trust. In addition, the foundation was responsible for the development of the highway signage program in New York and also provided assistance to other states in getting similar programs started. The foundation was not permitted by law to lobby, but it provided facts and information for the legislature and industry. Eight years after the foundation was established, the legislature had reached the point where it passed a law requiring state agencies to find ways making it easier for the wine industry to prosper.

Forging partnerships and bonds on many different levels has been important for the foundation's success, and the leadership provided by James Trezise has been important not only for the New York industry but nationally as well. In the mid-2000s his initiatives in promoting economic impact studies of the grape and wine industry in New York and elsewhere proved to be important tools in working with government bodies at all levels.

Figure 10.1: The Ohio Wine Producers Association published this brochure in the mid-1980s to promote the Ohio wine industry. Included in the brochure were maps and winery information. Author's collection.

Another statewide organization that has had an importance far beyond its own borders was the Ohio Wine Producers Association, founded in 1975 by a small group of winery representatives in a meeting with Garth Cahoon of the Ohio Agricultural Research and Development Center in Wooster, Ohio.[3] One of its first projects was to produce a brochure.

In 1978 the association hired Donniella Winchell as a part-time executive secretary and charged her with the job of revising the brochure, beginning some communications work, and lining up publicity contacts. Her first office was her dining room table. The annual budget was $700 a month out of which they bought her a used copy machine for $50 and paid her $3.00 an hour for working a few hours three days a month. At that time it was necessary to find out who the grape growers were or who was interested in opening a winery so that everyone could share ideas and become involved in an organization.

The funding needed to make the Ohio Wine Producers Association a significant force came from the Ohio Grape Industries Program, which was created by the Ohio legislature on December 29, 1980. This program was the idea of Robert Gottesman, president of Paramount Distillers in Cleveland and Meier's Wine Cellars in Silverton, and was created with the express intent of generating funds for basic research and developing a marketing approach that would sell Ohio wines in the state's major markets. Gottesman sold the idea to a former director of the Ohio Department of

Figure 10.2: Robert Gottesman was president of Paramount Distillers in Cleveland, Ohio, when it entered the wine business in 1976 with the purchase of Meier's Wine Cellars in Cincinnati and the subsequent acquisition by Meier's of three additional wineries in the Sandusky area. Because of his vision and political connections, he took a leadership role in revitalizing the Ohio wine industry. Photo by author, 1988.

Agriculture, enlisted a lobbyist, and with them decided on how to get the necessary legislation passed. This was not an easy task as it called for a tax on all wines sold in Ohio. The bill had to be introduced twice before it was passed. Initially, 70 percent of the funds raised went for basic research and 30 percent for product and marketing development, promotion, or education.

The first grant to the Ohio Wine Producers Association was $15,000, but it was eventually increased to between $35,000 and $50,000 a year. Winchell became the executive director and began channeling the money in a grassroots direction, starting by training winemakers on how to hold wine and cheese tastings. By 1984, tastings directly sponsored by the Ohio Wine Producers Association reached 30,000 to 40,000 people and had generated momentum that led to hundreds of other tastings throughout the state.

The Wine Council of Ontario had its origin in 1940 as an association of Ontario wineries formed under the name of the Canadian Wine Institute. In 1965, British Columbia wineries were invited to join. The organization soon proved to be too cumbersome to deal with provincial problems in Ontario, and the wineries in Ontario withdrew and became the Wine Producers Association. When the association was incorporated in 1974, the name was changed to the Wine Council of Ontario.

As a trade association, the council has played an important role in setting policies and directions for the Ontario wine industry and acting as a liaison and coordinating body between Ontario wineries, grape growers, and government bodies.[4] In addition to its political involvement, the council has been active in the export of Ontario wine including setting up trade booths and coordinating tastings worldwide. Some domestic projects were a "wine and dine" program to showcase Ontario wines in restaurants, industry promotions at the Liquor Control Board of Ontario, generic marketing programs, and the preparation of wine route maps, brochures and a *Wine Trails* newsletter.

The council has also had a role in the establishment each year of the minimum prices to be paid for Ontario-grown grapes through negotiations with the Ontario Grape Growers' Marketing Board. Under the auspices of the Farm Products Board, negotiations are carried out by a six-person committee, three of whom are appointed by the council and three by the board.[5] If negotiations are not completed by August 20, each side presents its final best offer and a Board of Arbitration accepts one or the other.

The Ontario Grape Growers' Marketing Board was established in 1947 with a primary goal being to negotiate grape prices rather than establish them. Over the years it took on the role of an association representing the grape industry. It worked with the Horticultural Research Institute of Ontario in their grape variety improvement program and with Agriculture Canada on phytosanitary requirements that led to a provincial virus-free grapevine program known as the Cooperative Project with Industry (COPI) program. Working with several groups, the board established the system of sugar bonuses and penalties that are negotiated each year as part of the terms and conditions of the sale of grapes. On January 4, 2003, there was a name change, and the Marketing Board became the Grape Growers of Ontario.

Marketing Comes of Age

In the 1980s, more attention was paid to marketing wine as people began to realize its importance. Looking back at that period in a 1994 interview, Winchell said that was the time when the transition from a farmer's to a businessman's mentality began to achieve success. By the early 1990s people had learned not only how to sell wine but to become marketers.[6]

By the mid-1980s, state organizations started to obtain the funding needed to attract competent marketing people to create programs that would benefit the industry. Television and radio, for example, were known to be an effective way to promote wine, but their use was limited because of the expense involved. In 1986, the Ohio Grape Industries Program, which had been formed a few years earlier, had a promotion budget of $325,000. It was decided that the first statewide television campaign would take place during Ohio Wine Month in June. An advertising agency was retained to develop both print advertising and commercials for radio and television. Two thirty-second commercials were prepared for Ohio Wine Month, one of which had a ten-second segment that individual wineries could use. More than 250 commercials were aired during a three-week period, and they were backed up by full-page four-color ads in major magazines. Radio commercials were prepared for use during the harvest season, also with tags for individual wineries, and two more television commercials were produced for the holiday season in November and December.[7]

Among the marketing tools used in the early 1980s were winery club memberships that increased wine sales and built a customer following. Private and custom labels also proved to be profitable. Sakonnet Vineyards in Rhode Island created custom labels for restaurants. Nonprofit organizations found that private labels could be used successfully during fund-raising campaigns. In 1987, in Michigan, nearly one-third of the total sales at Fenn Valley Vineyards came from privately labeled wine sold in stores. Some wineries developed specific custom label programs for use with real estate brokers or automobile distributorships who wanted to thank customers for attending an open house or taking a test drive.[8]

In 1986 the Washington Redskins celebrated their fiftieth anniversary. Two wineries marked the occasion. The team had its training camp at Dickinson College in Carlisle, Pennsylvania. The college ordered eighteen cases of wine with a special gold label from Blue Ridge Winery in Carlisle to give to the staff and players as a memento. At the start of the season, Meredyth Vineyards in nearby Middleburg, Virginia, released a Meredyth Burgundy and Meredyth Gold, naming the wines after the official colors of the Redskins. The wines were made available first to season ticket holders and then to the general public where the demand was high for the commemorative wines. Just as the winery was hard pressed to meet the demand, the existence of the wines was announced on the stadium scoreboard. By the time the Redskins played in the conference championship game, winemaking operations were stretched to the absolute limit. Meredyth, however, had its biggest single promotional event ever.[9]

Wine glasses inscribed with the name of a winery became more common as it was realized they were a method of advertising. That they could also make money was shown in 1987 when the New York Wine and Grape Foundation ordered eleven-ounce glasses from Libby Glass with the name of the winery on one side and the Foundation's logo on the other. More than 200,000 glasses were sold or distributed by forty-three wineries and by restaurants and other organizations.[10]

Meredyth Vineyards in Middleburg, Virginia, became one of the first wineries in the United States to hold a murder mystery dinner on two nights, June 21 and 22, 1985. The concept of inviting guests to play detective had originated about seven years earlier and had been held as weekend events at resort hotels. A capacity crowd of 100 each night paid $55 to attend.[11]

A close relative of Benmarl's Société, was an "Adopt a Barrel" plan at Woodbury Vineyards in Dunkirk, New York, that helped build an oak aging cellar. For $350, a customer could adopt a French oak barrel, be given adoption papers, and have his or her name embossed on the barrel. In addition to full visitation and sampling rights, the customer would receive each year for four years two cases of Chardonnay aged in his or her barrel.[12]

Winchell has been firm in her conviction that there are few really new ideas in marketing wines, just ones that are stolen and adapted. To her, good ideas are worth sharing, and in November 2004 she organized the first "License to Steal" National Wine Marketing Conference held in Geneva-on-the-Lake, Ohio, where people could get together to explore and share their best ideas on how to market wines. A steering committee from seven states arranged a program that included both expert speakers and breakout sessions for the exchange of ideas. Approximately 100 people came to the initial conference. One of the speakers was the owner of a computer company, and his appearance on the program underscored the importance of computers as an important tool for marketing in the new computer age.[13]

Tastings

As the industry grew, wine tastings in the East were held more frequently to promote eastern wines. One early tasting took place on April 14, 1981, at Windows on the World in New York City when the Association of American Vintners held a tasting of forty-three wines made by sixteen of their member wineries from ten states. This was the first time that eastern wineries had come to New York as a group for a media day. The wines were selected by two local wine media organizations, the Wine Writer's Circle and the Wine Media Guild. There were two tastings, the first at 1:30 p.m. for the media and a second at 3:00 p.m. for wholesalers, distributors, restaurateurs, and retailers. Nearly everyone attending was being exposed to a large number of eastern wines at one event for the first time, and the fact that they were favorably impressed with the quality of the wines made the media day a success.[14]

One of the landmark tastings of the second half of the twentieth century was a comparative tasting of wines from California and France that took place in Paris in May 1976, during which the California wines outscored the French. The result was a giant publicity coup for the California industry and permanently changed the quality perception of California wines. From time to time in the East there have been preference tastings of eastern and French wines. None has had the same impact on the wine world as the Paris tasting, but when eastern wines show well, it improves their image.

The Chaddsford Winery of Chadds Ford, Pennsylvania, held such a tasting at a black tie event on April 26, 1986, at the Downtown Club in Philadelphia that included six Chardonnays from the East and five outstanding Chardonnays from France. More than ninety invited people took part in the tasting conducted by Robert Perna, director of L'Ecole de Vin in Philadelphia. First place went to a 1983 Catoctin Vineyards Chardonnay from Brookeville, Maryland, that outscored such wines as a 1983 Pouilly-Fuisse, a 1983 Puligny Montrachet, and a 1981 Corton-Charlemagne. The publicity in the aftermath of the tasting was favorable not only for the wineries but for the eastern industry in general.[15]

Another tasting that attracted attention was the first New York Barrel Tasting held at Pierce's 1894 Restaurant in Elmira, New York, on March 28, 1980, which was attended by 200 people. Modeled after the annual California barrel tasting held in New York each spring, twenty-seven table wines were served along with a seven-course dinner.[16] What distinguishes a barrel tasting dinner from other wine dinners is that the wines served are not yet released to the public, and often are taken out of the barrel or tank just for the dinner. Wine dinners held by restaurants, often called winemakers' dinners when the wines served are from one winery with the winemaker in attendance to present the wines, are common promotional events with the food showcasing the restaurant and the wines advertising the winery.

From the time wineries first opened their doors in the East, visitors were welcomed into their tasting rooms to sample their wines in hopes that they would purchase some to take home. There were exceptions, however. In earlier days, dating back to the end of Prohibition, archaic laws restricted access to wine. When Melvin S. Gordon opened his Conestoga Vineyards in the monopoly state of Pennsylvania in 1963, he could not sell his wine at the winery and legally he could only drink or serve the wine he made by purchasing it at the state store. In the Finger Lakes in the 1960s most wineries offered tastings and tours but did not sell wine in their tasting rooms to avoid offending local retailers.[17] Even at the end of the twentieth century some wineries located in dry areas were unable to have tasting rooms.

Today it is rare to find a winery where one cannot sample wines, although by the mid-1990s it was becoming increasingly common for a winery to charge for a tasting. Visitors might be required to buy a souvenir wine glass, the cost of which was sometimes applied to a purchase of wine, or asked to pay extra to taste the winery's most expensive wines.

Figure 10.3: In October 1989, a "between seasons" Apple Wine Weekend at the Chaddsford Winery in Chadds Ford, Pennsylvania, allowed visitors to enjoy chilled apple wine outdoors and hot mulled apple wine inside the winery. Photo by author.

Competitions

By the mid-1980s, competitions that would become well known in later years allowed eastern wineries to enter their wines. The first annual San Diego Wine Competition was held on June 3, 1980, and the Dallas Morning News Competition held its inaugural competition in 1985.

In September 1983 the Beverage Tasting Institute of Ithaca, New York, held its first American Wine Competition at the Culinary Institute of America in Hyde

Park, in what competition director Craig Goldwyn termed "the Superbowl of wine competitions in America." The competition was limited to four varietals, and entries from California dominated the awards list in Chardonnay and Cabernet Sauvignon, Oregon took half of the awards in Pinot Noir, and New York showed best in the Rieslings. Four platinum medals were awarded to "quintessential, extraordinary wines." Three of them were from California. The fourth, and the highest scoring wine in the competition, was a 1982 Select Late Harvest Johannisberg Riesling from Glenora Wine Cellars in Dundee, New York, but this wine was disqualified after the competition when it was discovered that the winery did not meet the minimum production requirement of 300 cases. After the competition, Goldwyn noted that the results were a surprise to many people. "They prove that all of the wine made in America does not come from California; and it proves what those of us watching the East have known for a long time, that there are many fine wines being made in the East."[18]

What came to be the first appellation judging in the United States was the Finger Lakes Appellation Wine Competition held on July 27–28, 1983, in Ithaca. A total of ninety-three Finger Lakes appellation wines were entered by twenty-one wineries. An unconventional hedonic judging system sparked a lot of discussion about the results. Instead of a conventional score sheet, judges were asked to mark their response to seven judging criteria by using a sheet with seven horizontal lines without gradations. The ends of the horizontal lines represented a range from unappealing to appealing, and the judges were asked to put a slash mark on the line whenever their response "felt good." One group of scores stood out from the others, and these wines were awarded gold medals; the second group that stood out received silver medals. The judging was administered by Tom Cottrell, then extension enologist for New York, who at the end of the competition stated that the judges had done a good job of recording their impressions of the wines entered.[19]

Competitions are always fertile ground for controversy: judging systems, scoring methods, criteria for awarding medals, the percentage of medals to be awarded in relation to the number of entries; all of these are matters of opinion on which feelings can run high. Early competitions in the East not only had the usual organizational problems encountered by people new to the task of running competitions, but they also had to contend with the wide variety of wines made in the East.

The first Eastern Wine Competitions held at Wineries Unlimited illustrated the kinds of problems that early competitions in the East could face. The 1978 competition was strongly criticized when it was announced that out of thirty gold medals awarded, twenty-two went to wines made from native American grapes, six to wines made from the hybrids, and two to vinifera wines. The criticism raised, of course, was directed at the heavy preponderance of gold medals being given to the native American variety wines.

Best of category awards were made that year but, for the purpose of awarding medals, the top scoring 8 percent of the wines received gold medals, the next 8 percent were awarded silver medals, and the third 8 percent bronze medals. It turned out that there was a simple explanation for what had happened. One of the key elements in judging wine is to compare a given wine to others of its type. The labrusca wines were judged against other labrusca wines, and the scores they received reflected what in the judges' opinion the standard for labrusca wines was. Many of the judges who were not from the East had a preconceived opinion of the labruscas as being rankly foxy. They were surprised at the lack of what they considered foxiness in the wines they were judging and accordingly gave them top scores for their perceived high quality. When it came to the vinifera wines, the reference standard for these same judges was the California wines they were familiar with, and their scores for eastern vinifera wines tended to be lower.[20]

The chief judge in the 1978 and 1979 competitions at Wineries Unlimited was Philip Jackisch, a widely known authority on the analysis of judges and judgings. Adjustments were made in the scoring system the following year, and in an interview after the 1979 competition he talked about benchmarks:

> The basic philosophy I've operated under is that, first of all, we're establishing some benchmarks—we don't yet really have them; we don't really know what the best possible wine is that we can make in any given category. It's especially important to remember this in the East where we make more different wines than any comparably sized area on earth— many more. . . . But yet we don't have benchmarks for a lot of the varieties because we're the only ones making them. Nobody knows what the ultimate Vidal Blanc is going to taste like, whether or not we've really made the best that can be made; we're sort of feeling our way on this.
>
> Getting back to the Wineries Unlimited judging, for people to say after just two years that it isn't being done to perfection is unrealistic. The California judgings and the judgings in other parts of the world never grew this fast. We're the second largest competition in the country now [630 entries, a 70% increase over the previous year] and we can't—with the budget and with the sudden growth of the thing—do everything to perfection all at once. It takes time. It's tough to get judges, for example, that are familiar with all the wine types. For instance, we had 14 Muscadines, and how many people do we have that are really familiar with those? Some of the people that were familiar were invited to become judges but couldn't make it—so we did the best we could.[21]

Later in the century, when major California competitions solicited entries from the East, the problem of familiarity of wines from the East also arose. Increasingly, these competitions asked judges from the East to become part of their judging panels. These judges helped other judges to become more familiar with eastern wines, and it was not long before eastern wines were winning top awards.

Figure 10.4: When California wine competitions began to allow entries from the East, *Wine East* editor Linda Jones McKee was often sought after as a judge because of her knowledge of eastern wines and her ability to teach others to understand them. Photo by author, 1991.

The number of competitions open to eastern wines increased with time. In 1991 there were twenty-nine state, national, or international commercial competitions that were willing to accept entries east of the Rockies in North America. That number increased to forty-six in 2008.[22]

Canadian wineries have won top awards in European competitions. In 1977, Brights won two gold medals at Le Monde Selection in Brussels, Belgium. Photos of the winning wines, a 1975 Baco Noir and a 1976 Villard Noir were published on the cover of the winery's 1978 annual report. A major triumph came in June 1991, when Inniskillin's 1989 Vidal Icewine won Le Grand Prix d'Honneur at VINEXPO in Bordeaux. The award was important in accelerating the development of Ontario's icewine industry.

Vinifera grape varieties have always held a favored position in the grape and wine industry in the East. Two examples already mentioned in chapters 3 and 9 were Dr. Frank's pro-vinifera crusade and the resulting vinifera-hybrid controversy, and the decision in Ontario to reclassify labrusca varieties as juice grapes rather than wine grapes as a way of promoting their vinifera wines.

A strong prejudice against nonvinifera wines, especially wines made from native American varieties, also exists in the East. This prejudice, sometimes called "grape racism," is found in its most virulent form among wine snobs and others who do not want to be associated with any wines other than vinifera.[23] Wine competitions have been affected by this prejudice.

For many years, Willard Robinson ran the annual wine competition at the New York State Fair. In an article for *Wine East,* published in 1982, he wrote: "Prejudices among judges are rampant. When I announce to a team that the next class to be judged will be the sweet Concords, there will invariably be a chorus of groans. Lecturing the team on judging a wine for what it is supposed to represent helps very little. So you'll find that most of the medals are given to the dry, white prestige wines."[24]

Robinson found that the judges not only balked at being asked to serve on panels judging wines made from native American grapes, but began accusing him of discriminating against them. Traditionally, three best of show awards were given at the New York State Fair, one each for the vinifera, hybrids, and native American wines. The situation got so bad that the award for wines made from native American grapes was discontinued in 1984.

The Eastern Wine Auction

One promising promotion that got its start in the 1980s was the "Celebrity Wine Auction and Exposition of Eastern Wines." Early on in the decade, Robert F. Pliska, president of the Robert F. Pliska Winery and executive director of the Homes for the Mentally Handicapped, in Purgitsville, West Virginia, was looking for a way to raise funds to benefit his charitable enterprise, better known as the Vineyard. He discussed his idea of holding a wine auction with Hudson Cattell, who suggested that it would be nice to hold the auction exclusively for eastern wines. This, Cattell said, could become a venture that could one day prove to be a headline-getting attraction for the eastern wine industry as well as a financial success for a deserving charity.[25]

In the fall of 1983 Pliska decided that he was ready to begin. He enlisted the help of Chris Smith, the wine buyer for Morris Miller Wine & Liquors in Washington, DC, who had held an Eastern Wine Day at the store for several years. The event, held on May 3, 1984, at the Marriott in Gaithersburg, Maryland, began with a tasting hosted by the wineries who had contributed wines to the auction. Approximately 250 people turned out to bid on the ninety lots up for sale. Actor Tony Randall had agreed to be honorary sponsor of the auction, and several bottles of Bully Hill wine autographed by him brought up to $30.00 each. The high bid was $150.00 for a magnum of Brights President champagne with a unique artist's label. A Chardonnay in the Hargrave Vineyard Collector's Series signed by the artist Willem de Kooning brought $25.00. Most wines with the exception of special bottlings brought close to their retail price. Wines from as far away as Massachusetts, Michigan, and Texas were offered for sale. The ninety lots sold for a total of $2,945.00 and raised just under $1,000 for the Vineyard.

The second auction was held at the same location on May 5, 1985, and the sixty-three lots sold for $5,700. A Tucquan Vineyards Chancellor opened at $50 and was knocked down at $90. A twenty-liter bottle of Polish Polka Party Chancellor from Pliska's winery brought $300. A Mount Hope decanter honoring Korean War pilots sold for $80. Some of the lots were accompanied by autographs of famous people. A lot of four Massachusetts wines with Senator Edward Kennedy's autograph brought $105. Although celebrity autographs generally did not raise prices significantly, they were of great help to auctioneer John Connery in keeping bidders interested. Wines from eleven states were auctioned, and the high bid of $1,600 was for a donation of sixty-five bottles from the Sonoma County Wine Growers' Association.

Auction number three moved to the Commissioned Officers' Club at the U.S. Naval Hospital in Bethesda on May 4, 1986, and raised more than $7,500. The fourth auction, unfortunately, was postponed for a year due to illness in the Pliska family and when it was held on May 1, 1988, at Georgetown University, the number of participating wineries declined slightly as did the realized prices. A highlight of the fifth auction on May 7, 1989, at the Capitol Hilton in Washington, DC, was a case of wine tracing Bob Lyon's career as a Maryland winemaker at Byrd Vineyard in the late 1970s and Catoctin Vineyards in the 1980s that sold for $250. On this occasion additional monies were raised through a raffle and the sale of crafts and wine-related items. The sixth and final auction was held on May 6, 1990, at the Capitol Hilton. Approximately ninety lots of wine from more than sixty eastern wineries were sold at the auction. The preauction tasting attracted 383 people and gross receipts exceeded $15,000. For the second year in a row, a large number of volunteers were in evidence who helped keep the tasting and auction running smoothly. Sadly, the Eastern Wine Auction became too much for Pliska to handle himself, and an event that might have become a showcase for the entire eastern wine industry came to an end.

CHAPTER ELEVEN

⟡

TEMPERANCE, NEO-PROHIBITION, AND THE FRENCH PARADOX

The eastern wine industry has had to live with the aftermath of Prohibition ever since Repeal in 1933. Although its impact has lessened, even decades later, there are still dry counties in the East and a plethora of restrictive laws on all levels governing the distribution, sale, and consumption of wine and other alcoholic beverages. Anti-alcohol sentiment remains strong in many areas, and those who wish to oppose drinking find many reasons to do so ranging from morality and religious beliefs to putting an end to drunken driving.

The term Neo-Prohibitionist is applied to those in or out of government who seek to reduce alcohol consumption, although not necessarily by reinstating Prohibition. They believe that the problems associated with alcohol are best solved by limiting the availability of alcohol, and that the most effective means of doing that is through legislation by government. All forms of alcohol abuse from crime to drunken driving are pointed to as reasons to reduce consumption, and for them there is little difference between social drinking and binge drinking. To achieve their ends, increases in excise taxes, the imposition of exorbitant fees or unduly restrictive label requirements are among the weapons that have been used.

In the early 1960s a consumer health movement started in the United States with such publications as *Silent Spring* by Rachel Carson, which pointed out the danger of insecticides, and the Surgeon General's report on smoking. Concerns about nuclear power plants and a growing awareness of other environmental issues followed. David F. Musto, professor of the history of medicine at Yale University's School of Medicine, has called what has happened in the United States since the late 1960s and early 1970s a temperance movement.[1] Each of the two previous ones, one that peaked in the 1850s and the other in the 1920s, started as a strong health movement and created the perception that alcohol causes all kinds of social and health problems. By the 1980s, anti-alcohol campaigns had begun in earnest.

Drinking during pregnancy became a health issue in the 1970s, and in 1977 Commissioner Donald Kennedy of the Federal Drug Administration requested that the Bureau of Alcohol, Tobacco and Firearms (BATF) require the use of warning labels on alcoholic beverage containers to warn against fetal alcohol syndrome. In 1979, BATF decided it would prefer a public awareness campaign to the imposition of a warning label.[2] All of the known cases of the classic syndrome were caused by heavy drinking, and a study commissioned by the National Institute on Alcohol Abuse and Alcoholism showed that there was no evidence of damage to the fetus when a woman drank less than one ounce of absolute alcohol a day. Yet a fear campaign with misleading information grew steadily.

Mothers against Drunk Driving (MADD) was started by Candice Lightner after her thirteen-year-old daughter was killed in 1980 by a drunken hit-and-run driver. In the early 1980s the lobbying group she founded claimed to have a membership of almost 300,000 and attracted the attention of Congress, especially Senator Frank R. Lautenberg of New Jersey. This helped the passage by Congress of the National Minimum Drinking Age Act on June 28, 1984.

The advertising of alcohol was another area under attack by anti-alcohol groups. By 1985, "Project SMART" (Stop Marketing Alcohol on Radio and Television) had collected more than 500,000 signatures on a petition to either ban all alcohol-related ads or impose an equal time requirement devoted to health measures on the dangers of alcohol. In June 1977, members of California's Wine Institute had created a "Code of Advertising Standards," a series of voluntary guidelines for the responsible advertising of wine. It was a voluntary code for antitrust purposes, and was submitted in September of that year to the Federal Trade Commission for review. While confining itself to antitrust aspects, the commission commented, "Wine Institute's objective of encouraging the promotion of wine in a socially responsible way may well be laudable." When a Senate committee began hearings on alcohol advertising in February 1985, the Code became a major point that ended SMART's request for legislation.[3]

What Musto called a new temperance movement was termed the "New Puritanism" by Keith I. Marton, chairman of the Department of Medicine at Pacific Presbyterian Medical Center in San Francisco, who pointed to the negative attitude on the part of the public toward seatbelts in cars as well as pesticides and smoking. Columnist Ellen Goodman called it "The New Morality," and she wrote that in crusades, dedication turns to intolerance, and that drinking in moderation becomes no more acceptable than smoking in moderation or having an occasional abortion.

One would think that various segments of the alcoholic beverage industry would unite to confront the attacks against alcohol. However, this did not happen this time, leading to negative long-term consequences that further encouraged the Neo-Prohibitionists.

Seagram's Alcohol Equivalency Campaign

In early 1985, Joseph E. Seagram and Sons launched an alcohol equivalency campaign with a blitz of full-page newspaper ads that divided the industry. "It's Time America Knew the Facts about Drinking," the headline read in heavy, black, ninety-six-point type. Underneath the head was a mug of beer, a glass of wine, and a glass of spirits each separated by an = sign. A caption below stated "12 oz. of beer, 5 oz. of wine and 1¼ oz. of liquor all have the same alcohol content." Subsequent ads were changed to "A Drink Is a Drink Is a Drink" with the message: "It's Not What You Drink but How Many Drinks You Have."

A press release from the House of Seagram on August 13 quoted its president, Edgar Bronfman, Jr.: "Equivalence is not only a Seagram message, it is a message used by those who sincerely care about responsibility in the use of beverage alcohol. Equivalence is not only valid, it is a vital piece of information for drivers, pregnant women, people with the disease of alcoholism, and any other adult. We will continue to use every possible form of communication to get this message to the public."[4]

Why was Seagram willing to spend so much money on this campaign? One speculation in the press was that sales in the spirits industry were slumping and Seagram was hoping to lure customers back to spirits. Another reason was more likely. In a press release dated March 1985, *Wines and Vines* noted that "the distillers face a federal tax increase of $2 a gallon next October 1—to $12.50 a proof gallon (50% alcohol), whereas the federal wine tax remains at 17 cents a gallon. The spirits people are calling for 'equity,' basing the tax on the percent of alcohol in a beverage and ignoring the traditional status of wine as a table beverage of moderation."

Both the wine and beer industries called the equivalency campaign misleading. Robert Hartzell, the spokesperson for the Winegrowers of California, responded in a press release that it was not just the amount of alcohol that mattered but other issues as well. Wine is used very differently in the United States when contrasted with liquor. It is consumed with meals three times more often than liquor, and food is a major factor in lowering blood alcohol in the body. Wine, beer, and spirits affect people differently depending on many complex and variable factors. Blood alcohol levels are significantly higher after drinking liquor than after drinking wine.[5]

Hartzell and others questioned whether the servings of wine, beer, and liquor as depicted in the Seagram ad were even typical in normal usage. They pointed out that Seagram was actually saying that there is no such thing as a beverage of moderation.

Both sides had their supporters. In addition to the Winegrowers of California, the opponents of the equivalency campaign included the Wine Institute and the Beer Institute. Seagram lined up as many groups as possible to support the concept of equivalency. The list was extensive and diverse and included the California Highway Patrol, Pennzoil Products, Inc., and the U.S. Public Health Service among others.

Seagram had the ability to finance the campaign to whatever extent was needed to reach its goal. On March 3, 1986, they took out double full-page newspaper ads to thank their supporters. The headline read, "Last Year the Number of Americans Aware of Alcohol Equivalence More Than Doubled." A list of sixty-five supporting groups followed along with the results of a poll conducted by Market Opinion Research. Their findings showed that 59 percent of American adults now know the fact of alcohol equivalence, up from 27 percent a year ago; 80 percent find the fact of equivalence to be believable; and 75 percent rate knowing the fact of equivalence as "very important."

On November 5, 1986, before more than 1,000 members of the National Licensed Beverage Association in Las Vegas, Bronfman announced that Seagram would immediately discontinue its public education program on alcohol equivalence.[6] Although not retreating from his company's stand on equivalency, he stated: "a backlash developed within our industry against the equivalence campaign and against Seagram directly. Clearly, the public campaign of equivalence has become an unbearable divisive influence. The interest of the industry as a whole demands that the divisiveness end. If ceasing our campaign will end it, then we will cease."

The next day, James Sanders—president of the Beer Institute—applauded Bronfman's announcement and said the beer industry would help restore unity in the industry. He cautioned that the equivalency issue was far from over and cited numerous anti-industry groups that had incorporated equivalence ideas into their calls for higher taxes, bans on radio and television advertising, and imposition of warning labels.

It is not known why Seagram made the decision to end the campaign. Perhaps the company thought that the idea of equivalency had been promoted as far as would be practicable to help attain the spirits industry's goal of excise tax equality or, perhaps because at this time Seagram was in the process of selling its portfolio of wine holdings. As for a backlash, it would more likely be due to the inroads that the Neo-Prohibitionists were making. Sanders was right: the consequences of equivalence were just beginning.

Neo-Prohibitionism Gains Ground

In March 1986, Senator Robert Packwood of Oregon, chairman of the Senate Finance Committee, called for the enactment of three excise tax proposals affecting wine, and wine only, as part of a larger tax reform package. The first proposal was to increase the excise tax on table wine from 17 cents a gallon to 87 cents a gallon. Proposal number two would eliminate all excise taxes as business deductions, and the third would index future taxes tied to price changes.[7] None of these proposals was original with Packwood. The Congressional Budget Office had sent him a long list of tax options to help trim the federal deficit. Among them were two alcohol-related items. One would raise the taxes on liquor from $12.50 to $15.00 per gallon, a measure that would raise $3.5 billion over the next five years. The other would affect beer and wine through taxing their alcohol content at the same rate as liquor, and this would raise $31 billion over the same five-year period.[8] Although the nondeductibility issue and the indexing provisions were not part of equivalency, they were probably the result of Seagram's political lobbying.[9]

On May 9, 1986, John De Luca, Wine Institute's president, sent out a memo "To All Friends of Wine" stating that the Senate Finance Committee had taken its final vote and reported a tax reform bill without any excise tax increases. "We've been engaged in the political equivalent of trench warfare," he wrote. "With this note I want primarily to express our deep appreciation for your help and cooperation.... But there can be no complacency. The Finance Committee and the full Congress could turn around and raise our taxes in order to lower deficits."[10]

De Luca also said, "We still have quite a distance to go before anyone can run up a victory flag." Less than three weeks later, on May 25, 1986, the *New York Times* published an article by George A. Hacker, director for alcohol policies and Michael F. Jacobson, executive director of the Center for Science in the Public Interest. Equalizing tax rates at the current liquor rate, they said, would reduce the economic and social cost of alcohol abuse. It would also save lives through decreases in the rates of liver cirrhosis and automobile fatalities.

Michael Jacobson and two other scientists, James Sullivan and Albert Fritsch, established the Center for Science in the Public Interest (CSPI) in 1971, and in the early years their focus was on the food industry in the United States.[11] CSPI's interest in alcohol began in the early 1980s, and by 1988 its Washington office had twenty-eight employees, three of whom worked full time on alcohol issues. With 125,000 dues-paying members and an annual budget of $2.5 million, CSPI had become the most powerful campaigning body facing the alcoholic beverage industry.

First lady Nancy Reagan's "Just Say No" campaign in 1986 linked alcohol and drugs together.[12] Two years later this campaign led to the White House Conference for a Drug Free America. In 1988, CSPI and a broad coalition of health, medical, and social groups had succeeded in a campaign that culminated on November 18, 1988, when President Ronald Reagan signed the Alcoholic Beverage Labeling Act that required government warning labels on all alcoholic beverages bottled after November 18, 1989.[13] Two years earlier, a similar campaign had led to the required declaration of sulfites on wine labels whenever their content exceeded the threshold of ten parts per million established by the Federal Drug Administration and the Department of Health and Human Services.[14]

Jacobson often stated that he was not in favor of banning alcohol altogether. In an article by Lawrence M. Fisher in the *New York Times* on January 1, 1988, he was quoted as saying he did not preach abstention. "Still," he added, "because there is no effective way to lower just problem drinking, a viable alternative is to lower consumption across the board." When interviewed that fall, he said that cutting consumption by 50 percent would be a realistic goal and a tremendous advance if that percentage came from heavy drinkers. He then listed three goals that he would

Figure 11.1: Jacques Recht (*left*), winemaster at Ingleside Plantation Winery in Oak Grove, Virginia, poured a glass of wine for Michael Jacobson, executive director of the Center for Science in the Public Interest. By 1988, the center had become the most powerful of the neo-Prohibitionist groups the wine industry had to contend with. The event was the Great American Wine Tasting held on November 1, 1989, by the *Roll Call* newspaper and the National Vintners Association in the Madison Building of the Library of Congress. Photo by author.

like to achieve during the following ten years: greatly increased taxes, much better labeling with calorie information and ingredient listing, and a much greater volume of health information in advertising.[15]

Pressure increased on the wine industry. Despite the victory on the imposition of warning labels, the Neo-Prohibitionists continued their campaign by protesting that the size of type on the labels should be larger, that the warning statement should be on the front label, and that the warning should be expanded to require five different messages on a rotating basis. None of these was adopted.

An annual occupation tax bill passed Congress just before Christmas in 1987 as part of an omnibus budget bill.[16] For wineries with gross receipts over $500,000, the tax was set at $1,000; and for wineries with gross receipts less than that, $500. Then, in late 1989, an excise tax bill was finally passed, which on still table wines was an increase from 17 cents a gallon to $1.07.

How far the anti-alcohol movement could go became evident on December 14–16, 1988, when a Surgeon General's Workshop on Alcohol and the Impaired Driver was held in Washington, DC. The workshop brought together a panel that consisted mostly of control advocates in favor of restrictions on alcoholic beverages. The media, representatives of alcoholic beverage industries, and others were initially barred from the meetings, but a court order filed by the National Association of Broadcasters and the National Beer Wholesalers Association after the opening session required the admission of uninvited guests and observers.

"Proceedings" of the workshop were scheduled for release on May 31, 1989, and there was a strong suggestion that they might contain a viewpoint favoring the complete prohibition of alcoholic beverages. As the result of a consent agreement with the court, Surgeon General Everett Koop announced that he would accept and consider comments from interested parties until January 31, 1989. When the "Proceedings" were published, however, a lack of space was given as the reason for excluding nonparticipants' comments.[17]

The Industry Fights Back

Despite the virulence of the anti-alcohol campaign, the wine industry did not reply to the attacks in an effective manner. Seagram's equivalency campaign had split the alcoholic beverage industry to the point where unity was difficult. However, some individuals were outraged at what was going on. One of them was Gene Ford, who had spent seventeen years as a sales executive for the Christian Brothers Winery, taught alcohol beverage management at Washington State University and, as a member of the National Speakers Association, lectured widely on alcohol-related subjects including Neo-Prohibitionism. In January 1987, Ford started *The Moderation Reader,* a four-page protest paper that provided commentary on the tactics and agendas of the Neo-Prohibitionists and their activities.[18] His book, *The Benefits of Moderate Drinking: Alcohol, Health & Society,* was published a year later.

With the threat of higher excise taxes and fees, an increase in the occupational tax to $2,500 and $5,000, and more warning labels and signs, organizations began to form to provide a response. These included the National Wine Coalition, National Vintners Association, and American Wine Alliance for Research and Education (AWARE), all three formed in 1988 and 1989, and the Century Council in 1991. Already in existence was the Association of American Vintners, founded in 1978, which became increasingly influential following its name change to the American Vintners Association in 1992 and then to WineAmerica in 2002.[19]

The National Wine Coalition

On April 17, 1989, at a media luncheon at the Willard Inter-Continental Hotel in Washington, DC, Wine Institute president John De Luca announced the formation of the National Wine Coalition with initial funding of $200,000 by Wine Institute.[20] The Coalition, he said, is intended to "create a broad-based industry and consumer coalition that will develop an aggressive public education and information program to combat alcohol abuse, respond to critics, and increase public knowledge of wine's proper use in contemporary American society." Further, "the Coalition will fight to protect the individual's right to select their beverage of choice without undue imposition or control."

In addition to wineries, wine organizations, and allied industries, membership was open to wholesalers, retailers, the hospitality industry, growers, anti-alcohol abuse groups, food and wine interests, and the wine consumer. The initial executive committee consisted of Barry Sterling, Iron Horse Vineyards; Peter M. F. Sichel, H. Sichel Söhne; Frank Woods, Clos du Bois; Marvin Shanken, M. Shanken Communications; Jim Trezise, New York Wine Council; and Sam Bronfman, II, Seagram Classics Wine Co. Dr. John Volpe, executive director of the National Chamber Foundation, was selected to serve as executive director of the coalition.[21]

The National Wine Coalition established a newsletter, *Trends & Perspectives,* and in its first issue dated July 1990, it reported that the coalition's testimony was crucial in blocking the 500 percent increase in the occupational tax on wine producers. The lead article stated that the coalition was opposing several bills that were introduced to severely restrict the advertising of alcoholic beverages. The most threatening was the Sensible Advertising and Family Education Act of 1990, introduced in April by Representative Joseph Kennedy (D-MA) and Senator Albert Gore (D-TN), which would require five rotating health warnings to be added to print and broadcast alcohol advertisements. Another bill would not allow pictures, colors other than black and white, or slogans in alcohol advertisements. No action was taken on the Sensible Advertising Act of 1990, and it was reintroduced in 1991 by Kennedy in the House and by Strom Thurmond (R-SC) in the Senate.

Lead in wine became an issue in 1991 and the Food and Drug Administration was to determine tolerance standards and the Bureau of Alcohol, Tobacco and Firearms to issue regulations. The Center for Science in the Public Interest and other groups wanted to have warnings on lead put on wine labels and in advertising.[22] Following tests by the BATF and testimony by the National Wine Coalition, the less onerous result was to establish regulations on lead capsules.

The coalition also developed promotional programs to be used with consumers, methods to increase media awareness, and informational activities to address misinformation on wines. Sponsored research activities included measuring the impact of excise taxes on wine and the contribution of the wine industry to the U.S. economy. By July 1991, the coalition had 240 members.

Volpe resigned from the National Wine Coalition in 1993 to join Heublein, Inc., as their director of government affairs. As the new executive director, the coalition chose Gordon W. Murchie, president of the Vinifera Wine Growers Association, who had been elected to the board of directors on October 24, 1991. From 1958 to 1985, Murchie had served as a foreign service officer with the U.S. Information Agency, and from 1985 until his retirement in 1993, he was director of international development communications for the U.S. Agency for International Development.

Figure 11.2: Gordon W. Murchie became president of the Vinifera Wine Growers Association in 1989. From the time he took the position of executive director of the National Wine Coalition in 1993 until 2008, when he resigned from the VWGA, he was in the forefront of efforts to influence legislation in Washington, D.C., and to unite the wine industry around common goals. Photo by author, 1989.

His retirement became effective at midnight on March 31, 1993, and he took on the responsibility for the National Wine Coalition the following day.

In 1993, the National Wine Coalition opposed an increase in the federal excise tax, known as a "sin tax," as a funding source for the Clinton Administration's national health-care reform program. The Thurmond-Kennedy proposed legislation was still not resolved, and Representative Patricia Schroeder (D-CO) had reintroduced her bill requiring alcoholic beverage containers to list alcohol content, the number of servings per container, ingredients, and the number of calories per serving and per container. Her legislation brought back the equivalency issue that defined a serving as the amount of alcohol found in one beer, one shot of whiskey, and one glass of wine. On the positive side, the battle over user fees had been won, and the administration's plan to raise $5 million by charging a fee of $50 per label application and $250 per formula application was dropped.[23]

One of Murchie's earliest goals was to sponsor a symposium that would bring together people from every aspect of the wine industry, its allied businesses, wine organizations, wine enthusiasts, and wine consumers; in short, everyone interested in wine. After a year of planning, the First National Wine Issues Forum was held on September 26, 1994, at the National Press Club in Washington, DC. The one-day symposium was conducted by the National Wine Coalition and featured sessions on wine and health, taxes and regulations, issues in wine distribution, and international trade incentives and barriers. In addition to the National Press Club, sponsors of the event included the Vinifera Wine Growers Association, the New York Wine and Grape Foundation, and the Society of Wine Educators.

Approximately 125 people attended the symposium, and in the audience were 36 members of different associations, 17 vintners, 12 retailers, 17 people from government, and a number of people from the media. Among the speakers were Peter Sichel; Dr. R. Curtis Ellison, professor of medicine and public health at Boston University's School of Medicine; Becky Murphy, executive director of the American Wine Alliance for Research and Education (AWARE); and Walter Klenz, president of Wine World Estates Company. There were two luncheon speakers: Spencer Christian from ABC's *Good Morning America,* and Richard Mendelson, vice chair of the American Bar Association's Beverage Practice Committee, who gave the keynote address, "Neo-Prohibition Attacks on Wine."[24]

The First National Wine Issues Forum was thought to be the first of its kind held in the East and went a long way toward bringing the industry together. There was never a second forum, however. The National Wine Coalition, which had been criticized for its ties with Wine Institute, received diminished support from Wine Institute, and by 1995 the coalition was closed down. Murchie transferred directly to the Licensed Beverage Information Council as its executive director and stayed in that position until 1998. During that same time period he was also legislative chairman of the World Association of Alcohol Beverage Industries.

Murchie continued to be president of the Vinifera Wine Growers Association. Before he left the National Wine Coalition in January 1994, he had started the *Wine Exchange,* "The Vinifera Wine Growers Newsletter," and when the coalition folded, Murchie kept track of legislation on Capitol Hill in the *Wine Exchange* just as he had in the National Wine Coalition's newsletter.

The National Vintners Association

When the National Vintners Association (NVA) was formed in the early fall of 1988, executive director Richard J. Feeney told *Wines and Vines* in a telephone interview that the association was intended to represent wine growers and producers in states outside California, but that California producers could join.[25] He also said that the NVA would stress in Congress that wine is an agricultural product and that many independent growers and winery/vineyard operations qualify as family farms.

Feeney, who had years of experience as a lobbyist in Washington, saw the need for growers and wineries to have representation on Capitol Hill. One of the problems facing the wine industry in 1988 was finding out what was happening there in time to have input into proposed legislation. Through his long association with Congress, Feeney had quick access to Congressional offices and contacts with other government agencies, and one of the first things NVA did was to establish a wine hotline to provide instant response to news media, government, and individuals on current issues and crises.

NVA has been credited with being the leader in the farm product approach to wine, and Rick Feeney soon got NVA involved. The chairman of the House Agriculture Committee was Representative E. (Kika) de la Garza (D-TX), who was convinced that the government had focused on its responsibility to regulate wine for far too long and had paid too little attention to marketing wine. Wine is a farm product, he said, and American wine producers and consumers would benefit from having the U.S. Department of Agriculture (USDA) emphasize wine as a food beverage. When the NVA was founded, de la Garza was proposing a shift of jurisdiction over wine to the USDA with the exception of the tax aspects.

Feeney wasted no time in coming to the support of de la Garza. In December 1988, the House Agriculture Committee held a wine reception for members of Congress hosted by de la Garza, Representative Edward R. Madigan (R-IL), the ranking minority member of the Committee, and the NVA. The reception featured wine from eighteen states.[26] Unfortunately, this was not the time for people to pay attention to de la Garza's proposition that an expanding wine industry would find plenty of customers at home and abroad, and even less likely for his idea that teaching young people the proper and mature way to treat wine would help prevent abuse of an intrinsically good product.

Perhaps the longest lasting contribution Feeney made to the industry came in establishing wine tastings for Congress. On November 1, 1989, NVA and *Roll Call,* a private newspaper widely read by Congress, hosted "The Great American Wine Tasting" in the Madison Building of the Library of Congress for members of the Senate and the House, their spouses, and staff of key committees. About 500 people attended, wines from more than fifty wineries were donated, the majority of them from the East, and some enthusiastic legislators jumped in to pour wines from wineries in their districts.[27]

NVA held the first "Taste America: A Bounty of Fine Wines and Foods" on August 5, 1992, with Julia Child as hostess, in the Members' Private Dining Room of the U.S. House of Representatives in the U.S. Capitol. This was the first time that the dining room had been used for a trade event and was made possible by Feeney's friendship with Representative Charles G. Rose (D-NC). More than 275 members of Congress attended.

The impact of Taste America became evident in 1993 when House Speaker Thomas S. Foley asked Feeney when that year's event would be held. NVA had been taken over by the Association of American Vintners in late 1992 and Feeney was no longer affiliated with it. Feeney, however, recognized the value of the tasting to the wine industry and formed the Taste America Society to continue the event. On August 4, 1993, Taste America was held under the patronage of Les Dames d'Escoffier with twenty-nine wine and food trade organizations as sponsors. More than sixty wineries participated, two-thirds of them from the East, and more than 300 members of Congress attended.

Taste America became an annual event under Feeney's guidance, and the eighth annual event was held on August 5, 1999, just after Taste America was incorporated as an educational foundation with the name changed to the Taste America Foundation. There is no way to gauge the impact of Feeney's idea to promote wine to Congress, but it was a first. More important, it was followed by the founding in 1999 of the Congressional Wine Caucus by two members of the House, representatives Mike Thompson (D-CA) and George Radanovich (R-CA).[28] By 2004, the Caucus had 250 members of Congress from all fifty states.

From its beginning, the NVA had problems attracting members. Alan Barr, owner of Le Rêve Winery on Long Island had been elected the association chairman on January 23, 1989, and he was probably an unfortunate choice to head the organization. The April 30, 1989, issue of the *Wine Spectator* ran an adverse article about Barr and Le Rêve, under the headline "Nightmare at Dream Winery," citing such problems as unpaid bills, a foreclosure threat by a bank, a battle with the town of Southampton, and bad press. The NVA had also tried to start an insurance program for wineries, and this brought it into direct conflict with the Association of American Vintners (AAV), an older association with primarily eastern membership that had offered a comprehensive insurance program since its inception. In the absence of support from the eastern industry, there was little more the NVA could continue to do for free. In September 1992, the two associations merged to form the American Vintners Association. Feeney was specifically excluded from the new organization.

From AAV to WineAmerica

At the first Wineries Unlimited in 1976, some attendees expressed interest in forming an organization of eastern wineries.[29] During the next twelve months, support for the idea increased because ingredient labeling and appellation of origin issues surfaced in Washington. The larger wineries in the East saw the need to take effective action. They had the financial resources to undertake a lobbying campaign, yet they realized that an organization was needed if they were to be politically influential. The smaller wineries were somewhat skeptical of what the larger wineries might do, but they knew that the large wineries could provide the financial support they could not.

On December 1, 1977, at Wineries Unlimited, J. William Moffett and Hope Merletti of the trade magazine *Eastern Grape Grower and Winery News,* the sponsor of Wineries Unlimited, distributed a proposal to create an "Eastwine Producers' Advisory Council" to unite the eastern wine industry. There was sufficient support for the proposal to schedule a meeting in June 1978 to discuss bylaws and a budget. Peter L. Carp of Widmer's Wine Cellars was entrusted with the job of pulling everything together. At the organizational meeting held in Rochester, New York on

August 3, a sixteen-member steering committee was formed to develop the bylaws and budget. After considerable discussion, Nathan Stackhouse of Leelanau Wine Cellars in Michigan was responsible for naming the organization the Association of American Vintners.

Wineries Unlimited was held from November 29 to December 1 in 1978. The day before the conference, the full steering committee met in Philadelphia to finalize the bylaws and review the presentation that would be made to prospective members at Wineries Unlimited.[30] Elections were also held. All of the steering committee members were elected to become members of the board of directors for the first fiscal year. Carp was then elected president; James Mitchell of Sakonnet Vineyards in Rhode Island, vice president; Alcuin Wiederkehr of Wiederkehr Wine Cellars in Arkansas, secretary; and C. Frederic Schroeder of the Taylor Wine Company, treasurer. Moffett was named administrative director and his office at Watkins Glen the official headquarters of the association.

The earliest legislative priorities of AAV were to address the problems of ingredient labeling of wine and the proposal in Congress to disallow wine advertising as a business expense. Another priority was to advance the public's knowledge and appreciation of its members' wines, and the 1981 tasting at Windows on the World was an early major event.

According to Carp, AAV planned to have representation in Washington, although "we cannot be imprudent and budget ourselves a full time representative. The route we may go is that we acknowledge the fact that we have many parallel interests with California, and that in those issues we can work with them in Washington."[31] Over the years, as the Neo-Prohibitionist movement gained strength, AAV saw the need to work within a wider industry context and decided to form ties with the National Wine Coalition. As James G. Ashby, AAV's president, wrote in its newsletter, "During these times of insane Congressional proposals, which affect every American winery, it's just plain stupid not to unify." AAV asked for and got two positions on the National Wine Coalition board of directors and one slot on its executive committee.[32]

When the American Association of Vintners and the National Vintners Association merged in September 1992 to form the American Vintners Association, it brought the membership of AVA to more than 300 wineries in thirty-five states.[33] The AVA stated that it intended to present itself as a grassroots organization to influence federal legislation and public policy issues as they affected American wine and winegrowing. In 1995, a State Legislative Monitoring Program was established to provide assistance to wineries that were seeking to simplify laws and regulations that were impeding their ability to operate successfully and also to promote legislation that would enhance their profitability. A "State Wine Issues Network" was formed to engage AVA's grassroots strength to communicate and coordinate winery support. The grassroots mobilization proved to be very effective and in 1993 it was credited with killing BATF's $50 label approval user fee.

AVA was the beneficiary of a series of leaders who were successful in building an organization that would become WineAmerica in 2002. Robert G. Kalik, who was associated with the legal firm McDermott, Will and Emery in Washington, was appointed chief counsel for AAV in 1990, continued in the same position after the merger, and became the AVA president in January 1994. On November 1, 1994, Bill Nelson, executive director of the Oregon Winegrowers Association, became AVA's legislative vice president. In 2005, he became president of WineAmerica. Simon Siegl, executive director of the Washington Wine Commission, joined the AVA board in 1988 and became its first full-time president in 1996. David Sloane left his position as senior vice president of Wine and Spirits Wholesalers of America to become the president of AVA in 2002, eight months before the association was renamed WineAmerica.

AVA grew quickly. From about 300 members at the time of the merger, there were more than 500 member wineries in forty-two states when Kalik left and 650 in forty-four states when Siegl resigned in 2002. Among its major accomplishments was the development of the concepts for wine and grape research that were included in the passage of the 1996 Farm Bill. Significantly, there was an allocation of $500,000 for research that year, $800,000 in 1997 and over $1 million in 1998. This funding resulted in the formation of the American Viticulture and Enology Research Network (AVERN) which for the first time established national priorities for viticulture and enology research. In 1992, AVA created the Wine Market Council as its marketing research arm that was intended to grow, strengthen and stabilize the U.S. wine market. John Gillespie was named its executive director in 1994. The Council, as originally planned, became fully autonomous on January 1, 1995.

Another opportunity to influence Congress came on May 4, 1995, when the AVA and the Winegrowers of America held a joint board of directors meeting in Washington, after which fifty representatives of both organizations spread out on Capitol Hill for individual meetings with approximately 100 members of the House and Senate. On August 4, 1997, the AVA facilitated a meeting with several organizations to pursue the progress being made on legal direct-to-consumer shipments of wine, which led to legislation in 2002 that permitted consumers visiting out-of-state wineries to ship back to their homes the same amount of wine that they could have carried back on their own.

At the fall meeting in St. Louis on November 22, 2002, the board of directors gave approval to renaming the organization WineAmerica. One reason for the name change was that the new name would have a broad appeal and that it would "telegraph" that WineAmerica would be much more than a trade organization. New goals included the establishment of a council of state associations and the creation of a new category of consumer membership. From that time on, WineAmerica became the most influential association to promote and defend the interests of the wine industry nationally in the United States.

AWARE

One of the most important associations to be formed nationally at this time was not a self-described lobby but, rather, the American Wine Alliance for Research and Education, known primarily by its acronym AWARE. The bylaws, adopted on April 27, 1989, were prefaced by a mission statement stating that the purpose of the alliance would be "to develop an alliance among all segments of the wine industry and the public in order to fund research, produce educational materials, and develop programs regarding the economic, social, health, scientific, and cultural aspects relating to the production, sale and use of wine. It is expressly understood that the Corporation will not be an advocate of health claims, either pro or con, but will instead collect, evaluate and disseminate objective data and information concerning such claims in the public interest."[34] As a nonprofit organization, it had to avoid politics.

Allen C. Shoup, president of Chateau Ste. Michelle in Woodinville, Washington, was elected chairman of AWARE. Leading the alliance for many years were Dr. Keith I. Marton, who became president in 1990 and Rebecca Murphy, who succeeded Patricia E. Schneider as executive director in January 1992.

Increasingly, AWARE dedicated its efforts to providing a balanced view of alcohol science and issued regular peer-reviewed newsletter reports and health alerts for health and medical professionals. In 1995 it contracted with the AVA for its administrative and membership functions in order to concentrate on health provider education, the maintenance of its research data base on alcohol science, and special projects. Although AWARE could not engage in lobbying, the respect it won for its role in providing authoritative and balanced information about wine and health was important in reshaping the public perception of wine.

60 Minutes and "The French Paradox"

In the beginning of this chapter, David F. Musto of Yale University was quoted as saying that what had been going on since the late 1960s was a temperance movement rather than strictly an anti-alcohol campaign. He pointed out that health movements start with a fear and concern about the substances we take into our bodies, and there is a perceived need to protect the community. At the same time, however, there is a very strong positive side to the health movement that indicates concern over what you should take into your body. The growing strength of the local food movement in the first decade of the twenty-first century confirms his belief that what had been happening was a temperance movement.

In his 1986 interview, Musto also stated that "special events can occur that will greatly modify a trend or movement." Such an event took place in the 1990s as red wine began to be perceived as something beneficial to health. Gradually, during the course of the decade, the Neo-Prohibitionist campaigns against wine began to be blunted. The spark that started it off was a story on *60 Minutes*.

On Sunday, November 17, 1991, CBS devoted a segment of its weekly news program *60 Minutes* to what it titled "The French Paradox." The program focused on research that showed that the French have rates of heart disease 40 percent lower than in the United States despite having a diet higher in fat and cholesterol and an unhealthy lifestyle that included smoking more and exercising less. Moderator Morley Safer had three researchers on the program, two from France, Serge Renaud and Monique Astier-Dumas, and one from the United States, Curtis Ellison. They showed that there was an apparent relationship between moderate alcohol consumption, particularly of red wine, and a lower rate of heart disease.[35]

The program, watched by an estimated 55 million viewers, resulted in a 44 percent increase in the purchase of red wine during the four weeks following the broadcast, but otherwise there was little immediate reaction. There was nothing new about a link between heart disease and wine consumption. In the May 12, 1979, issue of *Lancet,* a British medical journal, A. S. St. Leger and two other researchers in Cardiff had shown that there was a negative correlation between ischemic heart disease deaths and wine consumption in a survey of eighteen countries. Edward Delnick had written an article, "Le Paradoxe Français" in the May–June issue of the U.S. publication *In Health,* which had been the basis for the CBS program. Ellison had spoken about the French Paradox at an AWARE forum not long before the broadcast.

What *60 Minutes* did was to stir up interest. Suddenly there was research in many countries looking into not only the role of red wine in the French Paradox but other practices followed by the French including the use of fresh fruits and vegetables, three meals a day without snacking, and drinking wine as a regular part of midday and evening meals. Two compounds that occur naturally in wine, quercetin and resveratrol, were discovered to have potential health benefits, a number of studies on the role of phenolic antioxidants in wine were conducted, and it was not long before it was shown that a diet including moderate wine consumption could provide more complete heart disease protection than a diet without wine. Also beginning to emerge were research findings that red wine could provide protection against many other health problems. As new facts became available, the media had increased interest in providing coverage.

Needless to say, there was strong reaction to the idea that there could be health benefits from drinking wine. The BATF prohibited wineries from quoting the *60 Minutes* segment in their newsletters and elsewhere as a violation of the Federal Alcohol Act. Nor would any advertisement containing references to the therapeutic or curative effects of alcohol be permitted. The Center for Science in the Public Interest questioned the validity of the studies. There was also a proliferation of junk science articles that attempted to refute the health values of wine. These included the unproven suggestions that pine bark or Vitamin E would be as good for health

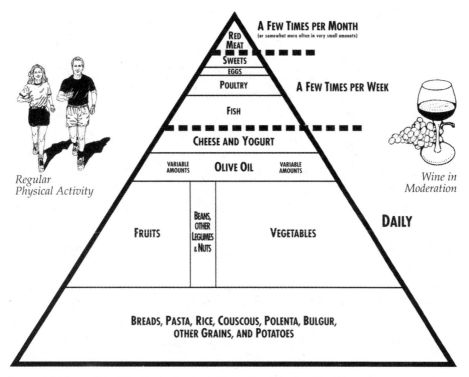

A FEW TIMES PER MONTH
(or somewhat more often in very small amounts)

RED MEAT

SWEETS

EGGS

POULTRY

A FEW TIMES PER WEEK

FISH

CHEESE AND YOGURT

VARIABLE AMOUNTS | OLIVE OIL | VARIABLE AMOUNTS

Regular Physical Activity

FRUITS

BEANS, OTHER LEGUMES & NUTS

VEGETABLES

DAILY

Wine in Moderation

BREADS, PASTA, RICE, COUSCOUS, POLENTA, BULGUR, OTHER GRAINS, AND POTATOES

Figure 11.3: The traditional Healthy Mediterranean Pyramid was developed by Oldways Preservation and Exchange Trust in Boston, Massachusetts, under the leadership of K. Dun Gifford. One way it differed from the USDA's Food Guide Pyramid released in 1992 was that it called for regular physical activity and wine in moderation. Reprinted with permission from Oldways Preservation & Exchange Trust, www.oldwayspt.org.

as wine or, on the negative side, telling readers not to forget that the French have significantly increased risks of stomach and esophagus cancers.[36]

Another attention-getting health development in the 1990s was the Mediterranean diet, which was closely tied to the traditional areas of olive oil cultivation in that region. Rates of chronic diseases there were among the lowest in the world and life expectancy among adults was one of the highest. With its emphasis on a variety of minimally processed, seasonally fresh, and locally grown foods, it fit right into the interest in the French Paradox and healthy living.

In 1988, K. Dun Gifford organized the Oldways Preservation & Exchange Trust in Boston for the purpose of preserving the healthy, environmentally sustainable food and agricultural traditions of many cultures and to make the lessons of these traditions more widely accessible. Oldways and the Harvard School of Public Health organized an international conference on Diets of the Mediterranean in January 1993, followed by the release of the Traditional Healthy Mediterranean Diet Pyramid in June 1994. Unlike the USDA food pyramid released two years earlier, the majority of fats included came from olive oil and oil from nuts rather than from meat and dairy products. The big difference in the Mediterranean Healthy Diet Pyramid was the inclusion of wine in moderation and regular physical activity, two factors that were involved in the French Paradox. A note to the Mediterranean Pyramid mentioned that wine was enjoyed in moderation, normally with meals and typically within a family context. It added: "From a contemporary public health perspective, wine should be considered optional in a Mediterranean-style diet and *avoided whenever consumption would put the individual or others at risk,* including during pregnancy and before driving."[37]

The message that drinking wine in moderation would be beneficial to health was promoted by other organizations. Women for WineSense was started in 1990 in the Napa Valley by Julie Williams, a partner in Frogs Leap Winery, and Michaela Rodeno, CEO of St. Supery Winery, to disseminate positive information to other women about moderate wine consumption. Gene Ford formed a group called Citizens for Moderate Drinking, and Robert Mondavi established the Mondavi Mission to convey the message that wine in moderation is healthy. Drink responsibly and drinking in moderation became increasingly used as watchwords in alcohol industry advertising.[38]

From the time that Seagram's began its equivalency campaign in 1985 when the wine industry first comprehended the magnitude of the danger it was facing, the response was to organize in opposition. But it happened gradually. Leaders had to step forward, wineries had to be convinced to act, Congress and state legislatures had to be educated to the fact that there was a growing wine industry across the United States and that wine was not a drug but a civilized part of society. A great deal of credit must be given to the people who founded organizations and worked hard in the cause of wine. How much further the temperance movement would have gone to restrict access to wine can never be known, but the Neo-Prohibitionist forces were strong and gathering momentum. The linking of wine to health was the main factor in slowing the anti-alcohol campaign. Subsequently there was the realization that it is one thing to tax something that is seen as a sin, but quite another to tax something that is perceived as beneficial to health.

There were times in the late 1990s when the Neo-Prohibitionists seemed to be making a comeback, and probably anti-alcohol sentiment will not disappear in the foreseeable future. One difference today is that there are strong organizations like WineAmerica that can warn and guard the industry in a way that was not possible in the 1980s.

Chapter Twelve

❧

Consolidation in the 1990s

THE REPRESSIVE ENVIRONMENT CREATED BY THE NEO-PROHIBITIONISTS IN THE 1980s continued to be an imminent threat to the wine industry into the mid-1990s. Winery growth slowed as some wineries closed and others that were planning to open were put on hold. The number of wineries in the East had increased by 153 from 1980 to 1985, but that increase from 1985 to 1990 dwindled to 66 and further to only 20 from 1990 to 1995 (see table 6.1).

The *60 Minutes* broadcast that highlighted the "French Paradox" in November 1991 proved to be a turning point in the fight against the Neo-Prohibitionists, but it took time for the health benefits of wine to become a compelling factor. For the remainder of the decade and beyond, the results of confirming research studies were published with increasing frequency. Adding to the positive image of wine was the publicity given to the Mediterranean diet in which wine was included.

Interest in wine on the part of the public increased during the decade. Wine events continued to be popular, the number of festivals grew, and attendance at them multiplied. After 1995, winery start-ups began to increase, and the number of wineries climbed from 565 to 803 in 2000.

In many ways the 1990s was a decade of consolidation where the industry was building on what was already in place rather than expanding. However, during the second half of the decade a momentum began to occur that resulted in an explosion of growth in the industry after 2000.

More Large State Festivals

The Maryland Wine Festival was first held in 1984. The following year the festival was expanded into a two-day event and was moved to the Carroll County Farm

Figure 12.1: At the second Nelson J. Shaulis Symposium held in Fredonia, New York in July, 1993, one of the exhibits was a shoot positioner/mechanical pruner developed by Tommy Oldridge of Lowell, Arkansas, in cooperation with Dr. Justin R. Morris of the University of Arkansas. By 2002 the Morris-Oldridge System for Complete Vineyard Mechanization was patented and licensed for manufacturing and marketing. Photo by author.

Museum, which became its permanent home. Attendance reached 25,500 for the eighth festival held in September 1991. At that festival "The Wines of Maryland Cup" was presented to Catoctin Vineyards of Brookeville, Maryland, for their Best of Show 1985 Cabernet Sauvignon.[1]

The inaugural Great Tastes of Pennsylvania called "The First Annual Wine and Food Festival" was held at Split Rock Resort in Lake Harmony, Pennsylvania, in June 1991, and brought in 7,500 paid admissions.[2] In addition to Split Rock Resort, the Pennsylvania Wine Association was a sponsor, and the festival management was by

Figure 12.2: Visitors to wineries are always interested in seeing vineyard and winery equipment in operation. This photo of a tractor and sprayer at Montdomaine Cellars in Charlottesville, Virginia, was taken in March 1993. Photo by author.

Barksdale, Ballard & Co. in Virginia, which had had festival management experience in connection with the Virginia Wineries Festival starting in 1988. As part of the festival there was a wine and food matching event held at four restaurants in eastern Pennsylvania. Eleven wineries submitted eighty wines and the restaurants prepared dishes to go with the wines. The public could sign up for any of the dinners and participate in the event.

The first Finger Lakes Wine Festival was held in August 1994 on the campus of the New York Chiropractic College just south of Seneca Falls along Cayuga Lake.[3] Doug Knapp, the event organizer, and his wife Suzie, owners of Knapp Vineyard

Figure 12.3: A bin dumper at the Chaddsford Winery in Chadds Ford, Pennsylvania, emptied grapes into a hopper during the 1989 harvest. Photo by author.

Winery and Restaurant on Cayuga Lake, had been planning such an event for four years. The festival was an immediate success and in 1995 the event outgrew the facility. Upon learning that the festival was looking for a new home, Watkins Glen International purchased it and after a year of planning moved it to their racetrack and the Seneca Lake Wine Trail became a major sponsor. A year later the New York Wine Country Professional Fencing Championship was held at the festival for the first time. After the 2000 festival, attended by nearly 15,000 people, it was announced that the Corning Museum of Glass would become a supporter of the festival.

Vintage Ohio started in August 1995, and was sponsored by the Cleveland *Plain Dealer* in cooperation with the Ohio Wine Producers Association, Lake Metroparks, and the Lake County Visitors Bureau. The festival was managed by Barksdale, Ballard & Co. and was held at Lake Farmpark in Kirtland. With the exception of the 1996 festival, which took place at the Lake County Fairgrounds in Painesville, the event has been held at Lake Farmpark, an outdoor living science center that includes a working farm. With an admission ticket to Vintage Ohio, visitors were able to explore the world of farming and children had the opportunity to milk a cow, see how a tomato grows, fish in a farm pond, or make ice cream.[4] A petting zoo and horse and tractor drawn wagons added to the promotional possibilities for Vintage Ohio. Attendance in 1995, the first year of the festival, was 17,000, and in its fourth year exceeded 30,000.

Wine Standards

The importance of setting standards for wine quality and finding effective methods for improving overall wine quality in various states in the East had long been recognized. In addition to the Augusta Wine Board, other attempts were made from time to time to establish wine standards that would usually result in a seal or other form of recognition or approval for qualifying wines.

In 1976 a Hudson Region Wine Council was formed by six wineries to provide direction for the quality of wines in the Hudson River Valley.[5] In 1979, William Wetmore of Cascade Mountain Vineyards announced the council's proposals to set and enforce standards for Hudson River Valley wines that would exceed those set by state or federal government.[6] Wines would have to be made only from selected varieties of grapes grown in the Hudson region and they would also have to be 100 percent varietals. After being approved by a panel of knowledgeable and experienced tasters, they would be entitled to carry a Hudson Region Wine Council seal.

No attempt to set up a judging panel or develop a seal was ever made.[7] A major obstacle arose over the question of who should pass judgment on the wines. There was tentative agreement that the New York State Agricultural Experiment Station at Geneva might be asked to do technical laboratory evaluations for basic soundness, but it did not go any further. Nor was there any agreement on finalized standards. One problem was that there were not enough grapes of the selected varieties available. Another was that some winemakers, including Wetmore, were in favor of making blends.

The Hudson Region Wine Council was too large and too diverse in makeup for cooperation to come easily. One reason why the Augusta standards succeeded was that only two wineries were involved at the start.

It is easy to see why it can be difficult for wineries to reach agreement. Not having one's wines approved can mean loss of competitiveness in the marketplace. Trust in the ability or fairness of those doing the judging is often a factor. Irrational as it might be, the fear that an unfavorable laboratory analysis would negatively influence the business and would override any idea that it might serve as a basis for improvement in future winemaking. Still, with the passage of time, there has been increasing recognition of the economic importance of wine quality that goes beyond one's own winery, an awareness that one bad wine in a state has the potential to affect the reputation of all the wines in that state.

In late 1992, Anthony P. Debevc of Chalet Debonné in Madison, Ohio, originated the idea of the Lake Erie Quality Wine Alliance.[8] He and a group of growers in Ohio, New York, and Pennsylvania who owned wineries along the shoreline of Lake Erie met several times to form an alliance that would promote the lakeshore region as a cohesive viticultural area producing quality wines. On June 17, 1993, the Quality Wine Alliance of Lake Erie was incorporated in Ohio by Debevc, Robert Mazza of Mazza Vineyards, and Alan E. Wolf of Conneaut Cellars. Mazza was elected the first president. The idea of creating a quality seal was discussed but was soon dropped. However, the twelve member wineries agreed on a logo that could go on a capsule as long as it was not used as an indicator of quality.

As an initial project, it was decided to develop a signature wine that would highlight the talents of their winemakers. Each winery would create its own blend, but their labels would share a name in common. The wines would have to be made from any or all of seven agreed-upon varieties of grapes with a sweetness range from 0 to 2 percent residual sugar.

A contest was announced to select a name for the wines, and "Reflections of Lake Erie" was the winning name. Three or four sensory evaluations were held by winery members, and in 1998 seven "Reflections of Lake Erie" wines were released. Demand for the wines was high, and it was decided to continue the project. In July 1993, the alliance had contracted with a firm for administrative services, and later an executive secretary was hired to help with marketing. The alliance was always dependent on its membership for funding and eventually, in the absence of outside financial support, the organization became dormant although it remains intact.

The success of the Vintners Quality Alliance (VQA) in Canada was a factor in the decision to set up the New Jersey Quality Wine Alliance (QWA).[9] In 1996, Dr. Joseph Fiola, the small fruit and viticulture specialist at Rutgers University, and Dr. Gary Pavlis, the cooperative extension agent for Atlantic County, discussed the idea of an alliance with a group of winemakers belonging to the Garden State Wine Growers Association. It was agreed that it would be desirable to ensure that all New Jersey wines met minimum standards.

When marketing and promotion money became available from Rutgers University in 1998, the logistics of a QWA were discussed. It was decided to link a QWA review with the New Jersey Commercial Wine Competition, and the idea was first tried experimentally with the 1999 competition held in February. This resulted in the establishment of an independent review board and a decision to inaugurate the program in February 2000. A QWA label was designed to identify wines passing the review. No provision was made for laboratory analysis.

The Ontario "Pull-Out" Program

The transformation of the Ontario wine and grape industry during the 1990s into a wine region recognized internationally for its quality was a remarkable accomplishment.[10] At the start of the decade the future did not look particularly bright in view of the problems remaining in the wake of the free trade and GATT settlements. The industry needed the promised assistance from both the provincial and federal governments and it was nearly two years before Ontario premier David Peterson and Canada's prime minister Brian Mulroney could reach agreement on a $145 million Grape and Wine Adjustment Program to be funded evenly by the two governments.

To cover the cost of removing uneconomic vineyards, price supports, and subsidy payments for grapes that were in surplus but not eligible for removal, $100 million was allocated for a Grape and Wine Adjustment Program, better known as the "pull-out program."[11] Approximately 8,000 acres, 50 percent of Ontario's vineyards, were pulled out in five rounds, most of them in a two-year period with growers being compensated at the rate of $1,100 an acre. No incentive was built into the program to encourage growers to replant, but some did and within four years 3,000 of the 8,000 acres had been replanted with vinifera. In 1990 the vinifera harvest was 4,000 tons; by 2000 it was 20,400 tons. By the mid-2000s the number of acres of vineyards in Ontario had reached 17,000, about what it had been fifty years earlier. The mix of varieties being grown, however, was much different.

The other $45 million was earmarked for a seven-year Ontario Wine Adjustment Program to help make the wineries competitive. Marketing was one intended use for these funds, but wineries that had been in existence at the time of the signing of the Free Trade Agreement could also use the money for capital expenditures.

Support for the industry came from the Ontario government. Before the 1988 harvest, Peterson opened the Niagara Wine Route as a way of increasing tourism and giving a boost to the industry. A brochure was prepared and blue and white markers were installed from Stoney Creek in the west to Niagara Falls in the east. It was the lifting of restrictions on the industry that proved to be most helpful.

As a start, the amount stores had to pay the Liquor Control Board of Ontario (LCBO) on sales in their own stores was reduced from 5 percent to 2 percent. In the early 1990s, approval was given for wineries to open their onsite winery stores for Sunday sales. Permission was also given for the use of credit cards for purchases at wineries and their retail stores. These two measures enabled wineries to double their sales.

Of great importance to the wineries later in the decade was authorization for direct delivery to restaurants. Until then, wineries could serve restaurants but had to sell to them through the LCBO. Now wineries could deliver wine and invoice restaurants directly and not through the LCBO. This meant that the wineries could keep the 58.6 percent LCBO markup and a $1.50 flat tax for themselves.[12]

During the third week of June 1990, Vineland Estates Winery opened the first "food deck," or wine bar, in Ontario. Customers could purchase wine samples, sit on the deck, and be served bread, cheese, and cold cuts—but no cooked foods because that would require a license.[13] This was the start of an important contribution to Ontario's wine image. Cave Spring Cellars opened its On the Twenty Restaurant and Wine Bar in 1993, and by the end of the decade several wineries had opened restaurants.

A rapid growth in the number of wineries occurred during the 1990s. Four new boutique wineries opened within two years after the Free Trade Agreement was signed, bringing the number of wineries in Ontario to eighteen. Included in this group were Henry of Pelham Estate Winery, Stonechurch Vineyards, Marynissen Estates Winery, and Magnotta Winery. By the middle of the decade there were twenty-three and more than sixty-five by the end of the decade. An estimated 3 million tourists visited the Niagara Peninsula in 1998. Hillebrand Estates Winery alone hosted 200,000 visitors and its restaurant served 70,000 meals.[14]

Improvement in wine quality, both in the vineyard and the winery, was certainly the most significant development of the decade. Money was available in the Grape and Wine Adjustment Program for research and technology. Increased awareness of the importance of clonal selection and drainage tiling in vineyards led to major changes in viticulture. As the industry grew, there was a pent-up demand for more research and training of people to work in vineyards and wineries.

In 1996, the Cool Climate Oenology and Viticulture Institute (CCOVI) was formed in St. Catharines as a partnership between Brock University and the grape and wine industry. To help CCOVI get started, Donald Ziraldo and John Howard of Vineland Estates Winery chaired a $4 million fund-raising campaign. The building housing CCOVI was named Inniskillin Hall in recognition of a $600,000 gift from Vincor International. Pledging support for a research chair were the Ontario Grape Growers' Marketing Board ($216,000) and the Wine Council of Ontario ($240,000). The first eight students were accepted into a three-year program in 1997.

Niagara College, located nearby in St. Catharines, began considering a grape and wine program in 1995 and, coordinating with Brock in 1998, set up a teaching demonstration vineyard. A year later an advisory committee was set up to survey the needs of the industry. A two-year undergraduate program was established in 2000 with twenty-five full-time students and a waiting list. A teaching winery opened on November 19, 2002, with Jim Warren in charge of the program.[15]

The dramatic improvement in the quality of Ontario wines was also due to the VQA, which had its rules and regulations in place by 1990. Adherence to these new standards by wineries making VQA wines was responsible for the increasing recognition of the quality of wines being made in Ontario. By 1994, sales of VQA wines had passed the million bottle mark and by the early 2000s, one million cases.[16]

One reason for the higher sales of VQA wines was the reputation established by Ontario icewines that had first been made commercially in 1983 (see appendix D). Five or six wineries had begun making icewine by 1985, but the event that caught everyone's attention came in 1989 when Inniskillin won the Citadelle d'Oro Grand Prix d'Honneur at VinExpo in Bordeaux. Suddenly, many wineries began to make icewine. Production in Ontario went from 2,000 cases in 1990 to 6,200 cases in 1992 to more than 10,000 cases in 1994. That number increased to 21,000 cases by the early 2000s. The success of Ontario icewine was a major factor leading to the treaty between Canada and the European Union (EU) in 2003 that gave Canadian wines free access to EU countries (see appendix D).

With so much promise in the future of the industry becoming apparent in the early 1990s, the rapid growth in the number of wineries was not surprising. The approximately 65 wineries at the end of the decade increased to about 150 in the next ten years. At the start it was mostly small wineries that opened, but by the end of the decade more and more money was invested in wineries. One of the first major building projects came in 1994 when Paul Bosc and his family opened the $6 million visitor-friendly Château des Charmes in the style of a Loire château. By 2001, several impressive wineries were built with the intention of attracting tourists: $7 million was invested in Peninsula Ridge Winery and comparable amounts in Andrés' Peller Estates Winery and Vincor's Jackson-Triggs Winery.

The 1990s also saw a consolidation of the large wineries. Donald L. Triggs was one of four investors who bought Château-Gai from the Canadian brewery John Labatt, Ltd. in 1989 and renamed it Cartier Wines, Ltd. Cartier and Inniskillin merged in 1992 and a further acquisition occurred in 1993 when Brights purchased all of the shares of Cartier-Inniskillin. The resulting company was named Vincor International, and Triggs became president and CEO. Vincor actively sought to expand and acquired wineries in the United States, Australia, and New Zealand. In 2003 it was the fourth largest winery in North America, and in 2006 it was bought by Constellation Brands for $1.27 billion in Canadian dollars.

A new wine region emerged in the mid-1990s when grape growing and winemaking began on the north side of Lake Ontario. Prince Edward County is a peninsula on the northeast corner of the lake extending south into Lake Ontario and is almost entirely surrounded by water. Early vineyard starts included 125 vines planted by Mike Peddlesden and Jamie Brauer in 1997 with 2000 more in 1998, and Geoff Heinrick's planting of 6,500 vines in 1996. The first winery was the County Cider Company opened by Grant Howes in 1996 in Waupoos.[17] By 2011 there were thirty-three wineries in Prince Edward County.

The VQA Program and Ontario Wine Exports

The "Rules and Regulations" that were approved in 1989 were applicable to a voluntary system. Wine standards were set and VQA labeling was used for certification purposes. On June 29, 2000, VQA Ontario was established as Ontario's wine authority after the passage of the Vintners Quality Alliance Act in 1999. Under an administrative agreement with the Ontario government, VQA Ontario is accountable to the Ontario Ministry of Consumer Services. As an independent regulatory authority, VQA was given the tools necessary to enforce its regulations, including the right to suspend or revoke VQA approvals and the power to prosecute violators with fines up to $100,000.

Two categories of appellation of origin have been established by the VQA: provincial and viticultural areas. Wines meeting provincial designation standards are permitted to use the word "Ontario" on their label. These wines must be made 100 percent from authorized varieties of Ontario-grown grapes, both vinifera and hybrids. This list consists of approximately seventy-two vinifera varieties, eight hybrids that may be given varietal designation, and another fifteen hybrid varieties that may be used in blends. Varietal wines must contain 85 percent of that grape variety and must exhibit the predominant varietal character of that variety as determined by the VQA tasting panel.

For a viticultural area designation, 85 percent of the grapes must come from one of three designated areas: Niagara Peninsula, Lake Erie North Shore, or Prince Edward County,[18] and 100 percent of the grapes must have been grown in Ontario. Only authorized vinifera varieties may be used. Varietal wines must be made from 85 percent of the designated grape variety, and the wine must show the varietal character of that grape.

A vineyard designated wine must be produced from authorized vinifera varieties only, and 100 percent of the grapes used must come from the designated vineyard, which in turn must be located in a designated viticultural area. Estate bottled wines must also be made only from authorized vinifera varieties and 100 percent from grapes grown in that vineyard. Further, the wine must not leave the winery before bottling. Varietal wines must meet minimum Brix levels.

Other quality standards have been set such as prohibiting the addition of water to any VQA wine. When the standards were finally established, it was decided to retain the European concept of the tighter the defined appellation of origin, the higher the standards for that wine. Thus, in what is called the hierarchy of standards, there is the provincial standard at one level, the designated viticultural areas one step higher up, and finally the estate bottled or vineyard designated wines at the top.

All VQA wines must be approved by the VQA Tasting Panel This panel is headed by the supervisor of quality control for the LCBO and has twenty-four permanent members, wine consultants employed by the board who have passed written and tasting tests. The wines passed by the tasting panel are then sent to the

LCBO laboratories for a regular analysis. Wines meeting all of the standards and tests are entitled to display the VQA trademark.

Most of the "Rules and Regulations" approved in 1989 were continued under VQA Ontario. One major change was the decision to reserve many geographical and winemaking terms exclusively for VQA use. Icewine, botrytized, late harvest wine, estate bottled, Niagara-on-the-Lake, and Niagara Peninsula were only a few terms that could not be used on the labels of any but VQA wines.

In 2000, Laurie Macdonald became the executive director of VQA Ontario. A major change occurred when increasing interest began to be shown in the creation of subappellations. After scientific research to set credible borders and studies of geology, soils, climate, topography, and growing conditions, twelve subappellations were added to VQA regulation in November 2005. Two of the twelve were based on the identifiable common use of terms, Niagara-on-the-Lake and Niagara Escarpment, where 85 percent of the grapes used to produce wine had to be grown there. Wineries in the other ten, which included such names as Twenty Mile Bench and Four Mile Creek, were required to use 100 percent of the grapes used in their subappellation.[19] In each case, except for Vidal for use in the production of icewine, the grapes used had to be entirely vinifera varieties.

During the next few years provinces other than Ontario began working toward the VQA appellation of origin system despite some disagreement about standards. While the impetus for starting a VQA system initially was to facilitate exporting wines to the EU, the latter began to insist that Canadian wine quality be determined by national rather than provincial standards. A new organization, VQA Canada, was created. In 2003 a trade agreement between Canada and the European Union gave Canadian wines free access to EU markets (see appendix D).

Minimum standards continue to be set in Ontario by the Wine Content Act, which is periodically reviewed and revised as necessary. VQA status is accorded to premium appellation wines only, and most Canadian wines are non-VQA wines.

Developments in Other Provinces

The Niagara Peninsula of Ontario was the earliest center of grape growing and winemaking in eastern Canada because its location between Lake Ontario and Lake Erie provided an ideal microclimate for growing grapes. Elsewhere in Ontario, and in other eastern Canadian provinces with similarly harsh winters, it took advances in viticulture and the identification of small microclimates for an industry to develop.

Nova Scotia

The first interest in growing wine grapes in Nova Scotia came in 1962 when Gordon B. Kinsman of the Nova Scotia Department of Agriculture and Marketing became

Figure 12.4: Robert A. Murray (*left*) Provincial Berry Crop Specialist in Nova Scotia, and Hans W. Jost conferred in 1984, the year in which Jost Vineyards had its first crush. Photo by author, 1984.

director of Horticulture and Biology Services and began reviewing the potential of various crops for the region. He felt that wine grapes should be considered, and he and Donald L. Craig, research scientist at Agriculture Canada's research station at Kentville, went to the Horticultural Research Institute of Ontario to discuss possible grape varieties for use in Nova Scotia with Ollie Bradt, the plant breeder at the institute.[20]

In May 1963, Robert A. Murray was appointed Provincial Berry Crop Specialist and was given the job of working with Craig on a wine grape program. Three test plots were established in three counties that year using grapes secured from Bradt. Among the varieties planted were the first French hybrids to arrive in Nova Scotia.

Two professors at Dalhousie University in Halifax founded the first farm winery, Grand Pré Wines at Grand Pré in the Annapolis Valley in 1980. Norman Morse had converted his vineyard to wine grapes in 1977 and Roger Dial planned to open a commercial winery. They planted the first of twenty-three acres of grapes in 1979 and delivered 200 cases of Maréchal Foch to the Nova Scotia Liquor Commission in the fall of 1980.[21] Production increased to approximately 20,000 cases in 1985. Unfortunately, a stock market plunge in 1987 led to the closing of the winery. It was subsequently purchased in 1993 by Hanspeter Stutz and reopened in June 2000 as Domaine de Grand Pré.

The second winery to open was Jost Vineyards by Hans W. and Erna Jost, who came from Germany and settled near Malagash along the Northumberland Strait. In Germany, Jost had studied viticulture and enology at Geisenheim and had owned the Christinehof Winery near Mainz along the Rhine. Jost met Craig in 1978 and was given a few vines and 750 pounds of grapes. At the time of the first crush in 1984 there were eighteen acres in the ground.

About this time Jost learned that he was seriously ill and in 1985 he sent his son Hans Christian Jost to Germany for six months to study under Helmut Becker, chief of the Geisenheim Grape Breeding Institute. Late that year the winery had its formal opening. After his father's death in 1987, Hans Christian Jost took over the management of the winery. By 2004 he and his wife Karen had forty-five acres of vineyards and were making 40,000 cases a year. In addition, in 1996, they bought property in the Gaspereau Valley where they planted thirty-seven acres of grapes. In 2004 the Josts opened a second winery, Gaspereau Vineyards.

Suzanne and Doug Corkum opened Sainte-Famille Winery in Falmouth in the Avon River Valley in 1990. The first of their thirty acres of grapes was planted in 1979, and their winery is considered to be one of the original "Big Three."

When Grand Pré Wines and Jost Vineyards first opened, their wines could not be sold at the winery. All wines in the province had to be sold through the Nova Scotia Liquor Commission stores. If they wanted to have tastings at their wineries, the wines had to be purchased through the commission's stores. The Grape Growers Association of Nova Scotia was formed in the fall of 1982 and began working with the provincial government and the Liquor Commission to liberalize the laws. The Farm Wine Policy that was passed in early 1986, allowed wineries that had a minimum of a ten-acre vineyard adjacent to the winery to sell on their premises 350 cases of wine for each acre of grapes, hold tastings, and deliver their wines to restaurants as well as Liquor Commission stores.

Wineries were allowed to serve food in 1991, and in 1993 Sunday afternoon sales were permitted. Farm wineries were not allowed to produce fruit wines until 1992 when a Cottage Winery Policy was adopted. Wineries had to have a minimum of ten acres of fruit in production and have the capacity to produce between 10,000 and 60,000 liters of wine annually. The 1986 Farm Winery Policy did not specify any minimum content of Nova Scotia grapes, and it was not until 1998 that farm wineries were required to have a minimum of 35 percent of Nova Scotia grapes in their wines.

In 2000, a new class of winery license was established, the Small Farm Winery license. The minimum acreage requirement was reduced to two, and the Nova Scotia content of their wines was set at 90 percent for grape wines and 100 percent for wines made from other agricultural products.

In May 2002, the Winery Association of Nova Scotia was formed, and its initial goal was to set Nova Scotia wine standards, which were adopted on June 28, 2005. The quality standards established included a range of permissible alcohol content from 8.5 percent to 14.9 percent, a minimum of 15°Brix for grapes at harvest, and regulations for the production of sparkling wines, icewines and other wines.

The Farm Winery Policy is revised from time to time, and the regulations are developed by the individual wineries working together with the Department of Agriculture, the Grape Growers Association of Nova Scotia, the Winery Association of Nova Scotia, and the Nova Scotia Liquor Corporation, which had changed its name from the Nova Scotia Liquor Commission on January 1, 2001. In July 2002, the Nova Scotia Liquor Corporation broke away from its strict monopoly by establishing four private wine and specialty stores. The Farm Winery Policy was revised in 2007 to set standards that would enable the farm wineries to enter into a contract with the Nova Scotia Liquor Corporation for the sale of their wines in the private wine stores. In 2010, there were fourteen farm wineries, thirty grape growers, and 475 acres of grapes in Nova Scotia.

Québec

Winter temperatures in Québec can drop below -30° Fahrenheit and temperatures stay below freezing from early December until the end of March. Two of the pioneers in viticulture in Québec who made the modern grape and wine industry possible were Christian Barthomeuf and Charles-Henri de Coussergues. Barthomeuf planted twenty-three acres of vines in 1980 and later founded Domaine des Côtes d'Ardoise in Dunham; and de Coussergues, who became one of four partners who founded Vignoble de l'Orpailleur in Dunham, planted a large vineyard in 1982. They identified wine grape varieties that could be successfully grown in Québec, notably Seyval Blanc, and began the practice of burying the vines in winter that enabled them to survive.[22]

In 1985 the government of Québec issued the first five cottage winery licenses. They were, in order of their license numbers: La Vitacée in St-Barbe, Vignoble Angell in St-Bernard de Lacolle, Domaine des Côtes d'Ardoise in Dunham, Vignoble de l'Orpailleur in Dunham, and Vignoble St-Alexandre (originally La Farma Abrutrezzi) in St-Alexandre.

The original five wineries in Québec were located in favorable microclimates south and east of Montreal. After 1992, vineyard plantings spread to the northern side of the St. Lawrence River between Montreal and Québec City, and the Québec City area itself. Very little vinifera is grown in Québec because of the climate. Although

Figure 12.5: Christian Barthomeuf (*right*) was one of the pioneering viticulturists in Québec and planted 23 acres of vines in 1980. He and Jacques Papillon founded Domaine des Côtes d'Ardoise in Dunham, the third cottage winery to open in Québec. Barthomeuf is credited with making the first ice cider in 1989. Photo by author, 1991.

French hybrid varieties such as Seyval Blanc and Maréchal Foch are still widely grown, there is increasing interest and plantings of Minnesota and Swenson hybrids such as Frontenac, Frontenac Gris, Marquette, Sabrevois, and Louise Swenson. A very hardy white wine variety developed in Québec, Vandal-Cliche, is also grown.[23]

Gilles Benoit, owner of Vignobles des Pins in Sabrevois, has been in the forefront of those experimenting with new varieties of grapes. His success with a red wine made from an Elmer Swenson cross, ES 5-2-1-9, led to an agreement to name the variety Sabrevois, and he has also experimented with growing vinifera in his vineyard.

Along with the first cottage winery licenses issued in 1985, wineries got the right to sell wine on their premises. In 1987, the Québec Association of Winegrowers was formed. By 2010, there were fifty-five wineries and about 650 acres of vineyards in Québec.

Tourism is expected to play an increasing role in the growth of the Québec industry. One winery that has become a showcase is Vignoble de la Chapelle Ste Agnès in Sutton. Founded by Montreal antique dealer Henrietta Antony, the winery has an eighteen-terrace vineyard, cellars on four underground levels, and a chapel built of solid stone in a Romanesque style.

Apple wine and cider are also important products made by a number of Québec wineries. Christian Barthomeuf is given credit for making the first cidre de glace, or ice cider, in 1989. He had made icewine in the 1980s and decided he could use the same technique by pressing apples frozen on the trees.[24] It takes eighty apples to make a 375-milliliter bottle of ice cider and a harder freeze is required than for icewine. The selling price for ice cider is comparable to icewine.

The Far Eastern and Western Provinces

Prince Edward Island has one winery, Rossignol Estate Winery in Murray River, which was opened by John and Lyn Rossignol in 1995. Their first vines were planted in 1993 and that same year John Rossignol began the process of getting the laws changed to provide for farm wineries.[25]

Newfoundland's first winery, Rodrigues Winery, was founded by Dr. Hilary Rodrigues and his wife Marie-France in 1993. Originally called Markland Cottage Winery when it opened in an historic cottage hospital, it went through a major expansion in 1998 and is now Canada's largest exclusive fruit wine winery with annual production of 25,000 cases. In 1997, Grant Young founded Auk Island Winery in Twillingate. In 2010, there were four wineries in Newfoundland.

In New Brunswick, the Department of Agriculture and other groups cooperated in 1998 to establish a winery program. Werner and Roswitha Rosswog of Baie Verte were a major force in the start of the New Brunswick wine industry. They received the province's first farm winery license and opened their Winegarden Estate Winery in 2002. By 2011, there were fourteen wineries in New Brunswick.

Wineries opened in the prairie provinces of Alberta, Manitoba, and Saskatchewan in the late 1990s and early 2000s. Most of the wineries primarily make fruit wines. In Saskatchewan, Banach Winery in Battleford opened in 1996 selling chokecherry wine. Marty and Marie Bohnet in Maple Creek became the first to plant grapes commercially in 2004 and opened their Cypress Hills Vineyard and Winery in 2007. Rigby Orchards Estate Winery in Killarney, Manitoba, planted fourteen acres of raspberries in 1987 and opened the winery in 1999. A second winery, D. D. Leobard, followed in 2000 in Winnipeg. In Alberta, the first cottage winery, Field Stone Fruit Wines, opened in Strathmore in 2005. The first certified organic cottage winery, en Santé Winery in Brosseau, was opened by Victor and Elizabeth Chrapko in 2006.

Fruit Wines of Canada

Fruit wines, a rapidly growing segment of the wine industry, cannot qualify for VQA status because in Europe wine is defined and recognized as coming only from grapes. Because of this qualification, a Canadian association called Fruit Wines of Canada was formed to create its own national quality standards for fruit wines.

In 1999, Sharon Burke, a senior trade officer with the Federal Ministry of Agriculture in Guelph, observed that Ontario's fruit wineries were suffering from both a lack of credibility and marketing. She suggested that the fruit wineries form an association to access government funding to help change the perception of fruit wines in Ontario. Provincial and federal funding were obtained, and the Fruit Wines of Ontario was started with twelve members. Within a year and a half it grew to twenty-two members. With Jim Warren as executive director, a second draft of rules, regulations, and quality standards was approved by the association members by October 27, 1999.

Fruit wine people from all over Canada met at the Toronto Wine and Cheese Show in March 2000. The first All-Canada Fruit Wine Competition had already been held in January of that year, and there was interest in establishing Canada-wide production and labeling standards. Christine Coletta from British Columbia, a consultant hired with federal funds, played a leadership role in providing organization, controlling dialogue, and attempting to arrive at a national consensus. The result was the creation of a national association of producers called Fruit Wines of Canada and the establishment of a Quality Certified (QC) program modeled on the VQA system for Canadian table wines. The Fruit Wine Quality Certified System was established at the end of the summer in 2000 and by the summer of the following year, 150 QC wines from three provinces had been approved and were for sale.

Included in the standards was a list of authorized fruit varieties that contained twenty-one varieties of fruits plus maple, honey, natural spices, cider, and rhubarb. Several categories of fruit wine were identified: iced fruit wine, fortified fruit wine, sparkling fruit wine, fruit table wine, cider, perry, and fruit coolers. Among other provisions, fruit wines were permitted to have a provincial or a Canadian geographic designation. Varietal fruit wines had to bear the name of an authorized fruit and have the appropriate character of that fruit. Blended fruit wines had to have the list of varieties used on the back label. Vintage dating was permitted along with both farm and estate bottled designations.[26]

In order to achieve QC status, a fruit wine must pass a sensory evaluation by the Fruit Wine Quality Certified tasting panel and laboratory analysis by the provincial liquor board. In Ontario the panel that does the tasting for VQA wines performs the same service for QC wines. Their tasting panel consists of the supervisor of quality control for the LCBO (or his or her designated alternate) plus six permanent members. The members must be wine consultants employed by the LCBO who have passed both written and tasting tests and, in addition, taken a one-day fruit wine training seminar conducted by the Fruit Wines of Canada. All wines are tasted blind in their various categories and are scored using a twenty-point scale. For varietal fruit wines, varietal character is an important part of the overall score.

All products passing the tasting panel are sent to the LCBO laboratories for routine analysis. Wines meeting all the standards and tests are entitled to display the QC trademark as part of their package and the letters FWQC (Fruit Wine Quality Certified) on the label. Wines that pass all the tests and score 14.0 or better may use the FWQC seal as part of their packaging.

CHAPTER THIRTEEN

❧

THE NEW CENTURY

THE TOP NEWS STORY OF THE FIRST DECADE OF THE TWENTY-FIRST CENTURY WOULD have to be the explosion in the number of wineries in eastern North America. In 2000, there were approximately 900 wineries in the eastern United States and Canada, and by the end of the decade, that number had tripled. During those ten years the number of eastern wineries in Canada increased by about 75 to 240 and in the United States by 1,735 to 2,538. At the end of 2011, according to the figures released by the Alcohol and Tobacco Tax and Trade Bureau (TTB), the eastern United States gained an additional 244 wineries for a total of 2,782.

Continued Trends of Growth

Table 6.1 provides a clear picture of the growth of the wine industry in the eastern United States, by listing the number of bonded wineries in each state at five-year intervals from 1975 to 2010. Between 2000 and 2005, 434 new wineries opened, and 1,104 more from 2005 to 2010. In 2000, only New York had more than 100 wineries; in 2010 there were eight states with more than 100 wineries each. The number of wineries in some states increased more rapidly than in others. New York had 363 wineries in 2010, up from 165 in 2000; Virginia, which had the second most number of wineries in 2010 with 237, moved up from 65 in 2000. In North Carolina, there was a 710 percent increase in the number of wineries during the decade, from 19 to 136.

Of the states that had over 100 wineries in 2010, New York, Ohio, Pennsylvania, Michigan, and Missouri ranked consistently among the top eight in numbers from 1975 to 2010. These were the states where the industry got off to its fastest start.

States with cold climates were slower to get their wine industry underway, but advances in viticultural knowledge enabled them to develop an industry quickly. New Hampshire went from one winery in 1990 to five in 2000 to thirty-four in 2010. Three other states had similar increases during the same time period—Vermont went from four to eight to thirty-one; Maine from five to six to thirty; Minnesota from five to fourteen to fifty-two.

In the South, where Pierce's disease has always been a continuing problem, the development of new grape varieties and planting grapes at higher elevations led to a similar pattern of growth in several states. Louisiana went from one winery in 1990 to seven in 2000 to eleven in 2010; Alabama from four to five to fifteen; Florida, seven to thirteen to seventy-five. Within the same time periods, two states west of the Mississippi River that got a later start soon made up for lost time. Kansas went from two wineries to seven to twenty-nine; and Nebraska, which had no wineries in 1990, had four in 2000, and twenty-nine in 2010.

The development of the industry in the East became much more uniform after 2000. In most states, the legal barriers to the establishment of wineries had been removed or substantially eased as the advantages of having a wine industry became more obvious. Viticultural knowledge had reached the level where techniques of dealing with low winter temperatures and the proper application of sprays had led to far fewer problems in the vineyards.

The increased interest in planting vineyards resulted in many workshops for beginners. In Nebraska, where the industry was just getting started in the late 1990s, more than 200 people attended the state's first annual grape and small fruit field day on August 12, 2000, the hottest day of the summer, to learn about trellising systems, end post assemblies, and sixty grape cultivars on trial. In Pennsylvania, Maryland, and Virginia extension agents worked together to hold workshops for new growers, often more than once a year with more than 100 people in attendance at each workshop.

The number of conferences increased, giving opportunities for people to learn at every level of experience. Viticulture 2000, held at Adam's Mark Hotel in Buffalo in February 2000, attracted more than 400 growers from New York, eleven other states, and Ontario. What was supposed to be a one-time event was subsequently repeated in later years. The first annual Cold Climate Grape and Wine Conference sponsored by the Minnesota Grape Growers Association was held in February 2005 in Rochester, Minnesota, and quickly established itself as a well-attended conference.

Other support services became more available. A greater number of consultants and laboratories started to do analytical testing. Those who wanted someone else to do the work could contract vineyard and winery services. Increasingly, assistance and services became available online.

Investment in Long Island

By 1999 the industry on Long Island had reached the point where investors were willing to make multimillion dollar investments in the future of the industry.[1] In that year the Hargraves sold their vineyard and winery to Marco Borghese, a member of a prominent wine family in Tuscany, and his wife Ann Marie for $4 million. The winery was renamed Castello di Borghese: Hargrave Vineyard. In the same year, Ray Blum sold Peconic Bay Vineyards in Cutchogue for $2 million to Paul Lowerre, a Manhattan investment consultant, and his wife Ursula; and Laurel Lake Vineyards in Laurel was purchased by a consortium of Chilean investors for $2.7 million. Michael Lynne, president and CEO of New Line Cinema, acquired two wineries— Corey Creek Vineyards in Southold for $2 million in 1999 and Bedell Cellars in Cutchogue a year later for $5 million. In 2000, telecommunications executive Vince Galluccio and his wife Judy bought Gristina Vineyards for $5.2 million.

Other very conspicuous start-up operations were also underway. Martha Clara Vineyards in Riverhead, owned by Robert Entenmann of the Entenmann baked goods family, planted 112 acres of grapes from 1996 to 2000 and spent an estimated $6 million on a tasting room and winery. In 1997, Raphael in Peconic, owned by John and Joan Petrocelli, planted the first of sixty acres of vineyards, over forty-three of them in Merlot. The $6 million winery, where the decision had been made to specialize in Merlot, opened in 2001 under the guidance of its consultant Paul Pontallier, the managing director of Château Margaux in Bordeaux, who first visited Long Island during the Bordeaux Symposium in 1998.

In 1978, Christian Wölffer, a German investment banker and owner of a venture capital company, bought fourteen acres of land in Sagaponack on the South Fork as a weekend getaway and started a horse farm that eventually developed into an equestrian center with the largest indoor riding ring in the East. The first grapes were planted in 1988 on what had become a 170-acre property, and when Wölffer Estate Vineyard celebrated its twentieth anniversary there were fifty-five acres of grapes and the winery was producing 16,000 cases of wine annually. Roman Roth was hired as the winemaker in 1992 and later, with Wölffer's blessing, he obtained his own farm winery license and made his own wines at Wölffer Estate under his own brand name "The Grapes of Roth."[2]

The first custom crush winery in the East was established in 2000 in Mattituck. The idea of starting the Premium Wine Group was that of Australian-born winemaker Russell Hearn, and in partnership with Mark Lieb and Bernard Sussman a state-of-the-art facility was built with a total capacity of 250,000 gallons.[3]

Education by Institutions

Opportunities for education by colleges and universities greatly expanded after 2000, in part to meet the growing need already established vineyards and wineries had for trained employees. Sometimes the support came from the industry as was the case when a wine technology program was started at Loyalist College in Belleville, Ontario, in September 2000, in cooperation with the Prince Edward County Wine Growers' Association. The College offered its research and laboratory facilities while the growers offered their vineyards to train students. In Dobson, North Carolina, Surry Community College began a continuing education program in viticulture in its Department of Agriculture, which became a Viticulture and Enology Technology Program in 2000. Initially it was thought that the program would serve students who were interested in being trained to work in the industry, but they found that many adults over the age of thirty from many walks of life enrolled because they wanted a new career. The North Carolina Center for Viticulture and Enology opened at the college in 2010. Starting in September 2001, Michigan State University in East Lansing created a two-year technical training program in grape growing and winemaking to prepare people to be qualified for jobs in the industry.

Missouri has a long history of helping the industry that dates back to 1986 when grape and wine research and an advisory program were established at Southwest Missouri State University at Mountain Grove with major funding assistance from the Missouri grape and wine industry. In 2000, the university established the Mid-America Viticulture and Enology Center to provide research, education, and service to Missouri and other Midwestern states. Three years later, in 2003, with a grant from the National Science Foundation (NSF), the center formed the Viticulture and Enology Science and Technology Alliance (VESTA) with three two-year community colleges in three other states to meet the need for trained industry workers.[4]

With a third grant from the NSF in 2011, VESTA was able to expand its partnerships to higher education institutions in seventeen states from coast to coast. Twenty-five online viticulture and enology courses were available and both certificate and applied science degree programs had been established. By 2012, more than 750 students had enrolled in online courses. In 2006, the Missouri Wine and Grape Board opened a second research center, the Institute for Continental Climate, Viticulture and Enology at the University of Missouri in Columbia, under the direction of Dr. Keith Striegler to serve Missouri with programs in research and extension.[5]

Changes also took place at the long-established research stations in New York and Ontario. At Cornell University's New York State Agricultural Experiment Station at Geneva, the retirement of Robert Pool on December 31, 2005, and the decision by Thomas Henick-Kling to leave the station a year later led to appointments of younger faculty members in both the viticulture and enology departments. In January 2007, Ramón Mira de Orduña Heidinger was hired as associate professor of enology; Gavin Sacks as assistant professor of enology; Justine Vanden Heuvel as assistant professor of viticulture; and, in February 2008, Christopher Gerling was appointed to the position of extension associate in enology.

To meet the demand for trained winemakers and viticulturists in New York and the East, Cornell created a four-year undergraduate program in 2004 with majors

Figure 13.1: Thomas Henick-Kling was the director of Cornell University's enology program at Geneva from 1987 to 2006. Among his many contributions was the creation of the Vinification and Brewing Technology Laboratory in 2000. Photo by author, 2006.

in enology and viticulture leading to a B.S. degree. The program, headquartered in Ithaca, utilized faculty from several departments in Ithaca, Geneva, and the U.S. Department of Agriculture's Plant Genetic Resources Unit in Geneva.[6] A teaching winery for use in the program was opened in Ithaca on April 1, 2009. (See appendix F about the first American wine course for credit at Cornell in 1953.)

Cornell's laboratory and grape research facility in Fredonia, New York, which had been under increasing development pressure, was relocated to Portland, New York, and renamed the Cornell Lake Erie Research and Extension Laboratory. The new facility opened on August 25, 2009, with Dr. Terry Bates as director.

As part of a budget-cutting move by the province of Ontario, the Ministry of Agriculture, Food and Rural Affairs transferred the operation of the Horticultural Research Institute of Ontario at Vineland to the University of Guelph on April 1, 1997. On February 1, 1998, the institute and three agricultural colleges became part of its Department of Agriculture—Vineland Campus. The province, however, retained ownership of the physical property including the land and buildings, and in August 2006, the Ontario minister of agriculture, food and rural affairs, Leona Dombrowsky, established the Vineland Renaissance Advisory Panel under the chairmanship of Donald Ziraldo to recommend ways to revitalize the Vineland Research Station. The panel recommended an expanded horticultural research

Figure 13.2: In addition to being the founding chairman of VQA, Donald J. P. Ziraldo was a leader in many projects that helped the wine industry in Ontario. He cochaired the committee to establish the CCOVI, chaired the capital campaign to found the Niagara Culinary Institute at Niagara College, and chaired the committee that established the Vineland Research and Innovation Centre and then served as its chairman. Photo by author, 2010.

institution capable of carrying out leading edge research and generating substantial revenues as a result of its research.[7]

In January 2007, the Vineland Research and Innovation Centre was established with Ziraldo as its chair. A partnership agreement was signed with the University of Guelph in August whereby the centre would take over the operation of the facility and work closely with the university on research related to the former's priorities. Research at the centre was not limited to viticulture but included many other aspects of horticulture.

At Brock University in St. Catharines, Debra Inglis was named the new director of the Cool Climate Oenology and Viticulture Institute (CCOVI) in 2008 and given the assignment of implementing changes that were already being planned. The CCOVI was for the first time permitted to expand into areas other than grape and wine research and services. Business and marketing were included, and Inglis had to develop a five-year plan that would also establish research priorities and measure research outcomes. In 2009, the CCOVI received major funding from the government and the Ontario industry that would allow for new research into winter hardiness and flavor chemistry and also develop outreach programs for Ontario grape growers and winemakers based on their priority needs.

The first step toward establishing a national grape and wine research network was in 2010 when the CCOVI and the Pacific Agri-Food Research Centre in British Columbia signed an agreement linking eastern and western Canada. In addition to strengthening cooperation and communications between researchers in the two provinces, joint research can be undertaken to address national priorities. Nova Scotia and other provinces are expected to become part of the network.

Niagara College in Niagara-on-the-Lake established a two-year Winery and Viticulture Technician Diploma Program in 2000, opened a teaching winery in 2002, and a culinary center with a teaching restaurant in January 2004. A Wine Education and Visitor Centre housing classrooms, labs, tasting counter, and space for meetings and seminars opened on November 5, 2009, with England's Prince Charles in attendance at the inaugural. In September 2009, prior to the harvest, the teaching winery moved into the Visitor Centre.

Also at Niagara College, a graduate program called Wine Business Management was started in 2008, a Brewmaster and Brewery Operations Management program was first opened to students in September 2010, and a teaching brewery was added a few months later. All of the culinary, wine, and beer programs were consolidated by Niagara College into their Canadian Food & Wine Institute created in September 2010.

Wine Quality

Recognition of the need to improve wine quality continued to grow with major initiatives in Pennsylvania and Ohio. In July 2003, an initiative started by Janet and Frederick Maki, owners of French Creek Ridge Vineyards in Elverson, Pennsylvania, resulted in the formation of the Pennsylvania Premium Wine Group by fourteen limited wineries in Pennsylvania.[8] The purpose of the organization was to raise the image of Pennsylvania wines in the eyes of sophisticated consumers by improving winemaking standards and increasing public awareness. A quality seal would be created for dry table and sparkling wines made by Pennsylvania wineries from Pennsylvania-grown vinifera grapes. An independent "blue ribbon" tasting panel would do the judging. On September 7, 2003, a panel selected forty-five wines as the first to receive Pennsylvania Quality Assurance seals. No chemical analyses were required in the early years but were later mandated to be performed prior to the wines being presented to the tasting panel.

On October 15, 2003, Stephen Menke was appointed to become Pennsylvania's first state enologist. A primary goal in hiring him was to establish a statewide Pennsylvania Wine Quality Initiative.[9] After funding for the program was secured from the Pennsylvania Wine Research and Marketing Board, he began a series of sensory evaluation training sessions. In 2008, he left Pennsylvania to accept a position at the University of Colorado and Mario Mazza of Mazza Vineyards in North East was asked to continue the training sessions. Denise M. Gardner, the state enologist appointed in 2011, is also involved in the program.

The idea of forming an Ohio Quality Wine Assurance Program began in 1999 when members of the Ohio Agricultural Research and Development Center (OARDC), the Ohio Wine Producers Association, and interested members of the Ohio wine industry discussed the idea and developed a rough draft as a proposal. Nothing happened until 2004 when the Ohio Department of Agriculture authorized a voluntary quality assurance program and gave the responsibility for its implementation to the Ohio Grape Industries Committee and the Viticulture and Enology Program at Ohio State's OARDC.

After examining programs in Ontario, New Jersey, and Washington state, a pilot quality seal program was initiated with the 2007 Ohio Wine Competition.[10] All wines had to pass both sensory evaluation and chemical analysis before achieving the Ohio Quality Wine seal designation. In later years three separate evaluation sessions a year were established—in February, July, and August. Todd Steiner, Ohio's state enologist and the enology program manager and outreach specialist at OARDC, has been in charge of the sensory evaluation and chemical analysis parts of the program. Moreover, the Ohio Grape Industries Committee administers a marketing component.

Other states have shown interest in establishing similar programs. With marketing and promotion being inseparable considerations, the trend toward increased quality will continue. As difficult as it has been sometimes, quality has to be the foundation on which the future eastern wine industry is built.

Economic Impact

The wine industry in the United States has always been subject to legislation in Congress for its survival and for its growth. When two wineries in North Dakota opened in 2002, all fifty states in the United States had wineries for the first time. This meant that each state had two senators with wineries in it and that each winery had a representative in its district. This gave the industry the chance to propose or influence legislation on its behalf, if the wineries were willing to back it, or lobby against it if the wineries were willing to organize to oppose it. At the state level, legislative action can also help its wineries out or cause them harm. Not every district in the state, however, is likely to have a winery.

From a political standpoint, the industry has stood to gain from its increased numbers. But politics can be fickle and carefully built friendships can be swept away by an election or public outcry. What the industry needed was a solid reason why it should be supported by government. That reason turned out to be the economic value of the industry.

On January 17, 2007, on Capitol Hill in Washington, DC, the Congressional Wine Caucus released the results of a comprehensive study by MKF Research

LLC of St. Helena, California, that showed that the United States wine, grape, and grape products industries were contributing more than $162 billion annually to the country's economy. This was the first compilation of reliable, credible figures documenting the national economic impact of the industry. Representative Mike Thompson (D-CA), cochair of the 182-member Congressional Wine Caucus, had this to say about the importance of the landmark study:

> Grapes, wine, and other grape products are truly an economic catalyst with tremendous growth potential in all 50 states. Policymakers can maximize these economic benefits by supporting legislation that enhances the wine and grape-product industry. Our support will ensure that this all-American industry continues to produce superior products and provide a strong contribution to our economy.[11]

Among the highlights of the study were figures that showed that the wine and grape industries were responsible for 1.1 million full-time equivalent jobs, $33 billion in wages, $9.1 billion in federal taxes paid, and $8 billion in state and local taxes. The nation's 4,929 wineries had $11.4 billion in revenues; the 23,856 grape growers with 934,750 bearing acres had grape sales of $3.5 billion. The retail value of grape juice and juice product sales was $2.8 billion, table grape sales $3 billion, and raisin sales $560 million. The retail and restaurant share of revenue from sales of U.S. wines was $9.8 billion, and the distributor share was $2.7 billion. An important result of the study was that there were 27.3 million wine-related tourist visits with estimated wine-related tourism expenditures of $3 billion.[12]

MKF Research published its first state economic impact study for the California industry in 2000 and followed it up with a study for Washington state. Jim Trezise, president of the New York Wine and Grape Foundation, saw the California study when it was first released and knew that a similar study would help him secure funding for the New York industry in Albany as well as in the interstate shipment battle described in the next section.[13] The Empire State Development Corporation provided a grant for the New York study. Barbara Insel, managing director of MKF, oversaw the study, which was published in 2005.[14] When the study was released, the foundation published a graph titled "What's in a Bottle of Wine? $6 Billion" and called wine "the ultimate value-added product (and pleasure of life)." A copyright symbol at the bottom of the graph was followed by the words "Please copy like crazy."

Trezise felt so strongly that economic impact studies of the kind developed for New York could make a difference in promoting the wine industry in other states and the nation that he embarked on a personal crusade to make it happen. Not only did he contact other states—about fifteen states contracted MKF for such studies—but he got four national organizations to sponsor a national study (with the foundation being a major financial contributor) and then provided the coordination to see that it happened. It was a triumph for Trezise when the national study was released by the

Congressional Caucus on January 17, 2007, and subsequently on February 7, 2007, at the opening plenary session of Viticulture 2007.

The major value of the MKF Research studies was to provide solid facts for national, state and local legislators, chambers of commerce, and other organizations with a vested interest in economic growth. With an independent research organization doing the studies using a standard and widely used methodology, the facts and figures released had credibility.

The Direct Shipping Issue

By its very nature, the wine industry has always been susceptible to attack by organized groups willing to spend money and influence to advance their particular agenda (see chapter 11). A different kind of threat to the success of the industry emerged at the beginning of the twenty-first century when the direct shipment of wine became an issue. On May 16, 2005, the United States Supreme Court handed down a long awaited ruling that states could no longer discriminate in the direct shipment of wine to consumers. They could no longer ban or restrict out-of-state wineries from shipping to consumers in their state if in-state wineries were permitted to do so. Direct shipping had been a controversial issue in the 1990s and continued to cause problems for the wine industry after the Supreme Court's decision.

When Prohibition ended, each state had to decide how to distribute wine and other alcoholic beverages within its borders. Some states established a state store system to handle the importation and sale of wine. More commonly, states created a three-tier system of distribution where a producer such as a winery could only sell to wholesalers who would then sell to retailers who in turn would sell to consumers.[15] There was no other legal way for wine to be distributed interstate.

It was convenient for large wineries to use wholesalers. In the mid-1950s there were more than 5,000 wholesalers in the United States, but by 2002 there were less than 400.[16] This meant that the remaining wholesalers represented more wineries and became less interested in handling wines from small wineries.

The small farm wineries founded in the 1970s and 1980s were generally permitted to sell wine in their own tasting rooms and to consumers within their states. As time went by, these wineries needed additional markets for their wines and, with the growth of tourism, their customers in other states wanted to have wines shipped directly to them. The wineries could not afford to sell their wines at half price to wholesalers, and the wholesalers had no interest in adding low volume accounts to their books.

A 1986 change helped smaller wineries when the state of California passed legislation providing for the two-way direct shipment of wine between states that signed an agreement to accept each other's wines. In states where the three-tier system was in effect, this became the only legal way wine could be shipped interstate without going through the wholesalers.[17] By 2004, there were thirteen states with reciprocal agreements, thirteen plus the District of Columbia that allowed limited direct wine shipments, and twenty-four that completely banned interstate shipment.

There were, of course, sales outside the three-tier system by individuals and even retailers who were willing to take a risk to get wines that were not available in their own state. In an article published in *Wines and Vines* in 2001, Russ Bridenbaugh estimated that, in 1995, 2 percent of what he called the "gray market" escaped the three-tier system.[18] Since the vast majority of wine sales were local, the gray market coexisted with the three-tier system until 1995 when the largest wholesaler in the South, Southern Wine and Spirits, decided to go after the 2 percent gray market. According to Bridenbaugh, "It funneled $60,000 to the state's legislators in the year and a half it took to get Florida's existing anti-shipping law upgraded to felony status." By the time Florida's felony law was passed in 1997, Kentucky had passed its own felony shipping law in 1996.

The penalties for violating the felony laws were severe and included heavy fines and possible jail time. Wineries, shipping services, and even consumers could be charged. For wineries, the worst scenario of all would be the loss of their winery license because the regulations of the Bureau of Alcohol, Tobacco, and Firearms stated that convicted felons could not hold federal bonded winery licenses. Intimidation and fear were enough to keep shipping services from handling wine. Preventing sales to minors and keeping the states from losing excise taxes were reasons given by wholesalers to get felony laws passed. Seven states had felony shipping laws by 1998 and wholesaler profits were at a record high.

In 1998, Indiana passed a felony shipping law that consumers almost immediately challenged in federal court as being unconstitutional.[19] For the first time, the grounds for the challenge were that the law violated the Commerce Clause of the U.S. Constitution, which would take precedence over the Twenty-First Amendment. The Indiana felony law was ruled unconstitutional in December 1999, but the legal argument continued on in federal court cases in other states. It became a battle between the Twenty-First Amendment, which gave states the right to regulate the control of alcohol, and the Commerce Clause of the Constitution, which gave Congress the power to regulate interstate commerce.

Wholesalers now had a new concern, the slow but rising sales of wine on the Internet, and they had the money to keep fighting direct shipping. Soon, in 2002 and 2003, federal courts had to decide if states could allow wineries to ship directly to in-state consumers while prohibiting out-of-state wineries from shipping wine to consumers in their states. In Texas, North Carolina, Virginia, and Michigan, laws banning interstate shipment were found to be in violation of the Commerce Clause, while in New York the ban on direct shipping was upheld.[20] Legislatures in Texas, North Carolina, and Virginia passed legislation to comply with the courts' decisions. Michigan and New York, however, chose to petition the U.S. Supreme Court to grant a *writ of certiorari,* and on May 24, 2004, the Supreme Court agreed to hear three cases, two originating in Michigan and one in New York.

Many in the industry hoped that having the Supreme Court take up the issue would clarify the direct shipping issue once and for all.[21] However, when the Court handed down its ruling on May 16, 2005, it was a 5–4 split decision that was very narrow in scope, and held that states cannot discriminate in the direct shipment of wine to consumers. In the majority opinion, Justice Anthony M. Kennedy wrote that "States may not enact laws that burden out-of-state producers or shippers simply to give a competitive advantage to in-state producers."[22] The decision left states with two options: to permit out-of-state direct shipment or prohibit in-state shipment. It was also probable that wholesalers and their trade associations would not take the decision lightly, and that a significant amount of lobbying money would be spent in an effort to persuade legislators in affected states to ban interstate shipping.[23]

It did not take long for state legislatures to react to the *Granholm* decision, as the Supreme Court ruling had come to be known, with varying outcomes.[24] Within a few months, New York and Connecticut passed favorable interstate shipping bills, and Louisiana and Rhode Island repealed shipment rights of local wineries. Court orders in Florida and Ohio opened their states to interstate shipping until their legislatures reconvened and new shipment rules could be debated. In Michigan, wholesalers tried to jam a bill through the legislature to repeal shipping and wholesaling rights of in-state wineries prior to the summer recess, but wineries and a well-organized consumer movement prevented passage of the bill.[25]

Minnesota passed a direct shipping bill in June 2005, permitting in-state and out-of-state wineries to ship not more than two cases of wine a year to Minnesota residents over the age of twenty-one and exempted these shipments from state tax. Strangely, one section of the bill called an "Advertising and Internet Speech Ban" favored Minnesota's liquor stores over wineries. Both in-state and out-of-state wineries were forbidden from accepting orders online from Minnesotans and, even though direct shipping itself became legal, wineries were prohibited from advertising their direct shipping services to consumers. Conversely, the state liquor stores were allowed to sell wine online and advertise their direct shipping services. This section was immediately challenged in court and was overturned in April 2006. Wineries could then sell wine on the Internet and advertise their services.[26]

In Virginia, where the direct shipping issue seemed to have been resolved favorably in 2003, wineries lost not only their shipping rights but the right to self-distribute their wines by using their employees or agents. They also lost their exclusive right to sell wine in the state's approximately 300 ABC stores. Wholesalers opposed every attempt the wineries made in the legislature to have their shipping rights restored until 2007. In that year, with wholesaler approval, a less than satisfactory solution was found. The General Assembly authorized the Virginia Department of Agriculture and Consumer Services to establish and operate a nonprofit corporation to provide wholesale wine distribution services to Virginia wineries and farm wineries for up to 3,000 cases a year.[27] The Virginia Winery Distribution Company began operations on April 17, 2008.

A year after the *Granholm* decision, progress could be summed up by saying that the decision had a mostly positive effect on the rights of consumers and wineries, and that the momentum created by it was noticeably moving state lawmakers in the right direction.[28] In the years that followed, new direct shipping laws were passed and others were modified. One solution in some states was to allow direct shipping for wineries producing less than a certain amount of wine such as in Illinois where the upper limit was set at 25,000 gallons. A similar solution was to establish a limit on the amount of wine that could be shipped to any one consumer. Some wholesalers began to realize that they really were not interested in low volume accounts and were willing to live with caps on direct shipping. Slowly the direct shipping issues in state legislatures began to be resolved.

The wholesalers, however, remained ready to change tactics to prevent further erosion of their profits. Legislation has been introduced more than once in the House of Representatives that would turn complete control of alcohol regulation from the federal government to the states. If this were to happen, wholesalers would have the opportunity to lobby state legislatures to pass laws in their favor with the possibility of putting an end to shipping to consumers. Legislation such as this in the name of states' rights always has a chance of being passed and can remain a threat to the wine industry in years to come. As was the case in the campaigns of the Neo-Prohibitionists, constant vigilance by the industry is a must for the foreseeable future to prevent harm to an industry vulnerable to special interests.

Trends and Prospects

The growth of the eastern wine industry since 2000 has been so rapid that only some of the major highlights have been summarized in this chapter. One way of lending perspective to what has happened during the first decade of the new century is to take a look back. Enough time has passed from the end of Prohibition to the present to identify trends that have developed in the eastern industry. Trends can be helpful in understanding what has happened in the past and why, and they may offer some insight into the future if they continue. Three major trends have helped the industry evolve into what it has become today.

The most enduring trend has been increasing wine quality. This was the motivation that led to the importation of the French hybrids, finding ways to grow vinifera successfully in the harsh climates of the East, and developing new and improved varieties of grapes through hybridization. In the first decade of the twenty-first century the search has continued. The Geneva Station has released five new varieties, Noiret, Corot Noir, Valvin Muscat, Arandell and Aromella; Frontenac Gris, La Crescent and Marquette have been introduced in Minnesota; and two Elmer Swenson hybrids, Brianna and Sabrevois, were named with Swenson's blessing by wineries that wanted to use them. For established vinifera varieties, the search for improved clones has become more widespread.

At the first Wineries Unlimited in 1976, a small number of wines were placed on three or four tables for tasting, and it was difficult to find a wine that one could drink with pleasure. Four years later more than 1,000 wines were put out for tasting and it was hard to find one that was seriously flawed. Today, wines from the East are winning gold medals and sweepstakes awards at major national and international competitions. The quality level has gone up dramatically throughout the industry. In addition to an increased knowledge of winemaking, experience that came with the passing of years was an important factor. The wines being produced today by wineries just starting out are on average of much higher quality than they were in 1976.

A second trend has been for wineries and the industry to operate on increasingly sound business principles. Many of the small wineries established in the 1960s and 1970s were started with little thought of making a profit. Their vineyard and winery operations were usually financed by earnings from a regular job, investments, or accumulated wealth. Although some wineries were much more attuned to making money than others, it was not until the mid-1980s that the trend toward running wineries for profit accelerated. Making money enabled businesses to expand. The increasing use of computers was also a factor.

Marketing wine in the early years necessarily took second place to growing grapes and making wine. The need to sell wine helped wineries develop marketing skills, which at first centered around ways of promoting wine in their own local markets. Later, wineries began to work with one another and formed wine trails; state associations started to promote wines of their member wineries. Although sporadic attempts were made to export wine prior to the 2000s, it has subsequently become more of a consideration and will undoubtedly increase in the years ahead.

A third important trend has been an increase in the ability of wineries to work together. Early growers in the East had an independent streak that encouraged them to rely on their own efforts. Together with the fact that growing grapes and making wine took so much time and energy, there was disinterest and even resistance to join with others in cooperative efforts such as working to change state laws. It took time for people to decide to become active in state or national organizations. The Neo-Prohibitionist movement that began to gain momentum in the mid-1980s helped bring wineries together on the political front, to contact their legislators, brief their local media, and educate their customers about the problems the industry was facing. A significant number of wineries did not become involved then, and even in 2010

Figure 13.3: Many wineries in the East draw on their region's history to help sell their wine. Ingleside Plantation Winery in Oak Grove, Virginia, made exact replicas of eighteenth-century wine bottles found five miles from the winery at Wakefield, George Washington's birthplace, for use in marketing their 1986 Pinot Noir. Photo by author, 1989.

with the continuing potential for trouble, WineAmerica should be able to recruit more winery members than it now has. If past history is any guide, there will be times when the well-being of the wine industry may depend on how effectively the industry can unite when it is under attack.

The trends that have been identified here are likely to continue in the future and contribute to the growth of the industry. New trends that will help shape the future of the industry may already be underway. In the wake of the *60 Minutes* broadcast linking wine and health, a broad concern for the environment and healthy food has taken hold.[29] As more and more wineries make these concerns part of their operations, the image of the wine industry and wine will change in the eyes of the public and in government circles.

In addition, an increasing number of visitors' centers in many states have helped educate the public about the industry. One of the largest was the New York Wine and Culinary Center that had its grand opening on June 17, 2006. The 19,745 square foot building, which cost $7.5 million to build, contained a theater, exhibit area, training kitchen, wine and food bar, and a tasting and sales room for New York wines.[30] Given that wine can be made once a year and that the history of winemaking

Figure 13.4: The New York Wine and Culinary Center opened on June 17, 2006, in Canandaigua as an educational center for New York wine and food. Major funding came from Constellation Brands and New York State. Photo by author, 2006.

in Europe goes back for hundreds of years, the development of the eastern wine industry is nothing short of remarkable. While the wine industry in the East was considered to be in its infancy in 1976, it is now being increasingly recognized as an important wine region of the world.

APPENDIX A

THE ORIGINS OF EASTERN WINE GRAPES

THE EARLIEST KNOWN REPRESENTATIVE OF VITIS, THE GENUS TO WHICH ALL grapevines belong, is the fossil species *Vitis sezannensis* dating back about 60 million years to the Lower Eocene epoch of the Tertiary period.[1] Over the millennia the ancestral grapevines evolved, and toward the end of the Tertiary period some 2 million years ago, the genera of grapes surviving today had become distinct from one another: the genus *Vitis* had separated into two subgenera—*Euvitis,* the bunch grapes, and *Muscadinia,* the muscadines.[2] One of the factors that allowed them to become distinct from one another was that they evolved with a difference in chromosome numbers, *Euvitis* with thirty-eight and *Muscadinia* with forty. This made interbreeding difficult.[3]

Also toward the end of the Tertiary period, the first distinct species began to develop. All species of *Euvitis* readily interbreed and can easily be hybridized. The development of species, therefore, requires some form of separation such as geographical or ecological barriers, or a simple biological mechanism such as flowering at different times. One important isolating factor may have been the glacial epoch called the Pleistocene, which lasted from the end of the Tertiary period until about 10,000 years ago. During this epoch the glaciers advanced and retreated four or five times and created major changes in climate and landscape.

Both *Euvitis* and *Muscadinia* existed in North America and Eurasia at the start of the Pleistocene. In North America the *Muscadinia* drifted southward away from the advancing ice, but in Eurasia the formation of the Himalayas and other mountain ranges prevented them from moving south, and they failed to survive in the Old World. The collapse of the land bridge between Asia and North America caused geographic isolation and the *Euvitis* vines in North America and Eurasia developed different characteristics.[4] The number of species of *Vitis* in the world today is estimated to be between sixty and eighty, thirty to thirty-five in North America, about the same number in Asia, and one important one—*Vitis vinifera*—in Eurasia.

Grapevine evolution has occurred naturally in the wild and also under domestication at the hands of man. The major evolutionary mechanisms—mutation, genetic drift, hybridization, and selection—are intensified and accelerated through the agency of man far beyond what is possible in nature. It is likely that the beginnings of agriculture date no further back in time than the start of the Neolithic period, or New Stone Age, about 10,000 years ago. The start of the domestication of grapevines is usually placed between 8000 and 6000 B.C.

Perhaps the first step in domestication came when early man selected the most fruitful vines in his native forest habitat and planted them where there was a dependable source of water and protection from animals. Then, by choosing the best performing vines and eliminating others, there was a gradual improvement in the vines and fruit. A major factor in the development of viticulture at a very early date was the transformation of the dioecious vines found in the wild—where the male and female reproductive organs are on separate plants—to hermaphroditic vines where the organs of both sexes are present in the same flower. Without this change from cross-pollinating to self-pollinating plants, which took place under domestication, it is unlikely that viticulture would have been possible on any large scale.[5]

Studies conducted in Europe comparing wild *Vitis vinifera* vines with similar varieties growing under cultivation nearby give an insight into some of the other changes that took place as a result of domestication. The wild vines, for example, had loose clusters with irregular set and variable berry maturity in the cluster. The berries were highly pigmented, astringent, high in acid, low in sugar, and had a high seed content. Under domestication the clusters became larger, longer, and more compact with berries uniform in maturity. The berries had a wide range of color with a decrease in pigment, few seeds, and moderate acidity and sugar content.[6]

The development of grape varieties started gradually following the domestication of the grapevine. Today it is estimated that somewhere between 8,000 and 14,000 grape varieties exist, of which only a small percentage make good wine. When the first settlers arrived in eastern North America the species of grapes that had developed over the millennia were growing in the wild. The first wines in the New World, strong and coarse, were made from the wild grapes. Many of the early colonists brought *Vitis vinifera* vines from Europe with them. Although none of these survived the harsh climates and diseases present in the East, some of them did hybridize with vines growing in the wild. These varieties are known as "chance hybrids" or "wilding" varieties. Some of the varieties such as Catawba, Isabella, and Delaware were found growing in the wild and simply transplanted into vineyards. Others were seedlings that were discovered and planted. Still others were the result of conscious crosses by man.

In the eastern United States in 1822, Professor Thomas Nuttall of Harvard University recommended the development of "hybrids betwixt the European vine and those of the United States [that] would better answer the variable climates of North America than the unacclimated vine of Europe."[7] The first attempts to improve the native grapes by hybridizing came in 1830 when William Robert Prince of Flushing, New York, grew 10,000 seedling grapes "from an admixture under every variety of circumstance."[8] Among the many hybridizers who followed during the nineteenth century were E. S. Rogers in Roxbury, Massachusetts, J. H. Ricketts in Newburgh, New York, and Thomas Volney Munson in Denison, Texas.[9]

The varieties of grapes known as the French hybrids, or sometimes as the French-American hybrids, had their origin in the second half of the nineteenth century when vine cuttings from the United States brought powdery mildew (oidium) and a root louse, phylloxera, to France for the first time. Hundreds of thousands of acres of French and other European vineyards were destroyed. It was eventually discovered that the classic French varieties could be saved by grafting them onto phylloxera-resistant rootstocks, but in another effort to cope with the phylloxera epidemic French hybridizers began crossing American varieties and species with European varieties in the hope of developing new varieties combining European wine quality with American hardiness and resistance.[10]

When early man went out into his garden and decided to throw out one vine in favor of another producing more or better fruit, he was doing in a primitive way what today's research stations are doing when they cross two vines in hopes of making an improved new variety. Today's breeders, however, have all of the tools of modern science available to them. They know, for example, that different species show resistance to various diseases as well as such stress factors as cold damage, drought, and iron chlorosis.[11] Advances in biotechnology including gene mapping and genetic engineering are enabling the evolutionary process to move ahead with even greater speed. Although the origins of the grape varieties found in the East today are diverse, they are all part of an evolutionary process leading in the direction of grapes or vines with improved characteristics for the benefit of growers, processors, and consumers.

Table A.1 lists the species of grapes that are of greatest importance for wine production in eastern North America today. Table A.2 includes the *Vitis vinifera* varieties that originated in Eurasia and were subsequently brought to eastern North America and used commercially for wine before 2000. These varieties are the products of evolution under domestication and the origin of some of them have been traced back as far as ancient Greek or Roman times. A great number of other vinifera varieties were used after 2000 as the number of wineries grew rapidly and the knowledge of how to grow them accelerated. Table A.3 lists the American varieties that originated in eastern North America mostly in the nineteenth century. Tables A.4 through A.8 list the varieties developed as the result of the work of the French and other hybridizers and modern breeding programs in North America and Eurasia. Wherever possible the listing includes the name of the variety, the breeder's designation number, the parents and/or species involved, the date the cross was made, and the date the variety was introduced.[12] On some of these lists there is an indication of whether the grapes would be used for white or red wine. The color of grapes used for making red wine was often described on the original lists as blue, black or red, but here they are given an "r" to indicate their use for red wine.

Many books on viticulture contain references to grape varieties that are suitable for the East. One book, however, is particularly recommended for information on grape varieties. *Wine Grapes* by Jancis Robinson, Julia Harding, and José Vouillamoz (New York, 2012), has updated and largely replaced an earlier book by Jancis Robinson, *Vines, Grapes and Wines* (New York, 1996). For information on grape varieties recommended for planting in the cold climates of the East, see *A Review of Cold Climate Cultivars* by Lisa Ann Smiley (Ames, Iowa, 2008).

TABLE A.1. Grape species most important for eastern North American wine production

Vitis Euvitis			Vitis Muscadinia
Asiatic species	European species	North American species	North American species
amurensis	*vinifera (vin.)*	*aestivalis (aest.)* *berlandieri (berl.)* *candicans (cand.)* *champinii (cham.)* *cinerea (cin.)* *labrusca (lab.)* *lincecumii* (linc.)* *riparia (rip.)* *rupestris (rup.)*	*rotundifolia (rotun.)*

Note: Grapevine classification: All grapevines belong to the genus *Vitis* of the family Vitaceae. Within the genus *Vitis* are two subgenera: Euvitis, the bunch grapes, and Muscadinia, the muscadines. Botanists recognize between sixty and eighty species, approximately half of which are native to North America. Listed here are those of greatest importance for the eastern wine industry.

*USDA taxonomy now accepts *lincecumii* as "*aestivalis* var. *lincecumii*." The older name is used here. The abbreviations following the species names are used in the tables that follow to identify the species involved in the parentage of the variety listed.

TABLE A.2. *Vitis vinifera*

Albariño (w)	Malbec (r)	Rkatsiteli (w)
Aligoté (w)	Malvesia (w)	Sangiovese (r)
Auxerrois (w)	Merlot (r)	Sauvignon Blanc (w)
Barbera (r)	Mourvèdre (r)	Sémillon (w)
Cabernet Franc (r)	Muscat Ottonel (w)	Sereksiya (w)
Cabernet Sauvignon (r)	Nebbiolo (r)	Sylvaner (w)
Chardonnay (w)	Petit Manseng (w)	Syrah (r)
Gamay (r)	Pinot Blanc (w)	Tannat (r)
Gewürztraminer (w)	Pinot Gris (w)	Tempranillo (r)
Grenache (r)	Pinot Meunier (r)	Trebbiano (w)
Grüner Veltliner (w)	Pinot Noir (r)	Viognier (w)
Lemberger (r)	Riesling (w)	Zinfandel (r)

Note: Varieties originating in Eurasia are the products of evolution under domestication and the origin of some of them has been traced back as far as ancient Greek or Roman times. This list includes only the principal varieties being used for wine in the East as of 2000. Then and now, wineries have been experimenting with other varieties.

TABLE A.3. American varieties

Name of variety	Parentage	Source
Agawam (r)	Wild labrusca x Black Hamburg (vin.)	Introduced 1869
Catawba (w)	Found in wild (lab., vin.)	Discovered 1802
Concord (r)	Chance seedling (lab., vin.)	Introduced 1853
Cynthiana (r)*	Chance seedling (lab., aest., vin.)	Introduced c. 1850
Delaware (r)	Seedling found in garden (vin., lab., aest.)	Discovered 1849
Delicatessen (r)	R. W. Munson x Delicious	Crossed 1902
Diamond (w)	Concord x Iona (lab., vin.)	Crossed 1873
Dutchess (w)	Concord seedling x Delaware (lab., aest., vin.)	Crossed 1868
Elvira (w)	Seedling of Taylor (lab., rip.)	First fruited 1869
Herbemont (r)	Propagated from old vine (aest., cin., vin.)	Crossed 1788
Isabella (r)	Chance seedling (lab., vin.)	Discovered before 1816
Ives (r)	Seed from uncertain source (lab.)	Grown c. 1844
Lenoir (r)	Named for man who grew it in S.C. (aest., vin.)	Named before 1829
Missouri Riesling (w)	Seedling of Taylor (lab., rip.)	Grown c. 1870
Muench (r)	Neosho x Herbemont	Introduced 1887
Niagara (w)	Concord x Cassady (lab., vin.)	Crossed 1868
Noah (w)	Seedling of Taylor (lab., vin.)	Grown 1869
Norton (r)*	Seedling (lab., aest., vin.)	Introduced 1830
President (r)	Seedling of Herbert	Introduced 1900
St. Vincent (r)	Discovered in Missouri	Introduced after 1973
Scuppernong (w)	Found in wild (rotun.)	Found before 1760
Stark Star (r)	Cynthiana x Catawba	Introduced 1892?
Worden (r)	Seedling of Concord	Introduced 1881

Note: These are varieties originating in eastern North America, but not as part of a modern breeding program.
*Research published in 1993 by Bruce Reisch et al. has shown that Norton and Cynthiana are the same grape.

TABLE A.4. French hybrid varieties

Name of variety	Original name and number	Parentage
Aurore (w)	Seibel 5279	Seibel 788 x Seibel 29 (linc., rup., vin.)
Baco Noir (r)	Baco 24-23; later Baco No. 1	Folle Blanche (vin.) x riparia
Le Commandant (r)	Bertille Seyve 2862	Bert. Seyve 822 x Bert. Seyve 872 (aest., lab., linc., rip., rup., vin.)
Cascade (r)	Seibel 13053	Seibel 7042 x Seibel 5409 (aest., lab., cin., linc., rip., rup., vin.)
(not named) (r)	Castel 19-637	Cinsaut x rupestris
Chambourcin (r)	Joannès Seyve 26-205	Seyve-Villard 12-417 x S. 7053 ? (rip., rup., vin., berl., aest., cin., linc.)
Chancellor (r)	Seibel 7053	Seibel 5163 x Seibel 880 (rup., vin., rip., linc., aest., cin.)
Chelois (r)	Seibel 10878	Seibel 5163 x Seibel 5593 (lab., rip., rup., vin.)
Colobel (r)	Seibel 8357	Seibel 6150 x Seibel 5455 (cin., lab., linc., rip., rup., vin.)
Couderc Noir (r)	Couderc 7120	Jaeger 70 x vinifera (rup., vin., linc.)
De Chaunac (r)	Seibel 9549	Seibel 5163 x Seibel 793 (vin., berl., linc., rup., rip.)
Florental (r)	Burdin 7705	Seibel 8365 x Gamay (vin., rup., aest., lab.)
(not named) (w)	Joannès Seyve 23-416	Bertille Seyve 4825 x Seibel 7053 (lab., rip., rup., aest., cin., vin.)
Landal (r)	Landot 244	Seibel 5455 x Seibel 8216 (aest., berl., cin., lab., rip., rup., vin.)
Landot Noir (r)	Landot 4511	Landot 244 x Seyve-Villard 12-375 (aest., berl., cin., lab., linc., rip., rup., vin.)
Léon Millot (r)	Kuhlmann 194-2	Millardet 101-14 x Goldriesling (rip., rup. vin.)
Lucie Kuhlmann (r)	Kuhlmann 149-1	Riparia/rupestris x Goldriesling (vin.)

(Continued)

TABLE A.4. French hybrid varieties   (*Continued*)

Name of variety	Original name and number	Parentage
Maréchal Foch (r)	Kuhlmann 188-2	Millardet 101-14 x Goldriesling (rip., rup. vin.)
Ravat Blanc (w)	Ravat 6	Seibel 5474 x Chardonnay (aest., cin., lab., linc., rip., vin.)
Ravat Noir (r)	Ravat 262	Seibel 8365 x Pinot Noir (vin., rup., aest., lab.)
(not named) (w)	Ravat 34	Unknown
Rayon d'Or (w)	Seibel 4986	Seibel 405 x Seibel 2007 (linc., rup., vin.)
Rosette (r)	Seibel 1000	Jaeger 70 x vinifera (rup., linc., vin.)
Roucaneuf (w)	Seyve-Villard 12-309	Seibel 6468 x Seibel 6905 (linc., rup., vin.)
Rougeon (r)	Seibel 5898	Seibel 880 x Seibel 4202 (vin., rup., linc., aest.)
(not named)	Seibel 8229 (w)	Seibel 5163 x Seibel 4989 (aest., cin., lab., rip., rup., vin.)
(not named)	Seibel 10868 (w)	Seibel 5163 x Seibel 5593 (lab., rip., rup., vin.)
Seyval Blanc (w)	Seyve-Villard 5-276	Seibel 4995 (or Seibel 5656) x Seibel 4986 (linc., rup., vin.)
Verdelet (w)	Seibel 9110	Seibel 5455 x Seibel 4938 (aest., cin., lab., linc., rip., rup., vin.)
Vidal Blanc (w)	Vidal 256	Ugni Blanc x Rayon d'Or (linc., rup., vin.)
Vignoles (w)	Ravat 51	Plantet x Seibel 880
Villard Blanc (w)	Seyve-Villard 12-375	Seibel 6468 x Seibel 6905 (vin., rup., linc.)
Villard Noir (r)	Seyve-Villard 18-315	Seibel 7053 x Seibel 6905 (vin., rup., linc.)

Note: These are varieties resulting from crosses made by hybridizers in France from the 1880s through the first half of the twentieth century.

TABLE A.5. North American breeding programs

Variety	Number	Cross	Date introduced	Date crossed
New York State Agricultural Experiment Station breeding program, Geneva, New York				
Alden (r)	NY 13035	Ontario x Grosse Guillaume (lab., vin., aest.)	1952	1926
Arandell (r)	NY 95.0301.01	NY 84.0101.03 x NY 88.0514.01	2013	1995
Aromella (w)	NY 76.0844.24	Traminette x Ravat 34	2013	1976
Canada Muscat (w)	NY 17806	Muscat Hamburg x Hubbard (lab., vin.)	1961	1928
Cayuga White (w)	NY 33403 (GW 3)	Seyval x Schuyler (Zinfandel x Ontario) (linc., rup., vin.)	1972	1945
Chardonel (w)	NY 45010 (GW 9)	Seyval x Chardonnay	1990	1953
Corot Noir (r)	NY 70.0809.10	Seyve Villard 18-307 x Steuben (lab., vin., aest.)	2006	1970
Fredonia (r)	Gladwin 15	Champion x Lucile (lab., vin.)	1927	1915
Golden Muscat (w)	NY 10303	Muscat Hamburg x Diamond (lab., vin.)	1927	1916
Geneva Red (r)[a]	NY 34791 (GR 7)	Buffalo x Baco Noir (rip., vin., lab.)	2003	1947

(Continued)

TABLE A.5. North American breeding programs   (*Continued*)

Variety	Number	Cross	Date introduced	Date crossed
Horizon (w)	NY 33472 (GW 7)	Seyval x Schuyler (Zinfandel x Ontario) (linc., rup., vin.)	1982	1945
Melody (w)	NY 65.444.4	Seyval x GW 5 (Pinot Blanc x Ontario) (linc., rup., vin.)	1985	1965
New York Muscat (r)	NY 12997	Muscat Hamburg x Ontario (lab., vin., aest.)	1961	1926
Noiret (r)	NY 73.0136.17	(NY 33277 x Chancellor) x Steuben (lab., vin., aest.)	2006	1973
Steuben (r)	NY 12696	Wayne x Sheridan (lab., vin., aest.)	1947	1925
Traminette (w)	NY 65.533.13	J.S. 23-416 x Gewürztraminer (vin., cin., aest., lab., rip., rup.)	1996	1965
Valvin Muscat (w)	NY 62.0122.01	Couderc 299-35 (Muscat du Moulin) x Muscat Ottonel (vin., rup.)	2006	1962

Horticultural Research Institute of Ontario breeding program, Vineland, Ontario

Variety	Number	Cross	Date introduced	Date crossed
L'Acadie (w)	V 53261	Cascade x Seyve-Villard 14-287	1995[b]	1953
Veeblanc (w)	V 53263	Cascade x Seyve-Villard 14-287	1977	1953
Ventura (r)	V 51061	Chelois x Elvira (lab., rip.)	1975	1951
Vincent (r)	V 49431	V 370628 (Lomanto x Seneca) x Chelois (cham., lab., vin., aest.)	1967	1949
Vivant (w)	V 63331	V 50154 x NY 25681	1982	1963

University of Minnesota breeding program, Excelsior, Minnesota

Variety	Number	Cross	Date introduced	Date crossed
Frontenac (r)	MN 1047	V. riparia #89 x Landot 4511	1995	1978
Frontenac Gris (w)	MN 1187	V. riparia #89 x Landot 4511	2003	Not crossed[c]
La Crescent (w)	MN 1166	St. Pepin x ES 6-8-25	2002	1988
Marquette (r)	MN 1211	MN 1094 x Ravat 262	2006	1989

University of Florida, Central Florida Research and Education Center breeding program, Leesburg, Florida

Variety	Number	Cross	Date introduced	Date crossed
Blanc Du Bois (w)	FLA H18-37	FLA D6-148 x Cardinal	1987	1968
Conquistador (r)	FLA L4-33	FLA E12-59 x FLA E11-40	1983	1969
Lake Emerald (w)	numbers not assigned at that time	Pixiola (V. simpsoni) x V. vinifera	1954	1944
Stover (w)	FES A4-43	Mantey x Roucaneuf	1968	1956
Suwannee (w)	FLA H15-13	FLA C5-50 x FLA F8-35	1983	1968
Welder (w)	number not assigned	Dearing x unknown muscadine	1977	early 1950s[d]

North Carolina Agricultural Experiment Station breeding program, Raleigh, North Carolina

Variety	Number	Cross	Date introduced	Date crossed
Carlos (w)	NC 57-56	Howard x NC 11-173	1970	1951
Noble (r)	NC 20-119	Thomas x Tarheel	1971	1946
Magnolia (w)	NC 60-60	[Hope, Thomas, Scuppernong] x [Topsail, Tarheel]	1961[e]	1954

(*Continued*)

TABLE A.5. North American breeding programs   (*Continued*)

Variety	Number	Cross	Date introduced	Date crossed
University of Georgia Agricultural Experiment Station breeding program, Griffin, Georgia				
Golden Isles (w)	GA 18-7-3	Fry x GA 19-6	1986	1969
South Dakota State University breeding program, Brookings, South Dakota				
Valiant (r)	SD 7-121	Fredonia x SD S9-39	1982	1967

[a]When GR 7 was introduced in 2003, it was named "Abundance." The name was withdrawn later that year because of a claimed trademark infringement and a new name, "Rubiana," was chosen. That name was dropped in 2004 after a winery claimed prior rights to the name. It was decided then not to rename GR 7, but in 2012 it was given its official name, Geneva Red.

[b]Joint introduction with the Grape Growers Association of Nova Scotia.

[c]Frontenac Gris was a single bud mutation of Frontenac.

[d]Developed by H. M. Welder of Tavares, Florida; planted at Leesburg in 1969 and introduced there.

[e]Joint introduction with the U.S. Department of Agriculture.

TABLE A.6. Independent breeding programs

Variety	Number	Cross	Date introduced	Date crossed
Elmer Swenson, Osceola, Wisconsin				
Brianna (w)	ES 7-4-76	Kay Gray x ES 2-12-13 (lab., rip., vin.)	2001*	1983
Edelweiss (w)	ES 40	MN 78 x Ontario (lab., rip.)	1974**	1949
Kay Gray (w)	ES 1-63	[MN 78 x Golden Muscat] x open pollinated (lab., vin., rip.)	1982	1968
LaCrosse (w)	ES 294	(MN 78 x Rosette) x Seyval Blanc (lab., linc., rip., rup., vin.)	1984	1960
Louise Swenson (w)	ES 4-8-33	ES 2-3-17 x Kay Gray (lab., rip., vin.)	1999	1980
Prairie Star (w)	ES 3-24-7	ES 2-7-13 x ES 2-8-1 (vin., rip., lab., aest.)	1999	1980
Sabrevois (r)	ES 5-2-1-9	(MN 78 x Rosette) x (MN 78 x Seneca) (lab., rip., vin., rup., linc.)	2002	1978
St. Croix (r)	ES 2-3-21	(MN 78 x Rosette) x (MN 78 x Seneca) (lab., rip., vin., rup., linc.)	1982	1972
St. Pepin (w)	ES 282	(MN 78 x Rosette) x Seyval Blanc (lab., linc., rip., rup., vin.)	1984	1960
Swenson Red (r)	ES 439	MN 78 x Seibel 11803 (lab., rip., vin.)	1974**	1966
Swenson White (w)	ES 6-1-43	Edelweiss x (MN 78 x Seibel 11803) (lab., rip.)	1999	c. 1980
Ed Swanson, Cuthills Vineyards, Pierce, Nebraska				
Temparia (r)	CV3M2E	Riparia x Tempranillo (rip., vin.)	2007	1996
David MacGregor, Lake Sylvia Vineyards, South Haven, Minnesota				
Petite Amie (w)	DM 8313.1	(ES 5-14 x Swenson Red) x (Suelter x Mario-Muskat) (vin., lab., rip.)	2004*	1983

*Named and introduced by Ed Swanson.

**Joint introduction with the University of Minnesota.

TABLE A.7. Foreign breeding programs: Germany

Variety	Station	Cross	Introduced
Bacchus (w)	Geilweilerhof	(Sylvaner x Riesling) x Müller-Thurgau	1972
Dornfelder (r)	Weinsberg	Helfensteiner x Heroldrebe	1956
Ehrenfelser (w)	Geisenheim	Riesling x Sylvaner	1929
GM 311 (w)	Geisenheim	Riesling x Seibel 7053 F2	not named
GM 318 (w)	Geisenheim	Riesling x Seibel 7053 F2	not named
GM 322 (w)	Geisenheim	Riesling x Seibel 7053 F2	not named
Kerner (w)	Weinsberg	Trollinger x Riesling	1964
Müller-Thurgau (w)	Geisenheim	Riesling x Madeleine Royale	1882
Optima (w)	Geilweilerhof	(Sylvaner x Riesling) x Müller-Thurgau	1970
Oraniensteiner (w)	Geisenheim	Riesling x Sylvaner	?
Orion (w)	Geilweilerhof	Bacchus x Seyve-Villard 12-375	1981
Ortega (w)	Würzburg	Müller-Thurgau x Siegerrebe	1971
Osteiner (w)	Geisenheim	Riesling x Sylvaner	1984
Pollux (w)	Geilweilerhof	[Oberlin 595 x (riparia x Gamay F$_2$)] x Foster's White Seedling	
Regent (r)	Geilweilerhof	Diana x Chambourcin	1996
Scheurebe (w)	Alzey	Sylvaner x Riesling	1964
Schönburger (w)	Geisenheim	Spätburgunder x (Chasselas Rosé x Muscat Hamburg)	
Siegerrebe (w)	Alzey	Madeleine Angevine x Gewürztraminer	1929
Zweigeltrebe (r)	Klosterneuberg	Blaufränkisch x St. Laurent	c. 1960

TABLE A.8. *Vitis amurensis* hybrids

Variety	Station	Cross	Date
Michurinetz	Novocherkassk	*V. amurensis* x Getsh (vin.)	c. 1940*
Saperavi severny	Novocherkassk	Severny x Saperavi (vin.)	1947**

*Michurinetz has also been considered to be a cross between *V. amurensis* and Sayanets Malengra.
**Severny is a cross between *V. amurensis* and Malengra.

How the French Hybrids Were Named

The varieties of grapes known as the French hybrids or the French-American hybrids originated in France during the last fifteen years of the nineteenth century and the first half of the twentieth century as one response to the phylloxera crisis in France.[1] They were originally identified in France by the name of the hybridizer (individuals like Albert Seibel, Maurice Baco, and Eugene Kuhlmann; or a firm such as that of Seyve-Villard and his son-in-law Bertille Seyve) and the number of the cross that created the variety. Some of the more popular hybrids acquired names very early. By 1929 Seibel 5279 was commonly referred to as "l'Aurore" because of its unusually early ripening date.[2] Others were later given names coined by a French official body during a classification of grape varieties to be permitted to be grown in France.[3] Sixteen red wine grape varietals and eleven white wine grape varieties were named by a decree dated February 27, 1964 (see table B.1).[4]

The vast majority of the French hybrids were not named and remained identified only by the hybridizer's name and number. Several of these were brought to North America, did well in the vineyards, and gained commercial importance in New York and Ontario. The use of hybridizer name and number for identifying varieties not only caused confusion among growers but was a problem in identifying varietal wines for consumers. In 1970 the Finger Lakes Wine Growers Association acted to select names for seven of the French hybrids that had not been named in France but which were important in New York.[5] By April 22, 1970, a list of suggested grape names had been compiled (see table B.2).

The final choice of names was published by the association in an eight-page leaflet titled "French-American Hybrid Names'" on August 24, 1970.[6] Included in

TABLE B.1. Varieties named in France in 1964

Red		White	
Baco No. 1	Baco Noir	Seibel 10173	Ambror
Seibel 14596	Bellandais	Baco 22A	Baco Blanc
Seibel 10878	Chelois	Ravat 6	Ravat Blanc
Seibel 8357	Colobel	Seibel 4986	Rayon d'Or
Couderc 7120	Couderc	Seyve-Villard 12-309	Roucaneuf
Joannès Seyve 26-205	Chambourcin	Seibel 11803	Rubilande
Burdin 7705	Florental	Seyve-Villard 5276	Seyval
Seyve-Villard 18-283	Garonnet	Seyve-Villard 23-410	Valérien
Landot 244	Landal	Seyve-Villard 12-375	Villard Blanc
Kuhlmann 188-2	Maréchal Foch	Vidal 119	Rami
Kuhlmann 192-2	Léon Millot	Vidal 9	Sainton
Oberlin 595	Oberlin		
Seibel 5455	Plantet		
Seibel 8745	Seinoir		
Seyve-Villard 23-657	Varousset		
Seyve-Villard 18-315	Villard Noir		

this list were Rosette (Seibel 1000), Rougeon (Seibel 5898), Chancellor (Seibel 7053), Verdelet (Seibel 9110), Cameo (Seibel 9549), Cascade (Seibel 13053), and Vignoles (Ravat 51).

Subsequent to the distribution of the leaflet the Canadian Wine Institute objected to having been left out of the naming process and specifically to the proposed name Cameo on the grounds that it was an infringement on a proprietary name used by one of their member companies. On March 9, 1972, a meeting was held at Vineland, Ontario, where it was agreed to set up a Great Lakes Grape Nomenclature Committee that would function in the naming of French-American hybrids that did not have names and that were commercially important. Oliver A. Bradt, representing the Great Lakes Grape Research Coordinating Committee, was named president; Dr. Ernest A. Kerr, representing the Horticultural Research Institute of Ontario, became the secretary. The other three members were Dr. John Einset, representing the New York State Agricultural Experiment Station; George Hostetter, representing the Canadian Wine Institute; and Seaton C. Mendall, representing the Finger Lakes Wine Growers Association.

The committee approved all of the names chosen in 1970 with the exception of Cameo (Seibel 9549). It was agreed to substitute the name De Chaunac in honor of Adhemar de Chaunac who had played such an important role in introducing many of the French hybrids into Canada.[7] On August 21, 1972, The Canadian Wine Institute held a black tie dinner at the Niagara Falls Club in Niagara Falls, Ontario, to celebrate the naming of Seibel 9549 for Adhemar de Chaunac.

TABLE B.2. Suggested grape names

Seibel 9110	Seibel 1000	Seibel 5898	Seibel 7053	Seibel 9549	Seibel 13053	Ravat 51
Verdelet	Rosette	Rougeon	Chancellor	Cameo	Cascade	Vignoles
Bon Verde	Premier	Regent	Valour	Cardinale	Vermillion	Americus
Autumn Gold	Titian	Crusader	Cavalier	Chroma	Pallisandre	Suzerain
Sonata	Glow	Hermitage Noir	Rosetta	Orion	Dawn Glow	Astarte
Savona	Blaze	Minerva	Carnellian	Suzerain	Elan	Vernal
Escort	Cerulean	Bon Bouquet	Adorn	Ceremony	Blue Luna	Cerulean
Accolade	Tantalus	Madrigal	Cascade	Ebony Blaze	Azure Blaze	Polaris
Tantalus	Lorelei	Serenata	Empyrean	Aztec	Midnight Opal	Dianthus
Empyrean	Fortune	Apollo	Blue Blood	Vigo	Consort	Luna
Apollo	Sibrel	Blue Sable	Medalist	Low Lights	Marvel	Petit Blaze
Nebulae	Blue I	Blue Finger	Escort	Velourais	Charmois	Perfecta
Silver Diana	Seibeloy	Lakes	Gravolle	Vedette	Chateau Lake	Ranier
Artemis	Mille Rouge		Sauvignon Seibel	Chevalier		Spindrift
Alabaster	Hardy Harvest		Keuka Park			Corona
Orion						Astral
Lorelei						Consort
Athena						Madrigal
Laguna						Seneca Wayne
Dulcinea						
Doreen						
Verdante						
Alpine Frost						

FIVE HISTORIC GRAPEVINE ACQUISITIONS DURING THE 1930s AND 1940s

THE FIVE ACQUISITIONS OF GRAPEVINES LISTED HERE DOCUMENT THE experimentation with grape cultivars that was taking place in the 1930s and 1940s to find the most promising varieties that would grow well in the difficult growing conditions in the East. Table C.1, showing the early acquisition of French hybrids at the New York State Agricultural Experiment Station at Geneva goes back in time to include the first group of hybrids received at Geneva on March 1, 1911. This handful of varieties plus those received in 1927, 1937, and 1939, was the extent to which French hybrids were accessed at Geneva prior to World War II.

Table C.2—an inventory of the grape varieties being grown at Boordy Vineyard in Riderwood, Maryland—illustrates the diversity of the varieties being tried. Many of the varieties tested were later discarded. Philip Wagner was adamant in giving

TABLE C.1. Early acquisitions of French hybrids by the New York State Agricultural Experiment Station at Geneva, New York

March 1, 1911	A number of hybrids received from George C. Husmann through the USDA via F. L. Husmann, Oakville, California	Castel 1028
		Seibel 14
		Seibel 78
		Seibel 215
		Seibel 2044
		Seibel 1XX
		Seibel 2XX
		Seibel 3X
		Alicante Ganzin
		Alicante x Rup. Terrace No. 20
		Chasselas x berlandieri 41B

(Continued)

TABLE C.1. Early acquisitions of French hybrids by the New York State Agricultural Experiment Station at Geneva, New York   (*Continued*)

February 28, 1927	A group of nineteen hybrids were obtained from Maclet-Botton, Villefranche en Beaujolais, France	Baco 43-23
		Bertille Seyve 2667
		Bertille Seyve 2862
		Cartier 1
		Malègue 2049-3
		Malègue 93-5
		Peage 5-10
		Seibel 14
		Seibel 1000
		Seibel 4629
		Seibel 4643
		Seibel 5163
		Seibel 5296
		Seibel 5437
		Seibel 5455
		Seibel 5898
		Seibel 6339
		Seibel 6905
		Villard 2-108
1937	A lot of fifteen was received from Maclet-Botton	Seibel 5163
		Seibel 5898
		Seibel 7136
		Seibel 7157
		Seibel 8365
		Seibel 10096
		Seibel 12583
		Seibel 13047
		Seibel 13680
		Seibel 14117
		Seibel 14189
		Seyve-Villard 5-276
		Seyve-Villard 12-622
		Seyve-Villard 14-287
		Seyve-Villard 18-315
March 16, 1939	Another shipment from Maclet-Botton	Baco 24-23
		Couderc 299-35
		Oberlin 595
		Seibel 4986
		Seibel 4995
		Seibel 5279
		Seibel 7053
		Seibel 8718
		Seibel 8745
		Seibel 8916
		Seibel 10146
		Seyve-Villard 3-160
1939	Received from Robert T. Dunstan, Greensboro, North Carolina	Seibel 4986
		Seibel 6468
		Seibel 7053
		Seibel 8357
		Seibel 8616
		Seibel 8745
		Seibel 8748
		Seibel 8916

Source: Information included in letter to Hudson Cattell from Dr. John Einset, of the New York State Agricultural Experiment Station at Geneva, New York, July 5, 1978. With reference to the hybrids received in 1911, Einset wrote: "Certain of these were sent before 1913 to the Vineyard Laboratory of this Station at Fredonia for testing. Name tags were lost resulting in temporary 'new' numbers, Seibel 3X, 2XX and 1XX." These "new" numbers were more than temporary, however, for Philip Wagner included two of them in his 1941 list of varieties being grown (see table C.2). Additional identifications may be found in a letter to Philip Wagner from Richard Wellington dated November 1, 1963.

TABLE C.2. Grape varieties being grown in 1941 by Philip and Jocelyn Wagner at Boordy Vineyard in Riderwood, Maryland

Old Varieties	Bacchus (r)
	Catawba (r)
	Delaware (r)
	Diamond (w)
	Eumelan (r)
	Iona (r)
	Norton (r)
Munson Hybrids	America (r)
	Bell (w)
	Brilliant (r)
	Champanel (r)
	Cloeta (r)
	Delicatessen (r)
	Lomanto (r)
	Manito (r)
	Rommel (r)
	Wapanuka (w)
	Wine King (r)
French American Hybrids	Baco No. 1 (r)
	Couderc 4401 (r)
	Seibel 128 (r)
	Seibel 1000 (r)
	Seibel 2056 (r)
	Seibel 5163 (r)
	Seibel 6339 (r)
	Seibel 1XX (r)
	Seibel 2XX (r)
New York State Hybrids	N.Y. 10608 (r)
	N.Y. 10839 (r)
	N.Y. 11407 (w)
	N.Y. 11417 (w)
	N.Y. 11456 (r)
	N.Y. 11683 (r)
	N.Y. 13774 (w)
	Westfield (r)
	Zinfandel x Ontario (r)
Vinifera Varieties	Cabernet Sauvignon (r)
	Franken Riesling (w)
	Petit Verdot (r)
	Pinot Chardonnay (w)

Source: This list was furnished by Philip Wagner and originally appeared as a mimeographed sheet titled "A list of grape varieties now being grown at Boordy Vineyard, Riderwood, Md., by J. and P. Wagner, Season of 1941."

the vines only routine care. If the vines could not handle that, they were discarded. For this reason, and because new varieties were constantly coming along, only one variety on this list, Baco No. 1, was still on the Boordy list 25 years later.

On September 9 and 10, 1941, Philip Wagner went to North Carolina to examine plantings by Robert T. Dunstan in Greensboro and Joe R. Brooks not far from Asheville. Table C.3 contains the thirty-eight varieties that Wagner considered to be promising, and cuttings of these were sent to Boordy Vineyard as soon as the wood could be propagated.

TABLE C.3. Thirty-eight grape varieties Philip Wagner found of importance during his visit to Robert T. Dunstan and Joe R. Brooks in North Carolina on September 9–10, 1941

Seyve-Villard	12303, 12309, 12327, 12358, 12364, 12417, 18315, 18402
Bertille Seyve	2667, 2862, 5563
Couderc	13
Seibel	4995, 5279, 5419, 5813, 6468, 6905, 7157, 9110, 10096, 10417, 11803, 13047, 13053
New York hybrids	12128, 16829
Dunstan crosses (no numbers)	Golden Chasselas x Edna, Edna x Muscat of Alexandria
Named New York hybrids	Athens, Buffalo, Hector, Ruby, Seneca
Munson hybrids	Beacon, Carman, Ellen Scott, Longfellow

Source: Philip Wagner, *Daybooks*, September 12, 1941.

When World War II ended, the first significant plantings of French hybrids took place in Canada. Of the twenty-one varieties received at Brights on April 11, 1946 (Table C.4), only thirteen were still in the ground in 1975. Table C.5 details the shipping list of three cases of plant material that was received at the Horticultural Research Institute of Ontario at Vineland Station in 1947. With the war over, vines could now be ordered freely from France, and this was done with increasing frequency.

TABLE C.4. Grape cultivars received on April 11, 1946, by Brights Wines, Niagara Falls, Ontario, from Maclet-Botton in Villefranche, France

French Hybrids	Bertille Seyve 2667 (r)
	Bertille Seyve 2846 (r)
	Couderc 29935 (w)
	Seibel 1000 (Rosette) (r)
	Seibel 4986 (Golden Ray) (w)
	Seibel 5279 (Aurore) (w)
	Seibel 5409 (w)
	Seibel 5437 (r)
	Seibel 5575 (r)
	Seibel 6468 (w)
	Seibel 6905 (r)
	Seibel 7053 (Chancellor) (r)
	Seibel 7157 (r)
	Seibel 8718 (r)
	Seibel 8745 (r)
	Seibel 9110 (Verdelet) (w)
	Seyve-Villard 5-276 (w)
Geisenheim Hybrid	Müller-Thurgau (w)
Vinifera	Perle de Csaba (w)*
	Pinot Chardonnay (w)
	Pinot Noir de Bourgogne (r)

Source: List obtained through vineyard records of T. G. Bright & Co., Ltd., courtesy of George W. B. Hostetter.

*Brights vineyard records show that Perle de Csaba was received on May 20, 1947. George Hostetter is certain that it arrived first in the 1946 shipment from Maclet-Botton.

TABLE C.5. Shipping list of grape cultivars sent from Producteurs Directs Nouveaux de Seibel in Montboucher (Drôme), France, to the Horticultural Experiment Station in Vineland Station, Ontario, dated January 28, 1947

	Cultivar	Number	Type
Bertille Seyve	2862 (r)	200	rooted
	2846 (r)	200	rooted
	2667 (r)	200	rooted
Seyve-Villard	3-160 (r)	200	rooted
	1-72 (w)	200	rooted
Seibel	4995 (w)	200	rooted
	5279 (w)	200	rooted
	5409 (w)	200	grafted/lot
	5437 (r)	200	rooted
	5455 (r)	200	rooted
	5575 (r)	5	cuttings
	6339 (r)	200	cuttings
	7052 (r)	200	rooted
	7053 (r)	200	rooted
	7157 (r)	200	cuttings
	8214 (r)	200	rooted
	8229 (w)	200	rooted
	8357 (r)	200	rooted
	8616 (r)	200	rooted
	8718 (r)	105	cuttings
	8745 (r)	200	rooted
	8916 (r)	200	rooted
	9110 (w)	200	grafted/3309
	9249 (r)	200	cuttings
	9549 (r)	200	cuttings
	10096 (r)	200	grafted/3309
	10868 (w)	200	rooted
	10878 (r)	187	rooted
	10878 (r)	15	cuttings
	11257 (r)	200	rooted
	11259 (w)	120	cuttings
	11259 (w)	80	rooted
	12583 (w)	200	cuttings
	13053 (r)	200	cuttings
	14514 (w)	200	cuttings
	14660 (w)	200	rooted
	14664 (w)	200	rooted
	14665 (w)	200	grafted/3309
	15062 (r)	100	grafted/3309
	15062 (r)	100	rooted

Source: Information taken from original shipping list dated January 28, 1947, courtesy of O. A. Bradt, Horticultural Research Institute of Ontario. The shipment was made under Import permit No. 4979 and had phytosanitary clearance.

APPENDIX D

EASTERN WINE TYPES

A WIDE VARIETY OF WINES HAVE BEEN MADE IN THE EAST SINCE PROHIBITION. Many of them have played a significant role in the development of the eastern wine industry. Some of the most important types of wine are reviewed here together with their early uses in the East.

Champagne and Sparkling Wines

The terms champagne and sparkling wine have often been used interchangeably in the East, and for most of the wine history of this region winemakers were free to use whichever term they wanted to describe their product. Champagne has been the name most used over the years because of the strong association it has had with celebrations of weddings, anniversaries, and other special occasions. Since Champagne originated in the Champagne district of France, the French have been very protective of the name. For more than a century, they have protested the use of the word champagne for any wine not produced in their own district. Champagne, however, was a name that customers in the United States were familiar with and, because it was felt that the word had long become part of the English language, there was resistance to yielding to French demands to discontinue its use. Unsuccessful court cases and French diplomatic initiatives are on record as far back as 1911 in the United States.[1] Out of respect for the French, some winemakers have chosen to use the term sparkling wine on their labels. Others have seen no reason to do so.

In 1934, the Federal Alcohol Administration, a predecessor of the Bureau of Alcohol, Tobacco and Firearms, was established within the U.S. Treasury

Department to create permit and licensing regulations. Charles Fournier of Gold Seal Vineyards became involved in the promulgation of regulations that legalized the term champagne. According to the regulations, an American champagne had to be "a type of sparkling light wine which derives its effervescence solely from the secondary fermentation of the wine within glass containers of not greater than one gallon capacity, and which possesses the taste, aroma, and other characteristics attributed to champagne as made in the Champagne district of France."

Fournier, who had been the winemaker at Veuve Cliquot Ponsardin, felt strongly that wines that met this standard should have the right to be called champagne and that any that did not should simply be called sparkling wine. In the early 2000s, Willy Frank, president of Chateau Frank in Hammondsport, took the same position as Fournier and stoutly defended his use of the word champagne on wines that were emulating the French.

It was different in Canada where nearly fifty years of political maneuvering and legal battles between the French and Canadians led to an episode in Canadian wine history that became known as the "Champagne Wars." On May 23, 1933, Canada had approved the Canada-France Convention Act under which the two countries agreed to honor the trademarks and trade names of the other. Despite the agreement, Canadian wineries continued to use the word champagne on their wine labels. The controversy started in 1955 when Alexander Sampson, the president of Château-Gai winery in Niagara Falls, Canada, placed a large display of his winery's champagne in a Paris store window.[2] This advertising caught the attention of the Toronto *Globe and Mail Magazine,* which ran a feature article under the headline, "He Sells Ontario's Wines in the Very Heart of France." The French protested, but the Canadian government simply responded by issuing a directive that permitted Canadian wineries to use the word champagne only if the product was labeled "Canadian Champagne."

The first French legal response came in 1964 when fifteen French producers went to court in Québec and asked that Château-Gai be enjoined from using the word champagne on its labels. When the French won, the decision was appealed and subsequently upheld in 1974 by the Québec Supreme Court. Other court cases were filed in Ontario in 1975 and 1976. In 1974, a newspaper article by Judy LaMarsh revealed that the 1933 trade agreement had never been ratified by both countries. The Canadian Parliament repealed the agreement in 1980 and Canadian winemakers could again use the term champagne legally.

The French, and later the European Union (EU), did not relent in their fight to protect the name "champagne." In a nonjury trial that started in the summer of 1987, sixteen French Champagne houses that had filed a lawsuit against five Canadian wineries using "Canadian Champagne" on their wine labels lost their case in a decision handed down by Ontario Supreme Court judge Wilfred Dupont.

The courts had left the Canadians victorious, but the victory was short-lived. Time had given the French and the European Union a weapon they had not been able to use earlier, and that was the ability to restrict imports into the EU. Canadian wines had improved rapidly in quality following the adoption of the Vintners Quality Alliance (VQA) appellation system in the late 1980s, and in the 1990s a new product produced in Canada, icewine, became a sensation in the wine world. Canada had not been able to gain free access to European markets and exporting icewines to the EU was economically appealing. A trade agreement between Canada and the EU signed on September 16, 2003, gave Canadian wines free access to EU markets in exchange for ending Canada's right to use "champagne" and twenty other generic wine names.[3]

The right to export wines into the EU was also one basis for an agreement between the United States and the EU that was signed on March 10, 2006. As was the case in the agreement with Canada, the use of "champagne" and fifteen other semi-generic names was ended in return for the mutual acceptance of winemaking practices that had hampered wine exports from the United States.[4] Unlike the Canadian agreement, however, the existing use of "champagne" was grandfathered to protect the long-standing investments of those wineries using the name before the signing of the agreement.

The first sparkling wine in the East was made by Nicholas Longworth in the Cincinnati, Ohio, area in 1842 when he discovered that a batch of his Catawba wine had not completely fermented. He marketed this wine as a Sparkling Catawba and attempted to duplicate it. By 1855 he was producing approximately 100,000 bottles by the *méthode champenoise* but continued to market it as Sparkling Catawba.[5] In 1857 the Missouri Wine Company in St. Louis also produced a sparkling wine with the same name. The Pleasant Valley Wine Company southwest of Hammondsport, New York, was founded in 1860 and in 1863 made its first sparkling wine, which was probably marketed as a Sparkling Catawba. In 1870, after the name Great Western was suggested to Charles D. Champlin, Pleasant Valley's sparkling wines were marketed as Great Western champagnes.

After black rot and powdery mildew devastated the vineyards in the Cincinnati area in the 1860s, the Lake Erie region became the center of the Ohio industry. By 1900, according to the 1902 U.S. Department of Agriculture Yearbook, Ohio ranked second only to New York in the production of sparkling wine, and these positions remained unchanged until the advent of Prohibition.[6]

According to *Wines and Vines*, the production of effervescent wines during the last year before Repeal was 118,491 bottles and 49,570 half bottles, based on figures published by the U.S. Tariff Commission. The first official post-Repeal champagne sale figures for the year 1934 showed that 425,854 gallons were marketed. Sales reached 1.1 million gallons in 1950, 3.4 million gallons in 1960, and 7.4 million gallons in 1966.[7] Champagne production figures at eastern wineries in 1966 were also given:

> Over 100,000 cases: (New York): Chateau Gay, Eastern Wine Corp., Gold Seal Vineyards, Monarch Wine Co., Pleasant Valley Wine Co., Robin Fils & Cie., and The Taylor Wine Company.

50,000 to 100,000 cases: (New York): San Marino Wine Co.; (Ohio): Meier's Wine Cellars; and (New Jersey): L. N. Renault.

15,000 to 50,000 cases: (New York): Hudson Valley Wine Co., Mandia Champagne Cellars, Marlboro Industries; and (New Jersey): Monte Carlo Wine Industries.

5,000 to 15,000 cases: (Illinois): Mogen David Wine Corp.; (Michigan): Bronte Champagne & Wines, St. Julian Wine Co.; and (New York): Hammondsport Wine Co.

Less than 5,000 cases: (New York): Brotherhood Corp; (New Jersey): Gross' Highland Winery; and (Ohio): Catawba Island Wine Co., George F. Lonz, and Steuk Wine Co.

Not all of the champagne sales in the United States consisted of wines made by the *méthode champenoise*. In 1928, Château-Gai in Niagara Falls, Canada, had become the first winery in North America to use the charmat process (bulk process) to make champagne; and when it opened its Chateau Gay winery in Lewiston, New York in 1934, it introduced the charmat process into the United States.[8] In 1966, less than half of the champagne and sparkling wine production in the United States was made by the *méthode champenoise*.[9] Also in 1966, a boom in sparkling wine sales was just starting with the introduction of Cold Duck, a fad wine that got its start in the East.

In 1963, Angelo Spinazze, winemaker and general manager of Bronte Champagne and Wines Company in Hartford, Michigan, was one of a group in Detroit that went to the Pontchartrain Wine Cellars restaurant.[10] At nearly every table in the restaurant people were drinking glasses of what they called "cold duck." Spinazze learned from the bartender that Cold Duck was a blend of champagne and enough sparkling burgundy to give it the color they wanted. The name Cold Duck came from the old German custom of *kalde ende* ("cold end") in which all the leftover wine on the last day of the Fasching, the carnival preceding Lent, was emptied into one bowl. At some point *kalde ende* came to be called *kalde ente* ("cold duck") and the custom extended to the end of any night of partying. What most impressed Spinazze was that sales of Cold Duck at the restaurant averaged 500 glasses a day at $1.00 each.

Spinazze and Robert Wozniak, president of Bronte, lost no time developing their own Cold Duck using champagne and 25 percent still burgundy, and fermenting them together using the charmat process. The resulting sparkling wine became the first commercial Cold Duck when it was released in 1963.[11]

Six months after Spinazze introduced Bronte's Cold Duck, it seemed to him as if everyone was making it. It was invariably made as a sweet wine with Concord for flavor, although Bronte used Delaware, Elvira, and white hybrids rather than Concord.[12] In 1968 the federal government ruled that to be so labeled the wine had to be made of equal portions of champagne and sparkling burgundy.[13]

Cold Duck was made by at least five wineries in Michigan, New York, and New Jersey in 1964 and, according to a *Wines and Vines* survey, by seventeen across the United States in 1968 and thirty-seven by 1970 including E. and J. Gallo, the Christian Brothers and Paul Masson.[14] Cold Duck was credited with most of the increase in consumption of sparkling wine from 7.7 million gallons in 1965 to 22.2 million in 1970 in the United States.[15] This was the peak of the Cold Duck boom; sales began a rapid decline in the early 1970s as the fad came to an end.

Eastern wineries led the way in the production of Cold Duck and had the opportunity to profit handsomely by marketing the product. However, they lacked the financing and the equipment needed to compete with the large California wineries. Cold Duck lived on in the East in the form of Baby Duck in Ontario.

The sharp rise in charmat process sparklers in California during the 1960s gave that state more than 70 percent of the sparkling wine market by 1970.[16] In 1978 the Canandaigua Wine Company introduced its J. Roget Champagne line, and in January, 1979, at the annual meeting of the New York State Horticultural Society, Marvin Sands, the winery's president, stated that "Champagne and sparkling wine market share has doubled from 3% in 1960, to over 6% today. This increase seems based in solid consumer interest, versus the Cold Duck fad of the early 1970s....Historically, New York State has been strongest in champagne and dessert wines. During the last three years, champagne has resumed its upward momentum and I believe New York State will share in this growth. Delaware grapes and Catawba grapes have been the foundation of New York State champagne, and I believe these grapes make a superior champagne compared to the average product produced in California."[17] Within ten years the sales of the J. Roget line made by the charmat process reached more than 1.5 million cases.

The early sparkling wines and champagnes in the East were made from native American grapes with Catawba being the grape variety most often used. At the beginning of the 1980s a blend of Catawba, Elvira, and Aurore was being used in Gold Seal's Marchant label, and Taylor's Great Western brand consisted of a blend of Catawba, Delaware, Dutchess, and Aurore.[18] Renault Winery in Egg Harbor City, New Jersey, used Noah as the base wine of its champagne in 1980. Gross's Highland Winery in Absecon, New Jersey, in the late 1960s produced its champagne from a blend of Niagara, Thompson, Adams, and Noah, with Niagara and Adams being the principal grapes. Other wineries used such varieties as Dutchess, Isabella, Elvira, and Iona. As the French hybrids became available, they were utilized to make champagne. T. G. Bright and Co. added hybrids such as Seyval Blanc, Rayon d'Or and Verdelet to its President Champagne in 1953. Bully Hill Vineyards in Hammondsport released its first brut champagne made from Seyval Blanc in 1978. Later, vinifera varieties were used, and Brights Pinot Champagne in 1955 was the first commercial vinifera wine to be produced in the East.

In the early 1980s approximately sixty-one wineries were producing sparkling wines and champagnes. More than half of them were making less than 5,000 cases.

Seven made more than 25,000 cases, Meier's Wine Cellars in Ohio and six in
New York.[19]

Coolers

Effervescence is a quality in a beverage that appeals to many people, especially
in a chilled drink, and many wines are made with light carbonation to give the
wine a "kick." In the United States, however, for the purposes of taxation, the
Bureau of Alcohol, Tobacco and Firearms declared a wine to be effervescent—
and therefore subject to a higher tax—whenever the carbon dioxide content of the
wine exceeds 0.392 grams per 100 milliliters. Wines below this level are considered
to be *pétillant* rather than sparkling, and many of the fad wines of this period had
a slight spritz to them. These wines have often played an interesting and profitable
part in eastern wine history.

Cold Duck was succeeded in popularity in the 1970s by an Italian import called
Lambrusco, a fruity, slightly sweet, lower alcohol red wine with a spritz to it. By the
early 1980s, in California, a new trend began with wines variously called "light,"
"soft," "low-alcohol," or "low-calorie."[20] Though these wines were not clearly
defined, they had lower alcohol content in common. In the summer of 1982, *Wines
and Vines* conducted a survey to see who was making these wines and about half of
the responses came from the East. Among the comments that were included was one
from Stephen Bahn of Stephen Bahn Winery in Brogue, Pennsylvania, who pointed
out that "many of the wines that have been produced in the East in the past have
been 'light wines,' by virtue of the fact that traditional high sugars are sometimes
unattainable, and we pick at lower sugars, yielding subsequent lower alcohol wines."[21]
In the *Wine Spectator* that same summer, under the heading "Native, Hybrids Make
Super Sippers," Lee Miller wrote: "With summer approaching, many of the wines
of the eastern United States and Canada seem especially appropriate for picnicking,
parties and sipping by the poolside on a hot July afternoon."[22] Above the head was
the line "Don't Forget Eastern U.S."

Coolers soon became part of the trend toward lower alcohol wines. They were
usually blends of white wine and citrus juices, carbonated, and often packaged
in beer-style bottles with crown caps and sold in cardboard carriers.[23] Bianchi
Vineyards in Kerman, California, is credited with putting the first two coolers, Red
Lite and White Lite, on the market in 1979.[24] The cooler boom really began with
the immediate success of Loretto Winery's California Cooler, which sold 700 cases
in 1981, 80,000 cases in 1982 and 2.4 million cases in 1983. There were approximately
sixty coolers on the market by the end of 1984 and total cooler production that year
was 25.2 million gallons. A year later production reached 51.7 million gallons.

One of the earliest coolers in the East was Steidl's Wine Cooler made in
Milwaukee, Wisconsin, in a 1983 joint venture between Thomas Steidl and the
Joseph E. Seagram Company. Seagram pulled out almost immediately and not

long afterward introduced its Seagram's Cooler. The Canandaigua Wine Company introduced its Sun Country Cooler in the spring of 1984 and by May marketed it in forty-seven states, aided by a multimillion dollar advertising campaign.[25] Other eastern coolers that came to market in the first half of 1984 included Silverton Wine Cooler from Meier's Wine Cellars, Island Cooler from Lonz Winery, Grape Vine Wine Cooler from Monarch Wine Co. in Brooklyn, Cask Great Lakes Cooler from Warner Vineyards, and Caribbean Cooler (Jamaica Red and Bahama White) from Bardenheier's Wine Cellars. The first cooler on the market in Ontario was Château-Gai's Canada Cooler.

On July 24, 1984, New York governor Mario Cuomo signed into law a bill that permitted New York wine coolers with no more than 6 percent alcohol to be sold in New York food stores. The bill, passed to aid New York's grape growers, specified that the wine base of the coolers had to be made entirely from grapes grown in New York.[26] By September, 20,000 permits had been issued to food stores and supermarkets and coolers began to reach the shelves. Loretto Winery in California, which made the California Cooler brand wine cooler, filed a lawsuit charging that the New York law was unconstitutional on the grounds that it stipulated that only coolers made from New York grapes could be sold in food stores. In January 1985, a federal district court ruled that the law was in fact unconstitutional, and in early May the Second Circuit Court of Appeals upheld the district court ruling. Soon after, the New York legislature passed a bill permitting out-of-state coolers to be sold in the state's food stores.[27]

A number of New York wineries marketed coolers through the food stores after the legislation was passed. One of them was Benmarl Vineyards, which made three coolers that were sold with increasing success in several grocery store chains including Grand Union and Red Apple supermarkets in New York City.[28] When the legislation was passed allowing all wine coolers to be sold, Benmarl found its shelf space crowded by E&J Gallo's Bartles & Jaymes Wine Cooler, California Cooler, and Sun Country Cooler, all of which were sold at a far lower price and were backed up by major national advertising campaigns. Benmarl's sales no longer continued to grow, and the crowning blow came when Benmarl, which could have sold the equivalent of its entire wine production as coolers, had a very large order cancelled. Soon afterwards, Benmarl discontinued its line of wine coolers.

The small wineries in the East found that the competition from the large wineries was not all they had to contend with. The success of the wine cooler market had attracted the attention of brewers who began marketing beer coolers. An early entry in the United States was Stroh's White Mountain Cooler, and in Canada John Labatt, Ltd. introduced a citrus flavored drink with a beer base called Twist Shandy, the "twist" referring to the twist cap.[29] Shandy, a combination of beer and lemon-lime soft drink, was popular in Europe at the time, and Pabst began marketing a similar product that they advertised as the American Shandy.

Malt-based beverages rapidly increased their share of the cooler market, and by the late 1980s the decline in wine coolers had begun. Like many other fads, it had had its share of colorful history.[30]

Spring Wine and Nouveaus

Two seasonal wines that originated in Europe and made their way to the East were spring wine and nouveaus. Both were first made in New York by Eric Miller, the winemaker at Benmarl Vineyards.

In the cooler white wine regions of Europe it is common to reserve part of the previous year's vintage to be released early for its immediate charm. An accident of nature, however, was responsible for Benmarl's 1976 Spring Wine.[31] The weather in the Hudson Valley turned cool earlier than usual after the Seyval Blanc grapes were harvested, and fermentation was still incomplete when the first cold wave in November stopped it altogether. When Miller tasted the wine, the noticeable spritz reminded him of the light, fragrant Vouvray wines he was familiar with from the Loire Valley. He bottled it in February and it was released at the winery's March tasting.

Other wineries in the East have made spring wines, often with woodruff added, as was commonplace in Europe. St. Julian Wine Company in Paw Paw, Michigan, was one of the wineries that marketed a May wine with woodruff in the 1970s.

The tradition of the Beaujolais Nouveau in France dates back to the early days of the twentieth century.[32] Beaujolais growers would take part of their crop, immediately put the grapes through carbonic maceration, and have a light refreshing wine for sale by November. Over time it became a sought after wine in several European countries, and festivals sprung up around its release. This *vin de primeur* was recognized by French law in 1951 and, in 1967, November 15 was established as its official release date.[33] It was then that the rush began to be the first to sell the Beaujolais Nouveau. In the United States the wine was brought in, sometimes by the Concorde supersonic jet, in order to meet the November 15 date. Gradually, as a way of promoting the Beaujolais Nouveau, there would be promotional activities such as racing the wines from the airport to hotels or restaurants where their customers would be waiting to be the first to sample the new wine.

Eric Miller made the first nouveau in the East as a wedding present for a friend, probably in 1971, and released it commercially in 1972.[34] The hoopla surrounding the arrival of the Beaujolais Nouveau did not escape eastern wineries. On November 9, 1982, the coastal schooner Pioneer docked at the River Café in Brooklyn with nouveaus from three wineries in the Hudson River Valley: Cascade Mountain Vineyards in Amenia, Benmarl, and Valley Vineyards in Walker Valley. "Wine lovers accustomed to awaiting arrival of the New Wines from France, the Beaujolais Nouveau, were stunned to learn that the Nouveau from Nouveau York had reached town first. In fact, many were surprised such wines even existed....Some of the best wines around are being made in New York nowadays and it's time people found out about them."[35] The initial press release stated that there would be photo and TV opportunities at the South Street Seaport Museum Dock from 1 to 2 p.m. and at River Café from 2 to 4 p.m. where transportation would be provided aboard the Pioneer.

In 1983 it was the Hudson River sloop Clearwater that brought the first nouveau wines to New York City. That same year, on November 14, one day before the French, nouveau wines from five Finger Lakes wineries arrived by runner at Turback's Restaurant in Ithaca where they were met by a large crowd including New York's commissioner of agriculture and markets.

During the next several years eastern wineries got a lot of favorable press coverage by beating the French to the marketplace and by using a wide variety of conveyances.[36] Bartlett Maine Estate Winery brought its first Nouveau Blueberry Wine to market by a 1941 Waco biplane. Seven Pennsylvania wineries brought their nouveaus to a tasting at a Philadelphia restaurant by, among others, horse and carriage, old-fashioned bicycle, and by baby carriage with a marching band escort. In 1986, Sakonnet Vineyards in Little Compton, Rhode Island, sold out its entire production of 450 cases of Aurore Nouvelle within a month after its first delivery by the scow schooner Vintage to Bannister's Wharf in Newport. Aurore Nouvelle was a white nouveau made from Aurore grapes and had a label that featured the goddess of the dawn being flown over the countryside by wild geese, presumably bringing the new wine in time for the holidays.[37]

The extravagant displaying of eastern nouveaus did not outlast the 1980s, but not before nouveau wines won a following on the wine lists of many wineries.

Ice Wine

The first record of Eiswein in Germany goes back to 1794, but ice wine was not widely recognized internationally until well into the twentieth century. As a traditional dessert wine, it is made from grapes that are left to be picked until they are frozen on the vine. When the grapes are pressed, the ice is removed and what remains after fermentation is a very concentrated sweet wine that sells at high prices to lovers of ice wine.

The first ice wine in the East, and the first in the United States, was made by Dr. G. Hamilton Mowbray in 1974 at Montbray Wine Cellars in Westminster, Maryland.[38] Mowbray had a wine tasting at the Cosmos Club in Washington, DC, on the night of October 4–5. He knew it would be getting cold, but not how cold. During the tasting he kept checking with the weather bureau, and when they told him it was 25° F, he knew it would be colder in Silver Run Valley. After giving his apologies to the group, he headed home. The temperature was down to 21° in the vineyard when the picking started at dawn. A year later, at Christmas, 1975, the wine was put on sale at $25.00, and on January 1 the price was raised to $50.00. Mowbray had made not only the first ice wine but the first Riesling ice wine as well.[39] In 1976 the second ice wine was made from Villard Blanc by Lucian Dressel at Mount Pleasant Vineyard in Augusta, Missouri.

In Canada ice wine is spelled as one word. Experiments in making icewine there began in British Columbia in 1973 and in Ontario in the early 1980s.[40] Three wineries in Ontario planned to make icewine commercially in 1983. At Inniskillin Wines, birds wiped out the entire crop the day before harvest. Pelee Island Winery had protected their vines with netting, but when the birds were caught in the nets, government officials arrived on the scene, ripped open the nets to release the birds and charged the winery with using dried grapes to trap birds out of season. Nothing came out of this legally, but the birds took advantage of the absence of netting to devour most of the crop. Hillebrand Estates Winery did not have a problem with birds simply because they were not relying on natural freezing. They harvested the grapes earlier, kept them in coolers, and then brought them back outdoors into the winter temperatures in December. In 1985 they concluded that natural freezing was preferable because of the increased concentration and improved flavor characteristics that came with letting the grapes hang on the vines for two additional months.

Icewines were included in the VQA's January 1987 draft of its rules and regulations. There was virtually unanimous agreement that natural freezing yielded the best product, and that became part of the standards including a provision that there could be no artificial refrigeration at any point. The VQA regulations required that the frozen grapes be harvested at temperatures no higher than 19° Fahrenheit and that the must (crushed grapes) remaining after pressing have a minimum of 32° Brix (degrees of sweetness). Since the grapes could not be allowed to thaw, which would lower the sugar content, the pressing had to take place outdoors or in a sheltered area with the doors and windows left open. A list of permissible grape varieties that could be used for making icewine was also drawn up. Most icewines today are made from Vidal or Riesling.

The uniqueness of icewine made it a natural for media coverage. Picking grapes in the middle of winter, putting netting over the vines, and the very idea of making something called "ice wine" attracted attention. It was not long before Canadian icewine gained more attention in the media by winning important awards. In 1991 it was announced at VinExpo in Bordeaux that a 1989 Vidal icewine from Inniskillin Wines had won a Citadelle d'Or Grand Prix d'Honneur, one of 19 accorded that honor from more than 4,100 wines entered. That same year saw all twelve icewines entered in the InterVin competition win gold medals. More and more wineries began to produce icewine and production soared from 2,000 cases in 1990 to more than 10,000 cases by 1994.

The prestige won by Ontario's icewines sold under the VQA appellation of origin system helped bring recognition to a much wider range of Ontario wines. In addition to sales in Canada, they won a place in the export market, particularly in Japan.

The cold winters in Canada make it possible to make icewine every year, often as early as December. In the United States ice wine can only be made in years when temperatures dip low enough to permit natural freezing, and for many years wines made from grapes that had been artificially frozen were marketed as ice wines. The Canadians long thought this was unfair to their naturally frozen icewines, and in November 2002, the Bureau of Alcohol, Tobacco and Firearms prohibited the use of the term *ice wine* or similar wording on all wines where the grapes used were frozen postharvest.

Kosher Wines

The first large Jewish communities in the United States were established in the East in the New York City area during the latter part of the nineteenth century. Most of the kosher wines were made for home consumption, and it was not until 1895 that the first commercial kosher winery operation was started by Sam Schapiro in a Lower East Side tenement basement. Concord grapes were the most readily available variety, and the enduring image of kosher wines began as that of a very sweet red wine with a Concord flavor.[41]

Outside of Israel, only three rules apply for making kosher wines commercially. "Once the grapes have reached the winery, the grapes and the wine must be handled by Sabbath-observant Jews; the yeasts and all other materials involved, such as those used in filtration and clarification in the winemaking process, must be kosher; and the equipment and machinery in the winery must be used exclusively for the production of kosher wines."[42]

In 1934, Leo Star began to produce a small quantity of kosher wines in New York City for sacramental purposes using grapes from western New York. He optimistically called his winery the Monarch Wine Company and gave his wine the name Manischewitz. Some stores carried it for the 1934 Passover season, but it was not until a year later that he began receiving rush orders for the wine. Much to his surprise, non-Jewish customers at the stores had tried the kosher wine and liked it. By 1938 Star had moved his plant to Brooklyn and it was not long before production exceeded a million gallons a year, more than 90 percent of which went into the non-Jewish market. An extensive advertising campaign at the end of World War II with the slogan "Man, Oh Manischewitz, What a Wine!" helped propel sales to more than 3 million gallons.

The success of Manischewitz led more wineries to market similar kosher wines. Chicago became another center of kosher wine production where the Wine Corporation of America sold 5 million gallons of Mogen David by 1952, mostly in the upper Midwest and the South.[43] There was never a requirement that kosher wines had to be either sweet or made from Concord grapes. The term kosher only applied to the way the wine was produced under rabbinic control. Increasingly, kosher wines were being made dry and semi-dry. By 1986, Royal Kedem Winery in Milton,

New York, was spending $1 million annually to tell consumers that kosher wines need not be sweet. Kedem also sent workers to California to produce kosher wines made from such varietals as Chenin Blanc, Sauvignon Blanc, White Zinfandel, Cabernet Sauvignon, and Chardonnay.[44]

Sales of kosher wines leveled off at about 10 million gallons in the 1960s. An era of sorts can be said to have come to an end in 1986 when the Canandaigua Wine Company bought the Manischewitz product line from Monarch Wine Company and moved the production facilities to Widmer's Wine Cellars in Naples, New York, which Canandaigua had acquired two months earlier.

Fruit Wines and Mead

Historically in the East, fruit wines in New England date back to 1632. In that year, Governor John Winthrop bought Governor's Island in Boston Harbor on the condition that he plant a vineyard there. The purchase price was an annual payment of "a hogshead of the best wine that shall grow there." In some years the payment was made in grape wine and in other years in apple wine. Many farms in colonial New England had orchards, and both apple wines and ciders were made. The Moravians, who settled in eastern Pennsylvania before the Revolutionary War, made communion wine out of currants. From colonial days to the present, fruit wines have been favorites of home winemakers.

In modern times one of the centers of the fruit wine industry has been the upper Midwest. Wisconsin and Michigan became known for their cherry wines, and the Amana area of Iowa for its rhubarb wines. A second center has been northern New England and Canada in places where cold winters made it difficult or impossible to grow grapes. As fruit wines have become increasingly popular, many wineries, especially smaller ones, started to make specialty fruit wines that sell out quickly; and other regions such as New Jersey are recognized as important fruit wine areas.

Among the more common kinds of fruits used for winemaking are apples, pears, strawberries and blueberries, bramble berries such as raspberries and blackberries, and stone fruits including peaches, apricots, plums, and cherries. Many other fruits are less frequently used such as elderberries, currants, loganberries, and cranberries.

It should be mentioned briefly that fruit wine production differs in a number of respects from making wine from grapes. Most fruits are much lower in sugar and much higher in acid than grapes and require amelioration with sugar and water. Special equipment has been devised for certain operations such as removing the pulp from the pits of the stone fruits. Clarification can also be a problem. On the plus side for wineries, many fruits are processed after they have been frozen, which means that winemaking for those fruits can be carried on throughout the year. Because fruit wines do not need to be aged, they can be released soon after bottling.[45]

The first wineries east of the Appalachians to produce fruit wines exclusively were located in New England. Each of the three described here achieved recognition far beyond their state borders. Nashoba Valley Winery in Bolton, Massachusetts, was started by Jack Partridge. He began his commercial career in 1978 by selling a few cases of wine in a store near his home in the Boston suburb of Somerville, opened his first winery in Concord in 1980, and three years later bought fifty acres of land with forty-five acres of orchards in Bolton. In 1983 he made 12,000 gallons of wine in ten different varieties and styles. As he wrote in 1983, "Compared to grapes, the world of fruit wines is unexplored territory. That's the way we like to think of it, and that's what we set out to do at Nashoba Valley Winery: explore that territory. There's no map."[46] Among his wines that year were a blend of apple and pear aged in oak, a dry cranberry-apple wine, and a sparkling apple wine.

Robert and Kathe Bartlett opened their Bartlett Maine Estate Winery in Gouldsboro, Maine, in 1983 and saw their production rise from 600 gallons in their first year to more than 14,000 gallons by 1990. Their wine list included wines made from apples, raspberries, and strawberries, but it was their blueberry and pear wines that attracted attention. Five different blueberry wines were made that ranged from dry to sweet with the dry wines aged either in American or French oak. The French oaks used were Navarre, Alliers, Tronçais, or Vosges. A nouveau blueberry wine was made using the traditional carbonic maceration. Four pear wines were made: dry, semi-dry, sweet, and a reserve aged in Limousin oak. Both the blueberry and pear wines were also made in blends with apple wine.[47]

The Joseph Cerniglia Winery in Proctorsville, Vermont, opened in 1986 and specialized in apple wines. As many as eight varietal apple wines were on sale at any one time. A spiced apple wine was produced as well as wines from other fruits. In addition, the winery made Vermont Hard Cider, a product described as more like a wine than a cider because its 12 percent alcohol content was much higher than the 4–6 percent alcohol ciders imported from France or England. By 1990 the winery produced between 50,000 and 60,000 gallons of wine and cider. A year later the winery developed a new product, Woodchuck Cider, which became an immediate success with production of 1.2 million gallons in 1996. In that year a partnership called the Green Mountain Cidery was formed with the Stroh Brewing Company of Detroit for the production of Woodchuck ciders. The Green Mountain Cidery was located in Springfield, Vermont, with a production capacity of 5 million gallons.[48]

Because of the emphasis he was placing on apple wine, Joseph Cerniglia was insistent on calling his winery an "apple winery." The first commercial winery in the United States to specialize in hard cider was West County Winery in Colrain, Massachusetts, which opened in 1984. Judith and Terry Maloney made an initial 300 gallons that year and increased their production to 3,500 gallons a decade later. Their orchard expanded from three acres at the start to 1,400 trees of English, French, and American varieties of cider apples.[49]

Those making fruit wines in early days were concerned about the image of their wines. Despite the history and tradition of fruit wines, the public associated them with Boone's Farm wines and a variety of mass-produced fruit-flavored wines. One of the keys in creating a positive image lay in getting people to try them and like them.[50] Another was to emphasize the affinity of fruit wines with food. In 1982, Nashoba Valley Winery published *A Partridge in a Pear Sauce,* a forty-eight-page book of fruit wine recipes, in which Partridge wrote that "because the range of fruit wine flavors is much broader than that of grape wines, a whole new field of cookery is now possible." The Bartletts worked closely with area restaurants to hold special dinners pairing Bartlett wines with gourmet dishes. Cerniglia made the decision to market varietal apple wines when he noticed that people shopping for apples did not just ask for apples, but for specific varieties such as Granny Smith, Golden Delicious, or Northern Spy. When they spot a bottle of wine labeled Granny Smith, they at least know what that apple tastes like.

Thomas Amabile of Cream Ridge Vineyards and Champagne Cellars in Cream Ridge, New Jersey, has pointed out that experimentation is the key to a winery's success with fruit wines and that it can involve contradictory approaches. On the one hand, there is great appeal for fruit wines that are fruity and taste like the fruit they are made from; on the other hand, oak can be used to create wines with a unique taste. It will be up to the customer to decide which wines are purchased, and these will be the wines the winery will continue to make. His successful experiments with fruit wines went beyond oak-aged cherry and pear wines to an attention-getting Cabernet Sauvignon-Chancellor blend with cherry wine added.[51]

Many wineries have shown that a specialty fruit wine can be profitable. By 1981, for example, Naylor Wine Cellars in Stewartstown, Pennsylvania, began making a holiday Sugar Plum wine that is placed on sale in early December and sells out before Christmas. Sometimes a signature wine can be created accidentally. The year 1992 was great for raspberries in Ontario, and Southbrook Farms in Richmond Hill had an excess they put in the freezer until they could decide what to do with them. Because Southbrook Farms also had a winery, they decided to make a raspberry wine. Their Framboise was a raspberry wine fortified with grape spirits to 14½ percent alcohol. What they did not expect was that 1,600 cases would be sold in 1995 after the winery won the Bordeaux Liquipak Trophy that year as the top fortified fruit dessert wine in the world at New Zealand's World Fruit Wine Competition.[52]

As noted earlier, most fruits contain much less sugar than grapes and amelioration is required to produce the correct amount of alcohol. Sugar is the most commonly used sweetener today although North River Winery in Jacksonville, Vermont, has used 10 percent maple syrup to sweeten its Vermont Harvest apple wine. Roger A. Morse, a former professor of apiculture at Cornell University, has traced the history of sugar from the first known sugar mill in China about 200 BC to its introduction in Europe about 600 AD.[53] At the time of the American Revolution there was little sugar production in America. The per capita consumption was about twelve pounds per year in the eighteenth century and only about fifty pounds by the mid-nineteenth century, both far short of the nearly 140 pounds in 1980. The scarcity of sugar may have been one reason why much more cider than apple wine was made in the colonies.

Other agricultural products have also been used for making wine. Dandelion wine, long a favorite of home winemakers, has been produced commercially. Vendramino Winery in Paw Paw, Michigan, introduced a dry 10 percent alcohol Onion Wyne in 1979. As of this writing, Peaks of Otter Winery in Bedford, Virginia, makes an Apple Pepper wine, a blend of 95 percent apple wine and a 5 percent chili pepper wine made from thirty varieties of peppers. In the early 1990s, Chatham Winery on Cape Cod in Chatham, Massachusetts, made flower wines from hibiscus, cactus, and honeysuckle. The list of unusual wines made commercially somewhere in the East is a long one.

Honey wine, or mead, is simply honey diluted and allowed to ferment. Morse believes it may have been one of the first alcoholic beverages made by man because in ancient times there was no sugar and relatively few fruits. The principal sweetener was honey, and honey was one of the few things from which an alcoholic beverage could be made. Cave drawings that show the harvesting of honey have been found that date back 12,000 years.

The tradition of mead in Europe never caught on in the United States because wine was already available when the country was very young.[54] The earliest winery in the United States to make honey wine exclusively was probably Little Hungary Farm Winery in Buckhannon, West Virginia, opened in 1985 by Ferenc Androczi, a native of Hungary.[55] He called his honey wines "melomel," a name for meads made with fruit. In 1996, the American Mead Association listed twenty-three wineries in the East, eight of them in Canada, that were making mead.[56]

Muscadine Wines

Muscadine grapes are native to the southeastern states and the Gulf Coast from Florida to Texas. Like the Niagaras and other labrusca grapes in northern states, they have distinctive, highly intense aromas and flavors that have made their wines favorites of generations of Southerners. Most muscadines belong to the species *Vitis rotundifolia* and are unlike other grapes grown in the East in that they grow in small clusters rather than bunches and have round berries the size of a cherry or marble.[57]

The best-known muscadine is the Scuppernong, a bronze muscadine known at first as the "Big White Grape" after it was discovered in 1755 along the Scuppernong River in North Carolina.[58] It was the dominant muscadine cultivar from that time through the middle of the twentieth century because the wine made from it was superior to that made from the more common dark-skinned muscadines. Modern breeding programs resulted in improved muscadine cultivars with increased yields and quality that largely displaced the Scuppernong in commercial production. The most important varieties today are Carlos and Magnolia for white wine and Noble for red.

Muscadine wines were made in quantity as early as 1565 in the Spanish settlements in Florida. Over the years, just as was the case with Concords in the North, the muscadines were important in the fresh fruit market and were used for jams and jellies. A traditional use for homeowners was to grow muscadines on backyard arbors and put the homemade wines in Mason jars.[59] Commercial use was primarily for wine, and before Prohibition 60 percent of muscadine production was used for wine. In 1880, census figures showed that Mississippi produced 210,000 gallons of wine; Alabama, 422,670; and Georgia more than 900,000, most of it from Scuppernong. There were 31 wineries in Mississippi and there were more than 100 wineries along the coast from North Carolina around Florida to Mississippi. Virginia Dare, a wine made by Paul Garrett, was the most popular wine in the United States prior to and just after Prohibition. Initially it was a 100 percent Scuppernong wine, but a shortage of that variety caused it to be blended later with vinifera wine from California, although care was taken to retain the distinctive Scuppernong flavor.

When Prohibition ended, the muscadine wine industry was not rebuilt primarily because prohibitionist forces remained strong in the South. It was not until the 1960s that muscadine production for wine was seen as a way to aid depressed state economies and provide an alternative profitable crop for farmers.[60]

In 1966, Mississippi became the last state to vote for Repeal, and in 1972 Louis Wise, the agricultural dean at Mississippi State University began looking for a way to boost his food and nutrition program. He found an ally in Dr. Boris J. Stojanovic, a former German prisoner of war from Yugoslavia, whose family had had a small winery. When the state legislature passed the "Native Wine Law" in 1976, making it legal to establish and operate wineries, seed money became available and the A. B. McKay Food and Enology Laboratory was established at Mississippi State with Stojanovic as director.[61] In 1977 Richard P. Vine became the cellarmaster and research assistant at the laboratory, and he was appointed coordinator in 1985. In the same year, Ellen Harkness (later Ellen Butz), joined the program as research analyst and microbiologist. Mississippi State University became not only the leader in muscadine research for the South but an early training center in enology and viticulture for the East. A degree-granting program in enology and viticulture was established in 1980.

Historically, most muscadine wines in the South were big, heavy, aroma-filled sweet dessert wines that were high in alcohol, but not fortified. As was the case with the labruscas in the North, it was difficult to make dry table wines from them. Again, as in the North, researchers in the South began working not only to create improved muscadine varieties and wine styles, but also to make hybrid crosses that would be resistant to Pierce's disease and that would make premium table wines in a more European style. One such wine was made from Blanc Du Bois, a white hybrid grape developed by Dr. John A. Mortensen at the University of Florida and introduced in 1987.[62]

Early Wine History, State by State

After Prohibition ended in 1933, wineries opened in the eastern United States as soon as it was legally possible and economically feasible to do so. Each state in the East has a wine history it can be proud of even though states that got an early start—such as New York and Ohio—receive more recognition. The early history of the modern wine industry in each state begins when the first wineries opened and usually continues to the point where the success of the industry is no longer in doubt.[1]

Alabama

Alabama's Farm Winery Act was signed on June 6, 1979, by Governor Fob James. Much of the credit for the passage of the legislation goes to Jim and Marianne Eddins who established Perdido Vineyards in Perdido. Jim planted the first fifty acres of muscadines in 1972. The grapes were sold to Bartels Winery across the state line in Florida until the owner died. With the loss of the market for his grapes, Eddins went to the legislature for help. At that time in Alabama, sales could only be made through state stores, wholesalers, or out of state. The resulting bill permitted a "native farm winery" to produce up to 100,000 gallons a year and sell not only to the ABC Board but also to wholesalers, retailers, and consumers for off-premise consumption. Perdido Vineyards opened on September 1, 1980.[2]

In the mid-1980s, two farm wineries got their start. Wayne Braswell opened Braswell's Winery in Dora, and Susan and Kelly Bryant opened Bryant's Vineyard in Talladega.

Arkansas

When Prohibition ended, the Arkansas legislature passed the Bonded Winery Act to ease a surplus of grapes that had built up during the Depression.[3] To encourage wineries to open, out-of-state wineries were taxed at the rate of 75 cents a gallon and Arkansas wineries 5 cents. More than 100 wineries opened, most of them making 20 percent alcohol wines from surplus Concords for sale to hillbillies. Reaction set in and many counties voted themselves dry as a way of closing down the wineries. By 1945 there were fifty-six wineries, and they dwindled further to thirty-three by 1950, ten in 1973, and five in 1977.

The wine industry that remained was centered in Altus where Swiss immigrants had settled in the 1870s. Two of them, Johann Andreas Wiederkehr and Jacob Post, opened wineries in 1880 that their descendants turned into large wineries. In the 1970s, Post Winery, operated by Matthew J. Post and his family, had storage capacity of about 400,000 gallons; and Wiederkehr Wine Cellars, with Alcuin C. Wiederkehr at the helm, had over 2 million gallons in storage capacity.

Wiederkehr was a graduate of Notre Dame and was studying law at the University of Arkansas when he joined the winery in 1958. From the beginning he knew that he wanted to be involved with the winery, and as an exchange student he went to Bordeaux to study winemaking and spent time working in a vineyard. He recognized the need for legislation to help the winery, and over the years he drafted thirteen bills. The first, which was enacted in 1961 and gave confidence to the industry, permitted a winery to continue to operate even if the county it was located in voted to become dry. A Native Dinner Wine Act in 1965 allowed restaurants for the first time to serve Arkansas wine with food in restaurants. That same year the Weinkeller Restaurant opened at Wiederkehr Wine Cellars, one of the first winery restaurants in the United States.[4]

Another winery at this time was the Henry J. Sax Winery, founded in 1934 and named after Alfred Sax, another of the Swiss immigrants who came to Altus in the 1870s. Eugene Post, Matthew Post's brother, started Mount Bethel Winery in 1956. In 1967, Cowie Wine Cellars opened in Paris, fifty miles south of Altus.[5]

In 1966, the University of Arkansas started a viticulture and enology program at Fayetteville. Leading the program from its inception was Justin R. Morris, who received his Ph.D. from Rutgers University in 1964 and began working in extension at the University of Arkansas that same year. Morris later became known nationally and internationally for the development of the Morris-Oldridge Mechanized Vineyard System that began in 1973 in cooperation with Lowell grape grower Tommy Oldridge.

Connecticut

Haight Vineyard in Litchfield was licensed in 1978, the same year that the farm winery bill was passed in Connecticut. Sherman P. Haight, Jr., the fourth generation of his family to operate the family textile mill in Georgia, planted 200 vines in 1974 and, encouraged by Dr. Frank and others, planted fifteen acres in 1975. An old post and beam tobacco barn was converted into a winery and he hired Shorn Mills, who had helped draft the farm winery act, as his winemaker. In five years production had reached 13,000 gallons. His daughter, Katie Haight, served as lab technician, bookkeeper, and winery representative.[6]

St. Hilary's Vineyard in North Grosvenor Dale was founded by Peter Kerensky, formerly the executive chef at Brown University. He started planting vines in 1962 and worked for years to get farm winery legislation passed. He was also the founding president of the Connecticut Grapegrowers Association. In May 1979, he opened his winery for sales to the public. He made wine only from the labruscas, some of which were aged in oak. When he died in 1989, his wife Mary and their children kept the winery open for a short time.[7]

Charlotte and Tom Young planted eight acres of grapes in 1977 and opened Stonecrop Vineyards in Stonington in 1980. Production probably never exceeded 1,500 cases. Illness in the family forced the closing of the winery within a few years of its opening.[8]

Joan and August W. Loos founded Hamlet Hill Winery in Pomfret. They planted five rows of French hybrids in 1975 and made their first 200 gallons of wine in 1978. In 1979, they sold their crop with the exception of the grapes needed for their legal 200 gallons as home winemakers. They produced 10,000 bottles in 1980 and opened the winery on November 15, 1981. Henry Maubert and John Spitzer acquired Hamlet Hill in 1986 but closed in June 1990 due to bankruptcy proceedings.[9]

William and Judith Hopkins decided to switch to grape growing and winemaking on their farm in New Preston when the dairy business began to decline in the late 1970s. They planted five acres in 1978 and added ten more in 1980. A nineteenth-century dairy barn was converted into a winery, Hopkins Vineyard, in 1979, and that same year they rushed grapes they bought in the Finger Lakes. In ten years they had twenty-five acres of vines and wine production had reached 7,000 cases.[10]

Another early vineyard and winery was that of Tom and Barbara Clarke. Tom was a founding member of the American Wine Society and planted a vineyard in 1965 in Marlboro, New York. For many years they lived in New Canaan, Connecticut, and on weekends Tom would go to Marlboro to tend the vineyards. When the Farm Winery Act was passed in Connecticut, the Clarkes bought a fifty-eight-acre property in Stonington and moved there in 1979. They sold their Marlboro vineyard to Allan and Judy McKinnon who renamed it Cottage Vineyards and started a winery. The Clarkes bonded Clarke Vineyard and Winery in 1983 and made 4,000 gallons. Tom Clarke died in May 1986 and, after his death,

Nick and Happy Smith bought the property and changed the name to Stonington Vineyards.[11]

Delaware

Nassau Valley Vineyards, Delaware's first winery, was founded in 1987 when Margaret I. Raley and her father, Robert A. Raley, Jr., began planting seven acres of grapes on the 116-acre family farm near Lewes. In 1991 they were responsible for the passage of farm winery legislation in the short space of two months and their winery opened in October 1993.

Florida

Interest in growing grapes and making wine in Florida started with the French Huguenots in the sixteenth century and continued into the wine grape boom of the Prohibition years. The Florida Grape Growers Association was founded in 1923, one of the oldest organizations of its kind in the United States. For more than 400 years winemakers were limited to using muscadines or citrus fruits because of

Figure E.1: Jeanne Burgess, wine-maker, and Keith Mullins, general manager, at Lakeridge Vineyards in Clermont, Florida. The winery originally started in 1982 as Lafayette Vineyards and Winery near Tallahassee. Photo by author, 1997.

Pierce's disease that precluded growing the vinifera and vinifera hybrids. Today's commercial farm wineries came into existence as a result of the passage of the Florida Farm Winery Law in 1979, due primarily to efforts put forth by the Florida Grape Growers Association, and by university research that followed.

Florida's Farm Winery Law reduced the license fee from $1,000 to $50, and eliminated the state tax on Florida wines. Researchers in Florida developed new bunch grape varieties such as Stover, Lake Emerald, and Suwannee that were resistant to Pierce's disease and could make quality table wines. Cooperative breeding projects with other southern states led to improved muscadine varieties such as Welder, Noble, and Magnolia.[12]

In 1979, prior to the passage of the Farm Winery Law, Joe Midulla, Sr., opened Fruit Wines of Florida in Tampa, primarily making citrus wines. The first farm winery to open was Alaqua Vineyard in Freeport by Foster and Rebecca Burgess. They built their winery in 1980 and it opened in 1981. Also in 1981, Florida Heritage Winery in Anthony was opened by Robert and Inge Price. Two wineries opened in 1983: Lafayette Vineyards and Winery in Tallahassee by Gary Ketchum and Gary Cox, and Wines of St. Augustine in Tampa by Ed Gogel.[13]

Georgia

When Georgia repealed its Prohibition law in 1936, Governor Eugene Talmadge sought a way to solve his state's peach surplus. He persuaded the state to lower the tax rate on wine made from fruit grown in Georgia and the Monarch Wine Company opened that same year. The winery was soon making more than a million gallons of wine a year, mainly peach wine.

Bill and Barbara Rosser planted the first of their thirteen acres of grapes in High Shoals in 1979. They and a number of other growers organized the Georgia Grape Growers Association and obtained passage of Georgia's Farm Winery Law in 1983. Under the new law wineries could sell wine on their premises and at up to five additional locations. The annual license fee was reduced from $1,000 to $50 and the tax rate per gallon dropped to 40 cents as opposed to $1.50 for out-of-state wines.

The second winery to open after the passage of the farm winery legislation was Château Élan in Braselton by Donald E. Panoz, the owner of pharmaceutical firms in Ireland and Georgia. Surrounding the French style château were 200 acres of vineyards, a conference center, restaurants, golf courses, and the winery, all on a 2,400-acre property.[14] The winery opened in 1984 with Ed Friedrich as winemaker.

Habersham Vineyards & Winery, founded in 1983 by Tom Slick in Baldwin, was the third winery to open. Slick had planted the first of his thirty acres of vineyards in 1979, and his location was a good one. The highlands of northeast Georgia offer some protection from Pierce's disease, and in the late 1990s and early 2000s new wineries began to plant grapes and open wineries in that region. Three were located in Dahlonega, the place where gold was first discovered in the United States in 1828. Three Sisters Vineyards and Winery, owned by Doug and Sharon Paul, was followed by Craig and Cydney Kritzer's Frogtown Cellars and Karl and Linda Boegner's Wolf Mountain Vineyards.[15]

Illinois

Early grape growing in Illinois centered around the town of Nauvoo on the banks of the Mississippi River. The first vineyard there was planted in 1847 by John Tanner from Bern, Switzerland, and Alois Rheinberger from Lichtenstein founded the first winery three years later.[16] In 1857, Emile Baxter opened a winery that has remained Illinois' oldest operating winery. After the winery closed during Prohibition, Cecil Baxter received the license for Gem City Vineland Company in 1936, the first winery to be bonded in Illinois and the only winery in the state at that time. In 1987, Kelly Logan and his wife Brenda, the fifth generation of Baxters, took over the business and renamed it Baxter's Vineyards.

Starting in the 1930s, most of the wine production in Illinois came from the large Mogen David Winery in Chicago, which made several million gallons of kosher-style wines from New York State grapes.

In 1963, Bern Ramey planted grapes in Monee, and he and Joseph Allen subsequently opened Ramey and Allen Champagne Cellars. Heavy damage to the vineyard from 2,4-D herbicide that had been sprayed on neighboring cornfields led to the sale of their operation in 1970 to Dr. John E. Thompson. Before the purchase, Thompson received assurances that the spraying would stop, and he then restored the vineyards and continued the winery as the Thompson Winery Company.

Legislation was passed in Illinois in 1976 that enabled a winery to sell part of its production at retail. Quick to take advantage of this were the Baxters, who opened a tasting room in 1977.

Fred and Lynn Koehler opened Lynfred Winery in Roselle in October 1979, as what they say was the result of a home winemaking hobby gone wild. The suggestion to open a winery was made by Lynn Koehler to her husband as he was planning to retire after twenty-five years of managing restaurants and country clubs.

Passage of farm winery legislation seemed to be a certainty in 1981, but a proposed hefty tax increase on alcoholic beverages to aid the financially troubled Chicago Transit Authority was piggybacked onto the farm winery bill.[17] The legislation did not pass. About this time, a Limited Wine Manufacturers License was created for wineries making less than 40,000 gallons exclusively from Illinois grapes. The fee was set at $120.

In 1985, the Lawlor family opened Galena Cellars Vineyard and Winery in Galena. Robert and Joyce Lawlor and their daughter Christina had opened their first winery, Christina Wine Cellars, in McGregor, Iowa, in 1976; and two years later they opened Christina Winery in LaCrosse, Wisconsin. Both of these wineries were closed in 1990 to permit them to focus on the Galena winery.

Also in 1985, Harry and Rita Hussmann opened Chateau Ra-Ha in Grafton and Mark Hendershot founded Waterloo Winery in Waterloo. The first winery in southern Illinois was Alto Vineyards in Alto Pass. Guy Renzaglia planted five acres of French hybrids in 1984 and opened the winery three years later.

Indiana

The earliest sites of grape growing and winemaking in Indiana were in the southern part of the state. During the first decade of the nineteenth-century the Swiss followers of Jean Jacques Dufour settled near Vevay along the Kentucky River after the vineyards of the Kentucky Vineyard Society began to fail. In 1814 George Rapp's Harmonists settled in New Harmony along the Wabash River where they grew grapes and made wine before returning to western Pennsylvania where they founded Old Economy in 1825.[18]

There were no wineries in Indiana when Prohibition ended, and the 1935 Liquor Control Act specified that wineries could not sell to consumers or retailers, but only to wholesalers. This restrictive legislation prevented new wineries from opening until 1971 when Indiana became the second state to pass farm winery legislation. Wineries then became able to produce up to 50,000 gallons of table wine and sell directly to consumers, restaurants, and stores. The annual license fee was set at $250 and no additional licensing by county authorities would be required.

It is not surprising that the first two wineries to open were by the two home winemakers most responsible for Indiana's small winery legislation. Dr. Donald L. MacDaniel, an optometrist in Connersville, formed a partnership that included three doctors and opened Treaty Line Wine Cellars near Liberty in August 1971, just four months after passage of the legislation. William W. Oliver and his wife Mary opened Oliver Winery in Bloomington in May 1973.

By 1975, there were five more wineries in Indiana. The first three of these were Villa Medeo Vineyards Winery in Madison by Mike and Elizabeth Mancuso, Swiss Valley Vineyards in Vevay by Alvin Meyer, and Easley Enterprises in Indianapolis by John Easley. Next to be licensed was Banholzer Winecellars in Hesston. Carl Banholzer had come to Indiana from Michigan where he and his wife Janet had been cofounders of Tabor Hill Vineyard and Winecellar. The last of the five was Golden Rain Tree Winery in Wadesville by a corporation that included Murli Dharmadhikari as vice president and winemaker.[19]

After retiring from the Navy in 1968, Ben Sparks and his wife Lee bought seventy acres of land in Brown County, planted grapes in 1969, and opened Possum Trot Vineyards in Unionville in 1978. In 1972, out of concern for the development of the industry, they began to organize a trade organization, and in 1975 the Indiana

Winegrowers Guild was incorporated. Ben was also primarily responsible for the first Indiana Grape-Wine Symposium held in 1974.[20]

The industry was helped in 1975 when the tax for small wineries was reduced from 45 cents to 25 cents a gallon. A major advance for the industry came in 1989 when the legislature established the Indiana Grape Market Development Program that was governed by a fifteen-member Indiana Wine Grape Council and administered by the Purdue University School of Agriculture. Among the people hired for research and extension were Dr. Bruce Bordelon, viticulturist; Dr. Richard Vine, enologist; and Ellen Harkness, wine quality lab overseer. Theresa M. Browning was appointed the first marketing specialist, a position that was subsequently held for many years by Sally Linton (later Sally Peart).

Iowa

The modern wine industry in Iowa got its start in January 2000, when Ron Mark, Paul Tabor, and Bill Brown formed the Iowa Grape Growers Association. At that time there were thirteen wineries in Iowa, eleven of them in the Amana Colonies, a religious communal society that had originated in Germany and settled in Iowa in 1855. A native wine law passed after Repeal allowed them to sell their wines to anyone. The other two wineries had opened in 1997, Mark's Summerset Winery in Indianola and Tabor's Family Winery in Baldwin. Bill Brown was a grower but had not yet opened his Timber Hill Winery in Leon.[21]

Prior to forming the association, the three men met to decide what was most needed for Iowa growers and winemakers. Along with favorable legislation, education was a basic need and no help was available from Iowa State University. By 2001, they were able to get the Iowa Department of Agriculture involved and some viticulture assistance was made available at Iowa State University. In February 2002, the Iowa legislature formed the Iowa Grape and Wine Commission within the state's Department of Agriculture, and needed funding for research and promotion became a reality through the allocation of the 5 percent tax on wine.

In 2003, a ten-year plan to provide for the sustained growth of the industry was started by the now renamed Iowa Wine Growers Association in cooperation with Iowa State University Extension. Helping develop the plan were legislators, retailers, and people from government, education, vineyards, and wineries. Within four years, Iowa had sixty-two wineries.

Kansas

Carry Nation and her hatchet are inextricably linked with Kansas in the lore of Prohibition even though her violent crusade against illegal saloons did not start until a decade after Kansas enacted statewide prohibition in 1880. Anti-alcohol sentiment was still strong in Kansas in 1948 when the legislature voted to permit county option. Other restrictions were slowly lifted, but there was a gradual interest in grape growing. In addition to hobby vineyards, there was a commercial venture that grew French hybrids for the table grape market. Kansas State University began varietal trials and research on grape hardiness and production in 1974.[22]

Robert G. Rizza, a pediatrician in Halstead, first planted three acres of grapes in 1978 and soon became instrumental in the passage of farm winery legislation.[23] What was usually part of a farm winery law in other states took three steps over a five-year period in Kansas. In 1983 farmers were allowed to make wine and sell it in bottles on their farms; in 1985 the license fee was reduced to $250 and they could sell wine to retailers; and, in 1988, they could sell wine for off-premises consumption and also to licensed wine distributors and others.

By 1987, there was sufficient interest in growing grapes to organize the Kansas Grape Growers and Wine Makers Association, and Rizza became its first president. The April 1988 legislation also authorized the State Board of Agriculture to establish a grape growing and winemaking advisory program to aid in the technology, promotion, and marketing of Kansas grapes and wine. It did not take long for the first winery to get started. On August 1, 1988, James E. and Eulalia Fair bonded their Fields of Fair in St. George, and the grand opening was held in May 1989.[24] In the same year, John E. and Luella Zibert opened Balkan Winery in Girard.

Les Meyer and his daughter Michelle Meyer Havey planted the first of their fourteen acres of vines in 1986 and opened Holy-Field Vineyard and Winery in Basehor in 1994. Also in 1994, a brother and sister, John and Merry Brewer opened Wyldewood Cellars in Mulvane. Their winery soon became the largest in Kansas with production of 40,000 gallons, 70 percent of it elderberry wine.

Villarizza, the winery planned by Robert Rizza, never opened.

Kentucky

In 1970, F. Carlton Colcord planted twenty-five acres of hybrids on his farm near Paris, and four years later he had expanded the acreage to fifty-five. The license fee to open a winery was $1,500 a year, and his first full crop was sold to wineries in Indiana and Ohio while he and other growers began working for legislation to have the license fee reduced.[25] Kentucky's powerful whiskey lobby prevented a bill from passing in 1974, but in 1976 when the Small Winery Act was passed reducing the license fee to $250, the wholesalers had the bill amended so that wineries could sell only to wholesalers, and not retailers; and limited sales to consumers to one quart at a time.

The Colcord Winery opened on November 11, 1977, and for a time Helen M. Turley was the winemaker. In 1982, the winery was put up for sale and, although Colcord attributed it to his long absences in London where he was involved in the oil business, the restrictions on the sale of wine were certainly a factor.

In 1981, the Kentucky Vineyard Society, founded by Jean Jacques Dufour in 1798, was reactivated by a group of people interested in grape growing and winemaking under the leadership of Colcord and Dr. Robert Miller of Eastern Kentucky University. One of their first successful efforts was to get the law changed to allow wineries to sell to retailers and increasing the limit on sales to consumers to a case at a time. Winery starts, however, did not happen until legislation was passed establishing a Grape Industry Advisory Committee. Through the efforts of the committee a farm winery bill was drawn up that created favorable provisions for establishing wineries. The Kentucky Farm Winery Law became effective on July 13, 1990.

By 1994, there were four wineries in Kentucky. Three of them were farm wineries: Barker's Blackberry Hill Winery in Crittenden, Bravard Vineyards and Winery in Hopkinsville, and Broad Run Vineyards in Louisville. The fourth, Springhill Vineyard and Winery in Springfield, opened in 1993 under the Small Winery Act.[26]

Louisiana

Winemaking in Louisiana dates back to the mid-eighteenth century when Jesuit priests made wine in that state. Among other winemaking endeavors was an orange wine industry that flourished for a time in Plaquemines Parish. The last of these wineries, Les Orangers Louisianais in Port Sulphur, closed three years before the native wine law passed in 1990. What put the Gottbrath family out of business was a combination of a freeze that wiped out their orange groves, the end of an exemption from the $1,000 state licensing fee, and the imposition of a law barring producers from selling their wines at the wholesale and retail levels.[27]

Leroy Harvey and Rupert Thompson, two of the founding partners of Feliciana Cellars in 1993, were instrumental in the passage of the 1990 Native Wine Act, which once again made it possible to sell wine at retail and at off-licensed premises. The first winery to be licensed was Casa de Sue Winery and Vineyards in Clinton by Mac and JoAnn Cazedessus in 1992. Their winery specialized in muscadine and blueberry wines. Feliciana Cellars was second, with Jim Hendrickson joining Harvey and Thompson. In addition to three muscadine varieties, they chose to grow Blanc Du Bois, a bunch grape, and Norton. Pontchartrain Vineyards, which opened in 1994 in Covington, started experimenting with French hybrids in 1978 but later concentrated on Blanc Du Bois and Norton.

Maine

In 1981, when Robert and Kathe Bartlett decided they wanted to open a winery making quality fruit wines in Gouldsboro, existing laws in Maine prevented them from opening a tasting room or selling wine on the premises. They researched laws

Figure E.2: Robert and Kathe Bartlett opened Bartlett Maine Estate Winery in Gouldsboro, Maine, in 1984. Photo by author, 1990.

in other states, became involved in drafting legislation for Maine, and lobbied for passage of farm winery legislation. Maine's farm winery law passed in 1983 and went into effect on July 26, 1984. Bartlett Maine Estate Winery opened on August 1, 1983 and quickly became known for its fruit wines, and particularly for its oak-aged blueberry and pear wines. The winery grew rapidly from 600 gallons in 1983 to 14,000 gallons by the end of the decade.[28]

During the summer of 1984, Don Mead and his wife Alison Wampler opened Maine's second winery, Downeast Country Wines, in Pembroke along the extreme eastern coast of Maine near Eastport. In 1987 they moved the winery south to Trenton, not far from Bar Harbor. Their four wines were made from blueberries and apples using old family recipes and methods of winemaking.

It would be seven years before the next winery was founded. Thomas E. Hoey opened Sow's Ear Winery in Brookville in the summer of 1991. Most of the early wineries made fruit and berry wines although there was some experimentation with grapes.[29]

Maryland

Despite the presence in Maryland of two pioneer growers and winemakers, Philip Wagner and Hamilton Mowbray, the wine industry got off to a slow start.[30] Wineries had to cope with highly restrictive state laws and other laws that varied from county to county. One such law restricted winery sales to one bottle of one label to one customer per year.[31] It was not until laws limiting production and sales at the state's wineries began to change starting with passage of the Class 4 Limited Winery Act in 1976.

Wagner encouraged grape growing and some of those who planted vineyards became his growers. Among them were John Ripley and Peter Black who planted five acres of French hybrids in 1973 at their Cedar Point Vineyard near Easton. Their grapes were used by Boordy Vineyard to make the first commercial wine produced from grapes grown on the Eastern Shore.[32]

Five new wineries opened in the 1970s: Provenza Vineyards by Tom and Barbara Provenza in 1974; Byrd Winery by Bret and Sharon Byrd in 1976; Bon Sporonza Winery by Ira Ross, also in 1976; Berrywine Plantation/Linganore Cellars by Jack and Lucille Aellen in 1977; and Ziem Vineyards by Bob and Ruth Ziem in 1977. A major event occurred in 1980 when Philip Wagner retired and sold Boordy Vineyards to the Deford family that for many years had supplied him with French hybrid grapes.[33] The winery moved to Hydes, and under the leadership of Robert B. Deford, III, the new Boordy Vineyards became the largest winery in Maryland.

Two organizations were formed that helped shape the industry, the Maryland Grape Growers Association in 1981 and the Maryland Wineries Association in 1984. Providing some of the leadership in the development of the Maryland industry at this time were Ann and Jerry Milne who had planted fifteen acres of vinifera in the Catoctin Mountains in 1975 and in 1983 partnered with Bob Lyon in opening a winery, Catoctin Vineyards, in Brookeville. In 1986, with the full support of the governor, legislation was passed to create a Maryland Winery and Grape Grower's Advisory Board and Ann Milne was named its first chair.

Massachusetts

Chicama Vineyards became the first winery in Massachusetts when George H. and Catherine Mathiesen planted their first five acres of grapes in West Tisbury on Martha's Vineyard, a ninety-five-minute ferry ride from Woods Hole on Cape Cod. The winery was licensed in 1973 and the first sales took place in 1974. In 1976, the farm winery bill they had worked for was signed into law and the license fee was reduced from $2,200 to $100 a year. By 1982, they were selling 13,500 gallons to summer tourists and year-round residents of the island. The Mathiesens had six children who helped out at various times, but Lynn was there the longest, starting full time in 1978. A graduate of Pratt Art Institute, she had spent nearly four years working at Hanns Kornell Champagne Cellars and Domaine Chandon in the Napa Valley and inaugurated Chicama's Sea Mist line of sparkling wines.[34] George Mathiesen died in 2005 and Catherine Mathiesen on October 21, 2007. A closing party was held on August 9 and 10, 2008, after which only thirty bottles remained unsold.[35]

After receiving a master's degree from Davis and getting two years of practical experience working in the Kaiserstuhl in Germany, David Tower leased an old library building in Cordage Park in North Plymouth for a winery in 1978. He bought grapes from the Lake Erie region and his Commonwealth Winery opened for sales in 1979. After buying grapes out of state for a second year, Tower began contracting for grapes in New England, and by 1985 he had helped plant over sixty acres in Massachusetts. In 1983, the winery moved to a larger location in Plymouth's waterfront district. Unfortunately, undercapitalization had been a problem all along and the winery closed in 1988 after failing to attract additional investment capital. When the winery closed, it was making 16,000 cases of wine, 9,000 of them cranberry wines, their biggest success.[36]

Nashoba Valley Winery got its start in May 1980, when Jack Partridge established the winery in an old woolen mill in Damonmill Square in West Concord. Partridge had been making highly regarded fruit wines at his home in Somerville since 1978 and the winery was an instant success. By 1981, he needed help in winemaking and hired Larry Ames and others in that year's production of 4,000 cases of seven different fruit wines. In 1983, he acquired fifty acres of land including forty-five acres of orchards in Bolton and moved the winery there in 1984. Health problems in Partridge's family necessitated a move to Arizona, and in 1995 the winery was sold to NVW, Ltd., with Rich and Cindy Pelletier becoming the active managing partners.[37]

The next three wineries to open were primarily fruit wineries. Plymouth Colony Winery in Plymouth, specializing in cranberry and cranberry blended wines, was opened in 1983 by Charles Caranci, Jr. Inn Wines in Hatfield was licensed in 1984 by Richard A. Phaneuf as a retirement winery. West County Winery in Colrain became the first winery in the United States to specialize in hard cider when Judith and Terry Maloney opened it in 1984.

Nantucket Vineyard on Nantucket Island could have opened in 1984 had Massachusetts not required a minimum production of 1,000 gallons before a winery could be licensed. Dean and Melissa Long founded Nantucket Vineyard in 1981 and opened for sales in 1986.

Michigan

All of the small wineries in Michigan that existed before Prohibition closed in 1919. Most of the thousands of acres of grapes in the state were Concords that had been increasingly planted after 1900 for the Welch Grape Juice Company. After Repeal, a combination of protectionist laws and consumer preference for sweeter fortified wines led to the creation of a new class of 16 percent "lightly fortified" wines made almost entirely from Concords. These wines dominated the wine lists of the large wineries until Michigan removed wine from the state monopoly stores in 1982.[38]

Figure E.3: Douglas Welsch, a member of the family that started Fenn Valley Vineyards in Fennville, Michigan, became the winery's winemaker. Photo by author, 1982.

It took more than thirty years from the time the first wineries got their start after Prohibition before a small boutique winery, Tabor Hill Vineyard and Winecellar, opened in 1972. In June 1969, the horticulture department at Michigan State University hired Dr. G. Stanley Howell for a combination of research and extension work in small fruits. Howell became interested in wine grapes in 1971 when he learned about the research that was taking place in Ohio and at Geneva, New York. He established an experimental winery, Spartan Cellars, in 1972, and the assistance that Michigan State University provided to growers and winemakers was important in the growth of the industry.

Several organizations helped advance the industry: the Michigan Wine Institute, which voted to provide funding for Howell's research; the Michigan Grape Society; and, most important, the Michigan Grape and Wine Industry Council created by the legislature in 1985 to fund grape and wine research.[39]

Fenn Valley Vineyards got its start in 1973 when William Welsch and his family moved to Fennville after buying a 230-acre property in southwestern Michigan. By 1977, fifty-two acres of grapes had been planted, mainly in French hybrids. The winery opened in 1975 with cherry and other fruit wines for sale, and in 1976 the first grapes grown at Fenn Valley were used for wine. A number of family members were involved from the start with Douglas Welsch as winemaker.[40]

In northern Michigan near Traverse City, two peninsulas extend into Grand Traverse Bay where the moderating influence on the climate provided by both Lake Michigan and the bay permitted early plantings of the vinifera. On Old Mission Peninsula, the first winery to be established was Chateau Grand Traverse in 1975 when Edward O'Keefe brought viticulturists from Geisenheim to plant forty acres of Riesling and Chardonnay, and by 1979 he had built a 50,000 gallon winery. Grape growing on Leelanau Peninsula began in 1965 when Bernard C. Rink planted the first twenty-six acres of French hybrids and opened Boskydel Vineyard in 1976. Two more wineries followed almost immediately on the Leelanau Peninsula: Leelanau Wine Cellars in Omena in 1977 and L. Mawby Vineyards in Suttons Bay a year later.[41]

Minnesota

Winemaking in Minnesota has always been a struggle to find grapes that would survive the harsh winters and also make a palatable wine. The modern history of wine in Minnesota began in 1943 when Elmer Swenson started to breed grapes in Osceola, Wisconsin. Swenson had taken an interest in grapes from his grandfather and was further encouraged by reading T. V. Munson's *Foundations of American Grape Culture*. In 1965 he took a few of his hybrids to a field day at the University of Minnesota's Horticultural Research Center, and in 1969 he became a member of its staff. In 1977, Swenson and the University of Minnesota released Edelweiss and Swenson Red, the first of many named Swenson's crosses that were to prove useful in winemaking.

Several vineyards were planted in Minnesota in the early 1970s, experimenting with French hybrid varieties and Swenson crosses, and in 1975 the Minnesota Grape Growers Association was established. The first winery to open was David MacGregor's Lake Sylvia Vineyard in Maple Lake in 1976. He became a member of the Minnesota Winegrowers Cooperative, which absorbed his vineyard and then in 1983 founded Northern Vineyards in Stillwater. In 1977, David Bailly opened the second winery in Hastings—Alexis Bailly Vineyard. He named the winery after an ancestor who had founded the town of Hastings.[42]

Minnesota passed a farm winery law in 1980. The license fee was reduced from $500 to $25, taxes were cut on in-state wineries, and an upper limit of 50,000 gallons placed on wine production. Peter R. Hemstad was hired to run the breeding program at the University of Minnesota in 1988. Frontenac and La Crescent were the first of a number of important new wine grape varieties to be released under this program.

Mississippi

Mississippi became the last state to repeal Prohibition in 1966. Mississippi State University began a program of enological and viticultural research in 1972, but it was not until 1976 with the passage of the Native Wine Act that there was an incentive for small wineries to open. That act reduced the license fee from $1,800 to $10, cut the wine tax from 55 cents to 5 cents a gallon, and allowed wineries to sell direct to retailers.[43]

In 1977, Otis Rushing and his son Sam opened Winery Rushing near Merigold. By 1980, they had a thirty-acre muscadine vineyard and were producing 25,000 gallons of wine. Thousand Oaks Vineyard, the second winery, was founded in 1978 by Bob and Peggy Burgin in Starkville. Their twenty-five-acre vineyard was planted half in muscadines and half in a combination of French hybrids and labruscas.

The third winery in Mississippi, Almarla Vineyard in Matherville, was founded in 1979 by the retired director of scientific services for the Bureau of Alcohol, Tobacco and Firearms, Alex Mathers. He began his vineyard by planting French hybrids, but soon changed it to twenty-five acres of muscadines. In the same year, veterinarian Scott Galbraith opened Old South Winery in Natchez after planting thirteen acres of muscadines.

Missouri

Missouri had more than 100 wineries prior to Prohibition, and it was from that state that Hermann Jaeger and George Husmann shipped rootstocks to France during the phylloxera epidemic. It was also where Cook's well-known Imperial Champagne got its start.[44] When Prohibition began, the wineries closed. Two monasteries, however, continued to make sacramental wines, one of which was St. Stanislaus Seminary in Florissant, founded by Jesuit missionaries around 1823.[45]

Most of the vineyards were torn out during Prohibition, with the exception of Concords grown by members of the National Grape Cooperative Association. Consumer preference was limited primarily to sweeter dessert-style wines such as those produced by Bardenheier Wine Cellars in St. Louis, a winery that had been founded in 1873 and reopened after Prohibition. The Missouri wine industry, however, was slow to revive even with the creation of a Domestic Wine License that had a sliding price of $5.00 for each 500 gallons produced up to a maximum license fee of $300.00.[46] There was also a stipulation that no more than 5,000 gallons of wine a year made from Missouri fruit could be sold retail at a winery.

The modern wine industry in Missouri goes back to a five-year period beginning in 1965 when several wineries opened their doors, all of them described in chapter 4. These included Stone Hill Winery in Hermann opened by Jim and Betty Held in 1965, Stoltz Vineyard Winery by William B. Stoltz in St. James in 1968, Mount Pleasant Vineyards by Lucian and Eva Dressel in Augusta also in 1968, and St. James Winery by Jim and Pat Hofherr in St. James in 1970.

By the early 1970s, the 5,000-gallon cap on wine that could be sold retail at the winery had become a limitation to Stone Hill's growth, and Jim Held with the help of his local representative in the legislature succeeded in getting the cap raised to

Figure E.4: The Stone Hill Winery in Hermann, Missouri, ceased wine production and the vineyards were abandoned during Prohibition. Jim Held and his wife Betty reopened the winery in 1965. Photo by Linda Jones McKee, 1981.

75,000 gallons. In 1980, the cap was increased to 500,000 gallons as part of a legislative package that amounted to a farm winery act, although it was not called that. Wineries could now use out-of-state fruit, but 95 percent of the wine had to be made from Missouri grown grapes. Only these farm wineries could have on-site sales and tastings, and only these wineries and certain restaurants could sell wine on Sundays.

Two years earlier David Kay, president of 905 International, owner of a chain of wine and liquor retail stores, persuaded the governor to form a task force to study the potential for the grape and wine industry.[47] One outcome was the formation of the Missouri Wine Advisory Board in 1980. An immediate result was the hiring of Dr. Bruce Zoecklein as the state enologist, and a year later Dr. Larry Lockshin was hired as state viticulturist. Both appointments were extension faculty positions at the University of Missouri–Columbia. Topping off the eventful year of 1980 was the creation of the Augusta American viticultural area, the first such appellation in the United States (see chapter 6).

In 1982, the Missouri Grape Growers Association was formed to mobilize support for legislation that in 1983 created the Missouri Grape and Wine Program in the Department of Agriculture. Funding for the program was provided by enacting a special tax of four cents a gallon on all wine sold in Missouri.[48]

Nebraska

The year 1985 marked the passing of Nebraska Farm Wineries Act.[49] Three years earlier, Jim Danielson, a wine retailer, planted wine grapes as a commercial venture at Rock Bluff Vineyards near Plattsmouth. Although he did not plan to open a winery himself, he encouraged others to plant grapes and to think about starting wineries. He realized that legislation would be needed to open wineries, and with the assistance of another early grower, Ed Swanson, and Senator Sandy Schofield, he drafted the farm winery bill.

Swanson started growing grapes experimentally on his mother's land near Battle Creek in the 1970s, and in 1983 he bought 15½ acres near Pierce where he planted more than sixty cultivars for evaluation and learned as much about viticulture and enology as he could. On November 15, 1994, Swanson and his wife Holly held the grand opening of their Cuthills Vineyards, Nebraska's first winery since Prohibition.[50]

The second winery to open was James Arthur Vineyards near Raymond. Jim Jeffers had purchased several hundred acres of land in 1992, and growing grapes on the land was the idea of his son-in-law, James Ballard. With the purchase of Rock Bluff Vineyards from Jim Danielson in 1996, plans for a winery moved quickly and the winery opened on August 30, 1997.

In 1997, a research program was started at the University of Nebraska as the result of a $111,000 grant from the Kimmel Foundation and support from the university. Under the leadership of horticulture professor Paul E. Read, four research vineyards were established starting in 1998, three in southeastern Nebraska and one in the western part of the state. Another major event was the formation in 1998 of the Nebraska Winery and Grape Growers Association for the purpose of encouraging the production and marketing of grapes.

New Hampshire

New England's first winery in modern times was White Mountain Winery in Laconia, New Hampshire. John and Lucille Canepa bonded their winery in 1969 after planting 800 French hybrid vines in 1965 and 1,000 more the following year. In 1982, when John Canepa was seventy-three, attempts were made to sell the winery, and after two changes in ownership Bill Damour bought the winery in 1991, renamed it the New Hampshire Winery, and moved it to Henniker. Financial problems developed and the winery closed a few years later.[51]

There were no wineries in New Hampshire in 1994 when Jewell Towne Vineyards in South Hampton became the first of the two new wineries to open. Peter D. Oldak and his wife Brenda bought a twelve-acre farm in 1977 with the state line between New Hampshire and Massachusetts running through their property. The

Figure E.5: John and Lucille Canepa opened White Mountain Winery in Laconia, New Hampshire, in 1968. Photo by author, 1984.

first grapes were planted in 1982 and by 1990 the sixty varieties of grapes under test were narrowed down to twenty. An eighteenth-century reproduction New England style post and beam barn was completed in 1999. Between 1994 and 2004, wine production increased from 40 cases to 2,000. Oldak has been a leader in encouraging others to grow grapes and make wine and was instrumental in starting the New Hampshire Winery Association in 2006.

Frank W. Reinhold, Jr., and his wife Linda established Flag Hill Winery in Lee in 1996. The first of twenty-one acres of grapes were planted in 1990 and the winery was opened six years later with production of 500 cases of four different wines. A distillery was added in 2004 and the winery was renamed the Flag Hill Winery and Distillery. Reinhold was also active in the development of the state's industry.[52]

New Jersey

With the coming of Prohibition, all of New Jersey's wineries closed with the exception of Renault Winery in Egg Harbor City, which remained open for the purpose of producing medicinal wines. When Prohibition ended, the state legislature permitted the issuance of one winery license for each one million residents.[53] Seven plenary licenses were granted with each winery being allowed to have limited retail sales on its premises. Qualifying wineries, in addition to Renault, included Tomasello Winery, which had vineyards going back to 1888. The winery was opened in 1933 by Frank Tomasello and passed along to his sons, Charles and Joe. A new winery licensed in 1934 was Gross' Highland Winery in Absecon, founded by a German winemaker John Gross. After Gross died, the winery was run by his grandson, Bernard F. "Skip" D'Arcy, who changed the name of the winery to Bernard D'Arcy Wine Cellars. In 1987, the winery was sold to developers.

Other wineries that opened prior to farm winery legislation in 1981 included Jacob Lee Winery in 1938 in Bordentown, Antuzzi's Winery in Delran in 1974, Balic Winery in Mays Landing in 1974, Polito Vineyards in Vincentown in 1978, and Tewksbury Wine Cellars in Lebanon in 1979. There were seven wineries operating in New Jersey when the Farm Winery Act was passed.

In 1980, six winegrowers in northwest New Jersey formed the Hunterdon Winegrowers Association and in the same year drafted legislation for a farm winery license. The Farm Winery Act was passed into law on September 10, 1981. In 1984, a second important piece of legislation that helped advance the industry was the creation of the New Jersey Wine Industry Advisory Council to serve in an advisory capacity to the New Jersey Department of Agriculture.[54]

Eight new wineries received farm winery licenses and opened wineries in the first four years following the enactment of the Farm Winery Act. Michael Fisher founded Amwell Valley Vineyard in Ringoes in August 1982, followed by Lou Caracciolo's Amalthea Cellars in December of that year.

James and Jonetta Williams established DelVista Vinyards in Frenchtown in July 1983. "Vinyards" is not a misspelling, Williams has explained, and was spelled without an "e" because he wanted to emphasize "wine"-yards. In December, 1983, Rudolf Marchesi established Alba Vineyard in Milford.

In October 1984, two more wineries opened—John and Marie Abplanalp's King's Road Vineyard in Asbury and, a month later, Four Sisters Winery in Belvedere by Robert and Laurie Matarazzo. Finally, in 1985, Franklin and Sylvia Salek established Sylvin Farms in Germainia in August, and Paul and Susan Tamuzza founded Tamuzza Vineyards in Hope in October.

New York

When the farm winery bill was passed in 1976, there were nineteen wineries in New York including the large wineries producing primarily kosher wines. In 1976, the wine industry was located in three areas of the state, all of them near large bodies of water that modify the wine growing environment: the Hudson River Valley, the Finger Lakes, and the western part of the state along Lake Erie.

The Finger Lakes

When the Farm Winery Act passed in 1976, Walter Taylor's Bully Hill Vineyards in Hammondsport was already in business in the Finger Lakes, as was Dr. Frank's winery. In 1973, the Villa D'Ingianni Winery in Dundee was opened by Dr. Vincente D'Ingianni, a medical doctor who came to the Finger Lakes from New Orleans. The winery was licensed in 1972 and opened in 1973. In the early 1980s, it was taken over by James and Carole Kilgore.[55]

One of the first wineries to open after the Farm Winery Act became law was Heron Hill Winery in Hammondsport on Keuka Lake in 1977. The principals were Peter Johnstone and John and Josephine Ingle, Jr. In 1968, the Heron Hill Vineyards had been planted, and Ingle Vineyards followed in 1972.

The first winery to open on Seneca Lake in modern times was Glenora Wine Cellars in Dundee in the spring of 1978. Its initial crush of 16,500 gallons was made in 1977. Gene Pierce, Eastman Beers, Ed Dalrymple, and Howard Kimball were the four partners who opened the winery. On April 8, 1987, it was announced that Glenora and Finger Lakes Wine Cellars were forming a partnership and both were being taken over by International Trading and Education Company (ITECO) based in Boston.[56] In 1991, Pierce, Dalrymple, and John Potter bought back the winery from ITECO. By 2000, the winery was making approximately 38,000 cases.[57]

A year later, another winery on Seneca Lake, Wagner Vineyards, was opened by Bill Wagner in Lodi. The winery building attracted attention because of its octagonal design. By 2000, the winery had 240 acres of vines and was producing 50,000 cases a year.[58]

Several other wineries opened in the late 1970s. Andrew Colaruotolo began planting the first of forty acres of grape in 1974 and licensed Casa Larga Vineyards in Fairport in 1978. John LeBeck renovated a 150-year-old Greek revival mansion and founded Chateau Esperanza in Bluff Point in 1979. Two wineries that were in business for a short time were Northlake Vineyards, founded by Fred O. Williams in Romulus in 1977, and Giasi Winery in Burdett, established in 1979 by Michael Giasi.

Also opening about this time was the Hermann J. Wiemer Vineyard in Dundee. Wiemer, who had been the winemaker at Bully Hill Vineyards until Walter Taylor fired him in 1980, had bought a 140-acre abandoned soybean farm on the west side of Seneca Lake and established a nursery operation. As of 2000, he was selling 200,000 vines and producing 12,000 cases of wine.[59]

Hudson River Valley

The Hudson Valley is known for the oldest continuously operating winery in the United States, Brotherhood Winery, founded in Washingtonville in 1839.[60] Also of importance in the wine history of the region, High Tor was opened thirty miles north of New York City in 1951 and, in 1971, farm winery number 1, Benmarl Vineyards, was started in Marlboro. Another winery with an early starting date was the Hudson Valley Wine Company, established in 1907 in Highland by the Bolognesi banking family based in Manhattan. The winery was sold to Herbert Feinberg in 1970 and was renamed the Regent Champagne Cellars in 1987.

After the passage of the Farm Winery Act in 1976, wineries opened quickly in the Hudson Valley. Ben Feder's Clinton Vineyards in Clinton Corners got its start in 1975 when he planted five acres of Seyval Blanc from vines he had obtained from Hermann Wiemer. Feder was so impressed with Bully Hill's first Seyval Blanc that he decided to grow that variety only. He followed up his initial planting with four or five acres more during the next three years. In 1977, he had his first vintage and, although he diversified his product line starting in the mid-1980s, his specialty remained Seyval Blanc.

William Wetmore planted his first vines in 1972 and built his Cascade Mountain Winery in Amenia in 1977. By 1980, he had fifteen acres of grapes and was making 15,000 gallons of wine. A restaurant was added in 1985 that specialized in foods of the region. He was active in the formation of the Hudson Region Wine Council in 1979.

Other wineries getting started at this time were El Paso Winery in Ulster Park, Cagnasso Winery in Marlboro, and North Salem Vineyard by Dr. George W. Naumburg, Jr., in North Salem. In the foothills of the Shawangunk Mountains on the west bank of the Hudson River, Walker Valley Vineyards in Walker Valley and Brimstone Hill Vineyard in Pine Bush were the first two wineries in what would become the Shawangunk Wine Trail.

In April 1975, a year before the farm winery bill was passed, John S. Dyson was named the New York state commissioner of agriculture and markets and in December of that year commissioner of commerce. In both positions he advocated passage of the farm winery legislation. He was impressed by the success Dr. Frank was having with the vinifera and decided that vinifera varieties might do well in the Hudson Valley. He planted an experimental acre on a family farm and the vines did so well that in 1979 he bought an old dairy farm in Millbrook where he began planting thirty acres of grapes. Millbrook Vineyards and Winery was founded in Millbrook in 1981. In 2000, after more than twenty-five years, John Graziano continued to be the only winemaker the winery had had, and wine production was averaging 12,000 cases a year.

Lake Erie

Chautauqua County, New York's westernmost county, is part of the Lake Erie Grape Belt that extends along the shores of Lake Erie from New York into Pennsylvania. In Chautauqua County alone there are 21,000 acres of grapes, making it the largest grape growing area in the state. Historically, most of the grapes grown there were Concords used for fresh fruit and grape juice, but by the early 1970s an increasing percentage of the acreage was being planted in wine grapes. Prior to the enactment of the Farm Winery Act, large wineries were established in Chautauqua County primarily for making kosher wines starting with the Welch Company in 1950. The Fredonia Products Company planted grapes in 1964 and began making kosher wines. In 1967, the Mogen David Wine Corporation of Chicago opened a large plant in Westfield to have a production facility closer to the vineyards.

The first small winery, Johnson Estate Vineyards and Winery was opened in Westfield in 1961 by Frederick S. Johnson when he inherited 125 acres of Concords from his father and had to decide what to do with them. After the passage of the Farm Winery Act, Merritt Estate Winery in Forestville became the fourth farm winery to open in New York. The decision to establish the winery in 1976 was to utilize the grapes being grown on the farm after the Taylor Wine Company canceled its contracts. James M. Merritt was instrumental in setting up the winery but died before the winery opened in 1977, and his son William T. Merritt took over as president.[61]

As the demand for table wines increased in the Finger Lakes and elsewhere, grapes from Chautauqua County were purchased by wineries outside the region. In 1967, Robert and Gary Woodbury, and Robert's wife Page took over the Woodbury family farm in Dunkirk. As a result of meeting Dr. Frank, they planted their first vinifera vines in 1970. Their vinifera plantings increased rapidly, and by the mid-1980s they had over 100 acres in the ground. Until their winery opened in 1980, their vinifera grapes were among those prized by other wineries.

Philip Wagner, Boordy, and Seneca Foods

In 1968, Seneca Foods Corporation, headquartered in Penn Yan, had a large grape juice operation in Westfield and a brand new plant in Prosser, Washington.[62] Its president, Arthur S. Wolcott, was thinking about adding winemaking to his operations when someone offered him a taste of Boordy Red made by Philip Wagner from French hybrids. Wolcott was so impressed that he went to Maryland to visit Wagner. In a letter to Maynard Amerine on August 19, 1968, Wagner reported that he had made an arrangement with Wolcott for regular consultations: "Five one day visits a year plus unlimited telephone consultation, $500 a month retainer going to $600 after the first vintage."

Seneca Foods made 15,000 gallons of wine in 1968. On January 18, 1969, Wagner wrote to Amerine that he was going up to New York to check on the Seneca wines and that he would be talking with Wolcott about the possibility of some sort of tie-in with Boordy Vineyard. The result was a written agreement signed on April 1, 1969, which authorized Seneca Foods to produce and market wine under the name of Boordy Vineyard and provided the terms and conditions under which Seneca would employ Philip and Jocelyn Wagner as business consultants.[63] There would be three Boordy Vineyards, one in each of three states, Maryland, New York, and

Washington. As Wagner envisioned it, it would be a concept new to the American wine trade, but familiar enough in Europe, that of several small regional wineries to be linked by a common name and point of view but with no intermixture of their wines.

In 1970, the winemaking operations at Westfield were moved to what was once Captain Paul Garrett's winery in Penn Yan and Raymond Knafo was hired as the winemaker. In 1971, 3,000 cases of wine were made and 20,000 cases in 1972. Three regional wines were produced in Washington's Yakima Valley in the fall of 1971. There was apparently only one vintage in Washington and two in the Finger Lakes. Sales never met expectations and letters to and from Wagner cite overproduction at Boordy, cutthroat competition as a result of overproduction in California, inflation, and consumer confusion over the name Boordy as reasons for ending the association between Boordy Vineyards and Seneca Foods Corporation effective July 31, 1977.[64]

North Carolina

In 1950, ten farmers in Onslow County planted twenty-five acres of Scuppernong as the result of the promise of a market made by an out-of-state winery. When the grapes came into production in 1955 and the buyer refused to buy them, Raymond A. Hartsfield, one of the growers, opened a winery, Onslow Wine Cellars at Holly Ridge. Then, in 1961, Richards Wine Cellars in Virginia encouraged North Carolina growers to supply them with grapes by offering them free vines and five-year contracts to buy their grapes at $200 a ton.[65]

There were 150 acres of muscadines in North Carolina in 1962, and as that acreage was doubling by 1965, the legislature appropriated $166,000 for research and extension. As a result of this funding, Dan Carroll and William Nesbitt were hired at North Carolina State University. Hartsfield sold his winery to Richards in 1968, grape prices dropped and again there were no wineries in the state. To help growers by encouraging wineries to open, the legislature cut the winery license fee from $1,000 to $100 and reduced the tax on native table wines from 60 cents a gallon to 5 cents.

In 1976, Duplin Wine Cellars in Rose Hill opened its doors with production of 3,000 gallons. There were now 2,000 acres of muscadines in the ground and with prices falling, eleven muscadine growers had begun planning the winery in 1972 as a cooperative venture. By 1982, production had reached 140,000 gallons.[66]

Another cooperative effort began in 1981 when six growers belonging to the Piedmont Grape Growers Association decided to open a winery, Germanton Vineyard and Winery in Germanton. To utilize eighty acres of muscadines, George and Benbury Wood opened Deerfield Vineyards Wine Cellars near Edenton in 1974.

In 1971, the vineyard and winery operation at Biltmore Estate in Asheville got underway. The 255-room mansion, built in the late 1800s by George W. Vanderbilt, had passed into the hands of his grandson, William Cecil, who thought that it would be fitting for his chateau to have a vineyard like those in France. Vineyard manager Tim Thielke planted three acres of French hybrids in 1971. Several years later, Cecil decided to open a winery and hired Philippe Jourdain, a sixth-generation French winemaker, first as a consultant in 1977 and then as the winemaker in 1980. One hundred acres of vinifera were planted by 1980. The first wines were sold in 1978, and in 1985 a 90,000 square foot winery and visitors center was opened in a converted dairy complex.[67]

Ohio

Nicholas Longworth arrived in Ohio in 1803 and the Catawba grape reached Ohio in 1825. The combination of the two in the Cincinnati area led to 2,000 acres of grapes and table and sparkling wines that won national and international attention before powdery mildew and black rot destroyed the vineyards in the late 1850s and 1860s. During the second half of the nineteenth century, when the center of the industry had moved to the Lake Erie region in northern Ohio, there were 33,000 acres of grapes and more than fifty wineries.[68]

Figure E.6: Arnie Esterer (shown here) and his business partner Tim Hubbard planted grapes at Markko Vineyards in Conneaut, Ohio, in 1968. Photo by author, 1977.

With the coming of Prohibition, many vineyards were converted to Concords for juice production, and after Repeal large volume sales were attempted through low-quality, low-priced wines that put them into competition with California.[69] The number of wineries in Ohio dropped from 161 in 1937 to 27 in 1963, with only about half of them making wine from Ohio-grown grapes.[70]

Several wineries founded in the last half of the nineteenth century survived Prohibition by making juice: Meier's Wine Cellars (1855), Lonz Winery (1862), Mantey Vineyards (1880), and Heineman Winery (1888). The Steuk Winery near Sandusky, founded in 1855, had to close during Prohibition but was unusual in that it maintained its vineyards throughout the thirteen-year period. Among the wineries that opened right after Repeal were Dover Vineyards in Westlake in 1934, Catawba Island Wine Company (also called Mon Ami Champagne Company) in 1934, and Klingshirn Winery in Avon Lake in 1935. In 1937, Anna and Nicholas Ferrante opened a winery in Cleveland called Nick Ferrante. The winery moved to Geneva in 1979, a restaurant was added in 1989, and in the hands of the third generation became known as Ferrante Winery and Ristorante.[71]

As a result of the test plantings starting in 1960 in southern Ohio, Wistar and Ursula Marting opened Tarula Winery in New Clarksville in 1967 and Kenneth and Jim Schuchter followed in 1970 with Valley Vineyard in Morrow. Two other wineries that started in the early 1970s were Chalet Debonné Vineyards by Tony J. and Anthony P. Debevc in Madison in 1971, and Cedar Hill Wine Company in Cleveland Heights by Thomas Wykoff in 1974. Arnie Esterer and his business partner Tim Hubbard made Ohio's first commercial vinifera wines in 1972 and opened Markko Vineyard in Conneaut a year later.

Although Ohio never needed farm winery legislation to aid its growth, two organizations were important in its success. The first was the Ohio Wine Producers Association, formed in 1975, when a small group of industry representatives met with Dr. Garth Cahoon of the Ohio Agricultural Research Development Center in Wooster. The first project the association undertook was to publish a brochure. Donniella Winchell, who became the association's executive director, began working part time in 1979 and full time in 1984. Over the years she directed marketing and promotion programs including the statewide festival Vintage Ohio, which started in 1995.[72]

The second organization was the Ohio Grape Industries Program, which Robert G. Gottesman was responsible for starting in 1980. Gottesman, the president of Paramount Distillers in Cleveland, bought Meier's Wine Cellars in Silverton after Henry O. Sonneman died in 1974. Subsequently he and Meier's acquired Lonz Winery on Middle Bass Island in 1979, Mon Ami Restaurant and Winery in Port Clinton in 1980, and Mantey Winery—which he renamed Firelands Winery—in Sandusky in 1980.

Gottesman had no experience in the wine industry when he bought Meier's, but he soon learned that selling wine in Ohio was more difficult than he had

Figure E.7: Tony P. Debevc opened Chalet Debonné Vineyards in Madison, Ohio, in 1971 together with his father, Anthony J. Debevc. Photo by author, 1977.

imagined. He found that the industry was so small that it would take a long time to generate enough revenue for it to become a significant force in the marketplace, but he had the vision and connections to make things happen. Working with the director of the Department of Agriculture and both political parties, he got the necessary legislation passed to create the Ohio Grape Industries Program and a new tax to fund it. The result was more than $250,000 a year available for research, marketing, and promotion. From that time until his death in 2000, he donated his time, resources and staff in one project after another to promote Ohio wines.[73]

Pennsylvania

The first winery in Pennsylvania after Prohibition was Conestoga Vineyards. Insurance executive Melvin S. Gordon planted French hybrids in the early 1950s and opened his winery in 1953 in Birchrunville in Chester County. Over the years the winery did not make more than 700 to 1,000 gallons a year and was sold in 1974 to David C. Fondots, who immediately applied for a limited winery license. Two brothers, Arthur and Martin Keen, joined the winery and a few years later took over the management of the winery. In 1987, a lawsuit brought by Fondots against the Keens led to the closing of the winery.[74]

Pennsylvania was the first state in the nation to pass a farm winery bill in 1968, known in Pennsylvania as the Limited Winery Act. The two wineries located in North East, Pennsylvania—Presque Isle Wine Cellars and Penn-Shore Vineyards—received their licenses on the same day in 1970 and they have both considered themselves to be the first wineries in the state.

Presque Isle Wine Cellars was established in North East in Erie County in 1964 by Douglas P. Moorhead and William Konnerth to sell home winemaking equipment and juice. When Konnerth retired in 1975, Moorhead's wife Marlene took his place as a partner in operating the business. With the passage of the Limited Winery Act, Presque Isle became a commercial winery. Selling winemaking equipment and juice to small wineries and amateur winemakers always took top priority and making their own wine took place as time permitted. Wine production at the beginning averaged 3,000 gallons a year.[75]

Three growers in Erie County, Blair McCord, George Luke, and George Sceiford needed a market for their grapes and joined Douglas Moorhead and others in working for passage of the Limited Winery Act. With the enactment of the legislation they founded Penn-Shore Vineyards. The winery made the legal limit under the law of 50,000 gallons, but they always had a need for new markets. In 1976, they opened an extension of premises called South Mountain Winery in Philadelphia, but a long standing zoning dispute forced the closing of the extension in January, 1978.[76]

In 1972, Pittsburgh dentist Dr. John D. Hart and Isabel S. Hart opened Harbrook Winery in Titusville. John Hart died within two years of the opening, but his widow kept the winery open for sales for a year or two before closing it.

The fifth winery in Pennsylvania, and the first in the eastern part of the state, was Pequea Valley Vineyard and Winery founded by H. Peterman Wood and his wife Alice on a sixty-six-acre farm in Willow Street, south of Lancaster. In 1972, they had their first crush using grapes they brought in from Erie County because not enough were available locally. The winery was opened in 1973 but sales did not meet expectations and the bank foreclosed on the property in 1978. A year later the bank sold it to Todd and Suzanne Dickel who renamed it Lancaster County Winery.[77]

In June 1974, Jerry and Kathy Forest opened Buckingham Valley Vineyards in Bucks County. Jerry Forest had made wine in Maryland since he was twelve years old and had visited Philip Wagner. The Forests moved to Pennsylvania in February 1966, and a test planting of thirty-seven varieties obtained from Philip Wagner was started that spring. The first permanent planting of ten acres was made two years later. Wine production went from under 1,000 gallons at the start to more than 30,000 gallons by 1998.[78]

Mazza Vineyards in North East opened in June of 1974 as a family enterprise involving Robert Mazza, his brother Frank, and their father Joseph. The family had long been in the construction business and the winery was built in Spanish Mediterranean style with the help of Gary Mosier, who became the cellar master and eventually the winemaker. He was trained by Helmut Kranich, a Geisenheim graduate, who joined the winery in April 1973. At that time Kranich was the only winemaker in Pennsylvania who had graduated from a major research station.[79]

Rhode Island

South County Winery had its start in 1973 when H. Winfield Tucker and Donald Seibert planted two acres of vinifera at Tucker's Tuckahoe Turf Farms in Slocum. The vineyards failed to survive and all of their wines were made from grapes purchased in other states. A Chardonnay was made in 1974 and 1975 from grapes bought from Woodbury Vineyards in Dunkirk, New York. Then there was a four-year period when no wines were made and in the early 1980s the winery closed.[80]

Prudence Island, after which Prudence Island Winery was named, is located in the middle of Narragansett Bay and is linked to the mainland by a ferry that runs to the island from Bristol. In 1972, after thirty years of living in Connecticut, William Bacon and his wife Natalie moved to Sunset Hill Farm on the island, a property that had been in her family for generations. With much help from George and Cathy Mathiesen at Chicama Vineyards in Massachusetts, they and their oldest son Nathaneal planted four acres of different varieties of vinifera in 1973 and thirteen acres of Pinot Noir and Chardonnay in 1974 and 1975. The first wines were sold at Prudence Island Winery in 1976, and in five years production had reached 2,500 gallons.[81]

Sakonnet Vineyards in Little Compton was licensed in 1975 by Jim and Lolly Mitchell who, after their marriage in 1973, decided they wanted to do something together. In 1975, they planted seventeen acres of grapes and an additional seventeen the following year. Their initial plantings were French hybrids; the vinifera came later. Sakonnet's first wines, 9,000 gallons in all, were made from purchased grapes and were placed on sale in 1977. Ten years later they were making 38,000 gallons. From the beginning the Mitchells had looked upon themselves as "starters," and in 1987 they sold the winery to Earl A. and Susan B. Sampson to take the winery to the next level. They hired Joetta Kirk as vineyard manager, the vineyards were expanded to forty-four acres, and within five years the winery was producing 70,000 gallons.[82]

Peter and Claire Berntson planted the first of their five acres of Pinot Noir at Diamond Hill Vineyards in Cumberland in 1976. Fruit orchards were also planted and the winery produced a wide variety of fruit wines. A private label operation began in 1989 and quickly became a major part of the winery's business.[83]

Figure E.8: Jim and Lolly Mitchell, the original owners of Sakonnet Vineyards in Little Compton, Rhode Island, started the winery in 1977. Photo by author, 1982.

South Carolina

For many years after Prohibition, the only winery in South Carolina was Tenner Brothers, established in 1953 in Patrick by Sal, Lukie, and Al Tenner. The winery, which had storage capacity of more than 500,000 gallons of wine, mainly produced muscadine wines and in 1966 was sold to the Canandaigua Wine Company.

James Truluck opened his Truluck Vineyards in Lake City on April 28, 1978. A graduate of the dental school at the University of Louisville, he served in the U.S. Air Force near the Loire Valley where he became accustomed to drinking wine with meals. With the help of his wife Kay, he began planting the first of fifty acres of vines in 1972 and making wine as a hobby. Their son, Jay, went to college for two years before returning home to become involved with the vineyard and winery full time.[84]

Jim Truluck was instrumental in getting a farm winery bill passed in the summer of 1980. The bill, intended to encourage the planting of wine grapes, reduced the tax from 57½ cents to 5 cents a gallon and permitted tastings and sales of wine on the winery premises. Although the winery grew from 1,400 gallons at the start to 20,000 gallons in 1989, Truluck made the decision to concentrate on his dental practice, and the winery closed in December, 1990.

Several other attempts were made to start wineries in the late 1970s, the most ambitious of which was a 600,000-gallon winery in Woodruff called Oakview Plantation. In 1975, Richard L. Leizear had a juice plant that he wanted to convert into a winery with the intention of providing a market for a large number of local muscadine growers.[85] Wholesalers opposed the winery and, because this was before the passage of the farm winery bill, all wines had to be sold through distributors, and the wholesalers were able to curtail winery sales. Oakview Plantation closed in 1979, but soon reopened under new ownership who renamed it Foxwood Wine Cellars. By the early 1990s it, too, had closed.

Most of the small wineries had closed by the time Montmorenci Vineyards opened in Aiken in July, 1990. Robert E. Scott, Sr., first planted sixteen acres of vineyards in 1987 as part of a larger farm operation and his son Robert E. Scott, Jr., became the winemaker. The winery is the oldest of the ten wineries that were open in 2009.

Tennessee

When Prohibition ended, grape growing and winemaking continued even though the first winery would not open until 1980. One of the most prominent amateurs who later became involved commercially was Judge William O. Beach, a county judge in Clarkesville, who first planted grapes in 1965 and became a home winemaker in 1968. He opened Beachaven Vineyards and Winery in partnership with his son-in-law Ed Cooke in 1987. Earlier, in 1977, he and Nashville attorney S. McPheeters Glasgow, Jr., played a major role in getting the Tennessee Grape and Wine Law passed. In addition to reducing the annual license fee from $1,500 to $50, the law allowed wineries to open to the public and operate tasting rooms in all counties, wet or dry. Favorable amendments were made to the law in 1983 and 1985.[86]

The oldest licensed winery was Highland Manor Winery in Jamestown, founded by Fay W. Wheeler and Robert Ramsey in 1980. The winery was sold in 1989, but two years later Stonehaus Winery in Crossville opened with Wheeler as president.

Also in 1980, Tiegs Winery opened in Lenoir City with Terry Tiegs as president. Smoky Mountain Winery in Gatlinburg, owned by Everett and Miriam Brock, was licensed in April and opened in 1981. Three years later, Laurel Hill Vineyard opened in Memphis and Tennessee Valley Winery in Loudon.

Two organizations have been important in the development of the industry. Seven people interested in growing grapes and making wine formed the Tennessee Viticultural & Oenological Society (TVOS) in Clarkesville. In 1982, with wineries beginning to open, the Tennessee Farm Winegrowers Association (TFWA) was organized for TVOS members who had commercial vineyards and wineries, and for others who were planning commercial operations.

A major step forward for the industry came in 1985 when the state legislature passed the Tennessee Viticultural Policy Act and established the Viticultural Advisory Board within the Department of Agriculture to help assure the stable development of the industry.

Vermont

Vermont reduced its license fees from $3,000 to $150 in 1971, the same year that Frank E. and Mitsuko T. Jedlicka founded their Vermont Wineries, Inc., in Danby, twenty miles north of Manchester. A former investment banker, Frank Jedlicka had become interested in wine while working with banks in France and the United States. His first wine, a 1971 apple wine, was being retailed in several states by 1973. Other wines followed including a maple wine and a dry rhubarb wine. The barn in which the winery was housed was destroyed by fire on September 30, 1976.[87]

Edward C. Metcalfe, Jr., and his wife Linda Cardone incorporated North River Winery in Jacksonville in 1985. Metcalfe came to Vermont from New Hampshire because Vermont did not then have a winery, and he wanted to create a tourist-oriented winery with an upscale image based on fruit wines. Within five years he was making 12,000 gallons of dry, semi-dry, semi-sweet and sweet fruit wines, half of which were sold at the winery.[88]

Joseph Cerniglia was the vice president of a New York brokerage firm when he took a ski trip to Vermont at the same time he was thinking about making a change in his lifestyle. He bought an orchard in Springfield in 1978 and the Joseph Cerniglia Winery opened for business on October 25, 1986. From the beginning he decided to specialize in apple wines, and it was not unusual for the winery to produce eight different varietal apple wines at one time. In 1990, he began marketing a 12 percent alcohol Vermont Old-Fashioned Hard Cider that was sold in a 375-millileter mug with a screw cap. This led to a new product, Woodchuck draft cider, that was an immediate success with sales doubling each year. On January 1, 1996, the Joseph Cerniglia Winery and the Stroh Brewing Company of Detroit, Michigan, formed a partnership called Green Mountain Cidery for the production of Woodchuck draft cider. In that year, 1.2 million gallons were sold.[89]

David and Linda Boyden founded Boyden Valley Winery in Cambridge in 1996, and in the same year Phil Tonks founded Grand View Winery in East Calais. Vermont's first vineyard and winery to use grapes only was Snow Farm Vineyard and Winery in South Hero founded by Harrison and Molly Lebowitz. Five-and-a-half acres of grapes were planted in 1997 and the first Vermont appellation grape wine, a 1998 Seyval Blanc, was placed on the market in 1999.

Virginia

Chapter 4 details the early plantings of the French hybrids and the vinifera from 1948 to the mid-1970s when the first wineries using these grapes opened. There were a few attempts to grow grapes and make wine in the 1930s, and during this decade a limited winery license was created under which wineries had to open until farm winery legislation was passed.

In October 1979, Archie M. Smith, Jr., and his wife Dody at Meredyth Vineyards began trying to get a bill through the Virginia legislature that would consolidate $2,200 in existing license fees and taxes that had to be paid under the old law into an umbrella license costing $100 a year. The opposition was "rather formidable," according to Smith, and passage came only after the Virginia Department of Agriculture and Consumer Services contributed lobbying support.[90] As a result of its assistance, liberalized marketing rules were added to the farm winery bill including the ability to sell wine by the glass at the winery and at one remote location. The governor signed the bill into law on March 24, 1980, and it became effective on July 1 of that year.

There were six wineries in Virginia in 1979 and 286 acres of grapes. The first farm winery to open in Virginia was Farfelu Vineyard in late May or early June, 1976. Meredyth Vineyards followed a month later on July 1, 1976. In addition to Farfelu Vineyard and Meredyth Vineyards, there were Piedmont Vineyards and Winery in Middleburg, Al Weed's La Abra Farm and Winery in Lovingston, Jim and Emma Randel's Shenandoah Vineyards in Edinburg, and Robert Viehman's The Vineyard in Winchester. Following the passage of the farm winery law, six more wineries were opened by 1981: Woolwine Winery, Rose Bower Vineyard and Winery, Barboursville Winery, Montdomaine Cellars, Ingleside Plantation Vineyards, and Oasis Vineyard. Seven years later, in 1988, there were a total of forty wineries and 1,220 acres of grapes.

Winemaking and viticulture got a boost during this period from two people. Jacques Recht, a Belgian enologist, became the winemaker at Ingleside Plantation Vineyards in 1980, and through teaching, consulting, and writing was instrumental in promoting quality winemaking in Virginia and other states.[91] Viticulturist Lucie T. Morton planted a three-acre experimental vineyard in King George in 1973, studied at the Ecole Nationale Supérieure Agronomique in Montpellier, and after her return in 1975 gave classes in grape growing and started her career as a vineyard consultant.[92]

The Virginia Wine Growers Association under the leadership of Robert de Treville Lawrence, Sr., had been active since the early 1970s in seeking legislative and financial support for the Virginia industry. Several other organizations followed, one of the earliest being the King George County Growers Association in May 1978. The Virginia Grape Growers Association came into existence in 1980, the Virginia Wineries Association in 1981 and the Jeffersonian Wine Grape Growers Society, also in 1981.

The founder of the Jeffersonian Wine Grape Growers Society was Felicia Rogan, who established Oakencroft Vineyard and Winery in Charlottesville in 1983. She arrived in Virginia in 1976 when she married John Rogan, owner of the Boar's Head Inn, and soon became involved in building the quality and reputation of the industry through serving as chairman of the Virginia Wine Advisory Board for several terms and promoting the industry in the statehouse, nationally and internationally.[93]

During the next few years grape and wine organizations working with the Department of Agriculture and Consumer Services succeeded in getting key legislation passed.[94] In March 1984, the General Assembly funded a wine marketing position in the Department of Agriculture and also enologist and viticulturist positions as well as a laboratory at Virginia Tech.[95] On June 8, 1984, Lou Ann Whitton (later Lou Ann Ladin) became the first wine marketing specialist and was followed in 1987 by Annette C. Ringwood. The Horticulture Department at Virginia Tech hired Bruce Zoecklein to fill the position of enologist on the main campus at Blacksburg in 1985 and, a year later, Tony K. Wolf to be the viticulturist working out of the Winchester Fruit Research Station. In 1984, a Viticultural Technical Advisory Committee was appointed to develop a grapevine certification program.

West Virginia

In the 1970s, the West Virginia Department of Agriculture began placing a strong emphasis on small family farms and specialty crops as an important part of the future of the state's economy. Stephen West planted the first vineyard in 1973 followed by Robert Pliska and Wilson Ward, all of whom would later open wineries. A farm winery bill passed the West Virginia legislature in 1978 and again in 1979 but both were vetoed by Governor John D. Rockefeller, IV, who stated that it would be an abuse of public office to foster the consumption of alcohol.

Late in 1979, the West Virginia Grape Growers Association was formed and passage of the farm winery bill became one of its first projects. The Department of Agriculture changed the emphasis of the bill from a "wine bill" to a "grape bill" and described grape growing as the basis for a state industry. There were indications that Rockefeller would sign the bill in 1980, but when the bill was passed there was yet another veto. On the fourth attempt, on March 5, 1981, the bill passed, was again vetoed, but became law when the legislature overrode the veto. A second bill that became law at the same time provided for the sale of table wine in larger grocery stores and specialty shops.[96]

The farm winery law set the annual license fee at $50, allowed wineries to produce up to 50,000 gallons of wine a year and permitted sales and tastings on the premises. Fisher Ridge Wine Company in Liberty was the first winery to open. Wilson Ward, a dentist, had anticipated the passage of the farm winery bill and bonded his winery in 1979. Because the farm winery law had not yet been passed, his wines could only be sold to the West Virginia state store system. He had a single large order of fifty-five cases. When the winery opened, production started at 1,000 cases.[97]

West-Whitehill Winery near Keyser was West Virginia's second winery, the result of a partnership between Stephen West, a Philadelphia attorney who had planted a vineyard in Fisher, and Charles Whitehill, a music professor at Potomac State College, who grew grapes at Keyser. The third winery, licensed in September 1983, was the Robert F. Pliska and Company Winery in Purgitsville. When Bob and Ruth Pliska planted their vineyard in 1974, they named it "Piterra," combining the Greek letter "pi" meaning "never ending" with the word "terra," meaning "land." The Pliskas also operated a home for mentally handicapped adults called The Vineyard, which was partially supported by sales from the winery

Wisconsin

The early wine history of Wisconsin centers on the Hungarian immigrant Agoston Haraszthy, who settled in what is now Sauk City, planted grapes, probably made wine and may well have dug the wine cave now on the grounds of Wollersheim Winery. When news of the discovery of gold in California reached Wisconsin, Haraszthy headed west and later achieved fame as the father of California viticulture. Peter Kehl bought Haraszthy's property in 1856, built a seventeen-room stone house and winery, planted grapes, and established Kehl Weinberg in 1867. After Peter Kehl died in 1870, his son Jacob took over the winery until 1899 when the coldest winter on record killed every vine in the vineyard, forcing the winery to close. The property remained in the Kehl family until 1972 when it was purchased by Robert and JoAnn Wollersheim.[98]

After Prohibition, the first winery to open was the Von Stiehl Winery in Algoma in 1967 by C. W. Stiehl, a Milwaukee surgeon, who in 1973 moved the winery to an old brewery building in Baraboo. At that time the winery was making about 35,000 gallons of fruit wine a year, half of which was cherry wine.[99]

Several other fruit wineries followed in the early 1970s. Stone Mill Winery opened in Cedarburg in 1971, Fruit of the Woods Wine Cellars in Eagle River in 1972, and Door Peninsula Winery in Sturgeon Bay in 1974. The region became best known for its cherry wines although wines were also made from other fruits. One winery, Fruit of the Woods Wine Cellars, was making 17,000 gallons of wine in 1980, one-third of which was cranberry wine.

Wisconsin did not have a farm winery law, and when Wollersheim Winery opened they simply renewed the Kehl winery license. Five acres of French hybrid grapes were planted in 1973 and the first vintage of 10,000 gallons was in 1976.

Figure E.9: Robert and JoAnn Wollersheim opened Wollersheim Winery in Prairie du Sac, Wisconsin, in 1976. Photo by author, 1980.

In 1984, Philippe Coquard came from France on a six-month internship and fit in so well that he became the winemaker in 1985 and subsequently married Julie Wollersheim. The Cedar Creek Winery in Cedarburg was acquired in 1990 and when Bob Wollersheim died in 2005, annual production had reached 216,000 gallons.[100]

THE FIRST AMERICAN WINE COURSE

THE FIRST WINE COURSE FOR ACADEMIC CREDIT AT AN AMERICAN COLLEGE OR university was held at Cornell University's School of Hotel Administration in Ithaca in 1953.[1] The one credit course was an elective open to juniors and seniors and, out of 150 eligible students, 80 signed up for the course.[2]

New York vintners had been occasional guest lecturers at the School of Hotel Administration for a number of years, and they thought that a course on wine should be offered on a regular basis. They enlisted the help of the Wine Advisory Board, which had been created by California's Wine Institute, and the Washington, DC-based National Association of Alcoholic Beverage Importers, Inc., which association selected Julius Wile to represent the importers. The director of the school, Howard Bagnell Meek, was receptive to the idea and agreed to institute a formal course on wine.

The five people responsible for the wine course who "pitched" the course to Meek were Julius Wile; George Lawrence of the Taylor Wine Company; John Longwell of the Urbana Wine Company; Tony Doherty, vice president of the Pleasant Valley Wine Company and the great grandson of its founder, Charles Davenport Champlin; and Legh Knowles, Jr., of the Wine Advisory Board. It was agreed that the purpose of the course would be to expose the students to all phases of wine used in hotels and restaurants.[3] Tony Doherty was named the first coordinator, and he was succeeded by Charles Fournier in 1957.

The first course was held in the fall of 1953, and the subjects covered were an introduction to wine by Doherty; wine grapes of the United States and Europe by Will H. Widmer, president of Widmer's Wine Cellars; chemistry of wines by Jim Ferguson of the Taylor Wine Company; the production of still wines by T. E. Carl of the Pleasant Valley Wine Company; sparkling wines and champagnes by Fournier; wines of California by Knowles; imported wines by Wile; and cooking with wine by Walter Tode, owner of The Inn in Ridgefield, Connecticut. Students also went on a field trip to three wineries—Pleasant Valley, Taylor, and Urbana. Several wineries hired wine course students during the summer to handle visitors.

From 1953 through 1961 a total of 641 students took the course. In 1962, the course became the three-credit Beverage Management Course.

American Viticultural Areas in the East

As of December 2012, the Bureau of Alcohol, Tobacco and Firearms and its successor, the Alcohol and Tobacco Tax and Trade Bureau, had approved 206 American Viticultural Areas (AVAs) in the United States, fifty-one of which were located in the East. An AVA may be as small in area as fifteen square miles or it may cover several million acres. It may be established within a particular state, within a larger AVA, or be part of a multistate AVA. In the list that follows, AVAs are listed by state in alphabetical order. Multistate AVAs have the initials of the states included in parentheses. The source of this list is the U.S. Department of the Treasury, Alcohol and Tobacco Tax and Trade Bureau.

Arkansas:
Altus
Arkansas Mountain
Ozark Mountain (AR, MO, OK)

Connecticut:
Southeastern New England (CT, MA, RI)
Western Connecticut Highlands

Illinois:
Shawnee Hills
Upper Mississippi River Valley (IL, IA, MN, WI)

Indiana:
Ohio River Valley (IN, OH, KY, WV)

Iowa:
Upper Mississippi River Valley (IL, IA, MN, WI)

Kentucky:
Ohio River Valley (IN, KY, OH, WV)

Louisiana:
Mississippi Delta (LA, MS, TN)

Maryland:
Catoctin
Cumberland Valley (MD, PA)
Linganore

Massachusetts:
Martha's Vineyard
Southeastern New England (CT, MA, RI)

Michigan:
Fennville
Lake Michigan Shore
Leelanau Peninsula
Old Mission Peninsula

Minnesota:
Alexandria Lakes
Upper Mississippi River Valley (IL, IA, MN, WI)

Mississippi:
Mississippi Delta (LA, MS, TN)

Missouri:
Augusta
Hermann
Ozark Highlands
Ozark Mountain (AR, MO, OK)

New Jersey:
Central Delaware Valley (NJ, PA)
Outer Coastal Plain
Warren Hills

New York:
Cayuga Lake

Finger Lakes
The Hamptons, Long Island
Hudson River Region
Lake Erie (NY, OH, PA)
Long Island
Niagara Escarpment
North Fork of Long Island
Seneca Lake

North Carolina:
Haw River Valley
Swan Creek
Yadkin Valley

Ohio:
Grand River Valley
Isle St. George
Lake Erie (NY, OH, PA)
Loramie Creek
Ohio River Valley (IN, KY, OH, WV)

Pennsylvania:
Central Delaware Valley (NJ, PA)
Cumberland Valley (MD, PA)
Lake Erie (NY, OH, PA)
Lancaster Valley
Lehigh Valley

Rhode Island:
Southeastern New England (CT, MA, RI)

Tennessee:
Mississippi Delta (LA, MS, TN)

Virginia:
Middleburg Virginia
Monticello
North Fork of Roanoke
Northern Neck George Washington Birthplace
Rocky Knob
Shenandoah Valley (VA, WV)
Virginia's Eastern Shore

West Virginia:
Kanawha River Valley
Ohio River Valley (IN, KY, OH, WV)
Shenandoah Valley (VA, WV)

Wisconsin:
Lake Wisconsin
Wisconsin Ledge
Upper Mississippi River Valley (IA, IL, MN, WI)

NOTES

Chapter 1

1. For a rationale of temperance movements, see "Understanding Today's Temperance Movement," an interview by Hudson Cattell with David F. Musto, *Wine East* 14:1 (May–June 1986), pp. 6–11, 21–22. According to Musto, the first temperance movement in the United States was cut short in the 1850s by abolition and the start of the Civil War. The second was to peak in the 1920s.

2. A short, but now dated, history of grapes and wine in eastern North America was published in "The Wines of the East" series (*The Hybrids,* 1978; *The Vinifera,* 1979; *Native American Grapes,* 1980; all Lancaster, Pennsylvania) by Hudson Cattell and H. Lee Stauffer/Lee S. Miller. An excellent history of wine in the United States prior to Prohibition is *A History of Wine in America: From the Beginnings to Prohibition* by Thomas Pinney (Berkeley, 1989). The early history in Canada is briefly covered in *Vintage Canada* by Tony Aspler (Scarborough, Ontario, 1983 and later editions); *The World of Canadian Wine* by John Schreiner (Vancouver, 1984); and *Wines of Ontario: An Industry Comes of Age* by William F. Rannie (Lincoln, Ontario, 1978). The early history of grapes and wine in the United States and Canada is woven into the text of various editions of *The Wines of America* by Leon D. Adams published in the 1970s and 1980s.

3. Cattell, "Recent Research Confirms Viking Discovery of Grapes," *Wine East* 33:6 (March–April, 2006), pp. 14–17, 53–54. Leif Eriksson's Vinland was located in the coastal area of the Gulf of Saint Lawrence and northeastern New Brunswick.

4. For many years, credit for planting the first vines in Nova Scotia has gone to apothecary Louis Hébert, who went by canoe up Deer River at the southern end of the Annapolis Valley in 1611 and planted vines he had brought from France. Although Hébert had shown an interest in a vineyard, it is known today that he went back to France in 1607 and did not return until 1617.

5. There is no direct evidence that wine was served at the first Thanksgiving held by the Pilgrims in Plymouth Colony sometime during the latter part of November 1621. A letter by Edward Winslow describing the feast does not mention wine although reference is made to the red and white grapes to be found growing there, which were described as "very sweete and strong." Given the harshness of daily life in the early settlements and the swiftness with which wine was made by early settlers, the idea that wine accompanied food at that first Thanksgiving cannot be dismissed.

6. Lucie T. Morton, *Winegrowing in Eastern America: An Illustrated Guide to Viticulture East of the Rockies* (Ithaca, 1985), p. 78.

7. A short history of Prohibition in the United States may be found in "The Whys of Prohibition," by Cattell, *Wine East* 11:1 (May–June 1993), pp. 10–19. For a readable book-length account, see John Kobler, *Ardent Spirits: The Rise and Fall of Prohibition* (New York, 1973).

8. Maynard A. Amerine and Vernon L. Singleton, *Wine: An Introduction for Americans* (Berkeley, 1965), p. 281.

9. Commercial wine production figures are from Pinney's *A History of Wine in America,* p. 436. The 1930 figure is from Richard Paul Hinkle, "Recollections of Repeal," *Wines and Vines* 74:10 (October 1993), p. 18.

10. Ruth Teiser and Catherine Harroun, "The Volstead Act, Rebirth, and Boom," in *The University of California/Sotheby Book of California Wine,* ed. Doris Muscatine, Maynard A. Amerine, and Bob Thompson (Berkeley and London, 1984), p. 57.

11. Amerine and Singleton, *Wine,* p. 282.

12. Kobler, *Ardent Spirits,* p. 227.

13. The term "intoxicating liquors" was not defined by the Constitution but by an act of Congress. It is interesting to speculate whether Congress could now choose to pass a law specifically exempting wine and/or beer from the category of "intoxicating liquors" and thus end the states' exclusive right to control those beverages.

14. Amerine and Singleton, *Wine,* p. 283.

15. Philip Wagner, "The Wines of California," *American Mercury* 29:14 (June 1933), p. 173.

16. A brief history of Prohibition in Canada may be found in John Schreiner, *The World of Canadian Wine* (Vancouver, 1984), pp. 202–205; and in Tony Aspler, *Vintage Canada* (Scarborough, Ontario, 1983), pp. 13–18. The most complete account of Prohibition in Ontario is *Prohibition in Ontario, 1919–1923* by Gerald A. Hallowell (Ottawa, 1972). *The Rumrunners: A Prohibition Scrapbook* (Scarborough, Ontario, 1980) by C. H. Gervais, describes the colorful days of the rumrunners and those who tried to stop them.

17. Marlene-Russell Clark, "Island Politics," in *Canada's Smallest Province, A History of Prince Edward Island,* ed. Francis W. P. Bolger (Prince Edward Island, 1973), pp. 319–320.

18. Prince Edward Island became the last province to end prohibition in 1948.

19. Schreiner, *The World of Canadian Wine,* p. 204.

20. William F. Rannie, *Wines of Ontario: An Industry Comes of Age* (Lincoln, Ontario, 1978), p. 67.

21. Schreiner, *World of Canadian Wine,* p. 204.

22. Percy Rowe, *The Wines of Canada* (Toronto, 1970), p. 48.

23. Hallowell, *Prohibition in Ontario,* p. 90.

24. "Report of the Ontario Wine Standards Committee" (Toronto, July 6, 1934), p. 22.

25. Schreiner, *World of Canadian Wine,* p. 204.

26. Rowe, *The Wines of Canada,* p. 49. The permissible limit today is 250 gallons per ton.

27. "Report of the Ontario Wine Standards Committee," p. 22.

28. James Warren, "Control and Taxation in Ontario," *Wine East* 14:1 (May–June 1986), p. 16.

29. Angus M. Adams, "'Ontario Superior' Means High Quality Wine," *Wine East* 9:3 (September 1981), p. 14. By contrast, today's limit is 0.13 percent.

30. Rannie, *Wines of Ontario,* p. 93.

31. Edwin R. Haynes, "45 Years in Wine," *Wine East* 11:3 (September–October 1983), p. 11.

32. U. P. Hedrick, "Native Grapes for Red Wines," *California Grape Grower* 15:1 (January 1934), p. 19; idem, "Native Grapes for White Wines," *California Grape Grower* 15:2 (February 1934), p. 20; idem, "The Champagnes of Eastern America," *California Grape Grower* 15:3 (March 1934), p. 20.

33. Harry E. Goresline and Richard Wellington, "New York Dry Red Wines," *Wines and Vines* 17:2 (February 1936), pp. 6–7; idem, "New York Dry White Wines," *Wines and Vines* 17:3 (March 1936), pp. 6–7; idem, "New York Champagnes," 17:12 (December 1936), pp. 5, 19.

34. Hedrick, "Native Grapes for Red Wines," p. 19.

35. "Eastern Wines Featured by Wine and Food Society," *Wines and Vines* 20:6 (June 1939), p. 12.

36. An earlier version of the next two sections was included in the first part of "Dry Table Wines for the East—The Roles of Fournier, Frank, Hostetter and Wagner," by Hudson Cattell and Linda Jones McKee, *American Wine Society Journal* 24:1 (Spring 1992), pp. 4–7.

37. A short history of Brights may be found in Schreiner, *The World of Canadian Wine,* pp. 41–50. See also Cattell, "The Pioneering Years at Brights," *Wine East* 14:2 (July–August 1986), pp. 10–11, 26–27. Brights Wines was incorporated under that name in 1939 as a wholly owned subsidiary of T. G. Bright & Company, Ltd.

38. According to Claude William Hunt (*Booze Boats and Billions,* 2nd edition, Belleville, Ontario, p. 186), "the firm of Hatch and McGuinness dominated rum-running on the Great Lakes. This enabled Harry to buy Hiram Walker in the deal of the year, raising him to the top of the Canadian distilling industry."

39. Schreiner, *World of Canadian Wine,* p. 45.

40. Cattell interview with Edwin Haynes, July 12, 1990.

41. Biographical information on de Chaunac was included in a Brights press release dated April 25, 1972. The capital "D" for the wine De Chaunac was chosen because the *Style Manual for Biological Journals* stated that a capital "D" should be used, and that spelling was registered officially. (Letter from O. A. Bradt to Cattell dated May 31, 1978.)

42. A brief biography of M. F. Jones is given in *Brights Wine Letter,* Vol. 1 (June 1982). Jones was responsible for the introduction of some of Brights best-known wines including the President line of champagnes and Canada's first vinifera wines (discussed in Chapter 2).

43. Some of the biographical information came from a Cattell interview with Fournier on November 3, 1979, and some from various Gold Seal Vineyards press releases.

44. Cattell interview with Philip Wagner, June 18, 1983.

45. The quote comes from a draft of an acceptance speech supplied to Cattell from Fournier when he received the Leon D. Adams Award at the 1982 Wine Industry Technical Seminar in Santa Rosa, California, on January 22, 1982.

46. Charles Fournier, "The Case for Quality," *Wines and Vines* 51:6 (June 1970), p. 47.

47. Ibid. The new regulations are also quoted here.

48. Ibid., p. 48.

49. Thomas L. Holling, "The Making of Fine Wines," *Monitor* 40:6 (December 1953), p. 7.

50. In an interview with Cattell on October 9, 1991, Philip Wagner recalled that the results of the competition were not announced for several weeks. The winning wines, still unidentified, were served at the banquet at the close of judging. During the banquet de Chaunac came up to him and asked, "Do you want to know what we're drinking?" He then opened his hand and showed Wagner the corks.

Chapter 2

1. The primary sources of information on Philip Wagner in this chapter are his *Daybooks,* two extensive interviews by Hudson Cattell on October 9, 1991, and May 3, 1995, and a number of shorter interviews dating back to June 23, 1977.

2. Letter to Ed Van Dyne, August 17, 1989.

3. Sheridan Lyons, "Founder of Boordy Vineyards Dies," *Baltimore Sun,* December 30, 1996.

4. There were various levels of editors on the Baltimore Sunpapers, the editor of the editorial page being one of the most important and entitling one to be called the editor. For most of Wagner's career his immediate supervisor was James Hamilton Owens, editor of the *Evening Sun* from 1922 to 1938, editor of the *Sun* from 1938 to 1943, and editor-in-chief of both papers from 1943 until his retirement in 1956. Wagner was known as Owens's protégé.

Most of Wagner's newspaper writing was on the opinion pages. When he was assigned to London it was to write feature material on English life. Yet it was while he was there that he had his one big news break. Britain's King Edward VIII had decided to give up his throne for Baltimorean Wallis Warfield Simpson. Wagner described how it happened in a letter to Sam Moore on January 28, 1989:

> "Bill Stoneman [of the *Chicago Evening News*] and I had the privilege (thanks to some detective work by Bill) of breaking the news of Mrs. Simpson's divorce suit to the waiting world. We had it exclusively because the suit was filed on a Friday in some such place as Norwich, so we held the story until the town hall was closed for the week-end. Then Bill filed for the final edition of the *Evening News* in Chicago, and a half-hour later I filed it for the first edition of the (morning) Saturday *Baltimore Sun,* and we locked ourselves in my office for a long and exclusive evening of refusing to answer the phone. All of which took place in another world more than half a century ago."

Wagner also managed to get a "noninterview" with Mrs. Simpson in which he reported that "Mrs. Simpson is not giving interviews."

5. Philip Wagner, *Vintage Books,* Vol. 1, July 23, 1932.

6. Philip Wagner, *Daybooks,* Vol. 1, Spring 1933 entry.

7. Frank Schoonmaker and Tom Marvel, *The Complete Wine Book* (New York, 1934), p. 194.

8. Wagner, *Vintage Books,* Vol. 1, May 25, 1934.

9. Letter from Philip Wagner to the Marquis d'Angerville, March 6, 1976.

10. Wagner, *Daybooks,* Vol. 1, entries from May 10–14, 1935. Among the wines served was Wagner's own Delaware, which he described as being "cool, beautifully clear, really superb in every way." Simon "remarked particularly on the bouquet, saying that it recalled some flower to him but that he couldn't remember what flower." The Wagners were not impressed with Simon, and Hamilton Owens took "a violent dislike" to him.

11. "'Wine Tasting' in New York," *Wines and Vines* 16:12 (December 1935), p. 4.

12. Cattell interview with Philip Wagner on October 9, 1991, during which Wagner admitted to being actually ashamed at having written *Wine Grapes.*

13. Lecture by Philip Wagner at the twenty-ninth annual meeting of the American Society of Enologists in San Diego on July 28, 1978; published as "The East's New Wine Industry," in *Wines and Vines* 60:3 (March 1979), pp. 24–26.

14. A considerable correspondence file exists on this order of Baco No. 1 vines. This transaction took place before the much more stringent regulations were adopted that would require that the vines actually be physically quarantined in the ground.

15. Wagner, *Daybooks,* Vol. 2, April 2, 1939.

16. *Baltimore Sun,* January 3, 1995. See also *Wine East* 22:6 (March–April 1995), p. 4.

17. Wagner, *Daybooks,* Vol. 3, September 6, 1940. The Wagners entered an exhibit at the State Fair on several occasions. A picture and description of their 1946 exhibit is on page 4 of *Wine East* 23:1 (May–June 1995).

18. Ibid., November 6, 1940.

19. Ibid., Vol. 4, December 31, 1941. In a letter to Gene Ford on February 11, 1997, Liza R. Rognas, historical consultant for the Washington State University Libraries, identified H. K. Benson as a chemist at the University of Washington, who probably bought the grapes for Belle Isle Winery on Stretch Island.

20. Ibid.

21. Most of the information on Dunstan comes from an interview held with him by Linda Jones McKee on July 18, 1983.

22. Ibid.

23. Wagner, *Daybooks,* Vol. 4, September 12, 1941.

24. Ibid., Vol. 5, September 19, 1942.

25. Ibid., Vol. 5, September 17, 1941.

26. For a comprehensive report on this tasting, see Cattell, "An Historic Wine Tasting," *Wine East* 25:1 (May–June 1997), pp. 26–29, 38. This article brings together Wagner's lengthy report on the tasting (*Daybooks,* Vol. 4, May 9, 1942) and an article Wagner subsequently wrote, "Tasting Wines of New Hybrids," *Wines and Vines* 23:8 (August 1942), pp. 24–27.

27. Wagner, "Tasting Wines of New Hybrids," p. 27.

28. Wagner, *Daybooks,* Vol. 4, May 13, 1942.

29. Ibid., Vol. 5, October 11, 1942.

30. Ibid., November 8, 1942.

31. Ibid., Vol. 6, September 8, 1943.

32. Ibid., Vol. 7, August 23, 1944.

33. Wagner, A.S.E. lecture, July 28, 1978.

34. Wagner, *Daybooks,* Vol. 10, July 10, 1947. The actual front and back labels are glued into Vol. 12 after the entry for February 25, 1950. One of Schoonmaker's major contributions to American wines in the late 1930s and 1940s was his belief that European names such as "Chablis" or "Burgundy" should be replaced by "honest, simple, straight-forward American names" with the emphasis on the grape variety and the region the wine came from. One of the names he influenced was Widmer's "Lake Niagara."

35. Ibid., Vol. 12, April 5, 1950. Included on the postcard were such items as saccharometers, acid-testing kits, small corker, hand pump, pruning shears, and grape shears.

36. Ibid., Vol. 13, August 12, 1951.

37. Wagner, "The President's House Crystal a Boordy Design," *American Wine Society Journal* 8:1 (Spring 1976), p. 7.

38. Wagner, *Daybooks,* Vol. 12, May 30 and 31, 1950.

39. Wagner, "President's House Crystal," p. 7.

40. Cattell interview with Wagner, June 23, 1977.

41. Wagner, *Daybooks,* Vol. 5, August 5, 1942. In a later entry dated September 8, Wagner reported that Richard Wellington had sent him the results of the tasting and that "the French hybrids ran away with the show."

42. Ibid., Vol. 8, September 13–16, 1944.

43. Wagner's recollection comes from a June 23, 1977, interview with Cattell. Richard Wellington would certainly not have been surprised; forty-five years later neither Nelson nor Lillian Shaulis could remember any special reaction on the part of the group. If anyone was actually stunned, it was Adhemar de Chaunac, on whom the tasting did make a deep impression. George Hostetter at Brights still recalls de Chaunac's emotional high when he returned to the winery. In his *Daybooks* (Vol. 8, entry dated September 22, 1945), Wagner wrote that the general average of the wines was low and most of the reds without interest with the exception that "ours were all good."

44. Among the books used in selecting which hybrids to order were the third edition of E. Pée-Laby's *La Vigne Nouvelle: Les Hybrides Producteurs* (Paris, 1929); and the third edition of J.-F. Ravat's *La Vigne: A Grand Rendement par les Nouvelles Méthodes de Culture et de Taille et par les Hybrides Producteurs Directs* (Besançon, 1942). The actual copies used were marked up, the first with markings in the margin relating to the selection process, and the second with Van Haarlem's initials.

45. Bright's vineyard records including "Variety Test Plantings: 1939–1945." Courtesy George W. B. Hostetter.

46. G. W. B. Hostetter, "Vinifera Grape Production in Ontario," in *Proceedings of Fourth Pennsylvania Wine Conference,* December 3–4, 1971 (University Park, PA), pp. 60–62.

47. Cattell interview with Ollie Bradt, September 23, 1977.

48. Cattell interview with George Hostetter, September 26, 1996. The statistics that follow are from this interview and from two publicity documents from Brights: "Brights Wines—Leaders in Canadian Wine

Making—Fine Canadian Wines Since 1874," dated October 8, 1981, and "Master Vintners Since 1874," undated but probably from around 1980.

49. John Schreiner, *The World of Canadian Wine* (Vancouver, 1984), p. 42. Philip Wagner's correspondence and diaries confirm Brights leadership during these early years. In his *Daybooks,* Vol. 15, June 13–17, 1953, Wagner wrote, "The Canadian industry has gone head over heels for the hybrids, but doesn't yet know which way it is looking or what to do (except de Chaunac). Jordan has sold all its 1,000-odd acres and kept only 35. They plan to work with the growers. The growers don't know where they stand."

50. Ibid., p. 47.

51. Tom Marvel, "Wines of the Finger Lakes," *Gourmet* 17:10 (October 1957), pp. 15, 42–48.

52. Richard Figiel, *Culture in a Glass: Reflections on the Rich Heritage of Finger Lakes Wine* (Lodi, NY), p. 23.

53. Richard G. Sherer, *Crooked Lake and the Grape* (Hammondsport, 1998), p. 37.

54. Ibid. There are other accounts of how and when Great Western got its name. Sherer's account, however, is documented by a letter from Wilder.

55. A short history of The Taylor Wine Company, Inc., can be found in "The History of Excellence," a four-page leaflet published by the winery in 1977.

56. Figiel, *Culture in a Glass,* p. 22.

57. Sherer, *Crooked Lake,* p. 116.

58. Much of the name and ownership changes come from "A Brief History of Gold Seal Vineyards, Inc.," a four-page handout published by Gold Seal Vineyards, Inc., probably in 1965. Keuka Lake was originally named Crooked Lake because it is shaped like a Y. When the Urbana Wine Company had its first labels made up in the mid-1860s, they did not like the name "Crooked Lake" on the label. They then petitioned the New York legislature for a name change, pointing out that all of the other lakes had Indian names. As a result, Crooked Lake was officially renamed Keuka Lake in 1868.

59. Thomas L. Holling, "The Making of Fine Wines," *Monitor* 40:6 (December 1953), p. 5.

60. According to a Gold Seal press release in December 1981, Alexander Brailow, a graduate of Montpellier, was hired by Fournier in 1946 as his assistant. He had come to the United States in 1940 after the fall of France in World War II and was employed at the New York State Agricultural Experiment Station in Geneva where he introduced the French technique of grafting in the vineyards. Brailow became chief winemaker in 1951 and retired in 1972 as vice president in charge of production.

61. In an interview with Cattell after Fournier's death on June 3, 1983, Wagner noted that financial problems plagued Gold Seal during the many changes in ownership. Fournier's greatest achievement, according to Wagner, may have been to hold Gold Seal together at times when the winery could have gone under.

62. Much of the history of Widmer's Wine Cellars comes from a Widmer's Wine Cellars *Fact Sheet,* a four-page handout prepared in 1988 for the one hundredth anniversary of the winery.

63. Cattell interview with Hostetter, September 26, 1996. Wagner, *Daybooks,* Vol. 8, September 13–16, 1944, noted that Fournier "is keen to try the hybrids, but clearly … is none too clear about their individual characteristics."

64. Wagner, *Daybooks,* Vol. 5, July 31, 1942. In Vol. 9 of the *Daybooks,* September 18–21, 1946, Wagner noted that Widmer's Rosette was just coming in for the first time. The grapes used in the early 1940s may have been purchased.

65. Letter from Andrew C. Rice to Cattell, June 26, 1978.

66. Cattell and H. Lee Stauffer, *The Wines of the East: The Hybrids* (Lancaster, PA, 1978), p. 16.

67. Wagner, *Daybooks,* Vol. 8, September 13–16, 1944.

68. Ibid., Vol. 9, February 24 and March 4, 1946.

69. Ibid, Vol. 9, September 18–21, 1946. John Brahm, a former vice president and vineyard manager at Widmer's, recalled in an interview with Cattell on October 27, 1995, that between one-and-a-half and two acres of S. 1000 were planted in 1945 or 1946. They surrounded a prisoner of war camp in the center of Widmer's vineyards and the German prisoners of war helped plant them. Between 1960 and 1962 Widmer's planted another nine or ten acres that were used to make the winery's Seibel Rosé. For more on the use of German prisoners of war at Widmer's, see Kari R. Smith, "Grapes of Wrath," *New York Archives* 6:1 (Summer 2006), pp. 6–7.

70. Philip Wagner, "Vintage in the Finger Lakes," *Wine East* 26:1 (May–June 1998), p. 16.

71. Cattell interview with Philip Wagner, October 9, 1991.

72. Wagner, *Daybooks,* March 3, 1946.

73. For more detail on the quarantine, see Cattell, "Zeroing in on Grapevine Smuggling," *Wine East* 11:6 (March–April 1984), pp. 6–9, 22–23.

74. Seaton C. Mendall, "A New York Vineyardist Evaluates French Hybrids for Wine in the Empire State," *Wines and Vines* 56:9 (September 1975), p. 60. "Zeke" had a number of titles at the Taylor Wine Company including vineyard manager, vineyard consultant, and vice president in charge of grower relations.

75. Greyton H. Taylor, "New York Wines: Their Place in the U.S. Market," *Wines and Vines* 35:11 (November 1954), p. 29.

76. Mendall, "A New York Vineyardist," p. 60.

77. Philip Wagner, "Profitable Wine Grapes for the Northeast," in *Proceedings of the New York State Horticultural Society,* Vol. 110, 1965, pp. 225–231. Reprinted in *Wines and Vines* 46:10 (October 1965), pp. 21–24.

Chapter 3

1. In an interview with Hudson Cattell on August 11, 1999, Willibald Frank, Konstantin Frank's son, stated that Dr. Frank's middle name is sometimes given as Damienovich, which literally means "son of Damien." In Russia, the use of the middle name is an honorary gesture. His wife Eugenia called him "Kotja," a Russian nickname for Konstantin. While he liked to be called Kotja, only relatives or a few close friends could call him that.

2. The main sources of information about Dr. Frank's European days came from a Cattell interview with Konstantin Frank on August 26, 1978, and interviews with Willy Frank on several occasions between 1985 and 1998. Two articles using these interviews have been published. See "The Young Konstantin Frank," *Wine East* 13:4 (November–December 1985), pp. 5, 21; and Cattell and Linda Jones McKee, "Dry Table Wines for the East—the Roles of Fournier, Frank, Hostetter and Wagner," *American Wine Society Journal* 24:2 (Summer 1992), pp. 41–44. The quotations in "Frank's Years in Europe" are from Frank's interview with Cattell. For a longer account of Frank's life and career, see Thomas Pinney, "Konstantin Frank: Zealot at Work," in *The Makers of American Wine: A Record of Two Hundred Years* (Berkeley, 2012), pp. 195–214.

3. At that time, in order to immigrate to the United States, there was a requirement that one had to have a sponsor who would guarantee the immigrant a job. Helen Schelling, Frank's oldest daughter, told Cattell in a telephone interview on May 29, 2007, that a friend of Frank's, Valentin Zahorsky, had come to New York City in 1949. When Frank expressed a desire to come to the United States, Zahorsky made the necessary arrangements for a sponsor who guaranteed a job for Frank at a Horn and Hardart Automat.

4. A useful summary of Frank's life at this time may be found in "Dr. Konstantin Frank" by Eunice Fried. *Vintage* 5:12 (May 1976), pp. 32–34, 58.

5. The author thanks the station director James Hunter for his efforts to locate and furnish photocopies of Frank's personnel files. There are several accounts of how Frank came to be hired at Geneva. The most widespread and easily refuted account is by Alexander Brailow (*American Wine Society Journal* 6:1 [Spring 1974], pp. 12–13, and *American Wine Society Journal* 13:4 [Winter, 1981], p. 88). Brailow claims to have corresponded with Frank in 1953 while he was working in a bakery in New York City and helped him first to get a job at Geneva and, a few months later, persuaded Fournier to give him a job working on Gold Seal's vinifera program. Though these dates and circumstances are in contradiction to Geneva's personnel records and Fournier's own accounts, the two men who both spoke Russian obviously knew one another. Ed Van Dyne, in "Dr. Konstantin Frank: A Retrospective," *American Wine Society Journal* 17:3 (Fall 1985), p. 70, quotes Brailow as telling him about one of the early days when Frank was staying with the Brailows: "The first morning [Frank] observed me making toast and coffee and inquired in astonishment if I got my own breakfast. I admitted that I did, whereupon he said, in Russian, 'In my house it is not the hen who crows.'"

6. Charles Fournier interview with Craig Goldwyn, May 20, 1981.

7. *Geneva Daily Times,* March 18, 1954. The Urbana Wine company was an earlier name for Gold Seal Vineyards. The *Station News* (62:11), in its March 17, 1954, edition, carried the same news.

8. Charles Fournier, "Birth of a N.Y. State Pinot Chardonnay," *Wines and Vines* 42:1 (January 1961), p. 32. See also "The Phylloxera Menace in Vineyards," *American Fruit Grower* 74:5 (May 1954), pp. 36–37.

9. Fournier, "Birth of a N.Y. State Pinot Chardonnay," p. 32.

10. Charles Fournier, "A Veteran Wineman's Second Look at Growing Vinifera in the Eastern United States," *Wines and Vines* 59:2 (February 1978), p. 30.

11. The figures that follow are from orders signed by Fournier and Frank and shipping records at Brights Wines, courtesy of George Hostetter.

12. Charles Fournier, "A Scientific Look at Vinifera in the East," *Wines and Vines* 42:8 (August 1961), p. 27.

13. Letter from Charles Fournier to Cattell dated October 8, 1979. A 1959 date is given by Fournier in his article "Birth of a N.Y. State Pinot Chardonnay," *Wines and Vines* 42:1 (January 1961), p. 32. It is likely that the grapes were harvested in 1959 and the wines released the following year.

14. Cattell interview with Willy Frank, August 28, 1998.

15. Seneca County Clerk's Office, Bath, New York.

16. Cattell interview with Willy Frank, August 28, 1998.

17. Fournier interview with Craig Goldwyn, May 20, 1981.

18. Brailow is quoted in "Dr. Konstantin Frank," by Ed Van Dyne, p. 70. See also Alexander Brailow, "An Eastern Look at Hybrids and Vinifera," *Wines and Vines* 55:5 (May 1974), p. 36.

19. In 1958, Lawrence Properties Co. sold its shares of Gold Seal Vineyards to a New York group. Robert Kimelman became Chairman of the Board, Fournier remained president, and Paul M. Schlem became vice president and treasurer. By 1963, Schlem was elected chairman of the board and, with the exception of Fournier,

all of the officers elected in 1958 were gone. See *A Brief History of Gold Seal Vineyards, Inc.,* a four-page handout prepared by Gold Seal.

20. Fournier interview with Craig Goldwyn, May 20, 1981. Stories have circulated for years that Frank took Gold Seal's planting records when he left. It seems likely that Fournier needed and got help in Gold Seal's vineyards after Frank left. Philip Wagner (*Daybooks,* Vol. 22, September 23, 1962) states: "Charles has been very much in the vineyards this year....(He) has a quarantine vineyard that is quite independent of Dr. Frank though Dr. Frank doesn't know it. He awaits a storm when it is made apparent to Dr. Frank that the vines in this vineyard belong to Gold Seal, not to him."

21. Konstantin Frank interview with Craig Goldwyn, May 20, 1981.

22. It is difficult to pinpoint the date Frank left Gold Seal, but it was clearly before April 1, 1962. In his *Daybooks,* Vol. 21, April 1, 1962, Wagner wrote that the Fourniers arrived "yesterday at 5:30 and left today at 4 p.m. The story of his difficulties—no trust in present owners, possibility of going to Widmer, Dr. Frank's resignation." The fact that Fournier even thought about leaving Gold Seal is evidence of the emotional stress caused by the rifts surrounding Frank's departure.

The most likely date for Frank's resignation would have been in March 1962. On December 22, 1961 (*Daybooks,* Vol. 21) Wagner wrote: "Fournier—worrying about Dr. Frank's typical reaction to my piece in November *Wines and Vines* ["The Four Approaches to Vinifera in the East," *Wines and Vines* 42:11 (November, 1961), pp. 45–47] about Eastern viticultural developments." Frank's comments about starting to dig the foundation for the winery points to a date closer to April 1 than the beginning of the year.

23. This was Dr. Frank's first crush for his own winery; the grapes had previously been sold to Gold Seal. (Willy Frank interview with Cattell, August 28, 1998.)

24. Elmer S. "Flip" Phillips has edited an abbreviated version of the Union's records titled *Ithaca Oenological Union,* privately published in October, 1990. The Ithaca Oenological Union, formerly known as the Tompkins County Oenological Society, was formed at Albert and Grace Laubengayer's home on December 10, 1966. According to Pete Scala, whose report of the meeting was dated December 31, 1966, a standard was set "that conveyed a wonderful balance of the science of oenology and a budgeted bacchanal. These were truly serious drinkers with high standards, and the basic requirement was met—all were true little wine makers." Membership in the Union was limited to home winemakers and their wives. Charter members who attended the first meeting were Albert and Grace Laubengayer, Andrew and Mary Schultz, Aldus and Lois Fogelsanger, Bob and Lucille Finn, Pete and Phyllis Scala, and Harry and Margo Kerr. Also considered charter members even though they could not attend were Roger and Mary Lou Morse and David and Lois Williams.

25. The form letter dated August 28, 1967, was obviously edited but was signed by Dr. Frank. Many of the invitations had a personal handwritten note penned by Dr. Frank.

26. Harry Kerr's account of the elections is given in Ed Van Dyne's "1967–1987: The American Wine Society—Twenty Years Old," *American Wine Society Journal* 19:3 (Fall 1987), p. 71. See also a handout by the American Wine Society in 1971 or 1972 titled *The American Wine Society,* which contains summaries of the October 7, 1967 meeting and an organizational meeting on December 3, 1967.

27. Letter from Dene Miller to Cattell, February 23, 1979. Her letter was printed in part in the *Pennsylvania Grape Letter and Wine News* 6:5 (February 1979), p. 6.

28. Ibid.

29. Minutes of the October 7, 1967, meeting of the Ithaca Oenological Society, p. 1.

30. Mark Miller, *Wine—A Gentleman's Game: The Adventures of an Amateur Winemaker Turned Professional* (New York, 1984), p. 131.

31. American Wine Society, *A Progress Report to the Members,* October 24, 1968, pp. 1–2.

32. *Vintage* (AWS) 1:4 (Fall 1969), p. 6.

33. Several interviews with people who attended the 1969 conference have elicited different accounts. It seems likely that Dr. Frank became upset by Walter S. Taylor's after dinner speech. One report has it that he became so enraged that he had to be driven home.

34. Minutes of the annual meeting at Erie, Pennsylvania, October 30, 1970.

35. Letter from Frank to G. Hamilton Mowbray, September 14, 1963.

36. The cooperators were under increasing pressure to grow only vinifera. For a time there was a classification of "secondary cooperators," but that was later dropped.

37. Quoted in Ed Van Dyne, "1967–1987," p. 73. A response to Edward Cloos, Jr., by Philip Wagner was published in the *American Wine Society Journal* 19:4 (Winter 1987), p. 136.

38. For a short biography of Lawrence, see *Wine East* 17:3 (September–October, 1989), pp. 7, 29–30, based on a Cattell interview with Lawrence on August 22, 1989.

39. Much of this section is based on an interview by Cattell with Dr. Willard B. Robinson of the New York Agricultural Experiment Station on June 1, 1982. This interview was the source of an article published in *Wine East* 10:2 (July–August, 1982), pp.12–13, 23, under the title, "The Strange Mystery of the Toxic Chicks."

40. For references to the de Leobardy and Breider publications, see "Review of Grape and Wine Toxicity Research," *New York's Food and Life Sciences Bulletin* 6 (January 1971).

41. Letter to Frank from D. Boubals of the Station de Recherches Viticoles in Montpellier dated June 18, 1965. Boubals added the comment that he thought Dr. Frank would be most interested in this research. By this time, however, Frank was well aware of Breider's publication. In a letter to G. Hamilton Mowbray on May 31, 1965, he refers Mowbray to abstracts already published on Breider's "embryonal damages after enjoyment of hybrid wines." On April 11, 1966, in a letter addressed to Mowbray and Charles Singleton, Frank mentions that he has given away twenty copies of Breider's article and "very badly" needs more.

42. Cattell interview with Robinson, June 1, 1982.

43. Letter from Gilbert S. Stoewsand to Cattell, October 30, 1989.

44. G. S. Stoewsand and W. B. Robinson, "Malnutrition: Cause of 'Toxic' Response of Chicks Fed Varietal Grape Juices," *American Journal of Enology and Viticulture* 23:2 (1972), pp. 54–57. See also "Station Scientists Test Wine's Effect on Chicks," *Geneva Times* (New York), February 4, 1971.

45. According to Paul Hodge, a staff writer for the *Washington Post,* this Anderson column was actually written by associate Leslie H. Whitten.

46. Paul Hodge, "Winemakers Angered by Columnist's Story," *Washington Post,* January 15, 1971.

47. Quoted Ed Van Dyne, "Dr. Konstantin Frank," p. 70.

48. Letter from Fournier to Wagner, July 23, 1982. Dr. Frank died on September 6, 1985.

49. Fournier, "Birth of a N.Y. State Pinot Chardonnay," p. 32; Keith H. Kimball, "Another Look at Vinifera in the East," *Wines and Vines* 42:4 (April 1961), pp. 63–67; Charles Fournier, "A Scientific Look at Vinifera in the East," *Wines and Vines* 42:8 (August 1961), pp. 27–29; and Philip M. Wagner, "The Four Approaches to Vinifera in the East," *Wines and Vines* 42:11 (November 1961), pp. 45–47.

50. Wagner, "The Four Approaches to Vinifera in the East," p. 45.

51. For a brief explanation of the vinifera-hybrid controversy in France, see Lucie T. Morton, "The European Attitude towards French Hybrids," *Vinifera Wine Growers Journal* 1:2 (Fall 1974), pp. 23–29. See also Lucie T. Morton, "The Vine of Gold," *American Wine Society Journal* 10:2 (Summer 1978), pp. 22–25.

52. Quoted in Morton, "The European Attitude," p. 25.

53. Philip Wagner; a heavily edited version of his speech appeared in the *American Wine Society Journal* 10:1 (Spring 1978), pp. 12–15 under the title "A Sham Controversy."

Chapter 4

1. This quote is taken from the manuscript copy of Wagner's lecture. Interestingly, Wagner's talk on the development of the French hybrids was not considered technical enough for publication in the *American Journal of Enology and Viticulture* despite being of "tremendous interest" (letter from editor A. D. Webb to Wagner, August 4, 1978). The lecture was subsequently published as "The East's New Wine Industry," in *Wines and Vines* 60:3 (March 1979), pp. 24–26.

2. H. C. Barrett, "The French Hybrid Grapes," *National Horticulture Magazine* 35:3 (July 1956), pp. 132–144.

3. Hudson Cattell interview with Joseph P. Milza, president of Renault Winery, July 31, 1980.

4. Principal sources for this section on Ohio include Garth A. Cahoon, James F. Gallander, and Carolyn Amiet, "Vineyards Return to Ohio River Valley after 100 Years," *Wines and Vines* 54:2 (February 1973), pp. 34–38; Garth A. Cahoon, "Grapes Stage a Comeback in Southern Ohio Counties," *American Fruit Grower* 89:5 (May 1969), pp. 17–18, 30; Cattell interview with Cahoon and Gallander published as "Garth Cahoon and Jim Gallander to Retire in Ohio," *Wine East* 19:5 (January–February 1992), pp. 4–6; and Garth A. Cahoon, "History of the French Hybrid Grapes in North America," in *Proceedings: Ohio Grape—Wine Short Course,* 1996, pp. 98–113 (also published in *Fruit Varieties Journal* 50:4 [1996], pp. 202–216).

5. Henry O. Sonneman, in partnership with his brother Cliff, bought Meier's Grape Juice Company in Silverton in 1928. After buying his brother out at the end of World War II, he turned Meier's from a winery making 50,000 gallons into a 2 million gallon facility. He thought Ohio should be producing some distinctive wines and the winery became known for its sherries and champagnes. With a need for additional vineyards, he bought Isle St. George (North Bass Island) in 1941. His extensive travels led him to believe that southern Ohio could once again become an important wine region. (Cattell interview with Meredith Lewis, November 10, 1994.)

6. The French hybrids were acquired from Boordy Vineyard, the Horticultural Research Institute of Ontario, and the New York State Fruit Tasting Cooperative Association. In addition to grapes to be used primarily for wine, juice grapes and table grapes were also included.

7. For the viticultural and enological evaluations, see two articles in *Proceedings: Ohio Grape—Wine Short Course,* 1972: Garth A. Cahoon and Donald A. Chandler, "Performance of Grape Cultivars and Selections at the Southern Branch of the Ohio Agricultural Research and Development Center," pp. 1–21; and James A. Gallander and J. F. Stetson, "Composition and Quality of Ohio Musts and Wines," pp. 22–30.

8. R. C. Moore and G. D. Oberle, "French-American Hybrid Grapes in Virginia," *Fruit Varieties and Horticultural Digest* 8:1 (Spring 1953), pp. 5–8.

9. Archie Smith [Jr.], "On the Scene in Virginia," *American Wine Society Journal* 9:2 (Summer 1977), p. 24. See also Harrison O'Connor, "Wine Country: Three Thousand Vines Nursed at Flint Hill," *Piedmont Virginian*, March 22, 1972.

10. According to the April 12, 1972 edition of the *Piedmont Virginian* published in The Plains, Maréchal Foch, Léon Millot, Aurore, and Rougeon vines came from the New York State Fruit Tasting Cooperative Association, and Rayon d'Or, Villard Noir and Villard Blanc vines were purchased from Boordy Vineyard.

11. Much of the biographical information about Lawrence comes from a Cattell interview with him on August 22, 1989.

12. Robert de Treville Lawrence, Sr., "Virginia's Budding Wine Industry," *Vinifera Wine Growers Journal* 9:2 (Summer 1982), p. 120.

13. Lawrence was impatient with those who urged caution. George D. Oberle in 1973, John R. McGrew of the USDA in 1973, and H. P. Olmo of the University of California at Davis in 1977 were among those who pointed out the special challenges of growing vinifera.

14. Among those interested was Ronald F. Cooper, who obviously believed in planning ahead. On June 1, 1972, he received permission from the Fauquier County Board of Zoning Appeals to locate a private landing strip on his seventy-one-acre property near Warrenton. He told the board that he was planning to build a very small and very slow airplane to be used for spraying "my future grape crop" (*Piedmont Virginian*, June 8, 1972).

15. Lucie Taylor Morton, "Elizabeth Furness: Virginia's Wine Pioneer," *Eastern Grape Grower and Winery News* 5:5 (October 1979), p. 55.

16. *Piedmont Virginian*, July 19, 1972.

17. Ibid., September 14, 1973. The *Piedmont Virginian* is an excellent source of information for events during this period. Most of the 1973 and 1974 dates that follow come from accounts in that weekly newspaper.

18. Cattell interview with Lawrence, August 22, 1989.

19. For an account of the early years of the winery, see Pamela Bearer and Linda Fleming, "Winegrowing on a New Hampshire Island," *Wines and Vines* 60:9 (September 1979), p. 86. For more on the difficulty the Canepas had in marketing their wines, see chapter 6.

20. "Meredyth Vineyards—Wine on the Five Year Plan," *Pennsylvania Grape Letter and Wine News* 5:7 (April 1978), pp. 4–5; and Harrison O'Connor, "Wine Country: Archie Smith Putting in a Vineyard Near the Plains," *Piedmont Virginian*, April 12, 1972. An account of Smith's life is available in *Wine East* 26:4 (November–December 1998), pp. 6–9.

21. Archie Smith, III, left Oxford to become the winemaker at Meredyth Vineyards in 1977 and wrote a highly regarded series of articles published in *Wine East* on how to grow different grape varieties in the East and how to make wine from them. Archie Smith, Jr., continued with a second five-year plan that included changing legislation in Virginia, and he and his wife Dody were instrumental in getting a farm winery laws passed in 1980. Father and son both held leadership positions in various Virginia wine organizations.

22. Charles Catherman, "Sleepless in Sandusky," *Proceedings: Ohio Grape—Wine Short Course*, 1995, pp. 36–37.

23. Cattell interview with Angelo Spinazze, July 19, 1998. See also Church, *Wines of the Midwest*, pp. 58–60.

24. For an account of a visit to Warner Vineyards and other Michigan wineries at the time, see "Michigan's Vineyard: *Wines & Vines* Visits a Midwest Fruit Basket" by Philip Hiaring, *Wines and Vines* 53:12 (December 1972), 19–23.

25. E. S. Phillips, "A Tour of Midwest Wineries: Taber [*sic*] Hill—Michigan," *Vintage* (AWS) III:3 (Summer, 1971), 6–7; and Philip F. Jackisch, "Tabor Hill '72," *Vintage* (AWS) V:1 (Spring, 1973), 13. For a longer account, see "Tabor Hill Vineyard and Wine Cellar," *Chicagoland Wine Scene* 1:4 (March, 1977), pp. 1–4. A short autobiographical sketch by Carl Banholzer, "Du Grand Cabernet Sauvignon des Indianas," was published in the *Vinifera Wine Growers Journal* 4:2 (Summer 1977), pp. 332–335.

26. Marshall C. Harrold, *The Ohio Winemakers* (privately published, 1976), p. 9. In *The Wines and Wineries of Ohio* (Franklin, Ohio, 1973), pp. 24–33, Philip R. Hines described the Bass Islands as one vast vineyard and that there were nearly five square miles of vineyards around Sandusky.

27. According to Hines, Lonz Winery on Middle Bass Island sold 100,000 gallons of juice each year during Prohibition, sometimes in 20,000-gallon lots. Some of the best customers were members of the Chicago Mafia who bottled it under a false label and sold it as sweet wine after putting a sliver of dry ice in the bottle to give it a fizz.

28. Hines, *The Wines and Wineries of Ohio*, pp. 94–97; Marcia King, "Goals and Family Leadership Pull Chalet Debonné Through Transition," *Vineyard and Winery Management* 14:2 (March–April 1988), pp. 30–36; Church, *Wines of the Midwest*, pp. 130–132.

29. Ruth Ellen Church, "Exciting Things Happen along Lake Erie Shores," *Chicago Tribune*, March 25, 1976; Craig Goldwyn, "The Restaurant That Crowns a Winery," *Wines and Vines* 62:9 (September, 1981), pp. 68–71. The

Cedar Hill Wine Company, Chalet Debonné, and Markko Vineyard were all covered in (Cattell), "Three Ohio Wineries Part of Lake Erie Grape Belt," *Pennsylvania Grape Letter and Wine News* 4:10 (July–August 1977), pp. 4–5.

30. Church, *Wines of the Midwest,* pp. 136–137.

31. James R. Treble, "A Tour of Midwest Wineries," Part 1, *Vintage* (AWS) III:1 (Winter 1971), p. 9. See also Adams, *Wines of America,* 2nd edition, pp. 174–175.

32. Church, *Wines of the Midwest,* pp. 105–107.

33. Two early sources of information about Stone Hill Winery are Linda Jones McKee, "Past and Present Meet in Missouri," *Wine East* 9:6 (March–April 1982), pp. 14–17; and Lucie T. Morton, "Winemaking Renaissance in Hermann, Missouri," *Historic Preservation* (December 1984), pp. 38–41. See also Ray Pompilio, "Home Grown in the 'Show Me' State," *Vineyard and Winery Management* 25:3 (May–June 1999), pp. 47–54, which also includes St. James Winery and Les Bourgeois Vineyards. A four-part series of articles dealing with the history of Stone Hill Winery appeared in the winery's newsletter, "Stone Hill Winery and Restaurant Gazette" (Awaiting Spring, 1995; Spring, 1995; Sizzlin' Summer, 1995; Holiday, 1995).

34. For an account of the early years at St. James, see Roy W. Taylor, "Missouri's Wine Scene: The 'Show-Me' State Is Looking Good," *Wines and Vines* 66:6 (June 1985), pp. 74–80. See also McKee, "Past and Present Meet in Missouri," pp. 16–17.

35. Everett Crosby, *The Vintage Years: The Story of High Tor Vineyards* (New York, 1973). This is an excellent and very readable account of the challenges and rewards that a pioneering grape grower and winemaker found in the early days in the East. See also Roger W. Christian and Arnold H. Epstein, "High Tor Vineyard, 30 Miles from New York City," *Vintage* 1:2 (April 1971), pp. 24–27.

36. Wagner, *Daybooks,* Vol. 13, entries for October 5, 1951, January 6 and September 26, 1952.

37. Peaceful Bend Vineyard was owned by Katherine Nott and Clyde Gill at the time of the Cattell interview with Nott on January 31, 2008. Additional information came from "Vinous Quest in Missouri," a talk originally given by Arneson to the American Wine Society that was later edited by Gill and preserved online together with an epilogue by Gill at the Peaceful Bend website, www.peacefulbend.com/tour/vinous.shtml.

38. See Leon Adams, *The Wines of America,* 1st edition (New York and San Francisco, 1973), pp. 70–71; and 2nd edition (New York, 1982), p. 87. The 1973 edition includes the fact that something went wrong with the 1963 vintage and it had to be poured down the drain. Additional information came from a Cattell interview with David Fondots on May 20, 1976, and a vineyard plot plan provided by Martin Keen, both of whom were later owners of Conestoga Vineyards.

39. Wagner, *Daybooks,* Vol. 21, May 4, 1962.

40. Hermann J. Wiemer came from a winemaking family in Bernkastel in the Mosel wine region in Germany and was a graduate of Geisenheim. Walter Taylor liked to say that he hired Wiemer when he visited Germany in 1967 and brought him to Bully Hill in 1968. Wiemer had in fact been working as vineyard manager at O-Neh-Da Vineyard in Conesus, New York, having been sponsored, probably in 1966, by Leo Goering, another Geisenheim graduate and the winemaker at O-Neh-Da (personal communication, William D. Edinger, July 8, 2008).

In 1973 while he was the winemaker at Bully Hill, Wiemer began experimenting with growing vinifera on an abandoned soybean farm he had bought along Seneca Lake. This led to Walter firing him by telegram on Christmas Day, 1979, while he was spending the holidays in Bernkastel. No clear reason has been stated for his dismissal, but his private preoccupation with the vinifera may very well have gotten to be too much for the prohybrid Walter. Wiemer later opened his own winery with fifty-five acres of vineyards and a large nursery operation on the western shore of Seneca Lake and became particularly well known for his Riesling wines.

For more on Hermann Weimer, see Frank Prial's column titled "Lakes' Success" in the *New York Times,* May 3, 1992; and Mort Hochstein, "Finger Lakes Winemaker Goes His Own Way," *Wine Spectator* 15:20 (February 28, 1991), pp. 35–36.

41. See chapter 8 for more on Walter, his flamboyant personality, and his much publicized feud with the Taylor Wine Company and the Coca-Cola Wine Company of Atlanta. An overview of his colorful life is presented in Cattell's article, "Walter S. Taylor, 1931–2001," *Wine East* 29:1 (May–June 2001), pp. 38–41, 54–55.

42. For an account of an early visit to the winery by James R. Treble, see "A Tour of Midwest Wineries," Part 2, *Vintage* (AWS) III:2 (Spring 1971), p. 12. Cattell interviewed Dressel on February 5, 2008. See also Ruth Ellen Church, *Wines of the Midwest* (Athens, Ohio), 1982, pp. 107–110. A combination of divorce proceedings and legal and financial problems led to the acquisition of Mount Pleasant Winery by Lucian Dressel's brother Phillip in June 1992.

43. The vinerights are discussed in more detail in chapter 8. For more information on Mark Miller and Benmarl Vineyards, see *Mark Miller: Wine—A Gentleman's Game* (New York, 1984) and Cattell's article "The Benmarl Story: Mark Miller and Benmarl Vineyards," *Wine East:* 34:1 (May–June 2006), pp. 20–31, 57–58.

44. Cattell interview with Douglas Moorhead in July 1977, used as "Winery Profile: Presque Isle Wine Cellars" in the *Pennsylvania Grape Letter and Wine News* 5:1 (September 1977) pp. 4–5; and subsequent interviews with William Konnerth and Moorhead on October 5, 1997.

45. A good source of information about John Moorhead is an article by Eleanor Heald and Ray Heald, "Grape-Challenges along Lake Erie," which appeared in *Practical Winery and Vineyard* 10:5 (January–February 1990), pp. 38–41.

46. "The Pioneer Spirit at Markko Vineyard," *Wine East* 12:1 (May–June 1984), pp. 8–11, 22. In the interview that led to this article by Cattell, Esterer voiced his confidence in the future of growing vinifera along Lake Erie: "I'm just disappointed that more growers and others in the business are still very scared and hesitant about making a change. We've been here 15 years, and we haven't seen more than just a little bit of additional interest in growing the vinifera. It will come, but it's a lot slower than I anticipated." See also "Arnulf Esterer Pioneers Vinifera in Ohio," *Vinifera Wine Growers Journal* 10:1 (Spring 1983), pp. 42–45.

47. The early history of Woodbury Vineyards was recounted by M. Page Woodbury in "Chautauqua Viticultural Region: Past, Present and Future" as part of her presentation at the annual meeting of the Society of Wine Educators in Stamford, Connecticut, on August 5, 1988, and was printed as a handout at the winery. See also "Chautauqua County Wineries," *Pennsylvania Grape Letter and Wine News* 8:2 (October 1980). pp. 4–5, 8; and Richard Figiel, "German Vineyard Management Techniques Give Woodbury Vineyards an Edge," *Vineyard and Winery Management* 16:3 (May–June 1990), pp. 39–41.

48. Cattell interview with Arnie Esterer, June 1, 1999. See also Adams, *Wines of America,* 2nd edition, pp. 181–182; and James L. Butler and John J. Butler, *Indiana Wine: A History* (Bloomington, Indiana), 2001, pp. 144–145. In 1995 it was decided that the time and effort to grow grapes and make wine had gotten to be too much and the vineyard was plowed under and replaced with pasture land.

49. For further information, see Roberta Grant, "Martha's Vineyard, the Island and the Vineyard," *Vintage* 6:5 (October 1976), pp. 28–29, 52. See also William A. Caldwell, "The Vineyard's Vineyard," *Country Journal* (September 1975), pp. 38–42; idem, "From Plymouth to Narragansett: Chicama—Not Martha—Has the Vineyards," *Wine East* 10:1 (May–June 1982), pp. 10–11, 20.

50. Cattell, "Surveying the Tennessee Grape and Wine Industry," *Wine East* 33:5 (January–February 2006), pp. 26–39, 58. Also helpful were the *Memoirs of Judge William O. Beach, Jr.* (privately printed, 1992), pp. 171–177.

51. Letter from Charles Singleton to Paul Hodge of the *Washington Post,* October 22, 1968. The details and reconstruction of these early years come from this letter and a Cattell interview with Phyllis Mowbray on August 19, 2000.

52. Wagner, *Daybooks,* Vol. 16, September 26, 1954, is the authority for the opening date. Jack Johnson of Copernica Vineyards and Phyllis Mowbray agree that 1962 was the probable closing date. Phyllis Mowbray added that Cároli meant "little Charles" and that Singleton named the winery after himself rather than the county.

53. An interesting account of Mowbray's early years in grapes and wine is available in Wayne J. Henkel's article, "Maryland Vintage 1979," *Baltimore Sun Magazine* (November 25, 1979), pp. 6–7, 13, 18.

54. In an interview with Cattell on November 13, 1979, Mowbray explained why he chose Montbray rather than Mowbray: "Well, actually it goes back to 1066. The name Montbray originated from the Norman 'de Montbray' who came in with William the Conqueror. Somewhere along the line the 'de' was dropped and after a while—well, the Anglo-Saxons couldn't handle that 'Montbray' bit—the name was changed to Mowbray, which is what it sounds like anyway. It became a fairly common name in England and then naturally it came over here. When it was my turn, I decided to go back to the French name rather than use my own. I would have used the 'de,' but, well, that seemed to be just a little too pretentious." The quote was used in "Montbray Wine Cellars," *Pennsylvania Grape Letter and Wine News* 7:4 (January 1980), pp. 4–5.

55. See Walter C. Elly, "Chateau Gay Ready to Take a New Look," *Wines and Vines* 46:6 (June 1965), pp. 39–40; E. S. Phillips, "Niagara Falls Wine Cellar," *Vintage* (AWS) 5:1 (Spring 1973), pp. 3–4.

56. Adams, *Wines of America,* 1st edition, pp. 57–58. The story as given here took eighteen lines in the first edition, was reduced to six lines in the second edition, and then vanished in the third edition. It would be nice to know the full story not only of Lewis and his winery, but others that have vanished over time.

57. The information on the Fedderman Wine Company comes from Frank W. Prial, "For the 'First Black Winery in the U.S.,' 1973 Was NOT a Good Year," *New York Times,* November 16, 1973, p. 43.

58. Feddernan also admitted to Prial that there was little interest in his wines and that his outright appeal to black consumers might not have been good marketing.

59. Harry Gordon, "The Wine and Grape Industry in Canada," *Wines and Vines* 24:7 (July 1943), p. 20.

60. Ibid.

61. Percy Rowe, *The Wines of Canada* (Toronto, 1970), p. 116.

62. Ibid., p. 117.

63. "Canadian Flavored Wines Selling Big in Canada," *Wines and Vines* 44:7 (July 1964), p. 7.

64. Philip Hiaring, "Baby Duck: No Babe in Canada's Sales," *Wines and Vines* 58:9 (September 1977), pp. 22–23.

65. A brief account of Andrew Peller's life and the founding of Andrés Wines may be found in John Schreiner, *The World of Canadian Wine* (Vancouver, 1984), pp. 30–38. See also *The Winemaker: The Autobiography of Andrew*

Peller, Founder of André's Wines Ltd. as told to S. Patricia Filer (Winona, Ontario, 1982). Additional information came from an interview by Cattell with Larry G. Gibson, vice president of Andrés, on September 24, 1999.

66. Schreiner, *World,* p. 73.

67. Peller, *The Winemaker,* p. 138.

68. Andrés Wines, "The Baby Duck Story," October 16, 1980.

69. Tony Aspler, *Vintage Canada* (Scarborough, Ontario, 1983), p. 24.

70. Hiaring, "Baby Duck," p. 23.

71. Cattell interview with Larry Gibson, September 24, 1999.

72. K. Helen Fisher, "Grape Growing in Ontario—1800–1990," mimeograph, Horticultural Research Institute of Ontario (Vineland, Ontario), p. 21.

73. An exception was made only in 1973 when 18,000 tons of concentrate were approved for importation to make up 80 percent of that year's shortage.

74. "Infrared Photography Helps Identify Frost-Prone Areas," *Pennsylvania Grape Letter and Wine News* 6:8 (May 1979), pp. 1, 4.

75. "Combating Vine Stress through the Use of Trickle Irrigation," *Pennsylvania Grape Letter and Wine News* 7:2 (October 1979), pp. 1, 4–5.

76. For the story of Schloss Laderheim, see Schreiner, *The World of Canadian Wine,* pp. 58–59.

77. Aspler in *Vintage Canada,* p. 26, noted that "the age of the packaged wine had arrived. The way the bottle looked was as important as what was in it."

78. Cattell interview with George Hostetter, September 23, 1977. This story is also told in Schreiner, *The World of Canadian Wine,* pp. 47–48. The same interview with Hostetter was responsible for the information on Brights House Wine and President Canadian Champagne.

79. Aspler, *Vintage Canada,* p. 21.

80. Schreiner, *World,* p. 49, attributes the name to a question posed by the wife of Brights president Edward Arnold, who asked her husband, "Why doesn't someone put out a house wine?"

Chapter 5

1. These statistics were reported in Leon D. Adams, *The Wines of America* (San Francisco and Boston, 1973), pp. 10, 28.

2. For an account of the adversarial role of the Pennsylvania Liquor Control Board, see Hudson Cattell, "70th Anniversary of Repeal—and the PLCB," *Wine East* 31:4 (November–December 2003), pp. 14–25.

3. James L. Butler and John J. Butler, *Indiana Wine: A History* (Bloomington, 2001), pp. 140–141. See also Ledford C. Carter and Dorothy Vitaliano, "Indiana Wine: Past-Present-Future," *American Wine Society Journal* 7:2 (Summer 1975), pp. 15–18.

4. The old wine law in Virginia is covered in two articles in the *Vinifera Wine Growers Journal:* "Virginia Wine Law" 3:3 (Fall 1976), p. 271; and "Wine Laws and Wineries in Virginia: Questions Most Often Asked" in 6:2 (Summer 1979), pp. 80–81. The exact date in the 1930s for the creation of this license is no longer on record at the Virginia Department of Alcohol Beverage Control, but it may have been for the benefit of Woburn Winery (see chapter 4). For the 1980 farm winery law, see "New Virginia Wine Law," letter to the editor by S. Mason Carbaugh, Commissioner of Agriculture, in the *Vinifera Wine Growers Journal* 7:3 (Fall 1980), p. 203.

5. Leon D. Adams, "The Future of Winegrowing in the Southeastern States: Farm Winery Laws Are Essential," *Vinifera Wine Growers Journal* 6:2 (Summer 1979), pp. 60–64.

6. H. C. George, "Behind the Scenes: How Alabama's Farm Winery Law Came to Be," *Wines and Vines* 60:12 (December 1979), pp. 37–39.

7. Robert G. Rizza, "Reviving the Kansas Wine Industry: A Model for Other States," *Vinifera Wine Growers Journal* 16:4 (Winter 1989), pp. 267–268.

8. Jenny Deam, "Kansas Ripens for Home-Grown Vines," *Vinifera Wine Growers Journal* 12:4 (Winter 1985), pp. 252–255.

9. "Kansas Bill Signed into Law," *Vinifera Wine Growers Journal* 15:3 (Fall 1988), pp. 156–157.

10. Amelioration with water to reduce the acidity of their labrusca wines was also a common practice and led to Walter S. Taylor's "Wine without Water" campaign to help sell Bully Hill wines. At one point, to protest the practice of bringing in blending wines from California, Taylor had a railroad tank car similar to those used to transport their wines to New York prominently placed on a hillside far above Keuka Lake where it could be easily seen.

11. Mark Miller, *Wine—A Gentleman's Game* (New York, 1984), pp. 80–82. Miller details his efforts in getting the 1976 bill passed on pages 177–180.

12. Frank Prial, "State's Smaller Vintners Press for Changes," *New York Times,* February 25, 1976.

13. "NY Lt. Gov. Tours Wine and Grape Industry to Highlight Need for Reform," *Eastern Grape Grower* 2:5 (October 1976), pp. 14–15.

14. These figures are from Adams, *The Wines of America,* p. x.

15. James R. Williams, "Diary of a Farm Winery Bill," *American Wine Society Journal* 16:1 (Spring 1984), pp. 22–24.The spelling of DelVista Vinyards is correct: Williams wanted to emphasize the connection between wine (vin) and vineyard.

16. A similar situation occurred in Tennessee in 1982 when Nashville attorney Mack Glasgow detected what seemed to be an innocent looking sentence in a proposed amendment to the 1977 Grape and Wine Law. If it had been enacted in the 1983 revision, wineries would have been prevented from operating legally in dry counties. Mack successfully campaigned to get rid of the problem sentence just in time. (Cattell, "Surveying the Tennessee Grape and Wine Industry," *Wine East* 33:5 [January–February 2006], p. 30.)

17. "Farm Winery Legislation Signed in Delaware," *Wine East* 19:2 (July–August 1991), p. 4.

18. The Pennsylvania Liquor Control Board was established in 1933 "to protect the public welfare, health, peace and morals of the Commonwealth," and for many years this meant strict control over anything having to do with wine and spirits. By the late 1960s and early 1970s, retirements and the arrival of a new generation of administrators gradually changed the concept of "control" to "merchandising" and "customer service." The hiring of Darryl S. Stackhouse as a management analyst in 1975 was an important step in identifying someone who could work with the wineries and legislature in making the changes that began in 1980. A much more complete account of the relationship between the PLCB and the limited wineries is given in Cattell, "70th Anniversary of Repeal—and the PLCB." Also, see Cattell and McKee, *Pennsylvania Wine* (Charleston, South Carolina, 2012), pp. 83–98, for the changes in the law.

19. "Report of the Ontario Wine Standards Committee" (Toronto, July 6, 1934), p. 22.

20. William F. Rannie, *Wines of Ontario: An Industry Comes of Age* (Lincoln, Ontario, 1978), p. 95. Walter Strawa died shortly after the winery opened and the assets of the winery were sold in 1965 to London Winery.

21. Two wineries received their commercial winery licenses in 1975, the other being the Podamer Champagne Company in Lincoln, which received its full production license on July 29, twenty-four days after Inniskillin. Podamer, however, had received a restricted license to produce samples in 1973 while Inniskillin did not receive its restricted license until April 1974. This was enough to give Podamer controversial bragging rights to being the first winery to open in modern times. There can be no question that Inniskillin was the more important.

The story of the start of Inniskillin and its founders, Donald J. P. Ziraldo and Karl J. Kaiser, is available in a number of places. Some sources for the information in this chapter include Donald J. P. Ziraldo, *Anatomy of a Winery: The Art of Wine at Inniskillin* (Toronto, 1995), pp. 10–11, 48; Rannie, *Wines of Ontario,* pp. 122–127; Schreiner, *The World of Canadian Wine,*(Vancouver, 1984), pp. 176–182; and Aspler, *Vintage Canada* (Scarborough, Ontario, 1983). pp. 53–56. For more on Major-General Kitching, see Linda Bramble, *Niagara's Wine Visionaries: Profiles of the Pioneering Winemakers* (Toronto, 2009), pp. 42–47.

22. The eight included Brights Wines, Château-Gai Wines, Barnes Wines, Jordan Wines (which became Jordan and Ste. Michelle Cellars in 1976), Andrés Wines, London Winery, Parkdale Wines and, although it closed at the end of 1977, Turner Wines in Toronto.

23. Schreiner, *World,* p. 178.

24. Aspler, *Vintage Canada,* p. 54.

25. Rannie, *Wines of Ontario,* pp. 124–125.

26. Aspler, *Vintage Canada,* p. 54.

27. Ziraldo, *Anatomy of a Winery,* p. 10.

28. A list of firsts was published in "Master Vintners Since 1974," a four-page mimeograph prepared at Brights Wines. See also Cattell, "The Pioneering Years at Brights," *Wine East* 14:2 (July–August 1986), pp. 10, 26–27. "George's Clone" was the name given to a superior clone of Baco Noir that was discovered by accident in Brights vineyard by George Hostetter.

29. For more on Paul Bosc and Château des Charmes, see Bramble, *Niagara Wine Visionaries,* pp. 82–101.

Chapter 6

1. Hudson Cattell, "Surveying the Tennessee Grape and Wine Industry," *Wine East* 33:5 (January–February 2006), pp. 28–29.

2. Philip Hiaring, "The Finger Lakes Wine Scene: Vintage 1969," *Wines and Vines* 50:11 (November 1969), p. 44.

3. Ivan Bass of the New Hampshire Alcohol Beverage Commission provided Cattell with the information that follows on the early laws affecting wine in New Hampshire on September 21, 2000.

4. When Cattell interviewed Reed on November 14, 2005, the latter added that this unpleasantness did not stop him from being a good neighbor. He could open the winery at 8 a.m. on Sunday, but he waits until 12:15 or 12:30 p.m. when nearby church services have ended. An increasing number of people leaving church have been stopping at the winery to buy wine on their way home.

5. A long account of similar opposition to the start of Alto Vineyards in Alto Pass, Illinois, was written by Gerry Dawes, "Heartland Blush: Wine and Religion in Southern Illinois," *Friends of Wine* 26:5 (October–November 1989), pp. 8–14. It was a two-year confrontation that began in January 1987, and lasted until December 1988, at which time the official opening of Alto Vineyards and Winery was covered by three television stations and several newspapers.

6. It is difficult to pinpoint the exact number of wineries in the East in any given year. The figures for 1975, 1980, and 1985 in the eastern United States were supplied to Cattell on microfiche by "Val the Librarian" at BATF and were identified as "Authorized-to-Operate: Wineries (Bonded)." These authorizations included bonded wineries, bonded wine cellars, distilled spirits plants, and tax paid bottling houses, and they were identified by a number and the initials BW, BWC, DSP, and TPWBH.

The second column in the table for each of these years is the number of BATF authorizations. These figures were adjusted in the first column in an attempt to get a more accurate count of the number of bonded wine producers. Because the distilled spirits plants and tax paid wine bottling houses were not wine producers, they were eliminated from the count. Whatever distinction BATF made between bonded wineries and bonded wine cellars is not evident. Wineries with a BW designation were considered to be wine producers; BWC designated wineries included both wine producers and wine bottlers. With the aid of *Wines and Vines* annual directories, statistical material published by *Eastern Grape Grower and Winery News,* and *Wine East* records, it was usually possible to resolve the question of which were primarily wine producers or wine bottlers. The bottlers were then subtracted from the BATF count.

From 1990 to 2010 only BATF and TTB figures have been used. At some point BATF may have changed their definition of bonded wineries, and the *Wines and Vines* directories eliminated most of the DSP and TPWBH entries and shifted some BWC designations to BW. Table 6.1 provides a reasonably accurate picture of the growth of wineries during these years.

Finally, it should be noted that BATF and TTB counts are based on the number of licenses that are open and not on the number of wineries in operation. Once a license is issued, the winery is counted whether or not the winery has actually opened, and a winery that has closed but kept its license open is also counted. No attempt has been made to change BATF or TTB numbers from 1990 on.

7. The two often went together. An interesting example is that of a poet, Tom O'Grady, who opened Rose Bower Vineyard & Winery in Hampden-Sydney, Virginia, in 1978. Tom was drafted in the late 1960s and trained for service in Vietnam. After being discharged from the military, he taught at a community college in Delaware while pursuing a doctorate. He and his wife Bronwyn decided to go back to the land, and after he joined the faculty at Hampden-Sydney College they bought property in 1973 and planted vines a year later. A sequence of thirty-three sonnets was published in 1977 under the title *Establishing a Vineyard,* and these poems were used in 1981 by Virginia filmmaker Charlotte Schrader as the soundtrack for scenes of grape growing and winemaking at Rose Bower in a twenty-eight-minute film *The Land Is a Woman.* O'Grady also founded the *Hampden-Sydney Poetry Review.* See Cattell, "The Artist as Winemaker and Poet," *Wine East* 17:3 (September–October 1989), pp. 16–23.

8. A chronological account of Rapidan River Vineyards from 1974 to 1981 is given in Richard Figiel, "Virginia's Two European Ventures," *Eastern Grape Grower and Winery News* 7:6 (December 1981–January 1982), pp. 20–23. See also James Conaway, "Vinifera in Our Own Backyard," *Vinifera Wine Growers Journal* 11:2 (Summer 1984), pp. 100–101.

9. The information on Joachim Hollerith in this chapter came largely from a Cattell interview with him on April 21, 2003. See also Ray K. Saunders, "A Taste of the 'Old World' Being Nurtured Near Culpeper," *Culpeper Star Exponent,* July 29, 1981; and Mort Hochstein, "Right Spot still Eludes Virginia Wine Pioneers, *Wine Spectator* 7:16 (November 16–30, 1982), p. 30.

10. Part of this section originally appeared in an obituary article, "Jean Leducq Dies in France at 82," *Wine East* 31:1 (May–June 2003), pp. 12–13. The sources for this obituary included a Cattell interview with Hollerith on April 21, 2003; an undated press release from Prince Michel Vineyards following Leducq's death on December 6, 2002; and various issues of *The Prince Michel Sun,* the winery's newsletter.

11. Richard Figiel, "Virginia's Two European Ventures," gives a chronological account of the early years of Barboursville Vineyards from 1976 to 1981. See also H. Christopher Martin, "Barboursville Enters Its Second Year," *Vinifera Wine Growers Journal* 4:3 (Fall 1977), pp. 388–391; Pino Khail, "Italians Grow and Make Wine in Virginia," *Vinifera Wine Growers Journal* 11:3 (Fall 1984), pp. 169–173; and Philip Hiaring, "It's Vinifera in Virginia," *Wines and Vines* 58:11 (November 1977), pp. 18–20.

12. For a story about Luca Paschina, see R. W. Apple, Jr., "Jefferson Gets His Wish: At Last, a Decent Bottle of Virginia Wine," *New York Times,* September 13, 2000.

13. "The French Connection at Glenora," *Wine East* 14:2 (July–August 1986), p. 4, and 15:1 (May–June 1987), p. 5. See also Mort Hochstein, "French Enter Venture in New York State," *Wine Spectator* 11:3 (May 1–15, 1986), p. 4. The involvement of the French was the subject of much interest and speculation in the Finger Lakes. One

attention getter was the fact that Glenora's winemaker, Ray Spencer, was required to wear a beret while working with Château Liberté.

14. Carl Cannon, "Paul Masson Looking to Eastern Vineyards?" *Wine Spectator* 4:21 (February 16–29, 1980), pp. 1, 3.

15. One of the most interesting careers is that of Jacques A. Recht, a professor at the Brussels Fermentation Institute in Belgium, an enologist who formed his own wine lab and who for many years was a consultant in a number of European countries and North Africa. As a boy, he was a courier for M15 (British Intelligence) in World War II, and later was the skipper of the Belgian Racing Syndicate boat. He was cruising around the world in a thirty-six-foot catamaran with his wife Liliane when he sailed up the Potomac River, met Carl Flemer of Ingleside Plantation Vineyards in Oak Grove, Virginia, and was persuaded to become the winemaker at Flemer's winery. For more on his career, see Jim Rink, "Jacques Recht: 2007 AWS Award of Merit," *American Wine Society Journal* 39:4 (Winter 2007–2008), pp. 18–19.

16. A short history of the Finger Lakes Wine Growers Association appeared on the last page of its annual reports for the late 1960s and early 1970s.

17. The percentage of total crop production in winery controlled vineyards in 1964 was 79.6 percent traditional native American varieties, 18.2 percent French hybrids, and 1.6 percent vinifera. By 1971 the percentages were 70.7 percent traditional native American varieties, 26.1 percent French hybrids, and 2.8 percent vinifera. (Hal Harry Huffsmith, "A Descriptive Study of the Premium Finger Lakes Wine Industry in New York State," M.S. thesis, Cornell University, 1973, table 12, page 24.)

18. Two articles that give a good overview of the Finger Lakes wine industry in the 1960s are Irving H. Marcus, "Report on a Visit to the Wineries of the Finger Lakes," *Wines and Vines* 45:12 (December 1964), pp. 16–19; and Philip Hiaring, "The Finger Lakes Scene: Vintage 1969," *Wines and Vines* 50:11 (November 1969), pp. 41–44. Two evaluations of suitable grapes for the region in the 1970s by Seaton C. Mendall are "A New York Vineyardist Evaluates French Hybrids for Wines in the Empire State," *Wines and Vines* 56:9 (September 1975), pp. 60–61; and "Prospects for Vinifera in the Northeast," *Eastern Grape Grower* 5:2 (April 1979), pp. 14–16. In the latter article, Mendall states that he does not consider any of the vinifera plantings in the Finger Lakes to be financially successful.

19. In an interview with Cattell on April 8, 2006, Monty Stamp recalled a visit by Beers and Mendall urging him to join their organization. He accepted and continued to be its secretary for the next thirty-nine years. Stamp and several other growers were important sources of information for its history.

20. Hal Harry Huffsmith, "A Descriptive Study," pp. 27–28. Taylor began issuing lists of prices they would pay for grapes, and these became the accepted prices for grapes not only in the Finger Lakes region but in many other states as well. This raised the question of price fixing, and in the mid-1970s it was made mandatory for each winery to release the prices it would be paying for grapes by August 15 of each year. The Taylor prices remained authoritative in other states and Cattell recalls that for a number of years following its inception in 1976 the *Pennsylvania Grape Letter and Wine News* would publish the Taylor price list in its September issue. As early as the third week in August there would be many telephone calls from wineries and growers in Pennsylvania and neighboring states requesting advance information on that year's Taylor prices as a basis for their own buying and selling.

21. *Rochester Democrat and Chronicle,* April 14, 1976.

22. William J. Sanok, "Vinifera Grapes for Long Island," Cooperative Extension of Suffolk County, March, 1977. See also Thomas E. H. Cottrell, "Smooth Sailing for Long Island Vineyards," *Wines and Vines* 65:11 (November 1984), pp. 100–103.

23. For an excellent account of the grape and wine industry in Long Island up to 2000, including a thirty-two-page chapter on the historical background, see Edward Beltrami and Philip E. Palmedo, *The Wines of Long Island* (Mattituck, New York, 2000). See also Louisa Hargrave, "A History of Wine Grapes on Long Island," *Long Island Historical Journal* 3:1 (Fall 1990), pp. 3–16.

24. An engaging interview with the Hargraves by Berton Roueché appeared in the September 20, 1976, issue of the *New Yorker* (pp. 123–133) under the title "A Natural Miracle." The Hargraves dated their newsletter by the number of years that had elapsed since the founding of their vineyard, not unlike the ancient Romans who dated events by the number of years that had passed since the founding of Rome. Cattell used their dating practice in the titles of two articles: "It's Year Nine on Long Island," *Wine East* 9:9 (November 1981), pp. 16–18, 21; and "It's Now Year Fifteen on Long Island," *Wine East* 15:3 (September–October 1987), pp. 18–23.

25. James Laube, "Long Island Finds Its Style," *Wine Spectator* 13:15 (November 30, 1988), pp. 24–32, ratings on pages 35–40. Le Rêve, which had opened in 1987, was a red brick, copper-roofed chateau near Southampton that cost $17 million. The enterprise soon went into bankruptcy, and in 1994 was purchased by Dr. Herodotus Damianos and renamed Duck Walk Vineyards.

26. *Federal Register,* Vol. 40, No. 138, July 17, 1975. The BATF dates of proposed rulings and rulings that follow are also the dates on which they were published in the *Federal Register.*

27. For a more comprehensive account of the establishment of the Augusta AVA, see "Augusta Viticultural Area: 20 Years Old," by Cattell in *Wine East* 28:2 (July–August 2000), pp. 22–28.

28. Cattell interview with Millard S. Cohen, secretary of the Augusta Wine Board, June 20, 2000.

29. U.S. Department of the Treasury, Bureau of Alcohol, Tobacco and Firearms, Public Hearing in the Matter of: American Viticultural Area Designations "Augusta," Augusta, Missouri, November 1, 1979, pp. 10–11.

30. For the complete standards, see Cattell, "Augusta Viticultural Area," p. 26.

31. *Federal Register,* June 20, 1980.

Chapter 7

1. Lucie T. Morton, *Winegrowing in Eastern America: An Illustrated Guide to Viniculture East of the Rockies* (Ithaca, New York, 1985), p. 17.

2. For a history of the first fifty years of the Vineland Station, see *Horticultural Experiment Station and Products Laboratory: The First Fifty Years* by E. Frank Palmer (Ontario Department of Agriculture, n.d.). In 2006 a history of the first 100 years of the station was published as *Celebrating a Century of Success, 1906–2006,* edited by Arthur Loughton, Richard V. Chudyk, and Judy A. Wanner (Horticultural Experiment Station, Vineland; University of Guelph).

3. K. H. Fisher, "Grape Growing in Ontario—1800–1990," Station mimeograph, pp. 16–17. See also "Grape Breeding and Production Research" by the same author in *Celebrating a Century of Success,* pp. 93–96.

4. In 2007, as the result of a government and industry-led initiative and financing by the federal and provincial governments, the Vineland Station was transformed into the Vineland Research and Innovation Centre with the intention of creating a world-class center for horticulture in Ontario (see chapter 13). The University of Guelph and the centre signed a research partnership agreement in 2009.

5. O. A. Bradt, "Reflections on the Eastern Grape Industry for the Past Forty Years," speech delivered on August 1, 1986, at the annual meeting of the Eastern Section of the American Society for Enology and Viticulture. Bradt credits Palmer with having worked with de Chaunac on deciding what vines to order; it was, in fact, van Haarlem at Palmer's request.

6. The practice of naming grapes and other fruits introduced at the station with the letter "v" at the beginning of the name or "vee" at the end was started by Palmer probably in the 1920s as a way of identifying the station with any varieties it introduced. In the mid-1960s, to celebrate Canada's centennial in 1967, the station's streets were also given names starting with the letter "v" (e.g., Veteran, Vedette, and Valentine).

7. For the circumstances surrounding the naming of L'Acadie and Vintinto, see "Two New Grape Varieties Named in Canada," *Wine East* 23:5 (January–February 1996), pp. 6–7, and "L'Acadie—A New Cold Climate White Wine Grape" by Hudson Cattell in the same issue, pp. 10–13.

8. "Infrared Photography Helps Identify Frost-Prone Areas," *Pennsylvania Grape Letter and Wine News* 6:5 (May 1979), pp. 1, 4.

9. R. F. Crowther and J. H. Lloyd Truscott, "Flor-Type Canadian Sherry Wine," report of the Horticultural Products Laboratory, 1955–56.

10. Tibor Fuleki, "Chemistry in Aid of Grape Breeding: The Vineland Grape Flavour Index," *Highlights of Agricultural Research in Ontario* 5:3 (September 1982), pp. 4–6.

11. Vicki Gray, "Ontario Wine Standards Tasting Committee," in *Celebrating a Century of Success,* pp. 171–172. The committee continued its work until the end of 1986 when it was taken over by the Vintners Quality Alliance.

12. Richard V. Chudyk, "Development of Ontario Grape Standards," in *Celebrating a Century of Success,* pp. 173–174. See also his articles "Quality Standards for Commercial Wine Grapes in Ontario," *Highlights of Agricultural Research in Ontario* 6:3 (September 1983), pp. 18–20; and "New Method of Forecasting Grape Quality," *Pennsylvania Grape Letter and Wine News* 6:7 (April 1979), pp. 1, 7.

13. Cattell, "Zeroing in on Grapevine Smuggling," *Wine East* 11:6 (March–April 1984), pp. 6–8, 22–23.

14. Two good accounts of the history of the Station are Paul J. Chapman and Edward H. Glass, *The First 100 Years of the New York State Agricultural Experiment Station* (Geneva, New York, 1999) and Roger D. Way, *A History of Pomology and Viticulture at Geneva* (unpublished, 1986, but available at the station's Frank A. Lee Library). A Cattell interview with Chapman on June 1, 1982, was also an important source of information for this section.

15. For complete details of this transfer, see the station's forty-second annual report, pp. 12–16.

16. At the request of grape growers in the western part of the state, the New York legislature established a grape research station at Fredonia in 1909 and made it a branch of the Geneva Station. The first viticulturist to be hired there was Fred E. Gladwin in 1913.

17. In a letter to Philip Wagner dated January 18, 1968, Wellington noted that Arthur J. Heinicke, who was the station director from 1942 to 1960, was not interested in plant breeding. Wellington's full role in grape breeding in that era will probably never be known primarily because he was not inclined to write about himself or his activities. He was a friend of Philip Wagner's and was very much interested in the French hybrids and other grapes that would make good wine. There was no support at the station for wine grapes, and he operated

his own private breeding program in his backyard. Cattell has talked with members of his family and others in an attempt to find out what he grew, the source of his grapes, and the wines that were made, but no one has been able to furnish any specific details.

18. Shaulis reviewed his career in an interview with Cattell on October 22, 1994, which was published as "New York Viticulture: Past and Present" in *Wine East* 22:6 (March–April 1995), pp. 8–15, 37–38.

19. Nelson Shaulis, E. S. Shepardson, and T. D. Jordan, "The Geneva Double Curtain for Vigorous Grapevines: Vine Training and Trellis Construction," Bulletin 811, New York State Agricultural Experiment Station, July 1967.

20. "Grape Harvesting Research at Cornell" by Shaulis, Shepardson, and Moyer was published in *Proceedings of the 105th Meeting of the New York State Horticultural Society,* 1960, pp. 250–254. In an article published two years later with "Mechanical Grape Harvesting" in the title, Shaulis recalled that someone wrote to him and asked what a mechanical grape was. He never used that term again; it was always the "mechanical harvesting of grapes."

21. Immediately after Prohibition, in an effort to support winegrowing as a national industry, Rexford Tugwell, assistant secretary of agriculture and a member of President Franklin D. Roosevelt's "Brain Trust," directed that two model wineries be constructed at two government research stations—in Beltsville, Maryland and Meridian, Mississippi. They were built and fully equipped; but, before they could go into operation, they had to be dismantled when Clarence Cannon, the anti-alcohol chairman of the House Appropriations Committee, found out about the project and threatened to block the entire appropriation of the U.S. Department of Agriculture if federal funds were used in the fermentation industry. Cannon died in 1964 and funding for wine-related projects was soon restored. For details, see Leon D. Adams, *The Wines of America* (Boston, Massachusetts, 1973), pp. 30–31; or Philip Hiaring, *"Wines & Vines* Takes a Historical/Viticultural Tour of Maryland Wine Country," *Wine & Vines* 55:8 (August 1974), pp. 24–26.

22. Cattell interview with Terry E. Acree on June 9, 2006, which was published as "Flavor Technology Past and Present at Geneva," *Wine East* 34:2 (July–August 2006), pp. 12–21.

23. D. W. Barton, "The Proposed Wine Research Program at Geneva," *Proceedings of the 109th Annual Meeting of the New York State Horticultural Society,* 1964, pp. 242–244.

24. The five key wineries, although several others were involved, were Canandaigua, Gold Seal, Pleasant Valley, Taylor, and Widmer's.

25. Cattell interview with Robinson, June 1, 1982. In this interview Robinson acknowledged that the Vineland and Geneva stations had a philosophical difference in their approach to research; Vineland was more consumer oriented. When it came to developing new grape varieties at Vineland, for example, part of the decision of whether to keep or discard a variety was based on taste tests that assessed the appeal of a wine to consumers. "Geneva has an industry council," Robinson said, "but Geneva decides what industry needs. We found that a great majority of industry people were perfectly happy with what they had, and their points of view were so diverse that there wasn't any industry position as such."

26. Jane E. Brody, "It's Wine Time Upstate in Search for Best," *New York Times,* October 9, 1973.

27. See "Two Decades in Wine at Geneva," a Cattell interview with Thomas Henick-Kling on October 5, 2006, published in *Wine East* 34:4 (November–December 2006), pp. 20–29, 50. The interview took place just before Henick-Kling left the station at the end of 2006.

28. "Dr. John R. McGrew Retires at Beltsville," *Wine East* 11:5 (January–February 1984), pp. 6, 27.

29. Some of Howell's preliminary findings were published as "Potential for Expanding Michigan's Grape Industry," in *Proceedings: Ohio Grape—Wine Short Course,* 1974, pp. 52–54.

30. "Missouri's Program for Development," *Eastern Grape Grower and Winery News* 8:2 (April–May 1982), pp. 33–34. Zoecklein moved to Virginia in 1985 to take the position of state enologist, and in the same year Lockshin left Missouri to become the executive director of the Ohio Grape Industries Program.

31. Way, *A History of Pomology and Viticulture at Geneva,* p. 46.

32. "Carl Haeseler Retires at Penn State," *Wine East* 21:6 (March–April 1994), pp. 4–5. In Erie County, part of the Concord Grape Belt, Thomas H. Obourn was hired as associate county agent in 1962 and was promoted to county agent in 1975. His extension work with wine grapes began in 1965 (personal communication with Cattell, July 26, 2006), and he recalls leading groups of growers on visits to wine grape growers in Ontario.

33. Two accounts of extension work during this period are Gilbert Smith, "Seaton Mendall: Taylor's Man in the Vineyards for 36 Years," *Eastern Grape Grower and Winery News* 5:2 (April 1979), pp. 36–38; and Richard Figiel, "Trenny Jordan…Changing Hats…Looking Back and Looking Ahead," *Eastern Grape Grower and Winery News* 8:3 (June–July 1982), pp. 18–22.

34. Cattell, "Bill Konnerth and *Cellar Notes,*" *Wine East* 25:4 (November–December 1997), pp. 12–19, 42–43.

35. On March 31, 1996, Gadek furnished Cattell with lists of courses and students, course descriptions, and other documents to supplement his oral accounts.

36. For a complete list of publication dates and name changes of these periodicals, see the bibliography.

37. For a more complete account of L & H Photojournalism, see "Anniversaries, Thanks, and a Bit of History," in *Wine East* 19:1 (May–June 1991), pp. 3, 28–30. See also "A Brief Chronology" in *Wine East* 36:2 (July–August 2008), pp. 6–8.

38. Cattell interview with J. William Moffett, February 10, 1992. See also Ed Van Dyne, "Bill Moffett & Enterprises," *American Wine Society Journal* 13:3 (Fall 1981), p. 67.

39. Bob Levine, "Wine Appreciation Instruction Comes of Age," *American Wine Society Journal* 9:2 (Summer 1977), pp. 26–27. See also Charles L. Sullivan, *The Society of Wine Educators: A History of its Inception and the First 10 Years* (Princeton, New Jersey, 2000).

40. The story of the founding of the Eastern Section was told with a good deal of humor by Andrew C. Rice at the tenth annual meeting of the Eastern Section at Mississauga, Ontario, on August 2, 1985. An edited version of the text was published as "Gestation, Birth, and Development of the ASEV/Eastern Section," American Society for Enology and Viticulture, *1989–90 News Edition and Directory,* pp. 15–23.

41. Peter McDonald, "The Viticulture Collection and Archive in the Cornell University Library," New York State Agricultural Experiment Station, *Station News* LXXX:14 (April 9–16, 1999), p. 2.

42. Many of the scholarship winners went on to hold prominent research or winery positions in the East including Andrew G. Reynolds, David Peterson, Charles Sims, William Edinger, Tony K. Wolf, and Thomas J. Held.

43. This quote is from a speech delivered by R. F. Crowther, secretary-treasurer of the CSO, on June 14, 1966.

44. Marlene Reimer, "CSO Back on Track," *Eastern Grape Grower* 7:3 (June 1981), pp. 47–49, 53.

Chapter 8

1. *Chicago Tribune,* March 3, 1977.

2. Philip Wagner, "Testing Direct Producers in the East," *Wines and Vines* 24:9 (September 1943), pp. 16–17.

3. "Eastern Wine Tasting," *Wines and Vines* 29:10 (October 1948), p. 18.

4. John R. McGrew, "Wine Ratings and Grape Varieties," *American Wine Society Journal* 17:2 (Summer 1985), pp. 47–48.

5. "Aging of Eastern Wines Subject of Tasting," *Pennsylvania Grape Letter and Wine News* 7:9 (June 1980), pp. 1, 6, 8.

6. *Eastern Grape Grower* 3:1 (February 1977), pp. 20–22.

7. Hudson Cattell, "Wine as Commitment at Canandaigua," *Wine East* 9:6 (March–April 1982), p. 10.

8. "Large Turnout for Legislative Tasting," *Pennsylvania Grape Letter and Wine News* 6:10 (July–August 1979), pp. 4–5.

9. *Pennsylvania Grape Letter and Wine News* 8:4 (May 1977), p. 1; and the *Philadelphia Daily News,* April 14, 1977, p. 7. One of the television cameramen covering the event was clearly unhappy at the hushed silence of the judging and audibly grumbled at the lack of sound. He settled for interviews with the judges. Bill Collins, food editor for the *Philadelphia Inquirer,* stated that he was the only city restaurant critic who had attended a German wine tasting school. He then added: "I graduated summa cum drunk," a remark that made the evening newscast. Another of his comments that made the press was, "Why they picked a bunch of sinners like us to choose the Pope's wine, I'll never know."

10. Frank J. Prial, "Going for the Gold," *New York Times Magazine,* October 15, 1989, p. 64.

11. The Host Eastern Wine Selections included the following varieties. Red wines: Millot-Chambourcin (Cedar Hill Wine Co., Ohio); Cabernet Sauvignon (Banholzer Winery, Indiana); and Concord (Bucks Country Winery, Pennsylvania). White wines: Cream White Concord, Manischewitz (Monarch Wine Co., New York); Muscato di Tanta Maria (Wiederkehr Wine Cellars, Arkansas); Cuvée Blanc (Tabor Hill Winery, Michigan); and Riesling (Markko Vineyard, Ohio). Rosé wines: Wendell Rosé (Golden Rain Tree Winery, Indiana); and New Hampshire Lakes Region Rosé (White Mountain Vineyards, New Hampshire). Sparkling wines: Brut Blanc de Blanc (Gold Seal Wine Co., New York); Chateau Imperial Extra (Monarch Wine Co., New York) and Cold Duck (Wiederkehr Wine Cellars, Arkansas). Dessert wines: Cocktail Sherry (Wiederkehr Wine Cellars, Arkansas); Cream Sherry (Great Western Wine Co., New York) and Celebration Port (Brotherhood Winery, New York).

12. The Maitre des Tastevins International, an organization headquartered in Rockville, Maryland, planned the Washington, DC, event to be the first of eight to be held around the country in 1978. Unfortunately, the enormous expenses incurred in putting on this initial event resulted in bankruptcy and the organization went out of existence.

13. This was the start of relaxing rules on the home winemaker. Until then, before producing wine for the exclusive use of his family, the head of the family had to register on Form 1541. Home winemakers were not allowed to take wines out of their homes nor could they permit guests in their homes to sample their wines. The Internal Revenue Service had not been enforcing these regulations, possibly because they were revenue-neutral. The first public judgings of homemade wines in the United States took place during the summer of 1972 at Mason City, Iowa, as part of the North Iowa Fair, and at the Indiana State Fair. For the Iowa reference, see Leon Adams, *The Wines of America* (San Francisco, 1973), p. 389.

14. *Vintage* (AWS) 5:2 (Summer 1973), p. 1. The American Wine Society was one of the sponsors of this first competition, which by 1977 became the AWS Amateur Winemaking Contest.

15. *Eastern Grape Grower* 1:7 (December 1975), p. 5. Seven years later, in 1982, what was called the First Annual Pennsylvania Wine Competition was held at the same time as the fourteenth Pennsylvania Wine Conference in Hershey.

16. *Pennsylvania Grape Letter and Wine News* 8:1 (September 1980), p. 6. Chief Judge Robert Mouser was questioned by Gerald D. Boyd of the *Wine Spectator* on a number of points about the competition, including the fact that the commercial and amateur wines were judged at the same time. See the *Wine Spectator* 5:14 (October 16–30, 1980), p. 2.

17. Philip Wagner, *Daybooks,* Vol. 8, September 24, 1944.

18. Ibid., Vol. 9, September 30, 1945.

19. *Benmarl Vineyards Vigneron,* Autumn 1982, pp. 1–2. This particular Fête du Muguet held on May 21, 1982, celebrated the twenty-fifth anniversary of the founding of Benmarl, and Mark was to offer a bouquet to his wife Dene. According to the newsletter, "At one point in the planning the traditional bouquet des muguets appeared impossible to supply. Then, 'au dernière instant,' a large bed of the little wild flowers was remembered by Vigneronne Edith Caywood Meckes tucked away in a corner of the old Caywood property to which Benmarl once belonged."

20. *Bucks Country Vineyard's Taster,* Vol. IV, No. 1, n.d.

21. Linda Jones McKee interview with Ken Schuchter, president of Valley Vineyards, July 28, 1993.

22. Denise Stary, "First Celebration in 1952 Featured Parade and Evening Dance," *Vintage Niagara* 2:3, pp. 5, 8–14. This issue of *Vintage Niagara,* published by the Niagara Grape and Wine Festival, was the 1981 Souvenir Booklet marking the thirtieth anniversary of the festival. Stary's article gives a history of the Festival from its inception through 1980. See also Peter Downs, "Celebrating 50 Years of Grape-ness," *St. Catharines Standard,* September 29, 2001.

23. When the moment came to crown Jeanette Lastowska, the first Niagara Grape Queen, her crown could not be found. Hostetter went looking for it while the mayor of St. Catharines presented her with a basket of grapes to keep things going. When Hostetter returned with the crown, which was in a box that a member of the orchestra had been sitting on, the emcee from the radio station CKTB announced, "George will now crown the Queen!"

24. *Maryland-Washington Beverage Journal,* September 1996, p. 55.

25. Cattell recalls visiting a start-up operation in Virginia and being told that the reason for opening a winery was to get a favorable review for his wines from Frank Prial of the *New York Times.*

26. The concept of making wines that customers in their local market would want to buy, however logical, was not immediately apparent to many winemakers. Surveying customers came even later.

27. New York Wine and Grape Foundation, *Annual Report, 2005–2006,* p. 22. The total number of tourist visits in New York State increased from 384,000 in 1985 to 1,439,000 in 1995 and 4,137,000 in 2003 (p. 19).

28. Cattell, "The Benmarl Story: Mark Miller and Benmarl Vineyards," *Wine East* 34:1 (May–June 2006), pp. 20–31, 57–58.

29. "The Benmarl Vineyards Vigneron: The Official Wineletter of the Benmarl Société des Vignerons" (Spring 1971).

30. For a look at Walter Taylor and Bully Hill Vineyards in 1976 just before the feud with the Taylor Wine Company began, see "Maverick of the Wine Business: Walter Taylor," by Glenn O'Brien. The article appeared in *New Dawn* and was reprinted in the September 1976, issue of Taylor's "Vineyard View."

31. Numerous articles have been published about the feud. The description that follows is taken in part from "Walter S. Taylor, 1931–2001," an obituary by Cattell that appeared in *Wine East* 29:1 (May–June 2001), pp. 38–41, 54–55.

32. "A Collector's Guide to the Bully Hill Labels," *Pennsylvania Grape Letter and Wine News* 5:9 (June 1978), pp. 4–5.

33. Linda Yglesias, "The Goats of Wrath: On the Front Lines with the Baron of Bully Hill," *Daily News Magazine,* September 18, 1988, pp. 16–18, 29.

Chapter 9

1. For the background of the Shenandoah Valley AVA controversy, see Hudson Cattell, "A Tale of Two Valleys," *Wine East* 9:2 (July 1981), pp. 8–12, 20–22.

2. Lou Ann Ladin was quoted in a *New York Times* article by Robert D. Hershey, Jr., November 3, 1985. As a result of this decision Leon Sobon decided to go with an Amador County designation on his labels. In order to keep his estate bottled label, it would have to have read "California Shenandoah Vineyards, Shenandoah Valley, California," which was too redundant for Sobon's liking (see Jeff Mapes, "Two Shenandoahs Get Official Nod," *Wine Spectator* 7:21 [February 1–15, 1983], p. 3.

3. *Vinifera Wine Growers Journal* 3:3 (Fall 1976), p. 248.

4. Cattell recalls that the extreme heat set in by late morning. Long lines formed to get a drink of water, people left early or did not come at all, and the only concession stand to do a booming business was the Linden Beverage Company whose cold sparkling cider Alpenglow was the only refreshing beverage in sight.

5. For a description of the feud that followed, see the *Fauquier Democrat* (Warrenton, Virginia), August 2, 1984.

6. Sources for this legal action are a letter from Randolph Parks, the attorney for Worrall and the Harpers, to Lawrence; the Decree of Injunction dated July 31, 1986 by Judge Carleton Penn of the Circuit Court for the County of Fauquier; and a subsequent Decree of Contempt of Court issued by Judge Carleton Penn on December 3, 1986. The controversy over the use of the appellation continued and was only resolved when it was announced in the summer 1990 issue of the *Vinifera Wine Growers Journal* (17:2, p. 139), that "The Annual Wine Festival" was being used with the number of the festival, and the word Middleburg was being used separately for the sole purpose of identifying the place of the festival.

7. *Wine East* 17:3 (September–October 1989), p. 7.

8. *Wine East* 20:3 (September–October 1992), p. 11.

9. Letter from the Vinifera Wine Growers Association to Virginia Wineries mailed on August 22, 1992.

10. In addition to holding the Eastern Wine Festival at Morven Park, Lawrence held two competitions in 1993. His final festival took place on June 22 and 23, 1996, after which the Eastern Wine Festival was dissolved. "I am moving back to my roots in Atlanta where I was born 81 years ago," he wrote to Cattell on November 23, 1996.

11. Zeke Mendall retired from Taylor in 1979. Ten years later, in a letter to Philip and Jocelyn Wagner on October 18, 1989, he wrote that when he retired most of Taylor's business was in the Lake Country series of wines and that by 1989 Taylor had lost 70 percent of that business. There had been no promotion of those products whatsoever.

12. These figures are from George L. Casler, "New York's Vineyard Industry," *Wines and Vines* 68:3 (March 1987), p. 26.

13. Letter from Mendall to the Wagners, October 18, 1989.

14. Cattell conversation with Neil Simmons, February 22, 2007.

15. The quotation by Edgar M. Bronfman, Seagram's chairman and CEO, appeared in the *Observer* (*Pennsylvania Liquor News*) on March 30, 1987.

16. Letter from Zeke Mendall to Philip and Jocelyn Wagner, December 30, 1990.

17. Monty Stamp interview with Cattell, April 8, 2006. For information on the cooperative in the Finger Lakes, see "Finger Lakes Growers Form Nucleus of State-Wide Cooperative," *Eastern Grape Grower and Winery News* 10:5 (October–November 1984), p. 61. Hearings were also held in the New York State Senate on ways to help the growers ("Hearings on Aid to NY Winegrowers," *Eastern Grape Grower and Winery News* 10:1 [February–March 1984], p. 39).

18. A major source for the information that follows was a Cattell interview with James Trezise on August 16, 1994, which was the basis of an article, "How a Foundation Helped Uncork New York," *Wine East* 22:3 (September–October 1994), pp. 10–15, 32.

19. Cattell interview with Trezise, April 3, 2008.

20. For many years, state support leveled off at $500,000 with the foundation raising the same amount through a combination of dues and program fees. For an account of the first decade of the New York Wine and Grape Foundation, see Cattell, "How a Foundation Helped Uncork New York," *Wine East* 22:3 (September–October 1994), pp. 10–15, 32.

21. A primary source of information about the winery is a biography of the winery by Richard and Rob Sands titled *Reaching for the Stars: The Making of Constellation Brands* (Napa, California, 2008). Two accounts of the earlier years are Philip Hiaring, "Canandaigua: A Success Story," *Wines and Vines* 52:9 (September 1971), pp. 47–52; and "Team Spirit at Canandaigua Wine Company," *Kansas and Oklahoma Beverage News,* July 1979. For a good overall account, see Thomas Pinney, *A History of Wine in America: From Prohibition to the Present* (Berkeley, California, 2005), pp. 255–58.

22. For Paul Garrett's story, see Leon Adams, *The Wines of America* (San Francisco, 1973), pp. 44–46; and Thomas Pinney, "Paul Garrett: American Wine for Americans" in *The Making of American Wine: A Record of Two Hundred Years* (Berkeley, California, 2012), pp. 107–126. What Garrett meant to the Sands can be found in Sands and Sands, *Reaching for the Stars,* pp. 31–34, 133. Garrett died in 1940.

23. Sands and Sands, *Reaching for the Stars,* p. 133. Leon Adams gives 1967 as the date Virginia Dare wines came back on the market.

24. Sands and Sands, p. 123. According to Richard Sands, Thunderbird never outsold Richards Wild Irish Rose.

25. The quote from Marvin Sands that follows came during an interview with Cattell on September 23, 1981, and was included in the article "Wine as Commitment at Canandaigua," *Wine East* 9:6 (March–April 1982), pp. 8–10, 17.

26. Linda Bramble, *Niagara Wine Visionaries: Profiles of the Pioneering Winemakers* (Toronto, 2009), pp. 67–68.

27. This was not the only task force to be formed. In addition to the long term Tanner Task Force, a shorter term task force had been established to look into problems of lost market share and the rapid increase in imports from abroad.

28. "Ontario Wine and Grape Industry Task Force Report," pp. iii–iv.

29. Ibid., p. 31.

30. Ibid., p. iii.

31. According to the August 3, 1988, newsletter of the Ontario Grape Growers' Marketing Board, the differential mark-up between Ontario and foreign wines sold through the LCBO was established in 1979 in response to grape and wine subsidies occurring in the EEC. At that time the subsidies were estimated at $200 million, but by the mid-1980s they had increased to $2.5 billion accompanied by a dramatic increase in the sales of EEC wines in Canada.

32. *St. Catharines Standard,* October 5, 1987. All week the *Standard* ran columns on what the Free Trade Agreement would mean for the industry. Cattell recalls the intense pessimism and gloom that prevailed. "It's all gone," said one industry executive. "Niagara will become the bedroom community for Toronto."

33. When the EEC countries got wind of the start of the free trade talks between Canada and the United States, it immediately occurred to them that there was a real possibility that the California wine industry could gain a competitive edge in Ontario and elsewhere in Canada. In the spring of 1985 the EEC filed an unfair trade practice with GATT, which found in favor of the Europeans and led to the preliminary ruling in 1987.

34. "GATT Ruling Adds Pressure on Canadian Industry," *Wine East* 16:1 (May–June 1988), p. 30, and "Ontario Update," *Wine East* 16:5 (January–February 1989), p. 8.

35. Part of this section originally appeared in "A New Quality Image for Ontario Wines," by Cattell in *Wine East* 22:5 (January–February 1995), pp. 4–10, 38–39. Much of the alliance's early history is based on a Cattell interview with Peter Gamble, VQA's first executive director, on September 22, 1994; and the later history on a Cattell interview with Laurie Macdonald, executive director from 2000, on June 9, 2007.

36. Angus M. Adams, "Evolution of Commercial Quality Standards for Ontario Wines," *Proceedings: Ohio Grape—Wine Short Course,* 1982, pp. 50–53. The training, tastings, seminars, and selection of panel members was delegated to the staff of the Horticultural Products Laboratory at the Horticultural Research Institute of Ontario and was carried out under the supervision of research scientist Vicki Gray. For a description of the tasting procedures, see Victoria P. Gray, "Quality Standards Improve Ontario Wines," *Ontario Fruit and Vegetable Grower* 34:1 (January 1984), pp. 7–8.

37. Angus M. Adams, "'Ontario Superior' Means High Quality Wines," *Wine East* 9:3 (September 1981), pp. 14–16.

38. *Pennsylvania Grape Letter and Wine News* 8:2 (October 1980), p. 6.

39. Cattell, "Sugar Standards for Grapes in Ontario," *Wine East* 14:5 (January–February 1987), pp. 24–25, 29.

40. John Schreiner, *The World of Canadian Wine* (Vancouver, 1984), p. 181. Schreiner did not specify the size of the order, but Ziraldo has told Cattell that the order was for 200 cases.

Chapter 10

1. *Pennsylvania Grape Letter and Wine News* 6:7 (April 1979). Subsequent "Wine Trails of Pennsylvania" appeared in April 1980 (7:7) and February 1981 (8:5).

2. For the early history of New York's wine trails, see Hudson Cattell, "New York's Wine Trails: A Success Story," *Wine East* 26:1 (May–June 1998), pp. 28–33.

3. See Donniella Winchell, "Two Decades of Promoting Ohio Wines: An Interview with Donnie Winchell," *Wine East* 23:2 (July–August 1995), pp. 10–15, 35.

4. For a good account of the role of the Ontario Wine Council during an important fourteen-year period from 1994 to 2007 when Linda Franklin was executive director, see Linda Bramble, *Niagara's Wine Visionaries: Profiles of the Pioneering Winemakers* (Toronto, 2009), pp. 170–191.

5. See Ronald C. Moyer, "Moyer Describes Ontario Marketing Board Function," *Eastern Grape Grower* 1:2 (March 1975), pp. 6–7; and "The Ontario Grape Growers' Marketing Board Turns 50: An Interview with Jim Rainforth," *Wine East* 25:3 (September–October 1997), pp. 14–21, 43.

6. Donniella Winchell, "Two Decades," p. 54.

7. *Wine East* 14:3 (September–October 1986), pp. 6–7.

8. Cattell, "Using Private Labels to Sell Wine," *Wine East* 15:1 (May–June 1987), pp. 16–21, 29–30.

9. *Wine East* 14:5 (January–February 1987), pp. 4–5.

10. *Wine East* 17:2 (July–August 1989), pp. 8–9.

11. *Wine East* 13:2 (July–August 1985), pp. 3–4.

12. *Wine East* 14:5 (January–February 1987) pp. 7, 30.

13. *Wine East* 33:1 (May–June 2005), pp. 55–56.

14. *Eastern Grape Grower and Winery News* 7:3 (June 1981), pp. 13–14.

15. *Wine East* 14:1 (May–June 1986), p. 4.

16. *New York Times,* April 2, 1980. This dinner was attended by Terry Robards, wine columnist for the *Times,* who created a stir when he wrote that the tasting showed that not all New York wines tasted like grape jelly, "but whether any New York wines have risen to levels of quality where they can compete with the better wines of California or Europe is another matter." He concluded by writing that "in the end I found myself thirsting for a well-made Chardonnay or Cabernet Sauvignon or Johannisberg Riesling from California to use as a benchmark, as a reminder of the quality levels that can be achieved in this country." There were angry reactions in the industry to the Robards column, for which see the *Pennsylvania Grape Letter and Wine News* 7:8 (May 1980), p. 2.

17. Irving H. Marcus, "Report on a Visit to the Wineries of the Finger Lakes," *Wines and Vines* 45:12 (December 1964), p. 18.

18. *Wine East* 11:4 (November–December 1983), pp. 16–17, 23.

19. *Eastern Grape Grower and Winery News* 9:4 (August–September 1983), p. 12.

20. For a further discussion of this judging, see the *Pennsylvania Grape Letter and Wine News* 6:3 (November–December 1978), pp. 2–3. Cattell, who interviewed many of the out-of-state judges immediately after the competition, was impressed with the way they freely and honestly expressed their opinions. As an example, Bob Morrisey, founder of the *Wine Spectator,* admitted that he did not know much about many of these wines and had tried many of them for the first time, but he very much enjoyed them and learned from the experience.

21. "The Wine Judging at Wineries Unlimited: An Interview with Philip Jackisch," *Pennsylvania Grape Letter and Wine News* 7:5 (February 1980), pp. 1, 4–5.

22. Competition listings in *Wine East* 18:5 (January–February 1991) and 35:5 (January–February 2008).

23. The first use of the term grape racism may have been by Lucie T. Morton in a speech delivered at the tenth annual conference of the American Wine Society in Arlington, Virginia, on November 4, 1977. "I decided to meet the issue of grape variety racism head-on," Morton stated. She ended her speech by saying, "I believe we should take pride in our native Eastern species …while at the same time welcoming the cultivation of European varieties as a great addition and asset to our uniquely varied viticultural region." ("The Vine of Gold," *American Wine Society Journal* 10:2 (Summer 1978), pp. 22–25.

24. Willard B. Robinson, "The Assessment of Wine Quality," *Wine East* 10:3 (September–October 1982), pp. 12–14, 22.

25. *Wine East* 11:5 (January–February 1984), p. 4; and 12:1 (May–June 1984), p. 3. The details about the six auctions described below were obtained from news stories in *Wine East.*

Chapter 11

1. "Understanding Today's Temperance Movement," an interview by Hudson Cattell with Dr. David F. Musto, was published in *Wine East* 14:1 (May–June 1986), pp. 6–11, 21–22. "One of the points I want to make very strongly," he said, "is that the wine industry may see this as an anti-alcohol or anti-wine movement in isolation from what is actually going on, a much broader health movement for both positive health and the great concern for what we take into our bodies. It isn't just directed at alcohol." No one could have foreseen in 1986 that alcohol and health, particularly wine and health, would become a very important issue in tempering the Neo-Prohibitionist crusade.

2. Warning labels would not be required until 1988. For more on fetal alcohol syndrome and fetal alcohol effects, especially during this period, see Gene Ford, *The French Paradox & Drinking for Health* (San Francisco, 1993), pp. 199–206.

3. The Code of Advertising Standards was updated and a revised text released in August 1987. As revised, the standards were extended to cover coolers as well as wine, advertisements were not to be directed towards pregnant women, and wine or wine coolers were not to be shown in conjunction with driving motorized vehicles. The text of the original code that was released in 1978 may be found in the *Pennsylvania Grape Letter and Wine News* 5:7 (April 1978), pp. 6–8; and the revised 1987 Code in *Wine East* 15:3 (September–October 1987), pp. 3–4, 30.

4. Billboards also became an effective tool. The August 13, 1985, House of Seagram press release was occasioned by a determination by the BATF that the message of equivalence was valid from a medical and scientific standpoint. How quickly Seagram's campaign was moving is evident from the press release which stated that the equivalence message was included in the drivers manuals of thirty-four states and by federal agencies.

5. The press release from the Winegrowers of California is undated but was written a week after the BATF determined that the equivalence message was valid. The release began by stating that "winegrowers note that the BATF decision was made before Federal Bureau saw full research evidence regarding major differences between wine, beer and liquor."

6. *Observer* ("Pennsylvania Liquor News"), November 24, 1986, page 2. The quote by Bronfman and the response by Sanders were taken from their coverage of the Las Vegas meeting.

7. Memo from John De Luca to All Friends of Wine, March 24, 1986.

8. *Wine East* 13:6 (March–April 1986), p. 4.

9. De Luca, Wine Institute memo, March 24, 1986.

10. Ibid., Wine Institute memo, May 9, 1986.

11. The background information on CSPI comes from an interview Tim Atkin, the editor of *Wine & Spirit International,* did with Jacobson in England in the fall of 1988. Atkin's article was published in *Wines and Vines* 70:5 (May 1989), pp. 29–35.

12. Wine law specialist Richard Mendelson has called "Just Say No" a fire and brimstone campaign. "During the two-term Reagan presidency," he wrote, "Americans came closest to re-creating the moral panic that had accompanied the march to Prohibition." (Richard Mendelson, *From Demon to Darling: A Legal History of Wine in America* [Berkeley, California, 2009], p. 163).

13. The implementation ruling by the BATF may be found in the *Federal Register* 54:3 (February 16, 1989), pp. 7160–7163. About this time, Proposition 65 passed in California, which required alcoholic beverages to be listed as carcinogens.

14. The BATF's final ruling appeared in the *Federal Register* 51:189 (September 30, 1986), pp. 34706–34710.

15. Interview with Tim Atkin cited in note 11.

16. The "annual occupation tax" was a further adaptation of the Special Occupation Tax originally enacted in 1862 to help pay for the Civil War. It was not repealed until 2005.

17. "Koop Report Squelches Industry Voice," *Observer* ("Pennsylvania Liquor News") 53:21 (June 19 1989), pp. 1–2. The workshop recommendations, including the issuance of a fact sheet stating that alcohol is an addictive drug, are given in this article, which concludes as follows: "The possible impact of this report should not be underestimated. Koop has announced his intention to have copies of it sent to every member of Congress, to officials in state and local government and advocacy groups throughout the country." Gene Ford's the *Moderation Reader* reprinted another evaluation: "The meeting was never intended to deal with drunk driving. Rather it was a bald attempt to put the prestige of the Surgeon General behind a series of drastic anti-alcohol measures."

18. The *Moderation Reader* soon became a forty-eight-page journal and was sent free to members of Congress and 90 percent of the states' legislators. Its circulation eventually reached 18,000. Ford's other books included *The French Paradox & Drinking for Health* (1993) and *The Science of Healthy Drinking* (2003). His high standards and objective reporting made his writings important for those who wanted facts.

19. An important source of information about these organizations has been the large number of press releases and newsletters they published.

20. *Wine East* 17:1 (May–June 1989), p. 8.

21. Wine Institute press release, September 1, 1989.

22. *Trends and Perspectives,* October 11, 1991, pp. 1–3.

23. *Wine Trends and Perspectives,* September 7, 1993.

24. *Wine East* (22:4) devoted most of its November–December 1994 issue to coverage of the National Wine Issues Forum including the text of two talks, "In the Wake of the 'French Paradox,'" by Curtis Ellison, and "Neo-Prohibition Attacks on Wine" by Richard Mendelson.

25. *Wines and Vines* 69:11 (November 1988), p. 16.

26. *Wines and Vines* 70:5 (May 1989), pp. 20–21. In April 1989, when the National Wine Coalition was formed, Feeney was quoted as saying, "So long as wine is lumped in with machine guns and cocaine, there will be an image problem" ("The National Wine Coalition is Launched," *Wines and Vines* 70:5, p. 18.) In its July issue (70:7, p. 6), the magazine endorsed de la Garza's proposal editorially: "If wine is to survive the attacks of zealots like the surgeon general—Koop—it must do it as a farm product. With the combined power of all 43 states."

27. This was not the first wine tasting for Congress. In 1980, the California Association of Winegrape Growers held its initial wine reception for Congress and a year later was joined by the New York Wine Grape Growers.

28. The idea of a Congressional Wine Caucus goes back to May 15, 1995, when Gordon Murchie invited Representative George Radanovich to meet with the National Wine Coalition board of directors to discuss ways in which key wine industry issues and Congressional support could be better tied together. At that meeting there was a proposal that a Congressional Wine Caucus be formed with Murchie as the "Secretariat" of the Caucus. No action was taken on the proposal until Mike Thompson was elected to the House. On March 22, 1999, an invitation signed by Radanovich, Thompson, and twenty members of Congress was sent to all senators and representatives to become charter members of the Congressional Wine Caucus and attend a reception on May 11, 1999, honoring them as charter members.

29. See *Eastern Grape Grower and Winery News* 4:4 (August 1978). "Association of American Vintners is Underway!" is on page 14, and editorial comment by J. William Moffett on page 6.

30. Interview with Peter Carp by Cattell and H. Lee Stauffer, November 30, 1978. Chairmen of standing committees were also elected: Nathan G. Stackhouse, Jr. (from Leelanau Wine Cellars in Michigan), Anthony P. Debevc, Robert Mazza, and Robert Wollersheim.

31. Ibid.

32. "AAV and NWC Form Ties," *AAV Winebrief* (March–April 1990), pp. 1–3.

33. "American Vintners Association Formed by Merger of AAV and NVA," *Vineyard and Winery Management* 18:6 (November–December 1992), p. 4.

34. *Report from the American Wine Alliance for Research and Education* 1:1 (June 1, 1989), p. 1. See also John A. Hinman, Esq., "How the Wine Industry is Meeting the Challenge," *Wines and Vines* 70:3 (March 1989), pp. 11, 44–49.

35. The panelists were Serge Renaud, an epidemiologist and director of Inserm; Monique Astier-Dumas, a nutritionist from Paris and the head of Lyon Center; and Curtis Ellison, a cardiologist and professor at the Boston University School of Medicine.

36. Ten specific junk science articles were mentioned in an address given by Lewis Perdue at a dinner meeting of the Society of Medical Friends of Wine on March 19, 1997, which was published under the heading "It's the Alcohol, Stupid!" in the *Bulletin of The Society of Medical Friends of Wine* 39:2 (November 1997), pp. 1–4.

37. For more information on the Mediterranean Diet Pyramid, see "Creating the Mediterranean Diet Pyramid: An Interview with K. Dun Gifford," *Wine East* 22:4 (November–December 1984), pp. 20–25, 34. Oldways Preservation & Exchange Trust may be contacted at its website address www.oldwayspt.org.

38. A nonprofit organization called the Century Council was formed in May 1991 to unite the alcoholic beverage industry in promoting responsible drinking. Its chairman was John Gavin, a former U.S. ambassador to Mexico.

Chapter 12

1. *Wine East* 19:4 (November–December 1991), p. 6. Governor William Donald Schaefer had suggested that a competition be held to help call attention to the Maryland grape and wine industry. The competition was held on September 14 and on September 22 he personally made the presentation.

2. *Wine East* 19:2 (July–August 1991), p. 5. The festival benefited public radio and television, which did a good job of publicizing the event well before it took place.

3. Festival brochure dated 1994 and subsequent press releases. There were earlier festivals in New York. For many years starting in 1961, the town of Naples held a grape festival. According to the August 5, 1977, "Vineyard Notes," written by Cornell extension specialist Thomas J. Zabadal, the New York legislature earlier that year had passed seven bills related to grapes. One of them provided for temporary permits to sell wine produced in New York "at functions such as fairs, carnivals, and the Finger Lakes Grape Festival." The newsletter announced that Governor Carey would personally attend a New York State Grape and Wine Celebration in Hammondsport on August 9 to comment on the passage of the seven bills.

4. Ohio Wine Producers Association press release, February 19, 1999.

5. Michael Bierbauer, "New York Trade Group Planning Special Seals," *Wine Spectator* 5:3 (May 1–15, 1980), p. 18. The six wineries were Benmarl Vineyards and Cagnasso Winery in Marlboro, Cascade Mountain Vineyards in Amenia, Clinton Vineyards in Clinton Corners, Northeast Vineyard in Millerton and Royal Wine Corp. headquartered in Brooklyn.

6. "A New Crop of Appellations of Origin," *Eastern Grape Grower* 5:5 (October 1979), pp. 16–17.

7. Cattell interview with William Wetmore, Cascade Mountain Vineyards, Amenia, New York, July 17, 2000.

8. Information on the Lake Erie Quality Alliance came from various Alliance press releases, the articles of incorporation, and Cattell telephone interviews with Arnulf Esterer, Douglas Moorhead, and Robert Mazza.

9. "Quality Alliance Program Begins in NJ," *Wine East* 27:3 (September–October 1999), pp. 9–10.

10. For a readable account of this decade, see Bramble, *Niagara's Wine Visionaries: Profiles of the Pioneering Winemakers* (Toronto, Ontario, 2009). An important source of information was a Cattell interview on September 25, 2002, with Art Smith, a former chairman of the Ontario Grape Growers' Marketing Board.

11. The pull-out program was designed to remove grapes, which at that time were in surplus. This included many acres of labrusca wine grapes, but not Niagaras or Concords because they were considered to be juice varieties. See Cattell interview with Jim Rainforth, secretary of the Ontario Grape Growers' Marketing Board, on September 25, 1996, published as "The Ontario Grape Growers' Marketing Board Turns 50," *Wine East* 25:3 (September–October 1997), pp. 14–21, 43.

12. Cattell, "New Trends in Ontario," *Wine East* 27:4 (November–December 1999), pp. 16–22. This article reviewed the progress the industry was making at the end of the decade.

13. Noreen Schmidt is credited with organizing the food deck. Vineland Estates Winery was founded in 1983 by German nursery owner Hermann Weis, and the Schmidt family has played an important role in the history of the winery. In the late 1980s, Noreen's husband, Lloyd F. Schmidt, was the winery's consultant before establishing his International Viticultural Services. By 2000, their two sons held top management positions in the winery:

Allan Schmidt as president and CEO, and Brian Schmidt as vice president of operations and winemaker. Both of them have been committed to building the food side of the business. Two years after John Howard purchased the winery in 1993, the winery put in a full-service restaurant, a carriage house for private parties, and three helipads for use by guests coming in from Toronto or Niagara Falls for dinner.

14. Cattell, "New Trends in Ontario," p. 19.

15. The Teaching Winery got off to an auspicious start. Production began in 2001 and 450 cases were made by students under the supervision of their instructor Jim Warren. In time for the opening ceremony, it was announced that the Niagara College Teaching Winery's 2001 Barrel-Fermented, Barrel-Aged Chardonnay had been selected as the White Wine of the Year at the 2002 Canadian Wine Awards, and that two other wines had received silver and bronze awards at the All Canadian Wine Championships. All of the wines produced at the winery are sold in-house and the proceeds reinvested in the program.

16. According to VQA Ontario, total production of all VQA wines was 1,250,000 cases for the year ending March 31, 2002, and 2,300,000 cases for the year ending March 31, 2009. In 2002, 21,900 cases consisted of icewine, and in 2009, 111,300 cases.

17. See Cattell, "North Shore Lake Ontario: An Emerging Wine Region," *Wine East* 28:4 (November–December 2000), pp. 26–31; and Lloyd F. Schmidt, "Realizing the Prince Edward County Dream," *Wine East* 30:4 (November–December 2002), pp. 10–13, 50.

18. The Prince Edward County appellation was approved on June 11, 2007 (*Wine East* 35:2 [July–August, 2007], p. 12). A fourth appellation, Pelee Island, was approved but deregulated on January 1, 2013.

19. The complete list of subappellations is as follows: Niagara-on-the-Lake, Niagara Escarpment, Niagara River, Niagara Lakeshore, Four Mile Creek, St. David's Bench, Beamsville Bench, Twenty Mile Bench, Short Hills Bench, Lincoln Lakeshore, Creek Shores, and Vinemount Ridge.

20. For more on the history of wine in Nova Scotia, see *The Tangled Vine: Winegrowing in Nova Scotia* by Chris Naugler, Bruce Wright, and Robert Murray (Bridgewater, Nova Scotia, 2004); Cattell, "Nova Scotia: Canada's New Wine Frontier," *Wine East* 12:4 (November–December 1984), pp. 6–10, 21–23; Philip Hiaring, Sr., "Wine Grapes a New Crop in Nova Scotia," *Wines and Vines* 68:5 (May 1987), pp. 38–44; and Robert Murray, "Celebrating L'Acadie in Nova Scotia," *Wine East* 32:5 (January–February 2005), pp. 12–18, 50.

21. Among the varieties that Craig was pushing for grape growers to use at that time (letter to Cattell from Craig, July 2, 1996) was V.53261, which he had obtained from Vineland in 1972. Craig had supplied grapes from V.53261 to Dial in 1975 and vines to Morse in 1977. When Grand Pré Wines opened in 1980, Dial gave V.53261 a proprietary name, L'Acadie Blanc. V.53261 became Nova Scotia's leading white wine varietal and Craig asked Helen Fisher at Vineland to name the grape, even suggesting the name Valée for it because grape varieties developed in Ontario traditionally began with the letter "V." V.53261 had not done well in Ontario and Fisher did not think it was worth naming. Its success in Nova Scotia, however, led to the formal naming of L'Acadie Blanc in a cooperative effort between Vineland and Nova Scotia (see *Wine East* 23:5 [January–February 1996], pp. 6–7).

22. For the early history of grapes and wine in Québec, see Roger Dial and Gale Dial, "The Historic Winemaking Tradition in Québec," *Wines and Vines* 69:6 (June 1988), pp. 67–70; Cattell, "Turning Acres of Snow into Vineyards in Québec," *Wine East* 19:3 (September–October 1991), pp. 10–17; and Harry Linnett, "Wineries? In Québec?" *Wines and Vines* 75:11 (November 1994), pp. 65–71, and 75:12 (December 1994), pp. 34–35. The wine scene in Québec in more recent years is described in Schreiner, *The Wines of Canada,* pp. 217–248; and Aspler, *The Wine Atlas of Canada,* pp. 209–241.

23. Joseph O. Vandal, a geneticist at Laval University in Québec City, began making crosses in 1947. After his death in the late 1980s, some of his research was carried on by Mario Cliche at the provincial agriculture station at St-Hyacinthe where Vandal-Cliche was released (Schreiner, *The Wines of Canada,* p. 222).

24. Marialisa Calta, "Where Cider Gets a French Kick," *New York Times,* November 11, 2007.

25. References for this section include "First Winery Opens on Prince Edward Island," *Wine East* 23:2 (July–August 1995), pp. 7–8; and "First Winery in Newfoundland," *Wine East* 23:6 (March–April 1996), pp. 9, 36. Information on wineries in New Brunswick and the prairie wineries was taken from various websites.

26. For more detail on Canadian fruit wine standards, see Cattell, "Quality Standards Set for Canadian Fruit Wines," *Wine East* 29:3 (September–October 2001), pp. 40–43, 58–59.

Chapter 13

1. See Frank J. Prial, "On the North Fork, Dreams of Napa," *New York Times* (July 26, 2000); and Hudson Cattell, "Major Investments Spur Long Island Wine Growth," *Wine East* 29:3 (September–October 2001), pp. 24–29.

2. A Cattell interview with Roman Roth was published as "The Wines of Wölffer and Roth" in *Wine East* 35:1 (May–June 2007), pp. 24–35, 58–59. "Wölffer Estate," an article by Richard Leahy, was published in the March–April, 2007 issue of *Vineyard and Winery Management* 33:2, pp. 2–12.

3. Russell Hearn, "How a Custom Crush Winery Operates," *Wine East Buyers' Guide* (2002), pp. 14–21.

4. Murli R. Dharmadhikari and Michelle L. Norgren, "An Educational Vision Expands in Mid-America," *Wine East* 32:4 (November–December 2004), pp. 16–21, 52. See also Michelle Norgren, "VESTA Localizes Education Across U.S.," *Wines and Vines* 93:1 (January 2012), pp. 150–153.

5. "Grape and Wine Research Restructured in Missouri," *Wine East* 34:4 (November–December 2006), pp. 6–7. Research in Missouri at this time also included the Center for Grapevine Biotechnology, headed by Laszlo Kovacs and WenPing Qiu at Mountain Grove.

6. "New Undergraduate Degree Program at Cornell," *Wine East* 32:1 (May–June 2004), pp. 8–10. See also Richard Leahy, "Cornell University Expands Wine Studies, Facilities," *Vineyard and Winery Management* 35:5 (September–October 2009), pp. 86–90.

7. "Steps to the Vision: A Five Year Business Plan, 2008–2012" (Vineland, Ontario: Vineland Research and Innovation Centre, June 3, 2008), p. 8. In its report, the panel provided a vision for Vineland: "Vineland will be a world-class institution and international hub for horticulture research, innovation and commercial activity."

Donald Ziraldo was one of the key people involved in most of the initiatives leading to increased research (see "Ontario Report" in *Wine East* 35:2 (July–August 2007), pp. 8–12.) In May 2007, a thirty-four-page report titled "Canadian Grape and Wine Research Strategy: Championing a Winning Example for Canadian Agriculture" was prepared under the direction of an advisory committee headed by Norm Beal, chair of the Wine Council of Ontario. Ziraldo was a member of the committee that consulted a wide range of industry stakeholders from across Canada as well as government agencies.

8. "PA's Premium Wine Group Starts Quality Seal Program," *Wine East* 31:4 (November–December 2003), pp. 6–8, and various press releases.

9. Stephen Menke, "A Proposed Enology Initiative for Pennsylvania's Wine Industry," a five-page undated printed proposal outlining his objectives.

10. See "Ohio Adopts a Quality Assurance Program," *Wine East* 34:6 (March–April 2007), pp. 7–8.

11. MKF Research LLC press release, January 17, 2007.

12. MKF Research, *The Impact of Wine, Grapes and Grape Products on the American Economy 2007: Family Businesses Building Value* (St. Helena, California, 2007). For background information on the study, see *Wine East* 34:6 (March–April, 2007), pp. 6–7, and in the same issue, "The Value of the MKF Research Studies," on page 4. The data for the study was compiled in 1995, and the methodology for the study was IMPLAN, the acronym for "IMpact Analysis for PLANing," the standard economic model used for impact studies developed by the University of Minnesota and the U.S. Forest Service and used by numerous government agencies, universities and businesses.

13. Jim Trezise, personal communication, November 9, 2010.

14. See "NY Wine Economic Impact Study Completed," *Wine East* 33:5 (January–February 2006), pp. 6–9, 56. This article included "Wine's Economic Impact: The Need for a National Study," by Trezise.

15. Thomas Pinney, in his *A History of Wine in America: From Prohibition to the Present* (Berkeley, California, 2005), has pointed out that the three-tier system was originally devised to forestall the development of monopoly practices by producers. What was not foreseen was that the system would eventually create monopoly conditions for wholesalers.

16. The number of wholesalers was given by James Trezise in the December, 14, 2002 issue of the *Wine Press* published by the New York Wine and Grape Foundation. Other estimates have placed the number of wholesalers as high as 10,000.

17. The legality of reciprocal shipping was assured on October 29, 2000, when President Bill Clinton signed Senate Bill 577, the "21st Amendment Enforcement Act," in which Congress for the first time recognized in a federal statute that the power of the states under the Twenty-First Amendment was not absolute (see Wine Institute press release dated October 29, 2000). It ensured that the legal framework already in place allowing consumers to receive interstate shipments would remain intact.

18. Russ Bridenbaugh, "The Direct Shipping Controversy," *Wines and Vines* 82:1 (January 2001), pp. 152–158.

19. Ibid., pp. 154–155. This was the first challenge to be brought by consumers in federal court. For a discussion of the participation of consumers in the direct shipping dispute, see Dante J. Romanini, "Wine and the Law: Gazing into the Future of Direct Shipments," *Wine East* 26:3 (September–October 1998), pp. 24–27, 46–47.

20. For an explanation of the rulings in the Virginia and North Carolina cases, see "Direct Shipping Bans Overturned in VA and NC," *Wine East* 30:1 (May–June 2002), pp. 8–10. Another way of resolving the in-state versus out-of-state controversy would be to ban intrastate shipment as well as interstate shipping, which would be devastating to wineries in that state. See Cattell, "Threat of Intrastate Shipping Ban Mobilizing Virginia," *Wine East* 29:5 (January–February 2002), pp. 19–25, 49–50.

21. A background article on the forthcoming Supreme Court decision examining the role of the Court, the participants involved, and the possible scope of its ruling was written by Dante J. Romanini, an attorney and a contributing editor for *Wine East*, as a way of putting the case in perspective ("Wine and the Law: Interstate

Shipping: Can We Predict What the Supreme Court Will Do?" *Wine East* 32:4 [September–October 2004], pp. 16–21, 48–49).

22. "Favorable Supreme Court Decision on Direct Shipping," *Wine East* 33:1 (May–June 2005), pp. 6–8, 10.

23. Dante J. Romanini, "The Supreme Court Has Spoken—But What Did It *Really* Say?" *Wine East* 33:1 (May–June 2005), p. 9.

24. The Supreme Court's decision came to be known as the *Granholm* case or the *Granholm* decision because one of the cases involved was Jennifer M. Granholm, governor of Michigan, et al., vs. Eleanor Heald, et al.

25. "Direct Shipping Update," *Wine East* 33:3 (September–October 2005), pp. 10–12.

26. See "Minnesota OKs Direct Shipping but Sparks Controversy," *Wine East* 33:4 (November–December 2005), pp. 8–9; and "Internet Wine Sales Approved in Minnesota," *Wine East* 34: 1 (May–June 2006), pp. 8, 57.

27. For the story of the direct shipping and self-distribution problems in Virginia, see two articles in *Wine East* by Terri Cofer Beirne, Esq., counsel to the Virginia Wineries Association: "Virginia Winery Rights at Risk in the Federal Courts," *Wine East* 33:3 (September–October 2005), pp. 16–19; and "'Virtually' Self Distributing in Virginia," *Wine East* 35:1 (May–June 2007), pp. 42–46.

28. Dante J. Romanini, "Wine and the Law: Update on Direct Shipment," *Wine East* 34:3 (September–October 2006), pp. 32–35.

29. One winery that has been active in all of these causes is Westport Rivers Vineyard and Winery in Westport, Massachusetts. When Bob and Carol Russell opened the winery in 1991, one goal was not only to educate people about wine but also about the importance of local agriculture and a balanced life style. Farmland preservation has been another one of their goals, and keeping and promoting the Heritage Farm Coast as a farm, fish, food, and wine region has regularly been the subject of fundraisers and other promotions since the winery opened. See Robert James Russell, II, "Moving Toward a Sustainable Future," in *Out of the Earth: A Heritage Farm Coast Cookbook* by Kerry Downey Romaniello (New Bedford, Massachusetts: Spinner, 1999), pp. 15–21.

30. "New York Wine and Culinary Center Opens," *Wine East* 34:3 (September–October 2006), pp. 14–15.

Appendix A

1. The origins and history of grapevines are complex and are still being revised as additional discoveries are made. The interested reader is referred to: "The Origin and Domestication of the *Vinifera Grape*" by Harold P. Olmo in *The Origins and Ancient History of Wine,* edited by Patrick E. McGovern, Stuart J. Fleming, and Solomon H. Katz (Luxembourg, 1995), pp. 31–43; "The Domestication of the Grapevine *Vitis Vinifera* L. in the Near East" by Daniel Zohary in the same volume, pp. 23–30; *Wine: A Geographic Appreciation* by Harm Jan de Blij (Totowa, New Jersey, 1983), chapters 2 and 3; and *Dionysus: A Social History of the Wine Vine* by Edward Hyams (New York, 1965), pp. 15–34.

2. The classification of grapevines is the subject of continuing study and proposals range from replacing the term *Euvitis* to reclassifying the North American species of *Vitis.* One recent study by Michael O. Moore of the University of Georgia is "Classification and Systematics of Eastern North American *Vitis* L. (Vitaceae) North of Mexico," *Sida* 14:3 (1991), pp. 339–367.

3. In modern times there has been limited success in crossing *Vitis* and *Muscadinia,* first by Robert T. Dunstan in North Carolina in 1955 and then by Harold Olmo at the University of California at Davis.

4. de Blij, *Wine: A Geographic Appreciation,* p. 11.

5. For a further discussion, see "Sex and the Single Vine" by John R. McGrew, *American Wine Society Journal* 11:2 (Summer 1979), pp. 27–30.

6. Olmo, "The Origin and Domestication of the *Vinifera* Grape," p. 33.

7. William Robert Prince, *Treatise on the Vine* (New York, 1830), p. 224.

8. Ibid., p. 252.

9. See *The Wines of the East: Native American Grapes* by Hudson Cattell and Lee Stauffer Miller (Lancaster, Pennsylvania, 1980) for a brief account of these early hybridizers. Thomas Pinney provides a useful summary in *A History of Wine in America: From the Beginnings to Prohibition* (Berkeley, 1989).

10. For a brief history of the development of the French hybrids, see *The Wines of the East: The Hybrids* by Cattell and Stauffer (Miller) (Lancaster, Pennsylvania, 1978). Two good book length studies are *The Great Wine Blight* by George Ordish (New York, 1972), and *The Botanist and the Vintner: How Wine Was Saved for the World* by Christy Campbell (Chapel Hill, North Carolina, 2005). For the names of some of the French hybridizers, see Appendix B.

11. For a report on modern grape breeding, see "Grapes" by Bruce I. Reisch and Charlotte Pratt in *Fruit Breeding,* Volume II: *Vine and Small Fruit Crops,* edited by Jules Janick and James N. Moore (New York, 1996), pp. 297–369.

12. It is impossible to list everyone who contributed to this list of grape varieties used in the East. Some of those who helped were Jeff Bloodworth, Hillsborough, North Carolina; Peter M. Cousins, USDA, ARS,

Geneva, New York; K. Helen Fisher, University of Guelph; Peter Hemstad, University of Minnesota; Pal Kozma, University of Pécs, Hungary; Ron Lane, University of Georgia; Valérie Laucou et al., INRA-Montpellier; John R. McGrew, Hanover, Pennsylvania; Lucie T. Morton, Charlottesville, Virginia; Bruce I. Reisch, New York State Agricultural Experiment Station; Andrew G. Reynolds, Brock University; Lloyd F. Schmidt, Grimsby, Ontario; Charles Sims, University of Florida; and Elmer Swenson, Osceola, Wisconsin.

Appendix B

1. For a detailed account of the naming of the French hybrids, and especially the Canadian involvement, see Hudson Cattell's article "Naming the French Hybrids," in *Wine East* 35:2 (July–August 2007), pp. 24–31, 58.

2. E. Pée-Laby, *La Vigne Nouvelle: Les Hybrides Producteurs,* 3rd ed. (Paris, 1929), p. 191.

3. Two table grapes were also named: Seyve-Villard 20365, Dattier de Saint-Vallier; and Seyve-Villard 20473, Muscat de Saint-Vallier.

4. "Arrêté du 27 février 1964 fixant les nouvelles appellations de variétés hybrides de Vigne," *Bulletin del'Institut National des Appellations d'Origine des Vins et Eaux-de-Vie,* No. 89, April 1964.

5. Grape varieties that are well suited to one region do not necessarily do well in another. Dr. John Einset has pointed out in his unpublished *Viticulture of Eastern North America* that many of the more commonly grown hybrids in France require a longer growing season to reach optimum maturity than is found in either New York or Ontario. This, in addition to the need for increased winter hardiness for grapes in the East, would explain why some of the hybrids most suited for the East have had little place in French viticulture and would therefore never have been named in France.

6. The leaflet contained a preface by Nicholas H. Paul of Naples, New York, president of the Finger Lakes Wine Growers Association. Included in the leaflet were technical descriptions and notes concerning each variety by George Remaily, experimentalist, and George L. Slate, professor emeritus, both of the New York State Agricultural Experiment Station in Geneva.

7. A short review of the naming process was given in an unsigned press release titled "French Hybrid Grapes Given Names," which was written after the names approved by the Great Lakes Grape Nomenclature Committee were submitted for publication in the *Register of New Fruit and Nut Varieties.*

Appendix D

1. For a history of the dispute over the term champagne, see William F. Heintz, "Champagne by Any Other Name," *Wines and Vines* 68:12 (December 1987), pp. 28–33.

2. John Schreiner, *The World of Canadian Wine* (Vancouver, 1984), pp. 21–25. See also Hudson Cattell, "In the Wake of the Champagne Wars," *Wines and Vines* 90:8 (August 2009), pp. 60–64.

3. *Wine East* 31:2 (July–August 2003), pp. 8, 52.

4. *Wine East* 33:4 (November–December 2005), pp. 6–7.

5. William F. Heintz, "Nicholas Longworth: The Father of U.S. Champagne?" *Wines and Vines* 65:12 (December 1984), 52–54. A more complete account of Longworth and the Cincinnati region may be found in two of Thomas Pinney's books: *A History of Wine in America From the Beginnings to Prohibition* (Berkeley, 1989), pp. 156–174; and "Nicholas Longworth," in *The Makers of American Wine: A Record of 200 Years* (Berkeley, 2012), pp. 22–38. See also "U.S. Champagne: Its Beginnings," *Wines and Vines* 48:6 (June 1967), pp. 27–30.

6. Kyle J. Johannsen, "The Winegrowing Industry of the Lake Erie Island Region," M.A. Thesis, Bowling Green State University, 1983, p. 153. Johannsen also mentions that the first American wine to christen a battleship, the USS *New York* in 1912, was produced by the M. Hommel Winery in Sandusky.

7. "U.S. Champagne: Its Present," *Wines and Vines* 48:6 (June 1967), pp. 33–35.

8. Leon D. Adams, *The Wines of America* (San Francisco, 1973), p. 356. The charmat process, named after Eugene Charmat in France, involved fermenting the champagne in large tanks and then bottling under pressure. This process was also known as the "bulk process" because large quantities could be made at one time. Also, but much less used, was the transfer method, or transfer process, which was developed in Germany and brought into the United States in the 1950s. In this method, fermentation still took place in the bottle, but instead of disgorging to remove the sediment, the contents of the bottles were emptied out, filtered to remove the sediment, and then rebottled and labeled with the wording "fermented in this bottle."

9. "U.S. Champagne: Its Present," p. 33.

10. Much of the information on Cold Duck came from a Cattell interview with Angelo Spinazze on July 19, 1998. See also Lynn Afendoulis, "Remembering Cold Duck," *Michigan Wine Country* (Fall/Winter, 1996), p. 7.

11. Other people have claimed to have been the first to invent, discover, or bottle Cold Duck, most of whom first encountered it at or through Pontchartrain Wine Cellars. There is little doubt that Robert Wozniak and Angelo Spinazze at Bronte were responsible for making and releasing the first Cold Duck in the United States.

12. Ruth Ellen Church, *Wines of the Midwest* (Athens, Ohio), p. 59.

13. *Wines and Vines* 49:12 (December 1968), p. 7.

14. "Flying Higher Than Ever," *Wines and Vines* 51:6 (June 1970), pp. 33–34.

15. "Cold Duck: A High Flier Levels Off," *Wines and Vines* 53:9 (September 1972), p. 38.

16. Louis Gomborg, "Wine Industry Dean Sees Growth Ahead," *Wines and Vines* 70:12 (December 1989), pp. 18–21. In 1967, California had 40 percent of the market, imports had 20 percent, and all other states had 40 percent. Interestingly, while the total U.S. sparkling wine market was climbing from 22 million gallons in 1970 to 47 million in 1984, bottle-fermented sparklers increased almost tenfold during those same years, from a few hundred thousand cases a year to more than 2 million cases a year.

17. Marvin Sands, "Current Trends in U.S. Wine Consumption and Marketing Outlook for Eastern Grapes and Wines," *Proceedings of the 124th Annual Meeting of the New York State Horticultural Society,* 1979, p. 129.

18. Paul Marks, "Variety of Grapes in Eastern 'Bubblies,'" *Wine Spectator* (May 1–15, 1981), p. 21.

19. *Arkansas:*   Post Winery, Wiederkehr Wine Cellars
   Connecticut: Haight Vineyards
   Florida: St. Augustine Winery
   Illinois: Thompson Winery
   Indiana: Banholzer Winecellars, Ltd.
   Maine: Bartlett Maine Estate Winery
   Massachusetts: Chicama Vineyards, Nashoba Valley Winery
   Michigan: Bronte Champagne & Wines Co., Fenn Valley Vineyards, Lakeside
                          Vineyard, Leelanau Wine Cellars, St. Julian Wine Co., Tabor Hill/Chi
                          Co., Warner Vineyards, Inc.
   Missouri: Ashby Vineyards, Bardenheier's Wine Cellar, Hermannhof, Rosati
                          Winery, St. James Winery, Stone Hill Wine Co., Winery of the
                          Abbey
   New Jersey: Gross' Highland Winery, Renault Winery, Tomasello Winery
   New York: Benmarl Wine Co., Brotherhood Corp., Bully Hill Vineyards,
                          Canandaigua Wine Co., Clinton Vineyards, Gold Seal Vineyards,
                          Hudson Valley Wine Co., Knapp Vineyards, Monarch Wine Co., Robin
                          Fils & Cie., Ltd., Royal Wine Co., Schapiro's Wine Co., Taylor Wine
                          Co., Wagner Vineyards, Widmer's Wine Cellars, Hermann J. Wiemer
                          Vineyards, Windsor Vineyards, Inc., Woodbury Vineyards
   North Carolina: Biltmore Co., Duplin Wine Cellars
   Ohio: Cedar Hill Wine Co., Mantey Vineyards, Inc., Meier's Wine Cellars., Mon
                          Ami Champagne Co., Moyer Vineyards, The Steuk Wine Co., Stillwater
                          Wineries
   Pennsylvania: Bucks Country Vineyards, Mazza Vineyards, Penn Shore Vineyards
   South Carolina: Truluck Winery
   Tennessee: Highland Manor Winery
   Virginia: Ingleside Plantation Winery, Oasis Vineyard, Rapidan River Vineyards.
   This list of wineries was compiled from the charts of champagne and sparkling wine producers published by *Wines and Vines* in 62:6 (June 1981), pp. 80–81; 63:12 (December 1982), pp. 25–31; and 65:12 (December 1984), pp. 35–38.

20. For a useful review of the characteristics that gave Lambrusco such widespread consumer acceptance, see Richard P. Vine's "The Lessons of Lambrusco," *Eastern Grape Grower and Winery News* 6:4 (August 1980), pp. 14–17. Some of the wines in the new trend were discussed in Philip E. Hiaring, "New on the Block: Low-cal Wines," *Wines and Vines* 62:9 (September 1981), pp. 25–26.

21. "A W&V roundup on who is producing light or soft table wines," *Wines and Vines* 63:9 (September 1982), pp. 32–34.

22. Lee Miller, "Native, Hybrids Make Super Sippers," *Wine Spectator* (June 1–15, 1982), p. 25.

23. An excellent article on the start of what he calls "one of the most incredible success stories in the wine industry" is Larry Walker's "Wine Coolers Are Hot Items," *Wines and Vines* 65:9 (September 1984), pp. 58–62. Another article highlighting early cooler producers in the East is Paul Schlein, "The Instant World of Wine Coolers…Who's Cool?" *Eastern Grape Grower and Winery News* 10:4 (August–September, 1984), pp. 16–17.

24. According to Gail Unzelman, editor and publisher of *Wayward Tendrils Quarterly,* tall drinks in California called "wine coolers" were referred to in Wine Advisory Board pamphlets dating back to the late 1940s and early 1950s. These recipes typically called for combining California wine with fruit juice, chilled soda or sparkling water, and ice cubes in a tall glass and garnished with fruit.

25. For an article on Canandaigua's Sun Country Cooler, see Terry Robards, "Coolers Keep One Winery Hot," *Wine Spectator* (March 16–31, 1986), pp. 18–19.

26. Richard Figiel, "NY Passes a Cluster of Wine Bills…Coolers but Not Table Wines in Groceries," *Eastern Grape Grower and Winery News* 10:4 (August–September 1984), p. 15. One of the other bills passed established the New York Wine and Grape Foundation.

27. See "All or Nothing for Coolers in New York," *Wine Spectator* (June 1–15, 1985), p. 3.

28. Cattell, "The Benmarl Story: Mark Miller and Benmarl Vineyards," *Wine East* 34:1 (May–June, 2006), p. 30.

29. The effect of beer cooler competition and other factors leading to a decline in cooler sales are given in "The Coolers: Here to Stay?" *Wine East* 13:12 (July–August 1985), pp. 7, 23.

30. Some of the names of the wine coolers were also eye-catching. Rattlesnake Cooler, advertised as "the cooler with a bite," was made by the Thousand Oaks Winery in Starkville, Mississippi, for Kershenstine Enterprises in Eupore, Mississippi, makers of Pappy Kershenstine's Beef Jerky. According to the December 1984–January 1985 issue of *Eastern Grape Grower and Winery News,* the jerky was marketed in thirty-three states by 103 independent Coors distributors, making it a ready-made network for a new wine cooler.

31. Cattell, "The Benmarl Story," pp. 29–30. See also "The Benmarl Vineyards Vigneron," the winery's newsletter (Winter–Spring 1977), p. 3.

32. For the early history of the Beaujolais Nouveau in France, the festivities that grew up around it there and its spread to other parts of Europe and the United States, see Bess Hochstein, "Beaujolais Nouveau is Back," *Wine Times* 1:2 (November 1988), pp. 12–13.

33. This date was changed in 1985 to 12:01 a.m. Paris time on the third Thursday in November.

34. Cattell, "The Benmarl Story," p. 29. See also "Building Excitement for the New Vintage in Nouveau York," *Eastern Grape Grower and Winery News* 9:6 (December 1983–January 1984), pp. 12–15, which credits Benmarl as producing the first American nouveau in 1971.

35. Cascade Mountain Vineyards news release, November 9, 1982.

36. "Those Charming Nouveau Wines," *Wine East* 14:5 (January–February 1987), pp. 8–10, 30; and "The Nouveau Wines Arrive in Philadelphia," *Wine East* 13:5 (January–February, 1986), p. 6.

37. "Aurore Nouvelle—A White Nouveau," *Wine East* 14:5 (January–February 1987), p. 9. In 1987, Boordy Vineyards in Hydes, Maryland, released Nouvelle, a blend of Seyval and Riesling (Donna Ellis in *The Owings Mills Flier,* November 5, 1987).

38. "Ice Wine—the 'First' of the First," *Pennsylvania Grape Letter and Wine News* 7:4 (January 1980), p. 5.

39. Mowbray's claim to being the first American ice wine did not go without dispute. Frank Prial's article in the *New York Times* in 1978 gave credit to Edmeades Winery in California for making the first American ice wine three years after Mowbray. When Mowbray objected, it was argued that Mowbray's 100 bottles could not be considered a commercial bottling when compared with a forty-four-case release. Mowbray retorted that any time he could sell a batch of wine for $5,000, it was commercial. The *New York Times* agreed and printed a retraction.

40. Much of the account of the early history of icewine in Ontario comes from Cattell's article, "Those Fabulous Ontario Ice Wines!" *Wine East* 22:5 (January–February 1985), pp. 8, 38–39. For a good account of icewine in Canada, see Tony Aspler's *The Wine Atlas of Canada* (Toronto, 2006), pp. 38–47. See also *Icewine: Extreme Winemaking* by Donald Ziraldo and Karl Kaiser (Toronto, 2007), and John Schreiner, *Icewine: The Complete Story* (Toronto, 2001).

41. For more on the history of kosher wines in the East, see Leon D. Adams, *The Wines of America,* 2nd ed. (New York, 1978), pp. 494–497; and Thomas Pinney, *A History of Wine in America: From Prohibition to the Present* (Berkeley, 2005), pp. 173–175.

42. Daniel Rogov, "The Long Winding Road to World-Class Wine," *Reform Judaism Magazine* online (Spring 2007), p. 6.

43. Irving H. Marcus, "The Case for Mogen David," *Wines and Vines* 33:7 (July 1952), pp. 11–12.

44. Stephen Frank, "Kosher Winemaking Comes of Age," *Times Union* (Albany), October 5, 1986, pp. G-1, G-10.

45. Two general articles on fruit winemaking are "Fruit Wines Deserve More Attention," by Richard Paul Hinkle, *Wine Spectator* (August 16–31, 1980), p. 10; and "Time for Fruit Wine: Winemaking Goes Beyond Vinifera," by Alison Crowe, *Vineyard and Winery Management* 32:2 (March–April 2006), pp. 46–53.

46. Jack Partridge, "Charting the Unexplored Territory of Fruit Wine," *Eastern Grape Grower and Winery News* 9:1 (February–March 1983), pp. 24–25. See also Linda Jones McKee, "Tradition Meets the Future at Nashoba Valley," *Wine East* 11:2 (July–August 1983), pp. 12–15, and Jack Partridge, "The Unique Fruit Wines of the Northeast," *Proceedings of the Eighteenth Pennsylvania Grape Industry Conference,* February 26–27, 1986, pp. 9–13.

47. See Cattell, "The Wineries of Northern New England," *Wine East* 18:4 (November–December 1990), pp. 23–24.

48. Cattell, "The Wineries of Northern New England," pp. 18–20. Philip E. Hiaring details the start of Woodchuck cider in "Is Cider the Next Lambrusco?" *Wines and Vines* 73:4 (April 1992), pp. 27–28; and the start of Green Mountain Cidery in a news item, "Green Mountain Cidery Opens in Vermont, "*Wine East* 25:1 (May–June 1997), pp. 8–9.

49. Judith Maloney, "Cider," *Shelburne Falls and West County News,* July 30, 1993; and Cattell, "It's Hands-On Selling that Pays Off," *Wine East* 21:4 (November–December 1993), pp. 8–9.

50. The proprietors of the three New England wineries shared their concerns about image in interviews with Cattell in 1990, which were the basis for an article, "The Fruit Wine Image in New England," *Wine East* 18:5 (January–February 1991), pp. 18–21, 30.

51. Cattell, "Focus on Fruit Wines at Cream Ridge Vineyards," *Wine East* 17:2 (July–August 1989), pp. 14–17, 28–29. Before opening his own winery in Cream Ridge, Amabile was the winemaker for Buffalo Valley Winery in Lewisburg, Pennsylvania. The winery opened in 1979 but by 1982, with the winery losing money, owner William Pursel decided to sell the winery. This happened to be the year that Amabile had added several fruit wines to the wine list. Customer demand for his strawberry wine exceeded his ability to supply it, and a nectarine wine put on sale later in the season brought customers to the winery from far beyond its normal marketing area. At the end of the year Pursel told Cattell that he could not believe it, but the winery made a small profit that year.

52. Cattell interview with William Redelmeier September 27, 1996. Framboise was the first dessert wine, but it was soon followed by Framboise Noir made from black raspberries, Framboise d'Or made from golden raspberries, and a Cassis from black currants.

53. Roger A. Morse, *Making Mead (Honey Wine)* (Ithaca, New York, 1980), p. 12.

54. James E. Tew, "Honey—The Basic Requirement for Mead," *Proceedings: Ohio Grape—Wine Short Course, 1986,* pp. 33–34.

55. See two articles by James E. Knapp: "West Virginia Wineries—A Re-Emergence," *American Wine Society Journal* 21:2 (Summer 1989), p. 55; and "Mountain Wineries," *Wonderful West Virginia* 51:1 (March 1987), p. 28. Androczi was a professor of Library Science at West Virginia Wesleyan College until he retired in 1981. West Virginia passed a farm winery bill in 1981 that did not include mead and, in 1985, after a long fight to cut through bureaucratic red tape, he sent a letter to President Reagan in which he wrote: "One reason there is so much stifling in the market is an inability to start a business." He received a personal reply and he was soon able to open his meadery *(Meadmaker's Journal* 6 [1995], p. 20).

56. *Inside Mead* 10:4 (August 1996), pp. 16–17.

57. A comprehensive book on the muscadines and their production is *Muscadine Grapes,* edited by Fouad M. Basiouny and David G. Himelrick (Alexandria, Virginia, 2001). Two interviews by Cattell with Ellen Butz in 2009 contributed to this section.

58. *Scuppernong: North Carolina's Grape and Its Wines* by Clarence Gohdes (Durham, North Carolina, 1982) is an important and very readable history of the Scuppernong grape.

59. Lucie T. Morton, *Winegrowing in Eastern America: An Illustrated Guide to Viniculture East of the Rockies* (Ithaca, 1985), pp. 66–67.

60. Basiouny and Himelrick, *Muscadine Grapes,* p. 8. Duplin Wine Cellars in Rose Hill, North Carolina, opened in 1976 as a farmer cooperative after a sharp fall in grape prices in 1972. During a seven-year period, production at the winery increased from 3,000 to more than 140,000 gallons. (Cattell, "Duplin Makes Wine the 'Old-Timey Way,'" *Wine East* 10:3 [September–October, 1982], pp. 8–11.)

61. See R. P. Vine, B. J. Stojanovic, J. P. Overcash, and C. P. Hegwood, Jr., "Mississippi's Model Laboratory for Southern Viticulture and Enology," *Eastern Grape Grower and Winery News* 6:1 (February 1980), pp. 36–38; Boris J. Stojanovic, "Mississippi's Distinguished Wine History: The East's Enology Teaching Center," *Vinifera Wine Growers Journal* 11:2 (Summer 1984), pp. 116–123; and Rob Levin, "School with Real Taste for the Grape: Mississippi State's Enology Lab," *Vinifera Wine Growers Journal* 14:1 (Spring 1987), pp. 17–20.

62. John A. Mortensen, "Origin of the Florida 'Blanc Du Bois,'" *Vinifera Wine Growers Journal* 14:1 (Spring 1987), pp. 5–8. An article by Julie Graddy, "Florida's First Premium Wine Grape 'Blanc Du Bois' Now Being Planted," appeared in the same issue, pp. 3–4.

Appendix E

1. References in these notes are good sources for further information. To avoid repetition, references to the histories by Leon Adams and Thomas Pinney have generally been omitted although they would otherwise be included. Some of the references, especially those for newspaper articles, are not included in the bibliography at the end of the book. When an author's name is known, it is used even though there was no by-line with the article.

2. H. C. George, "Behind the Scenes…How Alabama's Farm Winery Law Came to Be," *Wines and Vines* 60:12 (December 1979), pp. 37–39. This story, with emphasis on Jim and Marianne Eddins, is also told by Earl

Andrews and Rebecca Paul in "Next Door...Alabama Joins In," *Eastern Grape Grower and Winery News* 6:5 (October 1980), p. 17.

3. For a good history of Arkansas at this time, see Robert Schick, "The Arkansas Wine Industry," *Wine Review* 14 (June 1946) pp. 8–12, 18.

4. Two articles on Wiederkehr Wine Cellars and Alcuin Wiederkehr are "Arkansas Has Largest Winery in Southeast," by Philip Hiaring, *Wines and Vines* 54:10 (October 1973), pp. 22–25; and Tom Wood, "Wiederkehrs Grows into Award-Winning Winery," which first appeared in the Little Rock *Arkansas Democrat* on November 11, 1979, and subsequently was entered into the *Congressional Record* 125:182 (December 18, 1979) by Representative John P. Hammerschmidt (R-AR).

5. The Sax, Post, and Wiederkehr wineries are the subject of "Altus, Arkansas," by Frank R. Giordano, *Eastern Grape Grower and Winery News* 9:1 (February–March 1983), pp. 14–16.

6. Hudson Cattell, "The Good Foxes of Haight Vineyard," *Wine East* 10:4 (November–December 1982), pp. 8–11; and Georgia Sheron, "Making Wine History in Litchfield," *Connecticut Beverage Journal* (November 1987), pp. 43–44. For more on Connecticut wine history, see Eric D. Lehman and Amy Nawrocki, *A History of Connecticut Wine: Vineyard in Your Backyard* (Charleston, South Carolina, 2011).

7. John S. Rosenberg, "A Vintage Year for Connecticut," *New York Times,* February 11, 1979. See also Robert F. Valchuis and Diane L. Henault, *The Wines of New England* (Boston, Massachusetts, 1980), pp. 18–19, 41.

8. Valchuis and Henault, *Wines of New England,* pp. 24–25, 40.

9. Joe Cohen, "New Wine-Maker Enters Market with Gusto," *Hartford Courant,* November 13, 1981; Donald Breed, "Hamlet Hill Winery Battles Climate and Birds of Connecticut," *Vinifera Wine Growers Journal* 14:4 (Winter 1987), pp. 246–249.

10. Ricia Gordon, ed., *Wines of New England* (Brattleboro, Vermont, 1990), pp. 40–41; Elizabeth Lincoln, "Grapes and Wine in the Nutmeg State," *American Wine Society Journal* 20:3 (Fall 1988), pp. 84–87.

11. "Connecticut's First Pinot Noir," *American Wine Society Journal* 16:3 (Fall 1984), pp. 87–88.

12. An excellent introduction to what was happening at this time in the aftermath of the farm winery legislation may be found in R. P. Bates, "The Emerging Florida Wine Industry," *American Wine Society Journal* 17:2 (Summer 1985), pp. 41–44, 54.

13. Lafayette Vineyards and Winery started a second operation in Clermont in 1988 by planting a vineyard and opening the Lakeridge Vineyards and Winery. Both wineries were consolidated in Clermont in 1992 as Lakeridge Vineyards and Winery. See Cattell, "Finding the Best Market in a Tourist Area," *Wine East* 25:3 (September–October 1997), pp. 22–24, 42–43.

The best-known winemaker in Florida, and the long-time winemaker at Lakeridge, is Jeanne Burgess, the daughter of Foster and Rebecca Burgess. Two years before her parents opened Alaqua Vineyard in 1980, she entered the postgraduate enology program at Mississippi State University where she studied under Richard Vine. After graduating, she became the manager and winemaker at Florida Heritage Winery before joining Lafayette Vineyards and Winery in 1983. She was a pioneer in making commercial wines from the Florida hybrids and new muscadine varieties.

14. See "Wine Tripping in Georgia: A Day's Trip," *Wines and Vines* 73:2 (February 1992), pp. 16–18.

15. Cattell, "Exploring the Wineries of North Georgia," *Wine East* 30:4 (November–December 2002), pp. 22–31, 50; and Gayle and David Darugh, "The Georgia Wine Trail," *American Wine Society Journal* 34:4 (Winter 2002), pp. 111–120.

16. For the early history of Nauvoo, founded by the Mormons and later settled by the Icarians, see Leon D. Adams, *The Wines of America* (Boston, Massachusetts, 1973). Additional information about the Baxter family was furnished by Brenda Logan and the Baxter's Vineyards website.

17. *Wine East* 10:2 (July–August 1982), pp. 4, 6.

18. *Indiana Wine: A History,* by James L. Butler and John J. Butler (Bloomington, 2001) is an excellent source of information. See also Ledford C. Carter and Dorothy B. Vitaliano, "Indiana Wine: Past—Present—Future," *American Wine Society Journal* 7:2 (Summer, 1975), pp. 15–18; Philip E. Hiaring, "A Vinous Tour of Indiana, the Hoosier State; Wine Growing is Reviving after 160 Years," *Wines and Vines* 57:6 (June 1976), pp. 33–37; Ruth Ellen Church, "Indiana Wineries," *Vintage* 5:10 (March 1976), pp. 28–32; and Linda Jones McKee, "Making and Selling Wine in Indiana," *Wine East* 21:4 (November–December 1993), pp. 18–23, 31.

19. Linda Jones McKee, "A Touch of the Exotic in Southern Indiana," *Wine East* 10:1 (May–June 1982), p. 5.

20. *Wine East* 30:6 (March–April 2003), pp. 8–10.

21. Michael L. White and Murli R. Dharmadhikari, "The Iowa Wine Boom Includes Wine," *Wine East* 36:1 (May–June 2008), pp. 12–17, 53–55. Additional information was furnished to Cattell by Ronald Mark and Paul Tabor.

22. For an appraisal of the possibilities for grapes and wine at the end of the 1970s, see Thomas J. Schueneman, "The Grape in Kansas: Poised for a Winegrowing Comeback?" *Vinifera Wine Growers Journal* 9:4 (Winter 1982), pp. 225–230.

23. For more on Rizza and the start of the modern Kansas wine industry, see Robert G. Rizza, "Reviving the Kansas Wine Industry: A Model for Other States," *Vinifera Wine Growers Journal* 16:4 (Winter 1989), pp. 267–268; and Jenny Deam, "Kansas Ripens for Home-Grown Wines," *Vinifera Wine Growers Journal* 12:4 (Winter 1985), pp. 252–255.

24. Michael Martinez, "Harvest Puts Kansas Back in Winemaking: First State Winery in a Century," *Vinifera Wine Growers Journal* 15:4 (Winter 1988), pp. 246–247.

25. F. Carlton Colcord, "Small Winery Act for Kentucky," *Vinifera Wine Growers Journal* 2:1 (Spring 1975), pp. 34–36.

26. R. F. Sharp, "Made in Kentucky from Vine to Wine," *Lexington Herald-Leader Business Sunday,* July 13, 1997.

27. Mike Montgomery, "The Law Too Potent for La. Wine Makers," *Vinifera Wine Growers Journal* 15:3 (Fall 1988), pp. 206–207.

28. For Bartlett Maine Estate Winery, see "Blueberry is Best," *Maine Times,* November 22, 1985; and Michael Taylor, "Making Wine—and Having Fun too—in Maine," *Wines and Vines* 69:4 (April 1988), pp. 39–40. Both Bartlett Maine Estate Winery and Downeast Country Wines, which follows, are included in Cattell, "The Wineries of Northern New England," *Wine East* 18:4 (November–December 1990), pp. 16–25, 33–35.

29. According to an article by Peter W. Cox in the *Maine Times* for September 12, 1975, Dr. Bruce Trembly, a neurosurgeon at Thayer Hospital in Waterville, had a vineyard consisting of nearly three acres of Native American and French hybrid grapes near Lake Messalonskee. His Lakeside Vineyards sold grapes to White Mountain Vineyards in New Hampshire.

30. A good account of this early period is W. H. Earle, "Grape Expectations," *Baltimore Magazine* (November, 1980), pp. 66–70. See also Roger Morris, "The Wines of Maryland and Virginia Come of Age," *Washington Star Magazine "Home Life,"* September 30, 1979, pp. 14–19; and Regina McCarthy, *Maryland Wine: A Full-Bodied History* (Charleston, South Carolina, 2012).

31. Some wineries were said to have bottled the same wine under different labels to increase sales.

32. Lindsay Morris, "A 'French' Wine from Grapes Grown on the Shore," *Sun* (Baltimore), September 25, 1977, pp. 7, 10.

33. Cattell, "The *New* Boordy Vineyards," *Wine East* 9:1 (May 1981), pp. 10–12. See also Donna Ellis, "Vines to Wines," *Owings Mills Flier* (Maryland), November 5, 1987, pp. 19–22.

34. One early account of Chicama Vineyards is William A. Caldwell's "The Vineyard's Vineyard," *Country Journal* (September, 1975), pp. 38–42. See also Cattell, "Chicama—not Martha—Has the Vineyards," in "From Plymouth to Narragansett," *Wine East* 10:1 (May–June 1982), pp. 10–11, 20.

35. *Vineyard Gazette,* October 26, 2007; and *Martha's Vineyard Times,* August 14, 2008.

36. See Cattell, "The Winery in the Library," in "From Plymouth to Narragansett," *Wine East* 10:1 (May–June 1982), pp. 16–17; Melinda Logan Jones, "Commonwealth Is Rich in Wine," *Wines and Vines* 65:6 (June 1984), p. 73; and Donald D. Breed, "Struggling Massachusetts Winery to Close," *Vinifera Wine Growers Journal* 15:3 (Fall 1988), pp. 196–197.

37. Robert Temple, "New England Tradition Being Revived at Nashoba Valley Winery," *Massachusetts Beverage Journal* (December 1981), pp. 74–75; Linda Jones McKee, "Tradition Meets the Future at Nashoba Valley," *Wine East* 11:2 (July–August 1983), pp. 12–15; Anthony Spinazzola, "A New England Tradition: Fruit Wines," *Boston Globe,* March 9, 1983; and Melanie DuLac, "Fruit Wines Are All They Make at Nashoba Valley Winery," *Vineyard and Winery Management* 15:6 (November–December 1989), pp. 26–28.

38. For a good explanation of these laws and their consequences, see Thomas Pinney, *A History of Wine in America: From Prohibition to the Present* (Berkeley, 2005), pp. 175–178.

39. Gordon S. Howell, Jr., and Stephen S. Stackhouse, "Michigan's Wine Grape Research," *Wines and Vines* 55:9 (September 1974), pp. 45–47. For a later account, see "MSU Wine Research Facility Boosts State's Winegrape Industry," *Great Lakes Grape Growers News* 19:2 (July 1991), pp. 11–12. *The History of Michigan Wines: 150 Years of Winemaking along the Great Lakes,* by Lorri Hathaway and Sharon Kegerreis (Charleston, South Carolina, 2010) is a good resource.

40. Ruth Ellen Church, "A Tour through Fenn Valley Vineyards," *Chicago Tribune,* December 9, 1976; and George Cantor, "Family Winery Uncorks Winners," *Detroit Free Press,* September 11, 1977.

41. "Chateau Grand Traverse Specializes in Vinifera," *Great Lakes Grape Growers News* 16:1 (February 1988), pp. 4–5. Early wineries on the Leelanau Peninsula were covered in Cattell, "Wine in the Land of Delight," *Wine East* 9:5 (January 1982), pp. 6–10, 23.

42. Patricia Monaghan, *Wineries of Wisconsin and Minnesota* (St. Paul, 2008); John Marshall, "A Short History of Minnesota Grape Culture," *Vinifera Wine Growers Journal* 12:3 (Fall 1985), pp. 157–164; and Linda Jones McKee, "Where the Grapes Can Suffer" *Wine East* 10:5 (January–February 1983), pp. 8–11.

43. J. William Moffett, "New Wines in Old Miss," *Eastern Grape Grower and Winery News* 6:5 (October 1980), pp. 14–17.

44. Isaac Cook founded Cook's Imperial Champagne Cellar in St. Louis in 1859 after acquiring the property built by the Missouri Wine Company in 1832. Adolf Heck, Sr., reopened it after Prohibition as the American Wine Company. When Heck ran into financial problems, controlling interest in the company was sold to the German wine firm of Henkell & Co. in 1937 with a Swiss firm being used as a front for the transaction. Nazi foreign minister Joachim von Ribbentrop, a former salesman for the company and a relative of Karl Henkell, has been credited with making the deal that gave Henkell 52 percent stock control. During World War II the ownership of the winery was uncovered and the stock owned by Henkell was seized by the U.S. government under the trading-with-the-enemy act. On February 11, 1944, the stock was auctioned off in Chicago by the Alien Property Custodian to return the winery to American ownership. (See the *St. Louis Star-Times,* February 12, 1944, and February 18, 1944; and the *St. Louis Post Dispatch,* January 12, 1944, and August 18, 1944.)

45. Peter Joseph Poletti, Jr., "An Interdisciplinary Study of the Missouri Grape and Wine Industry, 1650 to 1989" (Ph.D. dissertation, Saint Louis University, 1989). Historical information is also included in Robert F. Scheef, *Vintage Missouri: A Guide to Missouri Wineries* (St. Louis, 1991).

46. Information from the Missouri Division of Alcohol and Tobacco Control and Cattell communication with Jim Held, May 27, 2010.

47. See "Missouri Plans Its Renaissance," *Eastern Grape Grower and Winery News* 6:2 (April 1980), pp. 16, 18.

48. The special tax, which was added to the existing wine tax of 30 cents a gallon, was passed despite heavy lobbying by California's Wine Institute.

49. Two good articles are Renée Cashmere, "Two Vineyards and Counting: Nebraska Sees the Birth of an Industry," *Wine Business Monthly* 5:8 (July–August 1998) pp. 35–37; and Paul E. Read, "Viticulture and Enology in Nebraska," *Wine East* 33:3 (September–October 2005), pp. 20–26, 54.

50. See Millie Howie, "Cuthills Vineyards: A Winery in Pierce, Nebraska," *Wines and Vines* 81:1 (January 2000), pp. 112–117.

51. For early accounts of White Mountain Vineyards, see "First New England-Made Wines on Sale at Easter," *Wines and Vines* 51:3 (March 1970), p. 28; and Pamela Bearer and Linda Fleming, "Winegrowing on a New Hampshire Island," *Wines and Vines* 60:9 (September 1979), p. 80. An account of the first attempted sale of the winery appeared in two issues of *Wine East:* "White Mountain Vineyard Changes Hands," (10:5 [January–February 1983], p. 7), and "White Mountain Vineyards Returns to John Canepa" (12:3 [September–October] 1984), p. 7. Both White Mountain Vineyards and the New Hampshire Winery were covered in two articles by Cattell: "The Wineries of Northern New England," *Wine East* 18:4 (November–December 1990), pp. 16–25, 33–35; and "The Wineries of New Hampshire," *Wine East* 31:5 (January–February 2004), pp. 28–32, 54–55.

52. Jewell Towne Vineyards and Flag Hill Winery and Distillery were both profiled in Cattell's "The Wineries of New Hampshire."

53. References for this section include Jacqueline Juster, "New Jersey's Wineries," *New Jersey Business* (June 1984), pp. 33–38; James R. Williams, "Central Delaware Valley Vines and Wines: A History and Guide," *Vinifera Wine Growers Association Journal* 12:4 (Winter 1985), pp. 228–232; E. A. Bonstein, "Grape Expectations: Future Looks Rosy for N.J. Wine Making," *Asbury Park Press,* March 13, 1988; Howard G. Goldberg, "Barnstorming New Jersey's Fledgling Wineries," *New York Times,* September 9, 1987; and Roger Johnson, "Farm Winery Prospects in New Jersey," *Eastern Grape Grower and Winery News* 7:6 (December 1981–January 1982), p. 10. Of value, also, are a series of undated, stapled, background information documents on the New Jersey Wine Industry that were sometimes but not always attributed to the Garden State Winegrowers Association. They were probably printed from the late 1980s to the early 1990s and included such topics as the history of New Jersey wine, association history, and information about member wineries.

54. In 1988, in recognition of the statewide role it had played, the Hunterdon Winegrowers Association changed its name to the Garden State Winegrowers Association.

55. Another winery that existed before the Farm Winery Act was the Barry Wine Company, operated by Skip and Ted Cribari on Hemlock Lake near Conesus. The original winery, called O-Neh-Da Vineyard, was founded in 1872 by Bishop Bernard McQuaid, and from 1924 to 1968 was maintained as a sacramental winery by the Society of Divine Word. From 1968 to 1982 it was operated as the Barry Wine Company. Ownership then passed to Michael J. F. Secretan who created Eagle Crest Vineyards to sustain the operations of O-Neh-Da as a sacramental winery while producing a wide range of Finger Lakes table wines.

56. Finger Lakes Wine Cellars in Branchport was opened on July 2, 1982, by Arthur C. and Joyce H. Hunt. Following the acquisition by ITECO, they formed Hunt Country Vineyards on August 8, 1987, and opened their winery on May 30, 1988.

57. Two articles on Glenora Wine Cellars are Cattell, "Glenora Wine Cellars," *Pennsylvania Grape Letter and Wine News* 7:5 (February 1980), p. 6; and Howard G. Goldberg, "Glenora Wine Cellars: Growth in New York's Finger Lakes," *Vineyard and Winery Management* 28:2 (March–April 2002), pp. 48–58.

58. J. William Moffett, "Wagner Winery: Designing for an Extra Margin of Control," *Eastern Grape Grower and Winery News* 5:3 (June 1979), pp. 26–29.

59. See Jane Perlez, "A Wine Innovator at Finger Lakes," *New York Times,* December 11, 1985; and Richard Figiel, "The Producer of Vines and Wines: Hermann J. Wiemer," *Vineyard and Winery Management* 18:1 (January–February 1992), pp. 36–38.

60. For a history of Brotherhood Winery, see Leon D. Adams, *The Wines of America,* 2nd edition (New York, 1978), pp. 155–158.

61. Cattell, "Chautauqua County Wineries," *The Pennsylvania Grape Letter and Wine News* 8:2 (October 1980), pp. 4–5, 8.

62. See Willard B. Robinson and Robin Pulver, "Boordy Vineyard Winery," *Geneva Times,* August 17, 1973; Ruth Ellen Church, "Boordy Wines Reach N.Y., Washington States," *Sun* (Baltimore), February 15, 1973; and a background article by Philip Hiaring, "The Wines and the Vines of Boordy Vineyard," *Wines and Vines* 50:5 (May 1969), pp. 19–20.

63. The terms of the April 1, 1969, agreement were included in the "Agreement to Terminate" dated June 27, 1977. It was at this point, incidentally, that an "s" was added to the name Boordy Vineyard.

64. In a letter from J & P Wagner to all Boordy Vineyards distributors dated July 11, 1977, it was stated that "after eight years of cordial association the arrangement between Boordy Vineyards and the Seneca Foods Corporation is being dissolved.... All future production will be concentrated in the original winery at Riderwood, under the ownership and management of the original proprietors, J & P Wagner."

65. Jeffery K. Morton, "North Carolina's Viticultural History," *Vinifera Wine Growers Journal* 15:4 (Winter 1988), pp. 248–252. See also Clarence Gohdes, *Scuppernong: North Carolina's Grape and Its Wines* (Durham, North Carolina, 1982), chapter 7. A good resource is *A History of North Carolina Wine: From Scuppernong to Syrah* by Alexia Jones Helsley (Charleston, South Carolina, 2010).

66. For more on Duplin Wine Cellars, see Cattell, "Duplin Makes Wines the 'Old-Timey' Way," *Wine East* 10:3 (September–October 1982), pp. 8–11; and Lucie Taylor Morton, "Contrasts in Carolina," *Eastern Grape Grower and Winery News* 5:4 (August 1979), pp. 14–17.

67. Tim Thielke, "A New Wine Image for the South: Biltmore Estate," *Eastern Grape Grower and Winery News* 7:2 (April 1981), pp. 16–17; and Larry Walker, "Biltmore Estate: Tourist Destination," *Wines and Vines* 76:3 (March 1995), pp. 46–48.

68. The early history of grapes and wine in Ohio is well covered by Thomas Pinney in *A History of Wine in America: From the Beginnings to Prohibition* (Berkeley, 1989).

69. Susan Katherine Sifritt, "The Ohio Wine and Grape Industries" (Ph.D. dissertation, Kent State University, 1976), p. 217.

70. Leon Adams, *The Wines of America,* p. 97.

71. Richard Leahy, "Ferrante Winery & Ristorante," *Vineyard and Winery Management* 34:2 (March–April 2008), pp. 60–70.

72. See "Two Decades of Promoting Ohio Wines," *Wine East* 23:2 (July–August 1995), pp. 10–15, 35.

73. For a portrait of Gottesman and his operating methods, see Cattell, "'The Lake Erie Islands: A Future to Match the Past?" *Wine East* 9:3 (September 1981), pp. 8–12, 22; and for an account of how the Ohio Grape Industries Program legislation was passed, and Gottesman's importance to the industry, see chapter 11.

74. "Winery Profile: Conestoga Vineyards, Inc.," *Pennsylvania Grape Letter and Wine News* 6:8 (May 1979), pp. 3, 7. See also *Pennsylvania Wine: A History* by Cattell and McKee (Charleston, South Carolina, 2012).

75. "Winery Profile: Presque Isle Wine Cellars," *Pennsylvania Grape Letter and Wine News* 5:1 (September 1977), pp. 4–5.

76. "Winery Profile: Penn-Shore Vineyards," *Pennsylvania Grape Letter and Wine News* 5:6 (March 1978), p. 3. For South Mountain Winery, see "South Mountain Winery Holds Press Reception," *Pennsylvania Grape Letter and Wine News* 4:2 (October 1976), pp. 1, 3.

77. "Pequea Winery," *Eastern Grape Grower* 2:4 (August 1976), pp. 15–17. A history of the winery was given in "Pequea Valley Vineyards to be Sold," *Pennsylvania Grape Letter and Wine News* 5:8 (May 1978), pp. 1, 4–5.

78. "Winery Profile: Buckingham Valley Vineyard and Winery," *Pennsylvania Grape Letter and Wine News* 6:2 (October 1978), pp. 3–8. See also Gerald C. Forest, "Stay Small, It Pays!" *Vineyard and Winery Management* 14:6 (November–December 1988), pp. 36–39.

79. "Winery Profile: Mazza Vineyards, Inc.," *Pennsylvania Grape Letter and Wine News* 6:4 (January 1979), pp. 3, 8.

80. Donald D. Breed, "Wine: Tasting Trips That Hit Close to Home," *Providence Sunday Journal,* August 9, 1981.

81. Cattell, "The Island Where Time Stands Still," in "From Plymouth to Narragansett," *Wine East* 10:1 (May–June 1982), pp. 9–15, 20–22.

82. Several useful accounts illustrating the growth of Sakonnet Vineyards include Roger Vaughan, "Building a Vineyard in Rhode Island 'Wine Country,'" *Horticulture* 55:9 (September 1977), pp. 20–26; Cattell, "From Spinnaker White to Compass Rosé," in "From Plymouth to Narragansett," *Wine East* 10:1 (May–June 1982),

pp. 9–15, 20–22; Cattell, "Five Coastal Wineries of Southern New England," *Wine East* 21:3 (September–October 1993), pp. 10–15, 29–30; Howard G. Goldberg, "This Rooster's Got Plenty to Crow About," *Vineyard and Winery Management* 23:5 (September–October 1997), pp. 34–40; and Carolyn Horan, "After 30 Years Sakonnet is still a 'Garden Spot' and an Industry Leader," *New England Wine Gazette* 17:4 (Winter 2005), pp. 12–13.

83. "Private Labelling at Diamond Hill Vineyards," *Wine East* 21:5 (January–February 1994), pp. 13, 33.

84. See Lucie Taylor Morton, "Contrasts in Carolina," *Eastern Grape Grower and Winery News* 5:4 (August 1979), pp. 14–17; James J. Cox, "A Bit of France in South Carolina," *Wines and Vines* 62:3 (March 1981), pp. 50–51; and Betty Lee Kuhn, "Dentist in the Vineyards: Dr. James P. Truluck," *Dentalpractice* (March 1982), pp. 70–72.

85. Richard L. Leizear, "Letter to the Editor," *Vinifera Wine Growers Journal* 2:1 (Spring 1975), pp. 46–49.

86. For a comprehensive overview of this early period, see Cattell, "Surveying the Tennessee Grape and Wine Industry," *Wine East* 33:5 (January–February 2006), pp. 26–39, 58.

87. "A Winemaker in Vermont Who Uses No Grapes," *Wines and Vines* 55:2 (February 1974), pp. 54–55. A news item in the June 1977 issue of the same magazine reported the closing of the winery in late 1976.

88. See Cattell, "The Wineries of Northern New England," *Wine East* 18:4 (November–December 1990), pp. 17–25, 33–34. Interestingly, according to Harvey Finkel (personal communication to Cattell), North River Winery was given bonded winery license number 1 for Vermont. Number 1 was originally assigned to the Jedlickas' winery, but the winery had been closed for almost ten years by the time Metcalfe was ready to start. Metcalfe thought it would be neat to have number 1 for North River, and he was able to persuade the federal office in New York to pass it along to him. Because number 2 had been set aside for North River, the Joseph Cerniglia Winery, which was just a few months behind, received number 3. Number 2 was never used.

89. In addition to Cattell, "The Wineries of Northern New England," see Anne Kipp, "A Toast to Vermont: The Joseph Cerniglia Winery," *Okemo Magazine* (Summer 1987), pp. 30–33; and "Is Cider the Next Lambrusco?" *Wines and Vines* 73:4 (April 1992), pp. 27–28.

90. Archie M. Smith, Jr., "Farm Winery Legislation a Boost," *Wines and Vines* 62:3 (March 1981), pp. 4–8. S. Mason Carbaugh was Commissioner of Agriculture during this period and M. W. Jefferson in the marketing division was responsible for the lobbying support. Carbaugh was a major supporter of the grape and wine industry from 1976 when he first visited the vineyards in Middleburg. In 1977 he formed the Virginia Grape Growers Advisory Committee to study the needs of grape growers and ways to encourage the development of the grape and wine industry. On September 8, 1977, he and his marketing staff headed the first Virginia Wine Grape Conference in Middleburg. See also *A History of Virginia Wines: From Grapes to Glass* by Walker Elliott Rowe (Charleston, South Carolina, 2009).

91. Lois A. Williamson, "A Belgian's Odyssey Has Vintage Ending for Virginia Wine," *Wall Street Journal*, September 30, 1986.

92. Howard G. Goldberg, "Wine Talk," *New York Times*, August 6, 1986.

93. Laura Rydin, "From 'Garage Wine' to Celebrated Virginia Standard Bearer," *Virginia Wine Gazette* 13:1 (Winter 2008/2009), pp. 4–5, 7, 9.

94. Getting a consensus from groups with strong personalities and diverse interests was not easy. It is a credit to the industry that while there were major disagreements, they were able to come together and present a united front when it counted. In 1983, Carbaugh dissolved the Virginia Wine Grape Advisory Committee and replaced it the next year with the Virginia Wine Grape Production Board. This lasted only until the beginning of 1985 when, with industry backing, the General Assembly created the Virginia Winegrowers Advisory Board under the Department of Agriculture.

95. See *The Grape Press,* the newsletter of the Virginia Vineyards Association, 1:1 (February–March 1985) through 1:3 (June–July 1985).

96. Cattell, "Ready for a West Virginia Wine? It's Coming!" *Wine East* 9:2 (July 1981), pp. 16–19.

97. See two articles by James E. Knap: "Mountain Wineries" in *Wonderful West Virginia* 51:1 (March 1987), pp. 24–33; and "West Virginia Wineries—A Re-emergence," *American Wine Society Journal* 21:2 (Summer 1989), pp. 53–56.

98. For an account of Haraszthy's years in Wisconsin, see Brian McGinty, *Strong Wine: The Life and Legend of Agoston Haraszthy* (Stanford, California:, 1998). The story of Peter Kehl and Kehl Weinberg is related in Carol DeMasters, "Wollersheim's Wine Adventures," *Milwaukee Sentinel* (July 1, 1976).

99. See "Wisconsin's Cherry Wine Producer," *Wines and Vines* 50:4 (April 1969), p. 20. Other fruit wineries at this time are discussed in Douglas D. Sorenson, "Wisconsin's Budding Wine Scene," *Wines and Vines* 61:8 (August, 1980), pp. 38–39. Another source is Patricia Monaghan, *Wineries of Wisconsin and Minnesota* (St. Paul, Minnesota, 2008).

100. Two early accounts of Wollersheim Winery are Andrew Martin, "Third Time is the Charm of Sauk City," *Wines and Vines* 59:9 (September 1978), pp. 66–68; and Cattell, "Wollersheim, Haraszthy and the Kehl Weinberg," *Wine East* 9:1 (May 1981), pp. 6–9.

Appendix F

1. The second course for credit was held several months later at the University of California at Davis.

2. Letter from Julius Wile to Harry L. Lourie, executive vice president of the National Association of Alcoholic Beverage Importers, Inc., dated December 16, 1953. Wile, who founded Julius Wile and Sons, a New York importer, told Cattell about the course on August 2, 1997, and subsequently furnished him with copies of letters and other documents, which in combination with their discussion became the source of information for this section. See also "'Wine 125' Now a Regular Course at Cornell," *Wines and Vines* 36:4 (April 1955), p. 9.

3. Interestingly, in a letter to Wile dated July 17, 1953, Lourie stated that Legh Knowles agreed with him that no controversial matters should be dealt with in this course. Lourie did not want Charles Fournier or anyone else to start the "interminable" fight between the "bottle fermented champagne people" and the "tank champagne" people.

BIBLIOGRAPHY

This is the first bibliography to be published that is entirely devoted to the history of the wine industry of eastern North America from Prohibition to the present. For this reason, it includes not only the sources referred to in the writing of this book, but other references that readers may find useful.

Included here are many of the relevant articles and books that were found for the period from the end of Prohibition to 2000 when the amount of literature began to proliferate. After 2000, the listings have been limited for the most part to direct references made in the text. Throughout, technical and scientific material has not been included unless it has been referred to in the text. Travel articles and other printed materials with little historical information have also been omitted. Because of the importance of several authors such as Philip Wagner and Konstantin Frank, a number of indirectly related articles by them have also been included. Finally, some of the works referenced in the notes have not been included in the bibliography when they pertained to one specific point being made.

Five periodicals are particularly important for tracing the history of the eastern wine industry since Prohibition. Because all of them have undergone at least one name change, it may be helpful to identify them. They are listed here alphabetically.

American Wine Society Journal
American Wine Society Newsletter (February 1969).
Vintage 1:2 (May 1969) through 5:4 (Winter 1973). The American Wine Society discontinued using the name *Vintage* after Philip Seldon's magazine *Vintage* started publication. References to the American Wine Society's *Vintage* in the bibliography are followed by the initials AWS.
American Wine Society Journal 6:1 (Spring 1974) to the present.

Vineyard and Winery Management
Eastern Grape Grower 1:1 (February 1975) through 3:3 (June 1977).
Eastern Grape Grower and Winery News 3:4 (August 1977) through 12:1 (February–March 1986).
Vineyard and Winery Management 12:2 (May–June 1986) to the present.

The Vinifera Wine Growers Journal
The Vinifera Wine Growers Journal 1:1 (January 1974) through 18:4 (Winter 1991). [The book *Jefferson and Wine,* edited by R. de Treville Lawrence, Sr., was designated as 3:1 and 2.]

The Wine Exchange, no. 1 (January 1994) through no. 30 (April–May–June 2001). [Nos. 23 through 28 were never published.]

Wine East
Southeast Grape Letter 1:1 (January 1974) through 1:12 (December 1974).
The Pennsylvania Grape Letter 2:1 (January 1975) through 3:8 (August 1976).
The Pennsylvania Grape Letter and Wine News 4:1 (September 1976) through 8:5 (February–March 1981).
Wine East 9:1 (May 1981) through 36:2 (July–August 2008).

Wines and Vines
California Grape Grower 1:1 (July 1929) through 15:12 (December 1934).
Wines and Vines 16:1 (January 1935) to the present.

Books and Articles
Some of the articles, primarily by magazine editors, were published without a byline. Where the author is known, the article is listed under the author's name. (In the late 1970s and early 1980s when editors did most of the writing, they were no doubt reluctant to have their names published multiple times in the same issue.)
Acree, Terry E. "Flavor Technology Past and Present at Geneva" [An interview with Terry E. Acree]. *Wine East* 34:2 (July–August 2006), 12–21.
Adams, Angus, M. "Evolution of Commercial Quality Standards for Ontario Wines." In *Proceedings: Ohio Grape—Wine Short Course,* 1982, 50–53.
———. "Ontario Wine Standards: A Progress Report in the Fifth Year of the Provincial Industry's Self-regulation." *Eastern Grape Grower & Winery News* 9:4 (August–September 1983), 16–19.
———. "'Ontario Superior' Means High Quality Wine." *Wine East* 9:3 (September 1981), 14–16.
Adams, Leon D. "The Future of Winegrowing in the Southeastern States." *Vinifera Wine Growers Journal* 6:2 (Summer 1979), 60–64.
———. "Southeastern Wine Progress." *American Wine Society Journal* 20:1 (Spring 1988), 17.
———. *The Wines of America,* Boston: Houghton Mifflin, 1973.
———. *The Wines of America,* 2nd ed. New York: McGraw-Hill, 1978.
———. *The Wines of America,* 3rd ed. New York: McGraw-Hill, 1985.
Adams, Leon D., with Bridgett Novak. *The Wines of America,* 4th ed. New York: McGraw-Hill, 1990.
Adamson, Robert W. "Wine Laws of Georgia." *Vinifera Wine Growers Journal* 5:2 (Summer 1978), 66–68.
Adolph, Carolyn. "Aid to Wine Industry Means Markup Changes." *Toronto Star,* March 10, 1989.
Alatorre, Dorothy. "You Grow *Grapes* in Texas?" *American Wine Society Journal* 13:2 (Summer 1981), 52–54.
Amerine, M. A., and V. L. Singleton. *Wine: An Introduction for Americans.* Berkeley: University of California Press, 1965.
Andrew, Earl, and Rebecca Paul. "Next Door … Alabama Joins In." *Eastern Grape Grower & Winery News* 6:5 (October 1980), 17.
Archey, Robert A. "Benmarl Vineyards: The Past and Future of the Hudson River Valley and the Société Des Vignerons." *Vintage* 6:3 (August/September 1976), 54–57.
———. "Boordy Vineyards: J&P Wagner: An Eastern Partnership." *Vintage* 6:12 (May 1977), 20–25.
"Arnulf Esterer Pioneers Vinifera in Ohio." *Great Lakes Fruit Growers News.* 10:2 (July 1982). Reprinted in *Vinifera Wine Growers Journal* 10:1 (Spring 1983), 42–45.
Aspler, Tony. "Salute to an Old Soldier." *Wine Tidings* 201 (September 1999), 4.
———. "Small Niagara Winery Makes Statement with Riesling." *Toronto Star,* October 29, 1988.
———. *Tony Aspler's Vintage Canada: A Tasteful Companion to Canadian Wine.* Toronto: McGraw-Hill Ryerson, 1993.
———. *Vintage Canada,* Scarborough, Ontario: Prentice-Hall Canada, 1983.

——. *Vintage Canada: The Complete Reference to Canadian Wines,* 2nd ed. Toronto: McGraw-Hill Ryerson, 1995.

——. *The Wine Atlas of Canada.* Toronto: Random House Canada, 2006.

Atticks, Kevin M. *Discovering Lake Erie Wineries.* Baltimore, MD: Resonant, 2000.

——. *Discovering Maryland Wineries.* Baltimore, MD: Resonant, 1999.

——. *Discovering New Jersey Wineries.* Baltimore, MD: Resonant, 2000.

Aylsworth, Jenn D. "Grape Grower Bucks Tradition in Kentucky." *American Fruit Grower* 117:9 (September 1997), 25, 28.

"'Baby Duck' … Will It Be the Toast of England?" *Wines & Vines* 60:4 (April 1979), 38.

Bailey, Liberty Hyde. *Sketch of the Evolution of Our Native Fruits.* New York: Macmillan, 1898.

Bailly, David A. "Developing the French-American Crosses." *Wines & Vines* 58:4 (April 1977), 44–47.

Ballard, D. Michael. "The Hows and Whys of Festivals" [An Interview with Michael D. Ballard]. *Wine East* 20:3 (September–October 1992), 12–18, 34.

Banholzer, Carl. "Du Grand Cabernet Sauvignon des Indianas." *Vinifera Wine Growers Journal* 4:2 (Summer 1977), 332–35.

Barber, David. "Missouri Wine Country." *American Wine Society Journal* 21:3 (Fall 1989), 95–97.

——. "Virginia Wines." *American Wine Society Journal* 23:3 (Fall 1991), 87–89.

Bardenheier, Joseph A. "The Wine Bottler Today." *Wines & Vines* 32:5 (May 1951), 10.

Barr, Henry M. *Lonz of Middle Bass,* Berea, OH: Henry M. Barr, 1982.

Barrett, H. C. "The French Hybrid Grapes." *National Horticulture Magazine* 35:3 (July 1956), 132–144.

Barton, Donald W. "The Proposed Wine Research Program at Geneva." In *Proceedings of the New York State Horticultural Society,* 1964, 242–244.

Basiouny, Fouad M., and David G. Himelrick, eds. *Muscadine Grapes.* Alexandria, VA: ASHS Press, 2001.

Bates, R. P. "The Emerging Florida Wine Industry." *American Wine Society Journal* 17:2 (Summer 1985), 41–44, 54.

Bates, Terry, "Shaulis Viticulture and Eastern Viticulture." *Wine East* 34:5 (January–February 2007), 26–30.

Baxevanis, John J. *The Wine Regions of America: Geographical Reflections and Appraisals,* Stroudsburg, PA: *Vinifera Wine Growers Journal,* 1992.

Baxevanis, John J. "The Wines of Michigan." *Vinifera Wine Growers Journal* 17:3 (Fall 1990), 201–206.

Beach, William O., Jr. *Memoirs of Judge William O. Beach, Jr.* Clarksville, Tennessee: privately printed (contact Louisa Cooke, Beachaven Winery), 1992.

Beadles, Jeanie. "Kansas Vineyards Rise Again." *Vinifera Wine Growers Journal* 14:1 (Spring 1987), 33–34.

Bearer, Pamela, and Linda Fleming. "Winegrowing on a New Hampshire Island." *Wines & Vines* 60:9 (September 1979), 80.

Beiley, Paul. "Questions Unanswered in Winery's Closing." *Niagara Gazette,* May 13, 1973.

Beltrami, Edward, and Philip F. Palmedo. *The Wines of Long Island.* Mattituck, NY: Amereon House, 2000.

Berberoğlu, Hrayr. *Canadian Wines and Wineries.* Toronto: Food and Beverage Consultants, 1988.

——. *Canadian Wines and Wineries,* 7th ed. Scarborough, Ontario: Food and Beverage Consultants, 2001.

Berger, Dan. "War of Wineries—and Grapes—Echoes in New York State." *Los Angeles Times,* August 3, 1989.

Beyers, Dan. "A Taste for Change: Overshadowed Md. Wineries Struggle to be Recognized." *Washington Post,* November 23, 1995, 1, 3.

Bierbauer, Michael. "New York Trade Group Planning Special Seals." *Wine Spectator* 5:3 (May 1–15, 1980), 18.

Boggs, Robert J. "Banquet Address." In *Proceedings: Ohio Grape—Wine Short Course,* 1983, 89–92.

Borrello, Joe. *Wineries of the Great Lakes: A Guidebook.* Lapeer, MI: (Raptor Press), Spradlin & Associates, 1995.

Botwin, Michael. "The Emerging Oklahoma Wine Industry." *American Wine Society Journal* 36:3 (Fall 2004), 94–96.

——. "The Wines of New England." *American Wine Society Journal* 8:3 (Fall 1976), 40–41.

———. "A Wine Tour of South Lake Erie." *American Wine Society Journal* 12:3 (Fall 1980), 52–57.

Bowes, Paul B. "How Renault Sells 1,500,000 Bottles of Champagne a Year." *Wines & Vines* 22:11 (November 1941), 30–31.

Boyd, Gerald D. "Chateau Morrisette." *Vineyard & Winery Management* 25:5 (September–October 1999), 48–55.

———. "Ivancie of Colorado: A Winery in the Rocky Mountains." *Vintage* 4:9 (February 1975), 26–30.

———. "Knapp Vineyards Bubbles with Activity." *Vineyard & Winery Management* 21:5 (September–October 1995), 22–26.

———. "Palmer Vineyards: A Star on Long Island." *Vineyard & Winery Management* 22:5 (September–October 1996), 26–31.

Bradt, O. A. "Notes on French Hybrids in Horticultural Research Institute of Ontario Vineyards." Mimeo, n.d.

Brady, Thomas A., Jr. "Oasis: Virginia's Largest Winery Features Versatile Cement Tanks." *Vinifera Wine Growers Journal* 10:3 (Fall 1983), 182–184.

———. "Resurgence of Colorado Winegrowing." *Vinifera Wine Growers Journal* 13:2 (Summer 1986), 115–117.

———. "Texas Invests $50 Million in Vineyard and Winery Program." *Vinifera Wine Growers Journal* 10:2 (Summer 1983), 89–92.

Brailow, Alexander. "An Eastern Look at Hybrids and Vinifera." *Wines & Vines* 55:5 (May 1974), 36–37.

———. "Wine Growing in the Finger Lakes." *American Wine Society Journal* 6:1 (Spring 1974), 12–14.

———. "Untitled AWS Awards Banquet Address, November 7, 1981." *American Wine Society Journal* 13:4 (Winter 1981), 87–88.

Bramble, Linda. "Cave Spring Cellars: Style and Elegance Keep Them Ahead of the Curve." *Vineyard & Winery Management* 29:2 (March–April 2003), 60–69.

———. *Niagara's Wine Visionaries: Profiles of the Pioneering Winemakers.* Toronto: James Lorimer, 2009.

Bramble, Linda, and Shari Darling, *Discovering Ontario's Wine Country.* Toronto: Stoddart, 1992.

Breed, Donald D. "Struggling Massachusetts Winery to Close." *Vinifera Wine Growers Journal* 15:3 (Fall 1988) 196–197.

Brody, Jane E. "It's Wine Time Upstate in Search for Best." *New York Times,* October 9, 1973.

Brown, Billie. "Wine's Missionary in the Bible Belt." *Wine Spectator* 12:6 (June 30, 1987), 41.

Brown, C. L. "The Home Winemakers of New York." *Wines & Vines* 16:3 (March 1935), 16–17.

———. "The New York State Wineries." *Wines & Vines* 16:7 (July 1935), 10.

Bryson, Stephen. "Minnesota—Grape Growing Frontier." *Eastern Grape Grower & Winery News* 3:1 (February 1977), 16–17.

Burchard, Hank. "Lorelei Vineyards of Luray: A Cautionary Tale." *Vinifera Wine Growers Journal* 4:2 (Summer 1977), 336–344.

Burgess, Jeanne. "Muscadine Wines." *American Wine Society Journal* 24:1 (Spring 1992), 16–19.

Burgess, Jeanne, and Wesley Cox. "Florida's Pioneering Vineyard Experiment." *Vinifera Wine Growers Journal* 14:1 (Spring 1987), 9–12.

Butler, James L., and John J. *Indiana Wine: A History.* Bloomington: Indiana University Press, 2001.

Cahoon, Garth A. "Grapes Stage a Comeback in Southern Ohio Counties." *American Fruit Grower* 89:5 (May 1969), 17–18, 30.

———. "History of the French Hybrid Grapes in North America." In *Proceedings: Ohio Grape—Wine Short Course,* 1996, 98–113. [Reprinted in *Fruit Varieties Journal* 50:4 (1996), 202–216.]

———. "New Grape Cultivars." *HortScience* 7:3 (June 1972), 214.

———. "The Ohio Wine Industry from 1860 to the Present." *American Wine Society Journal* 16:3 (Fall 1984), 82–86, 94.

———. "Status of Vitis Vinifera in Ohio." *Vinifera Wine Growers Journal* 3:3 (Fall 1976), 216–218.

Cahoon, Garth A., and Donald A. Chandler. "Performance of Grape Cultivars and Selections at the Southern Branch of the Ohio Agricultural Research and Development Center." In *Proceedings: Ohio Grape—Wine Short Course,* 1972, 1–21.

Cahoon, Garth A., James F. Gallander, and Carolyn Amiet. "Vineyards Return to Ohio River Valley After 100 Years." *Wines & Vines* 54:2 (February 1973), 34–38.

Cahoon, Garth A., James F. Gallander, and Carolyn F. Rife. "Ohio's Re-Emerging Grape-Wine Industry." *HortScience* 7:3 (June 1972), 229–232.

Caldwell, William A. "The Vineyard's Vineyard." *Country Journal* 2:8 (September 1975), 38–42.

Campbell, Christy. *The Botanist and the Vintner: How Wine Was Saved for the World.* Chapel Hill, NC: Algonquin Books of Chapel Hill, 2005.

Campbell, Edward D. C., Jr. "Of Vines and Wines: The Culture of the Grape in Virginia." *Virginia Cavalcade* 39:3 (Winter 1990), 106–17.

The Canadian Wine Institute. *Canada-U.S. Free Trade and the Canadian Wine Industry.* May 1987 report.

Carpenter, Reigh W., ed. *Winemaster: The Dr. Konstantin Frank Story.* Amsterdam, NY: Noteworthy Company, 1983.

Carroll, Daniel E., Jr. "North Carolina State Research Program." In *Proceedings: Ohio Grape—Wine Short Course,* 1979, 47–50.

Carter, Ledford C., and Dorothy B. Vitaliano. "Indiana Wine, Past—Present—Future." *American Wine Society Journal* 7:2 (Summer 1975), 15–18.

Cashmere, Renée. "Two Vineyards and Counting: Nebraska Sees the Birth of an Industry." *Wine Business Monthly* 5:8 (July–August 1998), 35–37.

Casler, George L. "New York's Vineyard Industry." *Wines & Vines* 68:3 (March 1987), 26–28.

Catherman, Charles. "Sleepless in Sandusky." In *Proceedings: Ohio Grape—Wine Short Course,* 1995, 36–37.

Cattell, Hudson. "Archie M. Smith, Jr. Dies at 78." *Wine East* 26:4 (November–December 1998), 6–9.

———. "The Artist as Winemaker and Poet." *Wine East* 17:3 (September–October 1989), 18–23.

———. "Augusta Viticultural Area: 20 Years Old." *Wine East* 28:2 (July–August 2000), 22–28.

———. "The Benmarl Story: Mark Miller and Benmarl Vineyards." *Wine East* 34:1 (May–June 2006), 20–31, 57–58.

———. "Bill Konnerth and *Cellar Notes.*" *Wine East* 25:4 (November–December 1997), 12–19, 42–43.

———. "Biltmore Estate—the 'Most Visited' Winery." *Wine East* 21:6 (March–April 1994), 16–17, 30.

———. "Boordy Vineyards Turns 50." *Wine East* 23:1 (May–June 1995), 16–19.

———. "Celebrating Riesling with History and a Tasting." *Wine East* 29:2 (July–August 2001), 24–27.

———. "Centennial in Geneva, New York." *Wine East* 10:2 (July–August 1982), 8–13, 23.

———. "Charles Fournier Receives Adams Award." *Wine East* 9:6 (March–April 1982), 12–13, 17.

———. "Chautauqua County Wineries." *Pennsylvania Grape Letter and Wine News* 8:2 (October, 1980), 4–5, 8.

———. "A Collector's Guide to the Bully Hill Labels." *Pennsylvania Grape Letter and Wine News* 5:9 (June 1978), 4–5.

———. "Combatting Prejudice Against Local Wines." *Wine East* 16:1 (May–June 1988), 24–28.

———. "The Coming Eastern Wine Boom." *Wine East* 10:2 (July–August 1982), 20–21, 23.

———. "Coping with Adversity in the Finger Lakes." *Wine East* 12:2 (July–August 1984), 8–9.

———. "Cows Make Way for Grapes at Piedmont." *Wine Spectator* 4:10 (August 16–31, 1979), 4.

———. "Dominion Wine Cellars: A Winery Cooperative." *Wine East* 15:2 (July–August 1987), 14–17, 29–30.

———. "Duplin Makes Wines the 'Old-Timey' Way." *Wine East* 10:3 (September–October 1982), 8–11.

———. "Eastern Vinifera Today: A Status Report." *Vinifera Wine Growers Journal* 13:3 (Fall 1986), 147–149.

———. "Exploring the Wineries of North Georgia." *Wine East* 30:4 (November–December 2002), 22–31, 50.

———. "Finding the Best Market in a Tourist Area." *Wine East* 25:3 (September–October 1997), 22–24, 42–43.

———. "Five Coastal Wineries of Southern New England." *Wine East* 21:3 (September–October 1993), 10–15, 29–30.

———. "Focus on Fruit Wines at Cream Ridge Vineyards." *Wine East* 17:2 (July–August 1989), 14–17, 28–29.

———. "From Plymouth to Narragansett." *Wine East* 10:1 (May–June 1982), 9–17, 20, 22.

——. "The Fruit Wine Image in New England." *Wine East* 18:5 (January–February 1991), 18–21, 30.
——. "Garth Cahoon and Jim Gallander to Retire in Ohio." *Wine East* 19:5 (January–February 1992), 4–6.
——. "Geneva Station Turns 125." *Wine East* 35:1 (May–June 2007), 48–53.
——. "The Good Foxes of Haight Vineyard." *Wine East* 10:4 (November–December 1982), 8–11.
——. "A Governor Tours Wine Country." *Wine East* 16:2 (July–August 1988), 8–11.
——. "An Historic Eastern Wine Tasting." *Wine East* 25:1 (May–June 1997), 26–29, 38.
——. "How a Foundation Helped Uncork New York." *Wine East* 22:3 (September–October 1994), 10–15, 32.
——. "It's Now Year Fifteen on Long Island." *Wine East* 15:3 (September–October 1987), 18–23.
——. "It's Seyval Only at Clinton Vineyards." *Wine East* 10:5 (January–February 1983), 14–16, 23.
——. "It's Year Nine on Long Island." *Wine East* 9:4 (November, 1981), 16–18, 21.
——. "The Journal of the Hybridizers." *Wine East* 16:3 (September–October 1988), 14–17.
——. "The Lake Erie Islands: A Future to Match the Past?" *Wine East* 9:3 (September, 1981), 8–13, 22.
——. "Major Investments Spur Long Island Wine Growth." *Wine East* 29:3 (September–October 2001), 24–29.
——. "Marketing the Unusual at Chatham Winery." *Wine East* 21:4 (November–December 1993), 15–17.
——. "Montbray Wine Cellars." *Pennsylvania Grape Letter & Wine News* 7:4 (January, 1980), 4–5.
——. "Naming the French Hybrids." *Wine East* 35:2 (July–August 2007), 24–31, 58.
——. "The *New* Boordy Vineyards." *Wine East* 9:1 (May 1981), 10–12.
——. "New Interest in Maryland Grapes: First Maryland Grape and Wine Conference." *Wine East* 9:2 (July 1981), 14–15.
——. "A New Quality Image for Ontario Wines." *Wine East* 22:5 (January–February 1995), 4–10, 38–39.
——. "Nova Scotia: Canada's New Wine Frontier." *Wine East* 12:4 (November–December 1984), 6–10, 21–23.
——. "The Ohio Village Vineyard." *Wine East* 16:3 (September–October 1988), 24–25.
——. "Organic Farming Practiced at Four Chimneys." *Wine East* 11:2 (July–August 1983), 20–21.
——. "Organic Viticulture in New York's Finger Lakes." *Wine East* 23:3 (September–October 1995), 10–23, 34–35.
——. "Pennsylvania Wine at the Crossroads: The Present Status and Immediate Future of Wine in Pennsylvania." In *Proceedings of the Seventeenth Pennsylvania Grape Industry Conference.* University Park: Pennsylvania State University College of Agriculture, 1985, 46–54.
——. "The Pesticide Dilemma: the New York Response." *Wine East* 18:1 (May–June 1990), 12–27, 30.
——. "Philip Marshall Wagner, 1904–1996." *Wine East* 24:5 (January–February 1997), 4–6.
——. "The Pioneering Years at Brights." *Wine East* 14:2 (July–August 1986), 10–11, 26–27.
——. "The Pioneer Spirit at Markko Vineyard." *Wine East* 12:1 (May–June 1984), 8–11, 22.
——. "Planning Pays Off at Horton Vineyards." *Wine East* 25:1 (May–June 1997), 10–17.
——. "A Question of Identity." *Wine East* 18:2 (July–August 1990), 11–15, 30–31.
——. "Quality Standards Set for Canadian Fruit Wines." *Wine East* 29:3 (September–October 2001), 40–43, 58–59.
——. "Ready for a West Virginia Wine? It's Coming!" *Wine East* 9:2 (July–August 1981), 16–19.
——. "Recent Research Confirms Viking Discovery of Grapes." *Wine East* 33:6 (March–April 2006), 14–17, 53–54.
——. "Remembering Leon Adams." *Wine East* 23:4 (November–December 1995), 3–4, 37.
——. "Rocket Symbolizes Progress for the Hunts." *Wine East* 11:2 (July–August 1983), 18–19, 22–23.
——. "The Search for Wine Grapes." In "Remembering the Contributions of Philip Wagner." *American Wine Society Journal* 29:1 (Spring 1997), 12–14.
——. "70th Anniversary of Repeal—and the PLCB." *Wine East* 31:4 (November–December 2003), 14–25.
——. "State Store Change Proposal Questioned." *Wine Spectator* 6: 1&2 (April 1–30, 1981), 1, 3.
——. "The Strange Mystery of the Toxic Chicks." *Wine East* 10:2 (July–August 1982), 12–13, 23.

——. "Sugar Standards for Grapes in Ontario." *Wine East* 14:5 (January–February 1987), 24–25, 29.

——. "Surveying the Tennessee Grape and Wine Industry." *Wine East* 33:5 (January–February 2006), 26–39, 58.

——. "A Tale of Two Valleys." *Wine East* 9:2 (July 1981), 8–12, 20–22.

——. "There's More Than Seyval at Clinton Vineyards." *Wine East* 32:3 (September–October 2003), 22–25.

——. "Those Charming Nouveau Wines." *Wine East* 14:5 (January–February 1987), 8–10, 30.

——. "Try Marketing Concord and Niagara as Fruit Wines." *Wine East* 18:5 (January–February 1991), 3, 29–30.

——. "Turning Acres of Snow into Vineyards in Québec." *Wine East* 19:3 (September–October 1991), 10–17.

——. "Using Private Labels to Sell Wine." *Wine East* 15:1 (May–June 1987), 16–21, 29–30.

——. "Vinifera Wine Cellars Turns 35." *Wine East* 25:4 (November–December 1997), 9–11.

——. "Walter S. Taylor, 1931–2001." *Wine East* 29:1 (May–June 2001), 38–41, 54–55.

——. "We Take the 21st." *Pennsylvania Grape Letter and Wine News,* 5:6 (March 1978), 2. [Reprinted as "Some People Still Need Educating." *Wine Spectator* 3:7 (July 1–15, 1978), 2].

——. "When a Winery Changes Its Name." *Wine East* 11:4 (November–December 1983), 8–9.

——. "The Whys of Prohibition." *Wine East* 11:1 (May–June 1983), 10–19.

——. "Wine as Commitment at Canandaigua." *Wine East* 9:6 (March–April 1982), 8–10, 17.

——. "Wine in the Land of Delight." *Wine East* 9:5 (January 1982), 6–10, 23.

——. "A Winemaker and A Grower Win Artistic Recognition." *Wine East* 20:6 (March–April 1993), 8–9, 28–30.

——. "A Wine Oasis Springs Up in Virginia." *Wine East* 9:5 (January 1982), 12–15.

——. "Wine Promotion on the Shawangunk Wine Trail." *Wine East* 19:4 (November–December 1991), 20–24, 30.

——. "The Wineries of New Hampshire." *Wine East* 31:5 (January–February 2004), 28–32, 54–55.

——. "The Wineries of Northern New England." *Wine East* 18:4 (November–December 1990), 16–25, 33–34.

——. "The Wineries of Pennsylvania." *American Wine Society Journal* 12:1 (Spring 1980), 10–13.

——. "The Winery That a Tugboat Built." *Wine East* 10:6 (March–April 1983), 8–10.

——. "Wollersheim, Haraszthy and the Kehl Weinberg." *Wine East* 9:1 (May, 1981), 6–9.

——. "The Young Konstantin Frank." *Wine East* 13:4 (November–December 1985), 5, 21.

——. "Zeroing in on Grapevine Smuggling." *Wine East* 11:6 (March–April 1984), 6–9, 22–23.

Cattell, Hudson, and Linda Jones McKee. "Dry Table Wines for the East—The Roles of Fournier, Frank, Hostetter and Wagner." *American Wine Society Journal* 24:1 (Spring 1992), 4–7; 24:2 (Summer 1992), 41–44.

——. *Pennsylvania Wine: A History.* Charleston, SC: History Press, 2012.

Cattell, Hudson, and Lee Miller. *Wine East of the Rockies.* Lancaster, PA: L & H Photojournalism, 1982.

Cattell, Hudson, and Lee Stauffer Miller, *The Wines of the East: Native American Grapes.* Lancaster, PA: L & H Photojournalism, 1980.

——. *The Wines of the East: The Vinifera.* Lancaster, PA: L & H Photojournalism, 1979.

Cattell, Hudson, and H. Lee Stauffer. *Presenting Pennsylvania Wines.* Lancaster, PA: L & H Photojournalism, 1976.

——. *The Wines of the East: The Hybrids.* Lancaster, PA: L & H Photojournalism, 1978.

Cawley, Peter. "Popping the Cork on Connecticut Grown Wines." *Vinifera Wine Growers Journal* 6:4 (Winter 1979), 228–232.

Chapman, P. J., and E. H. Glass. *The First 100 Years of the New York State Agricultural Experiment Station at Geneva, NY.* Edited by R. E. Krauss. Geneva: New York State Agricultural Experiment Station, 1999.

"Charles Fournier to Be Lauded." *Wines & Vines* 62:11 (November 1981), 24–25.

Chien, Mark L. "An Extension Educator Looks at the East." *Wine East* 34:5 (January–February 2007), 16–25, 53–54.

Chilberg, Joe, and Bob Baber, *New York Wine Country: A Tour Guide,* Utica, NY: North Country Books, 1986.

Christian, Roger W., and Arnold H. Epstein. "High Tor Vineyard: 30 Miles from New York City." *Vintage* 1:2 (April 1971), 24–27.

Chudyk, Richard V. "Grape-Wine Research Program in Ontario." In *Proceedings: Ohio Grape—Wine Short Course,* 1978, 8–15.

Chudyk, R. V. "Quality Standards for Commercial Wine Grapes in Ontario." *Highlights of Agricultural Research in Ontario* 6:3 (September 1983), 18–20.

Church, Charles F. "Wisconsin Wineries." *Vintage* 6:2 (July 1976), 44–45, 51.

Church, Ruth Ellen. "The Concord Grape Belt." *American Wine Society Journal* 8:2 (Summer 1976), 22–25.

——. "Exciting Things Happen Along Lake Erie Shore." *Chicago Tribune,* March 25, 1976.

——. "Indiana Wineries." *Vintage* 5:10 (March 1976), 28–32.

——. "Michigan Offers Aromatic Wine Options." *Wine Spectator* 6:16 (November 16–30, 1981) 13.

——. "Michigan Wines." *Vintage* 6:2 (July 1976), 33–37.

——. "Wineries of the Midwest." *Wine World* 9:5 (July–August 1980), 20–23, 44–45.

——. *Wines of the Midwest.* Athens, OH: Swallow Press, 1982.

Clark, Marlene-Russell. "Island Politics." In *Canada's Smallest Province: A History of Prince Edward Island,* ed. Francis W. P. Bolger, 1973, 289–327.

Clendinen, Dudley. "Trend Time in the South: 'From Shine to Wine,'" *Vinifera Wine Growers Journal* 13:1 (Spring 1986), 24–26.

Clifford, William. "The Hargraves of Long Island." *Vinifera Wine Growers Journal* 13:3 (Fall 1986), 172–175.

——. "New York Wines Come of Age." *Holiday* 43:5 (May 1968), 92–98.

Colcord, F. Carlton. "Small Winery Act for Kentucky." *Vinifera Wine Growers Journal* 2:1 (Spring 1975), 34–36.

"The Cold Country's Own Hybrids." *Wines & Vines* 59:7 (July 1978), 62.

"Cold Duck: Flying Higher Than Ever." *Wines & Vines* 51:6 (June 1970), 33–34.

Collier, Carole. "Winery Focuses on Organic Method." *Wine Spectator* 6:23 (March 16–31, 1982), 7.

Collison, Linda, and Bob Russell, *Rocky Mountain Wineries: A Travel Guide to the Wayside Vineyards,* Boulder, CO: Pruett, 1994.

Conaway, James. "After the Médoc ... Maryland?" *Washington Post Magazine,* July 12, 1987, 37.

Cooke, Michael J. "The Winegrowing Heritage of the New World: A Mixture of Eastern and Western Traditions." *Wines & Vines* 57:7 (July 1976), 30–32, 34.

Cottrell, Thomas E. H. "Smooth Sailing for Long Island Vineyards." *Wines & Vines* 65:11 (November 1984), 100–103.

——. "Winemaking on Two Coasts" [An Interview with Thomas H. E. Cottrell]. *Wine East* 22:1 (May–June 1994), 12–15, 34–35.

Cox, James J. "A Bit of France in South Carolina." *Wines & Vines* 62:3 (March 1981), 50–51.

Cox, Peter W. "The Grapes Are Ready." *Maine Times,* September 12, 1975, 17–19.

Craig, D. L., and R. A. Murray. "Wine Grapes Are Flourishing in Nova Scotia." *Wines & Vines* 67:6 (June 1986), 43–44.

Crosby, Everett. *The Vintage Years: The Story of High Tor Vineyards.* New York: Harper & Row, 1973.

Crowe, Alison. "Time for Fruit Wine: Winemaking Goes Beyond Vinifera." *Vineyard & Winery Management* 32:2 (March–April 2006), 46–53.

Crowther, Ralph. "The Ontario Wine Research Program." In *Proceedings: Ohio Grape—Wine Short Course,* 1974, 21.

Curry, John. "What Is Eastern Wine's Image?" *Eastern Grape Grower & Winery News* 8:3 (June–July 1982), 24–27.

Damastra, Carolyn. "The Great Grape State." *Michigan History* 85:5 (September–October 2001), 28–35.

Darrow, Terri L. "Winegrowing in Oklahoma." *Wines & Vines* 69:10 (October 1988), 42–43.

Daraugh, Gayle, and David Daraugh. "The Georgia Wine Trail." *American Wine Society Journal* 34:4 (Winter 2002), 111–120.

Dawes, Gerry. "Heartland Blush: Wine and Religion in Southern Illinois." *Friends of Wine* 26:5 (October–November 1989), 8–14.

Dawson, Evan. *Summer in a Glass.* New York: Sterling Publishing, 2011.

Day, Robert. "Carry Nation Did More Than Just Say No." *Smithsonian* 20:1 (April 1989), 147–164.

Deam, Jenny. "Kansas Ripens for Home-Grown Wines." *Vinifera Wine Growers Journal* 12:4 (Winter 1985), 252–255. [Reprinted from the *Kansas City Star,* Monday, August 19, 1985.]

Debevc, Anthony. "Wines of the Eastern Region." *American Wine Society Journal* 16:1 (Spring 1984), 29–30.

de Blij, Harm Jan. *Wine: A Geographic Appreciation.* Totowa, NJ: Rowman & Allanheld, 1983.

DeBord, Matthew. "Don Quixote on the Hudson: Benmarl's Mark Miller Dreams Big." *Wine Spectator* 26:11 (October 31, 2000), 100–104.

de Chaunac, Adhemar. "Canada, A Winemaking Country." *American Society of Enologists: Proceedings* 3 (1952), 23–26.

Dekowski, Daniel J. "The Wineries of Maryland." *American Wine Society Journal* 11:1 (Spring 1979), 3–7.

Denby, L. "Canadian Grape Mission to Russia." *British Columbia Orchardist* 14:2 (February 1974), 20–23.

Devaux, Guy. "Life in the Champagne Trade." *Wines & Vines* 73:6 (June 1992), 59–61.

"The Development of Grape Hybrids." *Wines & Vines* 27:12 (December 1946), 37–38.

DeWolf, Thomas. *P9–15: The Lure of the Vine.* Tucson, AZ: Hats Off Books. 2003.

Dial, Roger L. "Perspectives on Winegrowing in Nova Scotia." *Vinifera Wine Growers Journal* 6:3 (Fall 1979), 155–163.

Dial, Roger, and Gale Dial. "The Historic Winemaking Tradition in Québec." *Wines & Vines* 69:6 (June 1988), 67–70.

Dial, Tom. *The Wines of New York.* Utica, NY: North Country Books, 1986.

Doolittle, James, and Carol Doolittle. "What Is New in New York State Wines." *Friends of Wine* 14:6 (November–December 1977), 8–13.

Downs, Peter. "Celebrating 50 Years of Grape-ness." *St. Catharines Standard,* September 29, 2001.

Dresser, Michael. "Vintage Boordy." *Sun* (Baltimore), October 18, 1995.

DuLac, Melanie. "Fruit Wines Are All They Make at Nashoba Valley Winery." *Vineyard & Winery Management* 15:6 (November–December 1989), 26–28.

Dunne, Donnalee. "Growing Grapes in Minnesota—A Labor of Love." *Vineyard & Winery Management* 25:5 (September–October 1998), 92–94.

Dunne, Philip. "Michigan's Emerging Vinifera Region." *Vinifera Wine Growers Journal* 12:2 (Summer 1985), 73–76.

Durgin, Ted. "Challenging Napa? Maryland and Virginia Wineries Look to the Future." *Maryland Beverage Journal,* March 2004, 34–38.

Dyson, Cathy. "'Sour Grapes' Apparent in Va. Wine Country." *Fauquier Democrat* (Warrenton, VA), August 2, 1984.

Earle, W. H. "Grape Expectations." *Baltimore Magazine* (November, 1980), 66–71.

"Eastern Wine Tasting." *Wines & Vines* 29:10 (October 1948), 18.

"Eastern Wines Featured by Wine and Food Society." *Wines & Vines* 20:6 (June 1939), 12.

Einset, John. "Experience with the French Hybrids at Geneva." In *Proceedings of the New York State Horticultural Society,* 1964, 253–255.

———. "Viticulture of Eastern North America." Unpublished manuscript, Frank A. Lee Library, Geneva, New York.

Ellis, Donna. "Vines to Wines." *Owings Mills Flier* (MD), November 5, 1987, 19–22.

Elly, Walter C. "Chateau Gay Ready to Take on New Look." *Wines & Vines* 46:6 (June 1965), 39–40.

English, Sarah Jane. "Muscadine—The Pride of East Texas." *Wines & Vines* 68:6 (June 1987), 59–61.

———. *The Wines of Texas,* 3rd ed. Austin, TX: Eakin Press, 1995.

Ensrud, Barbara. *American Vineyards.* New York: Stewart, Tabori & Chang, 1988.

———. "New York Wine: Renaissance in the Making." *Wine Times* 2:1 (January–February 1989), 26–28.

Fagan, Brian. "Exploring the Ancient History of Wine." *American Wine Society Journal* 23:2 (Summer 1991), 39–41.

Fennelly, Donald J. "New Jersey Farm Winery Bill." *Vinifera Wine Growers Journal* 8:1 (Spring 1981), 31.

Ferrel, Ron. "Time for Georgia Wine." *Mountain Life* 2:5 (September–October 2003), 14–19, 42.

Figiel, Richard. *Culture in a Glass: Reflections on the Rich Heritage of Finger Lakes Wine.* Lodi, NY: Silver Thread Books, 1995.

———. "Dr. Frank & Willy: Rootstock & Scion?" *Vineyard & Winery Management* 18:3 (May–June 1992), 35–37.

———. "German Vineyard Management Techniques Give Woodbury Vineyards an Edge." *Vineyard & Winery Management* 16: 3 (May–June 1990), 39–41.

———. "NY Governor Honors Konstantin Frank." *Eastern Grape Grower & Winery News* 5:2 (April 1979), 23–24.

———. "'The Principal Place': Long Island's East End in Bloom." *Eastern Grape Grower & Winery News* 8:4 (August–September 1982), 16–18.

———. "The Producer of Vines & Wines: Hermann J. Wiemer." *Vineyard & Winery Management* 18:1 (January–February 1992), 36–38.

———. "Trenny Jordan … Changing Hats … Looking Back and Looking Ahead." *Eastern Grape Grower & Winery News* 8:3 (June–July 1982), 18–22.

———. "Virginia's Two European Ventures." *Eastern Grape Grower & Winery News* 7:6 (December 1981/January 1982), 20–23.

Fisher, K. H. "Grape Growing in Ontario—1800–1990." Unpublished manuscript, n.d.

———. "Vinifera Quality in Ontario Grapes." *Highlights of Agricultural Research in Ontario* 4:4 (December 1981), 1–4.

Foley, Alice J. "Messages on a Bottle." *Observer* (PA), October 28, 1985.

Ford, Gene. *The French Paradox & Drinking for Health.* San Francisco: Wine Appreciation Guild, 1993.

Fournier, Charles. "Birth of a N.Y. State Pinot Chardonnay." *Wines & Vines* 42:1 (January 1961), 32.

———. "The Case for Quality." *Wines & Vines* 51:6 (June 1970), 47–48.

———. "The Glorious Wine Bits of History." *American Wine Society Journal* 10:2 (Summer 1978), 19–21.

———. "The Importance of Hybrid Grape Vines." *Wines & Vines* 28:10 (October 1947), 28.

———. "A Scientific Look at Vinifera in the East." *Wines & Vines* 42:8 (August 1961), 27–29.

———. "A Veteran Wineman's Second Look at Growing Vinifera in the Eastern United States." *Wines & Vines* 59:2 (February 1978), 30–32.

Frank, Konstantin. "Early Experiments Vinifera Wine Cellars." *Vinifera Wine Growers Journal* 6:4 (Winter 1979), 198–209.

———. "Grapes and Wine in Eastern U.S.A." Unpublished manuscript, 1967.

———. "Our Experience in the Study of Rootstock/Scion Affinities." *Eastern Grape Grower & Winery News* 4:2 (April 1978), 32–33.

———. "Outlook for European Grape Varieties East of California." *Vinifera Wine Growers Journal* 4:2 (Summer 1977), 313–323.

———. "The Phylloxera Menace in Vineyards." *American Fruit Grower* 74:5 (May 1954), 36–37.

———. "Plowing for Winter Protection, Russia: Plows Designed in the 1930's." *Vinifera Wine Growers Journal* 7:4 (Winter 1980), 233–238.

———. "Possibilities for Vinifera Grapes for Wine and Dessert Purposes in New York State." Paper presented at Cornell University Agricultural College, Ithaca, New York, January 16, 1962 (mimeo).

Frank, Stephen. "Kosher Winemaking Comes of Age." *Times Union* (Albany), October 5, 1986, G-1, G-10.

Fried, Eunice. "Bully Hill Vineyards: On Target?" *Vintage* 2:10 (March 1973), 32–37.

———. "Dr. Konstantin Frank" *Vintage* 5:12 (May 1976), 32–34, 58.

———. "Eastern Wineries: A Profile of Fourteen American Wineries." *Friends of Wine* 15:6 (November–December 1978), 36–41.

———. "Hargrave Vineyard, North Fork, Long Island, New York." *Vintage* 7:5 (October 1977), 34–39.

———. "Traveling through the Finger Lakes: New York Wineries" *Vintage* 2:11 (April, 1973), 40–45.

———. "Willy Frank Initiates New Era That Stresses Vines, Not Wines." *New York Times,* November 27, 1985.

Fuleki, Tibor. "Chemistry in Aid of Grape Breeding: The Vineland Grape Flavour Index." *Highlights of Agricultural Research in Ontario* 5:3 (September 1982), 4–6.

Gallander, James F. "Ohio's Wine Research Program." *American Wine Society Journal* 18:2 (Summer 1986), 59–60.

Gallander, James F., and J. F. Stetson. "Composition and Quality of Ohio Musts and Wines." In *Proceedings: Ohio Grape—Wine Short Course,* 1972, 22–30.

Gentile, Roger L. *Discovering Ohio Wines.* Columbus, OH: Enthea Press, 1991.

George, H. C. "Behind the Scenes . . . How Alabama's Farm Winery Law Came to Be." *Wines & Vines* 60:12 (December 1979), 37–39.

Geracimos, Ann. "Wines of the Pleasant Valley Wine Company." *Vintage* 2:5 (October 1972), 26–31.

Gervais, C. H. *The Rumrunners: A Prohibition Scrapbook.* Scarborough, Ontario: Firefly Books, 1980.

Gifford, Jim. "Champagne and the Smaller Winery." [An Interview with Jim Gifford]. *Wine East* 19:6 (March–April 1992), 8–15, 31.

———. "Vitis Vinifera in the East: Its Booming Future." *American Wine Society Journal* 15:3 (Fall 1983), 67–69.

Giordano, Frank R. "Altus, Arkansas." *Eastern Grape Grower & Winery News* 9:1 (February–March 1983), 14–16.

———. "Charles Fournier." *Eastern Grape Grower & Winery News* 8:4 (August–September 1982), 26–28.

———. *Texas Wines and Wineries.* Austin: Texas Monthly Press, 1984.

———. "Vindication of Vinifera in New York—Dr. Frank's and Fournier's Dreams Come True." *Vinifera Wine Growers Journal* 9:4 (Winter 1982), 220–223.

Giorgio, Greg. "The Dyson Goblet: Revolution in Reds Eastern Vinifera." *Vineyard & Winery Management* 15:2 (March–April 1989), 30–31.

———. "Long Island's Future: Adaptation." *Vineyard & Winery Management* 16:4 (July–August 1990), 34–36.

———. "Virginia's Largest Winery, Prince Michel Still Growing." *Vineyard & Winery Management* 16:2 (March–April 1990), 43–50.

Giuca, Linda. "Following the Lure of the Grape." *Hartford Courant,* October 14, 1992.

Given, John C. "Windows on the World: Top Wine-Selling Restaurant." *Practical Winery & Vineyard* 10:3 (September–October 1989), 13–15.

Gohdes, Clarence, *Scuppernong: North Carolina's Grape and Its Wines.* Durham, NC: Duke University Press, 1982.

Goldberg, Howard G. "Finger Lakes Vintage Time." *New York Times,* September 15, 1985.

———. "Glenora Wine Cellars: Growth in New York's Finger Lakes." *Vineyard & Winery Management* 28:2 (March–April 2002), 48–58.

———. "New York's Wineries Chart Their Move Toward Vinifera." *Vinifera Wine Growers Journal* 16:1 (Spring 1989), 16–18. [Reprinted from the *New York Times,* June 29, 1988.]

———. "This Rooster's Got Plenty to Crow About!" *Vineyard & Winery Management* 23:5 (September–October 1997), 34–40.

———. "Touring and Tasting at L.I. Wineries." *New York Times,* August 9, 1996, C1, C18–C19.

Goldfarb, Alan. "Genetic Engineering and the Grape." *Wines & Vines* 76:9 (September 1995), 16–18.

Goldman, Daniel Franko. "Winery in the Basement." *Sun* (Baltimore), May 14, 1972, 14–15, 17, 19.

Goldman, Max. "The New York State Wine Industry as it Appears to a Former Californian." *Wines & Vines* 40:5 (May 1959), 18–19.

Goldwyn, Craig. "The Restaurant That Crowns a Winery." *Wines & Vines* 62:9 (September 1981), 68–71.

Goodman, R. N. "The Missouri Wine Grape Importation Program." In *Proceedings of the Tenth Annual Midwest Regional Grape and Wine Conference,* 1995, 21–24.

Gordon, Harry. "The Wine and Grape Industry in Canada." *Wines & Vines* 24:7 (July 1943), 18–20.

Gordon, Jim. "Champions for Their Vines." *Wine Spectator* 10:24 (March 16–31, 1986), pp. 20–21.

———. "A Tale of Two Marthas." *Wine Spectator* 9:21 (March 1–15, 1985), 25.

Gordon, Ricia, ed. *Wines of New England,* Brattleboro, VT: Whetstone, 1990.

Goresline, Harry E., and Richard Wellington. "New York Champagnes." *Wines & Vines* 17:12 (December 1936), 5, 19.

———. "New York Dry Red Wines." *Wines & Vines* 17:2 (February 1936), 6–7.

——. "New York Dry White Wines." *Wines & Vines* 17:3 (March 1936), 6–7.

Graddy, Julie. "Florida's First Premium Wine Grape 'Blanc Du Bois' Now Being Planted." *Vinifera Wine Growers Journal* 14:1 (Spring 1987), 3–4.

Grant, Roberta. "Martha's Vineyard, the Island and the Vineyard." *Vintage* 6:5 (October 1976), 28–29, 52.

"Grapes Are Busting Out All Over." *Wines & Vines* 51:3 (March 1970), 26–29.

Gray, Barry, Sam Aaron, Mrs. Philip Wagner, Everett Crosby, Murray J. Rossant, Trevor Howard. "Six Voices on Wine Over New York Radio." *Wines & Vines* 46:8 (August 1965), 17–26.

Gray, Victoria P. "Quality Standards Improve Ontario Wines." *Ontario Fruit and Vegetable Grower* 34:1 (January 1984), 7–8.

Greene, Christine. "Georgia Pioneers." *Eastern Grape Grower & Winery News* 8:1 (February–March 1982), 40–41.

Groff, Vernon. "The Wineries of Pennsylvania." *American Wine Society Journal* 14:3 (Fall 1982), 36–37.

Grover, Stuart. "Ohio Wineries: Back to the Good Old Days." *Buckeye Business Journal* 2:9 (September 1979), 1, 6.

Hacsclr, Carl W. "A Brief Chronological Development of the Pennsylvania Grape Industry up to 1968." In *Proceedings of the Seventeenth Pennsylvania Grape Industry Conference.* University Park: Pennsylvania State University College of Agriculture, 1985, 41–45.

——. "Grape and Wine Production in the East—A Vibrant Industry." *Vinifera Wine Growers Journal* 18:3 (Fall 1991), 141–143.

——. *History of the Pennsylvania Grape Industry.* Xlibris Corporation, 2009.

Haeseler, Carl W., George M. Greene, III, and John O. Yocum. "Experiences and Research with Wine Grapes in Pennsylvania." In *Proceedings, Ohio Grape-Wine Short Course,* 1982, 41–43.

Hagerman, William L. "Louisiana Proposes Major Program: 10-Yr. Project Could Add New Farm Industry." *Vinifera Wine Growers Journal* 14:1 (Spring 1987), 38–48.

Hall, Jay. "Tennessee's Wine." *Commercial Appeal Mid-South Magazine,* September 9, 1979.

Hallowell, Gerald A. *Prohibition in Ontario, 1919–1923.* Ontario Historical Society Research Publication No. 2. Ottawa: Love Printing Service, 1972.

Harbich, Richard T. "Vinifera Growing on Long Island—Success in Sight of New York City." *Vinifera Wine Growers Journal* 9:4 (Winter 1982), 215–219.

Hardy, Thomas K. *Pictorial Atlas of North American Wines.* Port Melbourne, Australia: Grape Vision Pty., 1988.

Hargrave, Louisa. "A History of Wine Grapes on Long Island." *Long Island Historical Journal* 3:1 (Fall 1990), 3–16.

——. *The Vineyard: The Pleasures and Perils of Creating an American Family Winery.* New York: Viking, 2003.

Harrison, Samuel F. *History of Hermann, Missouri.* Hermann, MO: Historic Hermann, n.d.

Harrold, Marshall C. *The Ohio Winemakers: A History of the Early Days; A Tour Guide for Today.* Dayton, OH, 1976.

——. "Some Ohio Prohibition Oddities." *Wines & Vines* 70:5 (May 1989), 7.

Hartsock, John C. *Seasons of a Finger Lakes Winery.* Ithaca, NY: Cornell University Press, 2011.

Harvan, Paula J. "Garden State Reviving Wine Industry." *Wine Spectator* 6:11 (September 1–15, 1981), 7.

Hathaway, Lorri, and Sharon Kegerreis, *The History of Michigan Wines: 150 Years of Winemaking Along the Great Lakes.* Charleston, SC: History Press, 2010.

Hauschildt, Leslie. "Amana's Craftsmanship Yields Good Wine." *Wine Spectator* 7:5 (June 1–15, 1982), 16.

Havill, Eric. "The Sober Truth about a Small Farm Winery." *Blair & Ketchum's Country Journal* 11:10 (October 1984), 32–40.

Haynes, Edwin R. "45 Years in Wine." *Wine East* 11:3 (September–October 1983), 10–11, 25–26.

Heald, Eleanor, and Ray Heald. "Firelands Winery—Showcase for Ohio *Vinifera* Wines." *Practical Winery & Vineyard* 14:4 (November–December 1993), 44–46.

——. "Grape-Challenges along Lake Erie." *Practical Winery & Vineyard* 10:5 (January–February 1990), 38–41.

——. "Michigan Wines—Striving for Regional Identity." *Practical Winery & Vineyard* 12:2 (July–August 1991), 35–41.

Hedrick, U. P. "The Champagnes of Eastern America." *California Grape Grower* 15:3 (March 1934), 20.

——. *The Grapes of New York.* Albany, NY: J. B. Lyon, 1908.

——. "Native Grapes for Red Wines." *California Grape Grower* 15:1 (January 1934), 19.

——. "Native Grapes for White Wines." *California Grape Grower* 15:2 (February 1934), 20.

Hefferman, William D., and Paul Lasley. *Missouri Grape Industry: Past, Present and Future.* Extension bulletin. University of Missouri—Columbia Extension Division MP500, 1977.

Hegwood, C. P., and J. P. Overcash. "Viticulture and Enology Research in Mississippi." *Vinifera Wine Growers Journal* 5:4 (Winter 1978), 191–199.

Heible, John J. "Wisconsin's Wollersheim Wines Successful: Local Markets Absorb All Their Wines." *Vinifera Wine Growers Journal* 14:2 (Summer 1987), 81–83.

Heinricks, Geoff. *A Fool and Forty Acres.* Toronto: McClelland & Stewart, 2004.

——. *Starting a Vineyard in Prince Edward County? A Viticultural Primer for Investors and Growers.* Picton, Ontario: Prince Edward County Economic Development Office, 2001.

Heintz, William F. "Champagne by Any Other Name." *Wines & Vines* 68:12 (December, 1987), 28–33.

——. "Nicholas Longworth: The Father of U.S. Champagne?" *Wines & Vines* 65:12 (December 1984), 52–54.

Heinze, Kirk, Ellen Casey, and Douglas Brinklow. *The Michigan Grape Industry: Transition, Progress and Challenge.* Special Report No. 8, March 1983, Michigan State University Agricultural Experiment Station, East Lansing.

Helsley, Alexia Jones. *A History of North Carolina Wines: From Scuppernong to Syrah.* Charleston, SC: History Press, 2010.

Henick-Kling, Thomas. "Two Decades in Wine at Geneva" [An Interview with Thomas Henick-Kling]. *Wine East* 34:4 (November–December 2006), 20–29, 50.

Henkel, Wayne J. "Maryland Vintage 1979." *Sun* (Baltimore), November 25, 1979, 6–7, 13, 18.

Hershey, Robert D. Jr. "Virginia and Maryland Winemaking Comes of Age." *New York Times,* November 3, 1985.

Hiaring, Philip. "Arkansas Has Largest Winery in Southwest." *Wines & Vines* 54:10 (October 1973), 22–25.

——. "Baby Duck: No Babe in Canada's Sales." *Wines & Vines* 58:9 (September 1977), 22–23.

——. "California Vintners Compare Four New York Varietals with Theirs." *Wines & Vines* 46:1 (January 1965), 18–20.

——. "Canandaigua: A Success Story." *Wines & Vines* 52:9 (September 1971), 47–52.

——. "Charles Fournier: The Man of the Year." *Wines & Vines* 63:3 (March 1982), 20–24.

——. "Coke's View: Things Go Better with Wine." *Wines & Vines* 58:9 (September 1977), 40–43.

——. "The Editor Evaluates Ole Miss Wine." *Wines & Vines* 60:12 (December 1969), 33–34.

——. "The Finger Lakes Scene: Vintage 1969." *Wines & Vines* 50:11 (November 1969), 41–44.

——. "In the Land of Enchantment They're Serious about Growing Wine Grapes." *Wines & Vines* 61:5 (May 1980), 58–62.

——. "Large Scale Winegrowing in the Peach State." *Wines & Vines* 64:5 (May 1983), 46–48.

——. "Long Island … the East's New Wine Outpost." *Wines & Vines* 58:3 (March 1977), 37–41.

——. "Michigan's Vineyard: *Wines & Vines* Visits a Midwest Fruit Basket." *Wines & Vines* 53:12 (December 1972), 19–23.

——. "New York Is No Stranger to 1975 Vintage Uncertainties." *Wines & Vines* 56:10 (October 1975), 27–31.

——. "The Renault Champagne Story." *Wines & Vines* 45:6 (June 1964), 28.

——. "Research on Grapes and Wine Guides Healthy Canadian Growth." *Wines & Vines* 54:10 (October 1973), 37–40.

——. "Texas Wine: Tall in the Saddle." *Wines & Vines* 66:9 (September 1985), 24–31.

——. "These Virginians Prefer Grapes to Cotton." *Wines & Vines* 57:2 (February 1976), 35–37.

——. "Two Wineries: Small in Size, Big in Promise." *Wines & Vines* 51:3 (March 1970), 19–20.

——. "Wine Grapes a New Crop in Nova Scotia." *Wines & Vines* 68:5 (May 1987), 38–44.

——. "The Wine Picture Is Changing in Ontario." *Wines & Vines* 57:6 (June 1976), 44–48.

——. "The Wines and the Vines of Boordy Vineyard." *Wines & Vines* 50:5 (May 1969), 19–20.

——. "*Wines & Vines* Takes a Historical/Viticultural Tour of Maryland Wine Country." *Wines & Vines* 55:8 (August 1974), 24–27.

——. "Wine's Comeback Continues in Ole Miss." *Wines & Vines* 60:12 (December 1979), 35–36.

——. "Wine Tripping in Georgia: A Day's Trip." *Wines & Vines* 73:2 (February 1992), 16–18.

——. "Wisconsin's Cherry Wine Producer." *Wines & Vines* 50:4 (April 1969), 20.

Hiaring, Philip E. "Covering the Wine Route in PA's Dutch Country." *Wines & Vines* 61:3 (March 1980), 20–22.

——. "In Maryland and Virginia, Wine Pioneers are Making Progress." *Wines & Vines* 60:6 (June 1979), 70–75.

——. "Is Cider the Next Lambrusco?" *Wines & Vines* 73:4 (April 1992), 27–28.

——. "Kentucky Weighs Wine Prospects." *Wines & Vines* 57:6 (June 1976), 64.

——. "The Lake Erie Wineries Are on the Move." *Wines & Vines* 58:4 (April 1977), 16–20.

——. "New York: Finger Lakes District." *Wines & Vines* 78:2 (February 1997), 16–32.

——. "A Vinous Tour of Indiana, the Hoosier State: Wine Growing Is Reviving After 160 Years." *Wines & Vines* 57:6 (June 1976), 33–37.

——. "Virginia Wine Festival Hosts 20,000." *Wines & Vines* 80:1 (January 1999), 23–24.

——. "Winegrowing Is Reviving in the Land of Longfellow." *Wines & Vines* 57:2 (February 1976), 32–33.

Hicks, Jim. "Yellow Rosé of Texas." *American Wine Society Journal* 7:3 (Fall 1875), 37–39.

Hines, Philip R. *The Wines and Wineries of Ohio.* Franklin, OH: Chronicle, 1973.

Hinkle, Richard Paul. "Friedrich Optimistic About Future of Georgia Wine." *Wine Spectator* (September 1–15, 1983), 14.

——. "Fruit Wines Deserve More Attention." *Wine Spectator* 5:10 (August 16–31, 1980), 10.

——. "Recollections of Repeal." *Wines & Vines* 74:10 (October 1993), 16–19.

Hochstein, Mort. "Bully Hill: A New York Pioneer with a Legacy to the Industry." *Vineyard & Winery Management* 27:5 (September–October 2001) 52–60.

——. "Finger Lakes Winemaker Goes His Own Way." *Wine Spectator* 15:20 (February 28, 1991), 35–36.

——. "French Enter Venture in New York State." *Wine Spectator* 11:3 (May 1–15, 1986), 4.

——. "Individuality Abounds in West New York." *Wine Spectator* 6:22 (March 1–15, 1982), 19.

——. "An Ivy League Education in Wine." *Wine Spectator* 17:4 (May 31, 1992), 69–71.

——. "Mississippi State Founds Wine School." *Wine Spectator* 4:22 (March 1–15, 1980), 8.

——. "New York Strives for Sparkling Success." *Wine Spectator* 15:17 (December 31, 1990), pp. 79–82.

——. "New York's True Believer." *Wine Spectator* 9:22 (March 16–31, 1985), 17–18.

——. "Tom Wykoff: Doctor/Restaurateur/Vintner." *Wine Spectator* 5:23 (March 16–31, 1981), 9.

Hoerneman, Cal. "Experts Toast Michigan Wines." *Vinifera Wine Growers Journal* 9:3 (Fall 1982), 194–197. [Reprinted from the *Detroit News,* September 9, 1981, 10F.]

Holling, Thomas L. "The Making of Fine Wines." *Monitor* (Official Publication of Associated Industries of New York State, Inc.) 40:6 (December, 1953), 5–8, 15.

Hollis, David W. "Marketing Is the Key at Wagner Vineyards." *Wines & Vines* 66:11 (November 1985), 64–65.

Hopkins, D. L. "Pierce's Disease of Grapevines." *American Wine Society Journal* 8:2 (Summer 1976), 26–27.

Horan, Carolyn. "After 30 Years Sakonnet Is Still a 'Garden Spot' and an Industry Leader." *New England Wine Gazette* 17:4 (Winter 2005), 12–13.

Hostetter, George W. B. "Our Experience with French Hybrid Grapes in Canada." In *Proceedings of the New York State Horticultural Society,* Vol. 109, 1964, 244–247.

——. "Stress Can Kill Your Vineyard." *American Wine Society Journal* 13:2 (Summer 1981), 47–50.

——. "Vinifera Grape Production in Ontario." In *Proceedings of Fourth Pennsylvania Wine Conference.* University Park, PA: College of Agriculture, Pennsylvania State University, 1971, 60–62.

——. "A Wine History of Niagara-on-the-Lake." *Wine East* 17:1 (May–June 1989), 24–28.

Howard, Richard. "New York's Wines and Wineries." (Restaurateurs' Guide to American Wines, Part II), *Dining* III:6 (December 1972–January, 1973), 31–34, 38, 40, 42.

———. "Wines and Wineries of the Great Lakes." (Restaurateurs' Guide to American Wines, Part III), *Dining* IV:1 (February–March 1973), 37–40, 42, 44.

———. "The Wines and Wineries of the Ozarks." (Restaurateurs' Guide to American Wines, Part IV), *Dining* IV:2 (April–May 1973), 58, 60. 63.

Howell, Gordon S., Jr., and Stephen S. Stackhouse. "Michigan's Wine Grape Research." *Wines & Vines* 55:9 (September 1974), 45–47.

———. "Potential for Expanding Michigan's Grape Industry." In *Proceedings, Ohio Grape-Wine Short Course,* 1974, 52–54.

Howie, Millie. "Cuthills Vineyard: A Winery in Pierce, Nebraska." *Wines & Vines* 81:1 (January 2000), 112–117.

Huffsmith, Hal Harry. "A Descriptive Study of the Premium Finger Lakes Wine Industry in New York State." M.S. thesis, Cornell University, Ithaca, 1973.

Hunt, Claude William. *Booze, Boats and Billions: Smuggling Liquid Gold,* 2nd ed. Belleville, Ontario: Billa Flint, 2000.

Hunter, David. "Ohio Valley Wines." *Cincinnati Enquirer Sunday Magazine,* June 8, 1980.

Hunter, James E., and Charles R. Krueger. "A Two-State Program for the Lake Erie Grape Industry." *Cornell Focus* 2:3 (1993), 10–13.

Hutchison, John. "Connecticut's Yankees are Courting the Vine." *Wines & Vines* 61:4 (April 1980), 38–39.

———. "Justin Morris: A Good Ol' Boy Who Talks Wine." *Wines & Vines* 68:11 (November 1987), 37–38.

———. "Sacramental and Kosher Wines: An Industry Godsend in More Ways Than One." *Wines & Vines* 57:9 (September 1976), 20–24.

———. "Wine Things are Happening in Arkansas." *Wines & Vines* 60:9 (September 1979), 68–70.

Hyams, Edward. *Dionysus: A Social History of the Wine Vine.* New York: Macmillan, 1965.

Irwin, Edward E. "Tennessee Passes Small Winery Law." *Vinifera Wine Growers Journal* 6:1 (Spring 1979), 27–29.

Jackisch, Margaret. "The Rebirth of Wineries in Southwestern Ontario … " *American Wine Society Journal* 14:3 (Fall 1982), 38–39.

Jackisch, Philip F. "Hybrids: The French Connection with an American Future?" *Vintage* 6:2 (July 1976), 26–32.

———. "Tabor Hill '72." *Vintage* V:1 [AWS] (Spring 1973), 13.

———. "Wine Competitions as Indicators of Quality Trends." *American Wine Society Journal* 10:1 (Spring 1978), 7–9.

Jefferson, M. W. "Virginia Promotes Marketing." *Vinifera Wine Growers Journal* 6:3 (Fall 1979), 130–132.

———. "Virginia's Vinous Future." *Wines & Vines* 60:12 (December 1979), 33–34.

Jenkins, Sylvia M. "Canada Vineyards May Be Reborn." *Wines & Vines* 55:2 (February 1974), 41.

Johannsen, Kyle J. "The Winegrowing Industry of the Lake Erie Island Region." M.A. thesis, Bowling Green State University, Bowling Green, Ohio, 1983.

Johnson, Ann. "Boordy Wines Produced at Seneca Foods in Westfield." *Westfield Republican,* February 24, 1971.

Johnson, Dirk. "Market Decline Threatens Upstate Grape Growers." *New York Times,* August 13, 1985.

Johnson, Sandra. "It's Getting 'Grape-ier' in Illinois." *Eastern Grape Grower & Winery News* 4:5 (October 1978), 44.

Jones, Melinda Logan. "Commonwealth is Rich in Wine." *Wines & Vines* 65:6 (June 1984), 73.

Jones, Richard. "Prospecting for Wine in the Southwest." *American Wine Society Journal* 8:4 (Winter 1977), 58–59.

Johnston, Jack. "History of Maryland Wine." In *Discovering Maryland Wineries* by Kevin M. Atticks, Baltimore, MD.: Resonant, 1999, 4–9.

Jordan, T. D. "Wine Grapes in Chautauqua County and the Role of Cooperative Extension." Pamphlet. Cooperative Extension Association of Chautauqua County—Agricultural Division, April, 1969.

Juster, Jacqueline. "New Jersey's Wineries." *New Jersey Business* 30:6 (June 1984), 33–38.

Kahn, Robert P. "Review and Analysis of Grapevine Certification Standards and Procedures and Recommendations Concerning the Entry Status of Grapevine Plant Materials, Animal and Plant Health Inspection Service." U.S. Department of Agriculture, 1977.

Kegerreis, Sharon. "Trends in Eastern Dessert Wines." *Vineyard & Winery Management* 35:6 (November–December 2009), 70–73.

Kegerreis, Sharon, and Lorri Hathaway. *From the Vine: Exploring Michigan Wineries.* Ann Arbor, MI: Ann Arbor Media Group, 2007.

Kender, Walter J. "The Geneva Fruit Breeding Program and the New York State Fruit Testing Cooperative Association." *HortScience* 15:4 (August 1980), 454.

Kenny, Sue S. "From a Wine Kit to a 2000 Case Winery." *Beverage Communicator* 21 (Summer 1983), 23.

Khail, Pino. "Italians Grow and Make Wine in Virginia." *Vinifera Wine Growers Journal* 11:3 (Fall 1984), 169–173.

Kierstead, Nancy. "Volunteer Labor Brings in the Harvest." *Wine East* 26:4 (November–December 1998), 18–19.

Kimball, Keith H. "Another Look at Vinifera in the East." *Wines & Vines* 42:4 (April 1961), 63–67.

———. "Remarkable Isle St. George." *Wines & Vines* 46:4 (April 1965), 57–60.

King, Marcia. "Goals and Family Leadership Pull Chalet Debonné through Transition." *Vineyard & Winery Management* 14:2 (March–April 1988), 30–33, 36.

———. "This Ohio Winery Thrives on Increased Efficiency." *Vineyard & Winery Management* 15:1 (January–February 1989), 25–28.

Kipp, Anne. "A Toast to Vermont: The Joseph Cerniglia Winery." *Okemo Magazine* (Summer 1987), 30–33.

Klees, Emerson. *Paul Garrett: Dean of American Winemakers.* Rochester, NY: Cameo Press, 2010.

Knap, James E. "Mountain Wineries." *Wonderful West Virginia* 51:1 (March 1987), 24–33.

———. "West Virginia Wineries—A Re-emergence." *American Wine Society Journal* 21:2 (Summer 1989), 53–56.

Kobler, John. *Ardent Spirits: The Rise and Fall of Prohibition.* New York: G. P. Putnam's Sons, 1973.

Koller, James. "On the Road to Rochester: The User-Friendly Wineries of New York State." *American Wine Society Journal* 24:2 (Summer 1992), 39–40.

Krauss, R. E. "Geneva … The Name of the Game is Wine." *Wines & Vines* 52:5 (May 1971), 20–21.

Krosch, Penelope. "Grape Research in Minnesota." *Agricultural History* 62:2 (Spring 1988), 258–269.

———. "Grape Research in Minnesota." *Vinifera Wine Growers Journal* 17:4 (Winter 1990), 231–242.

Krosch, Penelope, comp. *With a Tweezers in One Hand and a Book in the Other: The Grape Breeding Work of Elmer Swenson.* Lake City: Minnesota Grape Growers Association, 2005.

Kuhn, Betty Lee. "Dentist in the Vineyards: Dr. James P. Truluck." *Dentalpractice* (March 1982), 70–72.

Kurtz, Meg. "Rocky Mountain High: Winegrowing in Colorado." *Wines & Vines* 76:11 (November 1995), 53–55.

Ladurie, Le Roy Emmanuel. *Times of Feast, Times of Famine: A History of Climate since the Year 1000.* Garden City, NY: Doubleday, 1971.

Larsen, Roger. "The Desert Sprouts Winegrapes." *Wines & Vines* 64:11 (November 1983), 112–115.

Latimer, Patricia. *Ohio Wine Country Excursions.* Cincinnati, OH: Emmis Books, 2005.

Laube, James. "Long Island Finds Its Style." *Wine Spectator* 13:15 (November 30, 1988), 24–40.

Lawrence, Robert de Treville, Sr. "Georgia's Winegrowing Quantum Jump." *Vinifera Wine Growers Journal* 10:2 (Summer 1983), 185–187.

———. "Kentucky Pioneers a Premium Wine Industry." *Vinifera Wine Growers Journal* 11:4 (Winter 1984), 257–260.

———. "'Quality': The Essence of Wine-Growing." *Vinifera Wine Growers Journal* 5:1 (Spring 1978), 24–30.

———. "Quality Wine Growing Decline in New York." *Vinifera Wine Growers Journal* 4:3 (Fall 1977), 368–371.

———. "Tennessee's Beachaven Winery Opens." *Vinifera Wine Growers Journal* 14:2 (Summer 1987), 120–121.

——. "Viniculture Program in Georgia." *Vinifera Wine Growers Journal* 2:1 (Spring 1975), 25–26.

——. "Virginia Board Funds First Four Projects: A Major Step Forward for the Industry." *Vinifera Wine Growers Journal* 13:1 (Spring 1986), 12–15.

——. "Whiskey and 'Drys' Oppose Small Winery Act in Kentucky." *Vinifera Wine Growers Journal* 3:3 (Fall 1976), 219–221.

Leahy, Richard. "Barboursville Vineyards: 25 Years of Balancing Tradition, Continuity and Innovation." *Vineyard & Winery Management* 30:2 (March–April 2004), 48–58.

——. *Beyond Jefferson's Vines: The Evolution of Quality Wine in Virginia.* New York: Sterling Publishing, 2012.

——. "Childress Vineyards: A Drive for Success and Team Spirit." *Vineyard & Winery Management* 31:2 (March–April 2005), 42–50.

——. "Colorado Wines: High Altitude, High Expectations for a Dynamic Industry." *Vineyard & Winery Management* 32:5 (September–October 2006), 56–62.

——. "Ferrante Winery & Ristorante." *Vineyard & Winery Management* 34:2 (March–April 2008), 60–70.

——. "Prince Michel and Le Ducq: Ultra-Premium Wines with a Delicate Hand." *Vineyard & Winery Management* 25:4 (July–August 1999), 48–52.

——. "Viognier Leads This Virginia Winery to Market." *Vineyard & Winery Management* 19:4 (July–August 1993), 29–33.

——. "Wölffer Estate." *Vineyard & Winery Management* 33:2 (May–June 2007), 2–12.

——. "Wollersheim Winery: Continuing Tradition with Hardy Perseverance." *Vineyard & Winery Management* 32:2 (March–April 2006), 34–44.

Leaney, Rachel. "Message in a Bottle." *Hamilton Business Report* 7:1 (September 1992), 14–23.

Lee, Hilde Gabriel, and Allan E. Lee. *Virginia Wine Country.* White Hall, VA: Betterway, 1987.

Leech, William M. "Changing Tennessee Wine Laws." *Vinifera Wine Growers Journal* 4:1 (Spring 1977), 271–273.

Leedom, William S. "Memories of Frank Schoonmaker." *Vintage* 7:2 (July 1977), 48–52.

Lehman, Eric D., and Amy Nawrocki. *A History of Connecticut Wine: Vineyard in Your Backyard.* Charleston, SC: History Press, 2011.

Leizear, Richard L. "Letter to the Editor." *Vinifera Wine Growers Journal* 2:1 (Spring 1975), 46–49.

Levin, Rob. "School with Real Taste for the Grape: Mississippi State's Enology Lab." *Vinifera Wine Growers Journal* 14:1 (Spring 1987), 17–20.

Levine, Bob. "Wine Appreciation Instruction Comes of Age." *American Wine Society Journal* 9:2 (Summer 1977), 26–27.

Lincoln, Elizabeth. "Grapes and Wine in the Nutmeg State." *American Wine Society Journal* 20:3 (Fall 1988), 84–87.

——. "Grape Breeder of the North." *American Wine Society Journal* 20:4 (Winter 1988), 115–118.

——. "Minnesota—Where Grapes Can Suffer." *American Wine Society Journal* 19:4 (Winter 1987), 110–113.

Linnett, Henry. "Wineries? In Quebec?" *Wines & Vines* 75:11 (November 1994), 65–71; 75:12 (December 1994), 34–35.

Lippman, Thomas W. "Virginia Has Some Surprising Wines—Now Looks for Markets." *Vinifera Wine Growers Journal* 9:4 (Winter 1982), 247–250. [Reprinted from the *Washington Post,* November 9, 1981.]

Loubere, Leo A. "Wineries on the Niagara Frontier." *American Wine Society Journal* 12:2 (Summer 1980), 26–29.

Loughton, Arthur, Richard V. Chudyk, and Judy A. Wanner, eds. *Celebrating a Century of Success, 1906–2006.* Vineland Station, Ontario: Horticultural Experiment Station, Vineland, University of Guelph, 2006.

Lubic, Sherry, and Bill Lubic. "Missouri Winemaking: A Grape Renaissance." *Missouri* Magazine 17:6 (Spring/Summer 1990), 4–10.

MacLean, Galo. "An Ohioan's Case for Grafted Vines." *Wines & Vines* 57:4 (April 1976), 23–24.

Mansfield, Anna Katharine. "Winemaking in Minnesota." *Wine East* 33:1 (May–June 2005), 20–29.

Mapes, Jeff. "Two Shenandoahs Get Official Nod." *Wine Spectator* 7:21 (February 1–15, 1983), 3.

Marcus, Irving H. "The Case for Mogen David." *Wines & Vines* 33:7 (July 1952), 11–12.

———. "Continuous Fermentation Comes to the U.S." *Wines & Vines* 52:3 (March 1971), 25–26.

———. "Report on a Visit to the Wineries of the Finger Lakes." *Wines & Vines* 45:12 (December 1964), 16–19.

Marks, Paul. "A Voice in Favor of De Chaunac." *Wines & Vines* 62:11 (November 1981), 32–34.

Marshall, John. "A Short History of Minnesota Grape Culture." *Vinifera Wine Growers Journal* 12:3 (Fall 1985), 157–164.

Martell, Alan R. "The Reopening of Underhill Wine Cellars." *American Wine Society Journal* 26:1 (Spring 1994), 10–12.

Martell, Alan R., and Alton Long. *The Wines and Wineries of the Hudson River Valley,* Woodstock, VT: Countryman Press, 1993.

Martin, Andrew. "Third Time Is the Charm at Sauk City." *Wines & Vines* 59:9 (September 1978), 66–68.

Martin, Bernard. "Grapes in Kansas? Really!" *Vinifera Wine Growers Journal* 11:4 (Winter 1984), 244–246.

Martin, H. Christopher. "Barboursville Enters Its Second Year." *Vinifera Wine Growers Journal* 4:3 (Fall 1977), 388–391.

Martinez, Michael. "Harvest Puts Kansas Back in Winemaking: First State Winery in a Century." *Vinifera Wine Growers Journal* 15:4 (Winter 1988), 246–247.

Martini, John H. "New Laws, Products Offer Some Encouragement for NY Growers." *Wines & Vines* 67:10 (October 1986), 95.

Marvel, Tom. "Wines of the Finger Lakes." *Gourmet* 17:10 (October 1957), 14–15, 42–48.

Matthews, Thomas. "New York Globe-Trotter." *Wine Spectator* 15:10 (September 15, 1990), 80.

———. "Ontario Wines Come in from the Cold." *Wine Spectator* 17:6 (June 30, 1992), 35–41.

———. "Virginians Enjoy Some Down-Home Wine Tasting." *Wine Spectator* 16:8 (July 31, 1991), 9.

———. "A Wine Lover's Guide to Long Island." *Wine Spectator* 16:6 (June 30, 1991), 34–45.

May, Bess Ritter. "The Bad Old Days of Prohibition." *Wines & Vines* 69:10 (October 1988), 25–27.

Mazza, Robert. "Lake Erie Quality Wine Alliance—Its Mission and Present Status." In *Proceedings, Ohio Grape-Wine Short Course,* 1994, 147–149.

McCarthy, Regina. *Maryland Wine: A Full-Bodied History.* Charleston, SC: History Press, 2012.

McCloud, Jennifer. "Chrysalis Vineyards: A Personal Odyssey" [An interview with Jennifer McCloud]. *Wine East* 33:2 (July–August 2005), 10–20.

McDonald, Peter. "The Viticulture Collection and Archive in the Cornell University Library." New York State Agricultural Experiment Station, *Station News* LXXX:14 (April 9–16, 1999), 2.

McEachern, George Ray. "The New Texas Grape Industry." *American Wine Society Journal* 17:4 (Winter 1985), 122–125.

McGovern, Patrick E., Stuart J. Fleming, and Solomon H. Katz, eds. *The Origins and Ancient History of Wine.* Luxembourg: Gordon and Breach, 1995.

McGregor, Robert. "Vinifera in the Finger Lakes." *American Wine Society Journal* 10:1 (Spring 1978), 3–6.

———. "Vinifera in the Finger Lakes—Revisited." *American Wine Society Journal* 19:3 (Fall 1987), 78–80.

McGrew, John R. "A History of American Grape Varieties Before 1900." *American Wine Society Journal* 14:1 (Spring 1982), 3–5.

———. "Interspecific Hybrid Grapes Around the World." *Eastern Grape Grower & Winery News* 8:1 (February–March, 1982), 32–35.

———. *A Review of the Origin of Interspecific Hybrid Grape Varieties,* American Wine Society Manual #10. Royal Oak, MI: American Wine Society, 1981.

———. "Sex and the Single Vine." *American Wine Society Journal* 11:2 (Summer 1979), 27–30.

———. "Wine Ratings and Grape Varieties." *American Wine Society Journal* 17:2 (Summer 1985), 47–48.

McKee, Linda Jones. "Colorado: Eastern Wines in a Western Setting." *Wine East* 13:3 (September–October 1985), 8–9, 26–27.

——. "Making and Selling Wine in Indiana." *Wine East* 21:4 (November–December 1993), 18–23, 31.

——. "Past and Present Meet in Missouri." *Wine East* 9:6 (March–April 1982), 14–17.

——. "A Touch of the Exotic in Southern Indiana." *Wine East* 10:1 (May–June 1982), 5.

——. "Tradition Meets the Future at Nashoba Valley." *Wine East* 11:2 (July–August 1983), 12–15.

——. "Where the Grapes Can Suffer." *Wine East* 10:5 (January–February 1983), 8–11.

McKee, Linda Jones, and Richard Carey. *Pennsylvania Wineries.* Mechanicsburg, PA: Stackpole Books, 2000.

McKinney, Charles O., and John E. Crosby. "Vineyards in Texas—Past and Present." *Wines & Vines* 71:6 (June 1990), 55–57.

McLeRoy, Sherrie S., and Roy E. Renfro, Jr. *Grape Man of Texas: The Life of T.V. Munson,* Austin, TX: Eakin Press, 2004.

McRory, George. "Highlights of State Wine Laws." *American Wine Society Journal* 17:1 (Spring 1985), 16–21.

Meagher, Phyllis. "The Harvest of War." *Missouri Wine Country Journal* 5:1 (Spring 1994), 33–35.

——. "The Stark Star Shines Again." *Missouri Wine Country Journal* 2:1 (Spring 1991), 28–31.

——. "Wine from a Fruitful Valley." *Missouri Wine Country Journal* 4:2 (Fall–Winter 1993), 38–39.

Medders, Howell. "Mechanized Systems Streamline Vineyard Management." *Arkansas Land and Life* 4:1 (Spring/Summer 1998), 10–12.

Meister, R. T. "Viniferas in the East?" *American Fruit Grower* 81:4 (April 1961), 33–34.

Mendall, S. C. "An Eastern View of Mechanical Picking." *Wines & Vines* 56:2 (February, 1975), 24–28.

——. "A New York Vineyardist Evaluates French Hybrids for Wine in the Empire State." *Wines & Vines* 56:9 (September 1975), 60–61.

——. "Experiences with the French Hybrids in Taylor Wine Company Vineyards." In *Proceedings of the New York State Horticultural Society,* Vol. 109, 1964, 247–252.

——. "Prospects for Vinifera in the Northeast." *Eastern Grape Grower & Winery News* 5:2 (April 1979), 14–16.

——. "The Man Who Made it Happen: 1.5–4.5 T/A: Nelson Shaulis." *Eastern Grape Grower & Winery News* 5:1 (February, 1979), 12–15.

——. "Vineyard Operations at the Taylor Wine Company." *Wines & Vines* 41:2 (February 1960), 27–29.

Mendelson, Richard. *From Demon to Darling: A Legal History of Wine in America.* Berkeley: University of California Press, 2009.

Mendelson, Richard, Timothy Josling, John Barton, and Scott Morse. "The Canadian Role in Deregulation of the Wine Trade." *Wines & Vines* 70:12 (December 1989), 36–39.

Mielzynski-Zychlinski, Peter. *The Story of Hillebrand Estates Winery.* Toronto: Key Porter Books, 2001.

Milkus, B. J. Avery, M. Schoneboom, and R. Goodman. "The Missouri Wine Grape Importation Program: A Status Report for 1995." In *Proceedings of the Eleventh Annual Midwest Regional Grape and Wine Conference,* 1996, 69–74.

Miller, Eric. *The Vintner's Apprentice.* Beverly, MA: Quarry Books, 2011.

Miller, Eric, and Lee Miller. "The Chautauqua Wine Country." *Wines & Vines* 63:3 (March 1982), 40–43.

Miller, Mark. *Wine—A Gentleman's Game: The Adventures of an Amateur Winemaker Turned Professional.* New York: Harper & Row, 1984.

Mills, Joseph, and Danielle Tarmey. *A Guide to North Carolina's Wineries,* 2nd ed. Winston-Salem, NC: John F. Blair, 2007.

Mills, Steve. "Winegrowing in the Tarheel State." *Wines & Vines* 68:11 (November 1987), 63–64.

Mitchell, James A. "Wine Is Made in the Vineyard." *Eastern Grape Grower & Winery News* 8:5 (October–November 1982), 53–56.

Moffett, J. William. "Benmarl Vineyards: Developing the Hillsides in the Hudson Valley of New York." *Eastern Grape Grower* 1:1 (February 1975), 5–7.

——. "Eastern Winery Growth: Far Short of Demand by 1985 … " *American Wine Society Journal* 13:3 (Fall 1981), 63, 65–66.

——. "Geneva." *Eastern Grape Grower & Winery News* 6:5 (October 1980), 50–54.

——. "Lake Seneca is Finger Lakes' Newest Winery Site." *Eastern Grape Grower & Winery News* 3:4 (August 1977), 16–17.

——. "Lone Star on the Rise." *Eastern Grape Grower & Winery News* 8:6 (December 1982–January 1983), 14–18.

——. "A Look at Ohio's Grape Industry." *Eastern Grape Grower* 1:6 (September–October 1975), 18–19.

——. "Martini Means Ravat." *Eastern Grape Grower & Winery News* 8:3 (June–July 1983), 18–20.

——. "A New Crop of Appellations of Origin." *Eastern Grape Grower & Winery News* 5:5 (October 1979), 14–17.

——. "New Mexico: Land of Enchanting Investment." *Eastern Grape Grower & Winery News* 9:4 (August–September 1983), 22–27.

——. "New Wines in Old Miss." *Eastern Grape Grower & Winery News* 6:5 (October 1980), 14–17.

——. "NY Lt. Gov. Tours Wine and Grape Industry to Highlight Need for Reform." *Eastern Grape Grower* 2:5 (October 1976), 14–15.

——. "Out on the Islands of Erie." *Eastern Grape Grower & Winery News* 7:5 (October–November 1981), 16–22.

——. "Pequea Winery." *Eastern Grape Grower* 2:4 (August 1976), 15–17.

——. "Tennessee: Heading for a Wine Industry?" *Eastern Grape Grower* 3:2 (April 1977), 28.

——. "Virginia Vintners!" *Eastern Grape Grower & Winery News* 4:3 (June 1978), 18–20, 68.

——. "Wagner Winery: Designing for an Extra Margin of Control." *Eastern Grape Grower & Winery News* 5:3 (June 1979), 26–29.

——. "The Wollersheim Winery: Tradition with a Modern Twist." *Eastern Grape Grower & Winery News* 3:4 (August 1977), 18–21.

Monaghan, Patricia. *Wineries of Wisconsin and Minnesota.* St. Paul: Minnesota Historical Society Press, 2008.

Moore, James N. "Breeding Grapes for Cold Hardiness and Quality." In *Proceedings: Ohio Grape—Wine Short Course,* 1985, 3–6.

Moore, Michael O. "Classification and Systematics of Eastern North American *Vitis* L. (Vitaceae) North of Mexico." *Sida* 14:3 (1991), 339–367.

Moore, R. C., and G. D. Oberle. "French-American Hybrid Grapes in Virginia." *Fruit Varieties and Horticultural Digest* 8:1 (Spring 1953), 5–8.

Moore, Robert W. "Forecasting Florida's Bright Grape Future." *Vinifera Wine Growers Journal* 14:2 (Summer 1987), 116–117.

——. "Virginia Vineyards by Counties." *Vinifera Wine Growers Journal* 12:3 (Fall 1985), 169–175.

Moquin, Gabe. "Organizing a Connecticut Wine Council." *Vinifera Wine Growers Journal* 15:1 (Spring 1988), 57–58. [Originally published in the Connecticut Grape Growers Association *Newsletter* 1:1 (Winter 1988).]

Morris, Justin. "Successful Total Vineyard Mechanization." *Vineyard & Winery Management* 31:1 (January–February 2005), 84–90.

——. "Vineyard Mechanization—A Total Systems Approach." *Wines & Vines* 85:4 (April 2004), 20–23.

Morris, Lindsay. "A 'French' Wine from Grapes Grown on the Shore." *Sun* (Baltimore), September 25, 1977.

Morris, Roger. "The Wines of Maryland and Virginia Come of Age." *Washington Star "Home Life,"* September 30, 1979.

Morse, Roger A. *Making Mead (Honey Wine).* Ithaca, NY: Wicwas Press, 1980.

Mortensen, John A. "Developing Florida's Grape Industry from the Breeder's Viewpoint." *Vinifera Wine Growers Journal* 15:3 (Fall 1998), 183–186.

Mortenson, John A. "50 Years of Florida Research." *Eastern Grape Grower & Winery News* 9:1 (February–March 1983), 26–28.

——. "Origin of the Florida 'Blanc Du Bois.'" *Vinifera Wine Growers Journal* 14:1 (Spring 1987), 5–8.

Morton, Jeffery K. "North Carolina's Viticulture History: Home of America's 1st Cultivated Vines." *Vinifera Wine Growers Journal* 15:4 (Winter 1988), 248–252.

Morton, Lucie Taylor. "Contrasts in Carolina." *Eastern Grape Grower & Winery News* 5:4 (August 1979), 14–17.

——. "Elizabeth Furness: Virginia's Wine Pioneer." *Eastern Grape Grower & Winery News* 5:5 (October 1979), 55.

——. "The European Attitude Towards French Hybrids." *Vinifera Wine Growers Journal* 1:2 (Fall 1974), 23–29.

——. "Empowering Words and Deeds." In "Remembering the Contributions of Philip Wagner." *American Wine Society Journal* 29:1 (Spring 1977), 16.

——. "Goals and Plans for the AAV (An Interview with Tony Debevc and Donniella Winchell)." *Wines & Vines* 66:11 (November 1985), 67–69.

——. "The Prospects for Texas Wine." *Wines & Vines* 61:10 (October 1980), 26–33.

——. "The Robin Hood Grapes of the South." *Eastern Grape Grower & Winery News* 5:3 (June 1979), 16–20.

——. "An Update on Virginia Viticulture: Unmistakable Signs of Progress." *Wines & Vines* 62:10 (October 1981), 47–50.

——. "The Vine of Gold." *American Wine Society Journal* 10:2 (Summer 1978), 22–25.

——. "Will the Real Maréchal Foch Please Stand Up?" *American Wine Society Journal* 16:1 (Spring 1994), 14–15, 18.

——. *Winegrowing in Eastern America: An Illustrated Guide to Viniculture East of the Rockies.* Ithaca, NY: Cornell University Press, 1985.

——. "Winemaking Renaissance in Hermann, Missouri." *Historic Preservation* (December 1984), 38–41.

Moulton, Jane. "Andrew E. Rice." *American Wine Society Journal* 24:4 (Winter 1992), 131.

——. "A Brief Long Island Wine History." *American Wine Society Journal* 27:3 (Fall 1995), 86–87, 103.

——. "Chautauqua Vineyards and Winery." *American Wine Society Journal* 26:3 (Fall 1994), 83–84.

——. "Lake Erie Viticultural Area." *American Wine Society Journal* 17:3 (Fall 1985), 81.

——. "The Wines of Ohio." *Plain Dealer Magazine* (October 18, 1981), 4–19.

Mowbray, G. Hamilton. "Loud and Short!" *American Wine Society Journal* 9:5 (Winter 1978), 71–72.

——. "So, You Want to Plant a Vineyard and Start a Winery!" In *Proceedings of the Twelfth Pennsylvania Wine Conference* 1980. University Park: College of Agriculture, Pennsylvania State University, 1980, 44–50.

Moyer, Ronald C. "Moyer Describes Ontario Marketing Board Function." *Eastern Grape Grower* 1:2 (March 1975), 6–7.

Mueller, William. "A Midwestern Wine Dynasty: Lawlor Family Operation." *Wines & Vines* 67:11 (November 1986), 53–55.

Munzell, Michael. "On a Wine Tour in the Vineyards of the Heartland." *San Francisco Sunday Examiner and Chronicle,* August 16, 1992.

Murphy, George. "Walter Taylor and Bully Hill Wine." *Democrat and Chronicle* (Rochester, NY), June 22, 1975.

Murray, Robert. "Celebrating L'Acadie in Nova Scotia." *Wine East* 32:5 (January–February 2005), 12–18, 52.

Musto, David F. "Understanding Today's Temperance Movement." [An Interview with David F. Musto]. *Wine East* 14:1 (May–June 1986), 6–11, 21–22.

Naugler, Chris, Bruce Wright, and Robert Murray. *The Tangled Vine: Winegrowing in Nova Scotia.* Bridgewater, Nova Scotia: blue frog inc., 2004.

Naylor, Dick. "Small Eastern Wineries Feel the Market Pinch." *Wines & Vines* 72:7 (July 1991), 47–48.

Nelson, Richard R. "From Whence Came the Fox." *Pennsylvania Grape Letter and Wine News* 5:2 (October 1977), 3.

"New Bottling Room in Full Operation at Taylor." *Wines & Vines* 47:3 (March 1966), 14–16.

Newman, James L. "Vines, Wines, and Regional Identity in the Finger Lakes Region." *Geographical Review* 76:3 (July 1986), 301–316.

Newton, C. F. "Picture Perfection in Connecticut." *Wine Times* 3:4 (November 1990), 22–24.

New York Department of Agriculture and Markets. *I Love New York Wine Country.* Albany, NY: 1981?

Nixon, David E. "Colorado Embarks on Vinifera Planting Program." *Wines & Vines* 55:5 (May 1974), 25.

O'Brien, Glenn O. "Maverick of the Wine Business: Walter Taylor." *New Dawn* (September 1976), 62–65, 106, 110.

O'Brien, Karen. "Vineland Winery Grows but Keeps 'Estate' Image." *Lincoln Post Express,* July 22, 1987.

Ochs, Missy Brown. "Wines from the Wilderness." *American Wine Society Journal* 20:2 (Summer 1988), 53–55.

O'Neil, Theresa. "Virginia's Pre-eminent Vineyard: Prince Michel." *Vinifera Wine Growers Journal* 13:1 (Spring 1986), 30–33.

Ontario Grape Growers' Marketing Board. *Enterprise: The First 50 Years of the Ontario Grape Growers' Marketing Board, 1947–1997.* Vineland Station: Ontario Grape Growers' Marketing Board, 1997.

Ontario Wine and Grape Industry Task Force Report, May 12, 1986.

Ontario Wine Standards Committee Report, July 6, 1934.

Ordish, George. *The Great Wine Blight.* New York: Charles Scribner's Sons, 1972.

Overfelt, Robert C. "The Val Verde Winery: Its Role in Texas Viticulture and Enology." Southwestern Studies, Monograph No. 75, Texas Western Press, El Paso, 1985.

Owens, Christopher L. "Grapes." In James F. Hancock, ed. *Temperate Fruit Crop Breeding: Germplasm to Genomics,* 197–233. New York: Springer, 2008.

Palmedo, Philip F., and Edward J. Beltrami, *The Wines of Long Island: Birth of a Region.* Great Falls, VA: Waterline Books, 1993.

Palmer, E. F. *Horticultural Experiment Station and Products Laboratory: The First Fifty Years, 1906 to 1956.* Ontario Department of Agriculture, n.d.

Palmer, Jon. *Wineries of the Mid-Atlantic.* New Brunswick, NJ: Rutgers University Press, 1988.

Partridge, Jack. "Charting the Unexplored Territory of Fruit Wine." *Eastern Grape Grower & Winery News* 9:1 (February–March, 1983), 24–25.

——. *A Partridge in a Pear Sauce.* Concord, MA: Nashoba Valley Winery, 1982.

——. "The Unique Fruit Wines of the Northeast." In *Proceedings of the Eighteenth Pennsylvania Grape Industry Conference.* University Park: College of Agriculture, Pennsylvania State University, 1986, 9–13.

Patterson, J. T. "Wine Grapes in Texas." *Wines & Vines* 19:1 (January 1938), 14–15.

Peck, Ronald L. "Winegrowing in Missouri: the 'Show Me State.'" *Wines & Vines* 56:5 (May 1975), 26–28.

Pée-Laby, E. *La Vigne Nouvelle: Les Hybrides Producteurs,* 3rd rev. ed. Paris: Librairie J.-B. Baillière et Fils, 1929.

Pellechia, Thomas. "Teamwork for Success in New York." *Practical Winery & Vineyard* 12:1 (May–June 1991), 43–45.

Peller, Andrew. *The Winemaker: The Autobiography of Andrew Peller, Founder of Andrés Wines, Ltd.* Toronto: Alfin Publishers, Ltd. for Andrés Wines, Ltd. 1982.

Peradotto, Louis B. "N.Y. Wineries Now Require Licenses." *Wines & Vines* 26:9 (September 1945), 35.

Perdue, Lewis. *The French Paradox and Beyond.* Sonoma, CA: Renaissance, 1992.

Petuskey, Thomas J. "Wine in the Garden State." *American Wine Society Journal* 19:2 (Summer 1987), 39–41.

Phillips, E. S. "The Grape Industry in Virginia." In *Proceedings, Ohio Grape-Wine Short Course,* 1980, 4–7.

——. "Flip." ed. *Ithaca Oenological Union.* Ithaca, New York, 1990.

——. "New York State Wineries." *American Wine Society Journal* 11:3 (Fall 1979), 39–42.

——. "I Remember—Dr. Frank." *Eastern Grape Grower & Winery News* 11:5 (October–November 1985), 16.

——. "Niagara Falls Wine Cellar." *Vintage* V:1 [AWS] (Spring 1973), 3–4.

——. "A Tour of Midwest Wineries: Taber [*sic*] Hill—Michigan." *Vintage* III:3 [AWS] (Summer 1971), 6–7.

Phillips, Rod. *Ontario Wine Country.* North Vancouver, B.C.: Whitecap Books, 2006.

Pierce, C. Joseph, II. "Fourth Annual New York State Wine Barrel Dinner." *American Wine Society Journal* 15:2 (Summer 1983), 50–51.

Pierquet, Patrick. "Breeding Cold Hardy Grapes in Minnesota." *Eastern Grape Grower & Winery News* 6:2 (April 1980), 29.

——. "Grape Growing in Minnesota." *Vinifera Wine Growers Journal* 4:4 (Winter 1977), 435–440.

Pilla, Jen. "Why Does Florida Have Lots of Grapes but Few Wineries?" *Wall Street Journal,* October 18, 1995.

Pinney, Thomas. *A History of Wine in America From the Beginnings to Prohibition.* Berkeley: University of California Press, 1989.

——. *A History of Wine in America From Prohibition to the Present.* Berkeley: University of California Press, 2005.

——. *The Makers of American Wine: A Record of Two Hundred Years.* Berkeley: University of California Press, 2012.

Plane, Robert A., and Mary M. "A Scholar Talks to A.S.E.-East." *Wines & Vines* 60:2 (February 1979), 44–46.

Poletti, Peter Joseph, Jr. "An Interdisciplinary Study of the Missouri Grape and Wine Industry, 1650 to 1989." Ph.D. dissertation, Saint Louis University, 1989.

Pompilio, Ray. "Home Grown in the 'Show Me' State: Three Families Grow into the New Millenium." *Vineyard & Winery Management* 25:3 (May–June 1999), 47–54.

Porchon-Lynch, Tao. "Chateau Elan." *Beverage Communicator* 36 (Spring 1987), 14–15.

Prévost, Robert, Suzanne Gagné, and Michel Phaneuf. *L'Histoire de l'alcool au Québec.* Montréal: Société des alcools du Québec: Editions internationals Alain Stanké, 1986.

Prial, Frank J. "For the 'First Black Winery in the U.S.' 1973 Was NOT a Good Year." *New York Times,* November 16, 1973.

——. "The Game of the Name." *New York Times,* June 25, 1978.

——. "Lakes' Success." *New York Times Magazine* (May 2, 1992), 56.

——. "On the North Fork, Dreams of Napa." *New York Times,* July 26, 2000, 1, 6.

——. "Raising the Stakes for New York Wine." *New York Times,* December 4, 1991.

——. "Wine Talk: A Farewell to the Baron of Bully Hill." *New York Times,* May 2, 2001.

——. "Wine Talk: New York Wines Come of Age." *New York Times,* September 5, 1979.

Puckett, Carlotta, Carl C. Hilscher, and Steven Reeder. "Operating a New Winery Cooperative." *Vinifera Wine Growers Journal* 13:4 (Winter 1986), 252–259.

Rainforth, Jim. "The Ontario Grape Growers' Marketing Board Turns 50" [An Interview with Jim Rainforth]. *Wine East* 25:3 (September–October 1997), 14–21, 43.

Ramey, Bern C. "A Long Way from the Island of Madeira, Ohio Version Has 25,000-Case Goal." *Wines & Vines* 66:4 (April 1985), 28–31.

Rannie, William F. *Canadian Whiskey: The Product and the Industry.* Lincoln, Ontario: W. F. Rannie, 1976.

——. "From Days Gone By." *Canadian Wine & Cheese* (November–December 1985), 11, 13.

——. *Wines of Ontario: An Industry Comes of Age.* Lincoln, Ontario: W. F. Rannie, 1978.

Ray, Pamela. "Wineries of New Mexico." *Eastern Grape Grower & Winery News* 11:6 (December 1985–January 1986), 12–14; 12:1 (February–March 1986), 27–28, 38; *Vineyard & Winery Management* 12:2 (May–June 1986), 39–41.

Razee, Don. "Virginia Is Wine Country." *Wines & Vines* 65:6 (June 1984), 88–89.

Read, Paul E. "Viticulture and Enology in Nebraska." *Wine East* 33:3 (September–October 2005), 20–26, 54.

Read, Roy. "The Wine-Making Revolution Keeps Growing and Growing." *New York Times,* October 5, 1975.

Reisch, Bruce I., and Charlotte Pratt. "Grapes." In *Fruit Breeding,* Volume II: *Vine and Small Fruits Crops,* ed. Jules Janick and James N. Moore. New York: John Wiley & Sons, Inc. 1996, 297–369.

Reisch, Bruce I., Robert N. Goodman, Mary-Howell Martens, and Norman F. Weeden. "The Relationship between Norton and Cynthiana, Red Wine Cultivars Derived from *Vitis aestivalis.*" *American Journal of Enology and Viticulture* 44:4 (1993), 441–444.

Reissig, Harvey. "Old World Traditions: New Owner Follows Wiemer's Techniques." *Finger Lakes Times* (Sunday Taste), December 28, 2008.

Rexroad, William D. "Winegrowing in Kansas." *Wines & Vines* 57:6 (June 1976), 53–54.

Reynolds, Phil. "Lone Star Vino." *Wine Spectator* (October 16–31, 1984), 22–23.

Rice, Andrew C. "Gestation, Birth, and Development of the ASEV/Eastern Section." *1989–90 News Edition and Directory,* American Society for Enology and Viticulture, 15–23.

———. "The Small Winery at Taylor's." In *Proceedings of the Eighteenth Pennsylvania Grape Industry Conference.* University Park: College of Agriculture, Pennsylvania State University, 1986, 18–20.

Ringle, Ken. "Financier Joins Growing Virginia Wine Industry." *Washington Post,* September 27, 1976.

Rink, Jim. "Chateau Chantal: Room with a View." *American Wine Society Journal* 25:2 (Summer 1993), 48–49.

———. "Field of Dreams in Leelanau County." *American Wine Society Journal* 22:3 (Fall 1990), 99–100.

———. "Forks of Cheat—A West Virginia Winery." *American Wine Society Journal* 27:2 (Summer 1995), 64–65.

———. "Gentleman Farmer in Virginia." *American Wine Society Journal* 27:1 (Spring 1995), 26–27.

———. "Jacques Recht: 2007 AWS Award of Merit." *American Wine Society Journal* 39:4 (Winter 2007/8), 18–19.

———. "The Michigan State Man." *American Wine Society Journal* 35:1 (Spring 2003), 11–14.

Rizza, Robert G. "Kansas After Carry: A New Wine Industry in the Wheat State." *Vinifera Wine Growers Journal* 16:3 (Fall 1989), 161–164.

———. "Reviving the Kansas Wine Industry: A Model for Other States." *Vinifera Wine Growers Journal* 16:4 (Winter 1989), 267–268.

Robards, Terry. "Bleak Times for New York." *Wine Spectator* 10:24 (March 16–31, 1986), 12–13, 22–23.

———. "N.Y. Wineries on the Ropes." *Wine Spectator* (May 16–31, 1984), 22–23, 27.

Robinson, Jancis. *Jancis Robinson's Guide to Wine Grapes.* Oxford and New York: Oxford University Press, 1996.

———. *Vines, Grapes and Wines,* New York: Alfred A. Knopf, 1986.

Robinson, Jancis, Julia Harding, and José Vouillamoz, *Wine Grapes.* New York: ecco, 2012.

Robinson, Williard B. "Wine Research at Geneva Related to Trends in the N.Y. Wine Industry." In *Proceedings of the New York State Horticultural Society,* Vol. 126, 1981, 91–94.

Robinson, Williard B., and Robin Pulver. "Boordy Vineyard Winery." *Geneva Times,* August 17, 1973.

Rogan, Felicia Warburg. "The Emergence of Viticulture in Virginia." *American Wine Society Journal* 13:4 (Winter 1981), 96–99.

———. *Virginia Wines: A Vineyard Year.* Charlottesville, VA: Thomasson-Grant, 1987.

Rogov, Daniel. "The Long Winding Road to World-Class Wine." *Reform Judaism Magazine Online* (Spring 2007), 1–8. http://www.reformjudaismmag.org.

Rosengarten, David. "New England's New Vines." *Wine Spectator* 11:19 (February 15, 1987), 26.

Roth, Roman. "The Wines of Wölffer and Roth" [An Interview with Roman Roth]. *Wine East* 35:1 (May–June 2007), 24–35, 58–59.

Roueché, Berton. "Vinifera Growing on Long Island." *Vinifera Wine Growers Journal* 4:3 (Fall 1977), 400–407. [Originally appeared in the *New Yorker,* 1976.]

Rowe, Percy. *Red, White and Rosé.* Don Mills, Ontario: Musson Book Co. General Publishing, 1978.

———. *The Wines of Canada.* Toronto: McGraw-Hill Company of Canada, 1970.

Rowe, Walker E. *A History of Virginia Wines: From Grapes to Glass.* Charleston, SC: History Press, 2009.

———. *Wandering through Virginia's Vineyards.* Baltimore: Apprentice House, 2006.

Rydin, Laura. "From 'Garage Wine' to Celebrated Virginia Standard Bearer." *Virginia Wine Gazette* 13:1 (Winter 2008–2009), 4–5, 7, 9.

Sagle, Robert F., and Robert G. Kalik. "Trade Bill Can Help U.S. Wines in Canada." *Wines & Vines* 69:9 (September 1988), 42–45.

Sands, Marvin. "Current Trends in U.S. Wine Consumption and Marketing Outlook for Eastern Grapes and Wines." In *Proceedings of the New York State Horticultural Society,* Vol. 124, 1979, 128–130.

Sands, Richard, and Rob Sands with Paul Chutkow. *Reaching for the Stars: The Making of Constellation Brands.* Napa, CA: Val de Grâce Books, 2008.

Satterwhite, Bob. "Biltmore Winery's Goal: Quality European Style Wines." *Vinifera Wine Growers Journal* 12:2 (Summer 1985), 85–89.

Schandall, Wallace. "Modern Long Island Wines." *American Wine Society Journal* 27:3 (Fall 1995), 83–85.

Scheef, Robert F. *Vintage Missouri: A Guide to Missouri Wineries.* St. Louis: Patrice Press, 1991.

Schick, Robert. "The Arkansas Wine Industry." *Wine Review* 14 (June 1946), 8–12, 18.

Schmidt, Lloyd F. "Realizing the Prince Edward County Dream." *Wine East* 30:4 (November–December 2002), 10–13, 50.

Schoenwald, Irving. "Present Status of Arkansas' Wine Industry." *Wines & Vines* 22:10 (October 1941), 27.

Schoonmaker, Frank. "The Case Is Presented for Varietal Names." *Wines & Vines* 21:11 (November 1940), 8–9.

Schoonmaker, Frank, and Tom Marvel. *American Wines.* New York: Duell, Sloan and Pearce, 1941.

——. *The Complete Wine Book.* New York: Simon and Schuster, 1934.

Schreiner, John. *Icewine: The Complete Story.* Toronto: Warwick, 2001.

——. *The Wines of Canada.* North Vancouver, B.C.: Whitecap Books, 2006.

——. *The World of Canadian Wine.* Vancouver, B.C.: Douglas & McIntyre, 1984.

Schroeder, C. Frederic. "The Finger Lakes Wineries: 'We Offer a Choice,'" *Wines & Vines* 57:9 (September 1976), 63–64.

Schueneman, Thomas J. "The Grape in Kansas—Poised for a Winegrowing Comeback?" *Vinifera Wine Growers Journal* 9:4 (Winter 1982), 225–230.

Schwartz, Elizabeth. "Boordy Makes Good (on) Nouveau!" *Vineyard & Winery Management* 12:2 (May–June 1986), 14–17.

Scoblionkov, Deborah. "The Tiffany Touch." *Wine Spectator* 17:15 (November 30, 1992), 57–59.

Scott, Dan. "Turning the Corner in New Mexico." *Wines & Vines* 69:10 (October 1988), 38–39.

Shaulis, Nelson J. "New York Viticulture: Past and Present" [An Interview with Nelson J. Shaulis]. *Wine East* 22:6 (March–April 1995), 8–15, 37–38.

——. "Reflections on New York Viticulture." *Eastern Grape Grower & Winery News* 5:1 (February 1979), 18–20.

Shaulis, Nelson J., E. S. Shepardson, and T. D. Jordan. *The Geneva Double Curtain for Vigorous Grapevines,* Bulletin 811, New York State Agricultural Experiment Station, Geneva, July 1967.

Shaulis, Nelson J., E. S. Shepardson and J. C. Moyer. "Grape Harvesting Research at Cornell." In *Proceedings of the New York State Horticultural Society,* Vol. 105, 1960, 250–254.

Shaw, Robert D. Jr. "The Grapes of Hope." *Vinifera Wine Growers Journal* 1:1 (Spring 1974), 13–14.

Sherer, Richard G. *Crooked Lake and the Grape.* Virginia Beach, VA: Donning, 1998.

Sheron, Georgia. "Making Wine History in Litchfield." *Connecticut Beverage Journal* (November, 1987), 43–44.

Shulman, Eli. "The Wine Zealot of York County." *American Wine Society Journal* 25:4 (Winter 1993), 128–129.

Sifritt, Susan Katherine. "The Ohio Wine and Wine Grape Industries." Ph.D. dissertation, Kent State University, Kent, Ohio, 1976.

Simpson, Jerry H. Jr. "Duplin Wine Cellars: Civilizing the Southeast." *Vintage* 8:2 (December 1978), 26–27, 48.

Slate, George L., John Watson, and John Einset, *Grape Varieties Introduced by the New York State Agricultural Experiment Station, 1928–1961,* Bulletin 794, New York State Agricultural Experiment Station, Geneva, 1962.

Smiley, Lisa Ann. "A Review of Cold Climate Grape Cultivars." M.Ag. thesis, Iowa State University, Ames, Iowa, 2008.

Smith, Archie M., Jr. "Farm Winery Legislation a Boost." *Wines & Vines* 62:3 (March 1981), 4–8.

——. "Northern Virginia's Own Winery." *Northern Virginian* (April 1976), 18–19.

——. "On the Scene in Virginia." *American Wine Society Journal* 9:2 (Summer 1977), 24–25.

Smith, Gilbert. "Seaton Mendall: Taylor's Man in the Vineyards for 36 Years." *Eastern Grape Grower & Winery News* 5:2 (April 1979), 36–38.

Smith, Kari R. "Grapes of Wrath." *New York Archives* 6:1 (Summer 2006), 6–7.

Snell, Mary. "Raise Your Goblet to Fruit Wines." *The Original Maine Dining Guide,* 1986, 52–54.

Sonneman, Henry O. "Ohio State Wines: Their History and Production." *American Society of Enologists: Proceedings* 3 (1952), 17–22.

——. "The 'Specialty' Wines." *Wines & Vines* 32:5 (May 1951), 9.

Sorenson, Douglas D. "Wisconsin's Budding Wine Scene." *Wines & Vines* 61:8 (August 1980), 38–39.

Sparer, Dot. "What's Ahead for Georgia Vineyards." *Wines & Vines* 66:6 (June 1985), 83–85.

Spieler, Gerhard. "400 Years of South Carolina Wines." *Vinifera Wine Growers Journal* 11:3 (Fall 1984), 176–181.

Stary, Denise. "First Celebration in 1952 Featured Parade and Evening Dance." *Vintage Niagara* 2:3 (September 1981), 5, 8–14.

Steidman, Ben. "Managing Skill and Pride at Vineland Estates Wines." *Canadian Fruit Grower* 45:5 (May 1989), 3.

Stewart, Charles V. "Changing Wine Laws: The North Carolina Experience." *Vintage* 10:12 (October 1981), 24–27.

Stewart, Tod. "The Future of Prince Edward County." *Wine Tidings* 233 (September 2003), 18–21.

Stoewsand, G. S., and W. B. Robinson. "Malnutrition: Cause of 'Toxic' Response of Chicks Fed Varietal Grape Juices." *American Journal of Enology and Viticulture* 23:2 (1972), 54–57.

———. "Review of Grape and Wine Toxicity Research." *New York's Food and Life Sciences Bulletin,* No. 6, January, 1971, New York State Agricultural Experiment Station, Geneva, New York.

Stojanovic, Boris J. "Mississippi's Distinguished Wine History—The East's Enology Teaching Center." *Vinifera Wine Growers Journal* 11:2 (Summer 1984), 116–123.

Stone, Dee. "Georgia On My Mind … and in My Cellar." *Arbor Magazine* (Summer 1983), 20–22.

Stuart, Greenway. "Station Scientists Test Wine's Effect on Chicks." *Geneva Times,* February 4, 1971.

Stuart, Leonard. "Winegrowing in New Mexico." *Wines & Vines* 61:5 (May 1980), 30–31.

Subden, Ronald E. "The Odyssey of De Chaunac (Seibel 9549)." *American Wine Society Journal* 12:4 (Winter 1980), 80–84.

Subden, R. E., and A. C. Noble. "How the Hybrids Came to Canada." *Wines & Vines* 59:12 (December 1978), 42, 44.

Sullivan, Charles L. *The Society of Wine Educators: A History of Its Inception and the First 10 Years,* Princeton, NJ: Bob Levine, 2000.

Sun, Marjorie. "Mitchell Vineyard: Where Science and Wine Combine." *Morning Herald* (Durham, NC), September 19, 1976.

Swarthout, Joseph L. "The New York Wine Industry: Continued Prosperity." *Wines & Vines* 56:9 (September 1975), 62–65.

Swenson, Elmer. "An Interview with Elmer Swenson" [A 1982 Interview with Elmer Swenson]. *Wine East* 32:6 (March–April 2005), 25–31.

Tadevich, D. L. *Wineries of Indiana: A Guide to the Wineries and Vineyards of Indiana.* Carmel, IN: Publishing Plus, 2001.

Takahashi, J. Kenichi. "Vinifera Thriving on Long Island." *Wine Spectator* 5:9 (August 1–15, 1980), 2.

Taylor, Greyton H. "Eastern Wine Production and Distribution." *Wines & Vines* 32:5 (May 1951), 8.

———. "New York Wines: Their Place in the U.S. Market." *Wines & Vines* 35:11 (November 1954), 29–30.

Taylor, Michael. "Making Wine—and Having Fun Too—in Maine." *Wines & Vines* 69:4 (April 1988), 39–40.

Taylor, Roy W. "Missouri's Wine Scene: The 'Show-Me' State Is Looking Good." *Wines & Vines* 66:6 (June 1985), 74–80.

Teiser, Ruth, and Catherine Harroun. "The Volstead Act, Rebirth, and Boom." In *The University of California/Sotheby Book of California Wine,* ed. Doris Muscatine, Maynard A. Amerine, and Bob Thompson. Berkeley: University of California Press and London: Sotheby Publications, 1984.

Temple, Robert. "New England Tradition Being Revived at Nashoba Valley." *Massachusetts Beverage Journal* (December 1981), 74–75.

Tew, James E. "Honey—The Basic Requirement for Mead." In *Proceedings, Ohio Grape-Wine Short Course,* 1986, 33–34.

Thielke, Tim. "A New Image for the South: Biltmore Estate." *Eastern Grape Grower & Winery News* 7:2 (April, 1981), 16–17.

———. "Vinifera Success in Asheville." *Vinifera Wine Growers Journal* 7:2 (Summer 1980), 110–111.

"This Is the U.S. Wine Industry." *Wines & Vines* 34:11 (November 1953), 39–53.

Thomas, Marguerite. *Wineries of the Eastern States.* Lee, MA: Berkshire House Publishers, 1996.

——. *Wineries of the Eastern States,* 3rd ed. Lee, MA: Berkshire House Publishers, 1999.

"Thriving New England Wineries Facing a Bright Future." *Rhode Island Beverage Journal* (July 1981), 10–14.

Tiessen, Ron. *The Vinedressers: A History of Grape Farming & Wineries on Pelee Island.* Ontario: Pelee Island Heritage Centre, 1996.

Tracy, Dan. "Florida Wines Finding Place in Sun." *Vinifera Wine Growers Journal* 11:2 (Summer 1984), 98–99.

Treble, James R. "A Tour of Midwest Wineries" (Mount Pleasant), *Vintage* III:2 [AWS] (Spring 1971), 12.

——. "A Tour of Midwest Wineries—Stoltz Vineyards." *Vintage* III:1 [AWS] (Winter 1971), 9.

Trezise, James. "The Importance of Viticulture to the Winemaker ... and the Consumer." *American Wine Society Journal* 15:1 (Spring 1983), 23–25.

U.S. Bureau of Alcohol, Tobacco and Firearms. "Public Hearing in the Matter of: American Viticultural Area Designations 'Augusta.'" Transcript, Augusta, Missouri, November 1, 1979.

Valchuis, Robert F., and Diane L. Henault. *The Wines of New England.* Boston: Wine Institute of New England, 1980.

Van Dyne, Ed. "The American Wine Society Twenty Years Old." *American Wine Society Journal* 19:3 (Fall 1987), 71–74.

——. "Arizona's Embryonic Wine Industry: A Dark Horse?." *American Wine Society Journal* 15:2 (Summer 1983), 47–48.

——. "Bill Moffett & Enterprises." *American Wine Society Journal* 13:3 (Fall 1981), 67.

——. "Changes at Geneva." *American Wine Society Journal* 14:3 (Fall 1982), 40–41.

——. "Dr. Konstantin Frank: A Retrospective." *American Wine Society Journal* 17:3 (Fall 1985), 67–71.

——. "Philip Wagner at Boordy Nursery." *American Wine Society Journal* 21:4 (Winter 1989), 110–112.

——. "Reactions from Upstairs?" *American Wine Society Journal* 31:3 (Fall 1999), 93–94.

——. "A Resurgent Finger Lakes Wine Scene." *American Wine Society Journal* 20:1 (Spring 1988), 3–5.

"Varietal Wines: Boon or Burden?" *Wines & Vines* 31:12 (December 1950), 7–8.

Vaughan, Roger. "Building a Vineyard in Rhode Island 'Wine Country.'" *Horticulture* 55:9 (September 1977), 20–26.

Vine, Richard P. "The Lessons of Lambrusco." *Eastern Grape Grower & Winery News* 6:4 (August 1980), 14–17. [Reprinted from Proceedings of the 1980 Ohio Grape-Wine Short Course.]

——. *Wine Appreciation: A Comprehensive User's Guide to the World's Wines and Vineyards.* New York: Facts on File, 1988.

——. *Wine Appreciation,* 2nd ed. New York: John Wiley & Sons, 1997.

Vine, Richard P., B. J. Stojanovic, C. P. Hegwood, Jr. J. P. Overcash, and F. L. Shuman, Jr. "Developing a Wine Industry in Mississippi." In *Proceedings, Ohio Grape-Wine Short Course,* 1980, 8–11.

Vine, Richard P., B. J. Stojanovic, J. P. Overcash, and C. P. Hegwood, Jr. "Mississippi's Model Laboratory for Southern Viticulture and Enology." *Eastern Grape Grower & Winery News* 6:1 (February 1980), 36–38.

Wagner, Philip M. *American Wines and How to Make Them.* New York: Alfred A. Knopf, 1933.

——. *American Wines and Wine-Making,* 5th ed. New York, Alfred A. Knopf, 1972.

——. "Corks and Acorns." *Wine East* 16:1 (May–June 1988), 23.

——. "An Eastern Wine Analysis Laboratory ... the Need." *Eastern Grape Grower & Winery News* 8:1 (February–March 1982), 42, 45.

——. "Eastern Wine-Growing: Problems and Prospects." In *Proceedings of the Eleventh Pennsylvania Wine Conference,* University Park, College of Agriculture, Pennsylvania State University, 1979, 47–53.

——. "The East's New Wine Industry." *Wines & Vines* 60:3 (March 1979), 24–26.

——. "Facing an Epidemic." *Wine East* 17:2 (July–August 1989), 12–13.

——. "Federal Aid, Private Research, State Experiments, State Laws and the Winery." *Vinifera Wine Growers Journal* 2:2 (Fall 1975), 17–19.

——. "The Four Approaches to Vinifera in the East." *Wines & Vines* 42:11 (November, 1961), 45–47.

——. "The French Hybrids." *American Journal of Enology* 6:1 (January–March 1955), 10–17.

——. *Grapes into Wine.* New York: Alfred A. Knopf, 1976.

——. "The Great Wine Boom." *Fortune* 23:5 (May 1941), 88–90, 95, 122, 124, 126, 129.

——. "The History of Wine Growing in America." In *Wine in American Life*. San Francisco: Wine Institute, 1970, 7–17.

——. "A Letter from Hong Kong." *Wine East* 16:2 (July–August 1988), 21.

——. "Marketing Grapes and Wine." In *Proceedings, Ohio Grape-Wine Short Course,* 1977, 1–3.

——. "New: French Hybrid Grapes." *Farm Journal* 78:4 (April 1954), 88–90.

——. "New White Hybrids." *Wine East* 18:5 (January–February 1991), 22–24.

——. "On the Trail of St. Vincent." *Wine East* 15:6 (March–April 1988), 8–9.

——. "The President's House Crystal a Boordy Design." *American Wine Society Journal* 8:1 (Spring 1976), 7.

——. "Profitable Wine Grapes for the North East." In *Proceedings of the New York State Horticultural Society,* Vol. 110, 1965, 225–231. (Reprinted in *Wines & Vines* 46:10 (October, 1965), 21–24.]

——. "Science on the Farm." *Evening Sun* (Baltimore), September 24, 1937.

——. "A Sham Controversy." *American Wine Society Journal* 10:1 (Spring 1978), 12–15.

——. "Steps in Making Table Wine." In *Proceedings, Ohio Grape-Wine Short Course,* 1977, 78–80.

——. "Tasting Wines of New Hybrids." *Wines & Vines* 23:8 (August 1942), 24–27.

——. "Vintage in the Finger Lakes." *Wine East* 26:1 (May–June 1998), 10–19.

——. "Wagner's Question: Better Name for Hybrids?" *Wines & Vines* 59:5 (May 1978), 54.

——. "Wine from American Grapes." *American Mercury* 28:111 (March 1933), 360–367.

——. *Wine Grapes: Their Selection, Cultivation and Enjoyment.* New York: Harcourt, Brace, 1937.

——. *A Wine-Grower's Guide.* New York: Alfred A. Knopf, 1945.

——. *A Wine-Grower's Guide,* rev. ed. New York: Alfred A. Knopf, 1972.

——. "The Wines of California." *American Mercury* 29:114 (June 1933), 165–175.

——. "The Wines of the U.S." *Fortune* 9:2 (February 1934), 44–51, 118, 121–122.

——. "Wines, Grape Vines and Climate." *Scientific American* 230:6 (June 1974), 106–115.

Wagner, Philip M., and J. Wagner. "Testing Direct Producers in the East." *Wines & Vines* 24:9 (September 1943), 16–17.

Walker, Larry. "Biltmore Estate: Tourist Destination." *Wines & Vines* 76:3 (March 1995), 46–48.

——. "Brotherhood Winery: The Oldest Winery Learns Some New Tricks." *Wines & Vines* 79:9 (September 1998), 52–53.

——. "Canada Wines in Export Hunt." *Wines & Vines* 76:4 (May 1995), 18–20.

——. "Roundup of Texas Wine Producers: Sales Strong in State." *Wines & Vines* 66:9 (September 1985), 31–34.

——. "Southern Wines: Vinifera Looking Good but Muscadine Brings in the Dollars." *Wines & Vines* 71:6 (June 1990), 53–54.

——. "Stone Hill Winery: Credo: Give the People What They Want." *Vineyard & Winery Management* 20:3 (May–June 1994), 30–35.

——. "Virginia Wines Thrive Through Hurricanes, Rain and Spring Freeze." *Wines & Vines* 71:4 (April 1990), 20–22.

Walsh, Taylor. "Maryland's Promising Wine Industry." *Maryland* 11:1 (Autumn 1978), 2–5.

Wamboldt, Philip, Christopher Naugler, and Bruce Wright. *Nova Scotia Winegrower's Guide.* Bridgewater, Nova Scotia: blue frog inc., 2002.

Warren, Jim. "Control and Taxation in Ontario." *Wine East* 14:1 (May–June 1986), 16–17, 21.

——. "Living with Taxes, Controls and Brisk Wine Sales" [An Interview with Jim Warren]. *Wine East* 21:1 (May–June 1993), 8–15, 29–30.

——. "Thirty-Five Years of Winemaking in Ontario" [An Interview with James D. Warren]. *Wine East* 35:3 (September–October 2007), 20–32, 55.

Wasserman, Sheldon, and Pauline Wasserman. "New York State Sparkling Wines." *Vintage* 11:1 (November 1981), 19–23.

Waters, Christopher. "Vineland Estates Winery." *Vineyard & Winery Management* 33:6 (November–December 2007), 52–61.

Watson, Pamela. *Carolina Wine Country: The Complete Guide.* Greenville, NC: Woodhaven, 1999.

Way, Roger D. *A History of Pomology and Viticulture at Geneva,* Geneva. New York: New York State Agricultural Experiment Station, 1986.

Weinhardt, Leslie. "The Rise and Fall of Two Virginia Cooperatives." *Virginia Wine Gazette* 8:3 (Summer 2004), 6.

White, Michael L., and Murli R. Dharmadhikari. "The Iowa Boom Includes Wine." *Wine East* 36:1 (May–June 2008), 12–17, 53–55.

Whitman, William. *The Wines of Virginia: A Complete Guide*. Warrenton: Virginia Heritage, 1997.

Wiener, Susan. *Finger Lakes Wineries: A Complete Tour Guide to Central New York's Acclaimed Wine Country*. Ithaca, NY: McBooks Press, 1990.

Wiley, William F. "Geographical Study of the Winery Establishments in Southern Ontario." Honors B.A. thesis, University of Waterloo, Waterloo, Ontario, 1967.

Williams, James R. "Central Delaware Valley Vines and Wines: A History and Guide." *Vinifera Wine Growers Journal* 12:4 (Winter 1985), 228–232.

———. "Diary of a Farm Winery Bill." *American Wine Society Journal* 16:1 (Spring 1984), 22–24.

Williams, Robert C. "Texas Growers Ponder Future Directions." *Vineyard & Winery Management* 12:4 (September–October 1986), 33–35.

Willoughby, Malcolm F. *Rum War at Sea*. Washington, DC: United States Coast Guard, 1964.

Winchell, Donniella. "Two Decades of Promoting Ohio Wine" [An Interview with Donniella Winchell]. *Wine East* 23:2 (July–August 1995), 10–15, 35.

Winchell, Jim. "New Mexico Vineyard History & Future—Plantings 100 Years Before California." *Vinifera Wine Growers Journal* 10:4 (Winter 1983), 256–258.

———. "New Mexico Vineyards Yesterday & Tomorrow." *Eastern Grape Grower & Winery News* 9:6 (December 1983–January, 1984), 19–20.

"Wine Action Heating Up in Missouri." *Wines & Vines* 62:2 (February 1981), 40–40C.

"'Wine Tasting' in New York." *Wines & Vines* 16:12 (December 1935), 4, 17.

Winiarski, Warren. "A Grateful Reflection." In "Remembering the Contributions of Philip Wagner." *American Wine Society Journal* 29:1 (Spring 1977), 14–16.

Winkler, Wendy. "Cincinnati Winemaking—An Old Art Renewed." *Vintage* IV:3 [AWS] (Fall 1972), 10–11.

Wise, Alice V., and Robert M. Pool. "Wines and Winegrapes: A Success Story for Long Island Viticulture." *New York's Food & Life Sciences Quarterly* 19:1 (1989), 25–27.

Wolff, Katalin. "Toujours Wollersheim." *On Wisconsin* 100:3 (Fall 1999), 18–23.

Wood, Sean P. *Wineries & Wine Country of Nova Scotia*. Halifax, Nova Scotia: Nimbus, 2006.

Wood, Tom. "Wiederkehr Grows into Award-Winning Winery." *Arkansas Democrat* (November 11, 1979). [Reprinted in *Congressional Record* 125:182 (December 18, 1979), E6197–E6198.]

Woodbury, M. Page. "Chautauqua Viticultural Region: Past, Present and Future." Mimeograph prepared for the Society of Wine Educators Annual Meeting, Stamford, Connecticut, August 5, 1988.

Woods, Arthur. "If California, Why Not the East?" *Vinifera Wine Growers Journal* 7:3 (Fall 1980), 176–180.

Yglesias, Linda. "The Goats of Wrath." *New York Daily News Magazine* (September 18, 1988).

Young, Betty S. "Michigan Wines." *American Wine Society Journal* 8:1 (Spring 1976), 3–6.

Zabadal, Thomas J. "Grape and Wine Production: Historical Overview." In *Michigan Geography and Geology*, ed. Randall Schaetzl, Joe Darden, and Danita Brandt. New York: Pearson Custom Publishing, 2009, 602–604.

Ziraldo, Donald J. P. *Anatomy of a Winery: The Art of Wine at Inniskillin*. Toronto: Key Porter Books Limited, 1995.

Ziraldo, Donald, and Karl Kaiser. *Icewine: Extreme Winemaking,* Toronto: Key Porter Books, 2007.

Zoecklein, Bruce, and Larry Lockshin. "Missouri Grape Wine Industry's New Direction." *Vinifera Wine Growers Journal* 10:1 (Spring 1983), 32–36.

Index